Children's
Literature
Review

Guide to Gale Literary Criticism Series

When you need to review criticism of literary works, these are the Gale series to use:

If the author's death date is:

You should turn to:

After Dec. 31, 1959
(or author is still living)

CONTEMPORARY LITERARY CRITICISM

for example: Jorge Luis Borges, Anthony Burgess,
William Faulkner, Mary Gordon,
Ernest Hemingway, Iris Murdoch

1900 through 1959

TWENTIETH-CENTURY LITERARY CRITICISM

for example: Willa Cather, F. Scott Fitzgerald,
Henry James, Mark Twain, Virginia Woolf

1800 through 1899

NINETEENTH-CENTURY LITERATURE CRITICISM

for example: Fedor Dostoevski, Nathaniel Hawthorne,
George Sand, William Wordsworth

1400 through 1799

LITERATURE CRITICISM FROM 1400 TO 1800
(excluding Shakespeare)

for example: Anne Bradstreet, Daniel Defoe,
Alexander Pope, François Rabelais,
Jonathan Swift, Phillis Wheatley

SHAKESPEAREAN CRITICISM

Shakespeare's plays and poetry

Antiquity through 1399

CLASSICAL AND MEDIEVAL LITERATURE CRITICISM

for example: Dante, Homer, Plato, Sophocles, Vergil,
the Beowulf Poet

Gale also publishes related criticism series:

CHILDREN'S LITERATURE REVIEW

This series covers authors of all eras who have written for
the preschool through high school audience.

SHORT STORY CRITICISM

This series covers the major short fiction writers of all nationalities
and periods of literary history.

ISSN 0362-4145

volume 21

Children's Literature Review

Excerpts from Reviews,
Criticism, and Commentary
on Books for Children
and Young People

Gerard J. Senick
Editor

Sharon R. Gunton
Associate Editor

Gale Research Inc. • *DETROIT* • *NEW YORK* • *LONDON*

STAFF

Gerard J. Senick, *Editor*

Sharon R. Gunton, *Associate Editor*

Jeanne A. Gough, *Permissions & Production Manager*
Linda M. Pugliese, *Production Supervisor*
Jennifer E. Gale, David G. Oblender, Suzanne Powers, Maureen A. Puhl, Linda M. Ross, *Editorial Associates*
Donna Craft, *Editorial Assistant*

Victoria B. Cariappa, *Editorial Research Manager*
H. Nelson Fields, Judy L. Gale, Maureen Richards, Mary D. Wise, *Editorial Associates*
Paula Cutcher, Alan Hedblad, Jill M. Ohorodnik, *Editorial Assistants*

Sandra C. Davis, *Permissions Supervisor (Text)*
Josephine M. Keene, Kimberly F. Smilay, *Permissions Associates*
Maria Franklin, Michele M. Lonoconus, Camille P. Robinson,
Shalice Shah, Denise M. Singleton, Rebecca A. Stanko, *Permissions Assistants*

Patricia A. Seefelt, *Permissions Supervisor (Pictures)*
Margaret A. Chamberlain, *Permissions Associate*
Pamela A. Hayes, Lillian Quickley, *Permissions Assistants*

Mary Beth Trimper, *Production Manager*
Evi Seoud, *Assistant Production Manager*

Arthur Chartow, *Art Director*
C. J. Jonik, *Keyliner*

Laura Bryant, *Production Supervisor*
Louise Gagné, *Internal Production Associate*
Michelle M. Stepherson, *Data Entry Associate*

The paper used in this publication meets the minimum requirements of American National Standard for Information Sciences—Permanence Paper for Printed Library Materials, ANSI Z39.48-1984. ∞™

Library of Congress Catalog Card Number 76-643301
ISBN 0-8103-4645-1
ISSN 0362-4145

Printed in the United States of America
Published simultaneously in the United Kingdom
by Gale Research International Limited
(An affiliated company of Gale Research Inc.)

Contents

Preface

As children's literature has evolved into both a respected branch of creative writing and a successful industry, literary criticism has documented and influenced each stage of its growth. Critics have recorded the literary development of individual authors as well as the trends and controversies that resulted from changes in values and attitudes, especially as they concerned children. While defining a philosophy of children's literature, critics developed a scholarship that balances an appreciation of children and an awareness of their needs with standards for literary quality much like those required by critics of adult literature. *Children's Literature Review (CLR)* is designed to provide a permanent, accessible record of this ongoing scholarship. Those responsible for bringing children and books together can now make informed choices when selecting reading materials for the young.

Scope of the Series

Each volume of *CLR* contains excerpts from published criticism on the works of authors and illustrators who create books for children from preschool through high school. The author list for each volume is international in scope and represents the variety of genres covered by children's literature—picture books, fiction, nonfiction, poetry, folklore, and drama. The works of approximately twenty authors of all eras are represented in each volume. Although earlier volumes of *CLR* emphasized critical material published after 1960, successive volumes have expanded their coverage to encompass criticism written before 1960. Since many of the authors included in *CLR* are living and continue to write, it is necessary to update their entries periodically. Thus, future volumes will supplement the entries of selected authors covered in earlier volumes as well as include criticism on the works of authors new to the series.

Organization of the Book

An author section consists of the following elements: author heading, author portrait, author introduction, excerpts of criticism (each followed by a bibliographical citation), and illustrations, when available.

- The **author heading** consists of the author's full name followed by birth and death dates. The portion of the name outside the parentheses denotes the form under which the author is most frequently published. If the majority of the author's works for children were written under a pseudonym, the pseudonym will be listed in the author heading and the real name given on the first line of the author introduction. Also located at the beginning of the introduction are any other pseudonyms used by the author in writing for children and any name variations, including transliterated forms for authors whose languages use nonroman alphabets. Uncertainty as to a birth or death date is indicated by question marks.

- An **author portrait** is included when available.

- The **author introduction** contains information designed to introduce an author to *CLR* users by presenting an overview of the author's themes and styles, occasional biographical facts that relate to the author's literary career or critical responses to the author's works, and information about major awards and prizes the author has received. Where applicable, introductions conclude with references to additional entries in biographical and critical reference series published by Gale Research Inc. These sources include past volumes of *CLR* as well as *Authors & Artists for Young Adults, Contemporary Authors, Contemporary Literary Criticism, Dictionary of Literary Biography, Nineteenth-Century Literature Criticism, Short Story Criticism, Something about the Author, Something about the Author Autobiography Series, Twentieth-Century Literary Criticism,* and *Yesterday's Authors of Books for Children.*

- **Criticism** is located in three sections: **author's commentary** and **general commentary** (when available) and within individual **title entries,** which are preceded by **title entry headings.** Criticism is arranged chronologically within each section. Titles by authors being profiled are highlighted in boldface type within the text for easier access by readers.

The **author's commentary** presents background material written by the author or by an interviewer. This commentary may cover a specific work or several works. Author's commentary on more than one work appears after the author introduction, while commentary on an individual book follows the title entry heading.

The **general commentary** consists of critical excerpts that consider more than one work by the author or illustrator being profiled. General commentary is preceded by the critic's name in boldface type or, in the case of unsigned criticism, by the title of the journal. Occasionally, *CLR* features entries that emphasize general criticism on the overall career of an author or illustrator. When appropriate, a selection of reviews is included to supplement the general commentary.

Title entry headings precede the criticism on a title and cite publication information on the work being reviewed. Title headings list the title of the work as it appeared in its first English-language edition. The first English-language publication date of each work is listed in parentheses following the title. Differing U.S. and British titles follow the publication date within the parentheses.

Title entries consist of critical excerpts on the author's individual works, arranged chronologically by publication date. The entries generally contain two to six reviews per title, depending on the stature of the book and the amount of criticism it has generated. The editors select titles that reflect the entire scope of the author's literary contribution, covering each genre and subject. An effort is made to reprint criticism that represents the full range of each title's reception—from the year of its initial publication to current assessments. Thus, the reader is provided with a record of the author's critical history. Publication information (such as publisher names and book prices) and parenthetical numerical references (such as footnotes or page and line references to specific editions of works) have been deleted at the editor's discretion to provide smoother reading of the text.

Entries on authors who are also illustrators will occasionally feature commentary on selected works illustrated but not written by the author being profiled. These works are strongly associated with the illustrator and have received critical acclaim for their art. By including critical comment on works of this type, the editors wish to provide a more complete representation of the author's total career. Criticism on these works has been chosen to stress artistic, rather than literary, contributions. Title entry headings for works illustrated by the author being profiled are arranged chronologically within the entry by date of publication and include notes identifying the author of the illustrated work. In order to provide easier access for users, all titles illustrated by the subject of the entry will be boldfaced.

CLR also includes entries on prominent illustrators who have contributed to the field of children's literature. These entries are designed to represent the development of the illustrator as an artist rather than as a literary stylist. The illustrator's section is organized like that of an author, with two exceptions: the introduction presents an overview of the illustrator's styles and techniques rather than outlining his or her literary background, and the commentary written by the illustrator on his or her works is called illustrator's commentary rather than author's commentary. Title entry headings are followed by explanatory notes identifying the author of the illustrated work. All titles of books containing illustrations by the artist being profiled as well as individual illustrations from these books are highlighted in boldface type.

• Selected excerpts are preceded by **explanatory notes,** which provide information on the critic or work of criticism to enhance the reader's understanding of the excerpt.

• A complete **bibliographical citation** designed to facilitate the location of the original book or article follows each piece of criticism.

• Numerous **illustrations** are featured in *CLR*. For entries on illustrators, an effort has been made to include illustrations that reflect the characteristics discussed in the criticism. Entries on major authors who do not illustrate their own works may also include photographs and other illustrative material pertinent to the authors' careers.

Other Features

• An **acknowledgments,** which immediately follows the preface, lists the sources from which material has been reprinted in the volume. It does not, however, list every book or periodical consulted for the volume.

• The **cumulative index to authors** lists authors who have appeared in *CLR* and includes cross-references to *Authors & Artists for Young Adults, Contemporary Authors, Contemporary Literary Criticism, Dictionary of Literary Biography, Nineteenth-Century Literature Criticism, Short Story Criticism, Something about the Author, Something about the Author Autobiography Series, Twentieth-Century Literary Criticism,* and *Yesterday's Authors of Books for Children.*

• The **cumulative nationality index** lists authors alphabetically under their respective nationalities. Author names are followed by the volume number(s) in which they appear. Authors who have changed citizenship or whose current citizenship is not reflected in biographical sources appear under both their original nationality and that of their current residence.

• The **cumulative title index** lists titles covered in *CLR* followed by the volume and page number where criticism begins.

A Note to the Reader

When writing papers, students who quote directly from any volume in the Literature Criticism Series may use the following general forms to footnote reprinted criticism. The first example pertains to material drawn from periodicals, the second to material reprinted from books.

[1]T. S. Eliot, "John Donne," *The Nation and the Athenaeum,* 33 (9 June 1923), 321-32; excerpted and reprinted in *Literature Criticism from 1400 to 1800,* Vol. 10, ed. James E. Person, Jr. (Detroit: Gale Research, 1989), pp. 28-9.

[1]Henry Brooke, *Leslie Brooke and Johnny Crow* (Frederick Warne, 1982); excerpted and reprinted in *Children's Literature Review,* Vol. 20, ed. Gerard J. Senick (Detroit: Gale Research, 1990), p. 47.

Suggestions Are Welcome

In response to various suggestions, several features have been added to *CLR* since the series began, including author entries on retellers of traditional literature as well as those who have been the first to record oral tales and other folklore; entries on prominent illustrators featuring commentary on their styles and techniques; entries on authors whose works are considered controversial or have been challenged; occasional entries devoted to criticism on a single work by a major author; explanatory notes that provide information on the critic or work of criticism to enhance the usefulness of the excerpt; more extensive illustrative material, such as holographs of manuscript pages and photographs of people and places pertinent to the authors' careers; a cumulative nationality index for easy access to authors by nationality; and occasional guest essays written specifically for *CLR* by prominent critics on subjects of their choice.

Readers who wish to suggest authors to appear in future volumes, or who have other suggestions, are cordially invited to write the editor or to call our toll-free number: 1-800-347-GALE.

Acknowledgments

The editors wish to thank the copyright holders of the excerpted criticism included in this volume, the permissions managers of many book and magazine publishing companies for assisting us in securing reprint rights, and Anthony Bogucki for assistance with copyright research. We are also grateful to the staffs of the Detroit Public Library, the Library of Congress, the University of Detroit Library, Wayne State University Purdy/Kresge Library Complex, and the University of Michigan Libraries for making their resources available to us. Following is a list of the copyright holders who have granted us permission to reprint material in this volume of *CLR*. Every effort has been made to trace copyright, but if omissions have been made, please let us know.

COPYRIGHTED EXCERPTS IN *CLR*, VOLUME 21, WERE REPRINTED FROM THE FOLLOWING PERIODICALS:

American Indian Quarterly, v. 8, Spring, 1984. Copyright © Society for American Indian Studies & Research 1984. Reprinted by permission of the publisher.—*The American West,* v. XVIII, March-April, 1981 for "Children's Books Open Bright Frontiers" by Nancy Bell Rollings. Copyright © 1981 by the American West Publishing Company, Tucson, AZ. Used with permission of the publisher and the author.—*Appraisal: Children's Science Books,* v. 13, Fall, 1980. Copyright © 1980 by the Children's Science Book Review Committee. Reprinted by permission of the publisher.—*Best Sellers,* v. 32, December 15, 1972. Copyright 1972, by the University of Scranton. Reprinted by permission of the publisher.—*The Book Collector,* v. 23, Autumn, 1974. Copyright © 1974 by Justin G. Schiller. Reprinted by permission of the publisher and the author.—*Book Window,* v. 5, Spring, 1978. © 1978 S.C.B.A. and contributors. Reprinted by permission of the publisher.—*Book World—The Washington Post,* January 14, 1968. © 1968 Postrib Corp./ May 19, 1974; July 14, 1985; February 7, 1988; November 6, 1988; November 5, 1989. © 1974, 1985, 1988, 1989, *The Washington Post.* All reprinted by permission of the publisher.—*Books for Keeps,* n. 34, September, 1985; n. 44, May, 1987; n. 45, July, 1987. © School Bookshop Association 1985, 1987. All reprinted by permission of the publisher.—*Books for Young People,* v. 2, October, 1988 for a review of "Architect of the Moon" by Catherine Osborne. All rights reserved.—*Books for Your Children,* v. 5, Summer, 1970; v. 7, 1971; v. 11, Summer, 1976; v. 16, Autumn-Winter, 1981; v. 17, Spring, 1982; v. 20, Spring, 1985; v. 23, Spring, 1988. © *Books for Your Children* 1970, 1971, 1976, 1981, 1982, 1985, 1988. All reprinted by permission of the publisher.—*Books in Canada,* v. 15, December, 1986 for "The Young and the Naked" by Mary Ainslie Smith. Reprinted by permission of the author.—*The Booklist,* v. 70, November, 15, 1973; v. 71, June 15, 1975; v. 72, May 15, 1976; v. 73, February 1, 1977; v. 74, September 15, 1977; v. 76, November 1, 1979; v. 76, April 15, 1980; v. 77, January 1, 1981; v. 77, March 15, 1981; v. 78, June 15, 1982; v. 81, March 1, 1985; v. 82, September 15, 1985; v. 82, November 1, 1985; v. 82, February 15, 1986; v. 83, November 15, 1986; v. 84, March 1, 1988; v. 84, April 1, 1988; v. 84, August, 1988; v. 85, January 15, 1989; v. 85, March 1, 1989; v. 85, April 1, 1989. Copyright © 1973, 1975, 1976, 1977, 1979, 1980, 1981, 1982, 1985, 1986, 1988, 1989 by the American Library Association. All reprinted by permission of the publisher.—*British Book News Children's Books,* Autumn, 1982; June, 1986; Autumn, 1986. © The British Council, 1982, 1986. All reprinted by permission of the publisher.—*Bulletin of the Center for Children's Books,* v. 24, December, 1970; v. 26, March, 1973; v. 27, February, 1974; v. 31, January, 1978; v. 32, July-August, 1979; v. 33, July-August, 1980; v. 34, January, 1981; v. 34, March, 1981; v. 34, June, 1981; v. 36, January, 1983; v. 36, February, 1983; v. 36, June, 1983; v. 37, November, 1983; v. 38, September, 1984; v. 38, October, 1984; v. 38, January, 1985; v. 38, July, 1985; v. 39, October, 1985; v. 39, April, 1986; v. 39, June 1986; v. 39, July-August, 1986; v. 40, December, 1986; v. 40, April, 1987; v. 41, September, 1987; v. 41, December, 1987; v. 41, January, 1988; v. 41, April, 1988; v. 41, July-August, 1988. Copyright © 1970, 1973, 1974, 1978, 1979, 1980, 1981, 1983, 1984, 1985, 1986, 1987, 1988 by The University of Chicago. All reprinted by permission of The University of Chicago Press.—*Canadian Children's Literature,* n. 15 & 16, 1980; n. 54, 1989. Copyright © 1980, 1989 Canadian Children's Press. Both reprinted by permission of the publisher.—*Canadian Literature,* n. 112, Spring, 1987 for a review of "Zoom Away" by Jon C. Stott; n. 118, Autumn, 1988 for "Dummies & Children" by Adrienne Kertzer. Both reprinted by permission of the respective authors.—*Children's Book News,* Toronto, v. 2, June, 1979. Reprinted by permission of The Children's Book Centre, Toronto, Canada.—*Children's Book Review,* v. I, February, 1971; v. II, February, 1972; v. II, June, 1972; v. II, October, 1972; v. III, April, 1973; v. III, December, 1973; v. IV, Autumn, 1974; v. V, Summer, 1975; v. VI, October, 1976. © 1971, 1972, 1973, 1974, 1975, 1976 by Five Owls Press Ltd. All rights reserved. All reprinted by permission of the publisher.—*Children's Book Review Service,* v. 16, April, 1988. Copyright © 1988 Children's Book Review Service Inc. Reprinted by permission of the publisher.—*Children's Literature: Annual of the Modern Language Association Seminar on Children's Literature and The Children's Literature Association,* v. 2, 1973; v. 8, 1980. © 1973, 1980 by Francelia Butler. All rights reserved. Both reprinted by permission of Yale University Press.—*Children's Literature Association Quarterly,* v. 7, Summer, 1982; v. 8, Winter, 1983; v. 11, Spring, 1986. © 1982, 1983, 1986 Children's Literature Association. All reprinted by permission of the publisher.—*Children's literature in education,* July, 1970; n. 3, November, 1970; v. 9, 1978; v. 16, Spring, 1985. © 1970, 1978, 1985, Agathon Press, Inc. All reprinted by permission of the publisher.—*The Christian Science Monitor,*

1981. Copyright © 1981 by Duke University Press, Durham, NC. Reprinted by permission of the publisher.—*The Southeastern Librarian,* v. XX, Spring, 1970 for "Tell It Like It Is: New Criteria for Children's Books in Black and White" by Ann Allen Schockley. Reprinted by permission of the author.—*The Spectator,* v. 256, April 26, 1986; v. 261, December 10, 1988. © 1986, 1988 by *The Spectator.* Reprinted by permission of *The Spectator.*—*The Times,* London, April 12, 1972; April 24, 1972; April 28, 1972; May 1, 1972. © Times Newspapers Limited 1972. All reproduced from *The Times,* London by permission.—*The Times Educational Supplement,* n. 3269, February 2, 1978; n. 3425, February 19, 1982; n. 3558, September 7, 1984; n. 3577, January 18, 1985; n. 3685, February 13, 1987; n. 3776, November 11, 1988; n. 3778, November 25, 1988. © Times Newspapers Ltd. (London) 1978, 1982, 1984, 1985, 1987, 1988. All reproduced from *The Times Educational Supplement* by permission.—*The Times Literary Supplement,* n. 3274, November 26, 1964; n. 3378, November 24, 1966; n. 3404, May 25, 1967; n. 3484, December 5, 1968; n. 3536, December 4, 1969; n. 3555, April 16, 1970; n. 3583, October 30, 1970; n. 3640, December 3, 1971; n. 3672, July 14, 1972; n. 3687, November 3, 1972; n. 3709, April 6, 1973; n. 3742, November 23, 1973; n. 3774, July 5, 1974; n. 3864, April 2, 1976; n. 3879, July 16, 1976; n. 3900, December 10, 1976; n. 3931, July 15, 1977; n. 3979, July 7, 1978; n. 4000, December 1, 1978; n. 4018, March 28, 1980; n. 4086, July 24, 1981; n. 4121, March 26, 1982; n. 4156, November 26, 1982; n. 4200, September 30, 1983; n. 4252, September 28, 1984; n. 4270, February 1, 1985; n. 4282, April 26, 1985; n. 4334, April 25, 1986; n. 4391, May 29, 1987; n. 3701, June 5, 1987; n. 4447, June 24-30, 1988; n. 4472, December 16-22, 1988. © Times Newspapers Ltd. (London) 1964, 1966, 1967, 1968, 1969, 1970, 1971, 1972, 1973, 1974, 1976, 1977, 1978, 1980, 1981, 1982, 1983, 1984, 1985, 1986, 1987, 1988. All reproduced from *The Times Literary Supplement* by permission.—*The Use of English,* v. 23, Winter, 1971; v. 23, Summer, 1972. Both reprinted by permission of Scottish Academic Press, 139 Leith Walk, Edinburgh EH6 8NS.—*Voice of Youth Advocates,* v. 4, June, 1981; v. 5, February, 1983; v. 10, April, 1987; v. 11, February, 1989. Copyrighted 1981, 1983, 1987, 1989 by *Voice of Youth Advocates.* All reprinted by permission of the publisher.—*Wilson Library Bulletin,* v. 62, January, 1988. Copyright © 1988 by the H. W. Wilson Company. Reprinted by permission of the publisher.—*The World of Children's Books,* v. III, Spring, 1978; v. VI, 1981. © 1978, 1981 by Jon C. Stott. Both reprinted by permission of the publisher.

COPYRIGHTED EXCERPTS IN *CLR,* VOLUME 21, WERE REPRINTED FROM THE FOLLOWING BOOKS:

Arbuthnot, Mary Hill. From *Children and Books.* Scott, Foresman, 1947. Copyright 1947, renewed 1974 by Scott, Foresman and Company. Reprinted by permission of the publisher.—Bader, Barbara. From *American Picturebooks from Noah's Ark to the Beast Within.* Macmillan, 1976. Copyright © 1976 by Barbara Bader. All rights reserved. Reprinted with permission of Macmillan Publishing Company.—Bader, Barbara. From "Picture Books, Art, and Illustration," in *Newbery and Caldecott Medal Books: 1966-1975.* Edited by Lee Kingman. Horn Book, 1975. Copyright © 1975 by The Horn Book, Inc. All rights reserved. Reprinted by permission of the publisher.—Bader, Barbara. From "The Caldecott Spectrum," in *Newbery and Caldecott Medal Books: 1976-1985.* Edited by Lee Kingman. Horn Book, 1986. Copyright © 1986 by The Horn Book, Inc. All rights reserved. Reprinted by permission of the publisher.—Becker, May Lamberton. From *First Adventures in Reading: Introducing Children to Books.* Revised edition. J. B. Lippincott Company, 1947. Copyright, 1936, renewed 1975 by May Lamberton Becker. All rights reserved. Reprinted by permission of Harper & Row, Publishers, Inc.—Birtha, Jessie M. From "Portrayal of the Black in Children's Literature (excerpt)," in *The Black American in Books for Children: Readings in Racism.* Edited by Donnarae MacCann and Gloria Woodard. The Scarecrow Press, Inc., 1972. Copyright 1972 by Donnarae MacCann and Gloria Woodard. Reprinted by permission of the publisher.—Chambers, Nancy. From a review of "Games," in *The Signal Selection of Children's Books 1988.* Edited by Nancy Chambers. Thimble Press, 1989. Copyright © 1989 The Thimble Press. Reprinted by permission of the publisher.—From "Picture Books: Berlie Doherty," in *The Signal Selection of Children's Books 1988.* Edited by Nancy Chambers. Thimble Press, 1989. Copyright © 1989 The Thimble Press. Reprinted by permission of the publisher.—Crouch, Marcus. From *The Nesbit Tradition: The Children's Novel in England 1945-1970.* Ernest Benn Limited, 1972. © Marcus Crouch 1972. Reprinted by permission of the author.—Crouch, Marcus. From *Treasure Seekers and Borrowers: Children's Books in Britain 1900-1960.* The Library Association, 1962. © Marcus Crouch, 1962. Reprinted by permission of the publisher.—Dixon, Bob. From *Catching Them Young: Sex, Race and Class in Children's Fiction, Vol. I.* Pluto Press, 1977. Copyright © Pluto Press 1977. Reprinted by permission of the publisher.—Eaton, Anne Thaxter. From *Reading with Children.* The Viking Press, 1940. Copyright 1940 by Anne Thaxter Eaton. Renewed © 1967 by Anne Thaxter Eaton. Reprinted by permission of Viking Penguin, a division of Penguin Books USA, Inc.—Egoff, Sheila A. From *Thursday's Child: Trends and Patterns in Contemporary Children's Literature.* American Library Association, 1981. Copyright © 1981 by the American Library Association. All rights reserved. Reprinted by permission of the publisher.—Elledge, Scott. From *E. B. White: A Biography.* Norton, 1984. Copyright © 1984 by Scott Elledge. All rights reserved. Reprinted by permission of W. W. Norton & Company, Inc.—Eyre, Frank. From *British Children's Books in the Twentieth Century.* Revised edition. Longman Books, 1971, Dutton, 1973. Copyright © 1971 by Frank Eyre. All rights reserved. Reprinted by permission of the publisher, E. P. Dutton, a division of Penguin Books USA Inc. In Canada by Penguin Books Ltd.—Field, Rachel. From "Acceptance Paper," in *Newbery Medal Books: 1922-1955.* Edited by Bertha Mahony Miller and Elinor Whitney Field. Horn Book, 1955. Copyright © 1955, renewed by The Horn Book, Inc., Boston. All rights reserved. Reprinted by permission of the publisher.—Fisher, Margery. From *Classics for Children & Young People.* Thimble Press, 1986. Copyright © 1986 Margery Fisher. Reprinted by permission of the publisher.—Fisher, Margery. From *Matters of Fact: Aspects of Non-Fiction for Children.* Thomas Y. Crowell Co., 1972. Copyright © 1972 by Margery Fisher. All rights reserved. Reprinted by permission of Hodder & Stoughton Children's Books.—Fisher, Margery. From *Who's Who in Children's*

PERMISSION TO REPRODUCE ILLUSTRATIONS APPEARING IN *CLR*, VOLUME 21, WAS RECEIVED FROM THE FOLLOWING SOURCES:

PERMISSION TO REPRODUCE PHOTOGRAPHS APPEARING IN *CLR*, VOLUME 21, WAS RECEIVED FROM THE FOLLOWING SOURCES:

Children's
Literature
Review

Helen Bannerman

1862-1946

Scottish author and illustrator of picture books.

The following entry emphasizes general criticism on Bannerman's career. It also includes a selection of reviews to supplement the general commentary.

Praised as an author and artist whose works reflect both her gifts as a storyteller and her understanding of what appeals to young children, Bannerman is best known as the creator of *Little Black Sambo* (1899), one of the most popular and controversial books in the history of juvenile literature. A comic fantasy about a little boy who cleverly avoids being eaten by tigers in the jungle near his home by giving them his clothes, *Little Black Sambo* is acknowledged for introducing a new kind of picture book to the genre, one which uses short, rhythmic sentences to form an action-filled narrative which Bannerman depicts in vivid, childlike illustrations; like Beatrix Potter, to whom she is often compared, Bannerman placed her story and pictures in a format which small children could hold easily in their hands. *Little Black Sambo*, which critic Anne Thaxter Eaton calls "that miracle of simplicity and drama," is also regarded as the first story with a sympathetic black hero to become both a household book and a classic of children's literature. Bannerman's subsequent books also reflect her formula of simple language, repetitive sentences, suspenseful plots, and satisfying conclusions presented in tiny books. In these works—*The Story of Little Black Mingo* (1901), *The Story of Little Black Quibba* (1903), *Little Degchie-Head: An Awful Warning to Bad Babas* (1903; U. S. edition as *The Story of Little Kettle-Head*), *Pat and the Spider: The Biter Bit* (1904), *The Story of the Teasing Monkey* (1906), *The Story of Little Black Quasha* (1908), *The Story of Little Black Bobtail* (1909), *The Story of Sambo and the Twins* (1936), and the posthumous *The Story of Little White Squibba* (1966)—Bannerman describes the adventures of both black and white protagonists who encounter the world alone, as did Little Black Sambo, and succeed through their own ingenuity. Peppering her texts with the Indian words she learned as the wife of a doctor in the Indian Medical Service, and setting her books in a landscape that, although invented, includes many Indian characteristics, Bannerman created works which are recognized as among the first to which English children living in India could successfully relate. The books also contain some violent, sensational elements in both text and picture, such as the depiction of human and animal villains being blown up. Although these works were popular and widely imitated, *Little Black Sambo* is often acclaimed as the most successful example of Bannerman's talents.

Initially considered a positive influence on young children, *Little Black Sambo* prompted criticism by educators in the mid-twentieth century as a work which reinforces white supremacist attitudes. Perhaps no other piece of juvenile literature has generated such emotional intensity: as racial issues became more prevalent and social awareness grew, *Little Black Sambo* was designated as a book which caused feelings of inferiority among black children due to the charge that Bannerman depicted her characters as objects of ridicule. Denigrated for its stereotyped, caricatured illustrations, de-

grading names, exaggerated dialect, and primitive jungle setting, *Little Black Sambo* was dropped from many libraries and professional lists of recommended books for children both in the United States and the United Kingdom. In 1972, the newly-formed English group Teachers Against Racism sent letters both to Bannerman's British publisher, Chatto and Windus, and to the London *Times* regarding the negative attributes of Bannerman's works. This incident began a controversy centering on *Little Black Sambo* that reached worldwide proportions and is still being resolved. Bannerman's defenders point to the fact that since she wrote *Little Black Sambo* for her daughters, and not for publication, she chose an imaginary jungle land as the setting for her book, peopling it with characters which represented an exotic type of people and drawing them in an untrained style which contained no underlying racial messages. In addition, Bannerman's supporters contend that, since she did not retain the copyright for *Little Black Sambo,* she is not responsible for the proliferation of U. S. editions which contained illustrations by other artists reinforcing a distorted view of blacks. Current assessments of *Little Black Sambo* acknowledge her innocence, but note that Bannerman's works should be used carefully and with sensitivity in the home or classroom. However, many observers acclaim as perfect the blend of text and picture which Bannerman achieved in *Little Black Sambo* and point to the fervor with which children continue to respond to her works as a demonstration of their suitability as literature for the young.

(See also *Something about the Author,* Vol. 19 and *Contemporary Authors,* Vol. 111.)

THE SPECTATOR

[*The Story of Little Black Sambo* is a] most attractive little book. . . . [Little Black Sambo's] history was not written with one eye on parents and guardians, or the inconsistency of mixing up the African type of black with delightful adventures with tigers in an Indian jungle would never have been allowed to pass. As it is, Little Black Sambo makes his simple and direct appeal in the great realm of make-believe without paying the slightest attention to the unities or caring in the least about anything but the amusement of the little boys and girls for whom he was so obviously created. Every parent should at once get the book and give it both to the nursery and the schoolroom. It is impossible to deny that among this year's Christmas books *Little Black Sambo* is, to use his own classic phrase, far and away "the grandest tiger in the jungle." (p. 842)

"Modern Nursery-Books," in The Spectator, *Vol. 83, No. 3727, December 2, 1899, p. 841-42.*

ELIZABETH M. BACON

What about *Little Black Sambo?* Is it simply an amusing and harmless little story for young children? Or does it have more serious implications—which are not harmless at all? This is a question on which there are the widest differences of opinion. Even among progressive educators, there are many who take the point of view that this is a story which just happens to be about a Negro child (it could just as well be any other nationality, they say) and in itself has no implications of white superiority. They are influenced too, by the fact that the book has become almost a classic, a traditional part of children's literature.

Let us look at *Little Black Sambo* more closely. First of all, at the title. The name "Sambo" in our present-day American society is in itself an insult. It is deeply rooted in the tradition of Southern white chauvinism. And if you think that little children are unconscious of these implications and so it really makes no difference to them, let me tell you the story of a kindergarten group in a midwestern city. The book was read to the children. For several days nothing happened. Then one of the little Negro boys in the class was found on the playground in tears because several of the white children had taunted him by calling him "Little Black Sambo."

And Sambo's parents, "Black Mumbo," his mother, and "Black Jumbo," his father—how "quaint" they are! Black Mumbo is rather like the picture of the "Southern mammy" on the Aunty Jemima Pancake box, and the importance of pancakes in the story brings this all the more vividly to mind. And if you say, "Well, can't we separate the story from the pictures," there still remains the question of these names themselves. Aren't they funny? But the humor in them is not just the fun of playing with amusing sounds; rather it makes fun of the people they designate.

There is also the question of Little Black Sambo's clothes—the blue trousers, the red coat, the green umbrella, and the

purple shoes with crimson soles and crimson linings. It is certainly true that children love bright colors. Surely, there can be no objection to this! But wait a minute. Isn't it also true that one of the main arguments of white chauvinists who wish to prove that Negroes are uncultured and tasteless is the untruth that they have an indiscriminate and primitive love for bright-colored clothes? Actually, it is a fact, scientifically proved by the anthropologists, that taste in clothes has nothing to do with race. Yet certainly *Little Black Sambo* tends to establish the false idea very firmly in the child's mind.

Finally, there is the ending of the story. How satisfactory it seems, when the tigers have been reduced to butter, to have Sambo and his parents sit down to a feast of pancakes. And what a magnificent number they eat—Mumbo twenty-seven, Jumbo fifty-five, and Sambo himself a hundred and sixty-nine. You may say that this exaggeration is just the sort of thing to delight and amuse a child. But is this particular exaggeration an accident? Doesn't it actually reinforce the white chauvinists' false contention that Negroes are people of inordinate physical appetites? It reminds one of the recent flood of newspaper stories exaggerating the amount Joe Louis eats.

In short, Little Black Sambo is one of the first stereotypes a child meets in literature. However unconsciously, the book presents a picture of the Negro that tends to reinforce prejudice, to make the white child feel that he is superior and the Negro child feel that he is being made fun of. Some people will tell you that Negro children like *Little Black Sambo,* and so it must be acceptable. But all Negro children do not like *Little Black Sambo.* In fact, one library in a northern city with a large Negro population could not keep the book on the shelves because the children continually defaced it.

It is not coincidence that *Little Black Sambo* presents this kind of stereotype. In the original edition, Little Black Sambo is not a Negro at all, but a little Hindu boy. . . . [The book] reflects the philosophy of the "white man's burden," British imperialism's vicious doctrine of white superiority over any and all darker peoples. But whether the white chauvinism is directed against Hindus or Negroes makes no difference in principle. Today, as far as American children are concerned, Little Black Sambo is a Negro.

It is argued that the particular edition of the book which contains the original illustrations is all right, that the book has fallen into disrepute simply because some of the later pirated editions have illustrations that are so degraded and insulting as to beggar description. . . . In the first place, this contention is untrue. The original illustrations use all the usual stereotypes found in malicious cartoons of Negroes—the thick lips, the rolling eyes, the bony knees, the fuzzy hair. They make Sambo and his parents look ugly and ridiculous. In the second place, the chauvinism lies in the text itself, and while different pictures might mitigate this to some small degree, they cannot possibly erase it altogether.

Little Black Sambo cannot be considered in a vacuum. We cannot separate the story from its social effects; and in general, given the prevalence of white chauvinism in our society, these effects undoubtedly strengthen racial discrimination. . . .

It is hard to relinquish a "classic," to banish it from the bookshelf. Yet allowing *Little Black Sambo* to stay will only help to spread the ugly disease of white chauvinism and racial discrimination.

Elizabeth M. Bacon, "What About 'Little Black Sambo'?" in The Worker, Vol. 12, No. 11, March 16, 1947, p. 7.

MAY HILL ARBUTHNOT

[The story of *Little Black Sambo*], which might almost have come out of some folklore collection, has about it an effortless perfection which baffles analysis. Its extreme simplicity is deceiving. Just try to duplicate it! . . . How Sambo gets his clothes back and eats 169 pancakes into the bargain is certainly the best substitute for getting "the princess and half the kingdom" ever invented for children. The formula is: extreme simplicity of language, short, cadenced sentences with enough repetition to give the pleasant rhythm little children enjoy, a plot full of mild and funny surprises, considerable suspense, and complete satisfaction at the end. Still, the easy charm of this unaffected, convincing little tale eludes us.

In this age of color and race consciousness, some people wish that Mrs. Bannerman had not woven the word *black* into her repetitional cadence, but its presence should not blind us to the merits of the story. Nor should it give offense, for *black* is used as a part of the name, and *blue* coat and *red* trousers continue the cadenced pattern of colors. Moreover, Sambo is the first and most loved hero of young children. Isn't it desirable that the first association of many children with people of a different color should be by way of a lovable character like Little Black Sambo? He has the right kind of parents, just the kind every child would like to have. Sambo outwits the tigers over and over. He is happy and completely triumphant, the envy of all young hero worshipers. That his euphonious name associates racial color with all these desirable attributes should be a basis for racial pride and interracial admiration. (pp. 287-88)

May Hill Arbuthnot, "New Magic," in her Children and Books, *Scott, Foresman and Company, 1947, pp. 276-359.*

MAY LAMBERTON BECKER

Little Black Sambo is second only to [Beatrix Potter's books] in popularity—indeed, considering the various pirated versions, it may have been read by a greater number of delighted children. I cannot imagine a childhood without it now. For it has fun, hilarious, rollicking fun, and that is rare enough in books of any size for any-sized children. The gift of being funny for little children is one of the rarest to be bestowed upon authors or artists: Helen Bannerman is both at once, and her tiger in blue trousers, her tiger with shoes on his ears—how they touch off the bright spark of laughter! Never let yourself be misled into getting this blessed book with any illustrations but the author's: indeed, once you let your child see them he will "accept no other." (p. 33)

May Lamberton Becker, "Two Laps and Little Bits," in her First Adventures in Reading: Introducing Children to Books, *revised edition, J. B. Lippincott Company, 1947, pp. 26-42.*

FRANK EYRE

Almost as good, in her own way, as Beatrix Potter, but less prolific and less able to sustain her output (and also less of an artist) is Helen Bannerman, whose *The Story of Little Black Sambo* was published a few years before *Peter Rabbit*. Helen Bannerman's gift for robust story telling is unique and her economy of words combined with the unusual ingredients of her plots and the gaiety of her drawings to make *Little Black Sambo* a riotous frolic that has entertained children and parents for fifty years and shows no sign of losing its popularity. Her other books are not quite so good, although children who love reading will always take *Little Black Quasha* to their hearts, for the idea of the tigers waiting until the book was finished has that inspired "rightness" that children immediately recognize. (p. 26)

Frank Eyre, "Books with Pictures," in his 20th Century Children's Books, *Longmans, Green and Co., 1952, pp. 25-39.*

MARCUS CROUCH

Throughout the history of children's literature, books have appeared which have had a success out of all proportion to their artistic merits. *Little Black Sambo,* crudely drawn, unpretentiously written, struck a chord to which children's hearts responded. It was, and is tremendously popular, producing four sequels and a host of imitators. It is difficult to consider *Little Black Sambo* as 'literature', but there can hardly be one children's writer working today whose childhood dreams were not coloured by this absurd, delightful, unforgettable tale. (pp. 27-8)

Marcus Crouch, "The Edwardian Age," in his Treasure Seekers and Borrowers: Children's Books in Britain 1900-1960, *The Library Association, 1962, pp. 12-31.*

ROGER LANCELYN GREEN

A trifle of logical fantasy, *Little Black Sambo* . . . , had appeared as early as 1899, a tiny booklet catching the absurd for one eternal moment that is still much loved when read with exaggerated emphasis to a small child. There were sequels such as *Little Black Mingo* and *Little Black Quasha,* but the moment could not be recaptured, though these are longer and more artistic tales, and better value from the point of view of simple little adventure stories. (p. 256)

Roger Lancelyn Green, "Kenneth Grahame and A. A. Milne," in his Tellers of Tales, *revised edition, 1965. Reprint by Kaye & Ward, Ltd., 1969, pp. 249-57.*

ANN ALLEN SHOCKLEY

Undoubtedly, a dark and backward step in publishing history with regard to Negro children was taken in 1900 when Helen Bannerman's *Little Black Sambo* was first published. Even though some defending white librarians may contest this by saying that the book was actually about a little *Indian* boy, the ludicrous illustrations of thick red lips, and kaleidoscopic clashing colors of red coat, blue pants, purple shoes with "crimson soles and crimson linings," overtopped with a green umbrella, and replete with the name of Sambo, marked the model stereotyped caricature of Negroes to white children for generations. The devastating effect of this story has without question cast a long ugly shadow on the developing minds of white children by giving them a model caricature that demeans and ridicules black children. The Sambo infamy is well illustrated in the book titled *Call Me Charlie* by Jesse Jackson which came out in 1945. A white boy's mocking taunt to a Negro boy, who had just moved into a white neighborhood, of "Move on, Sambo," caused the Negro boy to reply indignantly: "My name is Charlie." Four words heavily distilled with potent meaning. (p. 30)

Ann Allen Shockley, "Tell It Like It Is: New

Criteria for Children's Books in Black and White," in The Southeastern Librarian, Vol. XX, No. 1, Spring, 1970, p. 30.

ELIZABETH GARD

[The following excerpt is from an article that originally appeared in Books for Your Children, Volume 5, Number 4, 1970.]

When my son passed the ABC, nursery-rhyme, stage, and began to need real stories, I was gratified, as I expect many other parents have been, to find so many of the familiar books of my own childhood still available and popular. . . . [The] most enjoyable rediscovery for me—the books which have come best through the second-time-around test—have been Helen Bannerman's Little Black Sambo, and his successors, Little Black Mingo, Quibba, Quasha and Bobtail.

Little Black Sambo is one of the most successful books ever written for the two-to-five age-group. It sells an average of 25,000 copies a year, and the others aren't far behind. The more I read them to my own and other children, and the more I discuss them with other adults, the more convinced I am that their success owes more to the enthusiasm of children than their parents.

Some children's classics, Christopher Robin certainly, and perhaps even some of Beatrix Potter's mild little pastel creatures, I suspect are persistently offered to children by sentimental adults who probably didn't enjoy them all that much when they were at the receiving end. Whereas with the Little Black books, I think it's the other way round—children keep on asking for them, but adults often shy away from them. There's a certain amount of to my mind rather ludicrous, liberal unease about the portrayal of 'little blacks'. Also, even parents who take the modern view that children should not be too protected, often recoil from the savagery of the stories. It was this unease I encountered which first aroused my curiosity about Helen Bannerman. Compared to Beatrix Potter, or even Enid Blyton, she seemed an unaccountably unknown figure.

The only clue on the title page was—"First Published 1899". That confirmed my original guess that she was part of the British Raj. The vocabulary gives her away—words like bazaar, chatty, mugger, and ghi (the melted tiger butter). But the setting is a puzzling jumble. The vegetation is tropical jungle, but the mud-hut villages look completely African. The animals are all Indian, but the humans look as if they've come straight off the plantation. They have the clothes and the features of Southern States cotton-pickin' Negroes. (pp. 184-85)

The Bannermans led very much the conventional life of British people in India. They travelled about with their entourage of servants, mainly in Bombay and Madras. Nothing particularly exciting seems to have happened to her. She herself had had none of the hair-raising encounters with fearsome beasts that she described so convincingly in her books. . . . But in her approach to the job of entertaining and amusing her children, Mrs. Bannerman was far from conventional. She made up her own stories and drew her own pictures. Her daughter, Dr. Davie Bannerman, had kept a marvellous collection of letters from her mother, written in a clear script and illustrated with engaging ink and watercolour sketches. (She could draw Indians beautifully when she wanted to.) Dr. Bannerman also remembers how Little Black Sambo came to be written and published:

Dr. Bannerman: My mother when she was a small child had always wanted a little book that was small enough to hold in her own hands, because she'd been often ticked off for not handling books carefully enough, and she wanted a little book that had the picture and the letterpress on opposite pages, so that she didn't have to look forwards and backwards and I think it was with the idea of realising this ambition for my sister and me that she originally made Little Black Sambo into a book. She just wrote them—the first one anyway—for my sister and me. We had been left alone, at least without our parents, in the hills because it was considered more healthy and children were very apt to die off in India at that time if they were kept too much in the plains. And so we were no doubt missing her, and she made this little book to sort of comfort us (she just bound it by hand and sent it to us in the hills.)

Interviewer: And was she surprised at its success?

Dr. Bannerman: Yes, I think she was. I don't think she would have expected it to catch on really at all, especially when all the publishers refused it to begin with.

Interviewer: Who suggested to her that they should be published?

Dr. Bannerman: She was somebody who visited our house and she and her husband were going home on leave, and she said she thought it ought to be published, and my mother was a bit doubtful whether anybody would want it, but she said 'Let me have the manuscript to take home with me,' and she went round the various publishing houses to see if she could get it taken on.

Interviewer: And her subsequent books?

Dr. Bannerman: Her subsequent books got in quite easily because as soon as Little Black Sambo had been a success, you see, the publishers were quite willing to have the later ones. The later ones brought in a great deal more money because the copyright had to be sold of Black Sambo before it was published, but he opened the door for the later books.

Elizabeth Gard: It's not difficult to see why Little Black Sambo has always been the favourite. The story is simpler and less gruesome than in the later books—yet it is eventful enough. Each picture exactly illustrates a moment in the story. There is none of the self-indulgence one finds in so many modern children's books, where a whimsical insubstantial text wisps around illustrations of great beauty but little narrative point. The simple words, and the highly effective repetition—each tiger growling identically "Little Black Sambo, I'm going to eat you up" rivet the attention of both reader and listener. Mrs. Bannerman seems to have fallen completely instinctively into just the right style for children.

Dr. Bannerman: Well, of course, she was accustomed to talking to us children in language that we could understand, and I suppose that made it so that other children could too.

Interviewer: But if you compare them with other children's books of that period, at the turn of the century, even Beatrix Potter contains a lot of words which children didn't understand, and which obviously she realised they wouldn't, like 'soporific' and words like this that your mother always seems to avoid.

Dr. Bannerman: Well, my mother always tried to avoid writing for grown-ups; she said she was quite aware that grown-ups prefer other pastel colours and that sort of thing but that she had found that children liked bright and garish colours, and so she always painted the pictures to suit the children and not to catch the eye of the grown-ups. And I suppose it was the same with the wording of it.

Elizabeth Gard: There's another important aspect in which I find Helen Bannerman's books are instinctively well judged, perfectly attuned to children's needs. They are all frightening—not frightening enough to upset or disturb children, but just frightening enough to excite them. One recurrent theme is the devouring of small and helpless creatures by large and savage beasts. The books are full of threatened and actual gobblings, and miraculous regurgitations.

There are one or two really violent episodes. In *Little Black Quasha* the tigers fight to the death over the right to eat her up. "Ears and tails were flying through the air, hair and blood were strewn upon the ground"—and strewn upon the printed page. In *Little Black Mingo,* the baleful crocodile (the old Mugger) swallows the cruel old woman Black Noggy, and the kerosene and matches she is carrying. The kerosene explodes inside the Mugger's 'dark inside' and both the wicked characters are blown into little bits. (All the wicked characters in these books end up in little bits). And there in the following illustration are all the gory fragments spattered across the page. In the last picture, Mingo and her friend the mongoose, without any sign of squeamishness, are sitting on the Mugger's fearsome head, having a cup of tea. David Holbrook, a well-known educationalist, considers it "a shattering story; Timon of Athens for toddlers", but advises parents not to flinch from it.

From The Story of Little Black Sambo *(1899).*

I agree with him. In my experience children relish a certain amount of gruesome detail. Savage instincts and frightening fantasies are already there in the child's imagination. Games about giants, witches and tigers, and stories like these, help to release and contain their fantasies. They also help children to place the violence they are more or less bound to see on television. And *Little Black Mingo* is nothing like, say, 'Struwwelpeter' or The Tinder Box. The innocent and helpless always escape, and the violence is confined to the animal world.

But Helen Bannerman did write one book, not now available, which I wouldn't want to show my children. Called *Little Kettle Head,* it is about a little girl (a little white girl), who pulls a pan of boiling water down from the stove, and has her head burnt off. A kind Indian servant makes her a new wooden head and fixes it to her truncated neck. "But she doesn't like it, and she cries and cries." That night as she lies miserably in bed, her own dear little head is miraculously returned to her. There it lies on a chair, with its fair hair spread out, and a faint smile upon its lips. It really is a grotesque book, and quite without the irony which marks others of the Cautionary Tale genre—Hillaire Belloc of course, and even that Edwardian curio *Ruthless Rhymes for Heartless Homes.*

It's an interesting fact that Helen Bannerman's books about animals only, and about white children—*Little White Squibba* was another—were comparative failures. I wonder why she usually chose to write about black children.

Dr. Bannerman: I think probably it was just she felt it made it more interesting to a child, and I don't think black had any unpleasant significance at that time. The Indians that we used to meet were quite prepared to talk about black, without feeling that there was anything derogatory in the word; I think the derogatory idea crept in later.

Interviewer: Because now there's so much uneasiness isn't there, that your mother's books are banned in the United States?

Dr. Bannerman: United States they are banned, and I did hear of some . . . out there where they've changed all the pictures of *Little Black Sambo* to make him a white child.

Interviewer: Little White Sambo.

Dr. Bannerman: I suppose they probably just call him Little Sambo. I don't know why if they object to his being a little black, because you'd never get a white child called Sambo.

Interviewer: No; well, it was a term of slightly patronising endearment I suppose, like 'piccanniny', wasn't it, and yet there is nothing of the slight feel of patronisation that you get in some other old-fashioned children's books about coloured children, like Epaminondas, and one very strange Victorian book called The Story of the Naughty Little Coloured Coon, which I can quite see why people might object to.

Dr. Bannerman: No, I don't think she had any sort of colour prejudice, and I think it was just to make it an interesting story for children. Perhaps she felt that a black child was a more romantic figure for a white child to read about.

Interviewer: I find that my children never even remark on this at all, and this is the experience of nursery-school teachers.

Dr. Bannerman: I think it's the grown-ups who are affected by that. And there again, it's probably this business of writing for the child rather than the grown-ups.

Interviewer: Were you ever given any reason by the American publishers as to why . . .

Dr. Bannerman: Well, there was one cutting that we got which said that it was rather apt to inculcate racial and religious intolerance, but I've never understood why that should be. I suppose it was because black was considered a derogatory word, and as far as the religious thing went, the only thing I could think of is that his parents are called Black Jumbo and Black Mumbo, and that Mumbo-Jumbo is connected with religious intolerance, but otherwise I can see no connection with religion one way or the other.

Elizabeth Gard: It seems absurd that an innocent production like Little Black Sambo should be fastidiously discarded—a ludicrously irrelevant gesture of apology for years of injustice. But **Little Black Sambo** will undoubtedly survive this muddled disapproval. He presides over the usual collection of by-products which surround popular children's classics. Dr. Bannerman remembers playing with toy figures of Sambo and the tiger. I remember sitting at a table-cloth with all the pictures blazoned round the edge. There have been cardboard cut-outs, gramophone records, and a Disney film, and now they're talking about nursery wallpaper. Little Black Sambo is big business. (pp. 185-90)

Elizabeth Gard, *"Bits Strewn All Over the Page,"* in Suitable for Children?: Controversies in Children's Literature, *edited by Nicholas Tucker, University of California Press, 1976, pp. 184-90.*

SELMA G. LANES

Once upon a time there was a little black boy and his name was Little Black Sambo. He enjoyed a mild success both in England, where he was first published in 1899, and, in translation, on the Continent. His truly remarkable success, however, came in the United States, where for a long while he was the only little black boy to appear as the hero of any book, for children or adults. Surprisingly, to those readers with a long-standing affection for Little Black Sambo, he has not been made an honorary member of the NAACP. In fact, for some twenty years now, he has been the object of a concerted cold-shoulder campaign by that organization and others, their aim being his exclusion from schools, libraries and publishers' juvenile lists throughout the land. The grounds are that Helen Bannerman, his creator, presents in her drawings an unflattering stereotype of black people, that her names are disrespectful, and that her protagonists therefore are meant to be objects of ridicule rather than genuine heroes or heroines. (pp. 158-59)

Little Black Sambo's ardent defenders are always quick to point out that his homeland is India. "After all," they say, "the story isn't even about Negroes." But if it is not, we may legitimately inquire why Mumbo, Jumbo and Little Black Sambo have such distinctly African features. Surely Mrs. Bannerman had Indians enough around her in Bombay or Madras to achieve better likenesses. The fact is, the book was conceived elsewhere.

Little Black Sambo was written not in India but in England during Mrs. Bannerman's trip home to place her two young daughters in school at Edinburgh. Feeling lonely on her return train ride to London, she wrote and illustrated **Sambo** to send as part of a letter. Why Mrs. Bannerman, sketching from memory, should depict black people as she did may well be explained by the fact that she herself had memories of a

different black population. As the daughter of a clergyman who was also an Army chaplain, she had spent the impressionable years of her childhood in various parts of the British Empire. Between the ages of two and ten she had lived on Madeira, off the west coast of Africa, where black Africans were a sizable element in a mixed population. Surely the dress of her Black Jumbo is more appropriate to a black man of such a semi-tropical, cosmopolitan locale (the West Indies suggested themselves before one knew Mrs. Bannerman's history) than to a native of remotest India. And the characters' names—Black Mumbo and Black Jumbo—which bring to mind the phrase "mumbo-jumbo" (a synonym for gibberish in English), again are more African than Indian in origin, a *mumbo jumbo* being the tribal medicine man of central Africa who protected his people from evil. There is little doubt that Mrs. Bannerman drew her characters as she did not out of malice but because she was a conventional product of her era. A proper English gentlewoman of the '90s, one of the sustainers if not builders of the British Empire, she no doubt saw one dark-skinned non-Englishman as looking much like another. Indians and African blacks were readily and innocently confused in her mind.

Beyond the names and drawings in **Little Black Sambo,** surely nothing suggests a white-supremacist attitude. There is neither dialect nor anything in the least demeaning in the behavior of any character. Sambo's quick wit in moments of dire stress would be the envy of many a diplomat today. In a subsequent story by Mrs. Bannerman—**Kettlehead**—a small white heroine is far less sympathetically drawn. A foolish and disobedient child, she loses her head, in actuality, because she persists in disobeying her mother's warning to avoid playing with fire. Given a kettle by a frightened Indian servant who wishes to help her conceal the disastrous loss, Kettlehead easily fools her dull-witted English parents. They merely find it odd that their daughter never removes her sunbonnet any more (it secures the kettle to her neck!). Perhaps in later years Mrs. Bannerman herself even comprehended something of the unconscious condescension of specifying Sambo as "black," for among her papers when she died was found another story, unpublished during her lifetime, titled **Little White Squibba** (as if to balance things on the eternal scales of Justice), in which a small English heroine follows exactly Sambo's course into the jungle but ends up, British-style, inviting all the hungry tigers home to tea.

Far more interesting than the Sambo story itself (a good one by any fair picture-book standards) are the reasons for its phenomenal success in the United States. Surely it had something to do with the fact that, for the first time, a story had caught American parents and children off their guard, allowing them to recognize freely the humanity of black people. . . . We could all approve of Sambo and his family without feeling either guilty or anxious. Quick wit and intelligence were no threat in a black boy from the primitive and faraway land of tigers, as they might have been in someone black walking down an American city street. Just as nature abhors a vacuum, so the human soul rebels against evasion and dishonesty. By the time Sambo arrived on these shores, the slaves had been free for some forty years. Thousands of blacks had left the plantations of the rural South to form an observable element in most cities' populations. Yet they might all have been invisible for the recognition they received as fellow human beings in white America. Sambo was taken to everyone's heart precisely because he allowed us to acknowledge what we knew inside but avoided confronting:

that black people were human beings just like us. In loving Sambo unreservedly, in some way every white had the feeling that he was also accepting the black man as a fellow human being. The nursery bookshelf was integrated, and no prejudice could be said to exist in a home where *Little Black Sambo* and *Peter Rabbit* stood side by side on the same shelf.

Because *Little Black Sambo* unquestionably helped white American children and adults to see black people in a new way, possibly for the first time, the book was, on the whole, a positive force. . . . (pp. 159-62)

As a teaching tool for white children, then, surely Sambo rated A-plus in his day. (p. 162)

[Sambo] was black, the hero of a beautifully satisfying picture book and, as such, justly loved in his time. Realities and even fantasies shift, however, and those of the 1970s, for parents and children, have moved a great distance from Sambo's lush green jungles to ones much bleaker, more menacing and closer to home. As a period piece—a relic of days when tigers roamed free outside of wild-animal refuges and mothers made pancakes from scratch—the work deserves to be preserved. As a fond memory of those of us over thirty, and white, it is unlikely to be forgotten. For the rest, one picture book is not worth a thousand angry protests. Let Sambo be consigned to literary history. (pp. 163-64)

> *Selma G. Lanes, "Black Is Bountiful," in her* Down the Rabbit Hole: Adventures & Misadventures in the Realm of Children's Literature, *Atheneum Publishers, 1971, pp. 158-78.*

BRIDGET HARRIS

[*The following excerpt is from a letter by Bridget Harris, the Honorary Organizing Secretary of* Teachers Against Racism (TAR), *to Ian Parsons, chairman of Chatto and Windus, Bannerman's British publishers. Dated 31 March 1972, the letter was prompted by an advertisement for a new boxed edition of Bannerman's books. TAR also sent a copy of their letter to Brian Alderson, the children's book editor of the London* Times, *who responded with the article "Banning Bannerman" on 12 April 1972. Bridget Harris's reply in the correspondence columns of the* Times *on 24 April 1972 stimulated a debate that caused a reassessment of Bannerman's works by librarians, teachers, and critics.*]

We wish to register a strong protest against (a) the continued publication and distribution of the Helen Bannerman books and (b) your recent issue of the boxed set of these books. In the multi-racial society which exists in Britain today, these books are both damaging and dangerous.

Teachers Against Racism is strongly opposed to the continued distribution of these books particularly *Little Black Sambo, Sambo and the Twins, Little Black Quibba, Little Black Quasha,* and *Little White Squibba.*

In all of these books the underlying racist message is made all the more sinister by their appearance of innocence and charm. Along with the whimsical stories the reader swallows wholesale a totally patronising attitude towards black people who are shown as greedy (Black Sambo eats 169 pancakes), stereotyped happy, clownish, irresponsible plantation "niggers"—they are shown giving their children away, and jumping for joy at the slightest provocation throughout all the books.

All black adults are portrayed as having the minds of chil-

dren, and the clear insinuation is that all blacks live in jungles with tigers etc.

The drawings in all the 'Little Black . . . ' books are racist caricatures; although they are supposed to take place in India (Ghee and Tigers) the people are shown as Kentucky Pancake House Niggers with rolling eyes, watermelon smiles, and comically fuzzy hair. Contrast this with *Little White Squibba* clearly written as a conciliatory sop, but failing utterly in so far as the illustrations are pictures and not caricatured cartoons.

The names of the characters throughout the series reinforce patronising and racist attitudes towards black people, viz: Sambo, Mumbo, Jumbo, Little Black Rag, Little Black Tag, Moof and Woof, etc.

We feel most strongly that these books which foster basic racist attitudes in children should be withdrawn at once from circulation and removed from children's libraries and schools.

We should be interested to hear your views on the subject. (pp. 165-66)

> *Bridget Harris, in a letter to Ian Parsons on March 31, 1972, in* Sambo Sahib: The Story of Little Black Sambo and Helen Bannerman *by Elizabeth Hay, Barnes & Noble, 1981, pp. 165-66.*

BRIAN ALDERSON

Commentators on modern children's books tend to be enthusiastic, if not always accurate, about *Little Black Sambo.* "A riotous frolic", says Mr Frank Eyre in his *British Children's Books in the Twentieth Century*, "that has entertained children and parents for 50 years"—(should be 70); and: "an absurd, delightful, unforgettable tale", says Mr Marcus Crouch in *Treasure Seekers and Borrowers*, noting its tremendous popularity and that of its four sequels—(should be six).

Chatto's share the critics' delight in the book—not uninfluenced by the fact that it sells thousands of copies each year—and they are now encouraging further interest in it by marketing complete sets of the "Little Black Sambo" series: seven volumes in a decorated box for £2.85.

The Little Black Sambo books are not without their detractors however. Even Frank Eyre regrets the appearance of *Little Black Quibba* "which was repetitive of earlier work", and some sensitive souls have found the battle of the tigers in *Little Black Quasha* a scene conducive to nightmares—heads, paws and tails flying about as though a bomb had hit a tiger-rug factory.

Coinciding with the appearance of the Black Sambo Box though has come an altogether more radical criticism: Mrs Bannerman's books have now been found to have an "underlying racist message" which is "made all the more sinister by their appearance of innocence and charm". They are books "which foster basic racist attitudes in children" and "should be withdrawn at once from circulation and removed from children's libraries and schools".

The tigerish zeal on this occasion comes from the Central Committee of Teachers Against Racism, who do not define very clearly what is meant by "fostering a basic racist attitude", but who are specific enough about the books' faults: "their patronizing attitude towards black people", their illustrations, which are "racist caricatures", and their use of such names as Sambo, Mumbo, Jumbo, etc. which "reinforce patronizing and racist attitudes towards black people".

All this concern over attitudes may appear surprising to those who had thought with Margery Fisher that *Little Black Sambo* was the "best of all repetitive tales for the young", or with Elaine Moss, that "this is a perfect story". Can such discriminating ladies really be so insensitive to "racist caricatures", or is the Central Committee of TAR (!) in danger of letting its passionate commitment to social justice distort its view of Helen Bannerman's intentions and achievement?

After all, once external considerations are allowed to affect our criteria for judging texts, critical anarchy supervenes. Billy Bunter is banned because there are fat boys in Ipswich, the Bastables are frowned on for their deplorable view of Woman's Place in Society, and, for all I know, Helen Bannerman is also condemned by conservationist associations for allowing such dreadful things to happen to her tigers, polarbears, snakes and crocodiles.

Nor, I fear, will modification do much good. The balance which an author achieves in a successful text, or an illustrator in a progression of drawings, is often a good deal more subtle than is credited, and latter-day Bowdlers are as ham-fisted among children's books as elsewhere.

The issue which TAR have raised is not really to be resolved by the banning of Bannerman, but by acknowledging the qualities that have given her books their popularity and by encouraging people to see the complete context in which they stand. For these unpretentious little stories do not take themselves seriously enough to warrant the use of such forcefully emotive accusations as "racist", and the pleasure which children (black as well as white) gain from them is a pleasure (*pace* the tigers) of friendliness.

Had the protagonists been white, and caricatured as whites are caricatured by such illustrators as Edward Lear and Tomi Ungerer, everyone would be delighted. But because there are so few books of any real character about black children, those which offer anything more than a safe, pallid domesticity are exposed to our social critics—who, like the old lady obsessed with obscenity, are not above standing on the dresser with a powerful pair of binoculars.

By focusing on *Little Black Sambo,* Teachers Against Racism are in danger of losing their wood behind a very innocent tree, and indeed, creating racism where none hitherto existed. If they really think that Mrs Bannerman is "sinister" they might do well to look at some of the tendentious "anti-authoritarian" children's books of Western Germany, or some of the anti-Semitic picture-books of Julius Streicher's hideous *Stürmer Verlag* of the 1930s.

> Brian Alderson, "Banning Bannerman," in The Times, *London, April 12, 1972, p. 15.*

IAN PARSONS

[*The following excerpt is from a letter to Bridget Harris from the director of Chatto and Windus, Ltd, the publishers of Bannerman's books in the United Kingdom.*]

At first, your letter filled me with amazement, mingled with despair. Can it really be true, I asked myself, that responsible people could be so utterly devoid of humour, so totally without imagination, as to put forward the views that you express. So my initial reaction was to send you a one-line reply in the form of a quotation—Honi soit qui mal y pense. But on reflection it seemed to me that, however intemperate and misguided your letter might be, it had been written with deeply held conviction and for a cause which I have supported all my life. . . . I therefore felt that it merited a considered reply.

First, then, your letter proceeds with a series of categorical statements, as if they were acknowledged matters of fact, when most of them are wide open to argument, if not highly tendentious, and some of them simply untrue. I refer in the first place to phrases like 'the underlying racist message', 'a totally patronising attitude to black people', 'the clear insinuation is that all blacks live in jungles with tigers etc.'; and in the second place the statement that *Little White Squibba* was clearly written as a conciliatory sop. It wasn't. It was written, like all Mrs. Bannerman's books were written, for the enjoyment of her own children, and far from thinking of it as a 'conciliatory sop' (in which case she would naturally have published it) she put it on one side and it was only discovered among her papers long after her death.

Secondly, there is the inescapable fact that generations of children have loved *Little Black Sambo.* After close on three-quarters of a century it is still as popular today as it was when it was first published: indeed much more so. All these thousands of children, have, I am sure, accepted it as an enchanting story, an enthralling fantasy. Little Black Sambo and his parents are no more like real people than the tiger is like a real tiger.

Could a tiger turn into butter with which to make pancakes, and could any child, black or white, eat 169 of them? It is all a flight of fancy. The sad thing is that in the deplorable climate of our times it can be twisted to seem, or so you would have me believe, an attack on coloured people. More's the pity. But that's no reason why countless children of this and future generations should be denied the pleasure which time has proved that these books provide.

There is another thing, too. Once you start operating a censorship (for that's what it amounts to) of the kind you and your colleagues advocate, there is no knowing where it will stop. I imagine that you will have written similarly to Frederick Warne protesting against the continuing publication of several Beatrix Potter titles—you'll recall that *Pigling Bland* runs away with a *black* pig, who is not very clever, and that in *The Tale of Mr Tod* one of old Benjamin Bouncer's daughters had committed the unpardonable sin of marrying a *black* rabbit. Terribly racist, I fear. And equally you would have to ban yet another children's masterpiece—Joel Chandler Harris's *Nights with Uncle Remus.* And this, before one could say Brer Rabbit, would lead the R.S.P.C.A. to demand the suppression of *Alice in Wonderland* and *Alice Through the Looking Glass.* For what could be more sadistically cruel than to make animals race each other round a pool, and a pool of tears at that; or to force a live dormouse head first into a pot of tea? The R.S.P.C.A. would then feel obliged to ban Kingsley's *Water Babies,* as unfair to chimney sweeps and fostering class distinction. One could go on indefinitely, but I hope I've made my point.

Seriously, though, I think you and your colleagues should stand back and take a long, slow look at yourselves and your attitude, and ask yourselves whether in fact it is not *you* who are the racists. You who, with the very best intentions but a crippling blindness to reality, import into the innocent and unsophisticated minds of little children the idea that there is something derogatory in having a coloured skin. Frankly, it appals me that people entrusted with the upbringing of children should think this way. For all you will succeed in doing, in the end, is to add fuel to Mr Enoch Powell's fire. Do you really wish to that?' (pp. 166-67)

> Ian Parsons, in a letter to Bridget Harris on April 12, 1972, in Sambo Sahib: The Story of Little Black Sambo and Helen Bannerman *by Elizabeth Hay, Barnes & Noble, 1981, pp. 166-67.*

BRIDGET HARRIS

[*The following excerpt is from a letter to the editor of the London* Times *in response to Brian Alderson's essay "Banning Bannerman."*]

We fail to understand Brian Alderson's attitude to the Teachers Against Racism campaign against **Little Black Sambo.** Had there been a book entitled "Little Jew Ikey" nobody in Britain today would fail to identify it as racist (whether they approved or disapproved).

Further, Brian Alderson, who we understand to be an expert on children's books, cannot by the same token be unaware of the 20-year-old campaign waged by the National Association for the Advancement of Coloured People and progressive teachers' groups in the United States of America against *Little Black Sambo,* which they hold to be "the epitome of white racism in children's literature". (United States Council on Interracial Books for Children.)

Helen Bannerman's books have become both dangerous and obsolete in the multi-racial Britain of 1972 where people of good will are trying to foster *respect* for black people amongst white children, in order to avoid the kind of terrible race tension and separatism which has occurred in the United States. The so-called "friendliness" which Alderson says **Little Black Sambo** generates is in fact the friendliness of paternalism towards a "child race".

> Bridget Harris, in a review of "Little Black Sambo," in The Times, *London, April 24, 1972, p. 13.*

J. KHALIQUE

[*The following excerpt is from a letter to the editor of the London* Times.]

It is not the violence of disjointed tigers which compels one to label Mrs Bannerman's **Little Black Sambo** as racist, as much as its title. The book depicts the Negro as an almost unclothed, illiterate and inferior savage from whose antics great humour can be derived. That, contrary to B. Alderson's article, seems to be racist.

Thirteen years ago in primary school, this book was read to the class I was in and being a coloured child from Pakistan, I suddenly became a "Little Black Sambo" to my classmates. Only the development of extraordinary defensive mechanisms prevented me from going home crying or getting regularly into fights over this. Consequently the book lost its innocence quite early for me. Nor did I gain much pleasure from reading it.

I am sure that even now thousands of immigrant children will unconsciously be building psychosocial defences to racialistic remarks like "Little Black Sambo".

The removal of such books would make words like Sambo, golliwog and darkie obsolete to small children.

That in itself would be a blessing as to coloured children such words give deep offence, and to their parents such words are obscene. Any harmonious multiracial society of the near future will find books like **Little Black Sambo** intolerable.

> J. Khalique, in a review of "Little Black Sambo," in The Times, *London, April 28, 1972, p. 15.*

IAN PARSONS

[*The following excerpt is from a letter to the editor of the London* Times.]

As the publishers for well over 50 years of Helen Bannerman's books we are obviously *parti pris* in the matter currently being discussed in your columns, but I hope you will allow me to make two points that seem to me relevant.

The first is that it all behoves the Secretary of Teachers Against Racism to quote the National Association for the Advancement of Coloured Peoples' campaign in America against **Little Black Sambo** in support of her own case. For it was one of these well-meaning organizations which, a few years ago, made an egregious ass of itself by having Mark Twain's *Huckleberry Finn* withdrawn from the New York public libraries because it contained the word "nigger", and was therefore *ipso facto* "racist".

The second is that according to Mrs Natalie Hodgson, the Children's Librarian of Wolverhampton, an area noted for its high proportion of coloured inhabitants, they "never have enough copies of **Little Black Sambo** to meet the local demand. Immigrants simply love it". *Verb sap.*

> Ian Parsons, in a review of "Little Black Sambo," in The Times, *London, April 28, 1972, p. 15.*

R. B. W. BANNERMAN

[*The following excerpt is from a letter to the editor of the London* Times *from one of Helen Bannerman's sons.*]

I have been following the correspondence with interest and for the most part with pleasure, discounting the charge of racialism as mere prejudice against which it is idle to argue—so I thought until I read Mr Khalique's letter. May I offer him my sincere sympathy, I do believe that his life could have been made quite intolerable by the little savages with whom he was forced to associate at the time and who cruelly nicknamed him "Sambo". . . .

I would like to assure Mr Khalique that it is my firm belief that my mother would not have published the book had she dreamt for a moment that even one small boy would have been made unhappy thereby. She would never allow us to "do evil that good might follow", however small the evil and however great the good. And I think good has followed, for more children like Sambo than hate him.

Nevertheless, I do not accept the charge that the book is racialist. Sambo is not held up to ridicule; he wore as many clothes as I did at his age; his parents were kind and good to him, just as mine were to me; he dealt adequately not only with a bunch of tigers but also with a heap of pancakes and returned home with his clothes intact. In fact he exhibited degrees of prowess and skill far in advance of my modest achievements at the same date.

R. B. W. Bannerman, in a review of "Little Black Sambo," in The Times, *London, May 1, 1972, p. 15.*

DOROTHY KUYA

[The following excerpt is from a letter to the editor of the London Times.]

As a black Briton, born and educated in this country, I detested **LBS** as much as I did the other textbooks which presented non-white people as living entirely in primitive conditions and having no culture. I did not relate to him, but the white children in my class identified me with him.

Helen Bannerman was a typical product of the age in which she lived: then the blacks were treated with at the most contempt and at the least paternalism. She may not have been malicious but she certainly was condescending.

Little Black Sambo along with many other such books must be removed from the classrooms if *all* our children, black and white, are to grow up with an understanding and respect for each other regardless of differences of colour, creed or religion. I would not suggest we burn the books, but rather put them in a permanent exhibition along with some of the jokes of *The Comedians,* the exhibition could be titled "Echoes of Britannia's Rule"—subtitled—"Information that made the British think they were great".

Dorothy Kuya, in a review of "Little Black Sambo," in The Times, *London, May 1, 1972, p. 15.*

JANET HILL

[The following excerpt is from an article that originally appeared in the 3 November 1972 issue of the Times Literary Supplement.]

No one, least of all a librarian, could deny that [Helen Bannerman's] books are popular with children, and this is perfectly understandable. The stories have an engaging mixture of simplicity and absurdity which cannot fail to appeal, and show how well the author must have understood young children. There seems to be fairly general agreement that **Little Black Sambo** is by far the best of them, and it is the title mentioned in every reputable bibliography of children's books for the very young. . . .

However, re-evaluation of books is a continual process. How do these books look in our multi-racial society in 1972? (p. 192)

[In his *Treasure Seekers and Borrowers,* Marcus Crouch] called the illustrations "crudely drawn". They certainly are. **Little Black Sambo** as shown in full regalia on page 18 is a grinning stereotype with clownish eyes and huge mouth; the old woman on page 11 of **Little Black Quasha** turns round with a horrified face and her face is horrifying; Black Mumbo and Black Jumbo on page 82 of **Sambo and the Twins** jump for joy on hearing that the twins are safe, looking for all the world like a caricature of two cotton pickin' niggers in their gaily striped clothes. Admittedly the illustrations in **Little White Squibba** are excruciatingly badly drawn, but they are nice and dainty. To compare Squibba in her full finery on page 18 with the previously mentioned picture of Sambo is to point up the difference. She is unmistakably flesh and blood; a real human being with a dignity and poise befitting her station in life. He is an unreal caricature, less than human, with matchstick legs and golliwog face. Certainly, as

From The Story of Little Black Mingo *(1901).*

the text claims, they both look grand. What is equally certain is that they inhabit different worlds.

Just as the illustrations are best discussed by contrasting **Little White Squibba** and the other books, so is the text. Not surprisingly the condescension of the writer is shown up most clearly by Squibba. She is sent books for her birthday "about little black children who had wonderful adventures in the jungle", and wants to follow their example. Imitation may be the sincerest form of flattery, but as the astute teenagers who discussed the books pointed out, her experiences, although superficially the same as Sambo's, are in fact quite different. She confronts each animal with aplomb, forestalls every move, and calmly invites them all, including the tiger, home to afternoon tea. They have pancakes, "because that was what most of the little black children had had after their adventures". Squibba is certainly secure in her tasteful and well-ordered home, where even the pancakes have a delicacy denied those served in the jungle. Meanwhile Sambo and his friends live on in their strange quasi-African jungle home, dancing around barefoot, surrounded by Indian tigers and eating mangoes and pancakes.

Seen in this light I believe that the stories are condescending and patronizing. I would not cite individual incidents so much as the entire ambience of the books, particularly as thrown into relief by *Little White Squibba.* The ambience of a book is sometimes a difficult thing to pinpoint, as anyone who has tried to prove that the ambience of so many English children's books is comfortably middle-class will realize. I freely admit that my own views about these books have changed, and that I championed *Little Black Sambo* in print some years ago, so that I can recognize that it is probably difficult for those of us who are white and care about children's books to see them as other than charming little stories. To call Helen Bannerman consciously racist is absurd. However, to recognize that her books are just another expression of benevolent paternalism, the more insulting for its benevolence, is merely to show awareness of the deep roots of racism in our history, culture and language. Her *outlook* is certainly racist in the context of today. (pp. 194-95)

Helen Bannerman's books have had a long life, and the time has come to consign them to oblivion. They should have no place in a multi-racial society. What was it Marcus Crouch said? "Throughout the history of children's literature, books have appeared which have had a success out of all proportion to their artistic merits." They have had a fuss out of all proportion, too. (p. 196)

> Janet Hill, "Oh! Please Mr. Tiger," in Suitable for Children?: Controversies in Children's Literature, edited by Nicholas Tucker, University of California Press, 1976, pp. 191-96.

JESSIE M. BIRTHA

[*The following excerpt is from an essay by a black librarian who acted as a children's books selection specialist for the Free Library of Philadelphia.*]

I think that the story of *Little Black Sambo* was and is an entertaining story for small children, *but* the development of circumstances concerning the Sambo tradition has been unfortunate. The usefulness of *Little Black Sambo* is dead. The acceptability of *Little Black Sambo* is dead. The story itself is not about an African child. It is about a child in India, and contains little in the slight plot that is objectionable, although as racial sensitivity and pride grew, the book has been dissected and all manner of symbolism attributed to its motivation, including sexual. However, a librarian will never offer this book to a black child if he stops to realize that the name Sambo has been used so often to refer to a Negro in a derogatory sense. . . .

The argument has been offered, children don't know or care about the background of a name. They only listen to the story. But it has been proved—and experienced—that if a story of this type is used in an integrated story hour or classroom, there is a certain amount of discomfort and—yes, inferiority feeling—for a black child when white classmates look at him and giggle, later teasing him by calling him Sambo. No matter how entertaining a book is, one group of children should never be entertained at the expense of another group's feelings. (p. 153)

> Jessie M. Birtha, "Portrayal of the Black in Children's Literature (excerpt)," in The Black American in Books for Children: Readings in Racism, edited by Donnarae MacCann and Gloria Woodard, The Scarecrow Press, Inc., 1972, pp. 153-55.

JUSTIN G. SCHILLER

[In] 1899 *Black Sambo* was a revolutionary-style picture book. Compared with its contemporary school of illustra-tors—Crane, Greenaway, Caldecott—the pictures are simple yet bold. The format of the book encouraged its handling by young owners, and the pages alternated between text and illustrations in a manner very appealing and appropriate to its compact size. It even seems probable that Beatrix Potter's animal books, which began in 1901 with the privately printed *Peter Rabbit,* were at least influenced by the overall design of this book. . . . (pp. 381-82)

> Justin G. Schiller, "The Story of Little Black Sambo," in The Book Collector, Vol. 23, No. 3, Autumn, 1974, pp. 381-86.

MARJORIE McDONALD

[*The following excerpt is from a paper presented by Dr. Mc-Donald at the conference of the American Academy of Child Psychiatry in 1973.*]

The power of *Little Black Sambo* lies in its roots in the unconscious regions of deeply repressed childhood fantasies and conflicts. . . . *Little Black Sambo* presents an appeal to unconscious wellsprings of prejudice while safeguarding against their eruption into consciousness. (At least until recently this was so.) (p. 514)

Sambo was written as a creative effort to master a most painful separation. Judging from the story [Mrs. Bannerman wrote for her daughters], I would assume that the children must have been very young and the pain of parting very acute. Although the separation was rationalized as necessary for the children's development, one of the mother's preoccupations on her lonely journey homeward probably concerned the adequacy of her preparation of her two small daughters for their venture alone into the world. (p. 515)

Disguised in [the] jungle drama of *Little Black Sambo* is the story of a small child's reactions to seeing the primal scene. Sambo, helplessly looking on at the fighting tigers, is the little child transfixed as he watches his parents in intercourse. No longer is he the manly little adventurer, the master of his own fate who can even outwit tigers. The final surrender of his umbrella—the symbol of his masculinity—marked the destruction of that illusion, and without his protective umbrella Sambo gets wet—for it is just then in the story that Sambo starts to cry.

In his regressed and frightened state, without his clothes or umbrella, Sambo hears a horrible "Gr-r-rrr" and fears the tigers are coming back to eat him up. But this clever little fellow does not even run away to save himself. Instead he hides behind a palm tree and "peeps" out to watch the tigers fighting over who is the grandest. This interpretation of the fight as a narcissistic struggle for power is the most likely explanation the little boy can think of for a fight. It also reveals that the child feels *himself* to be the instigator of the disturbance. After all, is it not Sambo's finery that causes the tigers to quarrel over who is the grandest?

The primal scene continues as the tigers take off their clothes and claw and bite each other. Then they come rolling and tumbling right to the foot of Sambo's tree. That is to say, the little onlooker feels himself being engulfed in the excitement. But Sambo is ignored as the tigers catch hold of each other's tails in their mouths, wrangle and scramble, and form a ring around the tree. This is a child's conception of intercourse, in which both parents, with their tiger tails, are portrayed as phallic and intercourse is performed using the mouth.

Next the reader is informed that the tigers appear "wee and far away," although strangely enough they are not in fact moving into the distance. It must really be the little child who feels "wee and far away," lonely and excluded from this strange fight that is going on between his parents. It is just at this moment of feeling deserted that Sambo jumps out of his hiding place and calls out to the tigers to ask why they have taken off their clothes (no—not *his* clothes!) and whether they don't want them any more. He must be the frightened child who feels his parents may not want *him* any more. The tigers hear Sambo call to them, but they will not let go of each other's tails so they respond to him with a "Gr-r-r-rrr." The angry parents growl at the child who is interrupting their lovemaking, but their growls must further convince the child that the parents are in a fight and that he has something to do with it because they are angry at *him.*

The tigers continue running round and round the tree, trying to eat each other up—"whirling around so fast that you couldn't have seen their legs at all." At the climax they all melt away "and there was nothing left but a great big pool of melted butter around the foot of the tree." But just as it was Sambo, not the tigers, who was "wee and far away," so it must be Sambo who has made the big pool of melted butter, for in his excitement Sambo must have lost control and urinated. He has lost his umbrella, the powerful phallus which would give him control and protect him from the rain of his urination. The author's illustrations intuitively expose this conflict by drawing the umbrella in a fully open position. In the scene where Sambo watches the fighting tigers he is hiding behind the open umbrella holding it with the handle extended in front of him, symbolizing his erection. (pp. 518-20)

After the primal scene has ended the parents in their undisguised form suddenly reappear in the story. The sexual excitement of the wild animals is over and once again they are human and civilized—"the right kind of parents, just the kind every child would like to have." To interpret [May Hill] Arbuthnot's remark, every child wants to deny his parents' sexuality.

Black Jumbo, on his way home from work, just happens to pass by with a big brass pot in which he collects the "lovely melted butter" to take home to Black Mumbo. Black Mumbo makes pancakes with flour, eggs, and sugar, and fries them in the melted tiger butter, which makes the pancakes "just as yellow and brown as little tigers." Black Mumbo ate 27 pancakes, Black Jumbo ate 55, "but Little Black Sambo ate a hundred and sixty-nine, because he was so hungry."

It hardly comes as a surprise to find that the aftermath of the primal scene is little tigers—babies. And these babies have been conceived, according to a child's theory of creation, by the father's urinating into the mother. The melted butter is symbolically put into the big brass pot. In a restatement, the butter is combined with eggs—in the pancakes—and the result is yellow and brown little tigers.

The eating of the pancakes, like the tigers' threats to eat Black Sambo, further symbolize oral conception. Probably the brown color in the yellow and brown little tigers symbolizes the completion of the child's gastrointestinal theory of creation. The orally conceived baby is delivered anally, like brown feces. That Little Black Sambo is the hungriest and eats the most pancakes is simply a child's longing to be able to make a baby himself. With the abundant gratification of

this wish 169 times over, the story comes to an end. At least it ends for about 40 years, until its sequel appears in 1936.

The small detail of why there are four, not two, tigers requires clarification. The changed number of course protects the disguised identity of the two parents. In addition, this multiplier of two seems to balance another numerical disguise which relies upon a divisor of two. The author's two little girls become the solitary Sambo of the story. The detail that Black Mumbo is illustrated as fat can now be interpreted as representing her pregnancy.

As Arbuthnot implies, the "repetitive cadence of colors" in the story is very important. The colors are vivid and cheerful, reflecting the good spirits of the story and contrasting with the black skin color of the characters. Whatever the racial implications (to be discussed later), the bright colors seem to achieve a reversal of affect which successfully defends against the intrusion of the author's underlying black mood of loneliness and sadness into the story.

Surely this psychoanalytic revelation of the concealed primal scene story can only enhance the reader's respect for *Little Black Sambo.* In the "extreme simplicity" and "effortless perfection" with which the story reaches to the depths of the human personality it well deserves its rating as a classic that could be mistaken for folklore. Moreover, it merits a further investigation—beyond the content of the story to the author who created it. How was Helen Bannerman able to write this story?

It is known that she produced *Sambo* following a painful separation from her two small daughters and also from Scotland, her native country and her home for the first two years of her life. When she wrote it she was traveling, something she had often done as a child, so that the traveling itself must easily have called up early separations. Furthermore, her loneliness must have been intensified by the fact that she was traveling alone; presumably her husband was in India awaiting her return.

The author's concern about having prepared her children for their new life without their parents underlies the opening of the Sambo story. But quickly the primal scene takes over. Is it not reasonable to suppose that in this primal scene the author, like any mother who has just sent a child off to school, is expressing a wish to replace her lost children with a new baby? The natural wish of the grown woman to return to her husband and to become pregnant then finds unconscious reinforcement in repressed primal scene memories from early childhood. No longer is it just the author's children, but now it must become the author herself who is the left-out and frightened little onlooker at the vividly portrayed primal scene. And it is her own childhood sexuality which then gives the compelling foundation to her story. The story reveals the typical coexisting wishes of a little girl to be a boy, but also to be able to have a baby herself. In the "*lovely* melted butter" there is the wishful denial of the loss of control and shame in the wetting that follows the masturbatory excitement of the primal scene. But in the loss of the umbrella and the ensuing wetting there is the crying little girl's recognition of her genitals as castrated. The masturbatory guilt at this castration, however, is not clearly identifiable in the story, and this omission will require an explanation later.

The question can be raised whether the *Sambo* story draws upon an actual witnessing of parental intercourse or only a childhood fantasy about it. The vivid technicolor portrayal and the quality of Sambo's ego state—he is an intense, frozen, peeping onlooker—leave little doubt, for me at least, that the author is indeed drawing upon her own childhood visual experience and not merely a fantasy. It is not possible to reconstruct more specifically the connections in the author's early childhood between primal scene exposure and separations. Both situations have in common the arousal of lonely, left-out, and lost feelings. *Perhaps* they might have occurred together, during the disorganization of family life that comes with moving. *Perhaps* a primal scene exposure could have happened at 2 years of age during the departure from Scotland—her birthplace and her homeland—but this is mere speculation.

However, I believe it is a reliable conclusion that it was the indispensable contribution from her own unconscious that enabled the author to write *Little Black Sambo.* It is a universal story of childhood sexuality, presented in palatable disguise. It holds an appeal not just for the author's children but for children everywhere, and especially *white* children in the United States. (pp. 520-22)

The impassioned rejection of *Little Black Sambo* by American Negroes, and more recently by sympathetic whites as well, cannot possibly be denied. Regretfully it has to be accepted that somewhere in this children's classic there must lie some justification for its "racist" reputation. . . . [There] is little overt racism in the story. But even when it is subjected to a psychoanalytic interpretation, there still appears to be no obvious evidence of racism. All that psychoanalysis reveals is a fascinating glimpse of childhood sexuality. *Sambo* is just a story of growing up, of separation, of a primal scene and conception, and of childhood excitement and castration anxiety. It is a story of childhood sexuality in disguise. *But it is just this unconscious childhood sexuality that underlies Sambo's racism!*

The book is the story of a little *black* boy's sexuality. That the author has "woven the word *black* into her repetitive cadence of colors" is not mere chance. The black skin color is an essential element in the story and the cadence of brightly colored clothing helps to underscore that the story is about *color.* The "racial" message of *Sambo* is that forbidden sexuality belongs to little *black* boys and their families.

The white reader uses this story to deny his own childhood sexuality. *Sambo* reassures him that the sexual thoughts and feelings of childhood belong just to primitive black people from the jungle, not to civilized white Americans. However, underneath the skin black people are no different from white, and they too would like to deny childhood sexuality. The story of *Sambo* is for blacks a blatant contradiction of that denial because it assigns the forbidden sexuality specifically to people with their own black skin color. Thus the black reader's rejection of *Sambo* resembles the impassioned rejection which greeted Freud's discovery of infantile sexuality.

Now the difficult question must be raised whether the author of *Little Black Sambo* was racially prejudiced. It has to be acknowledged that *unconsciously* this white woman, in racially segregated India, projected childhood sexuality onto a black figure. Furthermore, her story of "Little Kettle-Head," who suffers a castration for poking at forbidden fires, affirms that sexuality is taboo for a little *white* girl. (Probably it is more taboo for girls than for boys, too.) But is this evidence of prejudice?

Would it not be more reasonable to judge Mrs. Bannerman on the basis of her conscious thought and deed rather than her unconscious primary process displacement of sexuality onto skin color? The little evidence available suggests that she led a highly worthwhile life which was directly beneficial to India's dark-skinned poor people. It might even be that the creative discharge of her unconscious childhood conflicts in *Little Black Sambo* liberated her from their detrimental influence upon her conscious life, thus preventing the formation of a prejudice.

In the unlikely event that Mrs. Bannerman lived long enough to see the tragic fate of Sambo, by now a quite elderly gentleman, it must have caused her great agony. Like peace-loving Alfred Nobel, appalled at the destructive power of the dynamite he had discovered, Helen Bannerman would, I believe, be appalled at the destructive turn taken by the elemental forces in her story.

To achieve an understanding of a creative author is an enriching experience for a psychoanalyst. But in the case of *Little Black Sambo* the achievement is tempered by the frustration that enlightenment brings no solution. Indeed, it is not possible to improve on Arbuthnot's reluctant recommendation: "If 'black' applied to people is a cause of grief to some of our children, then the book should be omitted from school lists." It remains for future generations to abolish the color line and restore *Sambo* to its rightful position as a classic "modern fairy tale." (pp. 526-28)

> *Marjorie McDonald, " 'Little Black Sambo',," in*
> The Psychoanalytic Study of the Child, Vol. 29,
> *Yale University Press, 1974, pp. 511-28.*

MARGERY FISHER

[*Little Black Sambo*] has the simplicity and shapeliness of a folk tale and it is far removed from everyday life in India or anywhere else. Various elements in the story commend it for reading aloud—the artfully easy repetition, the enumeration of the little boy's grand new clothes and the suspense as he losses them one by one till his own safety is put in doubt; while the grotesque, primary-coloured pictures, with their exaggeration of facial expression and posture, seem congenial to children in the same way as the crude dramatic style of *Struwwelpeter.* The story has a clear literary form, the robbing of Sambo being balanced by the ending in which his enemies provide him with his favourite supper.

None of the books that followed has the stylistic inevitability of *Little Black Sambo,* though they have similar macabre and economically sensational plots. They have often been criticized for these elements but children continue to enjoy fantasy scenes of dismemberment and similar disasters.

A far more serious criticism of the stories [is] that they disseminate racist attitudes among children. . . . It is obvious that Helen Bannerman had no intention of drawing deliberately offensive stereotypes of black characters, verbal or visual; it is equally clear that she wrote from the point of view of her period and not ours. . . . Ideally one would hope that *Little Black Sambo* could always be read in the way it was originally written, as a comic and neatly planned cumulative tale whose characters belong to the world of fantasy and not to the world of the listener (whether an English child, an American, an Indian or a member of any race or colour). While the multi-racial societies of the world are still in the sensitive process of settling down, this seems an unsuitable book to read aloud to a class or to be presented in any way that will suggest its relevance to particular children. As a folk tale, it belongs in any case rather to the nursery, to be shared by mother and child in an atmosphere where, one could hope, misunderstanding and false impressions could be avoided, and where it could be enjoyed as a piece of comic fantasy.

> *Margery Fisher, "Who's Who in Children's Books: Little Black Sambo," in her* Who's Who in Children's Books: A Treasury of the Familiar Characters of Childhood, *Holt, Rinehart and Winston, 1975, p. 174.*

PHYLLIS J. YUILL

Over seventy-five years after original publication, **The Story of Little Black Sambo** holds a unique place in the history of children's literature, not only as an exceedingly popular story which fell into disrepute, but as a symbol of the value judgments faced by librarians, teachers, and parents when evaluating children's books in relation to heightened social awareness. (p. 1)

What is the special appeal that made **The Story of Little Black Sambo** such a phenomenal success? It has all the elements of a good story for young children: a sympathetic hero, simple and exciting plot, repetitive rhythm, abundant action, and a satisfying conclusion. . . .

[Its] innovative format has also been noted by British experts in children's literature and most recently by the U.S. bookseller and antiquarian Justin Schiller. . . . (p. 7)

Another point in the book's favor was its directness and lack of sentimentality. In an article in *Harper's* on the topic of superfluous emotion in children's books, author Phyllis McGinley commented:

> And at the very lowest age-levels there is no better book that I can think of than **Little Black Sambo,** which is no more sentimental than *The Way of All Flesh.*

An examination of all of Bannerman's stories reveals no gushy emotionalism or "sweetening" of any kind. In fact, the two Sambo stories are the mildest of the lot. In the others, there are gory and violent acts portrayed in text and pictures. In **Little Black Mingo,** a wicked old woman is swallowed by a crocodile and both are blown to bits in an explosion. **Little Black Quibba** includes a scene in which an evil snake and elephant are pulled apart and dropped onto sharp rocks from a cliff. **Little Kettlehead** is about a naughty white girl whose head is burned off in the kitchen fire. In **The Teasing Monkey,** falling rocks and coconuts injure a greedy bear and dangerous lions. Perhaps most gory is the scene in **Little Black Quasha** when a group of menacing tigers are provoked into fighting each other: "Ears and tails were flying in the air, hair and blood were strewn upon the ground." Even in the less violent **Little Black Bobtail,** a pursuing polar bear is shot by a cannon. In all of the stories with black children, the hero or heroine survives the threat of death by vicious animals.

Another appealing factor may have been that Sambo and the other children act alone, or with the help of friendly animals, but without adult intervention. Sambo is the only character with a happy home life; the others are orphans or have no visible parents, although one has a sick mother. The sense of independence and adventure may have stimulated young listeners or readers. (p. 8)

Possibly, the popularity of **Sambo** was due to an *acceptance*

of racism and a fascination with the distorted images of blacks presented by the entertainment industry. (p. 9)

Certainly [the] fascination with black people as naive, carefree, humorous characters must have had some influence on the popular regard for **Little Black Sambo,** especially since so many versions of **Sambo** (eleven were published in only five years between 1930 and 1935) changed the locale to Africa or the southern U.S. Rather than providing a more realistic basis for looking at black people, as [Selma G.] Lanes assumes, perhaps **Sambo** fit quite easily into the popular public image. (p. 10)

At first, **The Story of Little Black Sambo** was considered to be an exemplary model of a fresh, *positive* image for black children, when compared with the more negative books of the period, and in spite of the Indian locale of the original and "authorized version," its presence was accepted on lists of African American orientation. (p. 11)

Publicly stated objections to **Little Black Sambo** began appearing in professional journals in the mid-1940's. As Charlemae Rollins, Augusta Baker, and others spoke out against objectionable themes, stereotyped illustrations, degrading names, and exaggerated dialect, these criteria became more accepted in judging books in which blacks appeared. The seemingly innocent children's story about Sambo and tigers came under more demanding scrutiny. (p. 13)

The variety of illustrations in the multiple versions of **Little Black Sambo** produced in the U.S. during the 1920's, 30's, and 40's successfully served to confuse the locale of the story and the nationality of Sambo and his parents. Although it is never specifically stated in Bannerman's original version, the story seems to be set in India. Many illustrators changed the setting to Africa or the U.S; in spite of the prominence in the story of tigers, which are native only to Asia. (p. 15)

There are several theories about the inspiration for Helen Bannerman's original illustration, some more likely than others. One receiving popular credence among librarians is that Bannerman modeled them on minstrel-show characters. The "black-face" style of performing, which had begun in the U.S. in 1830, had become the rage of the British Isles in the 1860's and 70's, continuing in popularity until after the turn of the century. Minstrel performers appeared before Queen Victoria and were considered innocent family entertainment. (p. 16)

Another theory is that Bannerman conceived her characters as actual Africans, or a poorly defined Afro/Indian mixture, from memories of her youth. In proposing this opinion, Selma Lanes points out that Helen Bannerman may have had in mind images of non-Indian blacks:

> Why Mrs. Bannerman, sketching from memory, should depict black people as she did may well be explained by the fact that she herself had memories of a different black population. As the daughter of a clergyman who was also an Army chaplain, she had spent the impressionable years of her childhood in various parts of the British Empire. Between the ages of two and ten she lived on Madeira, off the west coast of Africa, where black Africans were a sizable element in a mixed population . . . There is little doubt that Mrs. Bannerman drew her characters as she did not out of malice but because she was a conventional product of her era. A proper English gentlewoman of the '90s, she no doubt saw

Cover of the first edition of The Story of Little Black Quibba *(1902).*

one dark-skinned non-Englishman as looking much like another. Indians and African blacks were readily and innocently confused in her mind.

Perhaps, but Portuguese Madeira is not as near to the African coast as is implied, and there is no evidence to suggest that Helen Bannerman lived in any other non-European part of the world until she went to India with her husband.

Finally, there is the unpublished theory that Bannerman crudely but fairly accurately depicted the 19th century British image of the features and dress of the peoples with whom she was familiar in India. Anna Pellowski, formerly of the New York Public Library and presently director of the Information Center on Children's Cultures (U.S. Committee for UNICEF), suggested this theory. She explained that some anthropologists believe there is evidence that ancestors of the southern Indians once intermingled with Africans who had traveled across the Indian Ocean from the west, producing Indians with darker skin and curly hair. (pp. 17-18)

Selma Lanes may have inadvertently found the true inspiration for Bannerman's Sambo when she recently discovered a remarkable similarity between the proudly parading Indian child and the "wooly-headed black-a-moor" in "The Story of the Inky Boys" in Heinrich Hoffmann's moralistic but popular picture book, *Der Struwwelpeter,* first published in Ger-

many in 1846. In this rhyming story, an unfortunate "black-a-moor" who goes for a walk with his green umbrella is teased unmercifully about his color by three young ruffians. Sympathetic Saint Nicholas intervenes. When his admonitions are ignored, he angrily douses the boys in an inkstand until they become as "black as crows." *Struwwelpeter* was translated into English by 1848, and one of the British publishers was Blackie & Son, with offices in London, Glasgow and Bombay. It is quite likely that such a highly-regarded moralistic book was available in young Helen's sternly religious home and that the impression was a lasting one. Although Hoffmann's "black-a-moor" wears only short pants, the pose of the two figures and the repetition of the green umbrella in *Little Black Sambo* seems like more than mere coincidence. In tone, also, many of Bannerman's stories resemble the violence and moralism of the *Struwwelpeter* assortment, especially *The Story of Little Kettlehead.*

Finally, as [May Hill] Arbuthnot points out, *Struwwelpeter* "marked the emergence in books of what can only be termed 'animated drawing,' the direct ancestor of the comic book of today." Bannerman may have been influenced by Hoffmann in this way also, for certainly her illustrations have a lively, active, animated quality. The proportion of pictures to text is very high when compared with other books of the period, and some, such as *Pat and the Spider,* have almost a flip-book quality.

Whatever the inspiration and forces working upon Bannerman as *The Story of Little Black Sambo* formed in her mind during that railway journey in India, her illustrations and those of the numerous other artists who depicted Sambo and his parents became the subject of increasing controversy. Depending upon the version of *Little Black Sambo* seen by children, it is not difficult to understand the impact of the illustrations on the feelings and attitudes of any child. Stereotypes and caricatures abounded in the various editions of *Sambo,* especially in those produced before the 1950's. (pp. 18-19)

By the turn of the [1960s], the majority of published opinion in regard to *Little Black Sambo* appeared to be that it could no longer be defended as a suitable story for children, no matter how innocent had been its original intent. Many concerned teachers and librarians seemed to agree [with Jessie J. Birtha] that,

> . . . the development of circumstances concerning the Sambo tradition has been unfortunate. The usefulness of *Little Black Sambo* is dead. The acceptability of *Little Black Sambo* is dead. . . .
>
> (p. 26)

The Story of Little Black Sambo has existed in the U.S. for over three-quarters of a century. The title has been dropped from most professional lists of recommended books, and it may be difficult or impossible to obtain in many school and public libraries, except in special reference collections. It is not the first book to have been seriously criticized and subsequently removed from libraries, but because of its place as a "classic," beloved by generations of whites in the U.S., it has aroused perhaps the greatest emotional reactions. (p. 28)

Attitudes in schools and libraries about *Little Black Sambo* are still decidedly mixed. (p. 30)

What is the future for *Little Black Sambo?* Its place in the history of children's literature as an innovative book in terms of format and style seems assured. Hopefully, research collections of children's books will endeavor to provide copies of the many variant editions for scholars, since they are such excellent examples of mass-marketed materials which significantly reflected white American interests and attitudes (in this case, toward blacks). As long as there are consumers creating a demand for the story in its various print and non-print forms, it will continue to be published. However, anyone involved with children should know the history of the story and the reasons for its offensiveness to African Americans and all Americans concerned with the elimination of racism.

The book's still-unsettled status in schools and libraries must be resolved. . . .

Whatever the author's intentions may have been, it is the demeaning results which are important. Educators and librarians can not ignore the existence of *Little Black Sambo.* Hopefully, consideration based on fact, historical perspective and desire for a pluralistic society can lead to fruitful discussion and constructive decisions. (p. 32)

> *Phyllis J. Yuill, in her* Little Black Sambo: A Closer Look, *The Racism and Sexism Resource Center for Educators, 1976, 52 p.*

DONNARAE MacCANN

Helen Bannerman's *Little Black Sambo* has been a bone of contention in the relationships of one librarian with another for a long time. To some it is a destructively offensive book. To others it is a literary "classic." Despite this disparity, libraries would not be affected if the book had been written for adults who have free access to every type of controversial reading matter. But a child, by the sheer fact of always being under the tutelage of others, is either aided or handicapped in the attempt to form a positive self-image. A book that impedes this process is of legitimate concern for all in our society.

Racism is a malady which has long been verified by psychologists and sociologists as a destructive force in the lives of children. Rather than a mere political opinion, racism is labeled a sickness because it distorts both the victim and those feeling superior to the victim. A Black child's self-image is severely affected when characters in a book—the very ones the child should be able to identify with—are degraded. A white child's sense of reality is severely affected when he or she is encouraged, by a book, to feel superior to a people from a different racial group.

Jessie Birtha, of the Philadelphia Free Library, has urged us to consider two questions when we select books. The first is, "How would I feel upon reading this book if I were a Black child?" Many librarians are not equipped to answer that question.

Those of us who are white are not equipped because we haven't experienced the hurtful socialization which would enable us to readily perceive all of the racist insults found in some books. Life, of course, has given a more heightened awareness to those who have been at the butt end of racism. For this reason it is especially necessary for white librarians and teachers to search their personal backgrounds for indifference or inexperience in this matter and then to make a determined effort to correct some of the harm done by racist books.

Of course it is not easy to say, "Place this book on a restricted shelf." Dr. Paul A. Miller, Omaha's Superintendent of

Schools in 1964, voiced the librarian's greatest anxiety about censorship when he said: "If you start here (withdrawing *Little Black Sambo*), where do you stop?" What do children's librarians reply to community groups when they insist that certain books are too anti-American, sacrilegious, or immoral for child readers? How would we answer other groups when they insist that *no* individual or group should be allowed censorship rights?

Attempting to judge a child's books as to their moral or patriotic qualities involves a difference of opinion, of taste, of political and social theory. These are matters which call for discussion, criticism, and the encouragement of children's books with unorthodox points of view to balance the preponderance of "establishment" materials.

But how can *Little Black Sambo* be "balanced" by another book? Can we imagine circulating a child's picture book which caricatured and insultingly stereotyped Italians or Irish or Jews? In recent years such books would never have passed through the screening process of white editors, publishers, reviewers and librarians. The pain and outrage such books would cause to white children would be more clearly understood by that same informal screening panel. Then why do we continue to ignore evidence of the pain caused to Black children by *Little Black Sambo?* (pp. 33-4)

Jessie Birtha's second question to be answered before selecting a book relates to aesthetic criteria: "If I were to borrow this book from the library, would I return to get another book like it?" Applying this standard, *Little Black Sambo* enjoyed a glowing reputation for a long time. But we should ask: To what degree is the book really distinguished for its rhythm, whimsy, imagination, humor, and compactness of form? Is it the professional duty or social obligation of a children's librarian to champion these elements *irrespective of other content?* Can literary elements counterbalance for a child the shock of self-rejection? The qualities of rhythm, imaginative invention, and so on, exist in so many forms and contexts that a child's early years are hardly sufficient to contain all the entertaining literary possibilities.

The history of *Little Black Sambo* negates its otherwise useful features. When children can be offered the joint pleasure of artistic form and humane content, why should we give them less? (pp. 34-5)

> *Donnarae MacCann, in an afterword to* Little Black Sambo: A Closer Look *by Phyllis J. Yuill, The Racism and Sexism Resource Center for Educators, 1976, pp. 33-5.*

BOB DIXON

[The illustrations of Little Black Sambo] in the many books in which he's featured show him as a racial caricature of a black boy. Here . . . we have the fuzzy hair, the large, round eyes and the wide (and simple) grin which give the game away, as much in respect of Sambo's race as of his relatives—the Kentucky Minstrels, the coons and the black servants of early Hollywood films. Here we have the condescending, the patronising end of racism, where the principals are merry, simple, childlike people—at best, amusing and at worst, stupid. In a racial context, they are the counterparts of working-class characters in a class context as portrayed in, for instance, *The Family From One End Street.* The two stereotypes are acceptable in this form: one to white racist sentiments and the other to middle-class attitudes. Children—

white children, that is—can laugh at Sambo's antics and feel superior. (pp. 100-01)

The book has been much criticised in recent years, but I think that not enough attention has been paid to the illustrations. After all, the story is almost identical with the Swedish folk tale, *Little Lisa*—so close that coincidence must be ruled out—and Bannerman must have got it from this source. Apart from changing the setting, she only added the pictures and the mumbo-jumbo.

All the stories in the series are about food and eating, and follow a basic pattern: firstly, animals threaten to eat up the children; then the animals are outwitted or fobbed off by some means; thirdly, there's the food, or a feast, which the children or friendly animals have and, lastly the hostile animals melt away, tear one another to shreds, are blown into fragments or dismembered or eat one another up and so cancel themselves out. (The order of the third and fourth elements may be reversed.) This pattern holds good, even for *Pat and the Spider: The Biter Bit* which is about a little white boy, not a caricature, dressed in a sailor suit.

Bannerman . . . lived in India for most of her adult life. A radio programme of a few years ago, which was concerned largely with the letters she sent to her children who were being educated in Britain, gave an interesting insight into her attitudes. At one point, she related how an Indian cook, who had been dismissed from the Bannermans' service, stayed on to impersonate (as she alleged) the new one, who hadn't arrived. 'They're all just alike,' said Dr Bannerman. 'So they are,' agreed his wife. (p. 102)

Bob Dixon, *"Racism: All Things White and Beautiful,"* in his Catching Them Young: Sex, Race and Class in Children's Fiction, Vol. 1, *Pluto Press, 1977, pp. 94-128.*

CONSTANCE B. HIEATT

Not long ago a prolonged controversy raged in the pages of the London *Times Literary Supplement* itself over the beleaguered small hero of . . . the venerable favourite *Little Black Sambo.* The opposition charged that Sambo is an insulting stereotype because he has a funny name, wears gaudy clothes, and eats a great many pancakes. No one noted the high incidence of funny names in the heroes of juvenile fiction: Bilbo Baggins, for example, and Huckleberry Finn. It was, however, noted for the defense that children like brightly coloured clothing and food high in calories, and that right-minded children would be likely to see Sambo as blessed with very kind parents who provided him with these delightful things. Of course, such right-minded children would also see that Sambo is noble, heroic, and resourceful. He deserves those pancakes: he turns the tables on the bullies who threatened to EAT HIM UP, but who were in fact turned to butter by their own stupidity.

No one has yet attacked this book for being frightening, which, in fact it is not—at least, at a distance from India. Its setting and exotic flourishes, such as butter labelled "ghi," distance it, as does the cartoonish aspect of Helen Bannerman's illustrations. Those who consider her pictures of "black" people insulting should be soothed by her later pictures of a white child, Little White Somebody-or-other, an insipid creation who has none of Sambo's character and appeal. Sambo is unquestionably the first black hero of English children's literature, but, ironically, he cannot be tolerated today

by those who misread this fantasy as a sociological document, or those who suffer from the misreadings of others. (pp. 9-10)

Constance B. Hieatt, *"Analyzing Enchantment: Fantasy after Bettelheim,"* in Canadian Children's Literature, *Nos. 15 & 16, 1980, pp. 6-14.*

ROSEMARY DINNAGE

[What I find in the *Sambo* books is] a wonderfully carefree access to the primitive, to eating and killing and destroying and surviving, within the prim and formal framework of the tale. Orality is rampant, not only where pancakes are concerned but in frogs jumping out alive from snakes or wicked Black Noggy striking a light in the crocodile's stomach and blowing them both to glory. Mouths gape viciously wide; but Sambo, Quibba, etc are *not* eaten, and always end up with something nice for tea. Nor is there any sentiment about disposal of villains: when the crocodile has exploded, his toothy head, with Scottish thrift, is used as a table where Mingo and his mongoose spread a checked tablecloth for tea every day; with his one eye still glazed open, Mingo's legs dangling over his fangs, it makes a perfect picture of safety in a jungly world. Ruthlessness, in this jungle, is innocent and presadistic. So long life to Sambo, Quibba, Mingo, and Quasha, and thumbs down on all who threaten their blameless existence.

Rosemary Dinnage, *"Taming the Teatime Tigers,"* in The Times Literary Supplement, *No. 4086, July 24, 1981, p. 834.*

ELIZABETH HAY

Little Black Sambo embodied nearly all the principles on which present-day books for young children are based and was revolutionary in its day. It was one of the first books small enough for a young child to hold comfortably. The pictures were direct and vivid, and were printed in primary colours. The story—a simple tale of a little black boy escaping from tigers which has the deeper symbolism of a child with a brave spirit going out to face the world alone—is action-packed and yet repetitive. It also lacked what had been considered essential in a children's book up till that moment: a moral purpose or improving tone. (p. 1)

Granted that the book was oustanding when it first appeared, why does it still sell today, over eighty years after it first appeared? Maurice Sendak . . . thinks *Little Black Sambo* is one of the great all time picture books for its perfect synchronisation of words with simple pictures. But that alone is not enough. There is also the pleasure a child takes in seeing him or herself as the hero setting out alone into a fascinating and dangerous world, and the satisfying climax where the tigers chase each other so hard that they turn into melted butter. . . .

It is a book that has been accepted so fully into the consciousness of generations of people, particularly in the U.S.A., that it has affected their images and thought processes. It is this power that has made the book matter, and matter to an extent far beyond the author's original intentions. As some liked the image of a primitive world which it offered, some came to hate it. Those who hate it do so with an intensity which amazes its admirers.

The critics of *The Story of Little Black Sambo* make many charges against the book. . . . The most serious charges, however, are that the name 'Sambo' has come to symbolise the depersonalisation of black people which was an aspect of slavery, and that the pictures, particularly in some of the unauthorised versions, offer demeaning stereotypes of black people in plantation or jungle settings. As the controversy has raged, with some librarians banning the book from their shelves and others shouting 'Censorship!', protagonists on both sides have lacked any but the barest biographical details about the author.

Much of the information which has been available is wrong. The first source was the preface in the first edition of 1899 [written by E. V. Lucas]. It said:

> There is very little to say about the story of ***Little Black Sambo.*** Once upon a time there was an English lady in India, where black children abound and tigers are everyday affairs, who had two little girls. To amuse these little girls she used now and then to invent stories, for which, being extremely talented, she also drew and coloured the pictures. Among these stories, ***Little Black Sambo,*** which was made up on a long railway journey, was the favourite; and it has been put into a DUMPY BOOK, and the pictures copied as exactly as possible, in the hope that you will like it as much as the two little girls did.

Helen Bannerman must have been very amused to hear herself described as English. She was a Scot, from Edinburgh, and, in the way of expatriates, a very Scottish Scot. But there is a more serious flaw in this publisher's preface: it implies that the story is set in India, which. . . . it certainly was not. (pp. 1-2)

The article in *Horn Book Magazine* in 1937 by Helen Dean Fish was an account of a visit to Helen in Edinburgh. The article [gives] Helen's view of the preface to the first edition: 'Well, that wasn't exactly true but something Mr E. V. Lucas gave out when the book was published.' The article then fails to go on and give what was the true version.

Fans of the book had to wait till 1942 for their next piece of biographical information. This appeared in the Publisher's Foreword to ***The Jumbo Sambo*** brought out in this year by Frederick A. Stokes Company, and was even more misleading. It is worth quoting so that the misconceptions it implanted in the minds of generations of children's book experts can be corrected straight away:

> In 1899 Helen Bannerman, a young English mother, wife of a British Army Surgeon stationed in India, was returning to her husband's post after leaving her two little daughters 'at home' in Edinburgh to be educated. Homesick for her little girls, on the long journey taking her away from them, she composed a story for their amusement and coloured the little drawings she made to go with each sentence. It was the now classic ***Story of Little Black Sambo***. . . .
>
> (p. 3)

Helen's husband, however, was not a British Army Surgeon. He was in the Indian Medical Service, and, apart from his early years which were spent on regimental duties, worked mostly in public health and medical research. More misleading still is the claim that the book was written in India while the author's children were left in Scotland. On this presumed fact a psychoanalist based a whole paper, explaining the book in terms of a traumatic separation.

The truth is that Helen Bannerman wrote her book in India and her daughters were at that time in India too. The story . . . is that they were left in the coolness of the hill resort of Kodaikanal while their mother rejoined their father, for a brief spell, in Madras. There certainly was a separation involved; but not a separation of continents. (p. 4)

It was against [the background of plague and plague research in Madras] that Helen brought up her two daughters. Quite apart from plague, there were other hazards for them. In those days, European children often failed to thrive in India. After the age of five or six they would grow thin and listless, without appetite and become very pale. They were subject in hot weather to prickly heat, an itchy body rash guaranteed to make the best-tempered child irritable. They kept getting stomach upsets, picking up parasites, and were at risk from various fatal tropical illnesses.

One of the things that did improve the health of such children was to take them to the hills. The hill station that [Helen and her husband Will] went to most from Madras was Kodaikanal. It was neither so near nor so fashionable as Ootacumund, but it was much favoured by missionaries, giving rise to jokes about the two communities there, known as Kodai spiritual and Kodai carnal. Helen and Will were always more on the side of the angels than of the Indian Civil Service, and Kodai became a second home. . . . (pp. 22-3)

Spending the hot weather up in the hills, though, put Helen in a dilemma. If she was to be there with the children for the entire season, she would be away from her husband for four or five months. . . . Helen never enjoyed being away from Will for long, and her solution was to leave the children with their Ayah at Kodai while she spent short spells with Will in the heat of Madras. The accepted wisdom in those days was that a man needed his wife more than children needed their mother.

It was on one of these journeys between Kodai and Madras that Helen wrote ***The Story of Little Black Sambo.*** (p. 23)

For Helen the entire journey took two days and two nights. As she travelled farther and farther from her daughters her thoughts were with them, and she wanted to do something for them. She had enough time on her hands to work out the story, and then to perfect it. One of the noticeable things about it is the economy of language and the perfect match between text and picture. The consistency and unity of the book may well have been helped by a long spell of uninterrupted concentration. It is likely that Helen worked out the book during the journey then finished the pictures and wrote the text out neatly when she got to Madras. She was careful to make the volume small enough for her daughters to hold easily in their hands themselves—something she had always wanted from books when she had been a child. Then, since she had her own book press, she bound it herself and sent it off to her daughters as a present.

With its pictures in bright primary colours and Little Black Sambo always on the point of being eaten, Janet and Day—then five and two—loved it. When their mother was there to terrify them with stories about tigers, they preferred her; but in her absence the little book was some sort of comfort and a reassurance to them of her love.

Other people who saw the book admired it too, particularly a friend of Helen's called Mrs Alice M. E. Bond. She thought it ought to be published and she asked Helen if she could take it with her on her next home leave to see if anyone was interested. Helen had not written it with any thought of publication, but, rather doubtfully, she agreed. She remembered from her childhood being told by R. M. Ballantyne, when he visited her parents' home in Edinburgh: 'Don't sell the copyright of your first book. That's the one,' he said, 'that you make the most on.' R. M. Ballantyne knew what he was talking about. He had suffered from the loss of the copyright of his early books, and the subsequent history of *The Story of Little Black Sambo* was to prove him right in the advice he had given to Helen when she was a child. Remembering this advice, Helen made one request to Mrs Bond, that she would not sell the copyright.

In London, Mrs Bond took the manuscript picture book to a publisher who was trying to bring in some quick income from a series of small books for children called The Dumpy Books. These were edited by E. V. Lucas, who was then a columnist on *The Globe* as well as the compiler of *A Book of Verses for Children* and literary adviser to [the publisher] Grant Richards. (pp. 24-5)

When shown Helen's bound and illustrated book *The Story of Little Black Sambo* he immediately offered Mrs Bond £5 for the copyright.

This put Mrs Bond in a quandary, as a letter she wrote to Grant Richards on 20 June 1899 shows:

> Could you manage to wait 6 weeks for an answer? I should very much prefer to ask my friend in India to decide about her own book, but, in case this would make the publishing of the book at all doubtful, I should have to make up my mind to decide something alone, but would *infinitely* prefer not to. Please answer me by return as, in *any* case I must write by next mail to Mrs Bannerman . . . In case of your obtaining the copyright, would Mrs Bannerman lose all future chance of a share in the book? . . .
>
> (p. 26)

This loss of the copyright was to work substantially to the disadvantage of the book and to the disadvantage of Helen's reputation. Not having an indisputable claim to the copyright she was unable to pursue the many versions, paying no copyright fees to anyone, which flooded the United States, adorned, in some cases, with damaging illustrations.

Grant Richards, however, was not prepared to move an inch on the copyright. His letters to Mrs Bond have not survived, but obviously he merely repeated his original offer. Two days later Mrs Bond wrote back to him. 'In answer to your letter of 21 June I have no option but to accept your offer, without reference to Mrs Bannerman, as I am anxious not to jeopardise the success of the little book.'

On that basis Grant Richards went ahead and prepared *Little Black Sambo* for publication. Helen, however, wrote to Mrs Bond indicating that she was reluctant to sell the copyright. This letter has not survived, but Mrs Bond wrote again to Grant Richards on 9 August 1899: 'I am sorry to find that Mrs Bannerman is somewhat disappointed as to the copyright, which she is most anxious to keep. She says, of course, if it is too late, she will abide contentedly by my decision but she would prefer you to pay her nothing for the book, and make what you can out of it, and let her retain the copyright. Can this be managed? If not, as I have given my word, the present arrangement must remain.' (pp. 26-7)

[There] the matter rested for many years—a *de facto* sale of the copyright for £5 by Mrs Bond, a sale to which Helen had never signed her agreement. (p. 27)

[Why] did a person who was both well travelled and scholarly write a book which contains aspects of both Africa and India? The explanation is that she was writing, not for publication, but for her own daughters. She wanted to set her story somewhere far away and exotic; she chose an imaginary jungleland and peopled it with what were to her daughters a faraway kind of people. To have made the setting India would have been too humdrum and familiar for them. Then, because she had a liking for terrifying tigers, she brought them in as the villains. She was far too good a naturalist not to be aware that tigers are found in India but not in Africa; no matter. Her jungle-land was an imaginary one, and tigers, which for her were symbolic dragons, were essential to the story.

The most Indian aspect of her books is the language. This again stems from the audience for whom they were written. Her daughters understood Hindustani words like 'ghi'; the English equivalent, 'clarified butter', would have been a mystery to them.

A question which has stimulated a lot of discussion in the U.S.A. is: why did she choose the name Sambo for her hero? . . . [It] is a name which came to have unfortunate connotations through its use in the United States as a generic title for any black male. . . . If it was used generically before 1899, Helen had no knowledge of this. She used it as a specific name. She was fond of puns and verbal jokes and many of her characters have names derived from common phrases such as—'Mumbo-Jumbo'; 'Rag Tag and Bobtail'. In this she was following in the footsteps of authors such as Charles Dickens, who invented amazing names for his characters and places, plucked from everyday words. . . . (pp. 29-30)

From [the various editions of *Little Black Sambo*] Helen made nothing—apart from her original £5. Nor did she make anything from sales of the book in the U.S.A. or from any other parts of the world. (p. 30)

Helen kept the copyright of all her subsequent books, though none of them—as she had feared—did anything like as well as her first one. (p. 36)

It is easy to see why Helen's books were far less 'vicarage tea party' than those of her contemporary, Beatrix Potter. Helen's life was a good deal less genteel. (p. 38)

[Beatrix Potter's] delightful pictures of animals are idealised and romanticised; compare her elegant Jeremy Fisher, a frog who sits on a water lily, fully clothed and sheltering under an umbrella, with Helen's natural frog in *The Story of Little Black Quasha*. Helen's animals are never dressed in clothes, are not anthropomorphised. The monkey in *The Story of The Teasing Monkey* makes himself a cloak or covering out of coconut husks; but this is in keeping with what a monkey could do. Nor do her animals have names, apart from Jacko the monkey. They are the frog, the snake, or the tiger. They also show in their behaviour the obsession of the real animal world—eating their prey, or at least trying to do so. It has been argued that to clothe animals in human garments, and tuck baby rabbits into little beds with sheets, and feed them with spoonfuls of castor oil, is misleading and harmful to a child. My faith in the power of children to grow out of any misconceptions such books may induce is total; but Helen Bannerman, though her animals do talk and show human emotions such as rage, portrayed them very firmly as animals and not as pseudo-humans. (p. 39)

In her study of *Little Black Sambo* Marjorie McDonald mentions that Helen lived in, 'racially segregated India'. There were, however, no laws forbidding the races to inter-marry or to mix with each other. The social intercourse between the Indians and the British was indeed limited; but it did take place. Helen's letters show that she went out of her way to entertain Indian women in her home. . . .

In 1916 Helen was asked to judge the flowers at the Madras Flower Show, jointly with the Hon Sir P. S. Sivaswamy Tyer. . . . Will and Helen attended weddings and other functions given by Indians, and Will was visited regularly by a Subadar-Major of the 64th Pioneers who had served with him in his very early posting, before he was married, in Baluchistan. (p. 140)

[The answer should] be evident to the question: was she a racist? . . .

A racist is someone who dislikes people of other races and is convinced of the superiority of his or her own. Two things about Helen's approach are clear: she approached other races with a very Christian approach: 'in God we are all one', and she had a deep sympathy and warmth towards the people of India. The Christian ideal is that the individual should approach all others, whatever their race or background, in a spirit of love. It is ironic that she, accused of being a racist, came nearer to the Christian ideal in her behaviour than some of those who make the accusation. Rob recalls that it was impressed upon him, when he was a child, that no one had any superiority *ab initio:* fundamentally they were all the same. What counted, he was taught, was effort.

It was because Helen was interested in other races, and could identify with their feelings, which she knew were much the same as hers, that she chose a black child as her hero. With the hindsight of history it is a pity she did not choose a brown child. Had she set *Little Black Sambo* in India the detail could have been authentic and the spurious connection with cotton plantations in the U.S.A. would never have developed. But she chose to set her book in a land of which she knew little. She had never visited Africa, and probably never knew any Africans. Her books were set in a vaguely African world of her imagination; it is not surprising if the detail is mixed. The reader can be assured, however, that the motive in setting her stories there was not to ridicule or demean black people in any way. She simply regarded them as part of the human race.

Someone with a similar approach today is Richard Scarry, author and illustrator of many children's books, including *Busy Busy World.* He offers caricatures or stereotypes of the races round the world, often unflattering. Russians are shown as bears, Indians as tigers and elephants, African as lions, and the Poles and Scots and Irish as pigs. So far as I know, there have been no complaints about this; nor should there be— though he does come under fire for alleged sexism. The animals are drawn with sympathy and humour; if a few stereotypes are reinforced, such as a peasant way of life in the case of the Irish or bagpipes that make an appalling noise in the case of the Scots, no matter. Richard Scarry is a story teller, and children delight in his stories and his funny pictures.

That is all that Helen would have claimed for herself. In her books, and her letters, she had an eye for a good story. Had

Cover of The Story of Sambo and the Twins *(1937).*

she wanted to make a serious contribution to our understanding of a particular area of human knowledge, she would have embarked on a massive tome, as her father had done. . . . Her ambition was much more modest: to amuse. (pp. 141-42)

Towards the end of her life, Helen was aware of criticisms of *Little Black Sambo* as racist.

As her son Robert was to say in answer to critics of his mother who attacked the book as racist in the columns of *The Times* in 1972: 'My mother would not have published the book had she dreamt for a moment that even one small boy would have been made unhappy thereby.' Nevertheless, a variety of charges were made against the book. Among the less substantial were accusations that eating so many pancakes made black people look greedy and that the garish colours for their clothes symbolised the artist's view of their childish minds. Among the more substantial complaints were charges that the pictures showed stereotypes or caricatures of black people, that the book showed black people in primitive jungle settings, or in demeaning slave plantation settings, and that the name Sambo had derogatory overtones for black people because it had come to be used in a generic way for any negro.

To understand the strength of feeling behind these charges we have to understand that when people in the U.S.A. speak of *Little Black Sambo* they are probably not thinking of the book with illustrations by Helen Bannerman. Though no figures are available, sales of the edition with her pictures were vastly outnumbered by sales of other editions with other illustrators. (p. 155)

Some of the pictures are horrifying. No wonder people took offence. Seeing the pictures by some of the other illustrators, the surprising thing is that the reaction took so long to find expression. . . .

If Helen Bannerman's friend Mrs Alice Bond had not sold the copyright of the book on her behalf in 1899, none of this would have been possible. The variety of versions, some with acknowledgement to Helen Bannerman and some without, were only possible because her claim to the copyright was very weak and she therefore could not pursue anyone who infringed it. . . .

All her best pictures were caricatures. She admitted it herself. She had had no instruction in drawing and she had developed the technique of 'heightening' the important aspects of a picture. When Sambo weeps, for example, his tears are as big as his hands, and when he is frightened his eyes open excessively wide. But this was how nearly all her pictures turned out. She caricatured her husband, her children, her friends, anyone within range—and herself. (p. 156)

Helen would have been an excellent cartoonist, given the opportunity—a better cartoonist than an artist. The way she could caricature people was, however, simply an aspect of her style. There was nothing racist about it.

Were her pictures stereotypes? A stereotype is something constantly repeated without change, a character without humanity. Helen Bannerman's *Little Black Sambo,* however, is an appealing child with individualistic parents. The same is true of the characters in her other books, with the exception of *The Story of Little White Squibba* in which Squibba significantly lacks personality. It was her daughter Day who was responsible for the major part of the Squibba drawings. So while I would accept the charge that there is an element of the caricature in her drawings, the charge that they are stereotypes cannot be sustained. It should be clear by now that I accept fully the charge that many of the pictures by other artists are blatant stereotypes.

Does Helen Bannerman make black people look greedy by showing them eating so many pancakes? Not all black people take themselves so seriously that they accept this charge. Most, like Helen Bannerman, have a sense of humour. . . . (p. 158)

In Helen's picture of eating the pancakes, mother, father and son are sitting politely at the table, set with a clean white cloth and plates and forks. In the Stoll and Edwards edition, however, Little Black Sambo, who is almost gross, is seen sitting by himself shovelling the food into his mouth off a plate on the plain wood. Like someone drinking alone, a child eating alone is not a happy sight.

Does Helen Bannerman's use of primary colours for the clothes of Little Black Sambo and his parents indicate that she thought they liked these bright colours because they had childish minds? Helen used primary colours because she wanted to appeal to the genuinely childish minds of her readers. The appeal of her pictures was that they were simple, direct and brightly coloured. Although this was revolutionary in its day, this is now a standard approach to pictures for young children. There is nothing derogatory in the clothes Helen Bannerman gives her characters—though the same

cannot be said about the clothes shown in, for example, the Reilly and Britton edition. Helen Bannerman's characters are nicely dressed, with a pride in their appearance; the opposite is true in the Cupples and Leon edition of 1917.

We come now to the question of the name 'Sambo'. . . . It appeared in comic strips and in black and white minstrel shows and was frequently used for a black person in a subservient position. It is no wonder that this label—for it had lost its original function as a name—came to be bitterly resented by black people. It typified the depersonalisation of slavery and the shame of the subsequent years of exploitation.

The question arises whether the use of the name would have developed in the way it did without the book. Certainly the book, in all its versions, had a very powerful impact on people's instinctive images. It was one of the very few books then available which even acknowledged the existence of black people. For generations it gave black Americans an image of themselves, and white Americans an image of black Americans. This is what gives the book an importance out of all proportion to its original significance. (pp. 158-59)

In Britain, protest against the use of the name Sambo in Helen Bannerman's book developed much later than in the U.S.A.. This was because the only edition available in Britain has been the Chatto and Windus edition with the original pictures. Britain has been spared the plantation images—and also the more recent Indian ones. The book is not available in bastardised versions in supermarkets; it can be bought in bookshops in the original edition or not at all. Nevertheless, in 1972, a protest against the book erupted with a virulence which made the British establishment sit up in astonishment.

Before the nineteen-fifties, Britain's black population was very small. But as immigration from the West Indies got under way, with West Indians being encouraged to come to Britain to work on London Transport and in the National Health Service, it increased substantially and quickly. On 31 March 1972 *Teachers Against Racism* triggered off by an advertisement for a new boxed edition of Helen Bannerman's books, sent [a] letter to the then Chairman of the book's publishers, Chatto and Windus. . . . (pp. 164-65)

TAR at the same time sent a copy of their letter to the Children's Books Editor of *The Times,* Brian Alderson. He brooded about it for a few days then on 12 April came out with a powerful article 'Banning Bannerman'.

[The] story became world news.

The correspondence in *The Times,* and the publicity surrounding it, changed the views of a number of figures in the children's books field. Janet Hill, for example, Children's Librarian in the London Borough of Lambeth, and influential as a champion of good books for black children, had up to this point supported *Little Black Sambo.* She had banned Enid Blyton's *Little Black Doll* from her shelves, and some of the Biggles books, but had always kept a place for Sambo. Now she changed her mind and explained her views in an article in *The Times Literary Supplement* of 3 November 1972, reprinted in 1980 in *Racism & Sexism in Children's Books,* edited by Judith Stinton:

> Helen Bannerman's books have had a long life, and
> the time has come to consign them to oblivion.
> They should have no place in a multi-racial society.

Talk of banning the books, however, drew the scorn of the

white establishment. Banning was a very blunt instrument, arousing a lot of resentment and ridicule; but the controversy did draw attention to the very real need for more books with a black character as hero. (pp. 170-71)

[A further accusation of racism in the book] is made by Dr. Marjorie McDonald, who feels there is a hidden sexual dimension to the book through which a subliminal racist message is offered. . . .

Dr McDonald interprets the tale as springing from Helen Bannerman's anxiety about her daughters as she journeyed away from them. (p. 172)

Dr McDonald is right to pinpoint Helen's separation from her children as the trigger or inspiration for *Little Black Sambo.* (p. 173)

I find Dr McDonald's interpretation of the symbolism of the gifts to Sambo very convincing. It is one of the most pleasing aspects of the book that Sambo, wearing the clothes his parents have given him, and carrying his umbrella, should go out into the wide world with perfect confidence in himself. This is indeed how we would all wish our children to behave when they go off on their own. That part of the analysis, however, can stand quite separately from Dr McDonald's interpretation of the tigers chasing each other as a child's eye view of intercourse. If there were an unconscious sexual parallel to the story, however, this could explain why people are inclined to describe *Little Black Sambo* as a *satisfying* book. But even if one accepts this, why should Helen Bannerman transfer imaginings from her deepest subconscious onto the form of a small child who was black?

There are many simple and quite possible explanations. She may have wanted a story for her children which took them away from the everyday routine of their life. Most fairy stories happen somewhere far away. Very few are set on the doorstep. She may have known they liked stories with tigers in them; certainly her sons did later on and she herself had enjoyed tiger stories from her own childhood. She may have been reading to her daughters from her copy of Heinrich Hoffmann's *Struwwelpeter*. This gory book of cautionary tales features a picture of a black boy striding out with an umbrella which could well have been the inspiration for Little Black Sambo. (*Struwwelpeter* is a book which Robert Bannerman confirms that he had as a child, and particularly disliked.)

Racism, however, is not about drawing pictures of black people. It is about denying people of another race their humanity. If Helen Bannerman chose Sambo as the vehicle for some of her most intimate feelings, what more could she do to acknowledge the common humanity of Sambo and of herself? We have come a long way since Freud first published *Creative Writers and Day-Dreaming* in 1907. We are not shocked by unconscious sexuality now. Just as the associations of the word 'black' have altered in recent years, so that it now has a positive image, so for many people sexual fulfillment, and even hidden sexual interests in children, are now understood as a matter for pride not shame. It may be that in the years ahead people will become less concerned with racial riddles and see the story for what it is, that of a child going out into the world and triumphantly overcoming its dangers.

Helen, too, in her day, had gone confidently into the world. She had met her first tiger at Mulkowal. After her death more tigers reared up accusing her of racism. Her letters are the gifts she casts towards them. Those who accept the message of her letters will have understood that the racial controversy has been chasing itself round a tree. Helen Bannerman was—as Will had said of her father—a good person, who deserves, at the end of the day, to be honoured by all. (pp. 174-75)

Elizabeth Hay, in her Sambo Sahib: The Story of Little Black Sambo and Helen Bannerman, *Barnes & Noble, 1981, 194 p.*

JOHN ROWE TOWNSEND

Little Black Sambo must be mentioned as a picture-story book of scant artistic merit but of instant appeal to large numbers of small children. It has always seemed to me that the story rather than the pictures accounted for its success. The tale of Sambo, his fine clothes and the tigers has everything that is needed. It is ingeniously repetitive-with-differences; the small hero comes out on top, the conclusion is absurd but satisfying, and the whole thing is so intrinsically pictorial that it needs little help from the artist. Even with Mrs Bannerman's own crude illustrations it could not miss. (p. 137)

John Rowe Townsend, "Pictures That Tell a Story," in his Written for Children: An Outline of English-Language Children's Literature, *third revised edition, J. B. Lippincott, 1987, pp. 125-42.*

Rhoda Blumberg

1917-

American author of nonfiction.

Called "one of the finest historians now writing for children" by critic Elizabeth Ward, Blumberg is the creator of a variety of informational books which are characterized by their unusual subjects, readability, lively style, and appeal to readers from the early grades to high school. Although she has written books about outer space, the sea and its inhabitants, and the occult as well as works which blend science and fantasy or give background on interesting facts, Blumberg is best known as the author of books on American and world social history which are recognized for their ability to make familiar events come alive for young readers. Several of Blumberg's works in this area are regarded as outstanding examples of their genre; perhaps her most acclaimed book is *Commodore Perry in the Land of the Shogun* (1985), in which she reenacts Matthew Perry's negotiations in Japan in 1853 while focusing on their effects on both the Americans and the Japanese. The confrontation between cultures is also the emphasis of another well-received book, *The Incredible Journey of Lewis and Clark* (1987), in which Blumberg explores the relationship between the explorers and the native Americans whom they encountered. Praised for investing these works and several of her other books with a balance of fascinating information and playful humor, Blumberg is also credited for adding to the accessibility of her works with well-chosen illustrations, photographs, and maps. Celebrated for her superior research, vivid descriptions, and enthusiasm, Blumberg is acknowledged for providing young readers with books that are both informative and entertaining. Blumberg has collaborated on several of her works with her daughter, Leda. In 1986, *Commodore Perry in the Land of the Shogun* received the *Boston Globe-Horn Book* Award for nonfiction and was named a Newbery honor book.

(See also *Something about the Author,* Vol. 35; *Contemporary Authors New Revision Series,* Vols. 9, 26; and *Contemporary Authors,* Vols. 65-68.)

AUTHOR'S COMMENTARY

[The following excerpt is from the acceptance speech Blumberg delivered in 1985 upon receiving the Boston Globe-Horn Book *Award for* Commodore Perry in the Land of the Shogun.]

Here is my magic passport to adventure—my library card. It enables me to travel through time and space. I'm a roving reporter, a foreign correspondent who was very happy commuting between the U.S.A., 1984, and Japan, 1854. It was exciting to be with Commodore Perry in the Land of the Shogun—to watch the Americans land in Japan and march past samurai warriors and feudal barons, to witness the signing of a treaty, and to participate in an American banquet and a Japanese feast that celebrated the historic occasion.

I have enjoyed outlandish assignments: in outer space, to write **The First Travel Guide to the Moon;** and in the depths of the ocean, to compile **The First Travel Guide to the Bottom of the Sea.** But my preference is traveling into the past.

I love history! I'm a compulsive researcher, obsessed with and addicted to ferreting out information that makes history come alive. Libraries are irresistible. It's heaven to wander around in the stacks, exploring, examining, and choosing books. What a joy it is to find information about a captivating subject that will eventually intrigue my readers.

However, I was not always addicted to history. At school, textbook history seemed a jumble of dull, dreary facts. It was tiresome memorizing names and dates and attempting to blow the dust off ancient information. My enthusiasm for history came after college, while working as a researcher and writer for CBS radio and spending most of my time going past those wise lions who guard the entrance to the New York Public Library on 42nd Street. Part of my job was to supply entertaining, historical material for radio programs. Nonfiction proved to be as gripping as fiction—a fantastic discovery. I am especially interested in social history and willingly endure monotonous diaries and poorly written manuscripts when they reward me with surprising information about people. (p. 41)

Rhoda Blumberg, "Traveling into the Past," in The Horn Book Magazine, *Vol. LXII, No. 1, January-*

February, 1986, pp. 41-3.

FIRE FIGHTERS (1976)

With a strictly business format and none of the personality of Beame's *Ladder Company 108*, *Fire Fighters* introduces slightly older children to such specialized vehicles as the smoke ejector and super pumper, to "slippery water" that flows faster through the hose, to "hookies" and "vollies" and "ripe workers" (smoky, difficult-to-extinguish fires). Women fire fighters are dutifully included, and even a hypothetical fire chief is conscientiously styled a "he or she." Not a spark of imagination, but the machinery is in working order.

A review of "Fire Fighters," in Kirkus Reviews, *Vol. XLIV, No. 5, March 1, 1976, p. 257.*

The romance of the fireman's job comes through strongly in this book filled with child appeal. Black and white illustrations stimulate the imagination. . . . Detailed descriptions are carefully selected and phrased for maximum interest and easy reading. Machines and devices also get plenty of attention. . . . (p. 91)

Complete with glossary and index, *Fire Fighters* provides science education as well as career information. As fire-fighting procedures are described, the child's natural questions are anticipated. The text explains why a hose must be held by no less than three firemen; how different kinds of fires receive special treatment; how horses were used to pull the fire wagons at the turn of the century; and, of course, how firemen dress in an instant and slide down the brass pole. *Fire Fighters* is a perfect information book for youngsters. (pp. 91-2)

A review of "Fire Fighters," in Curriculum Review, *Vol. 16, No. 2, May, 1977, pp. 91-2.*

SHARKS (1976)

Blumberg discusses the physical characteristics, feeding habits (e.g., shoes, documents, and the headless body of a knight in armor have all been found in shark's stomachs), reproduction, growth and habitats of various sharks. She also discusses the shark's relationships to other sea creatures and to man. Although the informative text is well-written, it is sometimes disorganized—e.g., information about shark physiology is interrupted by chapters on the enemies and companions of sharks—and some of the definitions in the glossary are unclear. The photographs are good, but they are frequently accompanied by sensationalized captions (e.g., "the jagged teeth in this sand tiger shark's mouth will finish off its victim very quickly."), and there are no explanatory drawings and diagrams. Zim's *Sharks* is written more simply and clearly and has many good explanatory diagrams, but this will fill the bill for libraries trying to keep pace with the "Jaws" craze.

Cynthia Richey, in a review of "Sharks," in School Library Journal, *Vol. 22, No. 9, May, 1976, p. 56.*

Long after Peter Benchley's *Jaws* is forgotten, *Sharks* ought to be of interest. The book follows the traditional format of the First Book series; but the language is vivid and the stories impressive. This is, perhaps, the sort of book that would inspire a student with an assigned report to continue to read. The first half of *Sharks* includes external anatomy, senses, enemies, and breeding. The rest is devoted to descriptions of major shark species. Most, but not all, of these are represented in the black-and-white photographs which are scattered throughout the book.

Sarah Gagne, in a review of "Sharks," in The Horn Book Magazine, *Vol. LII, No. 5, October, 1976, p. 525.*

When discussing this title with a children's librarian who had just read it, it emerged that the one part which had really stood out, for her, was the last paragraph which states: "The shark is not an evil, bloodthirsty, man-eating monster—Not fear but interest should make us want to know more about sharks, rulers of their world, the sea." and it is easy to see why that should have stood out. The author is almost encouraging readers of the book to get out and get to know sharks better, to make friends with them. It is true that one learns, in great detail, which sharks are man-eaters and which are not, but it would be extremely dangerous, to say the least, to swim close enough to a shark to find out exactly which species it was and therefore discover whether it was one in which one could, safely, take an interest. This rather unfortunate paragraph apart the book was excellent. Full of interesting and unusual stories about sharks, amply illustrated with photographs of them from the egg and embryo stage to the great whale sharks. . . . [Above] all, the text is extremely readable and makes the subject an interesting one. (pp. 105-06)

G. L. Hughes, in a review of "Sharks," in The Junior Bookshelf, *Vol. 41, No. 2, April, 1977, pp. 105-06.*

UFO (1977)

Although several privately supported organizations are still actively investigating new and old UFO sightings, the peak has passed and the Air Force has closed its UFO office. Blumberg has nothing new to report; the same events receive more extensive and stimulating coverage in David C. Knight's *Those Mysterious UFOs: the Story of Unidentified Flying Objects* which remains the best starting point for those interested in the subject.

Ovide V. Fortier, in a review of "UFO," in School Library Journal, *Vol. 24, No. 1, September, 1977, p. 121.*

Although a few pages at the end of the book suggest that many scientists have open minds about unidentified flying objects and wish to pursue observation and investigation, most of this book is devoted to reporting on the history and debunking of those reports that have been logged, both in the past and in contemporary sightings. Logical explanations are given for objects sighted, including some that have been photographed: odd cloud formations, flocks of birds or spiders, meteors and comets, aircraft seen at unfamiliar angles. Blumberg also points out some obviously invented reports by pranksters, or faked objects. While the subject is always intriguing, the book offers little that is new, reading like a popularized rehash of other material.

Zena Sutherland, in a review of "UFO," in Bulletin of the Center for Children's Books, *Vol. 31, No. 5, January, 1978, p. 74.*

[*UFO*] offers a dispassionate account of alleged sightings and landings and includes the classic case of Orson Welles's radio report of a Martian landing. Rational explanations are suggested for the various examples and there is an extensive list of adult books which take the controversial subject further.

Margery Fisher, in a review of "UFO," in Growing Point, *Vol. 16, No. 8, March, 1978, p. 3271.*

FIRST LADIES (1977)

The idea of showing the stresses placed on first ladies during the White House years, their reactions to these influences, and what measures they were able to effect while their husbands were in office is laudable; unfortunately Blumberg makes this her premise, then gives only superficial coverage. Granted, information on earlier women might be difficult to locate; not so later first ladies. Listed in chronological order, the short biographical sketches touch on the women's early lives, ways they met their husbands, and the strains of residing at the White House. . . . In addition to the reproductions of portraits or photographs, statistics tell place of birth, date of marriage, names of children, and length of term. The remarks, which provide basic data, are intriguing and hopefully will spark readers to more in-depth research. (pp. 158-59)

Barbara Elleman, in a review of "First Ladies," in Booklist, *Vol. 74, No. 2, September 15, 1977, pp. 158-59.*

An adequate biographical look at the wives (or, as in the case of James Buchanan, the niece) of each of the Presidents of the United States, from Martha Dandridge Custis Washington to Rosalynn Smith Carter. One or two page entries—the shortest is two paragraphs, the longest, ten—provide a picture or photograph (when available) and simple résumé data: birth and death dates (many of the women did not live to see their husbands inaugurated), length of marriage, number of children, period as First Lady, etc. Blumberg's coverage is more current than that of Kathleen Prindiville's *First Ladies* or of Jane and Burt McConnell's *Our First Ladies,* but that is the only advantage: not only is Blumberg less informative than the other two, but she directs most of her attention to superfluous details or to material about the Presidents, and uncovers few facts that cannot be located in encyclopedias.

Joe Bearden, in a review of "First Ladies," in School Library Journal, *Vol. 24, No. 5, January, 1978, p. 86.*

FAMINE (1978)

Overpopulation and unequal distribution of resources are targeted as the major causes of the current world food crisis. In contrast, accounts of historical famines in China, India, Europe, and Russia place more emphasis on war as the cause of famine. Unlike such titles as Pringle's *Our Hungry Earth: the World Food Crisis* and Archer's *Hunger on Planet Earth,* Blumberg's focus is purely famine, not hunger among the poor of famine-free areas. Both political and scientific solutions to famine are discussed, although Blumberg gives little attention to population control, a grave oversight. Although Pringle lacks Blumberg's information on past famines, he covers the causes and possible measures to alleviate world hunger problems in more detail. The illustrations in the Pringle book include more graphic photographs and charts, therefore making his the first choice for this age group.

Jo Ann Carr, in a review of "Famine," in School Library Journal, *Vol. 26, No. 1, September, 1979, p. 130.*

The author of this book for young adults paints a dismal picture of unstoppable world hunger. The book lacks an analysis of the root cause of hunger; it often presents only pieces of information and these are sometimes erroneous. For example, a discussion of the amount of grain fed to livestock states, "Even if we ate less meat the world would still not have enough food to prevent world starvation." However, according to the United Nations Food and Agricultural Organization, the world produces enough in grain alone to feed all people most of their protein needs and more than 3000 calories a day—as much as the average U.S. citizen eats.

Laurie Rubin, in a review of "Famine," in Interracial Books for Children Bulletin, *Vol. 15, No. 4, 1984, p. 7.*

WITCHES (1979)

Ancient beliefs about the power of witches led to horrendous witch hunts that lasted until late in the seventeenth century. Scores of people, including children, were accused, examined, and sentenced in Europe, Britain, and America with little cause or reason. Blumberg discusses these atrocities, detailing signs such as water tests, witch marks, and familiars that supposedly justified the arrests. Even now, witchcraft is not dead, as evinced by today's followers of Wicca, who worship a moon goddess and believe in doing good; the ministers of Satan, who hold black masses and serve the devil; and the number of books, kits, and gimmicks available in stores and mail order catalogs. This lively discussion presents the historical material matter-of-factly but switches to a skeptical tone in the final chapter on modern-day witch practices. Reproductions of old prints and descriptions of ancient tortures may perturb the fainthearted. (pp. 442-43)

Barbara Elleman, in a review "Witches," in Booklist, *Vol. 76, No. 5, November 1, 1979, p. 442-43.*

A survey of the history of witchcraft, from the violence of the early 1500s in Europe to witch hunting practices among the new settlers of America to today when witches far from being burned at the stake are popular practitioners of magical ceremonies and rites and have even taken to appearing on TV and to writing books. . . . As a quick take this is satisfactory, but it hasn't got the detail of *Witchcraft in America* by Clifford Alderman.

Linda Blaha, in a review of "Witches," in School Library Journal, *Vol. 26, No. 6, February, 1980, p. 52.*

BACKYARD BESTIARY (1979)

This begins by explaining what a bestiary is—a medieval book covering the natural history of both real and mythical creatures. Readers are then told to step outside to see the ". . . real creatures that are perfect subjects for a backyard bestiary . . . [and to] compare them with imagined monsters of long ago." Well, there is very little comparison but a good deal of juxtaposition. By alternately placing the description of a real creature right after the description of a fantastical one, the most potent quality of each is lent for a short time to the other; i.e., an aura of reality is given to the fantastic and an aura of wonder to the real. The book is a collection of curious facts on the small creeping, crawling and flying beasties found close to home. It is an appetizer. The text is enjoyable, but the information on spiders, snails, bees, etc. can be found in almost any book dealing with those topics. If, however, you had someone who wanted to get to the "far-out" facts without a lot of reading, this book would be fine. (pp. 127-28)

Cheryl Toth, in a review of "Backyard Bestiary," in School Library Journal, *Vol. 26, No. 7, March, 1980, pp. 127-28.*

Although this book delighted the children I showed it to, I have several reservations about it. Of the 15 animals considered, 11 are not found in most backyards. In addition, the fanciful accounts in the book leave one wondering which animals are the real creatures and which are fables. There are descriptions of the habits of an aphid-tending ant, spider, snail, dragonfly, monarch butterfly, ladybug beetle, bee, wasp and praying mantis. The ant-lion, considered a mythical creature in beastiaries, does in fact exist. Some of the fictitious creatures described are the amphisbaena, the great bird Roc, the Basilisk and the Dragon. . . . Recommended as collateral reading.

Yolanda Clapp, in a review of "Backyard Bestiary," in Science Books & Films, *Vol. 16, No. 1, September-October, 1980, p. 33.*

Although touted in the jacket description as "a blend of the world of nature and the world of fantasy," **Backyard Bestiary** is more of a hodgepodge. The premise promises intriguing possibilities—comparisons of creatures in your backyard with ancient monsters once thought to be real. But the comparisons are far-fetched and confusing. For instance, a legendary giant bird called a roc is described and compared to a dragonfly as an equally amazing creature. Yet the only similarity seems to be that both creatures fly. That insects were once brought into court and placed on trial is the lead in for an introduction to bees, who aren't in court but "are often killed by people who judge them nasty because they sting." Although a substantial amount of interesting information is presented in an attractive format, **Backyard Bestiary** fails to bring two appealing topics together in an organized, meaningful way.

Pamela R. Giller, in a review of "Backyard Bestiary," in Appraisal: Children's Science Books, *Vol. 13, No. 3, Fall, 1980, p. 13.*

THE TRUTH ABOUT DRAGONS (1980)

In picture-book format, a compendium of dragon lore presented as natural history and presumably taken from venerable sources. . . . In one- or two-page entries with headings such as "Habitat" and "Diet," Blumberg tells of dragon cures and charms (were iron horseshoes above the door really associated with dragons?) and of saints who conquered dragons with swords (St. George) or holy water (St. Martha). She distinguishes between the "ugly, nasty" Western dragons and the "beautiful, friendly and wise" dragons of the East, where they are respected and honored; and she divides the book into two parts, accordingly. In the latter we learn of the Japanese Emperor Hirohito's dragon ancestry, and of the fossils sold in China as dragon bones. Rather coyly, Blumberg presents the lore as fact—unlike McHargue in *The Beasts of Never,*

who also dealt with Western and Eastern dragons and alluded occasionally to the inconsistency (or whatever) of the beliefs. [Murray] Tinkelman's sinuous, blurry, cross-hatch dragon portraits don't reward the attention their full-page or double-page scale invites. This is, however, far more polished than the same pair's **Backyard Bestiary,** and it might enjoy a spill-over interest from the current fantasy fad.

A review of "The Truth about Dragons," in Kirkus Reviews, *Vol. XLVIII, No. 8, April 15, 1980, p. 514.*

Legends, fancifully presented as facts, about appearance, habits, and uses of Eastern and Western dragons are compared in a breezy text. Large, action-filled depictions of various dragons in Tinkelman's crosshatch style give life to the words. A scholarly bonus is the bibliography which includes rare, recent, foreign, and American sources. This should help fill the constant demand for monster books.

Ann G. Brouse, in a review of "The Truth about Dragons," in School Library Journal, *Vol. 26, No. 10, August, 1980, p. 60.*

You can discover everything you ever wanted or needed to know about dragons in **The Truth about Dragons.** The distinctions between Eastern and Western dragons are clearly given, including their appearance, diet, habitat, social order, mating habits, habits with treasure, enemies, cures, and charms. Sources for this fascinating book on dragon lore include Pliny, a first-century Roman. Pliny gave dragon hunting a 1500-year boost by mentioning that some dragons have a precious jewel inside their heads. . . . Every youngster should be prepared to encounter dragons after reading this definitive dragon treasure.

A review of "The Truth about Dragons," in The Reading Teacher, *Vol. 34, No. 3, December, 1980, p. 351.*

THE FIRST TRAVEL GUIDE TO THE MOON: WHAT TO PACK, HOW TO GO, AND WHAT TO SEE WHEN YOU GET THERE (1980)

This is a rather confusing book in that it gives off a number of contradictory signals: its format and artwork seem to be directed to a much younger audience than YAs. However, the information contained is outstanding. It is up-to-date, to-the-point, and accurate, which can't be said for all such books. Because of some doubts about the book, I tested it out with some of my 7th graders. To my surprise, they loved it. Many have asked to see it again, but I have to refuse them (it is still circulating to first-time readers).

The book is just what it says it is: a travel guide for someone who is planning to travel to the Moon. It is set in the year 2000 and has a matter-of-fact tone that really makes it seem as though it were written then. The great thing, though, is that in the process of describing the flight to the moon and things to do for the tourist on the Moon, Blumberg manages to impart a lot of information about space travel and the Moon, and in a manner that is nearly painless to the reader. It's a super way to inform and entertain at the same time. Sure to be a hit with a younger crowd and with minimal steering, it will be enjoyed by older kids as well.

Stephen Walker, in a review of "The First Travel Guide to the Moon," in Voice of Youth Advocates, *Vol. 4, No. 2, June, 1981, p. 36.*

Blumberg on a visit to China.

Organised visits of two or four weeks to the Moon started in 1992, according to the opening of *The First Travel Guide to the Moon,* and this handbook for tourists in the later years when booking has become almost commonplace includes advice about luggage, currency, hotels and details of the particular attractions offered by the craters or by Moon Town, 'founded in 1990 by twelve American Astronauts and twelve Soviet Cosmonauts'. . . . Cartoons of young travellers gazing at notices, buildings or moonscapes [by Roy Doty] and the deadpan 'advice to travellers' support the playful note of the book but this is not the only aspect to catch the attention. I would hardly expect it to be read for the space-details which, accurate as they are, could be found in any outline of what is known at present about the Moon. The surprise-element, and the most valuable one, is the consistent, unobtrusive emphasis on world co-operation. Young readers may not take particular note of the information on the 'Lingo translator' which they will enjoy using when they meet other tourists, 'whether they come from India, Scandinavia, Bolivia or Zambia'; they may not be more than casually interested in the location of the two main International Earthports, in Kenya and Sri Lanka, or by the fact that 'All announcements are in Arabic, Chinese, English, French, Russian and Spanish'—the official languages of the United Nations'. All the same, this amusing mock travelogue can only start children off with the right ideas, even if they hardly realise it at the time. (pp. 4465-66)

Margery Fisher, in a review of "The First Travel Guide to the Moon," in Growing Point, *Vol. 24, No. 2, July, 1985, p. 4465-66.*

SOUTHERN AFRICA: SOUTH AFRICA, NAMIBIA, SWAZILAND, LESOTHO, AND BOTSWANA (1981)

The author is most effective when describing life in contemporary South Africa and giving a graphic overview of the ways apartheid humiliates, impoverishes and oppresses the majority population. She does a creditable job of unmasking the phoniness of South Africa's so-called independent Black homelands and includes a lengthy critique of the regime's policies in mineral-rich Namibia. Unfortunately, the book contains serious flaws. The historical discussion is Eurocentric and insulting terms ("Bantu," "Hottentot," "natives," "bushmen") are used. Powerful African groups that mounted stiff resistance to the white settlers (like the Zulu) are described as "warlike"; the expansionist settlers are not. Government propaganda statements are occasionally presented without rebuttal; students could easily confuse the regime's distortions for truth. The final chapter on neighboring countries fails to include the historical reasons for the region's economic dependence on South Africa.

Brenda Randolph-Robinson, in a review of "Southern Africa: South Africa, Namibia, Swaziland, Le-

sotho and Botswana," in Interracial Books for Children Bulletin, *Vol. 15, Nos. 7 & 8, 1984, p. 21.*

DEVILS AND DEMONS (1982)

Blumberg goes through a veritable catalog of devils and their accomplices, including witches, demons, and sorcerers. Her breezy style will not appeal to those who take the subject seriously, but her coverage is certainly complete. Among the devilish activities she discusses are pacts made with the devil, the duties of demons, exorcism, and forms of devil worship. One of the book's strong points is its black-and-white photographs and illustrations, some of them quite scary.

> *Ilene Cooper, in a review of "Devils & Demons," in* Booklist, *Vol. 78, No. 20, June 15, 1982, p. 1366.*

THE FIRST TRAVEL GUIDE TO THE BOTTOM OF THE SEA (1983)

As she did in **The First Travel Guide to the Moon** Blumberg posits a voyage and describes the fictional accommodations, meals, entertainment, etc. This has rather less the format and style of a guidebook, since the passengers are not able to leave the submarine, but it gives a great deal of information about topographical phenomena of the sea bottom and about the creatures of the deep sea. The writing style is competent, casual, and direct; an index and a bibliography are included.

> *Zena Sutherland, in a review of "The First Travel Guide to the Bottom of the Sea," in* Bulletin of the Center for Children's Books, *Vol. 36, No. 10, June, 1983, p. 184.*

Blumberg is no match for Jules Verne in dramatic ability or in technical imaginativeness, but her account of a trip aboard an imaginary research submarine may interest children in learning more about the undersea world. The emphasis of Blumberg's tour is on strong, unusual parallels to life in our world. For example, one chapter describes "fish doctors' offices" where cleaner wrasse fish rid larger fish of dead flesh, parasites and bacteria infecting wounds. Coverage of this and other sights is brief and shallow, like a tour guide's spiel. The writing style is informal, accessible and clear, but she uses broad humor in naming the crew members (Hugo Down, Luke Spy-water, Sally Forth, etc.). . . . The standard works in oceanography are generally much better-written and illustrated and more informative, but they are also longer and more involved. Reed and Bronson's *The Sea for Sam* and Aksyonov and Chernov's *Exploring the Deep* could be used as follow-ups after Blumberg's brevity and flip humor has captured children's attention.

> *Jonathan R. Betz-Zall, in a review of "The First Travel Guide to the Bottom of the Sea," in* School Library Journal, *Vol. 30, No. 1, September, 1983, p. 118.*

By means of an imaginary journey through the sea in the research submarine "Sea Dragon," young readers are exposed to numerous and interesting features of the sea. Some of the subjects covered are: wrecks of the continental shelf, underwater sounds of shrimp, fishes and whales, features and organisms of the deep sea trenches, a shallow-water fish cleaning station, coral reefs and their inhabitants, the Sargasso Sea and its biota, the physical features of the mid-Atlantic ridge,

and vertical migration of fish and plankton. Each chapter is short and simple so as not to overwhelm readers. However, enough interesting facts are provided to maintain interest and give an appreciation for the wonders of the oceans.

> *J. Ross Wilcox, in a review of "The First Travel Guide to the Bottom of the Sea," in* Science Books & Films, *Vol. 19, No. 3, January-February, 1984, p. 156.*

MONSTERS (1983)

Aficionados of the monster genre will not be deterred by the loosely flippant scholarship in this dictionary. The alphabetical compilation includes historical and cinematographic entities. Forty-three black-and-white photos or illustrations, ranging from E. T. to recreations of medieval creatures, are included. Weak in comparison to Alison Lurie's lavishly beautiful *Fabulous Beasts* or Barbara Ninde Byfield's *Book of Weird*, this is still a welcome addition to the bestiary scene, if only to satisfy avid fans or those hunting for pictures of vampires, unicorns, mermaids and the like. If customer demand is high, buy an extra copy for your reference shelf.

> *Leslie Chamberlin, in a review of "Monsters," in* School Library Journal, *Vol. 30, No. 4, December, 1983, p. 63.*

THE SIMON AND SCHUSTER BOOK OF FACTS AND FALLACIES (with Leda Blumberg, 1983)

A fascinating examination of the numerous fallacies frequently quoted as facts. Each fallacy is succinctly stated and opposite it the corresponding factual information is provided, illustrating why the fallacy is inaccurate. The factual information, while concise, is detailed enough to explain the discrepancy of the related fallacy. Topics covered include animals, inventions, history, plants, insects, health, sports, weather and earth science. A tongue-in-cheek sense of humor adds an enjoyable element to the many straightforward factual analyses. This volume has a better layout and is more attractive than Gottlieb's *Science Facts You Won't Believe*. The addition of a comprehensive table of contents and index make this a unique and accessible reference book. And that's a fact.

> *Peter Roop, in a review of "The Simon & Schuster Book of Facts and Fallacies," in* School Library Journal, *Vol. 30, No. 8, April, 1984, p. 112.*

This remarkable little book is packed with answers to frequently asked questions in biology, zoology, earth science, and history. It uses a unique format that consists of well-defined leading questions or statements followed by answers and background information. . . . If you have ever tried to explain why flies can walk on ceilings, how many legs a millipede has, or whether fish can drown, you will thoroughly enjoy this book. Whether you are an elementary student or a full-fledged scientist, the book has facts that you can learn and apply everyday or incorporate into formal lessons in general science. The answers are not only scientifically sound but are easy to understand. Although the technical information is not referenced, it can be confirmed with an encyclopedia that can also be used to supplement the details for readers who are more scientifically inclined. In sum, this book is a valuable resource to stimulate interest in science and is a pragmatic source of information for students of general science or introductory biology. Every teacher who deals with young students will find this book a valuable resource in helping to stimulate interest in biology and earth science.

> *James A. Poupard, in a review of "The Simon and Schuster Book of Facts and Fallacies," in* Science Books & Films, *Vol. 19, No. 5, May-June, 1984, p. 295.*

COMMODORE PERRY IN THE LAND OF THE SHOGUN (1985)

Whatever they may say about a book and its cover, you can tell at first glance that this handsomely designed re-enactment of the 1853 East-West encounter is a winner. The Japanese illustration on the cover whets anticipation with its man and boy on shore exclaiming over the strange black ship in the harbor. Most of the treasury of pictures inside are from Japanese art of that time, including Japanese sketches of the American visitors. Other drawings, of the Japanese and their ways, are by official artists who accompanied Perry. All are meticulously chosen and seamlessly integrated with the text.

If the illustrations accentuate the Japanese view of the meeting, Blumberg's text follows American accounts. Blumberg plays down the threat inherent in Perry's militaristic strutting, and she ignores the expansionist context of his mission. With its background briefing on mid-nineteenth-century Japan's feudal rigidity, and its emphasis on the odd sights and customs that bemused the sailors—women who blackened their teeth and gums; guests who emptied the salt-cellar and sugar bowl into their equivalent of doggie bags—her human-interest account of the historic occasion risks reinforcing a nineteenth-century view of curious foreigners. Aware of this hazard, she explains "how mistaken Commodore Perry was in his belief that Japan was uncivilized." And she makes a point of balancing acts of ignorance—so that the sailors have a "belly laugh" when a Japanese guest on board drinks a glass of olive oil for wine, but "the tables are turned" weeks later when a navy man tastes and buys Japanese hair oil for liquor.

So, though one can't deny a sort of *King and I* sensibility, it is just as hard not to be captivated by the amusing details of official pomp and human circumstance on both sides. (pp. J46-J47)

> *A review of "Commodore Perry in the Land of the Shogun," in* Kirkus Reviews, *Juvenile Issue, Vol. LIII, Nos. 5-10, May 15, 1985, pp. J46-J47.*

Good books of history for young people are not as common as one would hope, so this album is especially welcome. Blumberg traces the impact of Commodore Matthew Perry on Japanese culture, using aptly chosen pictures and documents, and in the process provides a wonderful view of 19th-century Japanese culture. Her writing is clear, crisp and alive with fascinating scraps of information. A samurai, for example, wore two swords: the smaller one "was wielded when cutting off the head of a defeated rival. It was also used for *seppuku,* ritual suicide. . . . Seppuku was considered to be particularly well done if the samurai composed a poem before or while committing suicide. . . . The longer sword, the sharpest in the world, could cut through iron nails or split an enemy in two from head to foot." An accompanying sketch by Yoshitowshi depicts an angry warrior still intent on swordplay despite the two arrows in his back. Take that, Conan.

Most of Blumberg's book is not so sanguinary as this, but all of it is equally fascinating and informative.

> *Michael Dirda, in a review of "Commodore Perry in the Land of the Shogun," in* Book World—The Washington Post, *July 14, 1985, p. 8.*

In a book that uses many sources and a wealth of handsome illustrations, the fascinating story of Perry's dealings and difficulties in a country which had deliberately cut itself off from the Western world for several centuries is told with style and vitality, enabling the reader to feel a part of the great adventure. Using a large bibliography and, in particular, Perry's own memories, the author has drawn on material which lends full authority to the book and enriches it with the kind of detail that makes history come to life. The illustrations are especially well chosen, showing as they do the Japanese version of the Americans and the pageantry of the meeting in the Treaty House in Yokohama. The book offers a fine verbal account of the people, food, clothing, and traditions as they appeared to those who visited that virtually unchanged yet highly sophisticated country in the 1850s and a detailed visual interpretation by both the Japanese and American artists who followed and recorded the events with an equally avid interest. (pp. 576-77)

> *Ethel R. Twichell, in a review of "Commodore Perry in the Land of the Shogun," in* The Horn Book Magazine, *Vol. LXI, No. 5, September-October, 1985, pp. 576-77.*

Blumberg's book succeeds on two levels. First it is a well-written story of Matthew Perry's expedition to open Japan to American trade and whaling ports. The account is sensitive to the extreme cultural differences that both the Japanese and Americans had to overcome. Especially good are the chapters and paragraphs explaining Japanese feudal society and culture. The text is marvelously complemented by the illustrations, almost all reproductions of contemporary Japanese art, underscoring the unbiased approach of the book. On the second level, the book is a well-researched chronicle of the events of the trip. Blumberg has gone to the original sources to capture the sights, emotions, reactions and even tastes of both the Japanese and Americans. Yet she has not neglected the political and economic importance or mission of Perry's trip. The notes, appendixes and bibliography show a carefully thought out book which holds valuable information for sophisticated readers. There is no better book for students on this historical event.

> *John Buschman, in a review of "Commodore Perry in the Land of the Shogun," in* School Library Journal, *Vol. 32, No. 2, October, 1985, p. 168.*

Blumberg does an excellent job of explaining Commodore Perry's mission to Japan, while at the same time describing the rules and rituals of that then-mysterious country. An enlightening narrative, this begins with Perry's arrival in Japanese waters in 1853 and makes clear the people's initial terror as well as Perry's resolve to open Japanese harbors to American ships. Throughout, the author emphasizes the human side rather than the treaty negotiations, and it is this focus that makes the treatment so compelling. Particularly fascinating are the numerous graphics. . . . Quality nonfiction. (pp. 401-02)

> *Ilene Cooper, in a review of "Commodore Perry in the Land of the Shogun," in* Booklist, *Vol. 82, No.*

5, November 1, 1985, pp. 401-02.

THE INCREDIBLE JOURNEY OF LEWIS AND CLARK (1987)

The Lewis and Clark expedition, that staple of American history courses, is given a fresh account here. Blumberg explores a confrontation between two cultures, in a manner which is sympathetic to and revealing of the feelings of both peoples. She describes the experience of entering those lands west of the Mississippi, uncharted territory when President Jefferson proposed the expedition in 1803. The 16 chapters which follow the journey are arranged chronologically, concluding with the return of the explorers in 1806. The text is clear and often entertaining, with concrete details to bring historical events to life. Blumberg is refreshingly frank about the humanness of the expedition's members and the relationships that they had with some of the native Americans. The concluding chapter is a rather hasty summing up, but final sections, which include detailed chapter notes and an "Aftermath" about the later lives of prominent members of the expedition make up for this. Much care has been taken throughout the book to use and refer to primary sources, both in text and illustrations, which are generally well reproduced. Blumberg is not a great prose stylist—her text is often flat, and her people don't come to life. Where she shines is in the imaginative use of extensive research to tell, compellingly and entertainingly, stories from history. She respects her subject and her audience: an approach which makes this an outstanding choice to introduce young readers to this seminal American event.

Christine Behrmann, in a review of "The Incredible Journey of Lewis & Clark," in School Library Journal, *Vol. 34, No. 4, December, 1987, p. 90.*

The tale of an expedition into territory "mysterious as Mars," told with the Newbery Honor author's characteristic clarity and enthusiasm.

In the early 19th century, the interior of this country was thought to hide any number of oddities: strange monsters, mountains of salt, a lost Welsh tribe. In an effort to discover the facts, as well as to map out trade routes, President Jefferson dispatched a small party of soldiers westward on the Missouri River. Along with guides and interpreters (notably the young Shoshoni, Sacagawea) and Clark's black slave, York, this group collected samples of previously unknown wildlife, produced excellent maps and, most importantly, witnessed a panorama of Native American life and customs.

The author makes this all sound like the grand adventure it was, though she also carefully notes the drastic effects of trade, whiskey, and smallpox on native cultures. A large selection of 19th-century illustrations complements and extends the text; disappointingly, all are reproduced in black-and-white, and many are murky. Andrist's *To the Pacific with Lewis and Clark* may be more appealing visually, but this makes more engrossing reading. Index, bibliography, and excellent notes are appended.

A review of "The Incredible Journey of Lewis and Clark," in Kirkus Reviews, *Vol. LV, No. 23, December 1, 1987, p. 1672.*

[This] is a most impressive addition to the body of books about the three-year journey of exploration (1803-1806) led by Meriwether Lewis and William Clark. . . . Blumberg's writing is dignified but never dry, and her sense of narrative makes familiar history an exciting story. Maps are included, as are a bibliography, an index, chapter notes, and an "Aftermath" that describes participants' lives after 1806.

Zena Sutherland, in a review of "The Incredible Journey of Lewis and Clark," in Bulletin of the Center for Children's Books, *Vol. 41, No. 5, January, 1988, p. 82.*

Documented with extreme care from both primary and secondary sources, illustrated with early American paintings, and narrated with style, even humor, the book treats Lewis and Clark very well indeed. In an interesting and accessible text that can easily be handled by intermediate readers, Blumberg chronicles the nearly two-and-one-half-year, seven-thousand-mile journey of the Corps of Discovery from St. Louis to the Pacific coast. Excellent maps show very clearly the routes west and east as well as the locations of Indian tribes that were met and whose customs were studied. . . . The accomplishments of the expedition are notable, and the author clearly makes a case for their importance. The format works extremely well, with many illustrations of varying sizes inviting the reader to browse and then stop to discover details recorded by artists such as George Catlin, Charles B. King, Alfred Jacob Miller, and Charles M. Russell. Blumberg has real talent for extracting from reams of material those facts that will fascinate youngsters and then expressing them in an extremely readable text. An excellent history book. (pp. 220-21)

Elizabeth S. Watson, in a review of "The Incredible Journey of Lewis and Clark," in The Horn Book Magazine, *Vol. LXIV, No. 2, March-April, 1988, pp. 220-21.*

THE GREAT AMERICAN GOLD RUSH (1989)

Lively writing and careful use of primary sources make this a treasure trove; drawings and photos of the participants and extensive quotes from contemporary letters, diaries, speeches, and newspaper accounts also make the "gold fever" that drew hordes of adventurers to California in 1849 vivid and immediate.

Blumberg describes both sea and overland journeys, with the privations en route. Once in California, forty-niners faced high prices, shortages, disease, lawlessness, racial prejudice, swindlers, and quacks. "Seeing the elephant" was an expression that conveyed hardships endured: "Sick miners and disappointed prospectors wrote . . . that they had 'seen the elephant' and were ready to quit digging." Although $250 million in gold was dug between 1848 and 1852, most "argonauts" never found treasure. The Gold Rush did, however, increase California's population from 15,000 to 250,000; make businessmen and bankers like Levi Strauss and Heinrich Schliemann wealthy; and help the US become "one of the richest, most powerful nations in the world."

Compelling reading that brings a fascinating era to life.

A review of "The Great American Gold Rush," in Kirkus Reviews, *Vol. LVII, No. 17, September 15, 1989, p. 1399.*

An important and compelling period of our country's history is brought to life in Blumberg's account, with its exciting, "you-are-there" quality. Drawn extensively from primary sources, the material includes extracts and quotations from letters, diaries and newspapers, as well as reproductions of period cartoons, posters, ads and sketches. Footnotes and maps expand the text in which a handsome typeface is framed by wide margins on generously sized pages, creating an open, inviting look. Much information on 19th-century attitudes toward minorities and women—and the effects of those attitudes during the Gold Rush era—is presented. However, the inclusion of blacks and Indians in the "Foreigners" chapter subtly reinforces racist views. An excellent index and a bibliography are provided for this book which vividly illustrates the constant influences of history on our lives and times.

A review of "The Great American Gold Rush," in Publishers Weekly, *Vol. 236, No. 4, October 13, 1989, p. 55.*

A self-styled "compulsive researcher," Blumberg is one of the finest historians now writing for children. Rather than taking the wide-angled view of conventional historical narratives, she likes to zoom in on events or episodes in history that mark a turning-point or illuminate a place or period, as she did in her award-winning *Commodore Perry in the Land of the Shogun* and *The Incredible Journey of Lewis and Clark.*

The Great American Gold Rush—a subject that very much suits Blumberg's approach—is a straightforward, beautifully written account of the frenzied years when people from all over the world thought the roads of California were paved with gold. In fact, they were mostly dirt tracks, dusty in summer, treacherous with mud in winter. Beginning with the original discovery of a dime-sized nugget at Sutter's Mill in January 1848 (Sutter tried to keep it quiet, but "a secret of such brilliance was bound to radiate," Blumberg observes), the book goes back to contemporary newspapers, letters, journals and other eyewitness accounts to describe the hazards of the routes taken to California by goldseekers, whether overland or by sea round Cape Horn, and the lawlessness, bigotry and sheer physical misery of everyday life on the goldfields for the ordinary folk who in the end got very little of the quarter of a billion dollars' worth of gold dug up between 1848 and 1852.

Elizabeth Ward, "From a Flash in the Pan to a Glitter in the Sky," in Book World—The Washington Post, *November 5, 1989, p. 20.*

Ingri d'Aulaire
1904-1980
Edgar Parin d'Aulaire
1898-1986

Ingri—Norwegian-born American author and illustrator of picture books, fiction, and nonfiction and reteller.

Edgar—Swiss or German-born American author and illustrator of picture books, fiction, and nonfiction and reteller.

Hailed as major contributors to the establishment of the picture book as a legitimate art form, the d'Aulaires enjoyed a prolific and successful career which spanned four decades. The husband and wife team invested their works with distinctive lithograph illustrations and texts applauded for their sincerity and innocence in works directed to toddlers and readers in the early elementary grades. Often celebrated as the first artists to employ color lithography in books for children, the d'Aulaires are acclaimed for heightening the technical aspects of the medium to near perfection. Ingri's homeland of Norway figured predominantly in the d'Aulaires' books, not only in those on the lives of children of the North, but in works concerning Scandinavian myths, legends, and folktales. The first and most popular of these titles is *Ola* (1932), the story of a young boy's adventures over several months which range from a skiing accident to a fishing expedition. Imbued with information on Norwegian folklore, customs, and industry, the work received acclaim for both its landscapes and prose, which hover between realism and dreamlike fantasy. Avid travelers, the d'Aularies also composed works infused with facts about the lands they visited as well as their first-hand experiences, sensations, and childlike delight in discovery of the unexpected. Their immigration to the United States in 1929 sparked the couple's interest in major figures of American history; several of their subsequent titles feature such national heroes as Columbus, George Washington, and Benjamin Franklin. Of these biographies, the d'Aularies are undoubtedly best known for *Abraham Lincoln* (1939), which was awarded the Caldecott Medal in 1940. By gathering homey incidents from Lincoln's early life, the d'Aulaires created a portrayal noted for its simplicity, matter-of-factness, and appeal to children. Despite the d'Aulaires' comprehensive research and prearranged hiking and camping expeditions through the regions associated with their subjects to ensure the authenticity of their works, some critics feel *Abraham Lincoln* and the d'Aulaires' other biographies lack genuine American spirit. Nonetheless, the popularity of these books attest to their charm and the allure of the details which bring the past into focus for young readers. The biographies are also apt examples of the integration of the d'Aulaires' talents; the couple was frequently quoted as saying that Edgar brought the drama to their books and Ingri the humor. In their works on famous Americans, as well as their titles of a wide variety of subjects from Greek mythology to "The Star Spangled Banner," these two facets are in evidence.

As with their texts, the synthesis of the d'Aulaires special abilities is obvious in their illustrations, which merge Edgar's knowledge of architecture and landscapes and Ingri's experi-

ence in child portraiture. While the d'Aulaires have been extolled for their virtuosity in stone lithographic technique, their illustrations are also cited for their quaint folk art quality, humorous touches, luminosity of color, and primitive use of perspective typical of children's artwork. Much of the d'Aulaires' later career was spent redrawing their earlier illustrations; for example, *Abraham Lincoln* was redone on acetate in 1957 because printers were unwilling to handle the cumbersome stone slabs required for lithography. Separately and in collaboration, the d'Aulaires executed drawings for the works of other authors. Most notably, Edgar illustrated the Newbery honor book *Children of the Soil: A Story of Scandinavia* (1932) by Nora Burglon, and both d'Aulaires created pictures for Peter Christen Asbjørnsen's *East of the Sun and West of the Moon: Twenty-One Norwegian Folktales* (1938). The d'Aulaires were awarded the Regina Medal in 1970 for their body of work and *D'Aulaires' Trolls* (1972) was named a National Book Award finalist in 1973.

(See also *Something about the Author,* Vols. 5, and 24 [obituary]; 47 [obituary]; *Contemporary Authors,* Vols. 49-52; 102 [obituary]; and Vol. 119 [obituary].)

GENERAL COMMENTARY

MAY MASSEE

The [d'Aulaires's] finished books look so finished and sure that one might think that all the artists do is plan and draw—not so with the d'Aulaires for they make their own lithographs, using the old technique of the artist lithographer who had to do all his work by hand, without the use of the camera. This means that first of all the color drawings have to be sketched on paper the exact size needed—and these sketches are really complete color drawings for they have to be copied exactly on stones.

After a picture is complete on paper, Edgar makes the first drawing on the lithograph stone. He draws with crayon and his hand must be absolutely sure of every line, for there is no erasing or going over lines on a stone or zinc. What is put down is there to stay and if a drawing has to be changed a whole new drawing has to be made.

The first drawing is the black part of the finished picture. This means not only the lines, but all the shadows that need black and also some of the color spots that need a little black to deepen them. Only long practice and scientific accuracy (for the technique of an artist in his studio is as accurate as that of a scientist in his laboratory) have taught Edgar just how to make the key plate. And then the work of getting in the color begins.

The lithographer makes four impressions of that key plate on a large stone that weighs about two hundred pounds. One of these impressions is left just as it is to show the black part of the picture. Then the artists must look at their color sketch and pick out all the red places for the red plate, the blues for the blue and the yellows for the yellow. This would be comparatively simple if the colors were just flat and clear, but most of the time they are mixed—for instance, the greens are always part blue and part yellow, and to know just how heavy to make the blue and how heavy to make the yellow requires not only skill but infinite patience. And each of these colors must have a separate drawing for itself, so that the finished stone has four drawings on it,—one each for the black, the red, the blue and the yellow.

Now the lithographer must make the transfers and here, too, the artist must know what he wants and how to get it, for the wrong shade of color or the wrong etching of a plate may bring sea green on the meadows and grass green on the sea, or tomato red on the faces and easily spoil a picture. Multiply this process by the number of pictures in a book, and it is easy to see that any one of their picture books needs months of steady labor after the preliminary planning, the writing and sketching have all been done. (pp. 265-66)

In a book that Ingri and Edgar have made together, it is impossible to say what each has contributed, because it is all the work of both. Of course, *Ola* and *Ola and Blakken* came right out of Ingri's childhood. Norway, with its fascinating pine forests whose trees need only a proper amount of snow to turn into "a crowd of solemn creatures"—trolls, perhaps. Norway, the land in which you can ski into the gayety of a country wedding, made much more gay if you can hear Ingri say very fast, with a little twist of the tongue: "Siri and Turi, Randi and Guri, Mari and Kari and Gro." They are the little girls who take Ola to the wedding. It is a country where reality quickly meets fantasy and merges into it; a beautiful land, perfect for a sensitive child. It is all Ingri's by inheritance and living, but it has become Edgar's through his close association with Ingri's family, and many small nieces and nephews who live up to the family traditions for activity and enjoyment.

This sense of the joy of living is very real in their latest book, *Children of the Northlights,* where Lise and Lasse Lapp live in a white world whose sky flames into a strange beauty with the "Northlights." And whether it is playing bear or chasing reindeer, being buried in a snowdrift or helping the family to move, driving their own reindeer sleds, taking steambaths and diving into the snow, or sitting primly in school, these Lapp children are enjoying life every minute, and by the way, Ingri said they were some of the most beautiful children she has ever seen.

The d'Aulaires enjoy life themselves and are always ready to adapt themselves to anything that happens to them. They tell with glee that their first trip to America was the result of a bus accident in Paris. The damages were serious, but not too serious, and the accident insurance bought Edgar a tourist ticket to New York. Ingri came later, after Edgar had found work for them.

They had spent the year before in Kairawan in Tunis, and they were all ready and waiting to write a book about it. *The Magic Rug* is that book and it has given many children wings for their feet to take them far away. After that came *Ola* and *Ola and Blakken* and then *The Conquest of the Atlantic. The Conquest* is a combination history, exploration and discovery book. It is full of pictures, but the text is a rapid and true-to-fact record of hundreds of years of men's wanderings over the Atlantic, from the earliest Viking voyages to modern airplane conquests, and the text as well as the pictures is interesting to the old and the young, but not the too young. This book will make a new thrill for any voyager over the Atlantic, as it gives a vivid sense of one's being a discoverer, and leaves a reader very sure that there are still more worlds of discovery to conquer.

The d'Aulaires themselves do not know what may come next. When they were asked to make a picture book for The Lord's Prayer, they said it could not be done. And then Ingri thought of the way she used to love that prayer and decided to try to put into pictures what she had thought of it, as a little girl, and the resulting picture book is treasured by many like-minded little girls and boys. (pp. 269-70)

> *May Massee, "Ingri and Edgar Parin d'Aulaire: A Sketch," in* The Horn Book Magazine, *Vol. XI, No. 5, September-October, 1935, pp. 265-70.*

BERTHA E. MAHONY AND MARGUERITE M. MITCHELL

When *The Magic Rug* appeared in the fall of 1931, we knew that this book represented something new in the art of children's books. The drawings had the effect of being originals. We did not know that this book probably marked a new chapter in the marriage of two gifted people. From this time on they were to cease any concern about the interference of their marriage with their work. Their work was to be completely fused in their children's books, however much each might continue to paint separately and individually.

The Magic Rug grew out of a visit to North Africa where they had made more than two thousand sketches and paintings. In the fall of 1932 came *Ola,* a story of a little boy in Norway's winter, a book which has so endeared itself to our children that Ola lives for them; and in recent tragic happenings, they have asked over and over again in the Children's Rooms of Public Libraries, "Is Ola all right?" "Do you know where Ola is now? Oh, I hope nothing has happened to him." (p. 258)

Once children had had the story of Ola in winter, they must know what Ola was up to in summer. In 1933 came *Ola and Blakken*. And in this same year came another distinguished book from the d'Aulaires, *The Conquest of the Atlantic;* a book which to many of us symbolizes the ranging vision of this partnership. For this book the artists examined source material in the New York Public Library and the Library of the University of Norway in Oslo; the Musée de la Marine of the Louvre in Paris gave them accurate ship models, apparatus and costumes of the different periods. It is a picture-story book of the piercing of mysteries and the annihilation of ocean distances down through the ages. (pp. 259-60)

In 1934 came *The Lord's Prayer,* a book about which there will always be differences of opinion. We wish the artists had not seen fit to make it. As a matter of fact, when the plan for the book was first presented to them they thought it impossible. Later Ingri remembered her own images for the words as a child and they felt that they could undertake the picture book. We believe that on subjects like this prayer, a child's imagination should be left free to the ever-changing vision which comes with the years.

Before their next book was published, Ingri and Edgar d'Aulaire were to take one of the trips which are so much a part of their life and work. From Hammerfest, the most northerly town of Europe, they were to take a small boat to Bossekopp and from there proceed on horseback to Gargia in Lapland. From Gargia they started out on sleds drawn by reindeer, driving their own sled—a new experience for them. . . . The book which grew out of this trip was *Children of the Northlights.* It follows a little Lapp brother and sister, Lise and Lasse, through a year of their life. It was published in September, 1935.

When examining the d'Aulaires' *George Washington* and *Abraham Lincoln,* grown-ups should remember two things—1. That Edgar's mother was American. Her father had fought in the Civil War on the Northern side, although he had owned a plantation in the Southwest. Living in a foreign land, she had told the child Edgar stories of American heroes. Not only did Edgar have the bond of ancestry with America, but, as is characteristic of them, Edgar and Ingri walked over Virginia for their Washington material and camped for weeks with a car and tent in three states to gather their great portfolios of local color for the *Abraham Lincoln.* 2. That the d'Aulaires have made the drawings for these books from the standpoint of the children themselves. The horses do deliberately resemble rocking horses because the toy horse of childhood has been used as model. Toward the end of the book *George Washington,* turn to the picture of Washington taking command of his army in Cambridge. This is such a scene as a child might set up with his tin soldiers, toy buildings and trees. That is exactly what the artists had in mind as they drew.

Qualities which we feel in the two *Olas* and which some of us miss in the two American books have undoubtedly sprung from real roots of childhood wonder and joy cherished in long unconscious growth. Perhaps the American scene and material needed a longer period of assimilation. However we react to it, the work of artists always does something to

strengthen and clarify our critical point of view. These are adult concerns. The children take no heed of them. (pp. 260-62)

Just how do these two people work together? Edgar says, "When you find something amusingly expressed in our books, then it has been said by Ingri." Ingri says, "The dramatic quality of the story comes from Edgar." They both would say that Ingri contributes the intimate knowledge of children. They both would say that Edgar directs the methods of their work, for these artists draw their color illustrations directly on the lithograph stone as early craftsmen did. (p. 263)

Bertha E. Mahony and Marguerite M. Mitchell, "Ingri and Edgar Parin d'Aulaire," in The Horn Book Magazine, *Vol. XVI, No. 4, July-August, 1940, pp. 257-64.*

DOROTHY NEAL WHITE

In 1940 the Caldecott Medal for the outstanding picture book of the year was presented to Ingri and Edgar Parin d'Aulaire for their *Abraham Lincoln.* The award was a significant one, for Ingri, a Norwegian by birth, and Edgar, an Italian [sic], had in that particular book expressed all their feeling and affection for America, the country of their adoption. Both were European artists, who after their marriage, had painted landscapes in France, Italy, Germany, Dalmatia, and North Africa, each of them working separately as at that time like many young artists they were mortally afraid of being influenced by each other in any way. It does not seem to have occurred to them that their marriage had destroyed any real basis for such rugged individualism, and that whether they liked it or not, their art would alter by reason of their personal proximity.

When ultimately the peripatetic pair reached New York, Anne Carroll Moore of the New York Public Library, who has brought dozens of authors and artists of genius to children's literature, suggested to them that they might co-operate on a story book for younger readers. Unwilling at first, they agreed and found their métier. In *Children of the northlights, Ola,* and, *Ola and Blakken,* they gave American children three imaginative, exquisitely beautiful picture books about Norway, picture books which expressed the whole spirit of the north, lonely fjord, high mountain, remote valley, and the fantastic creatures of Norwegian folk lore who have their dwelling there. Ingri wrote and drew as a native does, from deep-rooted affection; Edgar wrote and drew as the newcomer does, with the sharp eye for what is unique to an individual country. Working as they do directly on a lithographic stone, a laborious process which gives a soft blurred tone which no other technique can produce, they make all their picture books with the same care and integrity which Ingri had formerly given to her child portraits and Edgar to his murals. They soon became established as two of the most gifted picture-book makers of this century.

Later they made distinctly American books, notably *George Washington* and *Abraham Lincoln.* Both these, as I have said, symbolized their Americanization. The two elder statesmen of the United States are described almost as legendary figures for the benefit of youngest readers, and the general result is charming. In preparation for these books, the d'Aulaires tramped and camped in the Lincoln and Washington country, but they did not come as close to it as to the country of the northlights. The Norwegian stories are fuller,

At the fireplace sat an old fiddler, playing and singing, and at a long table the wedding party was seated. The bride looked just like a princess with a huge silver crown on her head, and the groom had silver buttons wherever there was a place on his suit. The bridal feast was to last for several days, and this was just a light meal to give the wedding party strength for the long ride to church.

From Ola, written and illustrated by Ingri and Edgar Parin d'Aulaire.

richer, and more deeply rooted than the books about their adopted country. (pp. 39-40)

Dorothy Neal White, "Picture Books," in her About Books for Children, *New Zealand Council for Educational Research in Conjunction with New Zealand Library Association, 1946, pp. 13-44.*

MAY HILL ARBUTHNOT

[*George Washington, Leif the Lucky, Abraham Lincoln,* and *Pocahontas*] are a real contribution to the youngest. They are large books, eight by eleven inches, copiously illustrated with full-page lithographs in deep, glowing colors, on alternate pages, and with black and whites and innumerable small pictures in between. Some of the pictures have a certain stiffness which is not always pleasing. The *Washington* is the most unconvincing. There is one scene in which a field of grain looks like a river. You have to read the text to find out what the picture is about. Also, Mrs. D'Aulaire, a Norwegian, has a strong trend toward the peasant type of child in her illustrations. This is legitimate in their edition of *East of the Sun* and is also appropriate in *Leif the Lucky,* in which the Viking hero is of course the Scandinavian type. Many people have felt that it is not so happy a trend in the interpretation of American heroes.

These, however, are minor criticisms of work that is vigorous, alive with action, full of humor, and genuinely interpretative. *Pocahontas* is a gay book and the most winning story of them all. *Leif the Lucky* is the most rich and colorful, *Abraham Lincoln* the most humorous and revealing. Study the details

of the pictures in *Lincoln.* No need to talk about the doorless dwellings—in one picture a horse has stuck his head into the single room of the cabin and seems to be taking a neighborly interest in the new baby. Notice the little boys' single galluses upon which hang all the responsibility for holding up their scanty pants. Look at that three-sided shelter of the Lincolns, so hard to describe, but so completely re-created with all its pitiable details. You see for yourself the dangers of sand bars and fallen trees in the river. Abe's tallness is amusingly revealed over and over without the necessity for verbal descriptions. No need to say that Mary Todd was something of a termagant, nor that she had a few problems to contend with in Abe. That picture of the wildly disordered parlor, with Abe on the floor in stocking feet, and with Mary, arms akimbo, reflected in the elegant mirror, is a demonstration of their fundamental unlikeness. The book is full of just the sort of sly humor that characterized Abe himself, and every picture, including the small marginal sketches, will reward careful study. These are not merely ornamental illustrations but thoughtful and detailed interpretations of the man and the times. The D'Aulaires should continue this series of pictorial biographies upon which they have made so enlivening a beginning.

The text of these life stories is extremely simple, and the D'Aulaires have garnered episodes that young children can understand and enjoy, like the one about Abe's holding a child upside down to walk on the ceiling, or the one about Abe's riding a wild horse while successfully holding his stovepipe hat. A series of related dramatic episodes gradually reveals the maturing man and his achievements. This is the pattern of these picture books, which are introducing children easily and happily to the heroes they will learn more about later on. They can be read to children from six years old on, and children of eight or nine can read them for themselves. (pp. 481-83)

> May Hill Arbuthnot, "Biographies for Young Children," in her *Children and Books, Scott, Foresman and Company, 1947, pp. 480-84.*

BARBARA BADER

[Even] in the more finished drawings for *Ola,* there is a difference between the d'Aulaires' illustrations and those current in children's books. In disregarding, when it suited them, such conventions of post-Renaissance painting as perspective and proportion (part of what got the poster artists in trouble), the d'Aulaires had two alternative traditions to draw upon, one not long since revived, one still quite new—the decorative, often dramatic stylization of folk art and the willful, often expressive distortion of modernist art. In Ingri d'Aulaire's native Norway, which her husband adopted as his own, the folk strain had been renewed in the work, most notably, of Gerhard Munthe, while the modern idiom was theirs by training and prolonged contact. They made use of both, not so much in a formal, figurative sense as in reaching a rapprochement with children, extracting from folk art and modernist art the intensity and arbitrariness that cause them to be identified with the art of children. (p. 42)

Ola, Ola and Blakken and *Children of the Northlights* made the d'Aulaires' reputation as Norwegian emissaries to the United States. As spontaneous and almost as unstructured as [Maud and Miska Petersham's] *Miki* or *Miki and Mary,* they are ballasted more firmly by their background and forswear outright fantasy.

Beginning with *The Magic Rug,* the d'Aulaires' early books also established their medium, stone lithographs, as a brilliant new way of getting color into picturebooks; technically, they are as important in that respect as *Miki.* As the d'Aulaires explain, "It wasn't so much lithography in itself but color lithography which was the new idea, the complicated procedure of translating colors into infinite shades of blacks and grays and transferring the work to offset zincs to be printed in the right colors. This eliminates the photographic process, and gives the finished work a handdrawn look. (p. 44)

Because of cost, color appeared in the d'Aulaire books only at alternate openings, and half the illustration fell to the black and white pages (a scheme that predominated, in one way or another, until quite recently). It is well known that monochromatic prints or drawings can have as much 'color' as those in several hues, and lithographs, capable of the most complete gamut of tone of any graphic medium, have uncommon potential in this regard. And as they can be any of many things from the barest sketch to the equivalent of a finished painting, the artist has uncommon latitude. For *Conquest of the Atlantic,* done largely in black and white (with sometimes a second color, seldom several), the d'Aulaires designed solidly, keeping a close harmony between tone applied in rhythmic strokes and modeling, and composing in the deep blacks and luminous white that are another glory of the medium. Altogether different, the reindeer design from *Children of the Northlights,* abstracted after the fashion of prehistoric rock

images, is as beautiful as anything they have done and in its own way a consummate example of lithography.

There followed *George Washington, Abraham Lincoln, Leif the Lucky, Pocahontas, Benjamin Franklin, Buffalo Bill, Columbus*—the pictorial gallery of American heroes that children took to happily and some adults received with reservations. (pp. 44-5)

The ingenuousness of *George Washington* accounts for much of its charm as a children's book, that combination of gravity and gentle raillery that aligns the horses of Washington and his companions-at-arms like Rockettes, that stands G. W. upright through an arctic blizzard crossing the Delaware, that thrusts frostbitten feet into the picture of the commander-in-chief wrapped in his cloak at Valley Forge. Nor has Washington any the less luster for the owl looking over his shoulder.

Abraham Lincoln is a more dimensional and therefore a more difficult hero, and neither the treatment of the subject nor the treatment of the illustrations is as successful—the latter because they lack the broad simplicity that is the d'Aulaires' strength. But with *Leif the Lucky* they are not only on home ground, they are immersed in Norse myth and Nordic fire-and-ice. "He shall eat till he bursts," growls King Olav when one of his men fails to stop on signal, while the others quaff from horns, rats and mice consort under the table, and a trough of flames licks at the line of feet. It is all larger than life, and full-up with grinning demons and dramatic invention.

Unfortunately some of the d'Aulaire books have lost in the printing over the years, a fate not uncommon to picturebooks. But to work such as theirs, where matter is inseparable from manner, the damage is particularly destructive, and reminds us that the more illustration relies on realization of a complex intention, the more it is likely to suffer from error, penury or just unconcern. (p. 46)

> Barbara Bader, "Foreign Backgrounds," in her *American Picturebooks from Noah's Ark to the Beast Within, Macmillan Publishing Co., Inc., 1976, pp. 38-59.*

LEONARD S. MARCUS

The writing and illustration of biographies for children is most often an attempt at praise. Folk heroes like Johnny Appleseed and Joan of Arc, and inventors and statesmen like Benjamin Franklin recur in the lists, which change constantly with shifts in social awareness: many more children's biographies of women, black people, and American Indians have, for instance, appeared in the last few years than ever before. Infamous people do not receive attention, usually, except as moral foils. The psychology of evil—psychology as such—is not the underlying concern of most biographies for children. Rather, the central character's life in children's biographies is often offered as an exemplum, as a model for the child. Young George Washington, little readers have been told again and again, chopped down a cherry tree but never, never told a lie. (p. 15)

A biographer's praise . . . may take a variety of turns: it may focus on the uneventful and not especially promising times of a life as well as on the prophetic moments and recognized accomplishments. Praise that consists of a celebration of the ordinary details of experience remains more rare as a feature of biographies for children than of those written for the rest of us. Nonetheless, Ingri and Edgar Parin d'Aulaire, who published the first of their celebrated children's picture book biography series in the 1930s, managed to include such material, traveling as part of their research to many of the places their subjects—Washington, Columbus, Leif Erikson, and others—had lived, sketching and recording many small impressions of sight, odor, and sound for a documentation grounded in the immediacy of the senses as well as in objective historical fact. Thus in their biography of Christopher Columbus, they write: "the water [off Haiti] was so clear and seemed so safe that Columbus relaxed his watch and lay down to rest." When the Washington family (George having just become old enough to begin school) set out by carriage for a new home, "every now and then the wheels stuck in a mudhole, or a rotten tree fell straight across the road. The horses jumped over the tree and quite forgot that the carriage could not jump too. . . ." As a boy, George and the other Washington children sat around the fireplace each evening, listening to their mother tell Bible stories. "On the shiny tiles of the fireplace there were painted pictures of the stories she told. Thus George learned his Bible," the authors conclude, turning a precise bit of observation into the lead-in to a moral lesson of their own, "and he learned to be good and honest and never tell a lie." The human Washington turns to bronze—or stone.

The d'Aulaires do not recount the cherry tree anecdote, which is probably apocryphal. But they leave the thoughtful reader to wonder how, for instance, to reconcile their comment that the grown Washington's "hundreds of slaves and servants kept everything spick and span and in beautiful order" with their absolute faith in his goodness. An unquestioning determination to offer a moral example even when the facts (and complex moral issues involved) do not necessarily justify it has led to many such disturbing contradictions in biographies for children.

Illustration, for which the d'Aulaires perhaps remain best known, is itself a form of praise in picture book biographies. Pictures of course also serve the useful purpose of addressing children who do not yet know how to read. "Seeing comes before words," as the art historian John Berger has said. "The child looks and recognizes before it can speak"—or read. And in biographies and other books that largely deal with the past, illustrations put a face on the abstraction of *pastness,* placing this concept more readily within the reach of children whose more familiar experience of time is that of a continuing present.

But illustration also engages a more general condition of our ability—whether we are readers or not—to take in experience. "It is seeing," Berger says, "which establishes our place in the world; we explain that world with words, but words can never undo the fact that we are surrounded by it. The relation between what we see and what we know is never settled."

Illustrations, then, contribute more to a picture book biography than occasional picture-equivalents of the author's words. They traffic to some degree in unnameable objects, states and feelings. It is hard to say just what effect the visually rough-faced textural ground of the d'Aulaires' illustrations, lithographed on stone in five colors, has on our reading of these pictures—it suggests perhaps a "homemade" quaintness of expression that in the d'Aulaires' best work conveys a touching, delicate grandeur. But the experience of fine illustration remains irreducible. Along with what it tells us about the values, temperament and concerns of a biography's central character, fine illustration also puts us in contact with an individuality—and a form of praise—that is esthetic. (pp. 16-17)

The d'Aulaires' biographies keep to a regular pattern: large picture book format; a single full-page illustration or one or more small ones on every facing page; illustrations of alternating spreads in black-and-white and color; all illustrations lithographed; all colors more intense than in nature, as if to suggest an inner light or emotional resonance for every character and scene. Perspective is usually foreshortened, much modelling dispensed with in favor of a flat, "naive" story picture. Characters placed in these settings rarely seem larger-than-life and often look doll-like, well within the scale of a small child's sensible world. The image conveyed, of the past as a kind of toy world filled with animated toys (some of the time, it must be said, this impression arises mainly from an awkwardness in the illustrators' figure drawing), seems well suited to a young child's first encounters with the abstraction of "the past." And the d'Aulaires carry over into their writing this same assurance about the boundedness of the world in which such heroes as Lincoln and Washington live, as when the authors report that once, when Christopher Columbus was a boy, he "held an orange in his hand, and saw the tips of a butterfly's wings peeping up from behind it. He thought that just like this did the sails of a ship, far away, rise slowly over the horizon. It must be true that the world was round!"

In *Buffalo Bill,* the biographers' impulse to praise arcs off in the direction of the adventure story. Bill's capacity for horseback riding and buffalo hunting is glorified, his exuberance and evident joy in activity seemingly their own justification and reward. But what, the reader may ask, of all the Indians who got killed along the way? In one passage, a moral doubt concerning this question surfaces: "Soldiers were sent out to protect the white men and drive the Indians off their ancient hunting grounds. Buffalo Bill was sorry for the Indians. . . ." A sorrow, however, easily overcome: "But he knew that, vast as the plains were, there wasn't room for Indians and white men both. And as he knew the plains better than most other white men, he became an army scout." Bill, the tireless adventurer, will simply not be fenced into the role of moral hero, despite the d'Aulaires' best (and we now see, questionable) efforts. (pp. 18-19)

By far the best of their biographies both from the standpoint of illustration and writing is *Leif the Lucky,* the story of Leif Erikson. "A thousand years ago," they begin, "when the Vikings roamed the seas, led by their Norse gods, there lived a man in Norway called Erik the Red. He was able and strong but his temper was wild, and after a fight he was banned from Norway."

Epic forces have raised their heads and with them, apparently, a more subtle appreciation of human nature than the d'Aulaires usually show in their biographies. . . . A volatile, thrilling play of chance, nature, and fate makes Leif's world, as described by the d'Aulaires, less predictable and less morally contained than Washington's or Lincoln's: "[Leif's] ship swayed like a rocking horse. For a long time it was thrown about on the sea." After a treacherous voyage, he finds his rightful name, "Leif the Lucky," a hero of chance (even if, as the d'Aulaires suggest, his conversion from paganism to Christianity may have greatly improved his chances).

The d'Aulaires' drawings also take off with an energy and

fullness of vision not often matched in the series, or in picture book biographies generally. Wonderful rune-like ornamental figures, part-beast, part-tree or stone decorate the margins of the pages while further in the ice floes, Viking banquets, schools of whales, and fleets of ships pass in brilliant succession. Again and again, as in the text, isolated historical fact yields to an exuberantly drawn, interpretive legend-fantasy of what may have been: "Eternal ice and snow covered most of the land, but the banks of the fjords were green with grass. No men, no houses he found, but on the edge of the ice lay sleek seals and snoring walruses. And polar bears, foxes, and hares hurried silently, like shadows, over the icy wastes." Praise has become a heightened form of reporting, observation of a world that in all its variousness, beauty and terror, will outlast Leif, his parents, his own children. Leif's world is not a moral dollhouse but a truly vast place, to be measured, the d'Aulaires artfully suggest, by imagination.

The d'Aulaires' biographies, most of which are still in print today, remain very popular, if library borrowing provides any indication. Over the years the series has retained the status of a classic. Still, time has told for them in various ways as we have seen, leaving us aware of many shortcomings while also reminding us that over time biographies themselves become historical documents, casting light not only on their subjects' values and times but also on those of their authors and readers. (pp. 20-1)

> Leonard S. Marcus, "Life Drawings: Some Notes on Children's Picture Book Biographies," in The Lion and the Unicorn, Vol. 4, No. 1, Summer, 1980, pp. 15-29.

DONNARAE MacCANN AND OLGA RICHARD

George Washington and *Abraham Lincoln* by Ingri and Edgar Parin d'Aulaire, books from the 1930s, were reissued in 1987 as paperbacks. They are stereotypical in their portrayal of blacks and native Americans. In *George Washington,* there are numerous contented slaves—a misleading depiction of servitude that is perhaps not surprising in the cultural climate of the 1980s. The current decade has seen a variety of social regressions, and the children's book publishing industry is quick to reflect them.

> With beaming faces the slaves and servants, too, welcomed [General] Washington home. . . .
>
> He walked peacefully over his fields, where the slaves were singing and working.

Abraham Lincoln, a Caldecott prizewinner, presents Afro-Americans as obsequious and native Americans as clownish and cowardly. By showing ex-slaves bowing down to Lincoln, and an Amerind chief cowering, the d'Aulaires promote the notion of a "white man's burden." This point is made in the critical bibliography *Starting Out Right: Choosing Books about Black People for Young Children* (1972). Reviewers who worked on this publication for the Wisconsin Department of Public Instruction note that in the d'Aulaire text "the survival of the exploited is dependent on the mercy of a god in the form of Lincoln." They comment upon the way slavery is trivialized by the authors' description of Lincoln's neighbors: "They never tire of hearing about the river pirates and slave markets." The d'Aulaires' version of history, note the Wisconsin reviewers, transforms slavery into "a fairy tale rather than a social evil over which [Lincoln's] neighbors should have been indignant."

These two biographies are being advertised as "treasured classics," but by now librarians know better.

> Donnarae MacCann and Olga Richard, in a review of "George Washington" and "Abraham Lincoln", in Wilson Library Bulletin, Vol. 62, No. 5, January, 1988, p. 71.

THE MAGIC RUG (1931)

Here is a book whose simple chronicle of a magic rug which wafted two children to Africa serves as an excuse for incidental description of town and desert and offers opportunity for gay and interesting illustrations. Its pictures are, indeed, the striking feature of the volume to which lend it both originality and distinction. Reproduced directly from the artist's drawings in stone, they produce the effects of crayons with their clear colors and soft surfaces. Some of them are spirited sketches with many hues and varied detail, others sharply defined designs achieved with few lines, and in two or at most three tones. The grotesque figures we find less successful than the more conventional ones, but they will doubtless appeal to the childish eye. Altogether the book is one which should please the very young reader, and the child too young to read.

> A review of "The Magic Rug," in The Saturday Review of Literature, Vol. VIII, No. 6, August 29, 1931, p. 91.

John was a little boy who loved strange marvels and adventures. The cause of his strangest adventure was an Oriental rug that belonged to his father. John always had liked the rug because of its beautiful pattern and lovely colors. On the day of his great adventure John stretched out on the beautiful rug and fell asleep. At that moment the rug began to move gently along the floor, out through the open door, then high up into the air and faster and faster with the speed of the wind but still very gently so as not to awaken John.

Thus quite simply and easily little John and the reader are carried away into one of those regions of romance and adventure that lie quite close to every day. For the story tells how, after the rug has sailed to Africa, a sorcerer steals away its beautiful patterns, it becomes dull and gray and John and the little Arab girl, Ayesha, must bravely outwit the sorcerer and bring back the stolen figures in all their beauty and color. So well does the pattern of an Oriental rug lend itself to magic and enchantment that one wonders why it has not figured before in the numerous tales of flying carpets. It was fortunate, however, that the idea should wait for authors who are also artists, and whose text and pictures make such a harmonius whole that it would be impossible to think of one without the other. The illustrations, which are thoroughly oriental in color and atmosphere, are a delight and will interest adults and boys and girls of 10 to 12 as well as children of the picture-book age.

> Anne T. Eaton, in a review of "The Magic Rug," in The New York Times Book Review, September 27, 1931, p. 19.

In *The Magic Rug,* Ingri and Edgar Parin d'Aulaire have provided fun and rich intellectual entertainment for children who are at an age to enjoy wizardry and magic in a true Oriental setting. In a series of fine lithographic drawings in color accompanied by their own story they have not only given life

The deer did not like to be hitched up at all, and did what they could to get rid of the children. Snowwhitedeer ran around in a ring until Lise was dizzy and almost fell out.

Silverside tried to scare Lasse away and came toward him with lowered horns. But Lasse just laughed and hid under his sled, and Silverside drummed with his hoofs on the keel.

From Children of the Northlights, *written and illustrated by Ingri and Edgar Parin d'Aulaire.*

and meaning to the pattern of an Oriental rug but they have done it with rare imagination and selective skill. (p. 300)

> Anne Carroll Moore, "Bells and Balloons," in The Saturday Review of Literature, *Vol. VIII, No. XVII, November 14, 1931, pp. 281, 300.*

OLA (1932)

Out of feathery snow and silver ice, mountains and fjords and gleaming northern skies, this tale seems woven. It is put together with such delicate fancy and such complete understanding of children that its hero, the little Norwegian boy, Ola, will be taken by other children to their hearts at once as a new friend and very real companion. Ola goes skiing through a Winter forest where (as we can plainly see in the picture), the trees, under their heavy burden of snow, are transformed into a group of solemn creatures. While on his journey, Ola goes to a wedding. The reader turns the page and finds himself enjoying the full glory of the wedding feast; but outside, where the child reader will remember to look for them, the artist has not forgotten to show Ola and his companions looking in through the window. Ola joins a peddler and with him visits Lapland. In a fishing village he stops and fishes for cod, pulling them from the water all day long until Spring comes and the codfish go off to the great ocean. Then Ola finds a boat on the shore, climbs in and starts for home. On an islet he meets a little girl who shows him how to gather

eiderdown. As he watches the midnight sun from the top of a cliff he sees his friend the peddler sailing by and then Ola is off for home again with him, taking along his supply of eiderdown, codfish and codliver oil. Ola's journey is just such a journey as a child makes in his own imagination, but, as a background for the little boy, the authors have created, in effortless fashion, a picture of Norway—the land and its people, its customs, industries and folklore—so complete and vivid that a reader of any age can gain from the book real knowledge and understanding of the country. The illustrations are beautiful and deeply imaginative and have, as well, a color and humor that will delight both children and older readers.

> Anne T. Eaton, in a review of "Ola," in The New York Times Book Review, *October 9, 1932, pp. 16, 18.*

Here is a picture book light enough for little hands and large enough—the pages are 9×12—for everything in the pictures to be lovingly regarded. Everything will be; the first word that comes to mind for **Ola** is ingratiating. . . .

It takes a certain nostalgia to make a picture-book like this. The Petershams felt it in *Miki,* a book that left me with a disposition to like Hungary. In like manner the d'Aulaires paint from full hearts and make friends thus for their Norway. These color drawings were made directly on the lithographic stones; the reproductions so faithful that, though colors are clear and outlines definite, they keep the soft fairytale quality of a land of mist and cloud and high-piled snow. They are truthful, yet fantastic enough to fit a little fantasy all of whose features are true. Its influence may last longer than the picture-book period. It is not impossible that it may set the stage for the subsequent entrance of Hans Christian Andersen, and so to Björnssen and the Scandinavians on Parnassus.

> *May Lamberton Becker, "Far North," in* New York Herald Tribune Books, *October 16, 1932, p. 7.*

Space, light, and movement in harmony with a subject that lives in the artist's mind are the distinguishing characteristics of these three notable picture books [*Ola, Daniel Boone* (edited by the staff of the Bookshop for Boys and Girls in Boston), and *The Story of Noah* by Clifford Webb].

Totally different in theme and in the technique by which each one is consistently developed, the effect on the mind of distinct refreshment, and on the memory of recapturing that mood at the turn of a page, is common to all three and it is this which sets the books apart from other picture books of the year and assures them a place among the cherished possessions of children for years to come.

Ola is not merely another picture book to look at. *Ola* is a living character, a new friend whose adventures in a strange country—Norway—are as convincing as a child's own dream of adventure. *Ola* has been created out of great love of childhood and great sensitiveness to the atmosphere of a country backed by sound knowledge and accurate observation of material forms. It is a book to delight a four year old child with its quality of intimate companionship and zest for adventure and it is also a background book for later reading of Norse literature.

> *Anne Carroll Moore, "Spacious Picture Books," in* The Saturday Review of Literature, *Vol. IX, No. 18, November 19, 1932, p. 254.*

THE CONQUEST OF THE ATLANTIC (1933)

Ships from the days of the Vikings down to the present ocean liners and Zeppelin trans-Atlantic flights are all here. It is a book to conjure with, and one which makes us just a little envious that we came too late to have spent long, rainy afternoons poring over these lithographs instead of struggling with historical dates and geographies full of uninspiring maps. (p. 276)

> *Rachel Field, "The Gossip Shop," in* The Saturday Review of Literature, *Vol. X, No. 18, November 18, 1933, pp. 276-77.*

In size and shape it is like my last geography and it has oceans in it. The likeness ends there. That was heavy on the arm; this might go on letter-scales. That was crammed with dull, disconnected facts; this is the continuous and moving development of one idea—man's idea of the Atlantic from the medieval concept of horror of great darkness to its present position as one easy stage of airplane circuits of the globe.

From experience with Edna Potter's admirable *Christopher Columbus* I think the ideal audience for this book will be intelligent children ten years old. The narrative is good enough and the words long enough for any clear-minded adult who likes to find condensed and clarified statements of his ideas on any subject. But the pictures have the evocative quality likely to be most truly appreciated by a child or by such rare

men and women as retain the peculiar quality of ten-year-old vision. For a brief period this vision can see not only what is in a picture but what is beyond it. These full-page lithographs in color, and black and white are illustrations not only of events but of states of mind. They show not only what Leif and Columbus, Magellan and the clipper ship captains, Beebe and Balbo, did, but what they thought they were doing. It is a book to keep.

> *May Lamberton Becker, in a review of "The Conquest of the Atlantic," in* New York Herald Tribune Books, *November 26, 1933, p. 9.*

Here is a book that is unique in its dramatic presentation of the history of the Atlantic in an unbroken chain of events from the voyages of the Viking Dragon ships to General Balbo's twenty seaplanes flying from Italy to Chicago by way of Greenland. The opening pages make clear to us something of the mingled terror, mystery and fascination that the unknown wonderlands of the East held for Europeans in the days when the thought of exploring the Atlantic was beginning to stir in men's minds.

No child who sees them will forget these pictures that tell the story with imagination, with poetry and with a sense of the great drama that began when Prince Henry of Portugal gazed from his observatory and Columbus studied the maps that he thought were to guide him to India by a western route. With the pictures is combined a text that has the same vivid quality and the same touch of poetry. The account is brief and necessarily condensed; it can easily be rounded out, however, and amplified by other books, and for the boys and girls this is a fine introduction to the reading of history. It was with true understanding of children that the authors brought their tale of discovery and daring straight down the ages to General Balbo's silver planes, thus making the wonders of past accomplishment the more real to young people through the wonders of the present. The illustrations, which are magnificently reproduced, will be of great interest to the many boys and girls who like to make their own maps and pictures. A book which every American boy and girl from 10 to 12 should have the opportunity to enjoy.

> *Anne T. Eaton, in a review of "The Conquest of the Atlantic," in* The New York Times Book Review, *December 3, 1933, p. 18.*

OLA AND BLAKKEN AND LINE, SINE, TRINE (1933)

[In *Ola and Blakken*], Ola, Blakken, Line, Sine, and Trine leave in quest of new adventures which we trust they will find. The text of this second Ola book is clearer, better written, and more childlike than that of the first book, and it is a real adventure story. It is full of delightful thrills. There is a "big bad" troll bird with "big bad black eyes," a bird so big that it has (to the delight of the children) to sit on *two* roofs. *Ola and Blakken* is decidedly a six, seven, and eight-year-old book, it is rather stimulating fare for the average younger child. We have two very decided groups of picture books, one group with familiar happenings for the babies, and one group for the children who, with increased age, become bold and adventurous-minded.

> *Alice Dalgliesh, in a review of "Ola and Blakken and Line, Sine, Trine," in* The Saturday Review of Literature, *Vol. X, No. 18, November 18, 1933, pp. 279, 282.*

There was a welcome waiting for the reappearance of that Scandinavian little shaver, blue-eyed Ola, whom the D'Aulaires presented last year to an enraptured young audience. He had "something about him"—something that makes parents so pleased with pictures that they bring home the book for their own sakes and find the home audience just as happy over it. So here is Ola again in this new book, whose big light pages blossom with colors like the painted chests and furniture of his country, and adventures exuberant as the designs of Norwegian embroidery.

With him are not only three little girls who now get their names into the titles, but also a white horse so ingratiating he is worth his featured position there. Besides, there is a stronger plot-interest, so that children a trifle older enjoy it. This plot now involves a great Troll-Cock of magnificent color and a baleful eye, and two Troll giants who turn into mountains—you can see them doing it. The book has a childhood world in it. It does so much without appearing to try, and that is one of the best features of a book for children. Happily it ends—"But Ola with a Blakken and Line and Sine and Trine set off to look for new adventures . . ." I could do with another Ola book as good as this.

May Lamberton Becker, in a review of "Ola and Blakken and Line, Sine, Trine," in New York Herald Tribune Books, *November 19, 1933, p. 9.*

[This is] more delightful even than the first **Ola.** In the new volume, Ola with the help of the three little girls Line, Sine, and Trine and all the farm animals, save the beloved Blakken from the Troll Cock and capture the cock and celebrate his capture with a feast. The Norwegian land with its northern lights and mountains, its homes bright with gayly painted furniture and its creatures of farm and folk lore as presented by these young artists make one of the most fascinating picture books of our day. (p. 341)

Bertha E. Mahoney, "Apprentices to Life," in The Saturday Review of Literature, *Vol. X, No. 21, December 9, 1933, pp. 340-41.*

If proof were needed that in **Ola** Mr. and Mrs. D'Aulaire created a thoroughly convincing and lovable child character, it would be found in the attitude of boys and girls toward **Ola and Blakken,** which they seem to regard not as a new picture and story book but as another glimpse of a tried and true friend. "I know what book I want first," an eight-year-old was overheard to say. "I want that other one about Ola."

Both stories have a satisfying mixture of reality and fancy; in the second, however, fancy predominates. The story of Ola and Blakken, his beloved white horse, and the three little sisters and their adventures with the trolls and the troll-cock, has caught perfectly the folktale quality, with its directness, its rapid action and its humorous exaggeration. What child will not be delighted by the idea of all the farm animals hitched up together to the troll-cock to pull it up the hill, and the gay and convincing double-page picture to show them in the act? And what reader will not thrill to the thought of Ola, with great presence of mind, loading the old blunderbuss with a silver button and bravely aiming it at the troll-cock as it sits on *two* roofs? Ola whispering to the horse Blakken not to be afraid and the finely imaginative picture of the four children and the white horse setting off to look for new adventures in the boat made from the troll-cock's beak are among the illustrations that grown-ups will find particularly enchanting.

Pictures and story alike treat magic and wonders with the simple matter-of-factness that belongs to children and folklore, and the reader has the feeling that in these drawings he has at last the opportunity to see exactly what a Norwegian troll looks like. The illustrations are beautifully reproduced in gay and charming colors.

Anne T. Eaton, in a review of "Ola and Blakken and Line, Sine, Trine," in The New York Times Book Review, *December 10, 1933, p. 16.*

THE LORD'S PRAYER   (1934)

This new book by Mr. and Mrs. D'Aulaire is gay and Spring-like with its delicate colors and its touches of gold. As a picture book it has a certain appeal but since the artists so plainly intend their illustrations to be an explanation and interpretation of the Lord's Prayer, we must think of the pictures and text as a whole.

Once upon a time adults troubled themselves not at all as to what children were really thinking; boys and girls were told what it was right for them to think and their elders left it at that. Then came child study and adults grew interested in finding out what they could about a child's mental processes; "there were two kinds of papers," said the Little Old Woman Who Lived in a Shoe, referring to the "Solemn Symposium," described by Samuel Crothers in his "Miss Muffett's Christmas Party"; "one was about 'Obedience to Parents,' I used to have them when I was a little girl; the other kind is where you get at 'the Contents of the Child's Mind.'" We would shudder at the thought of a return to such disregard of children's individualities as that represented by the methods of Dotheboys Hall, but this illustrated Lord's Prayer is likely to make us wonder if, in the present day, the child's mind is not being subjected somewhat ruthlessly to the searchlight of publicity. If the adult must attempt an explanation let him do it in words, which are fleeting and readily forgotten; pictures shown to children at an early age make an impression harder to erase. It is to be feared that to the child familiar with this book the grave and measured music of "Lead Us Not Into Temptation, but Deliver Us From Evil" will evermore be connected with the thought of a rowboat and two children "resisting the temptation" to start out after the water lillies which their friends in another rowboat are already beginning to gather. The plump child whose hands wave temptation away in the preceding black and white drawing is an adult's picture, not a child's, though to some adults the idea of the Bible being made "cute" will be repellent.

It is surprising that two such understanding makers of books for children should, in this instance, put together a volume that fails to ring true. Is it because, knowing boys and girls as they do, they are not, after all, thoroughly convinced that adult symbolism and trivial pictures can explain great religious literature to children, who are themselves poets at heart? Children without doubt have their own secret symbolism but we can never know it, for their deepest feelings are inarticulate. These drawings lack the feeling of sincerity that we associate with Mr. and Mrs. D'Aulaire's work and border perilously on the sentimental. Here lies the great difference between this book and *The Christ Child* by Maud and Miska Petersham. The Christmas story is a perfect story for children and the Petersham pictures tell it with the beautiful simplicity and directness of the Gospels.

Something we must leave to the child, something untouched by blundering adult efforts to explain; there must be regions in the child's mind where, guided by the music and imagination of great literature, he will find his own way, bringing back something that he may not be able to put into words but that is a part of his inner life for all time.

> *Anne T. Eaton, in a review of "The Lord's Prayer,"*
> *in* The New York Times Book Review, *March 25,*
> *1934, p. 11.*

The first impulse on opening this gold-bound book, is to ask, now that it has been done so well, why it was never done before.

The answer is, of course, that in a way it has been—in the wrong way. The Lord's Prayer has been many times "embellished with woodcuts." But no one, so far as I know, has put its petitions, without a word of explanation or homily, into pictures that translate them directly in terms of a little child's experience. The result is a book a child can love and its parents find touching, pathetic, or satisfying, according as they have kept or departed from the spirit and the faith of childhood.

The only text is the words of the prayer—there is a Protestant edition and a Catholic edition—each petition separately in large clear lettering upon a fair large page. Turn the leaf and there is a double-page picture in the colors of spring, illustrating these words within the limits of a child's view of life.

The one I like best is Thy Kingdom Come. In a sunny suburban garden in whose trees birds in their little nests agree and on whose lawn a dog has curled up comfortably with a cat, children are happily at play. The gate is open and others in darker garments are being welcomed in to share the toys. A little girl nurses her baby brother; a woman opens a cottage window to look out on sunflowers turning intently toward the sun. It is so simple, so possible—so like that Land of the Righteous Gorky talks about in *Nachtasyl.* There was a man in Siberia, he said, who believed that somewhere on this earth there was a Land of the Righteous, where people were kind to one another and wished each other well. He could put up with his hard life because when things got too bad he could always pack up and start for that land. So when some one proved to him on the map that in all the world there was no such place, he destroyed the map—and then himself. There is something so humanly possible about the D'Aulaires' little kingdom of God that it may have, to some of us, the intolerable sweetness of a lost Paradise.

There are seven of these double-page color plates and two single pages; in between are black and white designs of birds and pets and children, often something amusing and always meaning something. In all the pictures gold is used discreetly and with uncommon success, whether to suggest sunshine or, more subtly, a sense of something precious. It is a distinguished and memorable picture book.

> *May Lamberton Becker, in a review of "The Lord's*
> *Prayer," in* New York Herald Tribune Books, *April*
> *1, 1934, p. 8.*

There have been many appeals for aid to children. Many of them still need it badly, whether in the form of milk, clothes or kindliness. But one must also not forget that little ones want food for their souls, prepared in a way both appetizing and nutritious. What could be better here than pictures—not the cheap, ghastly lithographs which still corrupt young imaginations, but honest art designed for children and fair to them?

Accordingly one may extend a hearty welcome to *The Lord's Prayer,* as illustrated by the D'Aulaires. . . . These pictures, drawn on stone, are exquisitely composed and reproduced. Homely, interesting symbolism applies the lesson to child life. (p. 642)

The value of the art work lies chiefly in the fact that it is a kind of sublimated child work. If youngsters could draw and color as well as the D'Aulaires, they themselves might make just such pictures. That is why they will seem to you (as they have seemed to me) so touching and tender. Practically all the illustrations could be copied by a somewhat talented child, and yet there is none which does not testify to genuine creative talent. It is in every way a splendid book, which I warmly commend. (p. 643)

> *George N. Shuster, in a review of "The Lord's*
> *Prayer," in* The Commonweal, *Vol. XIX, No. 23,*
> *April 6, 1934, pp. 642-43.*

CHILDREN OF THE NORTHLIGHTS (1935)

A book by the D'Aulaires is an event, and this is one for which they made unusually long and careful preparation. When I saw them last spring they had just returned from a journey . . . by reindeer sled to live with the Lapps, in itself no mean test of endurance and devotion.

These two young people, however, liked the Lapps immensely. Lasse and Lise, the two young Lappiets, with their relatives and their reindeer needed this frame of mind on the part of their interpreters. They belong to a race that has worked out by the survival of the fittest a system that not only permits them to keep on living but to enjoy life while holding the elements at bay. It is not so refined a system, but it is gorgeously robust. Children anywhere like robustious living. They can understand the doings of Lasse and Lise from the moment his star-shaped cap peeps out from the teepee-like tent straight through their busy day in the winter night.

School opens as soon as winter is well over; the schoolmaster gathers up his pupils over the hillsides, tossing them into the sled like berries into a basket. When the sun is getting high their parents come down from the mountain, driving the herds before them on the way to the coast; they pause to pick up school-sized boys and girls and have the babies christened, and are on their way to green grass before the sun has licked up all the snow and made the herd too lazy to travel. There is no more to the tale than this, not so much as has happened in earlier stories of the Far North from these author-artists; the story is about the Lapps in general, and the reindeer in which their wealth consists, and how little children enjoy being Lapps.

The pictures are droll and gentle, even in rough-and-tumble scenes, and not without the gay symbolic quality that sets these artists apart among children's illustrators. Their famous northern lights appear, stylized to the point of making some elders wonder whether children will understand what they mean—something that makes a sensible child chuckle. The full-faced sun licks up the snow with a jolly golden tongue. But the little Lapps are reproduced faithfully to the last bright bonnett, and the furry animals are all alive.

May Lamberton Becker, in a review of "Children of the Northlights," in New York Herald Tribune Books, *September 8, 1935, p. 7.*

The d'Aulaires are not ordinary travelers. On their journeys to Norway and Lapland they have looked about them with the clear-eyed pleasure that children take in new sights and strange lands, and into their book has gone the magic of the North and the romance of snow-covered countries. . . .

Boys and girls from 6 to 9 will thoroughly enjoy watching this brother and sister, as the pictures make it possible to watch them, herding the reindeer in the snow; driving Silverside and Snowwhite, their own special deer, harnessed to the narrow Lapp sleds like little boats; cooking and eating and sleeping around the great fire, while the pole star gleams through the top of the tent. . . .

The many pictures—there are more pictures than text—with their gayety and beauty and lovely color, seem to invite the reader to share the life they so vividly set before him.

Anne T. Eaton, in a review of "Children of the Northlights," in The New York Times Book Review, *October 6, 1935, p. 10.*

GEORGE WASHINGTON (1936)

George Washington has gay lithographs in color and in black and white. Some of the pictures are charming but others are stiff. The book as a whole is a disappointment, as it does not capture the American atmosphere.

Edith Rees, in a review of "George Washington," in Library Journal, *Vol. 61, November 1, 1936, p. 808.*

When I was little we had a *Life of Washington* that made me ever after regard him with a certain friendliness. This old book had not a trace of literary merit—this present one has plenty—but it did have many little pictures, and as these were chiefly of household and farm matters (battles being too big to get in) the Father of his Country was fixed in my little mind less as a military leader than as a gentleman whom everybody trusted and whom his family liked, who got us somehow through our troubles when we needed him, and then went back, once that necessity was over, to take up once more the conduct of a large and well-managed country estate and its industries. I have wished ever since that some one would make for little children a thoroughly good, illustrated life of Washington on this basis, and at last, to my wonder and delight, here it is. The D'Aulaires have given our newest generation material for true and joyous hero-worship.

Biography begins with hero-worship; every one knows that who introduces books to children. Washington would be more of a hero with young Americans had he not to contend with his postage stamps and with the glittering burden of remembrance of a recent year's continuous celebration of his good points. The wonder was that an American child emerged from that twelve months' ballyhoo convinced that he had good points at all. But now—one look at these truly enchanting pictures—in which patriotic red, white and blue softly predominate—and a rapid glance over the simple, graceful and dignified story, and it is clear that this is a book to put among a little American's picture-books even before he can read the text. He may be given it even if he is so little as to get from it his first idea who this lovable little fellow may be, hanging to the back of a plunging white pony. . . .

I like the book indeed as well as anything the D'Aulaires ever did, and that is saying a great deal.

May Lamberton Becker, in a review of "George Washington," in New York Herald Tribune Books, *November 15, 1936, p. 8.*

The full-page color lithographs are so decorative and amusing and the small paragraphs of text so well written that a child is given a very clear idea of Washington's life and of the Revolution. No nursery will be complete without it! (pp. 376-77)

Euphemia Van Rensselae Wyatt, in a review of "George Washington," in The Catholic World, *Vol. 144, December, 1936, pp. 376-83.*

ABRAHAM LINCOLN (1939)

AUTHOR'S COMMENTARY

[*The following excerpt is from the d'Aulaires's Caldecott Medal acceptance speech, originally delivered on May 28, 1940.*]

This book perhaps means more to us than any other book we have made. The more we studied Lincoln the closer he came to us, the greater he became, the more necessary for our present life, the closer related to us and our times. At last he was not an historical person any more, but a warm and kind and generous relative who had moved right into our studio with us. We became more and more convinced that if only we could give to our young readers a bit of the feeling we had about Abraham Lincoln we had perhaps done our tiny share to make the world a happier place, when those who are now children have grown up to run the world. And could there be any more sublime feeling for any one who had chosen for his vocation work with children and children's books?

Now, is there any vocation that could be richer and more fulfilling than work for children? You have a public with wide-open ears and eyes, without prejudices, and with a mind ready to be influenced by good or by bad. Grown-ups are hard to get at. They have their taste already settled; perhaps it is a good taste, perhaps it is a bad one. You just cannot do very much with it. But except for a very short period in every child's life where he has to go through a state of admiration for something that is sweet and pretty, without any inner meaning or relation to life, children have an excellent taste. You can fool grown-ups, give them something that is skimmed off your own surface, executed with great skill and taste and most will think—that is just wonderful. But you cannot fool a child. If a picture is cold he feels it, however beautiful the surface, and if you want to grasp and hold a child you have to give all there is in you, all your warmth and feeling. And as of course we, as does every other artist, sincerely believe that what we have to give is the only real art, we feel after having finished a book as if we had really done something to help build up society. The little book that we just have finished, we always hope, is going to help build up taste and artistic feeling in thousands of children who own this book, not only for the moment, but for the rest of their lives. (p. 248)

Ingri Parin d'Aulaire, "Working Together on Books for Children," in The Horn Book Magazine, *Vol. XVI, No. 4, July-August, 1940, pp. 247-51.*

The d'Aulaires at work.

Companion piece to the popular picture-biography *George Washington,* this brief story-life of the greatest American culture-hero, written and pictured for young children, follows the same general plan and uses the same arrangement of light, cheerful narrative and large lithographs on stone in five colors. Like that book, it is addressed to an age that enjoys pictures—especially large colored ones—more than text, unless it can get the latter by listening rather than by putting to work the lately attempted art of reading.

The effect, however, is bound to be less attractive to this very audience than that of the preceding book about the Father of his Country. There is—in the north at least—so strong a personal affection for Lincoln on the part of little boys, and it has made them conjure up—out of this affection as much as from any record—an image of him so lovable and benign, that any variation from their accepted image is likely to come in the nature of a shock. The element of the grotesque, latent in the actual appearance of Lincoln, will be emphasized by any artist at his own risk—as George Gray Barnard soon discovered. Many of these pictures do not emphasize it, but some of them do, and these our little boys are not likely to like. I think Lincoln himself might have enjoyed the humor of these designs; he had a liking for the grotesque, and the humor here is without malice and marked by evident affection. Time will tell whether our little children will enjoy them

in this way; they will not, I think, find them ridiculous and un-American, as some of their elders will. The story devotes itself more to pioneer phases than to darker scenes of Lincoln's later life, and it closes before he has started for Ford's Theater.

> *May Lamberton Becker, in a review of "Abraham Lincoln," in* New York Herald Tribune Books, *April 30, 1939, p. 10.*

There is nothing tentative about one's response to this book. It is love at first sight. Perhaps one's adult feeling is in part the remembrance of Robert Sherwoods' play, mixed with a conviction that now if ever American history needs to be cherished by American children. But apart from every other consideration the book has a thrilling quality. As for children's appreciation, we believe that they too will be stirred by the sincerity of these pictures and text, each telling with noble simplicity and inevitable pathos the story of Abraham Lincoln. Yet this story has natural humor and action. The author-artists have been successful in finding incidents that will appeal to children's imagination and satisfy their love of incident. Lincoln's boyhood is protrayed with deep understanding of the life of a gangling boy in a backwoods cabin. He grows taller by the page and his face shows the recognizable features before he is grown. This is no brief picture book, but a balanced story of Lincoln's life, up to the last beautiful page that shows the tired war-president seated in an armchair beside Tad Lincoln. Such a book would be important any year, but in 1939 it glows with special significance. As biography it is a finer interpretation than the d'Aulaire's *George Washington,* which it matches in size. The only possible flaw is that in the chain of events which during the Civil War made the nation's story Lincoln's story, the firing on the Federal Fort Sumter is omitted. Thus it might seem to older children who weighed the facts as given here that Lincoln's first step was offensive warfare, whereas southern guns did open the battle. Many of the lithographic drawings, generous in number, are in warm color; others both large and small are in black and white. For all children up to ten, and many who are older.

Irene Smith, in a review of "Abraham Lincoln," in Library Journal, *Vol. 64, May 1, 1939, p. 381.*

This book will probably be considered primarily in connection with its illustrations, but its true distinction, it seems to me, lies in the high standard it sets in the field of biography for children under 10. It is a rounded and well-proportioned outline of Lincoln's life which the d'Aulaires have given us, in an easy-running text unclouded by sentimentality. Thus, in describing Kentucky's most famous log cabin—"It wasn't much of a house in which he was born, but it was just as good as most people had in Kentucky in 1809"; and though the privations and poverty of Lincoln's early life are duly suggested they are presented, not as personal hardships, but as part of a frontier life which had also its moments of fun and adventure. The anecdotes beloved by every school child and others less familiar point out the various facets of Lincoln's character, yet there is no suggestion of the episodic in this narrative, which moves forward unhaltingly to the last page.

In the many lithographs, which range from small marginal illustrations to full pages of lovely color, one sees not only the boy growing into the man but the man in the eager-eyed boy. There is humor here, but very little of that sensitive imagination which illuminates the d'Aulaires' books of the Northland. Some of the pictures are quite beguiling but others are downright ugly, and the strong suggestion of primitive Scandinavian art strikes a false note.

Ellen Lewis Buell, "Lincoln's Life," in The New York Times Book Review, *June 18, 1939, p. 10.*

Readers from nine or ten deserve not only the truth but also the whole truth and nothing but the truth. For younger children, who lack historical perspective and are not as a rule interested in complex questions of character and motive, simplified stories of the great will inevitably take on the nature of legend, even of fairy-tale. The stiff figure of Lincoln, seemingly unsuited to fairy-tale treatment, is seen in the role of younger son turned prince. As Esther Moorhouse remarked, "there was no great difference between the cobbler's son who became a prince and the backwoods boy who became President of the United States of America."

The writer who introduces a very young reader to Lincoln may legitimately stress this aspect of the story, but he has a responsibility in that he is establishing a base on which later knowledge will rest. His portrait may be simple, but it must not be silly or trivial. Most obviously in the fairy-tale style is the disarmingly large and prettily coloured picture-book, ***Abraham Lincoln*** . . . Submitting to the picture-book form, the author-artists have chosen episodes with a suitable atmosphere. Looking at a picture of little Abe and Sarah after their mother's death, standing tearfully hand in hand in front of

a stylised forest and log cabin, a child might be forgiven for confusing the story with "Hansel and Gretel". What is offered of truth in the text is annulled, up to a point, by the prettiness of the pictures. Words may inform a child that Abe's childhood was hard, that he wielded an axe and carried water at an age when most children were playing, but the double spread of the Pigeon Creek dwelling hardly suggests a hard childhood. Here in a smooth forest enclave the child Abe chops at a tree in the foreground, father ploughs in the background, mother tends the fire in front of the half-faced camp; horse, cow and calf are neatly aligned in a lean-to, and Sally is glimpsed on her way to the spring with a yoke and buckets—all placed like figures in a toy village set. Similarly the picture of Lincoln saving the old Indian during the Black Hawk campaign suggests nothing more serious than a charade.

If there is nothing so ludicrous in the illustrations of Lincoln's later life, the choice remains a picture-book choice. We see the clerk finding Blackstone in a barrel, the President seized by grateful Negroes in the streets of Richmond. Since it fits the atmosphere of the book, the legend of Lincoln's tragic love for Ann Rutledge is perpetuated and gives rise to the first mention of his melancholy mood:

> She was sure he would become a great man some day, if he would just go on with his studies. And then they would be married, and be happy ever after.
> But one day Ann Rutledge took sick and nothing could be done to save her life. From that day on it was as if there were two Abes. The one was gay and full of funny stories, the other was so sad and sorrowful that no one dared to approach him. But he did his work and finished his studies, and one morning he took leave of his friends in New Salem. He borrowed a horse, and sad and penniless he rode off to Springfield, the capital of Illinois, to become a lawyer.

The implication here is that Lincoln rode off to Springfield almost on impulse to "become a lawyer"; no mention is made of the encouragement of his friends or the visits to local courts and "his studies" seem of brief duration. In a picture-book time and event are naturally telescoped and one cannot really quarrel with the concluding sentences, which accompany a portrait of Lincoln on the balcony of the White House listening to the band playing Dixie:

> . . . he sat down on his rocking chair to rest. He had done what he should do. He had held together the great nation brought forth upon this continent by his forefathers.

The purpose of the book—to establish early in life the figure of the greatest American—is a fair one. It may only be doubted whether this purpose is best served by making use of a picture-book form which constrains serious material. (pp. 370-72)

Margery Fisher, "Abraham Lincoln," in her Matters of Fact: Aspects of Non-Fiction for Children, *Thomas Y. Crowell Company, 1972, pp. 367-406.*

In general, this biography is an overromanticized portrayal of a man who is made to seem superhuman and flawless, even during his childhood. Its pictures seem unreal and do not reflect the hardships and struggles that were so much a part of this President's life.

The book does a disservice to Lincoln and his involvement with Black and Indian people. Both groups are depicted in the illustrations as the "white man's burden." After the Emancipation Proclamation is issued, Blacks are shown kneeling at Lincoln's feet while he maintains a detached, uncaring, arrogant posture. Earlier, Lincoln is shown as a strong man who protects what is illustrated as a timid, helpless Indian chief. The chief is about to be attacked by some white soldiers who are shown reeling with blood-thirsty rage, brandishing their swords in order to defend a land settlement with the Indians. The text corroborates the "white man's burden" concept. It implies that the survival of the exploited is dependent on the mercy of a god in the form of Lincoln. The incident, of course, is pure fiction and the way it is dramatized substantiates its falseness.

Blacks are illustrated as rigid figures, their immovable faces a dense, dark impenetrable mass, pierced slightly by two white dots. This is a ghost-like portrayal which will frighten children instead of invoking compassion and understanding for Black people who lived in agony. Still another picture of an Indian shows the "savage" image—he is jumping up and down in perpetual motion.

It is interesting to note that the story does not deal with violence except with the Indian incident. Indeed, it does not even cover Lincoln's assassination but ends after the Emancipation Proclamation.

We find that the entry of Black slaves into the story is abrupt and their condition is made to seem acceptable, not repulsive nor contradictory to the democracy that Lincoln was later to govern. After a New Orleans trip, Lincoln's neighbors "never tire of hearing about the river pirates and slave markets." Thus slavery is made to seem like a fairy tale rather than a social evil over which his neighbors should have been indignant. To add insult to injury, the authors continue by saying that Abe "was glad to be North again to his Indiana home where everyone was free." This is flagrant dishonesty. Among other atrocities, Blacks were disenfranchised at this time in Indiana. Furthermore, such a statement makes it seem as if slavery were a sectional issue—indeed a local color story—rather than a national issue of shattering proportions. Having the South absorb the full blame for the condition of black people is quite common; but it is an evasive technique. It distorts, is grossly unfair and should no longer be tolerated in literature and history.

This book also exemplifies a fault common to other books. It does not identify the slave master or trader as white. Two terms are used: "Negro (or Black) slaves" on the one hand, while everybody else is referred to as "people."

Because the authors are well known, we feel that the acceptability of this book will be taken for granted by many. Furthermore, it was awarded the Caldecott Medal for 1940 and libraries tend to have three or four copies currently on the shelves despite its age. This is unfortunate.

Overall this book makes a plastic hero of Lincoln instead of a thoughtful human being caught up in the politics of his time. We have pointed out some of the ways in which it mistreats Blacks and the issue of slavery as well as Indians and land treaties. As such, it will easily reinforce the classic myth of white superiority and we do *not* recommend its use under any condition. (pp. 144-45)

> *Bettye I. Latimer and Others, " 'Bright April' and*
> *'Abraham Lincoln' Reviewed," in* Cultural Conformity in Books for Children: Further Readings in Racism, *edited by Donnarae MacCann and Gloria Woodard, The Scarecrow Press, Inc., 1977, pp. 141-45.*

Five-color stone lithographs alternate with black and white illustrations of lithographic pencil on stone, and all reflect the wholesome qualities for which Lincoln was famous. (p. 242)

The crayonlike illustrations reveal much history regarding the time period and geographical settings surrounding Lincoln's life, and every page is filled with details revealing the life and culture of this pioneer President. The lack of realism in the style of the illustrations helps reinforce the brighter, lighter side of Lincoln's life, but it is the style that also prevents the audience from experiencing a true compassion for the primitive and adverse conditions which gave rise to such an important figure in the history of the United States. That Abraham Lincoln rose above these obstacles was what truly made him great; he was great in spite of them.

Subsequent reprints of this 1940 Medal Book include changes in the illustrations; compositions of pages, inclusion of details, features of faces, quality of color, and even the frontispiece vary in later editions. These changes, however, are subtle and do little to change the overall appearance or effect of the illustrations and the text. Slight discrepancies in the illustrations, open cabin doors and windows in February, and stereotypes of blacks and Indians, indicate that the d'Aulaires have taken some liberties with some details of their interpretation, and as an early biography, the book is subject to presenting so positive a picture that it ends without explaining the death of Lincoln, which, by its omission, evades some of the significance of Lincoln's life. (pp. 242-43)

> *Linda Kauffman Peterson, in a review of "Abraham Lincoln," in* Newbery and Caldecott Medal and Honor Books: An Annotated Bibliography, *by Linda Kauffman Peterson and Marilyn Leathers Solt, G. K. Hall & Co., 1982, pp. 242-43.*

ANIMALS EVERYWHERE (1940)

An apt description of this picture book for very young children is printed on the title-page: "In this book is unfolded the panorama of animal life from the tropics to the frigid North. It was made for the artists' little son, Per Ola. On one side crayon lithographs in rich color show the animals in their native settings, and on the other side the same animals appear with their backs turned. The calls and sounds of the animals are given in a simple text." The pages unfold to form a two-sided frieze. Although the folds turn like pages, their being unfastened does, of course, condition the book for library purposes. Its excellent coloring and fascinating variety make it perfect nursery property for children two to three years old. It should be useful also to pre-school teachers.

> *Irene Smith, in a review of "Animals Everywhere," in* Library Journal, *Vol. 65, No. 18, October 15, 1940, p. 878.*

Animals Everywhere is a gay panorama picture book showing animal life from the tropics to the Far North. Crayon lithographs in four colors display the animals of the cold, hot and temperate zones in their native surroundings. At the extreme left is a striking view of a hippopotamus in the group of animals that live far to the south because they like hot weather. The child can then follow along to the buffalo, horse, moose, beaver and others who "like weather that is neither too hot nor too cold"; after that he arrives at the polar regions where the reindeer, polar bear, seals and a great whale disport themselves among the icebergs and northern lights. On the other side in black and white one sees the animals with their backs turned. A touch that will delight children. Underneath these black and white pictures the calls and sounds of the animals are given in a simple text.

The title-page tells us that the book was made for the artists' little son, Per Ola, and the joy and fun that has gone into the making is very apparent. Most adults will feel an irresistible urge to give **Animals Everywhere** to some child and then to enjoy it with him. Children will take delight in spreading out this panorama on the floor and it will make a most effective decoration for a children's library or a nursery.

> *Anne T. Eaton, "Animal Pictures," in* The New
> York Times Book Review, *November 3, 1940, p. 10.*

[*The following excerpt is from a review of an edition of* Animals Everywhere *published in 1954.*]

This is a welcome reissue of a picture book which the artists made originally for their own little son, and which, though full of strange creatures, has the quality of being of the little child's own world. Published first in 1940, it has been succeeded by few if any animal picture books which the very young children have enjoyed more. Here are the familiar farmyard friends and the moose and buffalo and other less familiar animals of the temperate climates as well as the strange animals of the tropics and the arctic regions. The full color, double-page spreads alternate with pages in two colors which, amusingly, give pictures of the preceding animals in reverse. The descriptive text is brief and apt and very appealing to small boys and girls.

> *Ruth Hill Viguers, in a review of "Animals Every-*
> *where," in* The Saturday Review, New York, *Vol.*
> *XXXVII, No. 52, December 25, 1954, p. 26.*

LEIF THE LUCKY (1941)

Picture-books come and go, but some are permanent. This one will be. If the vocabulary is "older" than in most D'Aulaire books, so that children well beyond picture-book age will take it, the lithographs are so brilliant and humorous that the littlest will love them. The story antedates Columbus. Based on Viking sagas, story and pictures had their inception in Norway; surrounded with his own gear, under his own Northern Lights, Leif the Lucky, son of Erik the Red, appears from babyhood to his placid, retired old age.

The grotesque quality in Scandinavian folk art, the native blend of barbaric strength and Christian sentiment in this folklore, appear in full force in these pictures, at once strange and sympathetic. The lovely large head of the boy Leif, bringing in the ship's carved figurehead, or that of the boy asleep and vigorously dreaming; the jumping, dancing groups; the huddling animals; the flamboyant humor of practical jokes at King Olaf's banquet—these are among the highlights, but there is not a page that could not go into a folk museum. The story keeps to the record; kings and heroes, women and boys, dark Indians and fair-haired sailors, bring it across the ocean to "Vinland" and begin American history.

> *May Lamberton Becker, in a review of "Leif the*

Lucky," in New York Herald Tribune Books, *November 2, 1941, p. 7.*

In **Leif the Lucky** Mr. and Mrs. D'Aulaire are at their enchanting best. . . . The brief text is direct and spirited and childlike; the authors use a style that children enjoy. "Huge waves," they say, "rushed out toward the ships. Icebergs crashed into each other with a clang and a din as if all the glass in the world were broken to pieces. . . . Men shouted, girls cried, cows mooed, pigs squealed."

The pictures, with their glowing colors, their fine feeling of adventure on stormy seas and strange coasts, tell the story almost without need for words. These artist-authors understand a youthful audience and here in this true tale of the past for which they have faithfully explored ancient sources they include and touch with imaginative humor details which delight boys and girls, the thirsty voyagers drinking from a brook, the bones thrown under the table in the jovial banquet scene, and, particularly appealing to the child, animals, wild and tame, are shown everywhere. Through all the book gleams and sparkles that magic of snow and ice which gives a fairy tale quality to every chronicle of the North.

Leif the Lucky is an ideal first history book, for to young children records of the past mean most when centered upon a personality. Adults as well as children will enjoy the brilliance and beauty of these pictures. All school and public libraries will want it and it will be a volume of lasting interest for a child's own library.

> *Anne T. Eaton, in a review of "Leif the Lucky," in*
> The New York Times Book Review, *November 2,*
> *1941, p. 6.*

The d'Aulaires have here a subject close to their hearts and they have done it full justice in their most beautiful book. Such a portrayal of the days of the Vikings has long been wanted in libraries and schools, to make vivid children's impressions of the days of the discoverers. In a fuller text than that employed in their other books, Mr. and Mrs. d'Aulaire give a spirited and direct account of Leif's voyage with his father to Greenland and his own subsequent voyages to Norway and Vinland. But, naturally, the book's great distinction—and it is distinguished—lies in its stunning lithographs of dragon ships and Viking homes, of deeds of daring and zest for living, as they were known among the Norse heroes. Imagination and humor and a feeling for the details that children enjoy are combined with sound historical accuracy in a book that has lasting value for American children.

> *Alice M. Jordan, in a review of "Leif the Lucky,"*
> *in* The Horn Book Magazine, *Vol. XVII, No. 6, November-December, 1941, p. 469.*

THE STAR SPANGLED BANNER (1942)

Ingri and Edgar Parin d'Aulaire have built an unusual picture book around the text of the **Star Spangled Banner** giving a very interesting interpretation to passages which have been just words to many grown people as well as children. Ambitious as the task was, the feeling of the whole is very childlike. Some of the pictures are more successful than others, but all show imagination and deep patriotism.

> *Ruth A. Hill, in a review of "The Star Spangled*
> *Banner," in* Library Journal, *Vol. 67, October 15,*
> *1942, p. 882.*

Ingri and Edgar Parin d'Aulaire have made a beautiful book illustrating **The Star Spangled Banner.** The d'Aulaires have interpreted the words of the first verse with a charming set of lithographs. Theirs is the way a child itself might visualize the song while singing it—naive and gentle and a bit dim as to meaning. All four verses and the music of the anthem serve as end-papers.

Marjorie Flack, in a review of "The Star Spangled Banner," in The Saturday Review of Literature, *Vol. XXV, No. 46, November 14, 1942, p. 25.*

Children will share with their parents as they will the best of this year's books—the most beautiful, touching, ennobling picture book of those by which the D'Aulaires have enriched childhood. The words are those of Francis Scott Key; large colored lithographs take them line by line, bringing out their lasting meaning, translating them through the universal language of pictures into the idealism of our world's great hour. Here are children looking at Fort McHenry as if in a fireworks display of rose and blue, and here Key's spirit looks through the folds of the standard. But, with the second stanza comes a deeper thrill. "The deep where the foe's haughty host in dread silence reposes" is the ocean in whose silent depths lurks today's danger. A life raft laden with survivors catches the gleam on shore of today's banner, tomorrow's hope. The "band that so vauntingly swore" comes rank on rank to threaten the Statue of Liberty—all with hands raised in the dread salute of tyranny. But with each refrain, the Star-

Spangled Banner spreads its bright protection over some village street or city square—today.

They say we do not know the words of our national anthem. That will not be so any more.

May Lamberton Becker, in a review of "The Star-Spangled Banner," in New York Herald Tribune Books, *November 15, 1942, p. 7.*

DON'T COUNT YOUR CHICKS (1943)

Everyone has counted his chickens before they were hatched and that must be why this story with its rueful moral appears in the folktales of so many countries.

For this new presentation of it, Ingri and Edgar Parin d'Aulaire have taken the words of Hans Andersen's poem and made, on stone, the colorful, blandly humorous illustrations that reflect the country background of Scandinavia. The old woman stares out at us, solid-fleshed and naive. From the first page, we know that she will break her eggs in the end. But we follow her, step by step, on her journey to the fair to sell them. We follow her in her faith that she will make a fortune. And we go through with her disappointment and the rather comforting return to the farm—where, after all, she is quite content.

Joan Vatsek, in a review of "Don't Count Your Chicks," in The Saturday Review of Literature, *Vol. XXVI, No. 46, November 13, 1943, p. 25.*

This book, made by two artists who love both children and folklore, has all the freshness of a tale told when the earth was young and the joy that each new day holds for a child. . . .

Never has the story been presented with a more enchanting gaiety and a more childlike spirit. Beginning with the delightfully absurd endpaper, continuing with the proud cock and hen who started the train of events, and the old woman gathering her eggs and planning her rosy future, the reader follows the story breathlessly until, in a dramatic climax which children find delightful, basket and eggs go crashing to the ground.

Anne E. Eaton, in a review of "Don't Count Your Chicks," in The New York Times Book Review, *November 14, 1943, p. 6.*

Ingri and Edgar Parin d'Aulaire's delightful book, **Don't Count Your Chicks** [is] their finest work, we think, for little children. Thanks be, there is no cause for disappointment due to wartime economy in this generous large-paged book, teeming with fun-provoking, satisfying pictures in color, and a story to match. . . . [This] distinguished book . . . gives the reader some excellent advice and fun at the same time.

Florence Bethune Sloan, in a review of "Don't Count Your Chicks," in The Christian Science Monitor, *November 15, 1943, p. 12.*

WINGS FOR PER (1944)

In these troublous times, when we are all eager to give our children a feeling of security and a fair share of happiness and fun, it is good to know that new picture books are as gay and lovely as though all the world were happy. War comes into only two or three of the books for the youngest children, and

From Abraham Lincoln, *written and illustrated by Ingri and Edgar Parin d'Aulaire.*

then without sadness or bitterness, unless it be in Ingri and Edgar d'Aulaire's *Wings for Per.* Per, sturdy little towhead, grows up happy and carefree in a good world. The farm where he lives on a ledge in Norway is peaceful and remote. But suddenly his world changes. Swarms of warplanes spread destruction. Per and his friends hide a radio and carry on secret work. Finally Per is old enough to train as a flier and to take his part in the fight for freedom. All of this, the d'Aulaires have put into one of their large picture books. A tremendous conception for young children, a difficult thing to attempt, it has on the whole been well carried out.

> *Mildred C. Skinner, in a review of "Wings for Per,"* in Library Journal, *Vol. 69, October 15, 1944, p. 861.*

Even before Norway was invaded that nice round child, Per, wanted to fly. The freedom of his eyrie home, bleak desolation of wartime, grim escape, America's bright-colored security (which Per finally reaches)—all are strikingly expressed by the color and texture of D'Aulaire magic. This is all more vivid and believable than recent D'Aulaire contributions. Five to nine-year-olds will find something here to satisfy their sense of what the war is about.

> *Anne T. Eaton, in a review of "Wings for Per,"* in The New York Times Book Review, *November 12, 1944, p. 6.*

TOO BIG (1945)

It seems that when Ola—the d'Aulaires' little son, not the little Norwegian boy in their famous picture book who looks exactly like him—had reached the great age of four he was confronted with a difficulty not uncommon at that time of life. He was continually outgrowing his clothes, his shoes, everything. So his Uncle John wrote him a letter about it, so funny and so fitting that the little boy read it over and over, and the d'Aulaires, knowing that other little boys would enjoy it, made it into a picture book. Ola, whom first we see popping his head out from a patchwork quilt on which his dog and his cat are curled, begins to dress and finds "he could not get into his little coat because he was TOO BIG." He could not even put on his little hat for the same reason—always given with gay pictures and in capital letters. It even affected his conduct: He couldn't lift the cat by the tail because he was "too big," or ride his little dog (who just sat down under him); he could not ride the horse because the horse was "too big." "Never mind." he said, "I'll grow bigger and bigger" . . . and on the last page you see him grown up and riding a rampageous elephant!

The colors are particularly attractive, the animals as jolly as the little boy, and the simple little story comes soon after the d'Aulaires' animal parade for babies, making their first book for very little children.

> *May Lamberton Becker, in a review of "Too Big,"* in New York Herald Tribune Weekly Book Review, *September 30, 1945, p. 6.*

This year the Parin d'Aulaires have made a little book, square and sturdy. . . . The end-papers are enchanting and the drawings all through the book as lovely as those in the earlier books of these two artists. . . . Each picture has the details that little children love. Look under the table, for instance, in the picture where the boy is eating a huge meal in order

to grow bigger. See the cat playing with his shoe laces and the dog eating some of the scraps that have fallen from his plate. See how good that long loaf of crusty bread looks! His glass that holds the rich milk says "Good Boy" on its side. This would be a nice book to send abroad to the children who cannot yet read English. There are English words, but one could easily do without them. Certainly the little boy would grow up just as fast if there were no words at all.

> *Mary Gould Davis, in a review of "Too Big,"* in The Saturday Review of Literature, *Vol. XXVIII, No. 45, November 10, 1945, p. 52.*

POCAHONTAS (1946)

Whenever the d'Aulaires choose an American subject, I feel a distinct sense of disappointment. This is no exception. They have taken a hackneyed theme and done almost nothing to make it come to life. Pocahontas, her kindness to John Smith, her marriage to a white settler, her Indian background and the story of the Virginia colony are many times told tales, but safe merchandise. The illustrations in soft crayon lithographs have a static quality that offsets the essential drama of the story. But the d'Aulaires have a market, so don't overlook the book.

> *A review of "Pocahontas,"* in Virginia Kirkus' Bookshop Service, *Vol. XIV, No. 21, November 1, 1946, p. 541.*

The d'Aulaires have a special gift that gives their historical biographies for young children a lasting distinction in children's literature. It is the art of infusing historical fact with the atmosphere of fairy-tale, producing the frame of mind in which the hero is earliest and most memorably received. They seldom have had a subject more promising for the exercise of this gift, and the result in *Pocahontas* is one of the best of a series already highly honored. For while it keeps to the facts as we know them, we have always seen these facts—because they reached us first through Cap'n John Smith—through the atmosphere of somewhat standardized romance. I am myself a witness that whatever we were told about Pocahontas, it always began with her being an Indian princess who saved the life of John Smith, and as princesses were fairly grown up to fairy-tale readers, we did not think of her, whatever we were told, as a little child—the merry, strong, active, up and coming little favorite of her father that she was when she welcomed the big Englishman as a sort of marvelous new uncle. Here she is, to the life, a real little girl, red-skinned, muscular, quick as a wink, yet with something about her pictures and something about the turn of the words as her story is told, that puts it into the beautiful borderland where mythology and history get along so well together.

> *May Lamberton Becker, in a review of "Pocahontas,"* in New York Herald Tribune Weekly Book Review, *November 10, 1946, p. 8.*

The d'Aulaires have told the story of Pocahontas, and illustrated it lavishly in their own manner. The pictures are serious and formal in tone, correct in detail, and many of them are colored in poetic pastel shades. The story is presented rather flatly, with inverted sentences and little drama; in fact, it sounds like a translation from another language, done with more respect than knowledge of the possibilities of English.

Yet small children should enjoy the pictures and can certainly take the story in their stride.

Marjorie Fisher, in a review of "Pocahontas," in The New York Times Book Review, November 10, 1946, p. 3.

NILS (1948)

This is one of the nicest books the d'Aulaires have done, for it's a lovely looking book, as always, and a good lesson in basic Americanism. Nils is of Norwegian extraction, but determines to be an American and a cowboy. All goes well, until he wears to school a pair of long knitted stockings, brilliantly patterned, such as Norwegian boys wear at home. His schoolmates turned him into the butt of their jokes—the tragedy of being "different" was almost too much for him. But he learned—as did his schoolmates—that after all America is made up of what people of all backgrounds contribute. Gorgeous lithographs in full color reproduction for a charming book.

A review of "Nils," in Virginia Kirkus' Bookshop Service, Vol. XVI, No. 15, August 15, 1948, p. 396.

[Nils] is a lovely book in which these two artist-authors have fused their love of their Norwegian inheritance with a deep devotion to the U.S.A. as American citizens. The text seems to me more spontaneous and closer to their own home life than any of the fine contributions they have yet made to American history. Nils is a real boy with real parents who enter into his personal adventures and his problems as an American schoolboy. A book that presents truth to life whether lived in Norway or New England is worth tons of attempts to present racial customs and problems. It is the quality of naturalness in everyday living with a fine cultural heritage that gives distinction at this crisis in world history to a picture storybook which has been growing over the years. Peer Gynt is not just a strange name to the readers of **Nils.**

Anne Carroll Moore, in a review of "Nils," in The Horn Book Magazine, Vol. XXIV, No. 6, November-December, 1948, p. 435.

How fortunate the children are to have Ingri and Edgar Parin d'Aulaire still at work. They never repeat themselves, yet their books are unmistakable. They are real craftsmen, drawing their color illustrations directly on the lithograph stone.

The cover of their new book, **Nils,** shows an appealing little boy in a cowboy hat, his yellow scarf bright against the blue of the sky and the pattern of falling leaves. . . . Small boys will appreciate Nils' predicament, and, from the way he solved it, they will unconsciously learn something of tolerance and resourcefulness.

Frances C. Darling, in a review of "Nils," in The Christian Science Monitor, December 14, 1948, p. 16.

FOXIE (1949)

The d'Aulaires turn to a little mutt dog for a hero, and do a frankly funny book in black and white. Foxie's adventures will appeal to the picture-book age. They will know that a young master who teased his dog deserved to lose her for a while. They will laugh at the fat man who taught Foxie tricks

and took her into the circus act. When Foxie sings on the stage, dressed in lady's clothes, they will be delighted. Then, happy ending, Foxie's master calls her from the audience. She dives straight into the sea of faces and scrambles over the heads and shoulders into the arms of her master. A dozen little pictures without words, on both end-papers, introduce Foxie and a soup bone, and take her home to find it.

Louise S. Bechtel, in a review of "Foxie," in New York Herald Tribune Book Review, December 25, 1949, p. 8.

BENJAMIN FRANKLIN (1950)

I am—perhaps—out of step with the majority, in preferring those of the d'Aulaire picture books dealing with Norway to those with historical American figures. Their glowing and lavish illustrations—full page lithographs, and the decorative marginal drawings, many in full color, seem somehow particularly out of key with the character of the shrewd Dr. Franklin. There's considerable "color" too in the recounting of the boyhood, but the spirit of the telling will carry many small readers along—readers who are not ready for some of the shadings that make Franklin's life so overflowing.

A review of "Benjamin Franklin," in Virginia Kirkus' Bookshop Service, Vol. XVIII, No. 21, November 1, 1950, p. 655.

The oft told story of Benjamin Franklin is an unending source of pride and enjoyment to Americans of all ages. When given the d'Aulaires' magical interpretation, it should prove irresistible to 6 to 9 year olds—or to anyone who loves beauty in a book. In the tradition of their other biographies—of Washington, Lincoln, and Pocahontas—the illustrations form an integral part of this one. Full page pictures alternate with pages of text generously bordered with handsome Pennsylvania Dutch decorations, into which are woven a collection of Poor Richard's maxims to provide readers with both a hearty chuckle and food for solemn thought!

The story, as it should, begins in the small house on Milk st. in Boston, where Ben was born in 1706, and a gay picture shows it overflowing with father Josiah's 17 children, "all counted!" Then follows a fresh and lively recital of the colorful highlights of Ben's long, distinguished career, with accent on the qualities that made him loved by all—his wit and wisdom, his industry and common sense, and his devoted service to his country.

Polly Goodwin, "An Introduction to Ben Franklin," in Chicago Sunday Tribune, November 12, 1950, p. 5.

With the masses of children's books America produces, it never yet has had enough of the intelligent yet simple picture-story book to introduce its past to younger children. It took two Europeans to fill the gap dramatically, the d'Aulaires, with their big colorful books about Washington, Lincoln, Pocahontas, and the Star-Spangled Banner. Their new one is perhaps the best of this group. They have aimed it above their usual picture-book age, given it a longer, richer text and delightfully used on the margins many of Ben's brief maxims.

The biography is well condensed and Franklin's part in the shaping of our country clearly emphasized. Children of eight to ten will get a lively sense of our early history, as well as the more dramatic aspects of Franklin's printing and inventing. In big full-page pictures and in many fascinating marginal pictures a rich feeling for the period is developed. All is a bit humorous and boldly decorative in a Pennsylvania Dutch style. Yet Franklin himself emerges, real, friendly, dignified.

> *A review of "Benjamin Franklin," in* New York Herald Tribune Book Review, *November 12, 1950, p. 8.*

BUFFALO BILL   (1952)

[It] is difficult to put a finger on just why this book is not wholly satisfying. Perhaps because it is too pretty—too neat a package for days which demanded their fill of blood and sinew. However, it makes an excellent introduction to a popular figure in American folklore and history, with text and pictures (big effective lithographs in color) which play on imagination as well as facts of a glamorous life. There's something of the western march as background for this picture story of the famous rider-hunter-show man.

> *A review of "Buffalo Bull," in* Virginia Kirkus' Bookshop Service, *Vol. XX, No. 17, September 1, 1952, p. 546.*

A frontier boy like Bill Cody learned to look after himself, and little Bill could aim and shoot his father's big gun very, very early. Living beside the Oregon Trail, he frolicked and hunted with friendly Kickapoo Indian children, and he watched the traders, and the covered wagon families, and the ox-wagon strings rolling past toward the setting sun. Bill wasn't 12 when he got himself a grown man's job riding with an ox-wagon train across the plains. By the time dime novels and his traveling show brought fame and riches, Buffalo Bill had excelled at about every job the Wild West had to offer—buffalo hunting, stagecoach driving, riding in the Pony Express and Indian scouting for the Army.

In direct and vigorous style, Edgar and Ingri d'Aulaire depict Buffalo Bill's biography with bright sweeping illustrations that convey the breadth of the plains and the primitive drama of the times.

> *Miriam James, "Son of the West," in* The New York Times Book Review, *November 16, 1952, p. 39.*

THE TWO CARS   (1955)

The d'Aualires teach a solemn lesson in safe driving, but were it not for their accompanying colored lithographs, the unimaginative text would make a dull book. Two cars, one old and one new go for a ride one evening to prove which of them is the better. The new one breaks rules and is reprimanded by a policeman. The old car is about to get home first when he is stopped by the same cop, to be congratulated for safety performance, thus losing the race but gaining the glory. Rather uninspiring.

> *A review of "The Two Cars," in* Virginia Kirkus' Service, *Vol. XXIII, February 1, 1955, p. 76.*

Told originally to one little boy—the author-artists' son—this is a just-right picture story for all small boys who consider automobiles the most fascinating things in all the world. As the d'Aulaires tell and picture it, it seems perfectly reasonable that an old car and a new car should race through a

moonlit night to prove which is the best car on the road. This streamlined version of the hare and the tortoise clips along at high speed and ends in a reverse twist that doesn't offend a child's natural sympathy for the underdog. The theme of good road manners and safe driving is so closely integrated with the action that it doesn't sound like a moral at all. The pictures are amusing and the personification of the automobiles is done with a masterly use of mechanical detail.

> *Ellen Lewis Buell, "The Race," in* The New York Times Book Review, *February 6, 1955, p. 20.*

COLUMBUS   (1955)

The d'Aulaires' striking colored pictures and their narrative which paints the overtones of tragedy in Columbus' life would seem to command recognition as a good account of the first recorded discovery of America. The account of Columbus' life is full and carries the sequence of events further, for example, than the recently reported *The Columbus Story* by Alice Dalgliesh. The interpretation here also seems more complete for it describes Columbus as personally ambitious and frustrated rather than a solely selfless pioneer.

> *A review of "Columbus," in* Virginia Kirkus' Service, *Vol. XXIII, No. 19, October 1, 1955, p. 757.*

The d'Aulaires' **Columbus** is a longer, more detailed version [than Alice Dalgliesh's *The Columbus Story*] and is perhaps better suited to a child who has already heard the story and who has begun to want more information. Columbus' later voyages and discoveries are treated more fully than in Miss Dalgliesh's book and so are his last embittered days. The portrait of the aging, disappointed man who "wanted too much and so did not get enough" in no way detracts from the reader's sense of his greatness. Rather it adds to our understanding. Like the text, the pictures, in color and in black and white, are brilliant, stimulating to the imagination and filled with intriguing details.

> *Ellen Lewis Buell, "Admiral of the Ocean Sea," in* The New York Times Book Review, *October 9, 1955, p. 34.*

[The D'Aulaires' pictures] are striking and full of action and imagination that appeal to younger children. To the adult, their work seems like another Norse wonder-tale, instead of reflecting truly the lands they traveled far to see, to do this book. The text gives a full account of all the voyages and of Columbus' end, unknowing of his great achievement, proud and embittered that the Portuguese had found the way to Asia. It is a good telling for boys and girls of eight or nine, interesting, though not exciting. Families whose children liked the D'Aulaires' **Benjamin Franklin,** which also had an "older" text, will like this.

> *L. S. B., in a review of "Columbus," in* New York Herald Tribune Book Review, *November 13, 1955, p. 3.*

THE MAGIC MEADOW   (1958)

Swiss legend, custom, and atmosphere are deftly incorporated into this charming story of little Peterli. Episodic in form, this account of a child's life in Switzerland is made coherent by the use of a hero whose adventures and observations are happily at the disposal of the young reader. Brightly colored illustrations manage to blend fancy with fact and convey a feeling of that wonderful fresh, flowering country, whose clear air and peaceful atmosphere have for years made it a haven of travelers. Ingri & Edgar D'Aulaire, well-loved artist-writer team, . . . have written this book from on the spot observation and bring to the *Magic Meadow* the infectious enthusiasm of a voyage lovingly taken.

> *A review of "The Magic Meadow," in* Virginia Kirkus' Service, *Vol. XXVI, No. 18, September 15, 1958, p. 707.*

Despite its title, the only magic in this book is the magic of Switzerland, but that is magic enough. What we have is really a child's travelogue of that mountainous and picturesque country. From William Tell to tourists we see through the eyes of a little Swiss boy named Peterli. Peterli lives in a high remote village with his grandfather and around his simple story are woven some of the facts of Swiss life—its cheese making, its snowy winters and alpine rescues, its democracy and freedom, and inevitably its dependence on tourists. This may well whet the appetite of some 6-9-year-old to request his next school vacation in the Alps.

> *Marian Sorenson, "Other Faces, Other Lands— Knowledge for Nursery Naturalists," in* The Christian Science Monitor, *November 6, 1958, p. 16.*

A year of living, traveling, and sketching in Switzerland lies behind the careful creation of this work, which is at once a picture book, an elementary social study of Switzerland, and the story of a hard-working mountain lad. . . . A vivid, if brief, interpretation, with a pictorial richness that a child will not quickly forget. Here are the d'Aulaires' usual large full-color lithographs, striking in deep blues and greens, punctuated with the rainbow hues of Alpine flowers, and equally strong pages in black and white.

> *Virginia Haviland, in a review of "The Magic Meadow," in* The Horn Book Magazine, *Vol. XXXIV, No. 6, December, 1958, p. 463.*

INGRI AND EDGAR PARIN D'AULAIRE'S BOOK OF GREEK MYTHS (1962)

As usual, the D'Aulaires have given children a beautiful gift book, one that may well be a foundation volume for the child's home library. The old Greek myths are all here, from the Greek creation stories and the forming of the court of Olympus to the stories of the mortal descendants of Zeus like King Midas, Bellerophon and Pegasus, Jason and the Golden Fleece, ending with the apples of love and discord and the partly factual story of Troy. The myths are well told—direct, swift, not without humor—and the illustrations, many of them full page and in color, are interesting, often beautiful, always decorative, and frequently fascinating and whimsical. Parents, uncles, and aunts who have been searching for a big picture book that has good reading-aloud value for the younger ones and fine read-it-yourself value on up, have it in this volume that will probably take its place as a children's classic, to be pored over and reread, and finally handed down to their children's children.

> *M. J. T., in a review of "Ingri and Edgar Parin d'Aulaire's Book of Greek Myths," in* The Christian Science Monitor, *November 15, 1962, p. 8B.*

Children everywhere will welcome this lovely collection of

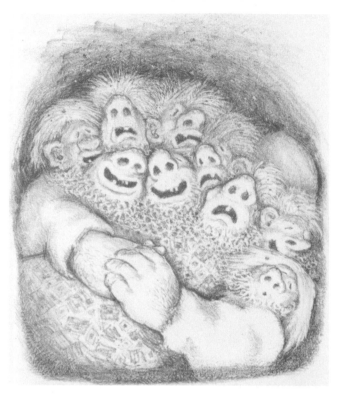

From D'Aulaire's Trolls, *written and illustrated by Ingri and Edgar Parin d'Aulaire.*

Greek myths. Written in a smooth, uncluttered style, the stories are brief, though not spare, and will probably have more appeal than the more ornate traditional retellings presently available in most libraries. Though the text is well written, this volume is most notable for its illustrations. Some of the lithographs are in soft colors, and a number are full-page. The d'Aulaires' distinctive stylized technique is ideally suited to the subject and captures the strength, grandeur, and heroism of these tales. Unfortunately, there is some unevenness of quality, and a few of the illustrations seem hurriedly executed. Nevertheless, a distinguished piece of bookmaking.

> *Marguerite A. Dodson, in a review of "Ingri and Edgar Parin d'Aulaire's Book of Greek Myths," in* School Library Journal, *Vol. 9, No. 4, December, 1962, p. 40.*

This *Book of Greek Myths* is for all ages; but it is particularly right for the middle group, whose imaginations are ready to soar, yet whose reading ability is not yet up to such excellent versions as Helen Sewell's or Olivia Coolidge's. (All too often nowadays, children are allowed to become too sophisticated before they encounter their rightful heritage of fairy tale, myth, and legend; feeling themselves beyond it when they do meet it, they may reject this heritage outright.) For any child fortunate enough to have this generous book, Zeus and the immortal members of his family, the lively minor gods, the kings and heroes of ancient Greek legend, will remain forever familiar figures. Wherever in literature, philology, or daily life he comes across their names—or derivations from them—it seems likely that fragments of the d'Aulaire pictures will flash through his mind. Faults loom small in a book so obviously the fruit of genuine enthusiasm for Greek mythology and delight in sharing this with children, whose responsiveness to integrity of workmanship, new experiences, bold color, and humorous detail the d'Aulaires have for so long respected by consistently giving their best. The style of the telling is relaxed and matter-of-fact; the pictures interpret the text literally and are full of detail and witty observation.

> *Margaret Warren Brown, in a review of "Ingri and Edgar Parin d'Aulaire's Book of Greek Myths," in* The Horn Book Magazine, *Vol. XXXIX, No. 1, February, 1963, pp. 59-60.*

In scope and purpose, ***Book of Greek Myths*** resembles [Jay Macpherson's] *Four Ages of Man.* The authors do not have, however, the same sure control of the subject. Their storytelling spins on (like Arachne, the spider's) without many dramatic highlights. There is too much exposition and too little dialogue. Some of the drawings, particularly the full-page ones in this oversized volume, are excellent and excitingly evocative. But others are poor, marred by awkwardness, and bad design.

> *Mary Louise Hector, in a review of "Ingri and Edgar Parin d'Aulaire's Book of Greek Myths," in* The New York Times Book Review, *April 28, 1963, p. 38.*

NORSE GODS AND GIANTS (1967)

It is not usual that a book which is essentially a good reference volume can be recommended as a storybook as well. But then, Ingri and Edgar d'Aulaire are not the usual author-illustrator team. They are fine artists, 1939 Caldecott medalists, and excellent retellers of old tales. In the ***Norse Gods and Giants*** they have turned their considerable talents to recreating the nine worlds of Odin in a lively prose style and colorful, imaginative pictures. The creation of the earth, the various Norse gods, many of the mythic stories, the final tragic destruction of that universe bound together by the roots and branches of Yggdrasil, the world tree, are here as brief but extremely readable stories. As an extra plus, there is a "Reader's Companion" that is both glossary and index in the end. The only thing missing is a map of the lands whose people believed in these wonders. The d'Aulaires' new volume is a big, handsome book and fit companion to their excellent volume of Greek myths.

> *Jane Yolen, in a review of "Norse Gods and Giants," in* The New York Times Book Review, *November 5, 1967, p. 46.*

Everything about this book, one which is uniquely appropriate to the talents of these artists—and certainly a work of great love—is notably lavish. Its outsized dimensions permit a striking breadth of lithographlike illustrations; sixty in rich full color and seventy-five in two colors are printed on excellent paper. The end papers, which show Odin's great ash tree, Yggdrasil, growing from the underworld to the high heaven above Asgard, and the initial design of each chapter reveal the d'Aulaires' intimate acquaintance with Nordic landscape and folk art and establish a brilliant pictorial atmosphere. The text is based on their deep knowledge of the Icelandic Eddas, the source of our information about Norse myths. The gods, the giants, the trolls, and the Midgard serpent, all the creatures in the mythological hierarchy, are clearly established, and their stories are told in a smooth, colorful prose.

> *Virginia Haviland, in a review of "Norse Gods and*

Giants," in The Horn Book Magazine, *Vol. XLIII, No. 6, December, 1967, p. 749.*

This big, dramatic picture story of the nine worlds of Norse gods, giants, men, gnomes and monstrous creatures may be worn out long before curiosity is satisfied, for it is one to be thumbed through forward and backward. It lures with pictures, challenges with facts and legends. It has some 38 powerful, full-page pictures in colors that speak of fjords, skies glittering with stars, and flaxen-haired maidens, while other pictures race up and down pages telling spirited stories which are augmented in the text. End papers map the relationship of earth to other worlds and a royal portrait of 29 gods stretches across title pages. Borders and ornamental initial letters carry wildly active, grotesquely comic symbols of beasts and men. Comic touches abound in scenes of battles and feasts. A four-page "Reader's Companion" gives phonetic pronunciations, recapitulations and cross references.

The book begins with the creation of the world by three Aesir gods, continues with stories of individual men and gods, and ends with "A New World" when the Norse gods perish and Christianity conquers. The tales have roots in the two great Icelandic books, *The Poetic Edda* of the 10th and 11th centuries A.D. and *The Prose Edda,* the collection of traditional myths and fanciful tales put down by Snorri Sturluson around 1200 A.D.

> *Martha Bennett King, in a review of "Norse Gods and Giants," in* Book World—The Washington Post, *January 14, 1968, p. 14.*

D'AULAIRES' TROLLS (1972)

Luminous, magical pictures of fearsome wild trolls and their sunless world transport readers deep into the mountains and forests of Norway and into the consciousness of old believers. There before us are frenzied, gluttonous trolls at their trampling revels, or gnome workers mining their resplendant gold and forging it at scattered bursts of fire, or the monstrous half-submerged heads of water trolls with their floating, tangled hair. But all is not rumble and ugliness: there are the lovely hudder-maidens, kin to the trolls, who lack souls and resemble humans from the front (but "when a young man heard an enticing song and saw a beautiful girl leading a herd of small black cows on the lonely highlands, he had better make sure one of the cowtails did not belong to her"), and then there is a charming scene of twelve captive princesses, mounted on golden pedestals, scratching a sleeping monster's twelve ugly heads. Stories and anecdotes—of the brave lad who rescued the 12 princesses, or the young fellow who stole the three trolls' single eye for some of their gold—are worked into the text, but mainly this is a robust and resonant natural history of the species: his need to hide from the sun, his habit of taking human babies and substituting squalling changelings, his eyes filled with splinters that made him see everything askew. And the authors never question the truth of it all, only mention in closing that "none have been seen walking around for over a hundred years"—which must be the book's only misstatement, for the D'Aulaires have surely seen trolls. (pp. 804-05)

> *A review of "d'Aulaires' Trolls," in* Kirkus Reviews, *Vol. XL, No. 14, July 15, 1972, pp. 804-05.*

There are children whose drawings of even the most ferocious monsters still reflect a quality of their own innocence and sweet temperament. The same is true of the artwork of the d'Aulaires. No matter how fierce their subjects, they can endow them with a kind of vulnerability that is both touching and—especially in the case of trolls—ridiculous. Seeing these great ugly creatures beset with problems related to health, hygiene and domestic tranquility reduces their power to horrify considerably.

For even though some trolls lived in halls of burnished gold and sat at tables of silver, their wives were hags, their babies screamed all day, and their hair was full of bugs. Even their own ferociousness could turn against them. "A twelve-headed troll had one great weakness. When he grew angry, all his mouths roared right into his twenty-four ears, and that gave him twelve splitting headaches. Then it was hard for him to keep his wits together." When he did marshal his (limited) mental forces, he would go foraging for high-born beauties to scratch his aching, itching heads. And the illustrations show a 12-headed giant picking up shrieking princesses like they were so many dressed-up matchsticks, then carrying them back into his mountain den, six distracted maidens under each shaggy arm.

Combining knowledgeableness with easy-going humor, the d'Aulaires work anecdote after anecdote into a kind of patchwork story-quilt. Each patch, while complete in itself, contributes to an over-all understanding of the Norwegian troll world, fragments of which have survived into today. In fact, after reading the book, the reader begins seeing troll-like manifestations everywhere. Five years ago, the d'Aulaires published a mythological tour de force, **Norse Gods and Giants.** Now, by limiting themselves to only one of the nine worlds of Norse mythology, they have written an authoritative book on trolls and created a nearly perfect picture book for children.

Sidney Long, in a review of "D'Aulaires' Trolls," in The New York Times Book Review, *September 10, 1972, p. 8.*

The d'Aulaires have drawn upon their knowledge of Norway and Norse legends to create a handsome picture book. Plentiful information about trolls, their habits and behavior, interspersed with three brief stories about trolls, make this more of a source book than a story book. Children are drawn to the subject and are sure to enjoy the black-and-white and color pictures, drawn in typical d'Aulaire style, which are of more substance than the text.

Margaret Maxwell, in a review of "D'Aulaires' Trolls," in School Library Journal, *Vol. 19, No. 3, November, 1972, p. 66.*

The book, crowning a lifetime of collaboration, represents the quintessence of the d'Aulaires' art. For, despite their wide interests, the roots of their creative work are deep in the landscape and folklore of Norway—originally inspired by Ingri's background and her living memories of a happy childhood. The authors present a kind of dissertation on trolls, and children will revel in the glorious array: forest trolls and water and sea trolls, along with their troll-hag wives and their troll-brat offspring; little, mischievous gnome-trolls; and the biggest, most nightmarish of all—the mountain trolls, often twelve-headed, which had magical powers and the strength of fifty men. All of the blunt earthiness of the traditional material—folk tales, beliefs, and superstitions—is worked into the text and pictures. "The old trolls were gruff and gnarled, and if they had ever washed it must have been very long ago."

Flies and moths swarmed around them and shrubs and weeds sprouted from their noses and ears. Many of them had tails as well, cowtails, pigtails or short, stubby bear tails. The troll-children weren't much prettier, and the troll-hags were uglier still. They had long, red, crooked noses, and some of them even carried their heads under their arms." The commodious pages—black-and-white stone lithographs alternating with full-color illustrations prepared on acetate overlays—are alive with vigor and imagination and a full measure of grotesque detail.

Ethel L. Heins, in a review of "D'Aulaires Trolls," in The Horn Book Magazine, *Vol. XLVIII, No. 6, December, 1972, p. 592.*

THE TERRIBLE TROLL-BIRD   (1976)

[The Terrible Troll Bird *is a revised version of* Ola and Blakken and Line, Sine, Trine, *which was published in 1933.*]

Some rooster that terrible troll-bird! After terrorizing the Norwegian valley the giant bird is brought down by a silver button shot from a blunderbuss. Not even 10 strong horses can move that mountain of feathers. Eventually the villagers get the fearsome fowl on the roasting spit and there's general merriment with humans, animals, gnomes and sprites joining hands and paws in a dance around the fire. But look out! Here comes Gygra and her husband, Jotun, two gigantic moss-grown old trolls to whom the bird belonged.

Don't be alarmed. The d'Aulaires are considerate of little minds and psyches and always have been. Out of the trolls' towering rage come all of those interesting rocks that dot the Norwegian landscape. Anyway, the children go to sleep on pillows and quilts made of troll-bird feathers. Words like homey, comfortable, old-fashioned and very pleasing characterize the illustrating and storytelling of the d'Aulaires in this remake here of their 1933 **Ola and Blakken.** The husband and wife team have, well, something to crow about once again.

George A. Woods, in a review of "The Terrible Troll-Bird," in The New York Times Book Review, *September 5, 1976, p. 16.*

In an unusual publishing venture, the d'Aulaires have created an exciting new edition of their 1933 picture book, **Ola and Blakken and Line, Sine, Trine.** The Norwegian story is for the most part unchanged. . . . Though Ola is still the dominant character in the story, the three girls are not quite as timid as they were in 1933. The writing has been revised: " 'I never heard of such stupid alarm' " becomes " 'I have never heard such silly talk.' " Both books contain black-and-white and full-color illustrations made by drawing directly onto lithographic stone, but the composition and style of the new book are typical of the artists' contemporary work. The sketchy, indistinct lines and mottled colors of **The Terrible Troll-Bird** are a far cry from the naïve but bold drawings of the earlier version. It is sad to lose the straightforward quality of the original art, but the new pictures transmit an exuberance of their own. A comparison of the two books offers a unique opportunity to study the evolution of two artists of great importance in the history of children's literature.

Sally Holmes Holtze, in a review of "The Terrible Troll-Bird," in The Horn Book Magazine, *Vol. LIII, No. 1, February, 1977, p. 69.*

Berlie Doherty

19??-

English author of fiction and picture books and scriptwriter.

Acknowledged as a writer of evocative works praised for their characterizations and delineation of setting, Doherty characteristically uses the perspectives of her young female narrators to provide young readers with insights into both the joys and sorrows of family life. Addressing the majority of her works to middle graders and young adults, she outlines how such elements as love, death, trust, and independence fit into the lives of both her narrators and their families. Doherty began her career with two collections of stories for young adults, *How Green You Are!* (1982) and *The Making of Fingers Finnigan* (1983), which describe the lives of the teenagers and adults who live on an urban English street. Her next work, *White Peak Farm* (1984), is a series of stories about a family who run a farm in Derbyshire; with *Children of Winter* (1985), Doherty retains her Derbyshire setting in a time travel fantasy which transports three contemporary children to plague-ridden England in the seventeenth century. Doherty is perhaps best known as the creator of *Granny Was a Buffer Girl* (1987), a young adult novel about three generations of a Sheffield working-class family which has gathered to celebrate the departure of their youngest member, Jess, for a year of study in France; from their stories, Jess learns about real love and accepts herself as a part of both her culture and the past. Underscored with comparisons of the social conditions of the characters, *Granny Was a Buffer Girl* presents readers with a bittersweet but ultimately positive view of life. Doherty is also well respected as the author of the "Tilly Mint" stories, delicate tales for preschoolers and primary graders which combine reality with fantasy as they describe how a little girl is sent on a series of magical adventures by her mentor, the ancient Mrs. Hardcastle. In her second book about Tilly Mint, *Tilly Mint and the Dodo* (1988), Doherty explores the issue of ecology; in this story, a wise female dodo takes Tilly back to the seventeenth century, where she sees the bird—the last of its species—become extinct. Doherty is the author of several radio scripts of her books and has also been a broadcaster. Formerly a social worker and teacher, she was also writer-in-residence at a Doncaster comprehensive in 1986, an experience that inspired the creation of *Tough Luck* (1987), a story for young adults about the events that occur to a group of students and their teacher during a snowy spring term. Doherty is also the author of *Paddiwak and Cosy* (1988), a picture book in verse about how two cats become friends. Doherty was awarded the Carnegie Medal in 1986 for *Granny Was a Buffer Girl.*

HOW GREEN YOU ARE! (1982)

Bee, Julie, Marie and Kevin are ordinary young teenagers, living in a street of terraced houses near the sea and Liverpool. Each chapter of this book is a separate episode, but it interlinks into a vividly written and strongly characterized picture of their lives, their friends and relatives, people who live in the street, and their schools.

The story lines are wide-ranging, varied and imaginative. A

Russian violinist defecting to the west, who in search of peace and rest, spends one night at Bee's home; Marie's birthday present—a little monkey—develops rabies, and the police have to shoot it; Donkey Man Mooney and Kevin are rescued by the lifeboat when they are caught by the tide; Weird George, the disabled boy, was finally accepted by the street; Catholic Julie wins a scholarship for a "snob" convent school. Her green uniform (of the title story) at first sets her apart from her friends, but they find out that she has not changed.

A thought provoking book, it will probably be more popular with older readers than young teenagers. Excellent descriptive writing, but the conversation tends to be too literary for reality, although the situations contain all the sadness, stress and problems of real life—strikes, death, illness, as well as the happier events. (pp. 150-51)

A. Thatcher, in review of "How Green You Are," in The Junior Bookshelf, *Vol. 46, No. 4, August, 1982, pp. 150-51.*

Convincing descriptions supported by line drawings by Elaine McGregor Turney ensure that Bee, Kevin, Julie and the rest of their friends could easily be the children you might expect to meet in your own neighbourhood. The stories are varied: some funny, some sad. They deal with relations, neighbours and friends; and with events such as the local fair, a wedding, a birthday and a haunting. This is an entertaining addition to the 'Pied Piper' series [published by Methuen].

> *Lucinda Fox, in a review of "How Green You Are!"*
> *in* The School Librarian, *Vol. 30, No. 3, September,*
> *1982, p. 232.*

THE MAKING OF FINGERS FINNIGAN (1983)

Narrator Bee grumbles about her contemporaries: nagging Marie, fanciful Nicola, half-witted George. But they are all neighbours in the run down seaside area near Liverpool where Bee lives, and instinctively she sticks by them.

The seven appealing stories about life in this community are linked by characters and incidents. Adults join children in an attempt to save the decrepit swimming pool, and fund raising activities for this project continue intermittently throughout the book. Julie's younger brother Robert, locked in the cinema, is rescued by Fingers Finnigan, a reluctant crook. Subsequently Fingers is removed from the domination of his criminally-minded mother and successfully installed as lodger and companion with another problem character, a sour and lonely old spinster.

The illustrations [by J. Haysom] in this book are small and rather sparse, but the text describes all the characters with sufficient verve for the reader's imagination to picture them without difficulty.

> *R. Baines, in a review of "The Making of Fingers*
> *Finnigan," in* The Junior Bookshelf, *Vol. 47, No. 6,*
> *December, 1983, p. 242.*

WHITE PEAK FARM (1984)

[The series of stories in **White Peak Farm**] are quiet, carefully observed and neatly crafted accounts of a farming family's life in Derbyshire. In keeping with a current trend, . . . the narrator is a girl. Her family lives in rhythm with the land and the seasons in a tightly netted community with its quirky characters, long-lasting feuds but ultimate supportiveness. Much of the life of the stories stems from the tension between the emerging young people and the claims of both the land and a brooding patriarch of a father (*not* a stock character). All this is evoked with an understatement typical of the conversation of the characters themselves. The satisfactions here are for the discerning reader, intrigued by complex relationships rather than insistent action, willing to work a little at what the writer leaves unsaid. It feels as though Berlie Doherty has drawn episodes and characters from factual observation and woven them into a single family's history; not that the research sticks out at the seams, but the other-than-fiction authenticity contrasts sharply with the more conventional narratives of the other two titles [reviewed here, Jane O'Connor's *Just Good Friends* and Joanne Webster's *Marigold Summer*].

> *Geoff Fox, in a review of "White Peak Farm," in*
> The Times Educational Supplement, *No. 3558, September 7, 1984, p. 29.*

A note of introduction tells us that chapters of this book were read on Radio 4's *Morning story;* and that the whole was written for BBC Radio Sheffield. Certainly, the first two chapters,

about Gran and about Aunt Jessie, are complete in themselves. We lose sight of Gran, but Aunt Jessie reappears briefly at the end to help a young couple in need of a home.

The central story is about a Derbyshire farm and the unusual family who own it. . . . Details of farm life are unsparing, as when the lambs have to be brought in at nightfall because of an unexpected snow warning. People speak convincingly and there is much concern for girls brought up in this environment, who are not reckoned to be farmers, and on whom advanced education 'is wasted'. Girls fall in love at the wrong moment, usually examination time; and boys seem far less disposed to give all for love.

I think teenage readers will enjoy this book, and the separate episodes—the mountain rescue, Easter snow, the hired hand—read aloud well in their own right.

> *Dorothy Atkinson, in a review of "White Peak*
> *Farm," in* The School Librarian, *Vol. 32, No. 4, December, 1984, p. 371.*

White Peak Farm is a collection of ten short stories about members of a single family; the stories are interrelated like the people so that by the end there is a portrait of the complete group. . . . Each character in turn learns how to be independent without destroying other people. The variations are delicately worked out and kept to scale, establishing the family as an uncomfortable but living structure without which growth, discovery and survival would scarcely be possible.

> *Dominic Hibberd, "Family Feelings," in* The Times
> Literary Supplement, *No. 4270, February 1, 1985,*
> *p. 130.*

TILLY MINT TALES (1984)

Tilly Mint's adventures have been broadcast on Radio Sheffield. Tilly is pre-school age but her friend Mrs. Hardcastle is 'the oldest woman in the world'—so she says. Tilly Mint loves her and when she hears Mrs. Hardcastle say 'I'm feeling right dopey' she knows that the old lady will soon fall asleep—and magic will happen to Tilly. All kinds of lovely things are possible then, she can fly, she can ride on a kind lion's back or visit the Land of Dreams and have a wish. One day Mrs. Hardcastle holds a grand party before breakfast and flies so high that Tilly never sees her again—but she can make magic on her own now.

These pleasant stories are an encouragement to children to use their imagination and so make their own magic, a timely stimulus in these days when children rely so much on passive viewing of television.

> *E. Colwell, in a review of "Tilly Mint Tales," in* The
> Junior Bookshelf, *Vol. 48, No. 6, December, 1984,*
> *p. 254.*

Tilly Mint Tales comes as something of a let-down after the author's brilliant **The Making of Fingers Finnigan.** In an excess of whimsy Mrs Doherty strains her inventive powers to creaking point. Her aim, presumably, is to effect a smooth blending of dreaming fantasy with humdrum reality but, alas, this doesn't always come off. There's no shortage of variety—from worms to lions, from sky-flights to frog-spawn—and most children will warm to the comforting and comfortable figure of Mrs Hardcastle. . . . They'll also take to the catchy verses which Mrs Doherty indulges in so liberally.

Stephen Corrin, in a review of "Tilly Mint Tales," in The Times Educational Supplement, *No. 3577, January 18, 1985, p. 29.*

CHILDREN OF WINTER (1985)

Time is bridged in **Children of Winter** in an entirely simple and successful way when three children visiting their grandmother in the Derbyshire hills enter light-heartedly into a game which brings them to a direct and startling view of the past. The time-slip is made possible because Catherine Tebbutt is a sensitive, dreamy girl, ready to respond to the influence of the old barn where they shelter from the storm and to the spirit of an earlier Catherine Tebbutt reaching out to communicate something of the terrible ordeal she and her brother and sister faced when, to save them from the plague raging in the village, their parents sent them to the barn to live through the winter in isolation. Catherine in the present finds herself directing Patsy and small Andrew, now called Tessa and Dan, in wood-gathering and water-carrying and the many contrivances by which the family in the past was able to survive and to emerge to join a sadly depleted village group in celebrating the end of terror. Re-enacting old events, the three children change completely to the attitudes and moods of former times and then, returning to the present, find time has stood still. The idea of a game turned to earnest is appropriate to a book designed to appeal to readers around nine or so who should not find it hard to imagine the feelings of children not too far removed from themselves faced with grim necessity.

Margery Fisher, in a review of "Children of Winter," in Growing Point, *Vol. 24, No. 1, May, 1985, p. 4432.*

The story is interesting and well told, which intensifies the bitter irony when an act of kindness brings plague to the barn. When the messenger arrives to take the children back to the village Dan is sick with it. A time slip back into the present cannot obscure the fact that this is a distressing end to a story for younger readers. (pp. 216-17)

R. Baines, in a review of "Children of Winter," in The Junior Bookshelf, *Vol. 49, No. 5, October, 1985, pp. 216-17.*

An old cruck barn was the inspiration for this adventure story set in the England of the Black Death. To make a time-slip story entirely plausible is no easy matter, but this one succeeds admirably. There is a present-day build-up of atmosphere as Catherine, Patsy, Andrew and their parents leave the bus and walk through the lonely countryside. They are caught in a sudden storm and take shelter in an old stone barn. From the time she leaves the bus, Catherine has a haunting sense of familiar and long-forgotten things, so when the children are left alone in the barn, with the door shut against the weather, the past takes over. The return to the present is equally skilfully arranged. The book may serve a two-fold purpose: for escape reading, or as a vivid picture of what might have happened to a family in plague-stricken England.

Lucinda Fox, in a review of "Children of Winter," in The School Librarian, *Vol. 34, No. 1, March,*

1986, p. 45.

GRANNY WAS A BUFFER GIRL (1987)

A Sheffield family, gathered for a young member of it about to serve a year in France, jumbles together the generations. They will sort themselves out and form the pattern of this story. Grandpa was a steel worker, Granny had served the buffing wheel: polishing spoons and plate, her chest, arms, stomach and legs protected from gritty dust by sheets of newspaper. Their son, Michael, had his heyday in the Teddy-boy years, and the good fortune to marry the right girl. As time goes by, one of their children will dwindle and die from a wasting muscular disease; the other will be Jess, with whom the everlasting circle started, as she set out for her year in France, her young man all ready for the next figure to start.

These family episodes are fascinating. Words come up that govern the generations; words about work, the boss and Cutler's Hall, about National Service and the Saturday hop, about redundancy, the pigeon-loft, and bowls, and the quietness of the house where one partner is left alone. Not expecting her to understand him, Grandad Albert tells seventeen-year-old Jess that love doesn't have much to do with kissing and cuddling. What it does have to do with is the substance of this story: family loyalties, disappointments, great griefs, and brief, vivid happiness. This is required reading for those who see grandparents as 'crumblies'. They may have been like that handsome couple who, in setting out on a motorbike to get married, defied both the cold repudiation of a Protestant mother and the anger of a Catholic dad. Attention must be paid.

Dorothy Atkinson, in a review of "Granny Was a Buffer Girl," in The School Librarian, *Vol. 35, No. 2, May, 1987, p. 148.*

The Carnegie Medal is given for 'an outstanding book for children'. Berlie Doherty's novel is indeed such a book.

Three generations of one very ordinary family come alive through a series of short highly readable tales, full of warmth and emotional appeal. The reader cannot help but be drawn into these vital and homely stories, with their mix of humour and heartfelt sadness. The characters are excellently portrayed with accuracy and empathy, so is their northern environment not only as it is today, but as it has been across three generations. From a basis of sound social history, here is a highly memorable insight into family life. The main audience is likely to be readers of twelve years and over, but this is a book which also made a lasting impression on the members of the [Carnegie Medal] selection panel.

Helen Pain, "Carnegie and Greenaway: The 1986 Winners," in Books for Keeps, *No. 45, July, 1987, p. 11.*

A series of bittersweet stories about the loves and marriages in three generations of a Sheffield family—framed by the reminiscences of Jess, the family's youngest member—adds up to a fine novel. . . .

In each generation there is love rewarded and love betrayed; the contrasts and parallels enrich the meaning of all. The love between parent and child is a second strong theme, most eloquent in the central story of Danny, Jess's older brother. . . .

Doherty with a group of English schoolchildren.

Vividly evocative of time and place, a poignant portrait of a dozen individuals whose joys and trials are universal.

A review of "Granny Was a Buffer Girl," in Kirkus Reviews, *Vol. LVI, No. 1, January 1, 1988, p. 53.*

On the eve of her departure for a year of study in France, Jess feels like "a snake shedding its skin . . . thrilled, scared," and incomplete. Her parents, brother, and grandparents come together, as is their custom, for one of their celebrations. They celebrate the life of her brother Danny, who died at seventeen, and of her grandmother Bridie, who lived to seventy, and they celebrate the small events which help them get on with their lives. As Jess watches them go through the bantering ritual which precedes their stories, she realizes that in sharing their secrets, their loves as well as their ghosts, they are helping her to understand "the strange thing that adults call love." . . . The author skillfully interweaves the industrial life and death of the Sheffield mills with the personal stories of four generations. The characters are drawn with sharp, unflinching honesty. Great-uncle Gilbert is a strange, terrifying giant of a man, reduced by a stroke to a hulk whose eyes "livid in a lifeless face, blazed black anger." Bringing together the family's stories gives Jess new insight into the bonds between them. As the train is leaving, she knows that "the snake had shed its skin." She is no longer a child and is able

to receive her mother's farewell gift—a photo of her brother Danny, laughing out of the past, "celebrating life." (pp. 357-58)

Hanna B. Zeiger, in a review of "Granny Was a Buffer Girl," in The Horn Book Magazine, *Vol. LXIV, No. 3, May-June, 1988, pp. 357-58.*

Nowhere is the case for historical fiction more effectively put than here. The stories that Jess hears on the eve of her departure for a year's study in France are the personal histories of three generations of her plucky Sheffield family. . . . She leaves with a symbolic gift: a photograph of Danny 'laughing out at [her] from the past . . . celebrating life'.

Readers who enter the past and join in this 'laughter' are made intimate with bygone lives that enable them to 'read' and celebrate the present anew.

"Elizabeth Hammill, Paperback Fiction: Berlie Doherty," in The Signal Selection of Children's Books 1988, *edited by Nancy Chambers, The Thimble Press, 1989, p. 66.*

TOUGH LUCK (1987)

AUTHOR'S COMMENTARY

When I suggested to 3P, a lively class of 13/14s at Hall Cross Comprehensive school in Doncaster, that I'd like to write a book with them, they responded with enthusiasm. In a secret ballot they voted for a book about "people like ourselves, the kind of things that happen to us"—which surprised and pleased me. . . .

I was at their school for one day a week for the spring term of 1986 on a writer's residency jointly financed by Hall Cross English department and Yorkshire Arts Association, and so would be spending a total of 11 double lesson periods with that particular group, and doing readings and poetry writing with others. It was snowing on that first morning. I had to travel by train and arrived late, in wellies. The snow persisted throughout the term, and became a feature of the book.

I spent the first session talking to the whole class about themselves, and then launched them into a quick-write on starting the term in the snow. Then I established the pattern of the project by dividing the class into random groups of five or six and taking the first group off to a quiet room to talk. I used a tape recorder, and we talked about home and school, hobbies, boyfriends, girlfriends, hates, pets etc. . . . I had no idea what would actually be written down, but was searching for something from within their own experience to start me off. We had agreed that the book would be about a class of third years in a comprehensive school—vaguely, while I was talking to them, I was listening out for an opener that would show the class as a microcosm. Jane did it. She told me about her last class building an igloo together. That was it. Next I was looking out for a way of singling out one member of the class. Donna dropped in the information that in Doncaster if someone's not turning up to school they're "twagging". We were off.

At home I read their writing, listened to their voices, and wrote the first chapter of the book that will probably always be referred to by them as "Twagger".

When I read it to them the next week we had some decisions to make. Were we writing a set of linked short stories or a novel? Did we want a narrator? Would that be a boy or a girl? After much discussion we decided on the sort of structure I often use, a girl telling the stories of the other characters. By the fourth week we'd changed our minds. We agreed that the strongly emerging central characters belonged to the novel form, and that the narrator was redundant. We had discussions about the use of violence and romance. We wrote sample chapters in class; I left them with strings of question to consider; every week we compared notes. Our small group sessions were invaluable; we talked our way through problem scenes; they offered me lively challenges and criticisms.

Our next big decision was the one that caused me the most problems. The two characters who claimed the most attention were boys—they had something in common that was of deep personal concern, though we agreed that they would never talk to each other about it. But we must have another strong girl. The whole class also wanted to take race on board.

This interested me. There were many children of ethnic minorities in the school; several in the class were of Asian origin. Everyone wrote about seeing or being the only Asian in a white school, and what they wrote impressed and worried and moved me. Here was an area that was so sensitive that I would never have dared to tackle it without their interest. By the time my short residency was finished and I was left to my own devices Nasim was the character I couldn't leave alone. . . .

It wasn't until I was at the stage of writing it all up for the class that I began to wonder whether the book might have a potential beyond teaching them to think about characterization and storytelling. Very quickly I drew together and resolved the main threads of the story into a book for the class to have, and then with the encouragement of my editor set about the long task of developing the novel *Tough Luck* from this embryo. . . .

Many, many hours have gone into the writing of *Tough Luck,* but those first eleven or so in the mobile classroom in the snowy school yard, when 3P gave me so much of themselves, are the life-blood of the book.

> *Berlie Doherty, "Snowy Story," in* The Times Educational Supplement, *No. 3685, February 13, 1987, p. 48.*

[In *Tough Luck,* Berlie Doherty] refuses to make her adults into easy caricatures; though, if you weren't a teacher, you might think the sour Mr Brown (Maths) a bit overdrawn, and the sympathetic Miss Peters (English) really deserves more than she gets when she says to a bunch of 3rd Years "late on Thursday afternoon", "I want you to write about a nuclear holocaust" ("They do that in the 5th Year," says one malcontent).

Her cast also includes a couple of sympathetic lively kids, along with Twagger (—sciver in Yorkshire patois) and Nasim, a Pakistani girl sent to England who settles in only to be whisked back to her homeland for an arranged marriage. Hill Bank Comprehensive shares some of the vigour of Grange Hill and has a touch of the *Kes* syndrome (caring teacher reaches difficult kid through wild birds—though here, neatly enough, they still mistrust each other). Twagger in particular is distinctively observed—wary, hunted, getting his retaliation in first, wounding with a tongue which knows where to hurt adults who invade him with kindness. This novel should be widely popular with individuals and as a class-reader.

> *Geoff Fox, "Through Teenage Eyes," in* The Times Educational Supplement, *No. 3701, June 5, 1987, p. 61.*

3B is a class of thirteen to fourteen year olds in a rough and ready comprehensive school. . . .

This book, rooted in experience, is told straightforwardly and with truth. For example, the author shows that the arrangement of a marriage for a thirteen year old can simultaneously appear shocking to an English mother, "tough luck" to another child, and the working of Kismet to the Pakistani bride herself.

> *R. Baines, in a review of "Tough Luck," in* The Junior Bookshelf, *Vol. 51, No. 4, August, 1987, p. 177.*

TILLY MINT AND THE DODO   (1988)

"Never sing on duty", says Berlie Doherty's Mole-rat Queen to one of her young guards after dismissing an older one for doing just that, and, as an ecological fantasy, *Tilly Mint and the Dodo* runs the risk of following her sententious instruction. The dust-jacket seems to be offering a health-warning to the imagination when it solemnly promises an "exploration of the conservation issue", and the dedication to "all children who love living things" strikes a further deliberate chord. But the story itself manages to slip past the guard of its own dutiful intentions and sing its way to the heart of the matter. The author instructs by pleasing, and knows that the wisdom lies in the delight.

Thanks to her dream-friend and mentor, Mrs Hardcastle, Tilly Mint comes into possession of a large, very old egg from which emerges a wise and witty female dodo. She seems to have been reborn in order to be taken home, and together this endearing pair return to the land of yesterday. They are constantly up against the humans—hunters and pirates—and Tilly is, of course, to learn what it really means for a species to become extinct. The three-way bond of affection which develops between Tilly, Dodo and the reader ensures that the story's climax is a moving one. For Dodo, inevitably, to go home means to meet her death, and the last Tilly sees of her (knowing that this is a *real* end) is when she is trapped: "She tried to rush forward to hug her again but all the jungle closed in a ring round Dodo and the pirates, keeping Tilly back so she couldn't see what was happening". The creatures all bow their heads in silence, and there is a finely achieved atmosphere of profound and resonant shame. Before she dies, though, Dodo has given Tilly an egg and sung her the song of the last dodo. Tilly wakes with the egg safe on her "special shelf" and the knowledge that she has been part of a "very important story".

It is largely because *Tilly Mint and the Dodo* is so full of affection and good humour that the uncompromising ending makes its impact. A friend has been lost and a lesson learnt. Even Dodo's response to being called extinct—"Dodo's eggs don't stink"—is an important part of the book's appeal. There is sometimes more in a bad-egg joke than is dreamed of in your ecology. The book's "on duty" message, voiced by Tilly herself, that "the world belongs to all of us" is proved on the reader's pulse by Berlie Doherty's light touch and Janna Doherty's gentle pictures.

> *John Mole, "A Friend Lost, a Lesson Learnt," in*
> The Times Literary Supplement, *No. 4472, December 16-22, 1988, p. 1406.*

Each of [the novels reviewed here, Hugh Scott's *The Shaman's Stone*, Dennis Hamley's *Hare's Choice*, Theresa Tomlinson's *The Water Cat*, and *Tilly Mint and the Dodo*,] is a story of the night in which, as Martha discovers in *The Shaman's Stone*, "something that usually anchors me to ordinary things is cut". Echoes of the supernatural, death, time and eternity sound through the stories, and like Tilly in *Tilly Mint and the Dodo*, all the fictional children have difficulty in dealing with the terrifying knowledge that "nobody's safe". Like the extinct and endangered animal species they befriend (two of these novels are written by conservationists), the children are shadowed by "a real deep sadness that only hunted animals know". A pulse of fear and danger throbs through the tales. . . .

At the same time, however, it is not merely hiding-behind-the-settee stuff that is at stake here. Amid the supernatural apparatus, the children and animals grow to learn equally about the importance of love and trust and risk-taking. . . .

The Water Cat and *Tilly Mint and the Dodo* are beautifully told through the voice of a child. Each portrays a deep desire to return "home"—the merman to the sea, and the Dodo to the land of his (now extinct) species. "Oh, Tilly, take me home," the Dodo says. Berlie Doherty's story about Tilly Mint and her magical adventure—this time to save the only surviving dodo from extinction—is poignant and delicately wrought. . . .

Tilly Mint and the Dodo ends with the important act of making a story into a book. . . . All four novels reflect the child's discovery of the act of writing: the need to "pour sadness on to paper" and "to fill the mind with words". It is this that keeps the night at bay, and that prompts the saving knowledge that "There is no fear unless I create it".

> *Sandra Kemp, "Mad and Magic Encounters: Keeping the Night at Bay," in* The Times Educational Supplement, *No. 3776, November 11, 1988, p. 52.*

[*Tilly Mint and the Dodo*] seeks unashamedly to enlist the support of children in the conservation movement. . . .

Berlie Doherty knows how to make her animal characters appeal to the reader's sympathy. . . .

A sympathetic reader will hold a class spellbound with this attractive excursion into the world of conservation.

> *D. A. Young, in a review of "Tilly Mint and the Dodo," in* The Junior Bookshelf, *Vol. 52, No. 6, December, 1988, p. 289.*

PADDIWAK AND COSY   (1988)

[*Paddiwak and Cosy*] rates top marks on all counts—text, pictures, and the real alliance of both. It's about that touchy subject, bringing in a new cat where a single favourite reigns. The beguiling telling, rich in words, runs like verse, with the right incantatory repetitions. The pictures [by Teresa O'Brien], some set in a stunning Pre-Raphaelite garden, are superb. (p. 37)

> *Naomi Lewis, "How Many Miles to Babylon?" in*
> The Listener, *Vol. 120, No. 3092, December 8, 1988, pp. 36-7.*

In her first picture book, the author of *Granny Was A Buffer Girl* describes a common event—a second cat's arrival in a comfortable household, as well as the first cat's initial dismay and eventual contentment with the interloper—with considerable artistry: lilting verse with cleverly echoing sounds; a series of actions that are both perfectly cat-like and a perfect parallel to human behavior ("The new cat ran upstairs,/lost and scared,/squeezing under dusty beds and sneezing there. /Paddiwak howled on the garden wall. 'I'm never, never, never going home at all'"). Illustrator O'Brien makes a splendid debut with her cats . . . ; she expands the text with many entrancing bits in the background, including the antics of mice and other small creatures. Much better than the familiar old cat book.

> *A review of "Paddiwak and Cozy," in* Kirkus Reviews, *Vol. LVII, No. 1, January 1, 1989, p. 48.*

In lilting verse, Doherty relates a woe-filled tale of feline usurpation . . . The story's verve is amplified by O'Brien's art, a wondrous riot of rich color evincing the artist's facility for capturing not only the cats' piercing green-gold gazes and graceful movements, but also the Victorian potted palm and the bric-a-brac-strewn interior. Keen eyes will spy the little mice tucked away in each scene—observers also of Paddiwak's rocky adjustment to sharing and being shared. A handsome presentation.

Phillis Wilson, in a review of "Paddiwak and Cozy," in Booklist, *Vol. 85, No. 15, April 1, 1989, p. 1382.*

Rachel Field

1894-1942

(Also wrote as Rachel Lyman Field) American author and illustrator of fiction and picture books, poet, dramatist, reteller, and editor.

The first woman to be awarded the Newbery Medal, Field is respected as a prolific and diverse writer who expanded the limits of juvenile fiction in the 1920s and 1930s by enriching her works with topics and emotions of complexity and depth. Unlike most other children's authors of her day, she created intimate portrayals of her characters and presented a more complete picture of life with all of its dangers and tragedies while accenuating decency, kindness, and the gratification in experiencing all facets of living. Field wrote fantasy, historical fiction, nonfiction, poetry, plays, and picture books as well as verse for adults and several popular adult novels. However, she is most often remembered for her juvenile fiction and poetry. Overflowing with adventure and pathos, Field's fiction for grade school to high school readers is considered remarkable for its avoidance of sentimentality and melodrama. Three of her titles—*Hitty, Her First Hundred Years* (1929), *Calico Bush* (1931), and *Hepatica Hawks* (1932)—are especially celebrated for recreating the past with realism and drama as well as for their admirable, spirited protagonists. *Hitty,* the story of a doll made from mountain ash in the early nineteenth century who writes her memoirs from her home in an antique shop, presents a survey of American social history through Hitty's multifarious adventures. In 1930, *Hitty* became the first book with an American theme to win the Newbery Medal.

Field's fiction is consistently noted for its sensitivity, a quality often alluded to in commentary on her other works for children. By fervently placing herself in the young reader's world, Field created her verse as impressions presented through the eyes of a child. Lauded for their freshness, her poems employ a moving, unassuming style to point out the delight of everyday experiences and the enthusiastic perceptions of common objects. In the collection *Taxis and Toadstools: Verses and Decorations* (1926), which is recognized as her best known book in this genre, Field explores the excitement of the city and expresses affinity with nature. She uses the language of childhood to describe elements of urban and rural life as she experienced them during the years in which she alternated between homes in New York City and Maine. Her picture books for the read-aloud and primary grade audiences, often fantasies about elves, holiday magic, and enchantment, or tales of problems presented and then resolved satisfactorily, are deemed beguiling for their innocence and optimism. Marked by the same hopefulness and quaint charm with which she invests her fiction, Field's dramas include a small number of characters, uncomplicated stage directions, and clear plot lines and are credited with being especially suited for performance by young players. Acclaimed for exhibiting the same contented mood as her texts, Field's illustrations—watercolor paintings and black and white or ink drawings and silhouettes which she created for her picture books and verse—are characterized by their joyful naivete and playful action. Field also produced collections of folk

and fairy tales, a book on the characters of Charles Dickens, and *Prayer for a Child* (1944), a work for which she received much attention. In 1932, *Calico Bush* was named a Newbery Medal honor book. *Prayer for a Child* won the Lewis Carroll Shelf Award in 1958, an honor also given to *Hitty* in 1961.

(See also *Something about the Author,* Vol. 15, and *Dictionary of Literary Biography,* Vols. 9, 22.)

GENERAL COMMENTARY

JOSIAH TITZELL

In [Rachel Field's] first book, *Pointed People,* she wrote **"May in Cambridge"**:

> How could I learn philosophy,
> Or read great books of history,
> When May came into Cambridge town,
> Sending the petals drifting down
> From tall horsechestnut trees alight
> With flower-candles, waxy white?

How could she, indeed? The answer, of course, is that she could because of her energy, mental and physical. All that and more. She could study with Professor Baker of Harvard's

47 Dramatic Workshop. Her first plays were produced there. Her love of the theater had asserted itself. She left Radcliffe to go to New York with material for her first two books, *The Pointed People* and *Six Plays.* The former is a book of bright poems—poems that are a first glimpse of a mind that delights in songs of thoughts and feelings, familiar things or distant, dim lands, elfin and fay, trees and characters, from the stage, the street in front of her house or from her imagination. The book is illustrated with charming silhouettes she herself made. In *Six Plays* appears the best of her first plays, which are also characterized by the variety of moods, from the happily fantastic to the more seriously dramatic. (pp. 24-5)

The stimulating, magic setting for which Rachel Field deserted [her hometown of] Stockbridge is actually a double setting. She is a double character. Under each division come subdivisions—true of all those who are sensitive, for sensitivity means reflection and adaptation—but primarily two people.

The double setting. Eight months of the year she lives in New York; four months she lives on an island off the Maine coast. Eight months she is a hurried, gay, impelling New Yorker, sensitive to skyscrapers, brightly-lighted taxis and ferries, florist shops and pretzel venders. Four months she is an islander and all that suggests: quiet and happy and content, with a constant awareness of a blue sky and white gulls; a blue sea and white, windy clouds; green islands, bright with berries and mushrooms; of salt in the air and the sound of the buoys and the surf; and the shadows over Sargent Mountain opposite that gallop like horse and hound. She responds fully to each, taxis and toadstools. (pp. 25-6)

[*Eliza and the Elves*] tells as much about elves as any one but Eliza can safely know. Three stories, from one of which the book gains its title, and many poems make up a delightful book. Elizabeth MacKinstry . . . decorated the book with an appreciation that makes it one of the nicest books about elves ever published. A month later *Taxis and Toadstools* was published. Here the promise of *The Pointed People* was fulfilled by a book of poems, about a city and an island that was filled with charming songs and thoughts you and I have wanted to sing and think for a long time and which we just haven't been quite able to. Here the author reappears as artist, with colored and black and white decorations that perfectly supplement the poems. At this time a "play" book appeared, *An Alphabet for Boys and Girls,* with a poem and drawing for each letter, both done by Rachel Field. It was a spontaneous creation—a fling—and won an admiring audience. It has just gained a companion volume, *A Little Book of Days,* again poems and drawings, this time one for each holiday. Together in their green and red bindings they make a most attractive pair.

To take its place on the shelf next to them one of Rachel Field's most perfect books has just appeared. It is called *The Magic Pawnshop* and is in the true Field *métier*, fantasy. It is a story of a pawnshop in New York on New Year's Eve and the happenings there—magical, fascinating happenings. It is done in a calm but spry mood, with an unusual ability for selection of material. And wisping its way through it, and hovering coolly over it, is a glowing golden mellowness.

By the time this appears in print [*The Cross-Stitch Heart and Other Plays*], charming pieces about Lady Jane Grey, and poetry salesmen, and wistful young violinists and Irish ped-

dlers, fantasies and rhymed dramas, will have appeared. This book of plays completes the published work of Rachel Field.

And completing her work, it completes this glimpse of her. There she is, a little girl who grew up in Stockbridge and was known as Rachel, an enthusiastic, impelling student known as Rachel Lyman Field, who swept through Radcliffe and took New York unto herself, and finally the person who lives in boisterous New York and the star-quiet Sutton Island, and is known as Rachel Field, the person who is gaily keen, aware of all she comes in contact with, and who loves old houses, patchwork quilts, roads, samplers, gypsies, elves and fairies, all animals, particularly dogs (her constant companion is a charming and devoted black-as-night Scotch terrier, Spriggin) and dancing bears, cuckoo clocks and merry-go-rounds, and night, with its stars and whispering mystery, or its wind and rain. Those who have heard her speak of the things she is thinking and writing, or who have seen her busy, strewn desk in her playhouse under the shadow of St. Mark's-in-the-Bouwerie, know that much that is glorious is yet to come from her. It may be poetry, prose, drawings or plays, and it may—and most probably will—be all four, but in any case it will possess that peculiar quality that distinguishes Walter de la Mare, James Stephens, Eleanor Farjeon, Barrie, A. A. Milne, and Rose Fyleman. Rachel Field is of their company, a troubadour company, whose eyes are deep and distant for all they see, whose songs are free and rich for all they feel, and whose imaginings glitter and tinkle with a crystal delight. (pp. 26-7)

Josiah Titzell, "Rachel Field: Portrait of a Troubadour," in The Horn Book Magazine, *Vol. III, No. 4, November, 1927, pp. 22-7.*

WALTER BARNES

Rachel Field is highly endowed and richly experienced in writing for children. In my judgment her poetry is superior to her stories, even to *Hitty:* and those parts of her stories are superior in which she is most descriptive, meditative, and imaginative. She has been writing too much for children, been bending her mind too steadily toward them; it is good to find in her last volume, *Branches Green,* many poems not aimed too pointedly at children—and for that very reason probably all the better as children's poems.

Taxis and Toadstools is the collection which made Miss Field known among children and lovers of children's poetry. It has perhaps as many admirable poems for children as any volume of original verse of these last ten years. Her poems have variety of theme, attitude, and treatment; they are well within the compass of children's experiences and yet do not condescend and patronize (I'd like to coin a word: "matronize"), they do not alienate the adult's respect nor affront the children's self-respect.

As the title would imply, this collection includes poems based upon city scenes and incidents. Here are the flower-cart man, the sandwich man, the blind beggar, the ice-cream and the pretzel-vendor; here are scenes at the theater, at chestnut stands, in the florist's shop, and the toy shop, the animal store, and even at the bank—a most unpromising spot to find a poem! Here is reality, but reality made poetry—though alas! not always—by the child's fancy, curiosity, freshness of vision, his sentience and sensibility. The blind man who "smiles at something all to himself "; the florists,

Quiet men and kind
With a sort of fragrance of the mind.

The uneasy impression that parrots' beady eyes give you;

They stare and shine, they shine and stare.
And you must stand before them there
And feel there's nothing in your mind
A wise old parrot couldn't find. . . .

In all these situations and many others there are the seeing eye and the sensitive, responsive heart, and, in most instances, the moving, unstudied utterance suggestive of the childlike idiom.

But if the city poems constitute Rachel Field's most distinctive contribution, they are not necessarily her best creations. Her poems on the "critters" and flowers, on the sea and seashore are equally fine. She has added the island to the poetical domains of children. There's a fanciful thing:

All the islands have run away
From the land which is their mother;

and the solemn assurance that

If once you have slept on an island
You'll never be quite the same.

and the grass-plot island at the road intersection which the child-explorer has landed upon:

The cars flash by and the hay carts pass
Like ships on a long brown sea
And the folk aboard them smile and nod
And wave their hands to me.

Well, there *is* something about an island.

Miss Field does not often write of fairies and goblins and creatures of that brood, but in the section which she calls **"Fringes of Fairyland"** are two poems I admire: **"The Elf Tree"** . . . and **"The Secret Land,"** reminiscent of Walter de la Mare, which has the true magic. (pp. 52-3)

I could wish that Miss Field had not been content with the careless, shoddy workmanship which mars many of her poems; the unnatural inversions, the padding, the lusterless prosaic phrases, the colloquialisms, the doggerel anapests; and in her latest collection [**Branches Green**] I find her technique much more nearly perfect. In **"Snow by Night,"** in **"Family Pew,"** in **"Anniversary,"** in **"A Northwest Window,"** in **"Gunga,"** in **"The Old Music Box"** the style more closely approaches the level of the mood and subject, though the exact, revealing phrase is not frequently found even here, the phrase which we utter over and over for sheer delight in its savor, to "make its English sweet upon our tongue."

Most of the poems in Rachel Field's earlier volumes are in the first person singular style, the "I" being the child. It is a little girl speaking most of the time; but though feminine, the poetry is not sissified; the poet makes no attempt to curry favor by talking down. Based on children's experiences and couched in language not too mature, the poetry often sounds overtones, often lifts and leads far, far away—it "goes somewhere and means something." (pp. 53, 57)

Walter Barnes, "Contemporary Poetry for Children," in The Elementary English Review, *Vol. XIII, No. 2, February, 1936, pp. 49-53, 57.*

ANNE THAXTER EATON

In *Calico Bush* Rachel Field has written a lovely story of early New England, with a freshness and beauty that is due both to the fine and stalwart characters so sympathetically described and to the pictures of the pine woods and rocky cliffs of Maine that the author knows so well. Miss Field's *Hepatica Hawks* is a fine study of a girl in the 1890's. Hepatica at fifteen was six feet four and one-half inches tall, and formed part of a traveling circus called "Joshua Pollock's Famous Freaks and Fandangos" until the discovery that she had a beautiful voice opened a way to a new life and opportunity. In this book Rachel Field has accomplished a difficult undertaking with ease and grace. Using material out of the beaten track, material that could easily lend itself to melodrama, she has handled it with delicacy and sincerity and so much sympathy and human understanding that the resulting story has both strength and sweetness.

Another book with an early American background by Rachel Field is one for younger readers, called *Hitty: Her First Hundred Years.* Hitty, who in Miss Field's book writes her own memoirs, was a doll carved from mountain ashwood by a peddler snow-bound in the Preble house in Maine. There her adventures and journeyings began, to continue for a century during which sturdy little Hitty passed from hand to hand. (pp. 172-73)

Not only is Hitty's story a good one, but the hundred years of the American scene which Miss Field describes in vivid and effortless fashion give to ten-year-olds a keen sense of what changes a century has brought. The characters in the story are alive and Hitty's sound commonsense and salty humor make her a welcome addition to book characters. (p. 173)

Anne Thaxter Eaton, "Stories Old and New," in her Reading with Children, *The Viking Press, 1940, pp. 156-92.*

JOSIAH TITZELL

[My essay "Rachel Field: Portrait of a Troubadour"] was written fifteen years ago and each paragraph shows its date. We don't think that way any longer; crystal clear were words Katherine Mansfield kept in the head, and after a recent pomposity A. A. Milne and Dhan Gopal Mukerji seemed refreshing. They had to prove themselves again, as Rachel did—to prove what could only be written in that way at that time and which had to be said differently after a while.

It has been proved that audiences do not grow with their author. They remain with the first success, remembering work which has been their discovery, which the author would like to forget, or, rather, to trade with newer effort. The hand-colored rhyme sheets and books of Lovat Fraser and Ralph Hodgson were being swapped for American primitives and the French Impressionists. Rachel's pixies were growing towards Vienna choir boys singing pizzicato polkas, her elves and fays were on their way to being Disney dwarfs and indigenous realities. And bound-out girls were looming to the Oakie Ora Larrabie of her short story, "Beginning of Wisdom," published in *The American Magazine* in March, 1942.

Fortunately for Rachel she continued writing children's books and she did not lose the audience she had. Yet she found a new one in her novels, some of those who grew from *The Magic Pawnshop* and *Hitty, Hepatica Hawks* and *The Calico Bush* to *Time Out of Mind, All This, and Heaven Too,* and *And Now Tomorrow.* (pp. 216-17)

In 1929 something new and exciting hit editors' desks, librarians' tables and the imagination of children everywhere—and many who weren't children. It was *Hitty, Her First Hundred Years,* the autobiography of an early American doll carved from mountain-ash wood, written by Rachel, magnificently illustrated by Dorothy Lathrop and gloriously presented by Louise Seaman. It was [a] triumph of a triumvirate, each contributing her inspired best. Anne Carroll Moore's *Three Owls* page in the New York *Herald Tribune*'s literary supplement, *Books,* was the yea or nay of all children's literature then, and *Hitty* burst upon the world through being granted by The Three Owls their full page on November 3rd, 1929. (p. 218)

Hitty was collaboration of the most brilliant sort. Illustrator and author were creating together, the one contributing as much as the other. They worked by long distance, correspondence, mental telepathy and occasional conventions with their publisher. When Louise Seaman molded the result into a whole and "presented" Hitty she was the débutante of the year. She was ready to prove a paraphrase of Miss Moore's welcome to her: "Still what is our lifetime to that of a doll's," particularly a sturdy, adventurous doll carved out of wood? (pp. 219-20)

1933 had three publications, *Just Across the Street,* with her own illustrations, starting as bravely Fraser as ever and ending more freely her own, and *Fortune's Caravan,* by Mme. Lily Javal, which she had adapted from a translation by Marian Saunders and which Maggie Salcedo had illustrated. The third was an important one to Rachel, as poetry always was. It was the reissue by Macmillan of a book published in 1930 by Brewer, Warren and Putnam, *Points East.* "Narratives of New England," the sub-title read. Designed by Priscilla Crane in the early 19th Century style, it explained that "the illustrations in this book are taken from early American and English chapbooks. Several are by Thomas Bewick, the famous English engraver, and others of his school. The wood-engravings appear again and again in 19th Century broadsides and pamphlets, an indication that the blocks were handed down from printer to printer and borrowed liberally." It was a handsome book and it had handsome things in it. No one, I think, can deprecate Rachel as a poet if he can step forward enough to accept poetry in the vernacular—which she assiduously aimed at—rather than in strained, lordly pentameters. In verse she was most eager and least sure of herself. She knew she was uneven in it—knew that she could write some things without working them out and thinking them through simply because she wanted to, and couldn't wait to bother with technique and philosophy. They showed their faults but they showed their spontaneity and feeling. She could say in a letter to a friend: "Do you think it gets over? I wrote most of it in my head as I drove back last week and stopped the car and dashed it down by the side of the road on an old envelope back. I could change the verses round, but I'd rather not." The enclosed verse was the title of one of her books, *Fear Is the Thorn,* published in 1936. The lines remain as they were first enclosed in the letter. But many verses would be reconsidered on criticism, weighed and shifted, never in any predictable way, in a way, by then, grown more poetically decisive. In 1934 she had already published *Branches Green,* with decorations by Dorothy Lathrop, there, too, letting her lines move from speech, not from rhetoric, from feeling rather than from rules. Her honesty in her verse is as touching as her own fear that she perhaps hadn't done it quite right. (pp. 220-22)

The popularity of her last novel [*And Now Tomorrow*] is al-

ready evident. With her other novels it will make her a well-known name to hundreds of thousands. But it is safe to predict that her books for children will make her a better-loved name, more faithfully remembered, in years none of us will ever know. In *Hitty,* the many miniature books, in all the others, to borrow a phrase from the above, early article: "She was—she is—Rachel Field." (p. 224)

Josiah Titzell, "Rachel Field: 1894-1942," in The Horn Book Magazine, *Vol. XVIII, No. 4, July-August, 1942, pp. 216-25.*

LOUISE SEAMAN BECHTEL

I wonder if I know why [Rachel Field] was a very good writer for children. In the years when I knew her, she did not see much of children, she had few theories about them, she never tried things out on them. But her kind of acute attention to the visual details of the outer world was like that of an alert child. This and her special loves in books, . . . and her love of the drama, all made her a good storyteller, and tended to a directness and simplicity of style that was inevitably appealing to children. If she had had any theory about it, it would have been spoiled. She had a very vivid and accurate and long memory. It was not accidental that she did not write of her own childhood, for she remembered much of it very exactly. But she used it all as approaches to stories. And they are all good stories. *Hitty* is perhaps the best, as a unique piece of Americana; to me a far better novel than hers for adults. But do re-read soon *Hepatica Hawks* and *Calico Bush,* for they are written with more emotion than *Hitty,* and each touches on feelings not frequently dealt with in books for girls. Are the children today missing that darling story of **"The Elfin Pup"** in *Eliza and the Elves*? and will *Little Dog Toby,* with its sights and smells of old London, be forgotten? No, the verses will be read and said and sung, and the stories pored over, and sometimes acted out, and essays about "My Favorite Author" will be written about her for many years to come.

Caring enough for the toadstool, the wild strawberry, the old toy; caring enough for all one's host of friends; this capacity to care so much, this kind of generous giving of oneself to the world—this is the source of all the memories that make writing, and brings the rich return that was Rachel's happiness. (pp. 234-36)

Louise Seaman Bechtel, "Rachel's Gifts," in The Horn Book Magazine, *Vol. XVIII, No. 4, July-August, 1942, pp. 230-36.*

MAY HILL ARBUTHNOT

Of Rachel Field's three books of poems for children—*The Pointed People, A Little Book of Days,* and *Taxis and Toadstools*—it is the third that children like best. Here are poems as direct and forthright as their author. They think and speak in terms of children, never talking down, never pretentious, but investing the everyday sights of city and country with the child's own sense of wonder and delight. (p. 121)

How could Rachel Field know so unerringly the child's sense of the miracle of islands? Over and over, she catches the curious wonderment of children. She shows a child turning back to look at the china dog with the "sad unblinking eye" and wishing for magic words to bring him to life; or a child wondering what the ring of the doorbell may bring forth; or feeling "strange and shivery" when a parrot looks at him with his "bead-bright eyes"; or wondering if skyscrapers ever want to lie down and never get up! These are authentic child-thoughts, and the children respond to their integrity with spontaneous pleasure.

Out-of-doors, the children of her poems voice that curious kinship with birds, beasts, and growing things that is part of the magic of childhood. Some people, like Rachel Field herself, keep this all their lives. In **"Barefoot Days"** the child is "glad in every toe," and the first verse is alive with the feeling of cool grass and curly fern under small, naked feet. Her children lie down in meadow grass and expect to hear the bluebells ring. They go to the woods for wild strawberries and forget that there is anything else in the world to do but "fill my hands and eat." They think that perhaps if they sit still long enough—the whole summer through—they may take root in the ground with the bay and the juniper trees. They understand the wild creatures, and when they see **"The Dancing Bear,"** they know at once something is wrong, for his eyes look bewildered "like a child's lost in the woods at night."

Rachel Field includes only eight fairy poems in her *Taxis and Toadstools,* but they make a colorful and convincing group. For the most part, Americans do not deal with fairies successfully. They are no part of the native tradition, and Americans approach them self-consciously. Rachel Field is an exception. Her few fairy poems are simple, sincere, and in good folklore tradition. (p. 122)

When you try to make a collection of children's poems about the city, you soon discover how few and inadequate they are. Rachel Field's unique contribution to children's verse is perhaps the three groups of city poems in *Taxis and Toadstools,* called **"People," "Taxis and Thoroughfares,"** and **"Stores and Storekeepers."** Of course the city child likes automobiles, just as a country child likes horses and cattle. (pp. 122-23)

The child who speaks in the first person throughout these poems likes people and watches them with friendly keenness even as Rachel Field must have done. Interest in people is characteristic of children, and it is recorded in these poems with sensitive perception. When the child sees **"Sandwich Men,"** there is a recognition of something wrong. The men are "dreary round the eye" with something about them that makes her "want to cry."

And this is not an unchildlike observation. Children study lame people or anyone who deviates from the normal with a passionate intentness that seems bent upon finding out why, at all costs. So this child perceives **"The Blind Man"** on the corner smiling to himself. She notices the keen blue eyes of sea captains, "trimmed round with lines," and how **"Old Man Cutter"** and his house seem to look alike. Florists are different from other storekeepers, for they have "a sort of fragrance of the mind."

Rachel Field's poetry never attains the power and sureness of her best prose, but the complete absence of artificiality or juvenile cuteness in these poems and her sincere reproduction of a child's point of view commend them to both children and adults. (pp. 123-24)

> *May Hill Arbuthnot, "Poetry of the Child's World,"*
> *in her* Children and Books, *Scott, Foresman and*
> *Company, 1947, pp. 100-30.*

MARGARET LANE

[Perhaps I have chosen to write about Rachel Field because] I feel a kinship with her in her love of Maine and islands, in

her appreciation of people, history, fantasy, in her zest for adventure. (p. 343)

The theater was always to mean much to Rachel. *Peter Pan* was the first play she saw. . . .

Her love of plays never languished. She had a sense for drama which even crept into her poetry, witness the dialogue with the elf in **"Elfin Berries"** or the play acting of the **"Quiet Child"** or **"My Inside Self."** These two poems picture a child, sturdy, prosaic in everyday life, but full of lightness, joy and mischief in imagination. (p. 346)

In [Rachel Field's] childhood days in Stockbridge we find the beginnings of another interest, an interest that was to influence her all her life,—her love of islands. . . . This early love of islands is reflected in the poem entitled **"The Grass Island,"** in *Taxis and Toadstools.* And again the same idea appears in her little book *The Yellow Shop* in which the children, Will and Rebecca, set up a lemonade and sandwich stand on a grass island where three roads meet.

Once a reporter asked Rachel Field if she believed in fairies. Her answer sheds light on how the practical and the imaginative were entwined in all she did as a child. She answered,

> I believed not so much in them as about them. I was willing to accept them as real characters in some of the stories I loved. When the story was finished the characters vanished just as characters that now come to life out of the pages of a good novel are gone as soon as some other interest takes the place of the novel. As a child I could pop out of Elfland into the kitchen as quick as a wink. A moment after a fairy tale had held all my attention I could be just as deeply entranced in the cook and what she was getting for dinner, and whether or not she was going to let me stir up something to bake in her nice hot oven. I always liked mussing around in the kitchen.

This same mixture of the practical with the imaginative is evident in her books and gives a special charm to many of her stories and poems. The Elfin Pup's lightness and springiness is contrasted to his size and clumsiness once he has tasted human food. Hitty tells her own story and yet keeps her doll-like individuality.

Years later when Rachel Field gave to the Stockbridge Historical Collection a copy of her book *The Pointed People* she marked four poems as being Stockbridge poems,—**"To See-Saw"** (her little dog), **"The Gypsies," "Blue,"** and **"The House in the Woods."** In these we catch glimpses of the child and what she will be, of her ever careful absorption in detail, her feeling for animals, her love of adventure; and we can share with her the thrill of the blueness of the bluebirds. . . . (pp. 347-48)

Her childhood in Stockbridge had to give way to school days in Springfield, but her awareness of everything around her was only to deepen in the years ahead. (p. 348)

[She] applied for admission to Radcliffe College, where she was admitted in 1914 as a special student because of her excellence in writing. . . . Three of Rachel Field's plays were produced there, **"Rise Up, Jennie Smith", "Time Will Tell",** and the outstanding one **"Three Pills in a Bottle",** which has been used constantly by amateur groups all over the country. It is a play very characteristic of her, combining whimsy with everyday life, the story of a very sick little boy, Tony, who meets the souls of three persons who pass by his window. Each soul is entirely different from its owner, and each has a pain. To them he gives the pills that were meant to cure him. It reminds one of her poem **"My Inside-Self."** (p. 349)

Later she lived in New York City on East 10th Street in the wintertime, and on a Maine island for four months in the summer, two places the antithesis of one another, but two places which she loved. She was sensitive to the beauty in city streets, to the many people as they went about their businesses, to the intimacy of little city parks, but when she came to her island—the island she had fallen in love with when at fifteen she spent a summer there studying water color with a cousin—then it was the sweep of sea and sky, the pointed firs, the wheeling gulls, or the mushrooms of many colors that caught her eye. (p. 350)

In *The Pointed People* the poems reflect her life in Stockbridge, her days in Cambridge, her love of Maine, and her feeling for the city. . . . These poems, as also the ones in her next volume, *Taxis and Toadstools,* bring to children today, as they did when she first wrote them, a glimpse into the world of fantasy, and an understanding of themselves. (pp. 350-51)

Her plays . . . show great variety, some of them skirting the realm of fantasy, others dealing strictly with everyday life. . . . Her first important play, **"Three Pills in a Bottle,"** is imaginative; **"Rise Up, Jennie Smith,"** is realistic, as is **"The Fifteenth Candle,"** a play of tenement life. These were her first copyrighted plays; the first of these was included with five other plays to make the collection *Six Plays.* All her plays are appropriate for children and young people to act, because the action and staging are simple and straightforward, full of vitality and imagination, giving the actor (or reader) an opportunity to experience varying aspects of life always with an insight into character. The plays are never melodramatic, but on the other hand, they are not dull. These plays and the ones that follow in *The Cross-Stitch Heart* and *Patchwork Plays* include themes that are characteristic of Rachel Field's interests,—those bordering on fantasy, such as **"The Sentimental Scarecrow,"** and **"The Cross-Stitch Heart,"** those based on her New England heritage, **"Polly Patchwork"** (an old-time spelling match), **"Greasy Luck"** (whaling days in Nantucket), and **"Little Square Toes"** (a child of Old Deerfield); plays giving a glimpse of English life a hundred years ago, **"Chimney Sweeps' Holiday"** and **"The Nine Days' Queen"** (Lady Jane Grey on the night before her execution); and those plays depicting various phases of modern life, **"At the Junction,"** **"Bargains in Cathay,"** and **"Wisdom Teeth."** Most of the plays have also appeared in acting editions and so have been easily available to amateur groups. **"Three Pills in a Bottle"** was so popular with amateur groups that it was acted week in, week out for a long time. (pp. 351-52)

Besides writing verse and plays she tried a novel. "It went the rounds," she wrote, "and was turned down as it should have been. But some of the editors wrote me letters about it and they all said that the first part, dealing with the heroine's childhood, was the best." This encouraged her to turn to children's stories, so that for the next ten years or so she devoted herself to this kind of writing. . . . (p. 352)

Later she explained her philosophy of writing for children:

> In writing books for children it is not necessary to have contacts with children. Of course it helps to know children. But if you have it in you to write children's books, you can write them anywhere,— alone on a desert island, if you have enough paper and pencils. . . . It seems to me far more important to be able to remember exactly how a thing impressed you when you were a child than to guess how it may impress another child. Children's natures do not change perceptibly from one generation to another. It is their dress, their speech and their manners that change, not their natures.

She felt that information for children should not be sugarcoated with story, that books of information and books of imagination are both wanted by the child but that they should be separate. An author should not write down for children. If an author writes a book "to please himself it's likely to have vitality and spirit and a lack of condescension and self-consciousness." She felt that she should be just as careful in her phrasing when writing for children as she was in books for adults, for "children are just as observant . . . and appreciate the right word and the apt description just as surely as grown people."

Her first stories for children were small books, some of them calling to mind the early chapbooks. *The Alphabet for Boys and Girls* and *A Little Book of Days* were two of these . . ., both illustrated with her own drawings, done with a reed pen and water colors, small figures of boys and girls very gay and childlike. The verses are fresh and appealing. (pp. 352-53)

[*Eliza and the Elves* and] *The Magic Pawnshop* are books which carry the young reader into the realm of fantasy, setting free the imagination, and yet always portraying characters who are true to life, and who stir one's sympathy and understanding. *The Magic Pawnshop* is somewhat longer than *Eliza and the Elves,* containing a sustained plot, and more characters, each one of whom is well drawn. (p. 353)

Little Dog Toby, written and illustrated by Miss Field, grew out of her trip to England in 1920 and her fascination with the Punch and Judy shows.

Two other little books were published at this time . . . , *Polly Patchwork,* and *Pocket Handkerchief Park.* In these, as in *Little Dog Toby,* she leaves fantasy for realism. *Polly Patchwork* is about an old-fashioned spelling match won by a little girl who had to wear a dress made from a patchwork quilt; *Pocket Handkerchief Park* pictures a tiny city park about to be auctioned off, a little park that means much in the lives of the children and grown-ups who play and work around it. In all of these books we enter intimately into the lives and feelings of the characters. Each one is an individual and through each one our understanding of people is broadened. We begin to know that people are the same everywhere.

And then in 1929 came *Hitty.* (p. 354)

Why was this book accounted a "most distinguished contribution to children's literature"? Perhaps because Miss Field was true to her conviction that no book for children should be written just for them. She commented on *Hitty* in a letter to her friend Mrs. Emerson, "I think it (*Hitty*) will amuse you more than the younger generation. I really wrote it for our age." But a child this spring commented: "There is never a dull moment. It's exciting, and so many things happen." There is swift sure movement from beginning to end, a plot well thought out and tied together. Hitty herself is well drawn, and tells her story with integrity. Each of the charac-

From Taxis and Toadstools: Verses and Decorations, *written and illustrated by Rachel Field.*

ters in the book lives in its own right and is distinct and true. Here is presented to the child a broad sweep of human nature, children with their varied interests and emotions from six-year-old Phoebe in her strict New England home to Little Thankful in Philadelphia ashamed of her tiny faded doll; and adults, including Phoebe's hardworking and fair-minded father, captain of the whaling ship, to delicate old ladies, and an Indian snake charmer. Here the child absorbs in detail life in many places and in many times. Rachel Field was a master of detail. . . . The child reader gains a sense of her New England heritage, but this is set against life in other parts of this country and elsewhere. It is not a narrow provincial view, but a world-wide view, with appreciation of many ways of living. It is a broad sensitive picture of life, but one full of many small and interesting details. *Hitty* is a book of integrity.

Because it is written ostensibly for ten- to twelve-year-olds, and yet is about a doll, the book must frequently be introduced to children. But once a child has started reading it, almost always she will fall under its spell, and finish it happily. Boys enjoy parts of it, too, especially Hitty's whaling adventures and her shipwreck on the cannibals' island, but in general it is a girl's book. (pp. 355-56)

But Miss Field did not rest on her oars just because she had won the Newbery Award. Again her creative urge pushed her forward and she wrote *Calico Bush.*

In *Calico Bush,* as in *Hitty,* Rachel Field has created characters who stand firmly on their own feet, people whom you might meet around the next corner. There is Maggie, the spirited French Bound-out Girl brought up in a French convent where she was accustomed to the niceties of living, but who is able to adapt herself to the hardships of life in early Maine and who is loyal to her new friends. There is slow-moving but determined Joel, and Dolly, his wife, worried and overworked. Across on Sunday Island there is lively Aunt Hepsa Jordan, well past seventy but smart as a whip. (p. 357)

Any child reading *Calico Bush* will come away with a new appreciation of the life in early days and a feel for the Maine coast with its islands and pointed firs and ever changing sea.

A girl will have identified herself with Maggie, or a boy perhaps with Caleb, and each will have grown a bit.

One more novel for young people Rachel Field wrote before she turned to adult fiction. This was *Hepatica Hawks*. . . . As a child she herself had been plump and so she wanted to write a story about an outsize girl who made good in her own right. The result is this sympathetic and understanding story of fifteen-year-old Hepatica Hawks, a freak, six feet four and a half inches tall, who is turning from childhood to adolescence with all the usual problems of that age intensified by her size. The various members of the freak show are all individually characterized, but it is Hepatica and the midget, Titania Tripp, thirty-two inches high, who stand out,—not because of their sizes but because they are so understandingly portrayed. In this story the reader gains insight into a way of life that is for the most part unknown to him, but one which turns out to be not as different as one might think. Human nature is the same everywhere.

No discussion of Rachel Field's books for children would be complete without mentioning that she illustrated some of her early books herself. Following in the footsteps of Lovat Fraser she frequently used a reed pen, sometimes with color, sometimes without. At other times she cut spirited silhouettes from black paper. . . . She could draw children better than adults. In fact there is a certain childishness about her adult figures, but always her tiny drawings are filled with life,—a child standing tiptoe against the sky, a dog capering with joy in the grass. (pp. 357-58)

Rachel Field has given us much. In her books for children, and for adults too, we gain perspective, a sense of history, and appreciation of how broad social changes affect individual lives, an understanding of our New England heritage against a world-wide background. We meet people, drawn so sympathetically and surely that we can identify ourselves with them, and understand ourselves the better. Her books for children frequently bring that breaking away from the staid and solid, that venture into the world of the imagination that today's matter-of-fact children need so much. And withal she does not write dully and stolidly. There is lilt, vitality, humor, vibrant action and integrity on every page. Her books will live, especially the best of her children's books. The world is richer for her sojourn here. We salute Rachel Field! (p. 366)

> Margaret Lane, "Rachel Field and Her Contribu-
> tion to Children's Literature," in The Hewins Lec-
> tures: 1947-1962, edited by Siri Andrews, The Horn
> Book, Incorporated, 1963, pp. 343-75.

RUTH HILL VIGUERS

Rachel Field was already known for her childlike verses and attractive little picture-story books when she and the artist Dorothy Lathrop made the discovery of an old doll in a Greenwich Village antique shop. "Hitty" immediately became a personality to them and her "memoirs" became *Hitty, Her First Hundred Years.* Author and artist worked closely together to make a perfect whole. . . . This is no doll fantasy, though the story is carefully kept within the framework of Hitty's experiences. It is an exciting period adventure story. People of all kinds pass through the pages and even the most briefly known becomes a complete character. The changes that a century brought to the American scene are arrestingly portrayed, and the adventures themselves reach heights of excitement. There are strong emotional scenes, such as willful Sally's repentance, and in few sea stories are fire and shipwreck more graphically described, yet Miss Field attained the ultimate artistry in the restraint that keeps this Hitty's story. (pp. 512-13)

From the time she was fifteen Rachel Field had spent each summer in Maine, enjoying particularly a small wooded island off the coast. *Calico Bush* derives from Miss Field's love and knowledge of Maine: the rocky cliffs, the pine woods, the pasture thick with the "green and springing" bayberry bushes, the cove at high tide where the spruces "seemed to be wading in their own dark reflections." Early in Rachel Field's writing career editors discussing a novel that had been turned down, remarked about her success in dealing with childhood. It was this encouragement that had started her trying to write for children, but she never could follow the suggestion to make her words as young as her ideas. She kept her artistic integrity and *Calico Bush,* which tells the story of a year in the life of a twelve-year-old French "bound-out" girl, has a nearly flawless structure that was not surpassed even in her widely successful adult novels.

In *Hepatica Hawks,* . . . Rachel Field further tested her skill. Hepatica was fifteen years old and six feet four and a quarter inches tall. Her father was a giant and her only friends were the other members of Joshua Pollock's "Famous Freaks and Fandangos," a traveling circus of the 1890's. Her story could easily have been melodramatic or at least sentimental but it is understated, moving, and beautiful. Rachel Field could see the people inside the odd-sized characters and handle an uncommon and difficult theme with delicacy and perception.

In the decades since Miss Field was writing for young people, new children's books by the hundreds have been published each year, yet her three novels stand out as colorful Americana and as living literature. (p. 513)

> Ruth Hill Viguers, "Adventure in the New World,"
> in A Critical History of Children's Literature by
> Cornelia Meigs and others, edited by Cornelia
> Meigs, revised edition, Macmillan Publishing Com-
> pany, 1969, pp. 511-30.

THE POINTED PEOPLE: VERSES AND SILHOUETTES (1924)

There is a subtle distinction between poetry about and poetry for children. Many people think they are writing one kind of child-verse when they are writing another, and it requires more than cleverness to produce a story or a poem that satisfies the child as well as grown-ups. Alice is the preeminent and immortal example, of course, of satisfactoriness all round, and other writers have been successful in combining the right qualities without apparent effort. Rachel Lyman Field, in a nice little volume of verses and silhouettes called *The Pointed People* displays this gift now and then, but she is not always certain of her audience. She too knows her Stevenson—**"Rainy Nights"** is very nearly a paraphrase of one of his poems—but she has her own ideas and her own style, and both are full of fun. **"Burning Leaves,"** for instance, with its silhouette of a bored young person in pigtails engaged in household duties, is a child-parody of the sort of lament—derived from the Irish—that fills all the coterie journals of the moment. . . .

"Gypsies" and **"If I were a Little Tree like You"** and **"The Old Postman"** are quite charming.

> Isn't it strange some people make
> You feel so tired inside

is very true, but a trifle sophisticated for infancy. **"Dust is such a Pleasant Thing"** and **"Venetian Beads"** are more within the ordinary child's range, and very nice too.

> A review of "The Pointed People," in The Times Lit-
> erary Supplement, No. 1192, November 20, 1924, p.
> 765.

SIX PLAYS: CINDERELLA MARRIED, THREE PILLS IN A BOTTLE, COLUMBINE IN BUSINESS, THE PATCHWORK QUILT, WISDOM TEETH, THEORIES AND THUMBS (1924)

That Miss Field's gift for writing fantasy is a real one is shown clearly in *Three Pills in a Bottle,* and even more clearly in *The Patchwork Quilt,* where a finely tender scene is written about a pathetic, muddle-brained grandmother, who revives memories of her youth and her children from patches in her quilt. In the other plays of the present volume Miss Field's fantasy is undisciplined in the needs of the theatre. It seems better suited to the story than the dramatic form. Her characterization in *Cinderella Married, Columbine in Business,* and all but a few scenes of *Theories and Thumbs* runs broadly to type, except in the wistful people who really interest her. *Wisdom Teeth* is a bad little comedy that has no place in a volume of thin but engaging fantasy.

> A review of "Six Plays," in Theatre Arts Monthly,
> Vol. IX, No. 2, February, 1925, p. 140.

ELIZA AND THE ELVES (1926)

Exploring with Miss Field is not perhaps . . . broadly amusing, for the fun of elves is a secret fun and shivers into tinkling particles at the touch of human fingers. But when the hearty chuckles of the outer world have died away and we become attuned to the eerie quiet of Elfland, we could wish for no more delightful interpreter than Eliza who, bewitched in her cradle by the little people, in turn bewitches us. The gates of

Elfland have swung ajar to her, and through them we hear silver songs, the "tinkle-tankle" of the sheep bells, and the baying of the Elfin Hound.

Constance Naar, "From Out Their World," in The New Republic, *Vol. 48, November 10, 1926, p. 352.*

What makes children like or dislike a book is a question modern publishers are going to great lengths to find out. In **Eliza and the Elves** there is at least one strong reason why they do. It is the personality of the author.

Who could write a story like **"What Happened to Eliza"** who did not herself have a knowing eye and a laugh up her sleeve for all the comical ways of elves, children and grown-ups? Eliza MacPann in her cradle, howling because the elves were tweaking her hair, is a young person such as the author herself might have been. Children will believe in the infant at once. . . .

The other two stories in the book, **"The Fairy Gentleman and His Dumpling Wife"** and **"The Elfin Pup,"** have this same quality of eerie reality. The gentleman who went courting in a "bottle green coat with swallow tails and upstanding collar," with "yellow bits of money that jingled pleasantly" all tied up in a red handkerchief, just to show that he had the wherewithal to provide for a wife, is a personage out of the author's own imaginative experience.

In **"The Elfin Pup"** children will recognize a real dog, bewitched to be sure, but none the less real, for he sniffs, cocks up his ears, succumbs to the delicious smell of good food cooking, and has all the most doggy traits imaginable. Yet, the elves have him in their toils, and his adventures in growing make lively reading.

Leonore St. John Power, "Elves and Humans," in New York Herald Tribune Books, *November 28, 1926, p. 8.*

TAXIS AND TOADSTOOLS: VERSES AND DECORATIONS (1926)

Certainly Rachel Field should write for children because of her ability to project herself into a child's world with joyous wholeheartedness. It is the world of the morning of which she writes,—the exuberant, highly colored world of an early autumn morning. The sun is up, the dew's on the grass, the apples are ripe, and life's a grand adventure fit for a king! The shadows and mystery of an elfin fairyland do not fall around us. Rachel Field's elves are happy, tangible companions to sit with us at table or accompany us to school during our first half dozen years. *Taxis and Toadstools* is a series of concrete pictures (in verse) of the people and things that form the vivid, glowing world of everyday to the child, be he from city or country. A number are, like **"The Flower Cart Man"** typical of New York. But although the author has her feet on the good green earth she is possessed of a bubbling fancy which runs like a fresh spring through such pieces as **"If Once You Have Slept On an Island,"** and **"The Green Fiddler,"** bless its heart. . . .

A review of "Taxis and Toadstools," in The Saturday Review of Literature, *Vol. III, No. 19, December 4, 1926, p. 403.*

Rachel Field is a romantic and much of her poetry for children was written under the consulship of Barrie. These verses

from the "Horn Book," "St. Nicholas Magazine," and other publications are now reprinted in England for the first time, and though anything from Miss Field's pen is welcome they are just too late for the best of the English fair. The child of her imagination has seldom been alone for long enough to have seen with sufficiently clear eyes the carousel, the flickering bioscope, and the harmonies of social life in America forty years ago. New York is visited, but seen from a safe window. Do witches spill neon lighting across Broadway? Miss Field does not tell us there is no magic in the city but she is at heart of the country. The pity is that there is so little of the American in these verses and so much of a comfortable fairyland. The best of the writing in this book owes most to solitude. **"The Lamb"** and **"The Old Schoolhouse"** might be found at some future date pressed like gulls' feathers between the pages of another "Golden Staircase."

The decorations belong to the same period of time and this is a pity, not because they are uneven, the best recalling those by Claude Lovat Frazer rejected so indignantly by A. E. Housman. But an illustrator working today might have placed the verses more evocatively during Rachel Field's own childhood and given us a dust-jacket—one thinks of Adrienne Adams instinctively—more immediately appealing to children of today.

A review of "Taxis and Toadstools," in The Junior Bookshelf, *Vol. 26, No. 6, December, 1962, p. 311.*

In some of the poems of *Taxis and Toadstools,* Rachel Field speaks as an adult to children; in a few, she speaks through the persona of a small boy; but in the majority, she seems to be speaking through the persona of a young girl. An examination of the poems reveals some interesting facets of Miss Field's young female persona.

Nearly all the poems have either rural or urban settings (hence the title), and the young girl shows herself to be a city-bred child. For example, in **"Taking Root,"** she wonders if she sat the summer through and never moved or stirred, "Could I take root on this pasture slope / With the bay and juniper?" Though it is a question that either a city or country child might ask, it is one that a country child probably would not have to ask. In **"Wood-Strawberries,"** the child picks strawberries "till my hands were red," and "It seemed there was nothing to do at all / But fill my hands and eat." As every country-reared child knows, strawberries are for sharing with the family in strawberry ice-cream or in strawberry shortcake and for preserving in jelly and jam for the winter to come. (p. 39)

Taxis and Toadstools is divided into ten sections, and in the seventh, **"Fringes of Fairyland,"** the persona, like many children, shows a bright imagination. In **"The Visitor,"** she prepares "bread and a sup of tea" for "an elfin gentleman," who is "Feather-footed and swift as a mouse. . . ." In **"The Elf Tree,"** a poem reflecting some of the folklore about fairies, the persona knocks her "knuckles three times three," just in case it should be the one "tree in all that wood . . . where the elves and fairies hide. . . ." In one of the longest poems, **"The Green Fiddler,"** the child imagines meeting a fairy and giving him "Four bright gold hairs" for his fiddle. The resulting music is so entrancing that "Stock still I stood in the shadowed wood, / Lest I should miss one note."

Nearly all children are disarmingly egocentric, and Rachel Field's is no exception. In **"The Peabody Bird,"** the young girl asks the bird why it keeps calling for someone named

"Peabody" when no one answers. Finally, she asks, "Couldn't you look for someone else? / And wouldn't I do instead?" The best example, however, of the child's egocentric nature is in **"I'd Like to Be a Lighthouse,"** where she wants to be one so that she can

    stay awake all night
   To keep my eye on everything
  That sails my patch of sea;
  I'd like to be a lighthouse
   With the ships all watching me.

One of the most appealing qualities of the persona is her sympathy. **"Skyscrapers"** shows her sympathizing with tall buildings, wondering if they "ever grow tired / Of holding themselves up high?" or if they "ever shiver on frosty nights" or if "they feel lonely . . . Because they have grown so tall?" She feels sorry for the little ceramic dog in **"The China Dog"** because he can never bark, tease for cake, or wag his tail; and if it were left to her, he'd be a real, live dog, barking, nipping her fingers, licking her hair, and "every single night he'd be / Snuggled up warm in bed with me!"

Another remarkable trait of the child is that she is nearly always cheerful. Rain to most of us can be somewhat depressing, but not to this child, who loves to "see it fall," making "Streets of shiny wetness" and "rumbling [a] tune that sings / Through everything I do." There's hardly anything that will depress her ebullient spirit. . . . One might well wonder why or how a child could be such a cheerful one, and the answer is in **"The Elfin Organ-Grinder."** It seems that if human children hear an elfin organ-grinder play, they "Will ever after have feet that dance / And hearts that are always gay." Surely, Miss Field's persona heard the organ-grinder play.

Though not all the young child's character traits are reflected here, these are some that reveal her personality. Rachel Field's persona is not as self-conscious as Christopher Robin in A. A. Milne's poems; she is not as contentious as the little girl sometimes is in some of Eleanor Farjeon's poetry; and she does not speak with the genuine cadence and language of childhood as does the little girl in Elizabeth Madox Roberts' *Under the Tree.* She is a city-bred child with a keen imagination, sometimes egocentric and sometimes sympathetic, nearly always pleasant and happy, joyfully going towards life, appealingly innocent. (p. 40)

> *Malcolm Usrey, "The Child Persona in 'Taxis and Toadstools'," in* Children's Literature Association Quarterly, *Vol. 7, No. 2, Summer, 1982, pp. 39-40.*

THE MAGIC PAWNSHOP: A NEW YEAR'S EVE FANTASY (1927)

An enticing book this, with its brilliant cover and occasional gay decorations in color by Elizabeth McKinstry, though its humor and fancy are in part of a kind more comprehensible to grown readers than to their juniors, who cannot be expected to follow its fanciful allusiveness. Children will doubtless enjoy the tale because its contains magic, romance, and a nice little girl; but it is related with one eye cocked for the smile of the adult listener.

In the matter of pretty Rose Martha's pawned conscience, too, while the assurance is general that consciences should never be pawned at any time, as they shrink and shrivel when separated from their owners, still, there is a certain tawdriness in the visit to a costume ball with the wrong man, which scarcely seems chosen in quite the best of taste for children, as the occasion for Rose Martha to pawn hers—not even though "Mr. Kit" with the dying conscience in a bird-cage in one hand and the sword of the reckless Kit Marlowe in the other, pursues her, defeats (and spanks) his supplanter, and restores it.

> *A review of "The Magic Pawnshop," in* The Outlook, *Vol. 147, No. 4, September 28, 1927, p. 122.*

You have read many a fantastic child's story, compounded of magic and nonsense, and you have read not so many naturalistic stories of real little girls in familiar situations,—not nearly so many, as a matter of fact, as the average little girl would like to read, for the magical tale seems to be far more frequent.

If you possess yourself of this little book of Rachel Field's, you will enjoy a very charming combination of both types, and that, too, in the continuous-story form which seems for some reason to be used less often for children than the short tale with which they are constantly supplied.

Not that even the most up-and-coming little girl could really involve herself in the delightful impossibilities that happen to Prinda during her visit to the magic pawnshop to secure a miracle for her sick uncle's use; but that they are all recounted with a running maintenance of realism in background, in character drawing, and in the logical following-out of a real plot—which even has two bits of love stories bound up in it. So a little girl reading will have the pleasures of recognition of many items of her own surroundings, combined with the surprises of a magic broomstick and its proprietress-rider, and all the goings-on in the magic shop over which she presides.

Especially delectable is the idea of the Conscience which one of the characters has pawned, and which appears as a luminous, colored Something in a wicker bird-cage, fading gradually to nothingness unless reinstated in its owner's bosom; and of the superfluous elderly aunt pawned by her family only to find a comfortable realm of usefulness in the pawnshop itself, so that she cheerfully repudiates their efforts to reclaim her when they find they have made a mistake and need her very dreadfully after all.

Full of suggestion are Miss Field's pawnshop shelves, and many real bits of understanding of human nature flash from her lines, as her ingenious little plot develops. A grown-up will not lack enjoyment in reading this story with a child. . . .

We hope Miss Field will give us more books in the same key.

> *"Magic and Realism," in* The Saturday Review of Literature, *Vol. IV, No. 12, October 15, 1927, p. 214.*

THE CROSS-STITCH HEART AND OTHER PLAYS (1927)

Rachel Field has solved a real problem in writing plays for amateur production—that of creating situations and writing dialogue that is neither insipid nor beyond the capabilities of inexperienced players. Miss Field excels in the light touch of comedy, fantasy, pathos; her characters have charm and originality, her sets are simple of execution. ***The Cross-Stitch***

Heart is one of the indispensable volumes for the amateur dramatic club's library. . . .

A review of "The Cross-Stitch Heart and Other Plays," in Theatre Arts Monthly, Vol. XII, No. 3, March, 1928, p. 226.

POLLY PATCHWORK; LITTLE DOG TOBY (1928)

A most lovable little book is **Polly Patchwork** with a gay cover jacket like an old patchwork quilt and quaint pictures in color of Polly in her patchwork dress and her companions of the spelling match.

The cottage in which Polly lives with her grandmother stands on the edge of Cranberry Common between Tumbledown Mountain and the sea, and at least one lover of the Maine coast feels sure that the story was born and bred on an island not far from North Haven Thoroughfare.

This, to my mind, is one of the most charming and authentic things Miss Field has done. It is for children a little older than those who claim her "Alphabet" and "Book of Days" for children just learning to spell and to sew, and also for grandmothers and all grown-ups who love old times and ways. It is just the book for a summer or early autumn birthday as well as the right size for a Christmas stocking.

Anne Carroll Moore, "A Little Girl's Book," in New York Herald Tribune Books, August 12, 1928, p. 6.

Books written expressly for small children are seldom interesting to the weary adult who is asked to read them aloud. But one finds in Rachel Field's work enough character, atmosphere, and charm to carry one through several repetitions to interested young listeners. **Polly Patchwork** has an exciting patchwork wrapper devised by Miss Field, and the illustrations by the author of the indomitable, gay little grandmother and the equally stout-hearted granddaughter, exactly bear out the spirit of the tale.

Little Dog Toby, also illustrated by the author, has many of the qualities of the most desirable English Christmas stories. The atmosphere of the English country side and early Victorian London with the rise of yellow dog Toby from the obscurity of the wrong side of the Park to the enviable position of the most celebrated Punch and Judy actor in the City, are interesting. But added to all this there is such a heartening description of a Christmas Party at Buckingham Palace, where Toby is bidden to entertain the children, that the book is sure to appeal to any young dog lover at Christmas time.

Dorothea Withington, in a review of "Polly Patchwork" and "Little Dog Toby," in The Saturday Review of Literature, Vol. V, No. 20, December 8, 1928, p. 482.

HITTY, HER FIRST HUNDRED YEARS (1929)

AUTHOR'S COMMENTARY

[*The following excerpt was taken from Field's Newbery Medal acceptance speech which she delivered in 1930.*]

Hitty, and how the book came to be written. First of all, I want to say that I feel as if I, myself, had very little to do with it. It is as if Hitty took things into her own mountain ashwood hands right from the start. Her very discovery was in the nature of what some of our ancestors might have called "a miraculous providence."

It is curious how books happen—those who write them often know least about this. Sometimes an idea comes all in a flash, for a whole book, or again one gathers material piece by piece and puts it painstakingly together like a patchwork quilt, or, as in this case, some concrete object will set a whole train of ideas in motion. Nothing was farther from my mind than writing the autobiography of an early American doll, until Dorothy P. Lathrop and I discovered Hitty in an antique shop in New York and found we had each wanted her. . . . Then one day Hitty was gone from the window and I wrote the news regretfully to Miss Lathrop. She replied by return mail, saying that we should have had sense enough to buy her together. "You could have written her story and I could have illustrated it." I knew she was right,—and in fact all sorts of ideas about Hitty's past life and adventures began to come to me, so it was a great relief to find she had only been taken out of the window to show a customer. That very night she was ours, with our only clue to her identity a yellowed slip pinned to her dress with "Hitty" written on it in faded Spenserian handwriting.

By such queer coincidences are books sometimes evolved!

Miss Lathrop's pictures are such an integral part of the story that I cannot imagine the text without them. Those of you who have seen the doll's six and one-half inches of wood will realize how impossible it would be to have shown her in proper proportion along with even a human forefinger. This meant much planning and ingenuity on the artist's part to keep the pictures varied and interesting. (pp. 86-7)

My problems in writing the story were of a different sort. They were chiefly connected with the element of time. I soon found that covering a hundred years of American life was more of a piece of work than I had expected. Incidentally, this accounts for the fact that the book is almost as long as a novel and required nearly as much care and research. But this also gave a cumulative effect and I was able to choose certain periods and things I already knew something about. I had for some years past been interested in reading old log books of whaling vessels, so it was natural for me to have Hitty go on a whaling voyage. Then after her New England, Philadelphia and New York days, I wanted to give a feeling of an entirely different life in another part of the country. This accounts for sending her down the Mississippi River and into the South.

Then there was the matter of style. I felt from the first that Hitty would have had a very prim but spicy way of talking, and so I tried to select every word and phrase carefully, for I think people don't give words half enough credit. Yet they are what really affect readers, children most of all because they are most impressionable. It seems to me we ought to remember what J. M. Synge said about dialogue: that "every phrase should be finely flavored as a nut or an apple." So many juveniles today are too evidently written down to children with the words so simplified that all the spirit is lost in commonplaces.

There is one thing Hitty and the Medal have in common and that is the past. I never get over that such things as old samplers, toys, and little tattered children's books should be here for us to see and touch long after those who made and handled them are gone. There is something singularly moving about them and I know that I can never see an old toy or one of those early chap books without this sense of the past. So perhaps, after all, it is appropriate that a little doll of a hundred years ago should be connected with John Newbery and his bookshop in old London. I cannot help feeling that she possesses qualities of character that would have pleased him and some of his distinguished friends and customers—Oliver Goldsmith, Charles and Mary Lamb, and others. (pp. 87-8)

> Rachel Field, "Acceptance Paper," in Newbery Medal Books: 1922-1955. edited by Bertha Mahoney Miller and Elinor Whitney Field, The Horn Book, Inc., 1955, pp. 86-8.

Hitty was born to high adventure and fortunately for us she has written her memoirs. The events of her life are varied in mood, sometimes wildly exciting, at other times quiet and a little sad for Hitty's life is not always a simple one. She is a doll carved from mountain-ash wood by an itinerant peddler while he is snowbound in the Preble house in Maine. She is no insipid, fluffy "Ma-ma" doll. She has an upturned nose and a serious manner and there is courage in her every peg— the sort of doll boys would allow their sisters to bring along on expeditions. This is perhaps accountable for some of Hitty's adventures and will certainly make the book one that boys will enjoy as well as girls. For Hitty is neither naive nor coy in her recital of her life. She is a New Englander, prim and gentle, yet ungiven to whimsical questionings or cautious side-steppings. Since the peddler endowed her with beauty and a delightful personality she can afford to be simple and direct in her attitude and her manner. Writing her memoirs is to her a serious business and pen in wooden hand she settles down to it.

There are slight episodes at first, such as getting lost under the pew at the meeting house and, on another occasion, being carried by crows to their nest. Her real adventures begin when Captain Preble takes his family (and Hitty) with him on a whaling expedition. Life now takes on that pace which keeps Hitty ever on the alert, for what can she not expect? The excitement of whaling from the sighting of the spout of water to the storing of the oil. The fire on board ship with the cargo of oil making it necessary to abandon the vessel. The long hours floating on the waves until she comes to rest in the South Sea rock pool. Nothing is too glamorous to happen to Hitty. She becomes the heathen idol of a tribe of savages. She is rescued by the cabin boy only to be taken to India where she is the companion of a snake charmer and a terrifying cobra. Missionaries save her on this occasion and she eventually finds her way back to America. Here she is acquired by an itinerant artist and begins her journeyings through the South. New Orleans and the Cotton Exposition are treated to the sight of Hitty in a wedding dress made of a beautiful old handkerchief. Her theft, her Moses-like abandonment in a wicker basket on the waters of the Mississippi, her rescue by the little Negro girl, all are incidents that Hitty tells about with varying amusement and remembered terror. Eventually, by a path that leads through the post-office's dead-letter department, a church bazaar and the Preble House in Maine, Hitty comes to the auction block. There are moments when she is afraid the large lady will get her but the kind old man with the white beard and the monocle is persistent to the extent of fifty-one dollars and so it is Hitty finds herself eventually in the antique shop in New York alone the long dark nights with Theobald the cat, and with nothing to do but write her memoirs.

Rachel Field in writing Hitty's story has surpassed anything

From Little Dog Toby, *written and illustrated by Rachel Field.*

she has done. Hitty is a real character, happily conceived and imaginatively and honestly developed. Miss Field's assimilation and reproduction of the 1800 American scene and mood add a rich background to the adventures of the doll. The scenes in the Preble household, those that introduce the etiquette of church and stagecoach, the descriptions of Boston and Philadelphia, are as complete and as veracious pictures of last century New England as can be found anywhere. It is this careful, yet unlabored re-creation of the period that adds to the value of the book and heightens the effect of Miss Field's keen characterization. The Preble family are as thoroughly New England in their mental processes as they are in speech and attitude. The Negroes and the Louisiana whites are as true as the Negro dialect which Miss Field has caught as only one person in twenty-five can. In this task of the writer, to project herself so thoroughly into the character and the period that she convincingly creates both, Miss Field has called on her hitherto proven powers as a dramatist. As a matter of fact, she has had occasion to employ here all her talents, combining, with her dramatic technique of self-projection and her narrative abilities, her poetic sensitivity and intense feeling. Yet with all this intricate selection and rejection, this conscious employment of varied and characteristic talents, the story as it is evolved is the doll's story, her memoirs which she and she alone could have written. Hitty is an important addition to our American cast of characters.

True, she was carved from mountain ash wood that the peddler brought from Ireland, but her heart was American.

Josiah Titzell, "Hitty's Odyssey," in New York Herald Tribune Books, *November 3, 1929, p. 8.*

Rachel Field and Dorothy Lathrop have done something more than achieve an original and altogether delightful story book for children in their joint record of Hitty's first hundred years. They have answered the oft-repeated question "Do Americans know how to play?" . . .

Hitty is not to be confused with any mere doll story, not even with *The Memoirs of a London Doll.* Reviewers and list-makers must lay aside the habit of classifying and pigeon-holing and give Hitty her own distinctive place among books embodying the American tradition.

Anne Caroll Moore, "The American Tradition," in New York Herald Tribune Books, *November 3, 1929, p. 8.*

I have always contended that the ideal children's book should approach in form as nearly as possible the adult novel. **Hitty** comes close to accomplishing this, and I personally found it far more arresting than the greater number of recent novels I have read. Hitty is a person of much character and originality, and to the reconstruction of her life history, from the Preble homestead in Maine over a hundred years ago to her honored old age in the Eighth Street antique shop, Miss Field had brought not only the invention, dramatic instinct, and happy use of the unexpected which color all her writing but also an amazing knowledge of certain phases of early American life—as in the description of the whaling voyage—and a feeling for the past which gives extraordinary vitality to her pictures. Children reading **Hitty** will have a clear and very intimate impression of a little girl's life in early New England, of sea-faring in the old days, of the Philadelphia Quaker household, of New York in the gay 'seventies, and of the quiet, shuttered existence of the two little gentlewomen in the old New Orleans house.

To read this book is like looking back not only on one's own childhood, but on a long perspective of other childhoods, each picture sharp and clear-cut, like something experienced rather than imagined. Phoebe Preble, the smug meanness of poor Little Thankful, wistful Clarissa, and gay daring Isabel, all stand before us vividly. They are living children. Each glimpse is admirable. And one of the best scenes in the book is when Sally, that strange, passionate child, who deliberately steals Hitty from the glass case in the Cotton Exposition and secretes her for many weeks, suddenly experiences religion at a negro camp-meeting and, overtaken by judgment in the shape of a thunderstorm, sacrifices her in terrified repentance to the black waters of the Mississippi.

> "Oh, God," she wailed, "don't let the lightning strike me dead and all of a heap, don't, please . . . I tell you I'll give Hitty back. I won't keep her another minute, Lord—look, here she is! You can have her, only just let me get back to Pa and the *Morning-Glory!*"
>
> She was sobbing hysterically now. I could hear her even above the storm. Now she was running pell-mell down the bank toward the river. I knew only too well what she meant to do with me.

It is rare to find writing like this between the covers of a children's book.

There is humor, tenderness, and a gentle irony in this portrait of the little doll who goes through fire and flood, suffers shipwreck, captivity, and man's ingratitude, whose very existence is at the mercy of those human friends with whose lives, in turn, her own is so closely associated, and who in the end is doomed to outlast them all. "She must be dead a good many years now, even if she lived to be an old lady," remarks Hitty, not without complacency, of little Phoebe Preble.

For like all imaginative writers who find freedom under the covering phrase, "a children's story," Rachel Field has spread her canvas far beyond its acknowledged bounds and created something real, truthful, and enduring—a philosophy of life.

Margery Williams Bianco, "Memoirs of a Lady of Quality," in The Saturday Review of Literature, *Vol. VI, No. 17, November 16, 1929, p. 392.*

Hitty's serene acceptance of adventure is partly, as she says herself, the result of being "made with a pleasant expression"—but not entirely. There may be a touch of satire in her consistent endurance through capture by savages on a desert island, days of floating in the sea, years of imprisonment down the side of an old sofa; this is an adventure story that takes a piquant view of well-used situations. At any rate, Hitty is just the right heroine for the book. She was made, she tells us, by a pedlar in Maine in the 1830's; the ashwood he used was enduring and so was her character. She serves (as many dolls had done before her) to introduce a panorama of American social history, as she becomes the property of Phoebe Preble whose father is a whaling captain, of Little Thankful, whose parents are missionaries in India, of Quaker Clarissa and rich Isabella Rensselaer and several other children. When she is finally housed in Miss Hunter's antique shop in New York she can look back over a century, notice social change, compare one owner with another and wonder what adventures may still await her—for "after all, what is a mere hundred years to well-seasoned mountain-ash wood?"

I don't know for a fact that Rachel Field had read Richard Horne's *Memoirs of a London Doll* but the course of her story is often very close to that early Victorian masterpiece. The mock-autobiography is a common enough form but there are parallels in some of the episodes. Like Maria Poppet, Hitty goes to the theatre, is partly burnt, sits for her portrait (but in daguerreotype, not in paint) and finds the children of humble homes kinder than those who are reared in luxury. Like Maria, too, Hitty has a certain tartness in the way she comments on the people she meets. And, like Maria, speech is almost her sole human attribute. She can't move by herself except occasionally, and then only by tumbling. The essentially passive nature of her actions is made clear in the illustrations, which unerringly interpret the doll's place in life and provide an amusing contrast to the "responsibility" she claims for herself through perilous times.

This is a splendid book—amusing in its mock-serious tone, endlessly varied in scenes and characters and with all the author's love of America's past to inspire it. Written in 1930, the story has matured with age and comes up as fresh and crisp now as the "watered-silk dress with draped skirt, fitted waist, and innumerable bows" which Miss Pinch the dressmaker contrived for Hitty's apotheosis as a "fashion doll". Her story would make a fine present for a girl of seven or eight, to read over a longish period, or it might go well as a family serial; wherever Hitty goes she should still, as always, be warmly welcomed. (pp. 2080-81)

Margery Fisher, in a review of "Hitty, the Life and Adventures of a Wooden Doll," in Growing Point, *Vol. 11, No. 7, January, 1973, pp. 2080-81.*

The mock-autobiography is a version of the domestic novel that goes back to the early nineteenth century in England. A certain piquancy is lent to a simple chronicle of domestic and social custom and event when it comes from a non-human narrator; a cat or a needle obviously see life in a refreshingly different way and it may be said that a doll character is particularly well suited to the form. The somewhat smug, enigmatic features of a wooden doll have inspired other writers before and since Rachel Field used the events of her heroine's life as the impetus for pictures of the world of merchants and seamen, city and country folk. Everything that happens is seen from the doll's rather caustic point of view. Among Rachel Field's many novels of America's past, graceful and authentic as they are, *Hitty* stands out as a literary triumph.

Margery Fisher, "Who's Who in Children's Books: Hitty," in her Who's Who in Children's Books: A Treasury of the Familiar Characters of Childhood, *Holt, Rinehart and Winston, 1975, p. 140.*

POCKET-HANDKERCHIEF PARK (1929)

The arrival of one of Miss Field's books is always welcome. Within a small compass, they have quite a character of their own, reminding one of that succession of charming little volumes by Kate Greenaway whose appearance so delighted another generation.

This story is about the tiny breathing space in a crowded city so much enjoyed and so passionately defended by the troup of little children who make it the center of their lives. There is found the merry-go-round with that so popular horse Christopher Columbus Lindbergh; there are the Pretzel Woman and "Pop" with his balloons; and, finally, there is the colored boy hitching post, cheerful survivor of the 'eighties. Would the children let so much color and romance fall tamely into the hands of the builders? No indeed! The story tells us what happened to prevent it.

A review of "Pocket Handkerchief Park," in The Saturday Review of Literature, *Vol. VI, No. 17, November 16, 1929, p. 431.*

PATCHWORK PLAYS (1930)

It would seem easy to write plays for children. In truth, it is woefully difficult, as is proved by the exceeding paucity of good plays for children to act. For the child play is not exempt from dramatic law. It must have a beginning, a middle, and an end. It must tell an entertaining story through cogent action and dialogue. It must be good, even though simple, theatre. And then there are other distinctive requirements. Neither in emotional content nor characterization should it lie outside the child's experience. It may deal with grown-ups, but as the child sees them, which is quite different from the way they view themselves. It should be pure in thought and word, without, however, mawkish goody-goodiness or false ethics. It should be brisk, vivid, and picturesque. Above all it must appeal to the imagination. It must have something

in it of wonder and magic. For to the child the world is not drab or tragic. Rather it is a kaleidoscope of colorful change and fascinating possibilities.

Rachel Field knows all these things. And, what is more rare, she has the ability to put them into practice. Therefore, she has already to her credit many deservedly popular books of stories and plays for children. In this volume she gathers together five new plays under a title suggested by the opening play, **"Polly Patchwork."** This is a dramatization in three scenes of her well-known story of the same name, and tells how Polly's odd patchwork gown worked a miracle and won for her a spelling match, thereby lifting its timorous little wearer to the pinnacle of school fame. **"Little Square Toes,"** a play for three girls, contrasts the naturalness and freedom of Indian life with the constriction and formality of the early Puritan, relating how seven-year-old Remembrance, stolen from her Deerfield home in King Philip's Wars, returns for a brief and disappointing visit to her former companions, whom she finds working industriously on intricate samplers. A gay little sketch is **"Miss Ant, Miss Grasshopper, and Mr. Cricket,"** which, "with a special bow to Mr. Æsop," portrays Mr. Cricket and his guitar as properly chivalrous to forlorn Miss Grasshopper in her plight of hunger and cold. With their *penchant* for animal, bird, and insect impersonation children will love to act this old fable in these new sprightly terms. **"Chimney Sweeps's Holiday"** is the most ambitious and longest play in the collection, and for that very reason perhaps the least successful, as it verges on the diffuse. However, it gives variety, and offers opportunity for old English folk songs and dances, while in its requirement of an all-boy cast it will meet a need. The last play, **"The Sentimental Scarecrow,"** is altogether delightful. It has whimsy and appeal.

Without resort, then, to sprites or witches, these little plays have a fairy-book ring that will prove enticing to the child actor. Moreover, children will enjoy reading the plays, or hearing them read.

Jane Dransfield, in a review of "Patchwork Plays," in The Saturday Review of Literature, *Vol. VII, No. 18, November 15, 1930, p. 334.*

It is a pleasure to welcome a book of plays for children so truly childlike and spontaneous, so well-written and with so much real atmosphere. . . . Words and music are given for the songs and the directions are clear and simple enough for children to use themselves. The author's illustrations give suggestions for costumes and settings.

Anne T. Eaton, in a review of "Patchwork Plays," in The New York Times Book Review, *December 7, 1930, p. 45.*

THE YELLOW SHOP (1931)

Probably every child has dreamed at one time or another of "keeping store" and every child who reads about the twins, Will and Rebecca, will envy them their little yellow shop. It had stood boarded up for years beside Miss Roxanna's gate and when she adopted the twins they decided to reopen it. . . . Just at their darkest moment, when it seemed as though the days of the little yellow shop were numbered, they were able to make a surprising sale that brought them enough money to pay for reshingling the roof on Miss Roxanna's house. And then, after all, Silas Bean was able to keep "Tony the Hot-Dog-Stand-Man at the Bridge" from turning them out of their place. A wholesome, jolly little story, thoroughly childlike and charmingly illustrated with the author's own drawings.

> *Anne T. Eaton, in a review of "The Yellow Shop," in* The New York Times Book Review, *October 25, 1931, p. 23.*

CALICO BUSH (1931)

Calico Bush is a story of the first rank. Adult readers as well as boys and girls will be grateful to Rachel Field for this fine and absorbing tale. Its roots go deep into the soil of that Maine which the author knows so well and the style suggests the strength and beauty of Winter woods and the northern Spring.

Marguerite Ledoux, a 12-year-old French girl, sets out for Canada in the year 1743 with her grandmother and her uncle, but the plague breaks out on the ship, "Oncle Pierre" dies, and the terrified captain hastily sets Marguerite and her grandmother ashore at Marblehead, the nearest port. The grandmother's death soon follows and Marguerite is then handed over to Joel and Dolly Sargent, to be their "bound-out girl" until she is 18. With them she goes to Mount Desert, at that time on the very edge of civilization, taking care of their five children and sharing in their pioneer life that meant the winning of crops from rocky soil, sheep shearing, spinning and weaving, and always the constant danger of attacks from the Indians.

Rachel Field has the imagination that can reconstruct out of a fragment of the past—a legend, a sampler, a quilt pattern—the life of another day and a whole circle of people in the surroundings where they carried on the affairs of everyday living. The characters in *Calico Bush* remain with the reader long after the book is closed. Aunt Hepsa, with her kindliness, sound common sense and humor, her terse, crisp talk which has the true New England flavor, is unforgetable. We learn to know the others, too, Joel Sargent, slow, sparing of words, utterly determined; Dolly, hard working, a devoted mother and kind, though lacking in imagination. Even the five little children have individuality.

Because she is a poet, Rachel Field shows us her characters against a beautiful and typical background which helps interpret them. There are the Maine firs and spruces crowding down to the shore in thick-set ranks of green, spicy bayberry bushes, distant hills faintly blue and rugged, straight gray threads of smoke that rise from the settlers' houses, night skies, with the first stars large and sharply pointed and, in the pastures overlooking the sea, sheep laurel, or calico bush, with its deep pinkish blossoms.

> *Anne T. Eaton, in a review of "Calico Bush," in* The New York Times Book Review, *November 22, 1931, p. 22.*

The success of *Hitty: Her First Hundred Years* placed upon an artist sincere and sympathetic as Rachel Field an obligation not lightly to be disregarded. There had been nothing in young literature like this rich autobiography of a self-respecting New England doll, keeping her essential qualities of doll and New England alive and robust through a century of domestic alarms and foreign excursions. Children everywhere clamored for another book exactly like it, that being

a way of children not unknown among older readers. This demand Miss Field has respected and fulfilled in the only way possible to a creative artist. Asked for another masterpiece about a doll, she has given another masterpiece about something entirely different. . . .

The strongest scenes [in *Calico Bush*] are near the close, and it leaves Marguerite in possession of her freedom and using it to choose the life of this place of which she is now a part. It has the qualities that make literature for any age—lyric beauty, high-heartedness, sincerity. It has not a trace of the most dangerous tendency in our fiction for young people, the tendency to be careful. There is even death, for babies do die on the frontier; there is what there should be in a work of art rising out of history. All that makes it distinctively a book for a young reader is that this wild and lovely world is seen through the eyes of a girl who has not yet heard the sharp imperative summons of sex. A book bringing back a world in which that clangor has not yet sounded may have a restfulness not incompatible with strenuous, even violent action. If, like *Calico Bush,* it brings it back in beauty, the book may qualify as literature.

> *May Lamberton Becker, "Like a Quilting Pattern," in* New York Herald Tribune Books, *November 29, 1931, p. 8.*

This is a really good book, simple in its narrative, meaty, sincere, and with that occasional thrill which is so much more effective when the story lifts you to it, than when some trick or irrelevant sensation spurs the jaded flank of narrative. Calico Bush is the name of the old ballad made on the sheep laurel flower and this story of a pioneer's family of 1743, settling on the mainland of Maine near Mt. Desert island, is woven in and out with authentic customs and folk poetry, both French and English. . . . The lives of the pioneers were chronicle, and the difficulty in writing their stories, especially for children, is to keep a nice balance between the routine of frontier life, interesting but still a routine, and the possibilities of adventure which lead the story teller for children into a melodrama of excitement where the hero always wins. Miss Field has got the texture of real life into her story without dulness on one hand or melodrama on the other. The island life flows with a genuine intensity but her touch is always sure upon the life and the family characters to which the adventures happen, and she never lets the episodes run off with the story. It is a skilful and rather touching book, with a remainder of good American experience for the child who reads it.

> *Henry Seidel Canby, "Pioneer Life," in* The Saturday Review of Literature, *Vol. VIII, No. 21, December 12, 1931, p. 369.*

One of the finest books Rachel Field ever wrote is *Calico Bush.* . . .

This book may well serve as a model of sound historical fiction. The picture of the times and the people is not only authentic but unusually well balanced. The hardships, the monotony, and the perils of pioneer life are there, unvarnished and frightening. The compensatory rewards may seem slight to young readers, but there can be no doubt in their minds about the sturdy, undismayed character of these early settlers. Here is no glamorized history, full of picturesque dangers in which the leading characters always triumph. Instead, the book portrays well-intentioned, hard-working human beings, whose plans sometimes go wrong, who make mistakes, who suffer grievous tragedy through their own weakness, but who persevere with fortitude and unwavering hope. So *Calico Bush* is no bleak tract on pioneer hardships; it is a heartening story of people helping each other and gratefully enjoying small blessings, brief interludes of happy companionship. The growing respect and affection of these people for each other and especially for the alien girl, Marguerite, give a warm emotional overtone to the whole story. Beautifully written, this book presents a brave, frank picture of early days and ways. (p. 398)

> *May Hill Arbuthnot, "Other Times and Places," in her* Children and Books, *Scott, Foresman and Company, 1947, pp. 396-421.*

HEPATICA HAWKS (1932)

The most individual and dramatic new story for girls in the teens is Rachel Field's *Hepatica Hawks.* Even more firmly rooted in the history of American life than the author's *Calico Bush,* this story has a deeper human appeal. Hepatica Hawks, six feet four inches and a quarter in height, is first introduced at the age of fifteen as a freak in a traveling show. Hallelujah Hawks, her father, stands eight feet four. Hepatica eventually becomes a famous opera singer. Plot and character present abundant opportunity for sensational treatment and sentimental development.

It is perhaps the most significant tribute one can pay to Miss Field's art to say that in reading the book one completely forgets the abnormal size of Hepatica Hawks and the giant father whose relationship is so sympathetically set forth. One becomes entirely absorbed in a very human story. A good deal of careful research must have gone into the writing of this book, and its subject has evidently been long meditated. The wider appeal to the intelligence and the sympathies of girls is clearly felt. I predict long life for *Hepatica Hawks.*

> *Anne Carroll Moore, in a review of "Hepatica Hawks," in* The Atlantic Bookshelf, *a section of* The Atlantic Monthly, *Vol. 150, No. 5, November, 1932, p. 24.*

In *Hepatica Hawks* Rachel Field has accomplished a difficult undertaking with so much ease and grace that it is hard to realize how difficult it was. . . .

Taking material that is out of the beaten track, material that could easily lend itself to melodrama, Miss Field has handled it with such delicacy and sincerity, with so much sympathy and genuine human understanding, that the result is a story that has both strength and sweetness. Hepatica is an appealing heroine, and there is no better test of the skill of Rachel Field as a writer than the fact that we are interested in Hepatica as a girl and not as a member of the freak circus. . . .

A story that will last.

> *Anne T. Eaton, in a review of "Hepatica Hawks," in* The New York Times Book Review, *November 13, 1932, p. 9.*

"A young novel," some one has called Rachel Field's new book. In the best sense of the word, it is a novel, for the book is a prose narrative of real beauty with characters and action out of real life portrayed in a plot. It may properly be called a "young" novel because all the action of the story occurs in the year Hepatica Hawks, its heroine, is fifteen. It will be liked by young people and many older ones as well. . . .

[The story] has a special delicacy and loveliness. A good story in itself, for grown-ups it might stand also as a symbol of those years when the spirit of youth—consciously or not—reaches out after beauty; is filled with yearnings; is troubled by imagined, if not real, oddity, and has little or no peace. *Hepatica Hawks* has no trace of a morbid quality, is free from sentimentality, and infused throughout with kindliness, generosity, and humanity.

> *Bertha E. Mahony, "A Young Novel," in* The Saturday Review of Literature, *Vol. IX, No. 19, November 19, 1932, p. 254.*

THE BIRD BEGAN TO SING (1932)

The Bird Began to Sing made us remember the concerns of our early Christmas Eves and prompted us to question others about theirs, for we realized that it was Tilda's solemn problem in the midst of the holiday scuffle and bustle that brought the story so appealingly close to us. Of course, no worry of ours ever was lifted from growing shoulders by a miracle, still . . . well, that the bird began to sing is certainly a miracle, and yet not at all an unlikelihood.

It was Grandpa Schultz's bird, a mechanical one which he had made for little Jakey. No one knew about it, not Frau Else, nor Aunt Mattie, nor Jakey, and certainly not Miss Louella Pollock. Only Tilda, and perhaps Pretzel, the dachshund. And then, the secret kept, Grandpa Schultz's work completed, the bird refused to sing. It would come out of its snuff box and move its head and wings, but it would make no sound. All the eagerness that was part of the excitement of Christmas Eve was forgotten by Tilda in her despair until. . . . It would hardly be fair to tell just how the miracle happened. Tilda did her ingenious best, and the bird did the rest. It is a charming story. . . . Perfectly free of all sentimentality, it has the courage to suggest (or was that the last thing in Miss Field's mind?) that Christmas for Tilda, as for most children, has almost nothing to do with good will and "God bless us every one." Individual excitement and enterprise are running too high to embrace historical significance. Rather are the sentiments of good cheer an echo of released personal exuberance. Of what first importance is it that the bird begin to sing! And sing he does, in a story which is not as ambitious as the familiar *Hitty* or *Calico Bush,* or this year's *Hepatica Hawks,* but which conveys so warmly its magic mood that it will be read and re-read regardless of the season of the year.

> *Josiah Titzell, "A Miracle on Christmas Eve," in* New York Herald Tribune Books, *November 13, 1932, p. 15.*

The story is full of Christmas as a child knows it. Rachel Field has the gift of seeing what a child sees and loves; for her, too, a little shop, gay with its Christmas stock, or a house with holly-trimmed windows, has something of magic and wonder. As she has already shown in *The Magic Pawnshop,* Miss Field can give to places a rare feeling of reality along with a fairy-tale atmosphere. Frau Else's little shop is as real as Miss Minerva MacLoon's strange little pawnshop, and children will feel that by looking they can find either one.

> *Anne T. Eaton, in a review of "The Christmas Tree in the Woods," in* The New York Times Book Re-

view, *December 11, 1932, p. 14.*

JUST ACROSS THE STREET (1933)

Thank Heaven there are still little streets in large cities where an author with so large a heart and so keen an eye as the author of **Hitty** and **Hepatica Hawks** can find real folks. The children who live in this one, for instance, can arrange to keep what might be called a companionate dog, barred from admission to the apartment into which his owner has moved but still eligible for a permanent visit to another child just across the street who yet possesses a personal yard.

In such a street anything can happen on a spring day. When the Sheffield horse and the flower-cart horse go by they are greeted by the neighborhood as local characters. For in this New York corner; believe it or not, there are real neighbors still. So when the antique dealer over the way fears lest his adored Indian Princess, the cigar-store sign standing in fine weather outside the shop, may have to be taken for debt, the neighborhood organises a garden party to raise funds for her relief. Midway of this festivity the fatal van draws up. When it goes away again, under the blanket in which the valuable effigy is swathed, huddles a determined small boy. Just how he is going to rescue the beloved he is not sure, nor indeed just where he is going, but something decisive must be done, and when he finds out what it is he'll do it. It turns out that he is being taken along with her to a moving-picture location—and it all turns out beautifully.

Whatever Miss Field writes is worth owning; this little book, slight as it may seem from so summary a condensation, has a wholesome human kindness that gives it depth and color. One thinks the better of a clamorous town for thinking there may be hidden away somewhere in the heart of its noise little streets quiet and kind as this.

A review of "Just Across the Street," in New York Herald Tribune Books, *November 12, 1933, p. 12.*

This is a city idyll. It tells of Joe and Katy's eight-year-old adventures in a neighborly city street. We suspect that the city *may* be New York. Mention is made of the elevated and the Avenue; but there is also a peacock who comes out of his house as a herald of spring, with the first warm days, and an Indian princess (wooden, it must be admitted) housed in an antique shop. A more exotic street, therefore, than most of us know.

In any case, New York or not, Miss Field has managed to make the street a pleasant one.

Miss Field's grave, humorous style brings the story to life. It is not as unusual a book as her **Hitty,** but it is one that her young readers will like.

A review of "Just Across the Street," in The Saturday Review of Literature, *Vol. X, No. 20, December 2, 1933, p. 308.*

SUSANNA B. AND WILLIAM C. (1934)

Here [is a tiny book] such as used to be offered to—and treasured by—little children, and would be more often now if experts such as Mr. Wilbur Macey Stone had their way: light little volumes "fitting a pinafore pocket," with clear type, wide margins and plenty of pictures. Rachel Field's **Susanna**

B. and William C. even carries out the time-honored habit of giving such books a cautionary character, though neither its cautions nor the conduct inspiring them need be taken too seriously. Miss Field is having fun with her subject—her two subjects, the girl whose passion is for shoes and the boy whose abnormal interest in locks and keys leads him to become at last so firmly wedged into a post-box that "not a doctor dared to hack the post-box from his youthful back, so William Cox, I weep to tell, must wear through life a square green shell." The accompanying pictures, whether of William walking abroad like a frisky sort of snail. Susanna garnished with her shoe collection, or the jolly balloon man, are gay with bright colors.

May Lamberton Becker, in a review of "Susanna B. and William C.," in New York Herald Tribune Books, *October 28, 1934, p. 10.*

Fortunate is the six or seven or eight year old who can boast on his own private bookshelf a set of Rachel Field's Lilliputian volumes, with their elfin gayety and charm. **The Alphabet for Boys and Girls, The Little Book of Days, Polly Patchwork, Pocket Handkerchief Park** and **The Yellow Shop** have already appeared in the same diminutive format as **Susanna B. and William C.,** with the author's own illustrations that are lively and humorous and have at the same time a charming touch of primness suggestive of the days when Jane and Ann Taylor were writing their *Original Poems for Infant Minds.*

That children enjoy a plainly pointed moral the long-continued popularity of Hofmann's *Struwelpeter* and of some of the Taylor's *Rhymes,* and, later, of Katharine Pyle's *Careless Jane,* have abundantly proved, so Susanna B., who was too fond of her shoes, and William C., who was too curious about locks and keys, are sure to find a welcome.

Anne T. Eaton, in a review of "Susanna B. and William C.," in The New York Review of Books, *November 4, 1934, p. 10.*

ALL THROUGH THE NIGHT (1940)

I do not know if this "stocking-size" book in green-and-white is for children or adults. I think it is for citizens of the Kingdom of Heaven, which does not inscribe ages on its passports. But because Rachel Field is one of childhood's beloved authors, her book belongs on this page.

It is the night before the first Christmas. The animals have it to themselves in the stable: man has left them the freedom of darkness. They see a man and woman take refuge there. They are first to greet the new baby. They do not know just what is going on, but they feel it, and talk about it among themselves. The lantern fails: a bright star, shining through crossed rafters, casts a strange shadow. In the morning the family goes its way. The dog catches up with them. "Wait, here I am!" he barks. "Let me come with you."

Perhaps if I read this story often enough I may be able to do so without choking up, I haven't yet.

In telling this story, the simplest way is always the best. It needs not to be made new; it never grows old. Miss Field tells how simple spirits welcomed the night that changed the world.

From Patchwork Plays, *written and illustrated by Rachel Field.*

A review of "All Through the Night," in New York
Herald Tribune Books, *November 10, 1940, p. 12.*

All Through the Night tells the Christmas story with a lovely
simplicity that makes us feel we are seeing the happenings of
that first Christmas night through the eyes of the gentle creatures who were there to greet the Child. Miss Field recalls the
gracious tradition of the animals in the stable who, finding
speech at midnight, were the first to worship.

Always we feel the animals playing their part in the story.
The night coming on when the birds and beasts and insects
of the stable knew that the world was theirs as the world of
day could never be, the darkness warm and alive with the familiar scents of fur and feathers, and grain and straw, doves
cooing sleepily and, as Mary and Joseph arrive, bright eyes
beyond the ring of light the lantern made, furry ears and
quivering nostrils.

This little book is just the right size to be loved and cherished
and carried about by small readers The drawings of manger
and stable, of lambs and oxen, and the Holy Child, have the
simplicity and childlike quality of the text.

*Anne T. Eaton, in a review of "All Through the
Night," in* The New York Times Book Review, *December 1, 1940, p. 10.*

Read every word of this moving tale, reverently and simply
told. This is the kind of book you would be happy to find in
your own Christmas stocking or you would love to tuck into
someone else's, for its beauty will appeal to any age. . . .

*Florence Bethune Sloan, in a review of "All Through
the Night," in* The Christian Science Monitor, *December 16, 1940, p. 7.*

CHRISTMAS TIME: VERSES AND ILLUSTRATIONS (1941)

Rachel Field is a writer who catches the spirit of time and
place, as those who know her **Little Book of Days,** her lovely
Christmas chapter in **Calico Bush** and the enchanted New
Year's Eve adventure of a little girl in **The Magic Pawnshop**
will testify.

Christmas Time, another tiny volume to match **All Through
the Night,** Miss Field's story of the first Christmas, which
was published a year ago, contains a dozen Christmas poems,
most of them new, a few previously published in the author's
Pointed People and **Branches Green.**

"The Legend," telling of the beasts at midnight on Christmas
Eve; **"When Mary Rode With Joseph,"** which shows us the
child surrounded by the humble animals, touch the deeper
meaning of the season; in **"Before Christmas," "City Christmas"** and others, we find the child's gleeful anticipation of
coming joys. . . .

*Anne T. Eaton, in a review of "Christmas Time
Verses and Illustrations," in* The New York Times
Book Review, *December 14, 1941, p. 10.*

Last year at this time a tiny book by Rachel Field, **All**

Through the Night, brought the feeling of Christmas to each of us. It is pleasant to have another such token this year, in appearance matching the first, and made up of eleven Christmas poems by Miss Field. She has also supplied the tiny sketches which are half the book's charm. Some of the poems are familiar, all are rich in the spirit of childhood and Christmas.

> *Irene Smith, in a review of "Christmas Time," in* Library Journal, *Vol. 66, No. 22, December 15, 1941, p. 1096.*

PRAYER FOR A CHILD   (1944)

This is sure fire. One of the loveliest books of the season—a beautiful piece of bookmaking, with the delicate coloring of Elizabeth Orton Jones' exquisite drawings perfectly reproduced; and the text, a prayer actually written for one child, but appealing to all, touching as it does on things common to every child's understanding and experience. The complete prayer is given at the start; then each step is illustrated with a full page picture, perfectly interpreting the reverent but childlike and human quality of the prayer. A modern classic.

> *A review of "Prayer for a Child," in* Virginia Kirkus' Bookshop Service, *Vol. XII, No. 19, October 1, 1944, p. 449.*

Here is the prayer of a loving heart for an actual child. Offered for [Rachel Field's daughter] Hannah . . . , because so directly meant for one dear child, it is for every child held dear. Any mother bending over the bed of a three-year-old, might say from the heart these words of Rachel Field leaning out from the gold bar of heaven.

From "bless this milk and bless this bread, bless this soft and waiting bed" its benisons go through the house, from "my little painted chair" to "other children far and near and keep them safe and free from fear." . . .

Many children will learn this—certainly the child for whom it was written—but it is less a prayer for a child to say than one *for* a child, to be said in his behalf. . . . [The] rhyme is a legacy, this book the casket in which the legacy is preserved.

> *A review of "Prayer for a Child," in* New York Herald Tribune, *November 12, 1944, p. 7.*

The lovely prayer that Rachel Field wrote for her own little daughter, out of a deep and sensitive understanding of childhood, has been illustrated by Elizabeth Orton Jones with so much tenderness and imagination that anyone who has ever known and loved a child will be touched and charmed. Here is childhood caught unawares, busy about its own affairs, artless and unselfconscious. The pictures and the prayer itself speak to children in a child's own language; older people will find this little volume beautiful, moving and deeply satisfying. A book for every household where there are children.

> *Anne T. Eaton, in a review of "Prayer for a Child," in* The New York Times Book Review, *November 12, 1944, p. 6.*

Rachel Field has left our boys and girls many a lovely poem and many a good story, but one of her greatest legacies to them has been this prayer. It was written for her own daughter, but now belongs to all boys and girls everywhere. It is a prayer, beautifully written . . . , bespeaking the faith, love, hopes and the trust of little children.

> *Marian A Webb, in a review of "Prayer for a Child," in* Library Journal, *Vol. 70, No. 1, January 1, 1945, p. 35.*

POEMS   (1957)

Piping childhood's refrains, Rachel Field found reason for rhyme in hurdy gurdys and music boxes, Christmas trees and bedtime prayers. Her even rhythms and clear expressions of mood and memory make a charming collection of verses with selections to please children of all ages. The black and white silhouettes which illustrate the book were done by the author. They attenuate the spirit and attitudes—now fey, now wistful—of her poetry.

> *A review of "Poems," in* Virginia Kirkus' Service, *Vol. XXV, No. 17, September 1, 1957, p. 634.*

Most of Rachel Field's lilting "poems" are tiny, about tiny things, bringing a mood with them—"not a little child but keeps some trace of Christmas secrets in his face." Their delicacy is admirably expressed in the agile, silhouetted figures that illustrate them. But all her poems were not written for children and we wonder why **"For Us in Wartime,"** for instance, was included.

> *Pamela Marsh, "Shining Surprises," in* The Christian Science Monitor, *November 7, 1957, p. 15.*

THE RACHEL FIELD STORY BOOK   (1958)

Three stories by Rachel Field [**"Polly Patchwork," "Pocket Handkerchief Park,"** and **"The Yellow Shop"**] serve as a pleasant reminder of that author's unique talent to combine homines with imagination and thus arrive at a peculiarly cozy brand of magic. A little girl in a patchwork dress of which she is ashamed finds within its bright patterns the key to the question in a spelling bee; a little boy's wish at midnight saves his beloved park; and a pair of energetic nine-year-old twins make it possible for their aunt, Miss Roxanna Robbins of Cranberry Common, to restore her gingerbread house. Adrienne Adams' quaint and diminutive illustrations suit Rachel Field's delightful style to perfection in their rendering of a tidy, bright little world of gentle events and fulfilled wishes.

> *A review of "The Rachel Field Story Book," in* Virginia Kirkus' Service, *Vol. XXVI, No. 12, June 15, 1958, p. 414.*

Teachers and librarians in search of good material for Story-Hours will find these three tales excellent. They are well-written, set in modern or Victorian times. . . . Their American origin gives just that "new and different" feeling, but these children, setting up shop to pay for much-needed home repairs, or banding together to save their little park, or turning a difficult situation at school into a success story, will be recognised by those who hear or read the tales as genuine boys and girls in "fixes" just like their own. (pp. 84-5)

> *A review of "The Rachel Field Story Book," in* The Junior Bookshelf, *Vol. 25, No. 2, March, 1961, pp. 84-5.*

POEMS FOR CHILDREN   (1978)

Rachel Field's poems are concerned in general with the smaller things of life: a china dog on a shelf, vegetables, and running barefoot through grass. Her style, which is clear and straightforward, suits them well, but the reader comes to hope she will pursue more complex themes: the poem about sandwich men almost catches that melancholy which is compounded of old age and poverty and anyone who has been bereaved will identify with Miss Lucinda's Garden, where the flowers bloom on though the one who planted them has gone. A danger of collecting the works of one author, that there will be a noticeable repetition of words and images, is not entirely avoided.

> *R. Baines, in a review of "Poems for Children," in* The Junior Bookshelf, *Vol. 42, No. 6, December, 1978, p. 299.*

GENERAL STORE   (1988)

Field's poem from another era inspires an affectionate display of the charms of an old-fashioned general store. "Someday I'm going to have—a store! / With a tinkly bell hung over the door, / with real glass cases and counters wide, / and drawers all spilly with things inside."

The spare text is set in large type, suggesting an ease that might attract beginning readers. But the best thing here is the book's absolute success in recalling the appeal of a store that barely exists today; this is a sweet celebration of simpler times.

> *Denise M. Wilms, in a review of "General Store," in* Booklist, *Vol. 84, No. 13, March 1, 1988, p. 1179.*

Even if the store in this book isn't one modern youngsters will recognize, all children have "played store" and fantasized about what they would sell in their own market. This book will fuel those imaginings. It is also a fanciful way to introduce today's children to the shops of yesteryear.

> *Heide Piehler, in a review of "General Store," in* School Library Journal, *Vol. 35, No. 8, May, 1988, p. 91.*

Leon Garfield

1921-

English author of fiction, nonfiction, picture books, and short stories, reteller, and editor.

Garfield is celebrated as a brilliant and original writer of works which characteristically use the content and background of English history to create an interpretation both modern and unique. Favorably compared to such authors as Henry Fielding, Jane Austen, Charles Dickens, and Robert Louis Stevenson, he brings a distinctive approach which relies on complex plots, larger-than-life characters, and a blending of the comic with the serious to such established literary forms as the adventure novel and the picaresque romance. Prolific and sophisticated, Garfield is generally considered the most innovative writer of historical fiction in the field of juvenile literature. Critic John Rowe Townsend has written, "Of all the talents that emerged in the field of British writing in the 1960s, that of Leon Garfield seems to me to be the richest and strangest." Garfield is often praised for defying categories, for using familiar literary ingredients in a fresh manner, for blurring the distinction between children's and adult literature, and for presenting the past to his readers in a distinctive and stimulating fashion. Addressing his works most often to a young adult audience, he takes the periods of the eighteenth and early nineteenth centuries and the settings of London and surrounding environs and adapts them to his imagination; although Garfield is accurate in his details, he uses his historical backgrounds to launch into explorations of human nature and morality. Most of his works are novels of experience, adventure stories which employ the journey motif to describe how a young orphaned or rootless hero becomes involved with characters and situations which lead him to understand his true identity. Garfield's heroes uniformly search for values that are solid and permanent in atmospheres of mystery and uncertainty; in their quests for love and truth, the protagonists encounter such realities as war, murder, slavery, and mental illness as well as ambiguous villains who are often not what they appear. Although his works often utilize conventional melodramatic devices, Garfield provides twists in narrative and characterization to show both hero and reader the deceptiveness of appearances, especially as they relate to good and evil; several of his books are also underscored by strong antiwar themes. Despite the maturity and unflinching realism of his works, Garfield is often acknowledged for investing his stories with humor and warmth as well as with a view of humanity which is ultimately positive and hopeful.

Garfield has made contributions to several genres with his books. Beginning his career with adventure stories set in the eighteenth century of which *Smith* (1967), the tale of a young pickpocket mistakenly accused of murder who thwarts his adversaries and comes into a fortune, is considered the most outstanding, Garfield intersperses these works with ghost stories, tales for younger children such as "The Boy and the Monkey" trilogy about an orphan and his pet who travel from London to Virginia, picture books which retell stories from the Old Testament, and novels which particularize actual events, such as the French Revolution in *The Prisoners*

of September (1975). He is also the creator of *The House of Hanover: England in the Eighteenth Century* (1976), a work of straight nonfiction which provides young readers with a guided tour of the National Portrait Gallery, and *Child O'War* (1972), a novel which uses excerpts from the actual memoirs of the youngest boy ever to join the British Navy, Sir John Theopilus Lee, to demonstrate the horrors of battle. Although Garfield has received much critical attention, many observers are especially delighted by *The Strange Affair of Adelaide Harris* (1971) and its sequel *Bostock and Harris; or, The Night of the Comet* (1979; U. S. edition as *The Night of the Comet*), comic novels about the adventures of two schoolboys in the Regency era which are filled with slaptick, farce, and irony, and by the twelve stories for younger children about boys and girls involved in various trades which are collected in *The Apprentices* (1978). With Edward Blishen, Garfield retold Greek myths in two works, *The God Beneath the Sea* (1970) and *The Golden Shadow* (1973), which describe the creation of the cosmos, its destruction, and the relationship between gods and humanity in the early mortal world. Although many reviewers lauded these books for capturing the spirit of the myths in contemporary language, others were less convinced of the success of this approach. Garfield has also written *Shakespeare Stories* (1985), a collection of stories based on twelve plays which attempt to provide young readers with the experience of seeing the plays performed. Throughout his career, Garfield has been lauded both as an exceptional storyteller and a writer of uncommon talent whose craftsmanship and strongly visual literary style add greatly to the evocative quality of his works. Garfield won the first Guardian Award in 1967 for *Devil-in-the-Fog,* the Carnegie Medal in 1970 for *The God Beneath the Sea,* and the Whitbread Award in 1980 for *John Diamond.* Smith was commended for the Carnegie Medal in 1967, while *Black Jack* was named a Carnegie Medal honour book in 1968 and *The Drummer Boy* received the same designation in 1970. Both *Shakespeare Stories* and *The Wedding Ghost* were runners-up for the Kurt Maschler Award in 1985. *Smith* was named a *Boston Globe-Horn Book* honor book in 1968, a designation also received in 1981 by *Footsteps* (U. S. edition of *John Diamond*). Garfield also received the Golden Cat Award in 1985 for his body of work. Two of Garfield's books have been commended for the Greenaway Medal for their illustrations, *The God Beneath the Sea* in 1970, with pictures by Charles Keeping, and *The Ghost Downstairs* in 1972, with pictures by Antony Maitland.

(See also *Contemporary Literary Criticism,* Vol. 12; *Something about the Author,* Vols. 1, 32; and *Contemporary Authors,* Vol. 17-18, rev. ed.)

AUTHOR'S COMMENTARY

[in] spite of all my research and caution over detail, I don't really write historical novels. To me, the eighteenth century—or my idea of it—is more a locality than a time. And in this curious locality I find that I can represent quite contemporary characters more vividly than I could otherwise. It seems to work in rather a strange way. For example, when you see someone you know intimately in new clothes . . . when you see, say, your husband or your wife in evening dress or even fancy dress, quite suddenly and fleetingly you see a fresher aspect of them. You see them stand out from the background that familiarity has consigned them to. For that brief moment they are no longer the comfortable furniture of your mind—the animated suit or gown—but something new and strange, yet at the same time something you know very well. I remember something like that happened to me once in a tube train. I was sitting watching someone I thought I knew; then I didn't know him; then I traced out each feature and was sure I did; then I didn't again. And at the end of the journey I discovered it was my father! I'd seen another aspect of him, a sort of double vision—strangeness and familiarity combined. In this way the historical romance is not, as some have accused, an attempt to escape from contemporary life, but an attempt to view certain aspects of it more clearly and with less clutter.

I admit I find the social aspects of contemporary life too fleeting to grasp imaginatively before they are legislated out of existence. And anyway, I don't think the novel is as suited to coping with them as is the television documentary or the newspaper. It was once, but not now. In the old days it was fine to take up arms in a social cause. But nowadays you're apt to find—thanks to some searching television series—that by the time your book is in print, your shining weapons have a quaint and antique air, rather like flypaper in a world of aerosols. From this point of view, a story set two hundred years ago has an enormous advantage. If you're up to date to the second when you write, you can't help being nearly two

years out of date when you're in print, and as any sensible woman will agree, to be two years out of date is to be faintly ridiculous but to be two hundred years out of date is to be really spectacular! Of course in time that two years will become two hundred but few of us have the time to wait. Fortunately for the novelist, human nature is more constant than fashion.

I did not choose the eighteenth century as my particular locality entirely by caprice. I preferred the discipline of classicism to the freedom of romanticism. Just as Alan Garner admits that he uses fantasy as a crutch, so I use classical form. But in this I'm far more alone. There does seem to be a general return to classicism, most obviously in music. Stravinsky and Britten seem to look back to Bach and Purcell rather than to the large orgies of Mahler and Strauss. In literature the romantic novel reached its apotheosis in the nineteenth century and achieved Wagnerian proportions. Then like the dinosaurs, it became extinct. The fruit became too heavy for the bough and the reader's hand could no longer sustain the weight. Now we are returning to a classical preoccupation with form and, consequently, more manageable lengths.

But the sad thing is that when we are abandoning the worst of romanticism, we are also abandoning much that was fine. Its large and attractive gestures and, above all, its marvellous narrative power. Oddly enough it is in children's literature that one still hopes to find a balance. Here romanticism is still alive because it has not courted the same dangers (inordinate length and overexpressiveness) that destroyed it elsewhere. (pp. 59-60)

> *Leon Garfield, "Writing for Childhood," in* Children's literature in education, *No. 2, July, 1970, pp. 56-63.*

GENERAL COMMENTARY

RUTH HILL VIGUERS

An outstanding English writer of the sixties is Leon Garfield, whose books have pace, humor, and unusually good characterizations. In each of his books mystery is focused on a strange, dominating figure. . . . **Smith,** the tale of a small pickpocket of the eighteenth century, is a triumph of story telling, characterization, and suspense. Few present-day writers combine the attributes that seem so effortless in Mr. Garfield's work: well-built plots, suspense, a writing style suited to the mood of each book, and characters that come to life. (pp. 491-92)

> *Ruth Hill Viguers, "Quests, Survival and the Romance of History," in* A Critical History of Children's Literature *by Cornelia Meigs and others, edited by Cornelia Meigs, revised edition, Macmillan Publishing Company, 1969, pp. 484-510.*

FRANK EYRE

> [British Children's Books in the Twentieth Century *was originally published in 1971.*]

[it] seems probable that children's books will eventually be read in three main groups only. First picture and 'read aloud' books for the very young before they are able to read; then the intermediate picture story and first reading books; and finally the 'young novel', a comprehensive category of fiction for the severely limited period during which children are still

prepared to read books specially produced for them, ending, probably, not later than fourteen. The better authors who have come into prominence in the past twenty years seem to have foreseen such a development and are writing books that might have been expressly designed for such a period. Not surprisingly they tend to be unclassifiable.

Leon Garfield is one author who has invented what is almost a new category of his own to fill this need. His books are not historical novels—though they are set in the past—nor are they simply adventure stories—it is even possible to see them, in some lights, as fantasies. But they are more likely to be read and enjoyed by those who like stories with plenty of action and excitement, than by lovers of historical stories or fantasy. . . . (p. 98)

Although Leon Garfield's work has strengthened with each book, his manner and method has remained unchanged and it is impossible to mistake any book by Garfield for one by any other writer. They are all set in a not too precisely defined part of the eighteenth century; a period which seems to have been chosen more for the opportunities it presents than for any special reason of historical interest or research. It is not an imaginary period, in the sense that Joan Aiken's settings are imaginary, but no serious attempt is made at historical accuracy. No doubt some reading must have been done to get the general picture of the period into the author's mind, but it would not be the kind of research that a Rosemary Sutcliff or a Stephanie Plowman undertakes before writing a historical novel and there are, as a result, occasional anachronisms and inaccuracies. But these are minor blemishes and it is clearly not Leon Garfield's intention to aim at an accurate historical picture. (pp. 98-9)

Leon Garfield's first book was *Jack Holborn.* It is the story of a foundling boy in search of his identity, told with fine gusto and decked out with a wealth of eighteenth-century trappings. . . . [Garfield has written that the story] was first written, and submitted to a publisher, as an adult book, but that—

> it lacked certain qualities that have come to be expected in an adult book. At the same time it possessed certain qualities that were not suited to a juvenile book. It was far too long and it had too many passages of reflection on self-explanatory action.

Jack Holborn was drastically cut and revised, under the guidance of an experienced editor, and was an immediate success, the unusual quality of the author being unmistakable. But the fact that this first book finally came into existence as the result of an editorial exercise and an obviously successful co-operation between author and editor is illuminating and no doubt partly explains the curious feeling that his books give to some readers that they are being stage-managed.

Leon Garfield's second book, *Devil-in-the-Fog,* is not his best book, but it is an excellent example of the author's manner and serves as a good introduction to his work. If the reader likes this he will like all the author's work, if he dislikes it he will probably dislike them all. It is the story of George Treet, the eldest son of a family of strolling players, who learns suddenly that he may be the son of a nobleman and the heir to great wealth. He is taken into Sir John Dexter's family, to find Sir John mysteriously wounded, Lady Dexter cold, haughty and withdrawn and a family of rivals seemingly as vicious as they are jealous. Eventually, after a series of events which read better in the book than they would if described

here, he discovers that he is Thomas Treet's son after all, that his supposed father Sir John Dexter has been the villain of the piece, and that the rivals are not so bad as he had thought. *Devil-in-the-Fog* is as stagey, theatrical and melodramatic as Treet's own performances no doubt were. The style of writing is high-pitched, inflated, with all the marks of the kind of historical writing which earlier had brought historical novels into disrepute. One almost expects a character to burst out with 'Gadzooks!' at any moment, and there are as many exclamation marks, leaders, and dashes as there ever were in Herbert Strang. . . . (pp. 100-01)

[Despite] this the book succeeds with most readers, who are carried along by the impetuosity and verve of the author's writing and attracted by the very theatricality and staginess of the period atmosphere which other readers find overdone. . . . Garfield is better at creating an impressionistic atmosphere from his writing than he is at describing an actual scene and the fact that the reader is made vividly aware of what the author is seeking to project is at least as much due to the artist [Antony Maitland] as it is to the author. (p. 101)

The book in which Leon Garfield comes nearest to making a complete success of the unique mixture of sinister characters, complex, sometimes obscure plots and macabre set-pieces that he has made peculiarly his own, is *Black Jack.* (pp. 101-02)

It would be difficult to imagine a more unlikely story. Yet Leon Garfield makes it not only readable, but compulsively so by the pace and tension of his writing and the almost frenzied 'come along quickly, let's get on with action and not bother too much about what is really supposed to be going on' that is the special mark of his manner.

His third book, *Smith,* is probably his best known, and is the one that has attracted most critical attention. It is a closely woven pastiche of the darker side of eighteenth-century London, with thieves' kitchens, pickpockets, hangings, the Old Bailey, Newgate, pox and plague all brought together in a witches brew of a book that seems to have about it the smell and sounds of the city that Garfield sees and to have hanging over it the darkness and fog and dirtiness that was at least one feature of the times. It is in many ways more like a miniature, and of course infinitely lesser, novel by Dickens than a children's book but there is no doubt at all that many children do read this, and all his books, with zest and find them both exciting and stimulating. His most recent book, *The Drummer Boy,* carries his strange tales even farther along the road to confusion. It is full of things that no other living author for children could achieve, but it would be an intelligent child indeed who could follow the author's tortuous threads to the true centre of his maze. Much as one has to admire his set pieces, and some excellent humorous writing, there is too much in this book that strikes false notes and too much that will mystify, confuse and unnecessarily distress young readers for it to be completely satisfying. Whatever may be true of *Jack Holborn, Devil-in-the-Fog* or *Black Jack,* or *Smith,* this book, one feels, should be in the adult section, because adults will be better equipped to get most value from it.

Leon Garfield's books, in fact, like those of some other writers, raise the question whether, in an age when the telling of straight narrative stories is no longer acceptable in adult novels, some writers may not be driven into children's books as the only way to make use of the gift that has been given them.

I remember hearing an Australian writer, Ivan Southall, tell a seminar audience that this was why he wrote children's books, and one wonders whether Leon Garfield and perhaps also another borderline writer, Alan Garner . . . , may not be novelists *manqués*.

Leon Garfield's work has been highly praised, and many good critics admire it, but it seems to me too early for a reliable judgement to be formed on it. His reputation is of very recent growth. . . . It is always difficult for an adult critic to be completely objective about children's books—so many of them are so much beneath notice to an informed mind that anything at all unusual stands out sometimes undeservedly—and this is particularly so with a writer like Leon Garfield who is, as he himself so shrewdly analysed, doing something that is neither quite for adults nor quite for children. But it seems unlikely that he can continue to produce at regular intervals a succession of the same kind of pseudo-historical firework displays. If he does, he will become type-styled and of less interest, but he has such obvious talent, as a born novelist of the true story-telling kind, that he may well develop his work along other lines that are of more interest to critics and readers like myself, to whom his present work does not greatly appeal because of its basic unreality. (pp. 102-05)

Frank Eyre, "Fiction for Children," in his British Children's Books in the Twentieth Century, *revised edition, Longman Books, 1979, pp. 76-156.*

JOHN ROWE TOWNSEND

Of all the talents that emerged in the field of British writing for children in the 1960s, that of Leon Garfield seems to me to be the richest and strangest. I am tempted to go on and say that his stories are the tallest, the deepest, the wildest, the most spine-chilling, the most humorous, the most energetic, the most extravagant, the most searching, the most everything. Superlatives sit as naturally on them as a silk hat on T. S. Eliot's Bradford millionaire. They are vastly larger, livelier and more vivid than life. They are intensely individual: it would be impossible to mistake a page of Garfield for a page written by anybody else. They are full of outward and visible action, but they are not just chains of events, for everything that happens on the surface has its powerful motivation beneath. And they create their own probabilities. Wildly unlikely it may be that the waif Smith should be rewarded with ten thousand guineas by the not-conspicuously-generous heirs to a fortune, but like many farther-fetched events this is entirely acceptable because nothing less would have matched the size of the story.

Although Garfield is endlessly versatile within his range, the range itself is narrow. His novels so far are all set in the eighteenth century, mostly in London and southern England. His themes are few and recurrent: mysteries of origin and identity; the deceptive appearances of good and evil; contrasts of true and false feeling; the precarious survival of compassion and charity in a tempestuous world. His characters, though never cardboard, are seldom of great psychological complexity as we understand the phrase these days, and often themselves appear to represent underlying forces or passions or even humours.

The choice of the eighteenth century is an unexplained mystery of the Garfield writing personality. It could be that it allows release from the realistic inhibitions that increasingly gathered round the novel from mid-Victorian times onwards. Garfield's is a lawless world; or, more precisely, a world in which the rule of law is itself a contender, is trying to assert itself but is not to be relied on for protection. Men are greatly dependent on their own quickness of hand, of foot, of eye, of wit. The world is one in which great and small rogues are forever busy and the Devil is there to take the hindmost. The author seems steeped in his period; even when writing in the third person he commonly puts 'mistook' or 'forsook' or 'forgot' for 'mistaken' or 'forsaken' or 'forgotten', and he will write 'twenty pound' rather than 'twenty pounds'. But this is not the eighteenth century that might be reconstructed by an historical novelist. It is original, organic, springing straight from the Garfield imagination; though I believe that the work of other writers, and artists, has provided an essential compost. You may well discern something of Stevenson in Garfield's first book, *Jack Holborn,* and something of Dickens everywhere. You may be sure that Garfield knows the work of Fielding and Hogarth, among much else from the eighteenth century itself. There are less obvious writers whose work can fruitfully be considered in relation to his: the great Russian novelists, especially Dostoievsky; even Jane Austen; even Emily Brontë. A rich literary soil is not simply constituted.

The first novel, *Jack Holborn,* showed many of its author's qualities already strongly developed, and immediately appeared remarkable when it first came out. In comparison with later books it has several weaknesses. On the surface it is a tale of piracy, murder, treasure, treachery, shipwreck and ultimate fortune, all in the best tradition of the sea adventure story. And so it will be read by children and by most other readers. There are also two separate questions of identity. One is simple: just who *is* the hero-narrator, the foundling Jack Holborn, so named from the parish in which he was abandoned? The other is disconcerting: how can it be that identical faces cover such different personalities as those of the distinguished Judge and the wicked pirate captain? Confusion between real and apparent good and evil is a recurrent Garfield theme; but the device used in *Jack Holborn*—the introduction of identical twins of opposite character—is crude in comparison with, for instance, the moral complexity of *The Drummer Boy* five years later. And *Jack Holborn* has other flaws. The story, of which the first three quarters are gripping, falls away in the final quarter; the narrator is brave, generous and well-meaning, but he is not interesting. Yet the Garfield style and vision are already unmistakable, and although the writing is not yet fully ablaze with metaphor in the later Garfield manner it rises at times to a staccato poetry.

Devil-in-the-Fog, the second novel, again revolves at length around questions of identity. The narrator George Treet, from being a member of a family of travelling players, is translated suddenly to the position of heir apparent to Sir John Dexter, baronet. In the misty grounds of the great house lurks Sir John's unloving brother, newly cut out of the succession. But who is the true villain, and is George really gentleman or player? The book shows one clear advance on *Jack Holborn:* the difficulty of making the narrator into an effective character in his own right is overcome. The artless George, in telling his story, allows us to see more of him than he can see of himself; we perceive, for instance, the honest vulgarity that makes him unacceptable to Sir John as an heir. And here enters another Garfield theme, that of true and false feeling; for we can contrast and appraise at their proper values the simple vanity of the Treets and the chilly pride of Sir John. But the story, although straightforward in theme and feeling, is complicated in terms of actual incident; and not even the Garfield energy is quite enough to drive it successfully through its own convolutions and lengthy denouement. Although it deservedly won the first *Guardian* award for children's fiction, *Devil-in-the-Fog* still seems to me to display outstanding promise rather than outstanding achievement.

Smith, the first of Leon Garfield's third-person narrations, was a stronger and more straightforward story than either of its predecessors. (pp. 97-100)

Once more there is a puzzle of identity: who is the mysterious Mr Black, and what has become of the long-departed son of the murdered man? There is also the confusion of good and evil; for the respectable young attorney who is paying his attentions to the magistrate's daughter is not what he seems, while it is the third-rate highwayman Lord Tom who saves the sum of things at the cost of his own life. In *Smith,* it seems to me that the forward progress of the story is no longer hindered by entanglement in complications; it knows where it is going and drives steadily towards its powerful climax. It is more unified, more of a novel than its two predecessors or its successor; it is not Garfield's richest book but it is the most obviously successful of his first four.

Black Jack is a more complex book than *Smith,* and, in its beginning and end, more powerful. It is however less satisfactory in structure. (pp. 100-01)

The love story here is fresh and touching. But the structure is perhaps more like that of a symphony—one with powerful opening and closing movements and quieter ones in between—than that of a novel, in which one might wish for a more continuous progress, a build-up of tension towards the climax.

Garfield's latest novel so far, *The Drummer Boy,* is the most ambitious of all and the most complex in ideas and feeling although not in plot. Its hero Charlie Samson is everyone's golden lad, the embodiment of all unfulfilled dreams and lost ideals. With Charlie the story moves from the field of battle, in which ten thousand scarlet soldiers have been mown down, to London, where the responsible General is trying to save his skin. In thrall to the General's beautiful and apparently dying daughter Sophia, Charlie is ready to perjure himself and shift the General's guilt to a haunted wretch of a scapegoat. He is brought to his senses by the cowardly, fat, pansy surgeon Mister Shaw and the common servant-girl Charity.

Clearly the book is concerned with the evils of false romanticism. The brief and doubtful glory of the battlefield is a poor exchange for the slow ripening of a lifetime which we see awaiting Charlie in the story's happy ending. The brief and doubtful glory of serving belle-dame-sans-merci Sophia and her exalted, hollow father is nothing in comparison with the warmth of an honest wench with twenty pounds in the bank and a loving nature. Again there is the bewildering interchange of good and evil; for the apparently natural love of Charlie for Sophia turns out to be a deadly menace, while the seemingly unnatural love of Mister Shaw for Charlie, though it is hopeless, pathetic, incapable of fruition, is beneficent. It would be possible to see Mister Shaw as the ambiguous hero of this story: himself the battlefield, with his healing gift at war with half a dozen ignoble purposes. Charlie as hero is so much a receptacle for the hopes and dreams of others that in himself he is an empty vessel. But at last he loses his drum, the symbol of his virginity of mind and body, and returns with Charity on his arm to the New Forest where he began.

The real story of Charlie Samson starts where the book leaves off.

I do not think *The Drummer Boy* is quite the major triumph that Garfield has been promising ever since *Jack Holborn,* but I am sure it will come. In the meantime, he has one small but perfect work to his credit in *Mister Corbett's Ghost,* which was published in England in 1969 as part of a triptych with two other stories. It is the tale of an apothecary's apprentice, Benjamin, who wishes his harsh master dead, and on New Year's Eve finds an old man who can grant the wish, at a price. But the ghost of Mister Corbett lingers with Benjamin and is more pitiable, more human even, than Mister Corbett was in life; and the boy is happy, in the end, to undo his bargain. Whether this is a story of the supernatural or an externalizing of inner processes is a matter of interpretation, or perhaps of the reader's own development. The themes are those of responsibility for one's actions and of the dreadful destructiveness of revenge; and in his dealings with Mister Corbett as corpse and then as ghost Benjamin goes through the stages of guilt: fear, shame, remorse, compassion. This is a tale told with total command; its temperature goes down, down, far below zero before returning all the more effectively to the warmth of living flesh. I would say, and not lightly, that it can be compared to *A Christmas Carol.*

The most obvious characteristic of Leon Garfield I have left until the end. He treats the English language with a mastery that sometimes verges on outrage. Effortlessly, page after page and line after line, he creates his individual and vivid images. . . . Garfield's metaphors tend to be strongly visual. But he does not only see; he touches, tastes and smells. (An analysis of the smells in his novels might be curiously illuminating.) As a man with medical knowledge he is well aware of the perishable human body, the too too solid, or sullied, flesh. In treating of life as it comes, more rough than smooth, he is not unduly fastidious. Yet he can be gentle, as in the love of Belle and Tolly in *Black Jack.* . . . Leon Garfield can do anything with words and his touch is very sure. . . . I do not believe in singling out a writer as 'the best'; books and their authors are only to a limited extent comparable, and should not be seen as competing against each other. But I have livelier expectations from Leon Garfield than from anyone else whose work is being published on a children's list in England today. (pp. 101-04)

> *John Rowe Townsend, "Leon Garfield," in his* A Sense of Story: Essays on Contemporary Writers for Children, *J. B. Lippincott Company, 1971, pp. 97-107.*

RHODRI JONES

Leon Garfield dislikes being described as a writer for children. He regards this as a publisher's convenience—a slot into which his books can be easily put. What interests him is the novel as narrative, and since the modern novel for adults tends to be concerned with psychological states and sexual exploration rather than with the telling of an intricate and neatly dove-tailing story, Garfield's novels are regarded as being more suitable for children. Certainly they appeal very strongly to young readers and a very important element of this appeal is the strong story-line.

Each of his novels is built on a complicated but firm plot, following the adventures of the main character through a series of clues and discoveries until the complications are resolved and the mysteries revealed as the novel comes to a close. The plots are usually based on a search of some kind—in *Jack Holborn* and *Devil-in-the-Fog* for the truth about the hero's origin, in *The Drummer Boy* for what is real and what is false. Always there is the search for knowledge.

Another factor which gives the novels an appeal for young people is the type of hero that Garfield depicts. Garfield's heroes are on their own. They have to make their own way in the bewildering adult world, finding out for themselves what is reality and what is illusion, learning by trial and error whom to trust and who is merely making use of them. There is Smith, for instance, the 12-year-old pickpocket stealing a living in fog-swirled 18th century London who learns that mere survival is not enough and that compassion is more important than wounded pride or self-interest. Or Charlie Samson, the golden drummer boy, whose goodness is taken advantage of and who learns that the adult world of pride and privilege is not all that it seems. It is through heroes like these that children can explore the strange adult world into which they are moving and against whom they can weigh their own experience.

The style Garfield uses also appeals to children. His language is highly coloured, full of imagery and humour, shot through with irony and ambiguity (which last may not always be grasped by children). Sometimes the imagery is used decoratively (the monkey 'stared out at the passing world with eyes like undertaker's buttons'; she laughed 'a merry tinkling sound, like a dish full of shillings'—from *The Boy and the Monkey*); often, it is used more organically as part of the meaning of the novel. In *Smith,* the dead eyes of the magistrate are a symbol of his inward blindness. In *The Drummer Boy,* the golden lad is in danger of having his innocence tarnished by the world.

Even in the most grim situation—for Garfield shuns little from murder to madness—humour keeps breaking through. (pp. 293-94)

The opening of *Smith* illustrates . . . the assurance with which Garfield establishes a style and a tone for his novels, a skill he may have learned from Jane Austen who has certainly influenced his use of irony. . . . (p. 294)

The other main influence on Garfield's writing seems to be Dickens, although he did not read Dickens until after he had written his first novel *Jack Holborn.* This can be seen partly in the characterization of the minor characters with their one easily recognizable catch-phrase or trait (Meg in *Smith* with her 'Learning? Give you a farthing for it!' or Pobjoy in *Jack Holborn* with his thirst for gin). It can be seen partly in the gusto and skill of the narrative. The whirling end of *Black Jack* is like a speeded-up version of the crescendo of crisis upon crisis at the end of *A Tale of Two Cities* or *Oliver Twist.* It can be seen partly in the use of symbolism. The travelling actors of *Devil-in-the-Fog* and the fair people of *Black Jack* with their casual, free and easy emotional world bear the same significance as the circus people in *Hard Times.* It can be seen in the way in which, once he gets going, Garfield's prose takes on a lyrical lilt and rhythm reminiscent of Dickens in full flight. . . . It is . . . exuberant exaggeration and vitality in the use of words that Garfield shares with Dickens. He also shares a warmth of heart and feeling. Virtue is triumphant. Goodness is seen to be good, without in any way descending to Dickens's sentimental excesses. This is not to say that Garfield is a greater artist than Dickens—merely that he has a better sense of proportion.

Garfield's novels are set in the 18th century. He has said (in an interview in *The Guardian*, 9.6.71): 'It's like science fiction in reverse: you take a moral problem out of context to observe it better; you have the reality of the past to latch on to.' Through the vividness of his writing, his choice of detail and the generosity of his characterisation, Garfield does bring a past age to life. *Smith* has the exuberance, the violence, the high spirits and the squalor of *The Beggar's Opera.* But his novels are more than costume charades. Moral questions and their reverberations loom very large. The search for identity is made concrete by having his hero literally search to find out who his father is in *Jack Holborn* and *Devil-in-the-Fog.* Moral choice is a very important element in *Smith.* Learning to distinguish between outward beauty, respectability or rank and inward corruption, self-seeking and wickedness is the basis of *Black Jack* and *The Drummer Boy.* Even in as slight a tale as *The Boy and the Monkey,* the value of a human life in terms of cash is considered.

And this is, perhaps, one of the most important aspects of Garfield's novels. They deal with the same kind of themes as adult literature, but in terms that children can understand. By identifying with the heroes, children can appreciate the moral choices that arise, and can see that the world is not entirely black and white but varying shades of grey. When they go on to read Shakespeare, Dickens, George Eliot or Jane Austen, they are prepared for similar complexities of feelings and responses to character and situation. If they do not go on to read these classics, they have had a valuable and easily approachable substitute. (pp. 294-95)

Rhodri Jones, "Writers for Children—Leon Garfield," in The Use of English, *Vol. 23, No. 4, Summer, 1972, pp. 293-99.*

MARCUS CROUCH

Leon Garfield seems to have had no 'prentice period. his first book, *Jack Holborn,* has all his characteristic qualities; indeed if one were to be unkind one might venture to say that he has gone on telling the same story ever since. . . . [The book contains] mutiny, shipwreck, jungle trekking, a slave-market and a great trial scene. The ingredients are all conventional enough. It is the author's expert chemistry—appropriately he is a biochemist by calling—which makes the unpromising materials react to produce tension and atmosphere.

Jack Holborn is sustained through great physical ordeals by the hope that he will discover his identity. . . . When the truth is made known . . . it is unspectacular. Jack's mother is not a duchess but a treasure of a housekeeper to a foolish Sussex knight. In *Devil-in-the-Fog* the situation is reversed. George Treet, one of a travelling showman's brood, discovers early on that he is in fact the long-lost son and heir to a wealthy Sussex knight. . . . At last it appears that he is not the heir, but that he has been called upon to play a part with innate professionalism.

What makes these absurd plots not merely acceptable but absorbingly fascinating is Garfield's craftsmanship. He has a gift for creating sharp larger-than-life characters, like Mister Solomon Trumpet in *Jack Holborn* and Mr Thomas Treet, genius and loving father who allowed his infant son to be scarred for life in return for payments down and to come, in *Devil-in-the-Fog.* He excels in equivocal characters, leaving the reader to puzzle through the course of a long story whether they are good or evil. More important than characterization is style. Written in conventional modern English, these stories would scarcely find a reader, let alone a publisher. But Leon Garfield tells his stories in an extraordinary evocative language all his own (it is no more the language of the Eighteenth Century than Jeffery Farnol's equally artificial stylistic mannerisms were). Garfield hypnotizes the reader, wooing him with strange sounds and haunting circumlocutions into a willing co-operation. The words are like an incantation. Archaisms abound, and common words are disguised as unfamiliar contractions—'to've' and 'so's'. The pressure never eases. Garfield has remarkable skill in focusing attention on a situation or a character by a telling description. When Jack Holborn sees for the first time the agent of Nemesis—characteristically in the fog—'he never spoke nor nodded nor waved to any living soul, but stared and stared across the dirty sea as if he was looking for a particular wave.' Here the device is effective and functional, but at times it seems a form of self-indulgence or exhibitionism. (pp. 34-6)

Leon Garfield's craft is at its most brilliant, and is most at the command of his theme, in **Smith.** In this story of a 'sooty spirit of the violent and ramshackle town' and of the London underworld the stylistic mannerisms are comparatively subdued, and the story moves almost as swiftly as Smith, beside whom 'a rat was like a snail'. Smith is a fine creation, a most complex blending of apparent contradictions who, having survived for twelve years 'the small-pox, the consumption, brain-fever, gaol-fever and even the hangman's rope', is destined for greatness of some kind, and greatness of a sort comes not only through his sly swiftness but because of courage and even kindness. . . . In this book there are qualities lacking in most of Garfield's work, compassion and involvement. It is not just a masterly exercise in story-telling, but a book through which the reader shares in the triumphs and disasters of Smith and his admirable sisters, Miss Bridget and Miss Fanny (pp. 36-8)

> *Marcus Crouch, "High Adventure," in his* The Nesbit Tradition: The Children's Novel in England 1945-1970, *Ernest Benn Limited, 1972, pp. 26-47.*

ANNE WOOD

All [Leon Garfield's] books deal in some way with an atmosphere of concentrated evil shot through with possibilities for good. . . . Leon Garfield's books are unique in children's literature.

He is as aware as any other author for children of the need for frequent action. Never a page is turned but something happens, and yet the overwhelming contribution of his books is that they deal in that old-fashioned quality, morality. At the centre of each story is a young person, a boy usually, whose life is impinged upon by mysterious forces for good and evil, their rightness or wrongness obscured by different shows and pretences or seemingly accidental occurrences. Is everything as it seems? Part of the fascination of reading Leon Garfield is penetrating the camouflage of his precision-made plots. These are not historical novels in the accepted sense. An interpretation of history is certainly not what they are about. An interpretation of life perhaps.

The young men in **Prisoners of September** involved in the bloodier side of the French Revolution could just as easily be young men caught up in the violence of the I.R.A. Pickpocket Smith has his modern counterpart and Leon Garfield's latest long novel, **The Pleasure Garden,** "a garden of dreams where the old and ugly imagine themselves to be beautiful,

the poor rich, and the damned saved—where all fantasies are played out" is as much a reflection of contemporary Britain as any part of eighteenth century London.

I therefore approached Leon Garfield's contribution to Andre Deutsch's Mirror of Britain series with heightened anticipation. I just didn't believe he could write a conventional general introduction to the Georgian Period. **The House of Hanover** proved my theory. Taking the brilliant device of viewing the period through the portraits of its leading figures, he proceeds to follow this through literally by making the entire book an account of a visit to the National Portrait Gallery. It is brilliantly done, never flagging for a second in breathless interest and amusement. It is entirely personal. Hogarth is featured on the front cover, Handel is lingered over, while Alexander Pope is gone over as quickly as is decent and Gainsborough comes a very poor second to Capability Brown. . . .

The House of Hanover must surely be one of the most entertaining introductions, not just to the artistic life of a particular period but to the relationship between art and life in any age, ever written. And if we seem to have moved away from the realms of childhood, consider for a moment the central question that a child on the point of growing up is concerned with, or for that matter, that the child that remains in all of us is concerned with. Who am I? Am I good or bad? The question does confront us and it needs audacity and a sense of humour to even contemplate it.

The line between good and evil is very thin and not always easily seen—it is a mystery to be probed. In his preoccupation on the grand scale with the devil's interference in the affairs of mankind, Leon Garfield does write the same book again and again. He has fabricated a totally convincing world dressed up in eighteenth century costume, endlessly fascinating to himself. Inside it he worries at dramatic situations presenting them to the rest of us with a flourish of style and wit. But more important than all of this, is that he presents them in terms that children, too, can enjoy and understand.

> *Anne Wood, "Portrait of an Author: Leon Garfield," in* Books for Your Children, *Vol. 11, No. 3, Summer, 1976, pp. 2-3.*

RONI NATOV

Leon Garfield has been hailed as one of the best contemporary writers for adolescents for his lively and unmistakable style, his ability to weave a series of endlessly fascinating plots, and for his quirky and unforgettable characters. He draws richly and with originality from our great masters of fiction: Fielding, Smollett, and Dickens. His debt to Fielding and Smollett is most obvious in terms of the settings of his novels, all of which take place in the 18th century. Many of them make use of the picaresque episodic structure and the complex combination of comedy and violence found in those early works. Encounters with all kinds of rogues, kidnappings, attempted and actual murders are not unusual in a Garfield novel. In fact, his own particular use of the adventure story, varied and expansive as it is, involves exploring and indulging in melodrama, which allows, of course, for suspenseful plots and characters that undergo extreme states of feeling.

But while any Garfield novel uses all the conventional melodramatic devices, his sense of humor tempers, refines, and adds complexity, so his novels don't feel corny or staged. Like

Fielding, Garfield seems to embrace humanity in all its pettiness and smugness, and is appreciative of man's ingenuity. He is interested in exploring what we do to survive—and how, in the direst of circumstances, we are often deprived of the luxury of being moral, upright, and clean. While Garfield takes us through slums, onto pirate ships, into prisons, his touch is always lightened by humor, and therein lies his chief debt to Dickens. It is obvious that at least two of his novels draw their style and format from Dickens' work. *Smith* is as much like *Oliver Twist* and *Prisoners of September* like *A Tale of Two Cities* as they could be without being actual copies or parodies of those earlier works. But chiefly Dickens' pervasive comic sense of character is what Garfield borrows and makes his own. His characters explode with idiosyncratic verbal tics and gestures, which become their signatures, though the characters rarely lose their complexity.

So Garfield comes to adolescents as a particularly rich writer, and one who defies categories. . . . [Garfield's adventure stories] are romances—sea stories, picaresque adventures, historical novels—which confront the same problems that all the "relevant" adolescent novels hinge on: the quest for identity, coming to terms with one's roots and heritage, learning to distinguish between authenticity and artifice, and finding a place for oneself in the world. Yet the use of the 18th century . . . allows a fresh look at these essential themes. The reader is glued to his seat, much in the way 18th and 19th century novelists held their readers in suspense, while Garfield plunges into these issues. He feels compelled to write about the quest for identity because, as he says, "I have a passion for secrets and mystery. And the secret and mystery of another individual seems to me the only mystery one can unravel endlessly. . . ."

So while his readers can revel in the sheer joy of good story-telling, Garfield is one of the few writers of adolescent novels who doesn't cheat them by ending his responsibility with suspenseful narration. Nor does he simplify the world in an attempt to satisfy the adolescent impulse toward closure. In other words, he does not make the world sweeter, or the obstacles in his stories darker, uglier, more or less threatening than they are. In his warmth and humor he urges an acceptance of humanity and a tolerance of ambivalence which is unique to the world of adolescent fiction. And it is this tolerance that allows for an honest, substantial, and mature point of view. (pp. 44-6)

> *Roni Natov, " 'Not the Blackest of Villains . . . Not the Brightest of Saints': Humanism in Leon, Garfield's Adventure Novels," in* The Lion and the Unicorn, *Vol. 2, No. 2, Fall, 1978, pp. 44-71.*

PHILIP HOLLAND

Garfield's novels appeal to young readers. . . . All his work has a strong narrative line and his books are worlds of violent adventure. Theatricality and melodrama are part of their fabric. The hero's search is not only for his identity but also for moral certainties in the shifting sands of good and evil. The hero is usually an adolescent boy, bewildered by the duplicity of the adult world. He is a valuable point of identification for the young reader. The moral choices he has to make are presented not in terms of psychological analysis (until we come to *The Pleasure Garden*) but in terms of action and discussion which offer a high level of vicarious experience. Garfield's style also has a wide appeal; its level of complexity varies, and while it is never easy for any other than the literate

child the vocabulary is not particularly unusual or difficult. The imagery is strongly visual and colourful and he appreciates children's curiosity for detail. He will thread an idea or an image through a story so that it becomes a signpost of the plot, providing a thrill of recognition or anticipation. Such detail contributes to the vividness of his writing and often to its humour, for even in the grimmest situation—and "the stench of Newgate gaol" pervades almost all the novels—an ironic humour breaks through. (p. 159)

Garfield's style is his unique characteristic. His highly coloured imagery and extravagant descriptions appeal to children even though not everything may be immediately accessible. His books are worth rereading to explore further the pictures he paints, or the thematic use of imagery such as that of the sea in *Black Jack.* (p. 168)

Very occasionally the imagery is merely decorative but usually it is an organic part of the writing. I think, to use Eliot's idea, Garfield possesses "a mechanism of sensibility" which can devour experience and turn it into effortless imaginative expression. I have heard him say that his style is not the result of endless reworkings, but the natural mode of expression of his subject matter. His war service, his seafaring experiences, his scientific training, his medical knowledge are all part of his imaginative reservoir. Of his character Bostock in *Adelaide Harris* he writes: "He did not have the creative imagination that seizes on matters, apparently of little use and far apart, and instantly divines the link between them." Garfield does have this quality and his creative imagination is fertile. (p. 169)

[Garfield] is a master of mystery and a master of style. The latter is probably seen to best effect in the short stories, where he polishes words like diamonds. (p. 170)

Different writers have different aims, but Garfield's attempt to produce books for the family is a notable one. It is commonplace to find him compared in reviews to Dickens. His literary antecedents include Stevenson and Fielding, but certainly he brings Dickens to mind. He creates a similar sort of London, he enjoys the theatrical and melodramatic nature of events, he constructs a stong narrative, he attacks materialism, he hates the law—"red in tooth and clause" he writes in one story—he loves eccentric characters. In *The Prisoners of September* he has given us his *Tale of Two Cities* and in *Mr Corbett's Ghost* a story that stands comparison with *A Christmas Carol*. As Dickens did, he seems to be moving from reliance on narrative strength to a compassionate observation of the meaning of life for an individual. Like Dickens, I think he is capable of creating his own audience, for a taste for the early novels can lead any reader to explore the latest works. We already have a rich set of novels and stories and his work with Edward Blishen on the retelling of the Greek myths as continuous narrative or his "fictional history" in *Child O' War* suggests that he is a writer of whom we can entertain great expectations. (pp. 170-71)

> *Philip Holland, "Shades of the Prison House: The Fiction of Leon Garfield," in* Children's literature in education, *Vol. 9, No. 4, 1978, pp. 159-72.*

NICHOLAS TUCKER

[Leon Garfield] usually sets his novels in the eighteenth century, and in *Smith*—one of his most exciting stories—there is plenty that an immature imagination can immediately understand and sympathise with, such as a melodramatic villain and at the other extreme, a saintly philanthropist. In between these two, Smith—a likeable pickpocket—almost perishes, but eventually fully deserves his happy ending. There are also in this seemingly black and white morality tale, several massive coincidences, sympathetic weather that darkens in accordance with the threat of evil, and even scenery that sometimes provides its own commentary on things—the pathetic fallacy so often used by Dickens, and a technique especially meaningful to children whose own imagination may also, not so long ago, have been quite willing to encompass the idea that clocks could sometimes frown, and buildings pull hideous faces.

This seems so far to be the kind of explicit, undemanding melodrama that children can appreciate without ever having to stretch their imagination, but this would be to underrate Mr Garfield's considerable subtlety. The blind, philanthropic magistrate who befriends the young hero also shares a type of moral blindness that Smith eventually is forced to expose. Minor characters who seem one thing, sometimes change on better acquaintance. In Mr Garfield's later books, this 'role-drift' becomes more pronounced. Readers who are ready to move on from the oversimplified parcelling up of characters into neat packages labelled either 'good' or 'bad' will respond to this type of subtlety, where even the appalling highwayman in ***Black Jack*** ends by appearing as a pathetic victim. In another fine novel, ***Drummer Boy,*** an allegory of innocence and corruption is followed through in a way that will bypass any reader happy simply to follow a good adventure story. Once again, it describes a situation where shabby, compromised characters at the start of the story eventually prove more worthwhile than superficially attractive but more sinister figures. (pp. 151-52)

> *Nicholas Tucker, "Literature for Older Children (ages 11-14)," in his* The Child and the Book: A Psychological and Literary Exploration, *Cambridge University Press, 1981, pp. 144-189.*

SHEILA A. EGOFF

Because the major writers of historical fiction deal with serious and profound themes, they very rarely indulge in the light touch. There is one outstanding exception, Leon Garfield, whose works serve to remind us that the comic side of life persists, even amid portentous events. (p. 177)

The eighteenth century, which is Garfield's specialty, lends itself particularly well to his often larger-than-life approach. His novels revolve around swashbuckling highwaymen and captains; eccentric doctors, teachers, and lords; a gentle, mad girl, and a Lillith-like general's daughter. Through them move his young heroes on a journey from innocence to experience. Other than ***The Prisoners of September*** his novels are not, strictly speaking, historical fiction, since ***Jack Holborn, Smith, Black Jack, The Sound of Coaches*** are completely fictional. ***The Drummer Boy*** does open with a battle scene (one of the most magnificent descriptions in children's literature), but we know neither where, when nor why the battle has taken place and it does not matter.

But Garfield's details are not fictional. When, at the beginning of ***Black Jack*** we read of the metal tube that the criminal inserted down his throat to prevent the suffocation of the hangman's noose, we know the scene to be accurate. When, in ***The Sound of Coaches*** we learn of the tradition of naming a coachman by the road on which he traveled (Mr. Dover, because of the Dover Road), its historicity can be accepted

because Leon Garfield's name is on the title page. Whether he is describing an eighteenth-century asylum, Newgate Prison, or a sailing ship, the details are completely convincing.

They do much more than carry conviction, they create atmosphere and it is perhaps Garfield's ability to create atmosphere that has led many critics to reach for comparisons of his work with Dickens and Fielding. Atmosphere is of course indefinable, but it is easily sensed, especially when it is created with the remarkable swiftness and economy that Garfield displays. . . . When Garfield's atmosphere moves into the macabre, which it does frequently, the spine actually tingles, the hair rises on the head, and one looks to see if the doors are firmly locked and the curtains drawn. He has provided many unforgettable episodes. . . . (pp. 178-79)

Although Garfield's plots are of the kind that keeps the reader turning the pages in the best tradition of storytelling, deeper themes do underly his work. He treats life as it comes—which is more often rough and uneven than smooth—and he is not afraid to describe plainly that which is ugly and grotesque. Usually however, Garfield is not so direct and plain in his treatment of evil, or of good. For to him the two are intermingled or disguised. Perhaps the most frequent and important choice his protagonists have to make is that between good and evil when neither is all that clear. Slowly, subtly, they must learn to unmask apparent good as evil or apparent evil as good. (pp. 179-80)

At the same time, Garfield's overall optimistic view of life has given us some of the tenderest passages in children's literature. ***Black Jack*** presents a macabre plot of a hanged man revived, his kidnapping of Tolly, the orphan boy, and the hold-up of a coach from which an insane girl escapes. It is also the story of the moving relationship between Tolly and the defective girl, Belle. Belle has never seen the sea:

> "Tell me about the sea," she begged. . . .
> "Water, Belle—as far as the eye can see . . . "
> "What noise does it make?"
> "It sighs and whispers and slaps and sometimes roars."
> "What's under the sea, Tolly?"
> "Green darkness—like a great forest. Strange flowers and weeds and fish and sunken ships and treasures."

It is probably the same delight in paradox that accounts for Garfield's sharp eye for the vulnerability even of villainy. (p. 180)

Among the many other interesting features of Garfield's work, not the least noteworthy is his unusual willingness, for these days, at least, to depart from the conventional novel format. His "Apprentice Series" offers twelve (one for each month of the year) vignettes of something fewer than fifty pages each, and it is a very real treat to see how adeptly he makes the short narrative form work for him. The apprentices are young teenagers who are both literally and figuratively in the apprentice stages of their lives, involved in learning the secrets and powers of a craft. They are also all linked by a symbol, that of light, both physical light and the figurative light of enlightenment, and the young people themselves and those who become involved with them eventually "see the light." The progress of Garfield's apprentices is the reverse of Hogarth's "The Rake's Progress." His characters are not only searching for the truths their individual craft might yield, but they also are struggling toward maturity. In their "rites of passage" they are initiated into the Vanity Fair of the London street life with its colorful characters, painful truths, and sordid ironies. Eventually the apprentices win through to a revelation of the good and an unmasking of the tawdry.

On one level the stories are straightforward, exciting, and, at times, comic narratives, the apprentice rivalry in *The Enemy* being a particularly good example of the latter quality. There are as well other levels of meaning—highly symbolical, often allegorical—and these are sometimes elusive. Thus *The Lamplighter's Funeral* is radiant with imagery of light that balances and transcends the raucous, dangerous, brutally jostling and mean-spirited street life that lies at the core of the story. (pp. 180-81)

The motifs of light and dark, or friendship and love, not romantic love, but the divine love of compassion, forgiveness, and rebirth, are creatively varied and skillfully interwoven very much like the contrapuntal lines of an eighteenth-century fugue.

In *The Enemy* a natural, comic, boyish rivalry is the surface theme, but both "enemies" as in other books, come to acts of extraordinary generosity. *Mirror, Mirror* is replete with a wealth of imaginative, inventive metaphors in which the daughter of the master carver of mirror frames uses her mirrors to visit ghastly, ghoulish torments on the poor apprentice. But once again, there is Garfield's perennial wit and good humor to lighten and vary the tone. The result is a story that has a medieval flavor, an eighteenth-century equivalent of some of the wry, whimsical, and sentimental anecdotes of Chaucer or the amorous jests of Boccaccio.

In format the "Apprentice" books appear designed to attract young readers, age nine or ten. They are not only brief, they have large type, a spacious look, and are perfectly illustrated by either Antony Maitland or Faith Jaques. The stories also have been issued in a combined one-volume edition, but lack the illustrations. The latter edition is probably intended for adults and if so, this publishing venture makes great good sense: Garfield is, for child or adult, a great storyteller. (pp. 181-82)

[The tradition of retellings] was broken and most dramatically with the interpretation of Greek myths by Leon Garfield and Edward Blishen, coauthors of *The God Beneath the Sea* and *The Golden Shadow*.

They pull no punches; they are true to the passionate spirit of the myths and respectful to the maturity, intelligence, and curiosity of their readers.

Essentially, *The God Beneath the Sea* is the sage of creation and destruction in the cosmos. It is the story of desire and conflict among the pantheon of gods and their involvement with the smaller but more poignant affairs of the frail mortals who tenaciously hold to their brief lives. The structure of the book is balanced on the life of Hephaestus, the hideous but visionary artist-smith who creates great beauty in metal and jewels out of his ugliness, pain, and inspiration. (p. 211)

The first part of the book is filled with wonderful vivacious tales of lust and humor; of Zeus's great loves and ubiquitous progeny, Hera's monumental jealousy, and Hermes's zestful trickery. Waiting to be answered is the question, "the earth—the sweet green earth. To whom would it be given?" The tone of raw primitiveness changes to one of almost modern realism

when Prometheus creates his mortals to inherit the earth. He "shaped the clay into images of the immortal gods" and sent them to seek their inheritance on the earth. With the mortals come pain and death.

The novelistic structure and the narrative flow is less intricate in *The Golden Shadow,* which deals on a more human scale with the early mortal world. It is the domain of heroes, peasants, and storytellers, and its central protagonists are Heracles and the Homeric Storyteller, both human and mortal, as opposed to the divine central figures of *The God Beneath the Sea* in the gods Hephaestus, Hermes, and Prometheus. Nonetheless, there is a striking link between the two books in the presence of art and artifice—the artist-smith, Hephaestus, and the Homeric Storyteller.

There is a strong sense of time passing, of death and aging in this second book; the passing of mortal life as compared with the glorious eternal youth of the gods in *The God Beneath the Sea.* It is also more of a whole, although closer to the form of a picaresque novel than the first; this because of the presence of the Storyteller, a Homer-like wandering bard traveling throughout Greece, gathering legends, and searching for a revelation of the truth of the gods. (p. 212)

Many of the basic Greek myths are woven into the Storyteller's life through his search for the gods, especially the stories of Heracles. Both books give a sense of immediacy, as if the reader were actually witnessing the events, but hidden and watchful, like the mortal Sisyphus hiding in the wood near Corinth and spying through a "grass keyhole on a divine secret," observing the passion and conflict of the gods. These are not events of the dim and distant past; they have happened only a moment before.

Garfield and Blishen have used a warm, romantic, and poetic style that gives credence to the fact that they wrote it by oral creation, chanting to each other. Far more than any other version of the myths, these books do lend themselves to reading aloud. (pp. 212-13)

Sheila A. Egoff, "Historical Fiction," in her Thursday's Child: Trends and Patterns in Contemporary Children's Literature, *American Library Association, 1981, pp. 159-92.*

NEIL PHILIP

Like Rosemary Sutcliff, he has been much concerned with the search for identity. But where Sutcliff's characters battle against real threats, Garfield's flounder among shadows of mystery and intrigue, in a world in which nothing is what it seems, where to a blind Justice in *Smith* "devils and angels are all one", and tormented Mister Shaw in *The Drummer Boy* can exclaim, "I believe in God, sir; but I must believe in a devil, too . . . you understand . . . otherwise how could I endure it? But I do not always know which is which, sir . . . "

Garfield's virtues are clear; perhaps because that is so he has not always been fully valued for them. His books are exuberant, densely-plotted, robust, bravura performances. There is nothing anaemic or prissy about them, and nothing brutal. He is not afraid of romance, of sentiment, of adventure. He can deal with moral questions without becoming ponderous; he can provoke both laughter and tears.

He can also be simply provoking. His is a rich talent, which has sometimes betrayed him into self-parody; with increasing frequency over the years he has passed the point where manner becomes mannerism. In books such as *The Pleasure Garden* and *The Confidence Man* his extravagant rhetorical flourishes, his elaborate and ingenious metaphors began to seem hollow, as he became increasingly drawn to allegory rather than character. But his most recent novel, *John Diamond,* shows a return to the less florid style of *Smith.* The convolutions of plot and the allegory are still there, but kept under control, with a corresponding sharpening of language. When a knock at the door heralds "Mrs Branch with a bowl of timid soup", one adjective does the work of three.

Garfield is nothing if not a stagey writer, drawn to melodrama and farce. He is a showman, like the irrepressible actor-manager Thomas Treet in *Devil-in-the-Fog,* who has "produced the most remarkable stage-effects our age has known". Like Treet, he is an original.

Neil Philip, "Romance, Sentiment, Adventure," in The Times Educational Supplement, No. 3425, February 19, 1982, p. 23.

MARY WADSWORTH SUCHER

Rarely can a teacher find an author such as Leon Garfield whose works will provide, almost in their entirety, promising fare for lackadaisical male readers. His books appeal to girls as well, but they contain so much that appeals to active, identity-seeking males that this aspect must be stressed.

Much of Garfield's writing seems to result from his own active, varied life—his scientific study, his Army Medical Corps experience, his interest in the eighteenth century and Shakespearean drama, and his fondness for language, along with "*much* reading of a very *few* books." His highly visual, colorful writing makes one think of Fielding or even Stevenson, but he is most often compared to Dickens and Thackeray in his handling of characters and intricate plots and in his propensity to use a definite time and place (eighteenth century London) as the setting for most of his novels.

His intent is not to write children's books, but rather to write "that old-fashioned thing the family novel, accessible to the twelve-year-old and readable by his elders." In fact several of his stories, such as *The Ghost Downstairs* and *Mr. Corbett's Ghost,* can be read on several levels so that the younger readers may enjoy the supernatural and more experienced readers will sense the wish-fulfillment aspect of the tales. . . . From the first, the difficulty in distinguishing good from evil has been a recurrent theme in his novels.

Not a serious historical novelist such as Rosemary Sutcliff or Hester Burton, Garfield only worries about details "unusual enough to be noticed and remarked on," such as the earthquake, which becomes an integral part of the plot in *Black Jack.* Thus he does not dwell on the politics or social customs. . . .

The unmasking of what appears as good, but which is really evil, along with the theme of puzzled identity recur in nearly all of the novels. . . . (p. 71)

Garfield's propensity for piling image upon image, usually concluding with a surprise tongue-in-cheek ironical climax, provides unexpected humor even in the midst of tragedy, notably in *Smith.* His delightful humor may be seen in the unbelievably funny *Night of the Comet.* Garfield can be wryly amusing, for example *The Pleasure Garden* and *The Sound of Coaches,* but the humor is often found in asides that char-

acters indulge in, much as in older stage comedies, notably in *Devil-in-the-Fog.* Another Garfield strength can be found in descriptive passages which frequently employ intricate, sometimes fanciful figures often followed by the obvious, powerfully expressed. And, along with his sometimes outrageous similes and intricate plots, Garfield is a strong delineator of unsavory, often diabolical, characters, especially in *Black Jack, The Pleasure Garden,* and *Smith.*

Garfield's robust, rich vocabulary and intricate picaresque plots will fascinate good readers from the middle school through senior high. The psychological overtones of *The Pleasure Garden, The Drummer Boy,* and *The Prisoners of September* make them especially suitable for high school. In *The Pleasure Garden,* all classes of Londoners frequent the eighteenth century Mulberry Pleasure Garden, unconscious of the little urchins hidden in the trees gathering evidence for the owner's blackmail enterprise. One night a young man is murdered at the feet of a clergyman/magistrate who suppresses evidence and is almost ruined in the aftermath. Love is the saving grace, however, just as it is in *The Drummer Boy* (the story of a young soldier disillusioned by war) and in *The Prisoners of September* (the story of two idealistic young adults unprepared for the depravity of the French Revolution as experienced at the LaForce Prison in 1792). (pp. 71-2)

Rich in atmosphere, character, and style, with the gusto of a Dickens or a Sterne, Garfield's elaborate and witty tales are full of surprises, courage of survival, and hope for the future. (p. 72)

Mary Wadsworth Sucher, "Recommended: Leon Garfield," in English Journal, Vol. 72, No. 5, September, 1983, pp. 71-2.

DAVID REES

All Leon Garfield's books are set in the eighteenth or early nineteenth century, but he is not a historical novelist in the conventional sense. There are few signs in his stories of painstaking research or attention to period detail; references to important political events are rare; and there is not much attempt to reproduce the language of the period. Indeed, many of his characters in their speech use modern idioms and slang. Garfield himself says in his essay, 'Writing for childhood', that 'the eighteenth century—or my idea of it—is more a locality than a time. And in this curious locality I find that I can represent quite contemporary characters more vividly than I could otherwise.' The comment is interesting, because Garfield does manage to suggest to the reader that he or she is entering an invented, imaginary locale—which is the technique used by the writers of fantasy, rather than the method of the historical novelist.

Garfield's sources are literary rather than historical. He has often been called the children's Dickens or the children's Stevenson, but only his first book, *Jack Holborn*—a tale of adventure and piracy on the high seas, with, almost inevitably, treasure as an important motif—could truly be labelled Stevensonian. As first novels go, *Jack Holborn* is superior to many, and it shows immediately Garfield's greatest asset—a gift for exciting, action-packed narrative. Few contemporary writers of children's fiction can tell a story as well as Leon Garfield. He subsequently wrote more complex, more subtle books than *Jack Holborn,* which is marred a little by the author being too concerned with what is happening now rather than what is going to happen next; but it certainly keeps the reader turning the pages. The Stevenson influence is there not only in the setting, but in the characterisation and in the style. The ambiguous, amoral figure of Solomon Trumpet recalls Long John Silver; Jack Holborn himself is a latter-day Jim Hawkins (though his adolescent emotional changes are entirely his own). . . .

The major influence in Garfield's second novel, *Devil-in-the-fog,* and in much of his later work, is Dickens. Garfield's London with its pickpockets, blackmailers, murderers, thieves and loose women, its teeming working class, its lawyers and judges, the fog, the smells, the exploited innocent child or the engaging street urchin at the centre of the action, is Dickensian, even though this London is usually eighteenth rather than nineteenth century. The themes of *Smith, Devil-in-the-fog, John Diamond,* and *The December Rose,* with their documents and heirlooms promising wealth or property, owe a debt to *Bleak House, Great expectations* and *Our mutual friend,* as does that favourite Garfield figure, the foundling child searching for his origins. Garfield often writes like Dickens, imitating him quite closely at times:

> From which I received a distinct notion that heaven was filled with a golden profusion of hoists, that never broke, nor stuck, nor poked young Treets through stained-glass windows.

This is from *Devil-in-the-fog,* but it could have come out of the first chapter of *Great expectations:*

> I am indebted for a belief I religiously entertained that they had all been born on their backs with their hands in their trousers-pockets, and had never taken them out in this state of existence.

There are other influences too. Many of the characters in *The strange affair of Adelaide Harris* and its sequel, *Bostock and Harris,* with their eccentricities and their grotesque appearances and habits, derive more from Thomas Love Peacock than Dickens; and the anarchists and bomb-throwers, as well as the vignettes of low London life in *The December Rose* are reminiscent of Conrad, particularly the Conrad of *The secret agent.* The world of the Red Lion inn in *The sound of coaches* is the Farquhar of *The beaux' stratagem:* the landlord with his catch-phrase 'As they say in the north' is very similar to Farquhar's landlord with his repeated 'As the saying is'. Henrietta Boston in *The prisoners of September,* with her penchant for Gothic horror novels and her talent for playing the piano frequently and badly, is from Jane Austen—a mixture of Catherine Morland and Mary Bennet. There are echoes of Fielding—the blind justice in *Smith,* Mrs Coker in *The prisoners of September*—and the coffin on the table at the beginning of *Black Jack,* with the apparently dead man coming to life, is used by Synge in the opening of *The shadow of the glen.* Smith's escape from gaol, hidden under his sister's skirts, is from Gunter Grass's *The tin drum.* 'We lay like a dead ship upon a dead sea'—*Jack Holborn*—is Coleridge (*Kubla Khan*); and from the same novel—

> 'What manner of man is he?' I asked uneasily. 'A wery bad mannered man . . .'

—is Shakespeare (*Twelfth night*).

Other echoes, parallels, and references could be quoted. Some are undoubtedly subconscious—the residue in the mind of one man's study of literature—but many are deliberate: the devices Garfield uses to give his created worlds their authenticity. One is not accusing him of plagiarism, or pallid imitations of the real thing. He has a remarkable ability to transmute these bits of other authors into something that is wholly his own; his style is in fact highly individual, and, at its best, an excellent instrument for his purposes. Parody (even self-parody), irony, a kind of grotesque humour, and a fine eye for the ridiculous are its hallmarks. (p. 43)

Garfield, however, can write very badly at times. As with William Mayne, the critical adulation he has received has led to overproductiveness and some third-rate work—as well as some near-masterpieces. . . . When he is not writing well, his work suffers from cliché—'black as sin' is a favourite, 'melancholy as sin', 'the sinful smile of crocodiles'—and, when he is not sure of what he is doing, often at the denouement of the story, he can be unconvincing or hysterical. Or he will reach for an improbable coincidence to solve a problem. Even the otherwise excellent *Smith* and *Black Jack* falter at their climaxes. (p. 44)

Garfield's best work is to be found in *Smith* and *Black Jack,* both exciting adventure stories set, for the most part, in eighteenth-century London; in *The strange affair of Adelaide Harris* and *Bostock and Harris,* the events of which take place in Brighton and in which we move forward in time to the period of the Regency; and in *The sound of coaches* and *The prisoners of September,* larger, more complex books in theme and scope, set in the rural England of the eighteenth century. (pp. 44-5)

Smith is by far and away Garfield's best known and most popular book. . . . It is a rare thing: a favourite with children, parents, teachers—and critics. Beginning with a quite spectacular murder—'Smith was only twelve and, hangings apart, had seen no more than three men murdered in all his life'—its narrative continues at a tremendous pace, doing what *Jack Holborn* does not, making the reader more concerned about what is happening next than what is happening now. *Jack Holborn* had little other than narrative, but *Smith* has much more. There are convincing, vivid characters, particularly Smith himself—faulty, engaging, and multidimensional. Even such a small part as the highwayman, Lord Tom, seems real: apparently romantic and generous, but actually a squalid crook. There is marvellous atmosthere—the descriptions of London brought to a halt by heavy snow are magnificent; and the chase through the snowbound countryside not only recalls *Bleak House* but is every bit as good as its original. The scenes of happy family life contrast very effectively with the episodes concerning villains, thieves and murderers. The combination of realism and symbol works well—the child, Smith, leading the blind judge is not just part of the narrative, but it represents justice tempered by compassion, the way the law should (but doesn't) work. Smith *is* Mansfield's eyes, guiding him to the truth. There are nice ironical touches—'a great many petitions had been got up' to save a popular highwayman sentenced to death, but 'none had succeeded, and no one in his heart of hearts was truly sorry, for the death of a hero (even though he was a murderous ruffian) was a vastly romantic thing'; and some fine comic moments. . . .

Smith is a rich and colourful novel; the author seems to be thoroughly enjoying himself, portraying the surface textures of urban working-class life as well as its undercurrents, in a narrative and prose style of immense gusto. It certainly deserves its high reputation.

Black Jack occupies much the same world as *Smith*—the grimy, crowded streets of London—and it has an equally spectacular opening, in this case a man being hanged at Tyburn. But the story moves away from London into the countryside when the central character, Bartholomew (Tolly) Dorking, meets some itinerant fairground people. (Travelling entertainers are often found in Garfield's novels: they are, for instance, important characters in *Devil-in-the-fog* and *The sound of coaches.*) Tolly is very different from Smith, not at all ebullient and self-sufficient; he is a quiet, gentle boy, an innocent adrift in a world of crooks of all sorts, and it is only his inner integrity and his love for the mad girl, Belle, that allow him to survive. Adolescent love is a major theme in *Black Jack;* it is the only novel of Garfield's in which it is seen as a great strength, incapable of being exploited and corrupted. Some of the most attractive parts of the book deal with Tolly's and Belle's feelings for each other. But dominating the entire story is the nightmare figure of Black Jack, the huge and terrifying robber who cheated the gallows. Seen at first as an ogre, almost a malevolent giant from a fairy tale, he finally helps Tolly because he comes to respect the boy's love for Belle.

Two themes Garfield explores in almost every book are central to *Black Jack:* the person who is the opposite of what he appears to be, and the unforeseen consequences of a chance meeting. The two brothers in *Devil-in-the-fog,* for instance, are the complete reverse of what George Treet originally thinks; Captain von Stumpfel in *The confidence man* is a petty trickster, not a hero; and there is more to Black Jack than a terrifying footpad. His chance meeting with Tolly alters both their lives, eventually for the better. . . .

Like *Smith, Black Jack* has a powerful narrative that holds the reader's attention; it is only towards the end of the book, when the earthquake occurs, that it becomes a little unstuck—too much happens too quickly here, and some of it is improbable. And also like *Smith,* there is a host of well-drawn minor characters, particularly the fairground folk: the blackmailer, Hatch; the astrologer, Mrs Arbuthnot, who, Cassandra-like, can only predict gloom and doom; and the quack doctor, Carmody, who befriends Tolly—a character who is reworked as Dan Coventry, the phoney actor, in *The sound of coaches.* (He is himself a reworking of Mr Treet in *Devil-in-the-fog.*) The same world as *Smith:* but *Black Jack* is no stale repetition. It's a fine novel, which does many new and interesting things, not the least of which is Garfield showing a central character who develops and changes, who moves towards maturity.

The strange affair of Adelaide Harris and *Bostock and Harris* stand apart from the rest of Garfield's work, not only because they are set in another period, but because their intentions, mood, structure and characterisation are very different. These are wholly comic novels, 'comedies of humour' in the Ben Jonson sense, in which the characters act out a kind of set-piece dance, with the dancing master (the author) directing and manipulating all the movements. . . .

The whole [plot] is treated as a huge joke, a sort of *danse macabre;* the manoeuvrings of the plot show Garfield at his most skilful and ingenious, and his treatment of the characters displays a gift for pleasing and apt caricature. Bostock and Harris are a delight. (p. 45)

Harris is . . . shifty, selfish, and only marginally more intelligent than Bostock, but Bostock has the redeeming virtues of innocence and honesty. They make a devastating pair, unwittingly causing a whole town to end up in a state of absolute chaos. The minor characters are no less deftly caricatured. . . .

Garfield's choice of Brighton during the Regency for the setting means a total departure from his usual 'world'. There is no squalor, filth, and overcrowding, and there are few working-class people, for the Prince Regent's Brighton was middle class—hypocrisy, gentility, vanity, keeping up appearances, and a false sense of honour are the vices displayed. Highwaymen, swindlers, thieves and murderers are noticeably absent. The same is true of the book's sequel, *Bostock and Harris,* which is a lesser achievement. *The strange affair of Adelaide Harris* would be hard to follow: it is a comic masterpiece, Garfield's finest novel. . . .

The sound of coaches has a more leisurely narrative than is usually found in Garfield's work, and the eighteenth century as observed here has a less grubby, more kindly feel to it than in the other novels, particularly in the opening chapters, which deal with the birth and childhood of Sam Chichester. Looking for a Dickensian parallel, one might say this is the world of *Pickwick papers,* rosier than the grim battleground of *Our mutual friend.* The goodness and generosity of people is emphasised; there is room at the inn when the pregnant woman is giving birth. As Sam grows up and wonders about his origins, we are shown many pleasant aspects of country life at this time, and there are some sharp observations of human behaviour. Sam's adopted parents, the dour old coachman and his devoted wife, are real, credible people—there is not a hint in this book of caricature. The subtleties of understanding and misunderstanding between parents and children are very well done. . . .

The sound of coaches is Garfield's most realistic novel, a straightforward account of a search for origins and identity, growing up, and solving the problem (or at least coming to terms with it) of what have I been put on this earth for? Sam's solution is exchanging a coachman's life for a career on the stage, his relationship with Jenny, and a reconciliation with his adopted father, who finally comes to see that actors do not necessarily inhabit 'a world of fraudulent dreams and pretence', that they aren't all 'the ever-willing bedfellows of lying, thieving and the crooked way'. (Though this is the life of Sam's real father, the hypocritical, drunken actor, Dan Coventry.) This is an impressive book: warm, unhysterical, convincing.

The prisoners of September is the only major work of Garfield's that has at its centre important political events that affect the lives and fates of the characters; it is therefore the only book of his that could be called a historical novel in the conventional sense of the term. The period is the French Revolution, and the events that dominate the plot are the September Massacres of 1792 in Paris. In this story Garfield makes audacious use of two utterly threadbare clichés of the historical novel—Lewis, the dashing young hero, saves a beautiful countess from death in a runaway coach; and the same young man rescues a family of French aristocrats from the Parisian mob and brings them to England. The clichés are brilliantly turned on their heads: the beautiful countess is a thief, and the aristocrats were not put in jail for political reasons, but because they are forgers. (p. 46)

[Despite] its wit, *The prisoners of September* is a sombre, tragic book. Lewis's comfortable background and obvious sex appeal do not help him at all. He is a victim of his own decency and a second-rate mind; drifting against his will into a marriage with the forger's daughter, he realises he is saddled for ever with his criminal in-laws, and he can do nothing about it. Love, once again, is seen as a weakness, exploited by the selfish and the greedy; 'amor' doesn't 'vincit omnia'—it drags people down into a morass of morally unacceptable actions.

This book has a glittering surface—the upper middle-class world of southern England—but it peels off that surface and reveals sham, nastiness and disillusion. Nothing is ever what it seems: as in *The pleasure garden* and *The strange affair of Adelaide Harris,* there is little about human nature that Garfield seems to admire. . . . Once again, the consequences of a single chance act become more far-reaching than anyone could expect. Innocent bystanders and mere acquaintances get caught up in the web of somebody else's life: all the characters in this novel are 'prisoners of September', affected by the massacres they had no direct, or even indirect, connection with. (pp. 46-7)

Leon Garfield finds it hard not to be an adult novelist. Books like *The strange affair of Adelaide Harris, The sound of coaches* and *The prisoners of September* stretch the young reader to his or her limits; though *Smith* and *Black Jack* remain very much within a child's concerns and grasp. At his best, when the wit and the storyline are at their most rumbustious, he is a great writer. His significant contribution to contemporary children's and young adult fiction is that he has given a new lease of life to the historical novel, and created a fresh interest in what was fast becoming an unpopular genre. (p. 47)

> *David Rees, "Blood, Thunder, Muck and Bullets: The Novels of Leon Garfield," in* The School Librarian, *Vol. 36, No. 2, May, 1988, pp. 43-7.*

JACK HOLBORN (1964)

[*Jack Holborn*] is not easy reading, for the plot is involved, and there are slight lacunae in its unfolding, as if the book had been cut and certain connecting links lost. Yet the brilliantly written episodes, of which the appearances of mad Taplow's "ghost" are among the most graphic, remain in one's mind, alight with promise for Mr. Garfield's future.

The foundling, Jack, ignorant of his birth except that he was left as a baby on the doorstep of St. Bride's in the City, runs away to sea, and becomes, through no fault of his own, a member of a pirate crew. There is no romanticizing of piracy here. Jack's shipmates, the gin-sodden cook, Pobjoy, treacherous Taplow, and mildewed Mister Morris, the sailing-master, are sharply drawn as the scoundrels they are, and play out their parts against a lurid background of storm and shipwreck. Disaster dogs the few survivors of the Charming Molly, and Mr. Garfield plays a fresh and original tune on an old theme: that ill-gotten gain brings a curse with it.

A book for rather older children, it requires some patience, even rereading in places, for the author does not always treat his plot expertly. He seems unable to control his main themes through the tortuous paths of shipwreck, slavery and mistaken identity. A firmer editorial hand might have clarified the issues. Nonetheless, a vividly painted rogue's gallery and a robust style that owes something to Smollett—a statement intended as a compliment—make Mr. Garfield an author worth watching.

"Period Settings: Civil War to Twentieth Century," in The Times Literary Supplement, *No. 3274, November 26, 1964, p. 1072.*

Jack Holborn is a picaresque novel, set in the mid-eighteenth century, with a brisk foundling hero, an enigmatic hero/villain with a past, pirates and storms at sea, African marshes and slave-trains, and a trial-scene to tie up all the threads. Fate and personality equally determine what happens in this superb story, which is written in a splendidly eccentric, richly modulated prose. . . . *Jack Holborn* is [a book] nobody should miss.

> *Margery Fisher, in a review of "Jack Holborn," in* Growing Point, *Vol. 3, No. 6, December, 1964, p. 423.*

Here is an excellent story of piracy and adventure. . . . (p. 98)

The book is considerably more than just another well-spun yarn. Mr. Garfield succeeds in creating an 'Ancient Mariner' aura throughout the story. The style has the true flavour of the period; the characters are clear and realistic and there is a really excellent mystery surrounding the pirate captain and Jack's real identity. This is the best piece of junior fiction I have encountered this year. (p. 101)

> *James Falkner, in a review of "Jack Holborn," in* The School Librarian and School Library Review, *Vol. 13, No. 1, March, 1965, pp. 98, 101.*

There is a type of book which operates both on an adult and a juvenile level. I am not thinking of books like *Robinson Crusoe* or *Gulliver's Travels,* which probe deeply into the human condition and to which the child may bring his own uncluttered and innocent responses, taking from the surface of the work an enjoyable fiction comprehensible within the limits of his own world. Nor do I have in mind those books . . . which have been written with professional competence for a specific market, but which hold within them a range of interpretation that may seriously activate and perhaps even tax the critical and intellectual faculties of an intelligent adult. I am thinking of a third and rarer type of book, one which may well have been written in ignorance of the readership it will eventually find, and which operates successfully on the adult and the juvenile level simultaneously.

I suggest as examples of this an acknowledged classic, Robert Louis Stevenson's *Treasure Island.* . . . and a modern story of adventure on the sea set in a similar historical period, Leon Garfield's *Jack Holborn.* . . . The former was produced when a writer of genius descended into the realm of juvenile fiction. Stevenson's integrity and devotion to his craft would not allow him to produce anything that was not the best he could write. The latter was written when an author whose talent in the field of juvenile fiction was shortly to be recognized set out to write an adult novel. Converging upon the dual level from opposite directions they appeal powerfully to the boy in man as well as the man in boy.

Superficially the two books appear to have a good deal in common. They both set out to tell a story crisply, clearly and with excitement. Involvement begins on the first page and our function as readers 'is to lay by our judgment', as Stevenson himself reminded Henry James, 'to be submerged by the tale as by a billow'. It is the familiar appeal of the romance, a willing suspension of all that may impede our enjoyment of the adventure and the journey. Thus the story is set in both cases in a world far removed from the one with which we are familiar, but a world, nonetheless, with whose outlines and general shape we feel a kind of distant blood-relationship. The pirates, the sea and the island in both cases spring at us from a dimmed past; they are something we half recognize and cannot fully forget. (pp. 113-14)

And as with setting, so with character. The people who are our companions on the voyage will be clearly enough delineated in their outlines for us to know who they are and what they stand for, but not so densely probed or explored that they will obscure the free flow of the story. 'Character', wrote Stevenson, in *A Humble Remonstrance,* 'to the boy is a closed book. For him a pirate is a beard, a pair of wide trousers, and a liberal complement of pistols.' The pirates who capture the Charming Molly in Chapter One of *Jack Holborn* swarm suddenly out of the dark, yelling and cursing into the night air and discharging muskets and pistols as they come. The details which give us our impression of Billy Bones on the first page of *Treasure Island* are vivid and shrewdly selected, but they add up to the child's idea of the standard pirate—the character is simply better done rather than different in kind from its predecessors. The narrator, in both cases, is adequate for the role he has to play but is seldom in danger of developing his own personality beyond the orthodox limits of the genre. And the assorted collection of squires, doctors, Trumpets and Morrises slide like greased counters around the set, every now and again erupting into a spasm of activity which rivets our interest, but never holding it at the expense of the progress of the story.

In the progress of the story, skilfully and effectively managed in both cases, one can observe an interesting variant of technique. In *Treasure Island,* as Mr. G. S. Fraser has pointed out in his afterword to the Signet edition, the heightened moments often occur, paradoxically, at moments when the action is arrested. The death of Pew, Jim in the apple barrel, Israel Hands up the mast—the situation is lingered over, the tension deliberately drawn out, and both are resolved violently and suddenly as breaking point is reached. With Garfield, by contrast, there seems a definite effort to keep things continuously on the boil, to move as quickly as possible through the many hazards of the plot to the dramatic climax of the story. The impression is of a series of scenes in pictures, almost like a succession of colour slides, and with the same heightened colour that one often associates with such slides. Noises are added, the picture is set moving, and at the resolution of the scene the next slide is already in place. With both writers the overwhelming consideration is the exciting flow of the action and there is clearly more than one way of achieving this.

The additional dimension in *Treasure Island* occurs as the character of Long John Silver develops and extends beyond the boundaries normally trodden by the villains of juvenile fiction. (pp. 114-15)

The devil-as-angel, villain-as-hero, good-man-as-bad-man strain is in the mainstream of nineteenth century romantic fiction and with psychological refinements has been at the centre of all sorts of twentieth century writing. It was also at the centre of Stevenson's own personal background and psychological make-up. (p. 115)

It gets into *Treasure Island* because Stevenson is *unconsciously* exploring the ambiguity of man as a moral animal. . . . As a literary man and storyteller, sensible of what was hap-

pening in his art, and innately fascinated by the 'doppelganger' theme anyway, Stevenson could not help but let it into any work in which his imaginative faculties achieved full play—even a boys' adventure story.

Garfield's *Jack Holborn* is an interesting comparison, for it approaches the territory we have been discussing from the other side. It was conceived as an adult book and the intention was to deal with problems of good and evil through the medium of an exciting and well told tale. The 'doppelganger' theme, treated here through the good and evil captains of the Charming Molly, is at the centre of the complicated plot and everything else in the story revolves around it. Indeed, the fact that there are two captains, though the reader may have guessed it earlier, is not explicitly revealed until the contrived and vivid courtroom scene which is the climax of the book. There is a strong element of the detective story in the tale and a marked difference of voice in the manner of telling it.

The basic register of Jack in narrating the tale is that of the unaffected raconteur, eager to give a straightforward account of the extraordinary adventure that has befallen him, relaxed in the knowledge that the events themselves are sufficient to enthral all who are willing to be held. But nothing less than the melodramatic mode will do as the story gets under way and climaxes succeed one another with bewildering rapidity. The professional storyteller takes over, and the rhetorical devices of the raconteur, the measured delivery of key sentences, the pause for effect, the writer's equivalent of the distended eyeball and the stabbing forefinger, make themselves felt through the prose.

Sometimes the lyrical is attempted, as in the description of Jack's diamond in the bartering sequences. Sometimes the horrible is vividly represented; one remembers, perhaps, the extended treatment of Mr. Trumpet's unfortunate experience in the swamp. And sometimes the lyrical and the horrible are fused in a single description, suggesting again how good and evil may be aspects of the same thing. The river, for instance, which leads the weary party through the weird experiences of the middle section of the book, runs 'directly out of the sun to wind its uncanny way through the dark of the world'. At one point 'it had sparkled like a necklace', while later it is revealed as 'a creeping hearse of dead branches, and rotted vegetation, endlessly slit by the sinful smile of crocodiles'. That last image, straight out of the nursery, is an excellent example of the way in which a child's range of reference is used throughout this section to create a deep sense of adult evil. In this way, and sometimes in the simple but effective juxtaposition of opposites, as in the river's 'silver treachery', the prose reflects the main intention. The voice is not, perhaps, as personal, as controlled, or as consistent as Stevenson's, but it knows clearly enough what it is trying to say, and it is trying to say something very similar.

Similar to what? Not, surprisingly enough, the child's adventure story, *Treasure Island,* which fashioned the literary tradition in which it can now clearly be seen to lie and which its author had not previously read. But *The Master of Ballantrae,* that adult novel of the struggle between a powerful, evil man and a weak, good man, which Garfield admired and which provided him with the idea of a book in which the weak rather than the evil go to the wall. To this he added another major theme taken from the nineteenth century romances—Melville in *Moby Dick* particularly, and Victor Hugo in a number of his novels—the idea of nature as an active, evil force.

The attempt to bring this out permeates the book. In addition to the river there is the extraordinary prominence given to the dark storm, which follows the ship throughout its voyage and is invariably described as a tiger. When the party lands on the African coast the image is again there to meet them as the trees crouch like an enormous animal. And the courtroom scene itself, the climax of the book, is carefully and quite deliberately presented as a kind of storm. Not all of this is, I think, successful, nor is it as obvious in the present version as its author might like to think. But in the original draft, twice as long and written as an adult book, the intention was clear enough. It is hardly surprising that the work carries with it to its different market at least some of the qualities which characterized the intention of the original. (pp. 115-17)

> *Clive Pemberton, "Aspects of 'Treasure Island' and 'Jack Holborn'," in* The Use of English, *Vol. 23, No. 2, Winter, 1971, pp. 113-17.*

DEVIL-IN-THE-FOG (1966)

Devil-in-the-Fog is 18th-century—not history, but luscious melodrama, complete with wicked baronet, missing heir, convenient recognition scar, the lot. And much more than the usual lot, because Mr Garfield has humour too and ingenuity in mixing old ingredients to produce something fresh. This is first-person narrative, with showers of exclamation-marks, a proliferation of parentheses, and enough lines of dots to demarcate the parish boundaries on an ordnance map. But the warmth and gusto are genuine enough, the characters swagger, the drama is riveting.

> *Geoffrey Trease, "Golden Age," in* New Statesman, *Vol. 72, November 11, 1966, p. 708.*

[*Devil-in-the-Fog* is] doubly disappointing after the author's *Jack Holborn.* Mr. Garfield's earthy, fantastic style, so at home in an exotic pirate setting, here seems altogether too clever. It was a mistake to make the young travelling actor George recount his own adventures. He speaks in character ("Oh God, I whispered, Why? Why?") and his eighteenth-century grammar, even if accurate, is difficult to read. When the mysterious stranger who overshadows the lives of the Treets pays his last visit and George takes up his apparently rightful position as son and heir to Sir John Dexter, strange characters crowd confusingly in. . . . The identity of the wicked Principal remains a fairly good secret until the end. There are humorous moments, like the seven little Treets perched on the stocks where their father sits, but that gentleman, reminiscent of both Vincent Crummles and Wilkins Micawber, scarcely merits George's extravagant adulation. The characters of eighteenth-century high life are unreal, and we feel little involvement until the end, when George finds himself back among those who love him for his own sake.

> *"Troubled Times," in* The Times Literary Supplement, *No. 3378, November 24, 1966, p. 1078.*

The dead little gentleman—what a title that would have been for this strange compound of mystery, violence and Dickensian humour. Did the infant George Dexter die in truth or was he really farmed out among the numerous progeny of Mr. Treet the itinerant actor? . . . The theme is implicit in the first lines ('My father is put in the stocks again! Oh, the injustice of it! My father is a genius—as are all of we Treets') as it is in the last ('For the dead little gentleman sleeps in the

churchyard close by his father . . .). Father and son, character inherited or acquired—the theme is carried like a refrain through the story. . . .

Artistry is a matter of painstaking work relaxed, finally, in personal ease. One of Leon Garfield's devices, implied in his title, is to sustain the image of fog all through the book. In the abstract, for everyone is in a fog about the meaning of events. In the everyday life of the Treets, since their claim to respect rests on the Lucifer's Smoke and Devil's Fire they are so adept at producing. And in event after event—the November fog that heralds the arrival of the Stranger; the mists of Sussex 'like clumps of wool from a giant's sheep' through which the Treet's waggon rolls towards the Hall; the mist-hung thicket where George ventures to meet his disreputable and perhaps murderous uncle. To notice this is a pleasure for the reader, but not an effort; every part of the book is natural and inevitable. Yet what a strange, almost tormented prose it is, really—a mass of asterisks and dots and exclamation marks, of whimsical detail and Joycean phrase (the footman has 'conspiracy-shaped eyes,' and the fumes of Mr. Treet's smoke jostle 'like a crowd at a wedding or a hanging'). It is all as closely suited to the late eighteenth century period as the drawings in which Antony Maitland suggests sinister mystery in high places. A strange book, more than life-size and yet life-like for the feelings and attitudes of the characters: a book to leave firmly out of categories and accept thankfully for what it is—a masterpiece.

> *Margery Fisher, in a review of "Devil-in-the-Fog," in* Growing Point, *Vol. 5, No. 6, December, 1966, p. 809.*

SMITH (1967)

Mr. Garfield is a difficult writer to praise highly—yet. His gift for language is remarkable and he can evoke a scene so vividly that you see, feel, hear and smell it, but his first novel, *Jack Holborn,* was a broken-backed story, and *Smith,* his third, suffers equally from Mr. Garfield's episodic treatment and the unlikeliness of his plot. The author's knowledge of the underworld of eighteenth-century London enables him to paint a splendidly convincing backcloth. He invents a set of characters to people his stage. They must, of course, talk and act, and so they do, in a series of episodes. Moreover, Mr. Garfield likes to give his characters typical catch-phrases, so that they are recognizable by what they say rather than by what they are. . . .

Mr. Garfield is fascinated by the mixture of romantic bravado and unutterable squalor that characterized eighteenth-century low life, but is he moved by those who lived in it? The alleys, taverns and rat-ridden dens that lay under the shadow of Newgate and the hangman's noose are brilliantly evoked, but the misfortunes of Smith, the waif whose very life hangs on the mysterious document he stole from a murdered man, hardly ever stir the feelings. Characters are drawn in bold, Dickensian strokes, and a wry humour pervades the writing. Indeed, there is so much to admire that one is impatient with the weakness of the plot, especially its sentimental ending.

Mr. Garfield can take his readers with him into the stench and filth of footpad London, across the snowbound heath where the pistols of the high toby, Lord Tom, flashed "blue daylight", into the sunless swarming warren of Newgate prison, and the cellar of the rickety old Red Lion tavern, but he cannot make them believe in the convoluted plot or involve them in the fortunes of those who partake in it. This is, perhaps, a basic weakness of many picaresque novels.

"Dark Doings," in The Times Literary Supplement, *No. 3404, May 25, 1967, p. 446.*

[*Smith*] crosses the line into brilliance.

Smith himself, a pickpocket by trade, 'a sooty spirit of the violent and ramshackle Town', has so far survived . . . to reach the age of 12. But can this luck hold out? For after he has taken—something—from a troubled-looking old gentleman, he sees his victim murdered and searched by two men in brown. His find is a document: but Smith cannot read. Nor can his two handsome older sisters, Miss Bridget and Miss Fanny, stitching away at *their* trade, the altering for hangman Mr Jones of the clothes of each day's clients. A blind magistrate and his daughter take a fancy to the urchin and start to teach him how to read. But the brown men move again. The tale leaps on in a series of dazzling scenes—a session in Newgate where Smith is held for the old man's murder; an eerie flight through a kind of ventilator; the reading at last of the script; the tomb with the black stone angel to which it leads; the extraordinary climax. Leon Garfield speeds with shrewd or crackling or poignant wit through the London of dark thieves' kitchen and gentleman's mansion, in and out of St Paul's, St Andrew's and the Old Bailey. To follow is an electrifying experience. (pp. 732-33)

Naomi Lewis, "Newgate Pastoral," in New Statesman, *Vol. 73, May 26, 1967, pp. 732-33.*

With this, his third novel, Mr. Garfield has not only established himself as a writer of distinction but also shown that the historical novel for the young can find its idealism in the humble as well as the highly-born, its insights in unromantic settings as well as in heroic deeds. . . . The plot is full of gripping incidents; Newgate gaol and a churchyard on Prickler's Hill are part of the scenery. . . . But the most distinctive features of the book are the dialogue and the prose, spare, unsentimental both, yet haunting in cadence and memorable as Dickens, no less.

Margaret Meek, in a review of "Smith," in The School Librarian and School Library Review, *Vol. 15, No. 2, July, 1967, p. 222.*

In Leon Garfield's *Smith,* the vigour, pace, and tearing high spirits of the prose suggest an instrument of strikingly inclusive powers. The description of Smith's first bath shows the bite and movement of which Garfield is capable:

> At last he crouched, naked as a charred twig, quivering and twitching as if the air was full of tickling feathers.
>
> 'Ready,' he said, in a low, uneasy voice, and the four footmen set to work.
>
> Two men held him in the tub; one scrubbed, and one acted as ladleman. This last task was on account of the water having been dosed with sulphur, and it consisted in spooning off Smith's livestock as it rushed to the surface in a speckled throng.
>
> From beginning to end, the washing of Smith took close upon three hours, with the scullery so filled with sulphurous steam that the footmen's misted faces grew red as the copper saucepans that hung

like midnight suns on the scullery's streaming walls. (pp. 52-3)

The trouble is that Garfield rests at the strictly external level of this example; it makes his novel a marvellous read, but he can only sustain the simple line and momentum of thrilling suspense. In spite of the strikingness of the image of Smith rescuing a blind Justice of the Peace, the allegory becomes a simple, necessary platitude purporting to justify a traditional treasure hunt for a Will, a Prodigal Son, and a casket of coins. Garfield is very good, there is no doubt: his imagining of Newgate is intensely picturesque, with the sentimentality of heartiness without which no child ever discovered a proper moral sympathy. What he takes from Victorian melodrama however is just the colour, and such novel-writing lends itself to the colour-charting which passes for academic criticism of the tourist office kind—'colour' and 'movement' are what Dickens was and is most praised for. (p. 301)

Fred Inglis, "Resolution and Independence," in his The Promise of Happiness: Value and Meaning in Children's Fiction, *Cambridge University Press, 1981, pp. 292-311.*

In a notable group of high adventures, historically based, *Smith* seems to me to exemplify especially the unique qualities of the Garfield package. Here is the idiosyncratic style, exclamatory and shot with bizarre images; the typically light-and-darkness atmosphere in an eighteenth-century London accurately in period but adapted to the author's needs; cliché characters and action jolted into new, exciting life in a complex, mystifying plot; men and women drawn with Dickensian sharpness and drollery; macabre happenings mitigated by compassion and moral questioning. There is something of *The Beggars' Opera* in this book. . . . Involved in an affair of murder and treachery through a document filched from a dead man (which he cannot read), Smith is whirled from one danger to another. There are new lessons for him to add to those of an active street life—not only how to read but also what value to put on justice, on gratitude, on pity. How can we know good from evil? How far can the law fairly represent human behaviour? These and other questions, which recur in Garfield's work, are integrated in a superbly organized narrative, entirely satisfying in concrete detail, startling in sardonic humour, rich in the quirks and quiddities of individuals. Children around ten should relish this as a rattling good story: I hope they will find time to go back to its layered pages later to discover more of its secrets. (pp. 57-8)

Margery Fisher, in a review of "Smith," in her Classics for Children & Young People, *Thimble Press, 1986, pp. 57-8.*

BLACK JACK (1968)

[*Black Jack*] is not for the squeamish. It opens gruesomely with a public hanging and a 'Tyburn widow' who claims strangers' corpses to sell for dissection. Garfield piles on the horrors with macabre gusto, body-snatching, a private madhouse, the lot, his rich poetic diction once more demonstrating that in this genre he can write his competitors under the table.

Geoffrey Trease, "History, Mystery," in New Statesman, *Vol. 76, No. 1964, November 1, 1968, p. 594.*

Leon Garfield's first book, *Jack Holborn,* marked him out at once as an historical novelist with an individual style. Mr. Garfield really knows the eighteenth-century scene and his background is impressively authentic. What gives this knowledge wings and makes him so readable is his command of a vivid, fast-moving prose. But there is something more than style and pace to his new novel. The progress from *Jack Holborn* to *Black Jack* shows that as Mr. Garfield's appetite for his chosen century grows, especially for the macabre elements in it, so does his skill in telling his tale, while his interest has shifted beyond the picaresque rogues' gallery of his previous books. Now he gives us a compassionate treatment of the emotions of his chief characters that brings real depth to his new novel. . . .

Mr. Garfield's prose style has always had distinction, but in this novel it is employed in service to a far better story than he has yet written. There is no disparagement intended in pointing out that it owes much of its vividness to a certain verbal device employed by Dickens, a constant cross-reference from material objects to human life. . . .

There is a richness about this book, both in physical detail and in human feeling, that makes it a notable contribution to the genre of the historical novel.

> *"Macabre but Moving," in* The Times Literary Supplement, *No. 3484, December 5, 1968, p. 1369.*

One has observed Leon Garfield's distinctive qualities develop through his four eighteenth-century novels; a mastery of gripping openings, the rich Dickensian characterization, the nightmare atmosphere of impending doom and threatening mystery which inform the narrative, the wryly humorous and vivid imagery. To these, in *Black Jack* he has added the moving portrayal of a human relationship, tender and demanding, as Tolly seeks to win Belle back from her world of fear and madness and unravel the mystery which surrounds her. Although based on fear, the boy's relationship with the Rasputin-like Jack is also complex and, towards the end, affecting as they develop a need for each other. . . .

A magnificent novel.

> *Gordon Parsons, in a review of "Black Jack," in* The School Librarian and School Library Review, *Vol. 17, No. 1, March, 1969, p. 84.*

MR. CORBETT'S GHOST AND OTHER STORIES (1969)

Leon Garfield has quickly established himself by general acclamation as one of the most gifted and individual writers for the older child. He has staked out a special corner for himself; one is tempted to say 'a graveyard plot', so macabre is his fancy, but that description would belie the vitality, the exuberant gusto, with which he claps his skeletal grip upon the bristling nape and sends his delicious frissons down the spine.

Those who seek absorption, and dislike short-story collections, need not be put off by the title of his new book, *Mister Corbett's Ghost and other stories,* for there are only three stories, and two are of novella length. Both have Mr Garfield's favourite period and setting, the seamier side of the 18th century. One is about the nightmare errand of a London apothecary's apprentice on New Year's Eve, and the other is laid in a convict-ship bound for the American Colonies. Both, and the short story between them, about a Dutch artist caught up in a sea-battle with the English, are related in Mr

Garfield's characteristic style, by turns humorous and horrific, earthy and fantastical, scintillant with new-minted phrases.

The style is superb. Of the content I am not so sure. It poses the question that always crops up at parents' meetings on children's reading tastes. Is horror undesirable, or does it provide a healthy release? Do we *need* to be frightened? In an epoch of continuous anxiety, sensed by the children as their elders sit listening to the news, is it not perhaps a relief to surrender to one vicarious terror that ends swiftly and is seen to be comfortingly imaginary when the book is closed? I rather incline to this homoeopathic dose of horror, but I wish now that Mr Garfield, having given us four books of this genre, would emerge from the shadow of the gallows and exercise his splendid powers in a wider historical field.

> *Geoffrey Trease, "Gore of Yore," in* New Statesman, *Vol. 77, No. 1992, May 16, 1969, p. 700.*

There are three separate stories here. In the title story the author is in his spine-chilling vein, and there is more of the wholly supernatural than in his previous books. Benjamin, an apothecary's apprentice, is driven by his master's peevish and provoking treatment to wish him dead. A sinister customer calls and grants him his wish, at a price. The dead man's ghost, however, transparent but visible to all, attaches itself to the boy, who then realizes that the price is impossibly high, and he spends a night of stark terror before the mysterious stranger is persuaded to restore the situation. Mr Garfield compels increasing admiration with each new work. He has already been mentioned in review in the same breath as Dickens, no less; in this story there is something of the quality of the Ibsen of *Peer Gynt.* The plot of the second story, *Vaarlem and Tripp,* is a slight one; the achievement here is a virtuoso performance in character drawing.

Romance is introduced into the third story, *The Simpleton.* The cruelty of mutineers at sea and the tenderness of the relationship between boy and girl are intensified and enhanced by being shown through the eyes of the simple, though not simple-minded, central character. Strongly recommended.

> *Robert Bell, in a review of "Mr. Corbett's Ghost and Other Stories," in* The School Librarian, *Vol. 17, No. 2, June, 1969, p. 195.*

The separation of mind and feeling is the theme of *Mr. Corbett's ghost,* the first of three stories which confirm the pattern of Leon Garfield's language and thought. He has never rendered atmosphere with as much power as he does in the scenes of his first story, making Hampstead Heath an expanding place of terror and possession. The bitter struggle of a young apprentice to free himself from a cruel master is shown, literally, on the frontiers of the human spirit. Is the old man who lends Benjamin the power of death human or superhuman or is he an emanation of Benjamin's own thoughts? Does the miserable apothecary appear to his former victim as a ghost with independent life or as something Benjamin himself has created, out of fear and compassion? To his chill and mysterious detail Leon Garfield adds a wry and mature understanding of the indignities of human nature. So finely is his story worked out that we are hardly aware that strong form and verbal dexterity have done their part in carrying the force of its theme. In a lighter vein but still with a sombre irony, *Vaarlem and Tripp* shows a glimpse of cowardice and genius in the setting of a seventeenth century sea battle. At sea again, in *The simpleton,* a boy transported through the trickery of evil associates finds himself in the company of jailbirds and unexpectedly protected by the worst of them. A pretty passenger further complicates his situation until the wheel of fortune brings him fortune and revenge in a way that provokes laughter and thought alike in the reader. The paradoxes and quips of this tale alone would be enough to mark Leon Garfield as a craftsman of the first rank; his serious comment on human beings is never allowed to extrude from a literary form which is part and parcel of it.

> *Margery Fisher, in a review of "Mr. Corbett's Ghost and Other Stories," in* Growing Point, *Vol. 8, No. 3, September, 1969, p. 1374.*

THE BOY AND THE MONKEY (1969)

Charming and sad are suitable adjectives for this slight tale of an orphaned boy of the mid-eighteenth century who culls a precarious livelihood by selling his melancholy pet monkey to gullible rich folk and later selling the proceeds of the creature's pilfering in the houses to which he is temporarily admitted. It is inevitable that he is caught, suffers the rigours of a harsh criminal law, rigours which are, however, relatively mitigated through the fascination which the monkey exercises on court and accuser. Indeed, the last third of the tale is heavy with an unusual kind of suspense which helps to make the story feel a good deal longer than thickness and format suggest. [Trevor Ridley's] illustrations, in black and white as much as in colour, make for a delightful gift book which could be re-read with continuing pleasure.

> *A review of "The Boy and the Monkey," in* The Junior Bookshelf, *Vol. 33, No. 6, December, 1969, p. 385.*

The Boy and the Monkey is the most original of the four [Long Ago Children's Books published by Heinemann], and carries the hallmark of his now recognizable prose style which is such a pleasure to read. This tale would have to be given to older children in the age group [seven to nine]. As always, Mr. Garfield makes no concessions. The trial scene will undoubtedly make demands on young readers, and in a series of this kind the author might perhaps, without watering down his words, have spared children too many crabbed legal terms.

> *"Long-ago Children," in* The Times Literary Supplement, *No. 3536, December 4, 1969, p. 1390.*

Written as one of a series of books intended for readers 7-9 years old, the story seems unsuitable for them because of the difficulty of the language and some of the concepts. It also imputes intention (at the level of human thought) to an animal. . . . The book is too slight for the reader old enough to comprehend it; it is strong only in the distinctive style of writing and Garfield's usual convincing evocation of the period.

> *Zena Sutherland, in a review of "The Boy and the Monkey," in* Bulletin of the Center for Children's Books, *Vol. 24, No. 1, September, 1970, p. 8.*

THE DRUMMER BOY (1969)

This is a book about illusions, not specifically the illusions of youth, for although the novel's hero is a young drummer boy, one of the most powerfully drawn characters, Mister Shaw,

is fat and middle-aged, but he has his illusions, too. The book is also about coming to terms with reality, but without the tarnish of cynicism or the bitterness of despair. It begins with a military engagement. The regiments advance up the hill in a blaze of scarlet, drummed by Charlie Samson. Just as his drum "has caught the rhythm of their hearts", so Leon Garfield's golden prose catches the brief excitement and splendour of the occasion. But disaster swiftly overtakes the army, and it becomes plain within the first few pages that Mr. Garfield has thrust his young hero face to face with the last reality, death. From that confrontation, Charlie goes on to learn something of the painful realities of life. At the end, illusions are stripped away, and the characters whom we have accompanied to the beat of Mr. Garfield's drum leave our minds for the ordinary day-to-day reality that all of us have to live.

This may be a misconception of the author's intentions. This is a book that could be read at several different levels. On the surface, it is an account of an appalling massacre during, presumably, the Napoleonic wars. The drummer boy survives unhurt, and so do a group of seedy fellows who have prudently hung back when their comrades advanced. Among them is a surgeon, Mister Shaw, and in a set piece of macabre which Mr. Garfield always does well, we see this unsavoury specimen of humanity poking his way from corpse to corpse, extracting teeth to fill a couple of bags that hang at his waist. All the drummer boy brings back from the field of carnage is a letter that he has taken from the hand of a supposedly dead officer, a farewell written to his sweetheart. The letter is directed to Sophia Lawrence, in Bruton Street, and Sophia is the daughter of General Lawrence by whose orders the attack was made, and upon whose conscience lies the death of 10,000 men.

At this point one questions why Leon Garfield must, it seems almost wilfully, strain the credulity of his readers. Ten thousand is a huge force to be drummed into battle by, apparently, *one* drummer boy. It is also an incredible number to be ambushed by enemies hiding in what the author himself describes as "a small wood". Furthermore, we are asked to believe that all but two of those who marched up the hill into the ambush perished within minutes. This is not the only incident in the book that seems unnecessarily puzzling, but it is the most important, for upon it hangs the story. It would be unfair to give away more of the plot, which each reader must unravel for himself, but genuine admiration for the writer's work should not blind one to what often seems a weakness in Mr. Garfield's novels—the handling of the plot. The wide range of characters and incidents are sometimes tied into such knots that only a melodramatic solution can be found, and in some cases it seems so unnecessary. But when complaint has been duly registered for the tortuous and unlikely turn of the plot, one must emphatically declare that there is so much to enjoy, so must first-class humorous writing, so much to stir the heart and sometimes move it deeply, that the reader is left the richer for having read the novel.

> *"At the Sound of the Drum," in* The Times Literary Supplement, *No. 3555, April 16, 1970, p. 411.*

Leon Garfield's imagination is disciplined so that the surprises and bizarre events in his stories are properly related to the whole. He makes it seem natural, and yet astonishing, that Charlie Samson the drummer boy, the "golden lad" of the regiment, should be the link between the General who gave orders (or said he did) in anticipation of ambush, his son-in-law who disastrously failed to carry them out and the young soldier whose remarkably unheroic death will deprive the General's daughter of life and love—unless Charlie is prepared to stand substitute. The handful of survivors of the slaughter, relying more than they realise on Charlie's innocent optimism, find their way from the battlefield of France to a port where English smugglers adopt them into their band. From a headquarters in the New Forest Charlie and an odd companion, fat, shrewd Mister Shaw the surgeon, make their way to London and experience the shock of Sophia's vampire beauty. What is heroism? What is love? How can a mere boy, trained to lead with the sound of his drum, learn to work out his own orders for life? Perhaps none of Leon Garfield's parables of innocence tarnished has been quite as moving or as sharply considered as this one. In his quick, pointed sentences he uses visual images to establish a mood or a scene or to make a point about character; the whole book is imbued with the red and gold of destruction so finely blended on Antony Maitland's dust-jacket. It is most particularly an artistic whole, this book, an enormously stimulating and touching one. It will not teach children historical fact but will open the past for them.

Margery Fisher, in a review of "The Drummer Boy,"
in Growing Point, *Vol. 9, No. 1, May, 1970, pp.*
1534-35.

Karl Kraus said: "There are two kinds of writers, those who are and those who aren't. With the first, content and form belong together like soul and body; with the second, they match each other like body and clothes." Leon Garfield in ***The Drummer Boy*** has become one of "those who are". It is no more a children's book than *Gulliver's Travels* is a travel book; but the fact that it had to be prepared for the children's market may be the reason why it is so perfect a work of art: enforcing compression of complex ideas within the accepted length of a children's novel, and enforcing exclusion of all that may not have been central to them. (p. 47)

[The] landscape of the book is, as in Lawrence, a real landscape, and a landscape of the inner world. (pp. 47-8)

The book is full of real objects that are the indirect, universalized expression of feelings which have analogous resemblance to them.

Each character is welded to one such object, objects often emotionally reinforced by their colour. With Charlie this object is, of course, his white-faced drum, the symbol of all his ideals. As he leads his regiment into battle, the prose mimes splendidly the forward movement of the zealous soldiers and the drum-beats: "The drúmmer bóy is théir gólden lád, and he's cáught the rhythm óf their heárts." All too soon afterwards, the prose again mimes in heavy stresses the miserable aftermath: "slów and heávy, he was thúndering oút the Fúneral Retréat for the glóry of the fállen in the grass." Charlie's military illusions are shattered, but he, like his drum, emerges from battle with a whole skin, and he gratefully recovers his drum. The next time Charlie nearly faces death, this time from water, the drum recovers him; the sailors throw it into the sea after him; it floats; he catches it "in full embrace" and it "sustains him". It also sustains Sophia, who has not lost her military illusions; to sustain her, Charlie has to compromise his own golden integrity by telling lies; the Retreat he beats in the London streets is for money, and for his own fall. At the end, in the Forest, when the ignominious survivors of the French battle finally part and say their farewells, Charlie beats a last defiant Advance into life. He beats

so hard he splits the drumskin. "He wept for his broken drum; he wept for his dream of Sophia Lawrence, and for the drums of all such as he; he wept for the ten thousand scarlet men who slept on the hillside and would dream no more." This is as Ralph weeps at the end of *Lord of the Flies* "for the end of innocence, the darkness of man's heart, and the fall through the air of his true, wise friend, called Piggy". But Charlie still has his true, wise friend, called Charity. She was never impressed by the drum which so thrilled Sophia; her first suggestion was that Charlie should sell it to a tinker for a shilling. When Charlie drums through his long vigil outside Sophia's house, Charity the maid tells him roundly "to give over that grisly row". Finally, she agrees to give the drum houseroom as a vegetable basket; so Charlie himself retains only the fading shell of his own ideals. The drum was empty before anyway.

Charity, of course, is charity; the name of this kind of love is mentioned several times in the book before she is. She is characterized simply by the often-mentioned white petticoat which keeps "dancing out of her gown as if it was putting its tongue out at the world". Sophia, the General's daughter, is characterized by her blood-red gown, which, as she stands at a window of the house, gives the impression "of a drop of blood clinging to the house's face". In the room, her gown "caught the sunlight and turned to blood". She is a vampire figure, living on other blood. When she is dying, Charlie observes a spot of bright red on her bosom; but it moves, and flies away, for it is only a *ladybird* "mocking blood". This image goes back to the book's opening, where in the battle that so thrills Sophia "grown men crash . . . bearing crimson medals on their scarlet chests" and sombrely lie wearing their scarlet "with a difference", like the soldiers of Wilfred Owen's *The Send-Off*. . . . (pp. 48-50)

Sophia is, as her name suggests, sophisticated; a town version of Hardy's Eustacia Vye, pining for emotion. . . . "To be loved to madness" is Eustacia's great desire; "love was to her the one cordial that could drive away the eating loneliness of her days." Eustacia's "high gods" were William the Conqueror, Strafford, and Napoleon Bonaparte. Sophia's gods would not be much different. By the time Eustacia had consumed Clym Yeobright, the native, who returned with so many fine ideals, he is stripped of them and reduced to the belief that "instead of men aiming to advance in life with glory they should calculate how to retreat out of it without shame". That other returned native, Charlie Samson, is similarly diminished by his service to Sophia; Charlie's only ambition at the end is "to undo what he has done, and leave the world without the stain of having lived in it".

Mister Shaw accurately diagnoses Sophia's complaint: "she sits in her little room at the top of the house quite shut away, feeding . . . feeding. . . . The father feeds her—and she feeds him. She feeds him on vanity; and he feeds her on death, endless, endless, death." Charlie's battle story, and the lie that her lover, James Digby, died bravely, nourishes her; on the third day of his lovelorn vigil outside her house, Charlie is said to be "fading". When he finally enters the house again, Sophia reproaches him for growing so pale, especially as she herself seems to be gaining in strength. "You fade while I bloom. It should not be so, drummer boy." This is exactly the situation of the male innocent in Blake's *Mental Traveller*. . . . And, as in Blake, the Male revives as the Female loses her strength. . . . Owing to Mister Shaw's frenzied, caring determination to make him see the truth of things, Sophia's spell is broken, and Charlie sees fear and hatred in Sophia's serpent eyes. Sophia says on her grimy deathbed: "Remember how we talked of my blossoming while you faded? Now it's changed about." (pp. 50-2)

All the imagery in the book is functional, never merely decorative. We are told, for example, that "the gathering clouds of the General's fall" will destroy Sophia; but nearly thirty pages before that, the author says: "it was the presence of Sophia Lawrence that brooded over the house like an ominous cloud." She is the cloud, the cause of her father's ruin and of her own; we are only permitted to see this through the linking metaphors, which are much more dark and powerful than finite statements.

Much of the imagery is "black", but set against this there is assertion of love in the sense of charity. The most eloquent assertion of charity is not made by Charity, but by Mister Shaw: "Oh God, Charlie—do you know what love is? It ain't just the spitting flicker of green wood catching. It's a mighty weapon, Charlie! It's the defender of the faith—it's the only thing we still have on our side! Even my talent, Charlie, only exists because of love!" (p. 54)

The human conflicts in the book are of great intensity, reminiscent even of Blake and Hardy. The recurrent images compress and universalize the human drama: birds, clouds, drum, flowers, teeth, wind and woods; these are reinforced by colour motifs: gold, silver, black, white and red. Never are the metaphors forced, and there is no moment when objects become awkwardly something inward and subjective; for their outward form and their inward meaning co-exist with no conflict, fusing into a perfect work of art. The body and the soul of the book are one.

Such a fusion is reached by nothing schematic, but by the imagination; the book answers perfectly Coleridge's definition of the imagination: "that reconciling and mediatory power, which incorporating the reason in images of the sense, and organizing (as it were) the flux of the senses by the permanent and self-circling energies of the reason, gives birth to a system of symbols, harmonious in themselves and consubstantial with the truths of which they are the conductors." (p. 55)

Richard Camp, "Garfield's Golden Net," in Signal, *No. 5, May, 1971, pp. 47-55.*

THE GOD BENEATH THE SEA (with Edward Blishen, 1970)

The pity of it. Like Sisyphus, whose story occupies no less than three chapters of this book, the authors sweat purple words as they roll their new version of the Greek myths by inches up the ascent, and what happens? The stone gets heavier the further they push it, only to roll back to the bottom, taking Messrs. Blishen and Garfield with it. It is difficult not to be influenced by the cloudy rhetoric of this book. Put plainly then, Edward Blishen and Leon Garfield conceived the idea of retelling a selection of Greek myths "not as a collection of separate tales but as a continuous narrative", written in "the literary voice of our time" (quoted from the Afterword). With them on the journey went the artist Charles Keeping. His contribution is magnificent. . . . From this book, it is Keeping's interpretation of the "enormous violent energy" of the Greek myths that will be remembered.

In contrast to the spare yet flowing line of the drawings, the text is lush, meandering and self-indulgent. It is larded with those lazy adjectives, "mighty", "terrible", "lovely", and weighed down under laborious similes. Simile was the stock-in-trade of the great classical poets, from Virgil himself to Milton and Pope. Similes suit a leisured book, but they have their dangers. Metaphor is cleaner, swifter, harder-hitting. The opening sentences of the book set the pace. Nearly fifty words containing two extended similes are used to describe a pinpoint of light moving across the sky. A further fifty lines of print follow to tell us that the infant Hephaestus, hurled out of Olympus, has arrived in the ocean grotto of Thetis and Eurynome. This opening is used—undoubtedly an excellent device in itself—to allow the book to start dramatically. What has gone before is then related to Hephaestus by his guardian goddesses. He learns of Chaos, of the rise and fall of the Titans, of mad Cronus and the rule of Zeus.

An attempt to "humanize" these primitive myths only ends in weakening their impact. The story of Demeter and Persephone, for instance, is reduced in power by anthropomorphism. . . .

In the story of Cronus and later of Prometheus, something of the grandeur of these myths does come through, even if only fitfully, and this increases one's bitter disappointment in the work as a whole. It could have been so splendid. At first, Keeping's awe-inspiring picture of Cronus swallowing his child dominates a slack text, but suddenly, when Cronus is forced to disgorge his children, the literary rope tautens. In a terse paragraph, the authors describe how the mad king "spewed out the fiery inhabitation of his belly" and "stared in dread at what he'd brought forth. They rose before him like columns of fire: the children he had consumed". This is true Garfield horror, as the death of the first man is told with the tenderness of the author who created "the poor thing" in ***Black Jack.*** We are genuinely moved as our first mortal ancestor is carried over the Styx, sadly questioning his escort, Hermes, "Why? Why?" But the authors cannot sustain the pace of the tension. The over-writing has become chronic, and it is only just to lay some of the blame upon an editor who did not see how urgently the book needed honing down, who did not notice upon page after page the plethora of empty superlatives. "Zeus", we read, "was overcome by the largeness of his gestures. The words are ominous for the reader. If this is "the literary voice of our time", God help us.

"Stones not Bread," in The Times Literary Supplement, *No. 3583, October 30, 1970, p. 1254.*

There have been many retellings of Greek myths for children but this interweaving of about twenty of them must be among the best. It is difficult to add authentic language and atmosphere to such old and familiar stories. These authors have succeeded.

Victorian moralizing dullness was more concentrated on the ancient Greeks, and on what children should be taught from them, than on almost anything else. This dullness is monumentalized in masses of poetry and literature for children. Very few writers have been able to touch, let alone release, the real life sealed up in those old shapes. The joint authors of this book deliberately set out to crack the Victorian plaster, and the result may be a surprise to some people. These stories are, after all, primitive revelations, the life they dramatize is not a little demonic. (p. 66)

Greek mythology presents a working anatomy of our psychic life in a very complete and profound way. In this sense, it is as useful to our knowledge of ourselves as a knowledge of physical anatomy is to a physician. It is more useful, in that it is a living thing, it enriches our sense of ourselves with genuine additions, new openings and recognitions. It is a whole system of keys and passwords and introductions to energies, and relationships between energies, within ourselves. As Plato suggested, it is the highest and most natural form of education for young children.

For such reasons, it is quite important that these myths are kept in readable form, and it is for such reasons—if I read their *Afterword* rightly—that Leon Garfield and Edward Blishen applied themselves and put such energy and imagination into this book.

Beginning with the birth of Hephaestus, they follow a developing series of about twenty stories through the war with the Titans, the creation of the main gods and of men, down to Hera's unsuccessful attempt to dethrone Zeus. These goings on—usually so cloudy and familiar and abstract—are made vividly new, interesting, often exciting. The authors obviously enjoyed the job greatly. Their zest sweeps you along. It is a real feat, to make everything sound so first hand. These are in fact genuine imaginative retellings—the dramatic urgency, the casual invention of many beautiful details, the characterization, the striking flashes of language, the hectic impressionistic scenes, are just what you get in very good retellings of folktales by practised traditional narrators. Everything jumps to life in front of your eyes. Some moments are really wonderfully visualized. The authors have stripped away the pseudo-classical draperies and produced an intense, highly coloured, primitive atmosphere. We are reading about the elemental gods of tribes just awakening—with their dreams fresh—from barbarism and animal unconsciousness. Frequently, they read like Norse myths, or like some African myths—with richer, more suggestive vistas. (pp. 66-7)

It will be a good thing if the authors can be persuaded to make another collection as shapely and vivid as this one. (p. 67)

> *Ted Hughes, in a review of "The God Beneath the Sea," in* Children's literature in education, *No. 3, November, 1970, pp. 66-7.*

With so many books published annually, and so little space available to a critic, it seems extravagant to pay attention to rubbish, but in this case there may be a lesson to be won from the experience. **The God Beneath the Sea** is very bad. It is almost impossible to read, let alone assess. . . .

Leon Garfield and Edward Blishen have fallen into the trap they tried to avoid. The prose is overblown Victoriana, 'fine' writing at its worst, cliché-ridden to the point of satire, falsely poetic, groaning with imagery and, among such a grandiloquent mess, intrusively colloquial at times.

Worst of all, the authors are so coy in their efforts to be 'frank' about sexuality that only the cumulative absurdity saves them from prurience: '. . . and in a white passion of wings, [he] quenched his restless heat'. 'The Titan's daughter was already quick with child'. 'Her time was at hand'. 'Her gown was torn, her hair awry and everything about her proclaimed her ruin.' All that is missing is, 'Afterwards, they slept.'

It's necessary to quote, because destructive criticism is cheap and easy, and the authors must speak for themselves—which

they do at length in an Afterword that is embarrassing in its hubris:

> . . . those re-tellings that now have most currency among the young form a haphazard sequence of tall tales often related in a manner which arises from certain conventions of translation from Greek poetry, and have little in them of the literary voice of our own time. We wondered if it might be possible to discover some new style of telling these stories—a language freed in some important respects from those conventions.

A statement such as that makes the book the more deplorable: to have been aware of what was wrong, and to have written a pastiche of all that was worst.

Some justification of form, if not of language, might have been pleaded if the book were an introduction to Greek cosmogony; but throughout there are stage asides that are meaningless if no background knowledge is to be assumed in the child reader. . . . (p. 606)

The text of **The God Beneath the Sea** demonstrates what is dead in our feeling for Classical myth. But if that were all, there would be no justification for wasting energy on the book, except to warn readers from being conned into buying it on the strength of the authors' prestigious names. The trouble is Charles Keeping and his illustrations. It's unbelievable that these clear statements are his reaction to, or have anything in common with, the fudge that surrounds them. They are a singular vision of what Classical myth must have been. They are what happens when great gifts are put at the service of the subject. . . .

If you want to see the survival of Greek mythology justified, buy **The God Beneath the Sea,** discard the text, take Charles Keeping's drawings, and frame them. (p. 607)

> *Alan Garner, "The Death of Myth," in* New Statesman, *Vol. 80, No. 2068, November 6, 1970, pp. 606-07.*

[Mr. Garfield and Mr. Blishen] have been unable to escape from a net of tradition as tight as that of Hephaestus. It is true that they have successfully exorcised the didactic treatment of the Gods (a kind of laundry-list approach supplementary to the compilation of classical cribs) but they have not fulfilled their aim of retelling these tales 'with the literary voice of our own time'. Throughout the book there is a straining after theatrical effect which is very wearing on the reader's nerves and the piling up of attendant clichés is too often punctuated by coy periphrases (the 'tender moans that dissolve into sighs' like any romantic magazine story) or just plain bathos ('Pan, the maker of panic'—which sounds like a television advertisement).

The authors' reaction to the size of these myths and the lushness of their prose has something in it reminiscent of Kingsley, but without his grace and his sense of total construction. Whereas Kingsley, though, elected to recount classical adventure stories, Mr. Garfield and Mr. Blishen have turned to the more difficult theme of the creation myths. It was brave of them to seek a means to unite these disparate tales of the birth of the gods into a single narrative, but again, the very intractability of the material has defeated them. In the first section on 'The making of the Gods' there is both too much diversity and too much sameness, and in the final section 'Gods and men' the book loses momentum among a series of very tenuously related stories (Deucalion, Demeter, Autolycus, Sisyphus). Only in the central section 'The making of men' does it really spring to life in a way that approximates to the authors' intentions. The linking of the stories of Prometheus and Pandora, the subtle dramatic interplay between Gods, Titans and men, is developed with strength and irony—modern narrative techniques in the service of ancient lore. (p. 22)

Brian W. Alderson, in a review of "The God Beneath the Sea," in Children's Book Review, *Vol. I, No. 1, February, 1971, pp. 21-2.*

[This] long and detailed book quivers with excitement. Its language is like a mosaic of fiery, precious jewels; and its interwoven plots are brilliantly handled. Beginning with the creation of the world, the book advances swiftly to the creation of the gods and then to the creation of man. The cast of characters is enormous, yet each god takes on a distinct personality. Nothing is omitted here, whether it be the agony of the bound Prometheus or the tragic fate of crippled Hephaestus or the wild lusts of Zeus. The making of mankind from a few handfuls of clay is perhaps the most moving part of the story, as the gods decide to limit him before his journey on earth has even begun. The death of the first pitiful man, the unleashing upon the world of evil and sickness by Pandora—all these episodes touch the heart quite strangely. They are only myths, yet they seem to be a total dream-history of the world. Authors Garfield and Blishen have written a strong, sensual and complicated book for adolescents, who are of course the very people that will appreciate it most.

Barbara Wersba, "Tales of Mortals and Immortals," in The New York Times Book Review, *May 2, 1971, p. 46.*

THE STRANGE AFFAIR OF ADELAIDE HARRIS (1971)

What is a children's book? What is a young adult? What pigeon-hole is big enough for Garfield? The answers to these questions must depend finally on each reader's discretion. Certainly this is a book for all to read—all, that is, from a reasonably sophisticated eleven years upwards, for an intricate plot, a devastating mock-heroic tone demand some such starting point of age. As for the top limit, this is a comedy, a superb comedy whose slapstick, irony and farce may be readily accepted by adults on its own terms. All the same, there is one respect at least in which this book is within the particular reach of young people; to use Blishen's phrase, there really is 'a child's eye in the centre'.

Imbroglio is the only word for the swift, bewilderingly intricate plot. It concerns the disappearance of Adelaide, infant daughter of Dr. and Mrs. Harris, and the far reaching effects of this disappearance on several households in Regency Brighton, including Dr. Bunnion's Academy, the Poorhouse, and the pub where the sinister detective Mr. Raven lurks spider-like, spinning webs entirely un-spider-like in their contorted absurdity. The original agents of the imbroglio are two schoolboys. Mr. Brett their schoolmaster, watching them with trepidation from the front of the class, decides 'Bostock was the larger of the two, but Harris was the deadlier. Though Bostock had caused more destruction and would, most likely, end on the gallows, Mr. Brett believed Harris to be his evil genius'. The ridiculous affair of Adelaide could not have happened if the boys had not possessed the appalling,

ruthless innocence of their years. Mr. Brett has been outlining to the class the Greek way of exposing female infants and this has become confused in Harris's mind with the legend of Romulus and Remus. Suppose they expose his baby sister on the Downs? Surely a vixen will come by to suckle her. No sooner said than done—but the excited boys, lurking nearby, see not a vixen but a pretty girl, Tizzy Alexander, come to Adelaide's rescue. And so it all begins. (p. 1817)

What I want to stress is that though this is a mature and extremely cultivated book, with a humour as sharp as a scalpel and as entertaining as the Marx Brothers, it is all the time subtly keyed to the boys. The animal passions evinced by Ralph Bunnion and the egregious Sir Walter, the monstrous drunkenness of Mrs. Bonney, are hilarious rather than sordid partly because we see them through the eyes of the two boys, naturally coarse and self-centred, who find the grown-ups splendid if inexplicable fun to watch. Even when the boys are not present their attitude still colours the story. When you have into the bargain a mock-heroic style worthy of *Tom Jones* that mitigates near-seduction and greed and stupidity just through ribaldry, you have a book which can be called 'for the young' or 'for the general reader' with equal truth.

Certainly Leon Garfield's talent in word-spinning and word-choosing are here exercised to the full. The book must be read slowly and often for the full richness of its flavour to be appreciated, and for the last ramification of the cunning plot to be properly noted. I doubt whether we shall see such a shrewd comedy for many years. (pp. 1817-18)

Margery Fisher, in a review of "The Strange Affair of Adelaide Harris," in Growing Point, *Vol. 10, No. 5, November, 1971, pp. 1817-18.*

Intrigued delight takes hold of one with the very first sentence of Leon Garfield's **The Strange Affair of Adelaide Harris** and never lets go till the hapless plottings of those old friends Bostock and Harris, having tangled themselves into a positive cat's cradle of complication, pull finally clear. It is a fourfold delight, deriving as much from the invention which can place at all the string-pulling vantage points such a variety of entertaining characters as from the author's dry comments on their thoughts and motives; as much from the ingenuity that twitches them round Brighton and its countryside in a dance of such fascinating intricacy as from the never-failing brilliance of Mr Garfield's style. Lighter and more pointed than ever, now deliciously witty too, it is a constant joy. . . . This new story gives the impression of being a contemporary engraving, first exquisitely drawn and then coloured vividly by hand.

Just as one can pore over a print of Cruikshank to find a new twist of expression or an unexpected aside of action, so here one can turn again and again from the musty, fly-droning classroom where Mr Brett intones about classic heroes to the chalky hollows of the downs where Bostock and Harris attempt to follow their example, from Tizzy walking out there in yellow muslin to the sprawling Ralph, measuring his length on the sward as he lunges after her, spoiling both handsome nose and embroidered waistcoat in the process and setting in motion the affair of honour which so embroils everyone connected with Dr Bunnion's Academy. . . .

The whole book sparkles with richness and to try and quote from it would be useless, for in searching for one felicity another yet more delightful would appear and so one would never stop.

Yet—and in spite of all these superlatives there is still a reservation, faint as a breath of wind across the downs, but persistent nevertheless—in the very way that one praises is implicit a faint regret. One talks of period prints rather than actuality, of characters that are skilfully manipulated rather than moving with their own life; one seems to see the whole story through a bioscope, or as though it were a picture in a frame and the characters at one remove. This new story of Leon Garfield's touches most delectably the fancy but not, as his earlier stories so notably have done, the heart. Perhaps it isn't meant to; after the white-hot intensity of *The Drummer Boy* he may well have needed the relief of a change, but one hopes that the change may be only temporary.

> *"High Comedy," in* The Times Literary Supplement, *No. 3640, December 3, 1971, p. 1509.*

It is Bostock and Harris who are responsible for 'the affair', they (or at least Harris) having decided to expose Harris's sister Adelaide on the downs above Brighton in the hopes that she will be adopted by a wolf. This decision sets in train a sequence of events of extraordinary complexity, their relationship to real life being a fragile one, but their existence for the sake of Mr. Garfield's art being amply justified. Casting aside the elements of romantic drama which characterised such books as *Jack Holborn* and *Black Jack,* and turning his back on the pretensions of *The Drummer Boy,* he has allowed full play to the ingenuity and wit that are also present in those books.

It is impossible to chart the convolutions of the story. . . . What can be singled out is the sureness of the comedy: the descriptions (Mrs. Bunnion asleep 'like a stately ship rising and falling at anchor'), the characterisation, even of the walk-on parts (poor Adam, the apostate monk from Basingstoke, who was too wet to burn) and a farcical cross-talk that is at times reminiscent of Christopher Fry. The book has its flaws—some of the jokes are repetitious, and there is superfluous hat tipping towards our newly-acquired freedom of expression in 'children's literature'—but it is a fresh and original addition to that rather rare species: the comic novel.

> *Brian W. Alderson, in a review of "The Strange Affair of Adelaide Harris," in* Children's Book Review, *Vol. II, No. 1, February, 1972, p. 14.*

CHILD O' WAR: THE TRUE STORY OF A BOY SAILOR IN NELSON'S NAVY (with David Proctor, 1972)

[Sir John Theophilus Lee] is portrayed in Leon Garfield's study in 'afternoon light' as an ingratiating nonentity. . . . His one substantial claim on the regard of posterity, apart from the memoir around which *Child O' War* is built, issues from a judiciously negotiated contract for the supply of lemon-juice to the navy.

A pretty slender target, you may think, for Mr. Garfield's bubble-pricking broadsides. But Lee's is by no means the only character to be raked, for little good is said of any of the actors in the revolutionary drama. Callous heads are hacked broadcast from fat, bemedalled bodies on both sides of the Channel; all politicians are pompous fools, or worse; only the First Consul himself is allowed—true to the multiple standards of our own time—to escape his due share of invective. Well, of course we all know that war is a rude game played by less elevated minds—but what would Mr. Garfield and his

able annotator, David Proctor, have done about Napoleon? Batter him into submission with adjectives, perhaps?

> *J. Allan Morrison, in a review of "Child O' War: The True Story of a Boy Sailor in Nelson's Navy," in* Children's Book Review, *Vol. II, No. 3, June, 1972, p. 86.*

[*Child O' War*] brilliantly presents excerpts from the memoirs of Sir T. Lee, a very young midshipman—he enlisted at the age of five—who served through the Napoleonic wars. It is [Leon Garfield's and David Proctor's] triumph that they have turned what was an endlessly boring document into a compassionate and witty short book which should do more to illustrate to the young what horror lies behind the brave front of war than all the diatribes contrived by moralists and preachers. (p. 758)

> *Catherine Storr, "The Spice of Life," in* New Statesman, *Vol. 83, No. 2150, June 2, 1972, pp. 758-59.*

Sir John Theophilus Lee, the youngest boy—at the age of five and a half—ever to join His Majesty's Navy . . . is shown to us not only as a snobbish old man reminiscing but through the eyes of his own children watching him; the stark facts of a British sailor's life and the peerless actions they fought in are shown in a fuzz of extemporization, through receding archways of fretwork, as it were.

Though Leon Garfield's inventive re-creation of the Victorian scene is as ingenious as ever, though, even at several removes and through the pen of Sir T. Lee, the clear facts of the sea battles compel their own lucid prose, the two do not mix; it is as though someone had spun a cocoon of candy floss round a piece of steel. There are two stories here, one of fanciful family life and the other of straight, unwhimsical action, and though both may be in the memoirs each would seem to be for an entirely different taste. It is difficult to believe that a young reader following Alexander and Swiftsure into action would want to be switched to Euphemia's predilection for jelly, or that anyone sharing Henrietta's romantic dreams would care much about the line of battle at Cape St Vincent. Between them the interest flickers hither and thither, like a compass needle gone mad.

> *"Captains and Boys," in* The Times Literary Supplement, *July 14, 1972, p. 807.*

THE GHOST DOWNSTAIRS (1972)

Splendidly logical is Leon Garfield's *The Ghost Downstairs,* with the spooky originality one expects from this writer. I'm not sure how old a child would have to be to appreciate the true meaning of its Faustian theme, let alone the chilling concept of selling one's own childhood: I suspect that this is really a tale for adults. But then so were some of the most enduring children's books ever written.

> *Gillian Tindall, "Dreams to Sell," in* New Statesman, *Vol. 83, No. 2150, June 2, 1972, p. 760.*

The nature of the aesthetic and intellectual experience this book offers is not quite clear. It is handsomely produced; text and [Antony Maitland's] illustrations complement each other in their eerie beauty. Mr Garfield has selected a high literary pedigree for this brainchild; Mr Fast sells seven years of his life for £1m. in Faustian manner, only to discover that his trick (he has bargained away his discarded childhood) deprives him of the power to enjoy his riches, since he no longer possesses his dreams. Ultimately he repents. One is reminded of *A Christmas Carol,* and the long tradition of moral fable in English literature. It is a complex notion; and the texture of the writing is dense—occasionally one's enjoyment of its quality is almost too keen. But the full sinister impact of the fable never quite emerges; the moral consequences of the bargain are never quite achieved. This is partly because the excellence of the writing is not matched by equally skilled plot manipulation (one can see a child demanding, 'But what *happens?*') and partly, I suspect, because the implications of the fable are not absolutely clear. For this type of writing to succeed, this is surely essential? The question is asked in disappointment, since something very fine has narrowly been missed. What remains is still of substance and quality; but for whom, now, does Mr Garfield write?

> *Patricia Stubbs, in a review of "The Ghost Downstairs," in* The School Librarian, *Vol. 20, No. 3, September, 1972, p. 254.*

The hallowed usage of the legal profession provides Leon Garfield with some memorable imagery. Never guilty of restraint of metaphor, he is at his distractingly brilliant best in this Dickensian mood. **The Ghost Downstairs** is a demanding narrative—and so full of words! The reader must be prepared to think between and further beyond the lines than Mr. Garfield felt it necessary to go.

> *J. Allan Morrison, in a review of "The Ghost Downstairs," in* Children's Book Review, *Vol. II, No. 5, October, 1972, p. 154.*

THE CAPTAIN'S WATCH (1972)

Pistol, a monkey in **The Captain's Watch,** is a thief, an embarrassment to his owner, Tim, who is in the process of being transported to America. Unable to dispose of the goods, Tim has to return them to their owners, claiming to have found them, and is amazed to find himself rewarded for 'honesty'. All goes well until the Captain's watch is stolen, whereupon a hanging is threatened; but a happy resolution is found.

So far, so good. Much of this is vintage Garfield, at home in the eighteenth century, with his story and characters giving plenty of scope to exercise his inimitable style. Unfortunately, the climax of the story comes some ten pages before the end of the book, the remainder being filled by an unnecessarily lengthy tying-up of ends to little purpose or impact.

> *Robert Barker, in a review of "The Captain's Watch," in* Children's Book Review, *Vol. III, No. 2, April, 1973, pp. 49-50.*

The Captain's Watch is another story of Leon Garfield's young eighteenth-century scamp Tim and his monkey, Pistol. . . . [The] wild and ebullient drama which they manage to create on the captain's well-regulated ship is more than worthy of them. But what particularly distinguishes Mr Garfield's comedy is the way in which the questions of heart and morality it raises belong completely to the period and are not imposed from without.

> *"Long Ago and Far Away," in* The Times Literary Supplement, *No. 3709, April 6, 1973, p. 383.*

THE GOLDEN SHADOW (with Edward Blishen, 1973)

In **The Golden Shadow** the authors have combined a number of stories from disparate sources into a literary whole. Gods, demi-gods and god-like humans strive, love, lust, inhabiting a landscape whose very rocks and stones, whose tides are alive with menace and promise. The stories are linked through the figure of an aged storyteller who wanders from place to place, always, like the hero of Ted Hughes's *Bedtime Story,* inattentive at the crucial moment; so that he is there when the events happen, but never sees them happen. . . . It is an interesting device, and a successful one, as if the authors had imaginatively become this archetypal figure, and tried to eavesdrop on the scenes they described.

Since so many stories are packed within 150 pages, some, inevitably, suffer. At times the authors try too hard to work up to a climax in too short a time. . . . The result at such moments is a sub-Keatsian, orgasmic kind of writing, overladen with imagery. Here for instance is Atalanta running her final race:

> The rushing wind painted her tunic against her breasts and flying thighs . . . she laughed aloud; she and the inquisitive air were one. She was a spirit—a dream in men's minds to be possessed only in sleep and death.

Good. Yes very. But you can have too much of a good thing.

However, when the authors settle down to the central episode, the story of Heracles, his childhood, his madness, his crime, punishment and expiation, his heroic act of mercy towards the chained Prometheus, and his eternal reward, the book becomes very good indeed, moving with remarkable narrative power. Here the myth is transmuted into something new: utterly modern in its writing and still Greek in feeling.

> *Gerard Benson, "Ancient & Modern," in* New Statesman, *Vol. 85 No. 2201, May 25, 1973, p. 782.*

In their first book **The God Beneath the Sea,** Messrs. Garfield and Blishen retold in a highly personal and consciously literary manner the early sequences in the cycle of the Greek Myths—the origins and rivalries of the Gods, and the creation of Man, as yet a puny and insignificant arrival on the scene. In their new book, the untimely creation of the Titan Prometheus has grown to people a world of kings and courtiers, nobles, princes, fishermen and others. Though the gods are still plentifully in evidence, it is man who now fills the centre of the stage. Through this world wanders the aged poet storyteller, a homeric figure, wearily seeking the vision of the gods he so longs for, yet seldom witnessing at first hand even the deeds of men. Nevertheless, it is from scattered accounts of these that he weaves his stories and constructs the pattern he sees in the interaction of men and gods. Towering over all others in his imaginings is the figure of Heracles, mightiest hero of them all, and the most pursued. He fills the storyteller's mind just as he dominates the pages of this book. We follow him from birth, through prodigious childhood: he is successively marvellous boy, golden youth, the murderer of his children, the tortured hero of the Labours, pathetic old man and finally a burnt out case, performing a last deed of heroism, mightier in its way than anything before. (pp. 182-83)

This is in no way a conventional retelling of the deeds of a strong-arm bully whose heroism is measured in monsters slain and enemies lying dead in heaps. It is every bit as idiosyncratic an interpretation as the previous book, concerned more with the hero as a man than a superman, and questioning the nature of heroism itself. If there are two ways into myths as has been suggested, it is true to say that this book takes the inward route, looking beneath the outer religious and moral purpose of the stories to their inner preoccupations. We feel Heracles primarily as a man, still larger than life, but in weakness as well as in strength; the archetype not of the hero as species, but of everyman's heroic suffering in his quest through life. It is this dimension—the massive humanity of Heracles—that the authors have added to the traditional story. It may be an interpretation nearer to our ways of thinking than to the original conception of the Greeks, and perhaps we lose here something of the old heiratic grandeur of the Myth, but we gain far-reaching insights, investing the story with a new and valid relevance.

To package such a book exclusively for children seems a mistake; not only does it predispose half its potential readership against it, it diminishes the achievement itself. *The Golden Shadow* is for all who will read and are of an age to understand. It is not an easy book; its narrative devices are as complex as the ideas it contains. Despite the moments of humour, of broad comedy even, it is a sombre story told as a tragedy with all the violence and blood-letting that implied for the Greeks as well as Shakespeare. The language of its telling, only, is simpler than in the earlier book, more nearly reaching the poetic than the often tortured prose of that other. (p. 183)

> *Judith Vidal Hall, in a review of "The Golden Shadow," in* Children's Book Review, *Vol. III, No. 6, December, 1973, pp. 182-83.*

"There is no doubt about it," wrote Thomas Mann in 1936, "the moment when the story-teller acquires the mythical way of looking at things . . . that moment marks a beginning in his life." And with this gem of a book to back me up, I would add: the moment the listener, in this case the young adult reader, is confronted with such a story-teller, this moment must mark a beginning of a deeper insight into the dark recesses of man's fantasy life.

Is this saying a great deal? I mean to. One should not underestimate the literary gift of a thoroughly successful work, one that is sure to influence the inner life of every child and adult who reads it.

The original story-tellers here already worked with myth. But the book would not be what it is, a re-creation of the Heracles legend that makes us feel witness to its birth, were Leon Garfield and Edward Blishen themselves not endowed with the mythical perspective. In the hands of those less skilled and less sensitive, such a re-creation would be hubris.

Here time flows. The tales are stunningly interwoven. And like a true poem, time flows in the round. Thetis, sea-goddess, whispers the haunting question: "Tell me—tell me, who will my lover be?" "You will bear a son who will be greater than his father. Does it please you?" comes back the answer. At the same time the vulture picks away at the liver of Prometheus Bound, and Zeus, assuming the form of her husband Amphitryon, sleeps with Alcmena. From this union Heracles, who in the end releases Prometheus, is born. . . .

Let's hope that the child of Thetis will soon be the project for another beautiful book. . . .

> *Shulamith Oppenheim, in a review of, "The Golden Shadow," in* The New York Times Book Review,

February 3, 1974, p. 8.

LUCIFER WILKINS (1973)

Lucifer Wilkins is Leon Garfield's third story about the eighteenth-century cockney convict boy, Tim, and his monkey, Pistol. In Garfield's previous volume in the series, Tim failed to buy his freedom after being transported to Virginia. He is now unwillingly forced by Pistol to run away with a huge forbidding Negro slave, Lucifer Wilkins. Like his namesake, Lucifer is a rebel against a kind master: "I needs to do an injury." The theme of the book is the search for freedom. Pistol, however, when offered his in a Brazilian forest, rejects it, and Lucifer exchanges the "stony servitude of the spirit" for the "excellent servitude of the heart" by admitting his need for Tim and Pistol. An interesting idea, it is all very lightly handled with Garfield's usual wit and style. The weird trio of Negro, boy and monkey is left walking away into the future—plenty of scope for another volume.

> *"Spearheads of History," in* The Times Literary Supplement, *No. 3742, November 23, 1973, p. 1430.*

The rebellious feelings of negro slaves in the New World, however saintly their masters, the Virginian background and the jungle scenes are vigorously, if slightly, drawn in, but what sets the story apart, as usual, is Leon Garfield's vivid poetic imagination, which sees the huge black Lucifer's grin "like a yard of calico", or lets him whisk the puny little London thief aloft "like a weed uprooted".

> *M. Hobbs, in a review of "Lucifer Wilkins," in* The Junior Bookshelf, *Vol. 38, No. 2, April, 1974, p. 112.*

THE SOUND OF COACHES (1974)

Leon Garfield's sense of the past is at once precise and imaginative, and his presentation of it is entirely convincing because his interest is concentrated, not on the accidentals of behaviour, but rather on the unchanging human heart. In his latest book, ***The Sound of Coaches,*** the world of highwaymen, travelling players and coaching inns is more or less incidental. The greatest attention is focused on complex aspects of the parent and child relationship and how it affects a child's developing sense of his own identity. Mr Garfield writes so convincingly of inner feelings that we are prepared to take his picture of the outer world on trust.

Nevertheless much of the energy, excitement and melodrama of the book derives from the setting—for the book is unashamedly melodramatic, as it is unashamedly Dickensian. The effortless narrative skill which holds the reader relentlessly from the storm-struck opening to the quiet coda owes much to Garfield's Victorian master. So do several leisurely chapter openings that take the form of brief essays on such topics as coach-proprietorship or the art of acting. There is above all Dickens's theatricality which permeates the book, and governs the complex plot, so full of reversals and coincidences, maintaining the suspense to the very end. Character creation, too, is handled with Dickensian humour and vitality. . . .

Sam [is] the foundling, torn between the stolid, conscientious coachman who is his adoptive father, and the mysterious "other pa" who has left him only a pistol and a pewter ring. In spite of his desire to please the old coachman, Sam is always in some scrape or another, and after crashing his coach, he runs away and joins a company of actors (theatrical motifs pervade the whole book). The coachman's love for Sam and his subsequent horror at the destruction of his old coach, the narrow morality which makes him dismiss the players as "trash" are movingly portrayed, and it is therefore something of a disappointment that the plot cannot be resolved happily without compromising his stiff-backed integrity. Mr Garfield's final solution is altogether too cavalier, but it is a measure of our involvement that the ending seems so disturbingly disengaged.

> *"Hard Times," in* The Times Literary Supplement, *No. 3774, July 5, 1974, p. 713.*

One must write two reviews of this novel: one for critics, teachers and followers who read Leon Garfield as our forebears read Dickens, and one for a young reader who might begin with this book and read all the Garfield novels in a month, if it were that reading month in his life.

For the adult reader I must say this is a book of self-pastiche. Having done it all before most successfully—coaches, highwaymen, inns, travelling players, the macabre mix of the tragical-comical, the preposterous reliance on coincidence and the novelist's right to warp and weave, the brilliant coruscations of language and extremes of bathos, Mr Garfield does it all again. But this time the marrow does not freeze. He is indulging himself, not us.

For the young reader who is making a beginning or extending a regard I say, learn from it how an accomplished storyteller goes to work; this time he keeps you outside just enough to show you how it's done.

> *Margaret Meek, in a review of "The Sound of Coaches," in* The School Librarian, *Vol. 22, No. 3, September, 1974, p. 248.*

The richly styled atmospherics of Leon Garfield form one of the salient literary features in the landscape of the last decade and a half of children's books. . . . [His] tales of misty derringdo, replete with coincidental encounters and nightmare villainies that work an insidious chemistry on the imagination of the reader, will remain on booklists for a long while. Nevertheless the strength of stories like **Devil-in-the-Fog** and **Black Jack** and **Smith** should be seen side by side with the pastiche heaviness of **Child O'War,** the manneristic parody of **The Strange Affair of Adelaide Harris,** and now the sense of self-imitation that arises in **The Sound of Coaches**. . . .

Episodes trickle along, description doing the work of action. The characters are not able to support this amplitude, for they thrive in the pell-mell that continually entertains and delightfully confuses the reader. The greater scope to show the hero's feelings is impaired by a hang-dog prolixity with none of the wry self-knowledge that exonerates, say, Tom Jones from being tiresome. **The Sound of Coaches** has few of the haunting harmonics one yearns to hear again: in fact it is rather a weary sound, going on a bit too long.

> *C. S. Hannabuss, in a review of "The Sound of Coaches," in* Children's Book Review, *Vol. IV, No. 3, Autumn, 1974, p. 110.*

THE PRISONERS OF SEPTEMBER (1975)

This book marks a turning-point in Leon Garfield's career.

It is not only that he has chosen to leave the strange never-never land of **Smith** and **Jack Holborn** in favour of the authentic historical past. He has abandoned too his standpoint of ironic detachment; if he does not identify with his characters now he certainly takes them very seriously indeed.

If this should seem too sober a view, it must be added that Mr. Garfield has a great sense of fun, and exercises all his old virtuosity in description and happy turns of phrase. (p. 263)

The story is of Sussex and of France under the Revolution. Mr. Garfield for once introduces historical figures, notably the Comtesse de la Motte-Valois, victim or villain of the Queen's Necklace affair, whose introduction to bourgeois Sussex society ends disastrously. The first scenes, freshly evoking the atmosphere of the Downs and introducing affectionately the naive and accident-prone hero, are delightful. The story is richly humorous, but seriousness breaks in very soon. The Revolution is no joke, especially to Lewis' aristocratic and radical friend Richard who, fired by Tom Paine and the eloquence of his foolish tutor, goes off to help the people of France and is duped into the role of agent-provocateur. The ugliness of the scenes in Paris is relieved by the character of Corporal Bouvet, anglophile and reluctant revolutionary, one of the very nicest of Mr. Garfield's offbeat characters. There is tragedy, but the hint of a happy ending, even for the gallant corporal, living it up in his prisoner-of-war camp.

This seems to me to be Mr. Garfield's best book to date. He writes as well as ever, and captures atmosphere with all his old mastery. It has sometimes seemed in the past that he exercised these crafts almost for their own sakes. Here his skills are at the service of a strong theme, a subtle and complex plot, and a gallery of very individual, entertaining and, for the most part, entirely credible characters. In writing **The Prisoners of September** he demonstrates once again, and this time most tellingly, the meaninglessness of classification into 'children's' or 'adult' books. This is a Book. (p. 264)

> *M. Crouch, in a review of "The Prisoners of September," in* The Junior Bookshelf, *Vol. 39, No. 4, August, 1975, pp. 263-64.*

A real reader's book. The plot is as nicely convoluted and ironically involved as one has come to expect; the characters have a touch of the eccentric excess that so delights: but the great fascination to the committed reader is that Mr. Garfield uses words so well, so prodigally, so precisely, so colourfully, powerfully, brilliantly. (p. 66)

Here are mystery and madness, violence and virtue, terror, conspiracy, coincidence, character, humour and surprise. . . .

Mr. Garfield has been accused of self-indulgence—there seems little here. And it is asked: For whom does Mr. Garfield now write? Surely he writes for those who love fine words and a strong story. However, it will be a well-schooled adolescent that copes easily with this. (p. 67)

> *C. E. J. Smith, in a review of "The Prisoners of September," in* Children's Book Review, *Vol. V, No. 2, Summer, 1975, pp. 66-7.*

This splendidly unclassifiable novel opens in a mood of exuberant mock-Gothic comedy, with a hero as gullible, though hardly as winning, as Catherine Morland: it ends in tragedy, in the victory of violence and compromise over idealism and innocence. Events of great moment in the past—the French

Revolution in general and the Septembrist massacres in particular—are treated with the opportunism of a Dickens or a Dumas, used to give a positive turn to the lives of two heroes who prove, in the end, to be anti-heroes. (p. 2679)

I have no doubt that *The Prisoners of September* will be read with an eye to its relevance to the present day, for the very direct look at the self-perpetuating nature of violence, the implied comment on political ignorance and uninstructed idealism, the negation of conventional heroics. I hope it will also be read as an excellent story. The twists of the plot are contrived through the two main characters but also through a great many minor characters delineated strongly and with an almost genial humour. Dialogue and description are managed with a skill and firmness which I do not think Leon Garfield has ever equalled. In particular, his predilection for the off-beat or unexpected verbal image is, in this book, kept in bounds and used only when it really contributes to the story in one way or another. At the beginning of the book the uneasy friendship of the two young men is upset, as so often, by one of Mortimer's half-intentional gibes. Lewis is offended, Mortimer is interested but remorseful:

> " 'I'm sorry', whispered Mortimer hopelessly towards the angular staircase, up which the unmistakeably offended Lewis had stalked like an animated stained-glass window.
>
> As the image occurred to him, Mortimer lapsed into his faintly contemptuous smile. Mockery of the Bostons seemed inevitable. Their mansion was even more Gothic inside than out. Pointed arches and fretted woodwork confronted the eye at every turn; the whole place so resembled a cathedral that it was to be wondered that the Bostons hadn't dressed their servants in vestments instead of livery."

The rapid changes of mood in the passage, its usefulness in stressing points of personality, can be enjoyed as one might enjoy a piece of music intricate and skilful and, above all, pleasing in sound. For, though I may have seemed to suggest otherwise, this is a pleasing book to read—pleasing because it does so well what it sets out to do, pleasing because of the conclusion on which the story rests, so unexpected and yet so right; pleasing, above all, because in it, Leon Garfield expresses once more, in the indirect way proper to a novel, his respect for humanity. (pp. 2679-80)

Margery Fisher, in a review of "The Prisoners of September," in Growing Point, *Vol. 14, No. 3, September, 1975, pp. 2679-80.*

THE APPRENTICES (also known as "Garfield's Apprentices"): *The Lamplighter's Funeral; Mirror, Mirror; Moss and Blister; The Cloak* (1976); *The Valentine; Labour in Vain; The Fool; Rosy Starling; The Dumb Cake; Tom Titmarsh's Devil* (1977); *The Filthy Beast; The Enemy* (1978)

Leon Garfield is always acutely aware of contrasts and his new series, "Garfield's Apprentices", opens with two stories—*Mirror, Mirror* and *The Lamplighter's Funeral*—which offer examples of cruelty and compassion, defeat and victory, far more stringent than those in *The Boy and the Monkey*. Though the tales are short and structurally simple, they will appeal mainly to children experienced enough to catch the tone of a writer's voice and listen to his unspoken message. Both tales are full of imagery—the brilliance of

jewellery and glass in the first, the revelations of torch light in the second. In the first a vain girl, tormenting after her custom a new and timid apprentice learning her father's trade of framing mirrors, is made to see, in one tense moment, that her beauty can be marred by her temperament. In the second a lamplighter acquires, not of his own volition, an assistant who forces him to see and take to heart the misery of vagrants lurking in the darkest corners of the city. These are stories intended not to teach children history but to surprise them into realising that time does not change humanity very much. Leon Garfield's particular version of the London of Fielding and Hogarth offers its own private, searching history lesson.

Margery Fisher, in a review of "Mirror, Mirror" and "The Lamplighter's Funeral," in Growing Point, *Vol. 15, No. 2, July, 1976, p. 2913.*

[*The Lamplighter's Funeral*] opens with one of Garfield's best set-pieces: the funeral ceremony—to the full flare of torches and the fumes of stinking pitch—of one Sam Bold, lamplighter of Cripplegate, "now conducted with flaming pomp to his last snuffing place". After the funeral feast, one of the fraternity, Pallcat, overcome with gin and emotion, takes unto himself as apprentice a skinny, homeless urchin called Possul. As a "link boy" Possul earns the odd penny by lighting the rich through the murky streets with a flaming fistful of tow dipped in pitch. Before long it is borne home to even the cynical old Pallcat that there is something otherworldly about this boy whose torch invariably reveals some act of cruelty or anguish better left unlit. "Just who *is* Possul?" asks the anxious publisher, and the reader is no less baffled. Who, indeed, is meant to read this inconclusive little story? The format suggests under-elevens, most of whom will revel in the macabre but jib at the symbolism and the self-conscious philosophizing which bedevils the whole book.

It is in *Mirror, Mirror,* however, that the author really runs amok. Here the apprentice is Daniel Nightingale, a country boy from the wilds of Hertfordshire, who comes to London to the home of Mr Paris, master carver of mirror frames. It is his daughter, Lucinda, who dominates the story—a wholly contemptible, malevolent girl whose heart is as corrupt as her face is angelic. Daily she sets traps for Daniel, always with mirrors. Nightly she summons him to her parlour in which there stands a shrouded easel. Each time she snatches the cloth away a different "reflection" confronts the boy in the false mirror behind it: a bleeding pig's head, the face of a newly hanged man, skulls, dead rats, worms. . . . He is unnerved, tormented, degraded. At last, a kindly glassmaker provides the demented boy with a simple remedy by which Lucinda may learn the bitter truth about her own nature. The message here is only too clear, though it is a sophisticated message for a child to accept. The way in which it is delivered is utterly distasteful.

Those with strong stomachs may be amused but others could well be revolted if not actually frightened by the surrealist overtones of this peculiar story.

Ann Evans, "Crusading Spirit," in The Times Literary Supplement, *No. 3879, July 16, 1976, p. 880.*

[In *Moss and Blister*, Leon Garfield presents] his simple people simply as they are, in a comic view that surprisingly avoids being patronizing while delighting in absurdity at every social level. His laughter is quite without contempt, despite the fact that his methods are akin to caricature. Inevitably Blister, the midwife's apprentice, with her protruding ears, saucer eyes and dream of an immaculate conception (her own), is a more memorable creation than Ben or Emmie [in Geoffrey Trease's *Violet for Bonaparte*]. ***Moss and Blister*** is the latest in Garfield's series of "apprentices", odd little books whose length suggests a slightness that their energy contradicts. Moss the midwife and her scrawny apprentice are a splendidly comic duo, plying their trade of delivering babies—itself seen as essentially comic, perhaps for the first time since Dr Slop—on Christmas Eve.

> *Julia Briggs, "Romantic Traditions," in* The Times Literary Supplement, *No. 3900, December 10, 1976, p. 1545.*

Each addition to Leon Garfield's *Apprentices* series, of which [***The Cloak***] is the third, is original and imaginative. It is not only a clever evocation of a period, but a study of relationships and a *story* with an unexpected ending. Two youths are apprenticed to the eighteenth century equivalent of a pawnbroker and are not averse to doing some unscrupulous business on their own account. It is the elegant cloak of the title which is their downfall, and it is through this cloak that they discover the meaning of the word 'redeemed.'

A brief vignette of the time, an allegory, or just a story? It all depends on the reader. (pp. 110-11)

> *E. Colwell, in a review of "The Cloak," in* The Junior Bookshelf, *Vol. 41, No. 2, April, 1977, pp. 110-11.*

Christmas Eve, and Moss [in ***Moss and Blister***], a midwife with the more endearing traits of Sarah Gamp, is answering a call with her foundling apprentice Blister, a bean-pole of a girl with immortal longings in her. For while Moss, conscious of the ancient dignity of her profession, yearns to be called to a Second Coming on this night of the year, Blister, fiercely jealous of the possible rival among their night's clients, hopes to be chosen as the second mother. Garfield's ***Apprentices*** seem cheerfully able to contain such metaphysical flights of fancy within the earthy confines of eighteenth-century London, the innocent but invincible ignorance, the weight of superstition and outward show which overlies Moss's expert knowledge of her job, the realistic births, and the none-too-attractive characters we meet. The ambitious mirror-silverer's apprentice Bosun is drawn to Blister despite himself, so for them at least Christmas Eve fulfils its promise. Of course, as always, much of the success is due to Leon Garfield's recurrent rhythms and phrases and the vital, close-packed language which, every so often, pulls the mat from under the words with splendid comic effect. Faith Jaques' line-drawings in the text enhance the Dickensian sense of wholesome happy vigour unbowed by the harshness of reality.

> *M. Hobbs, in a review of "Moss and Blister," in* The Junior Bookshelf, *Vol. 41, No. 2, April, 1977, p. 111.*

Linkboys and watermen, churchyards, winding alleys, and characters glimpsed in shifting perspectives—we are back in the unmistakable world of Leon Garfield. His marvellously detailed knowledge of social customs illuminates the love stories of two eighteenth-century apprentices, stories which have the charm of street ballads, or old prints of the Cries of London.

The Valentine is a masterpiece in miniature, a tale told with wit, and decorated with a wealth of appropriately funereal imagery. Hawkins, an undertaker's scraggy apprentice, loves

a rival undertaker's daughter, Miss Jessop, whose heart is pledged to the gentle youth she saw in his coffin before he was buried on St Valentine's Day. Dressed always in black, Hawkins and Miss Jessop are totally involved in the ritual of death. Phrases from the burial service slip from their lips, Miss Jessop's adolescent passion seeks its natural fulfilment in suicide, Hawkins poses before her like a churchyard monument; and only at the end is their formality shattered when, in pursuit of the urchins who have stolen Miss Jessop's wreath, Hawkins leaps recklessly over gravestones, life vanquishes death, and love is set free.

Wholly serious though they are, Leon Garfield invites us to smile at the young couple's solemnity. Undertaking is, perhaps, a "horrible, unfeeling trade", but in the midst of death life must go on—and does.

Labour in Vain is less elegiac, more robust. Snobbish young Gully, a cobbler's son, has acquired a horror of feet—and feet provide the dominant image of the book. Gully is a buckle-maker's apprentice, and just as he hopes, with plate and pinchbeck buckles, to embellish the sordid reality of shoes, so he tries to pretend that the stinking cobbler's shop is a prosperous "family leather business". Burdened by his shameful secret, Gully is driven to wild exaggeration, even according to his sweetheart's lamplighter father the dignity of an "oil and ladder business". Inevitably his house of cards finally collapses, springing a genuine surprise on the reader.

After the firecracker brilliance of Leon Garfield's early novels, these stories have a more sober tone. But an apprentice's life was sober, with his bed under the counter, and his scanty holidays.

> *Angela Bull, "Dead-End Jobs," in* The Times Literary Supplement, *No. 3931, July 15, 1977, p. 859.*

Leon Garfield's "Apprentice" stories are not for a young reading age, despite the somewhat misleading format and [Faith Jaques's] plentiful illustration. In these terse, ironic tales there is a concentration of imagery, an elusive technique of characterisation and a breadth of social comment which demand an alert reader (I suggest, ten and over) ready to accept an idiosyncratic but authentic view of the past. Like their predecessors in the series, the present books [***The Valentine, Labour in Vain, The Fool,*** and ***Rosy Starling***] contain several linking devices. The London scene shifts from one street to another within the City, from St. Martin's Churchyard in ***The Valentine*** to a dingy yard off Old 'Change in ***Labour in Vain,*** from a Jewish clockmaker's in Carter Lane in ***The Fool*** to Drury Lane and its alleyways in ***Rosy Starling.*** Each tale is marked by a festival. Ironically St. Valentine's Day casts its romantic spell on a melancholy young woman much obsessed by death and an undertaker's apprentice; Mothering Sunday marks the occasion, potentially disastrous, when buckle-maker Gully takes Miss La Salle, who works in silver thread, to meet his mother, whose cobbler's shop he has drastically misrepresented; on the Eve of Passover young Bunting collects his wandering wits to judge between his employer, Mr. Israels, scrupulous in his attitude to ritual, and old Levy, whose confidence trick is based on ancient truth; while blind Rosy the cage-maker listens to the sounds of Maypole dancing with a lad reluctant to obey his master and steal her lustrous hair for his wig-making. Beyond the links of place and circumstance there are deeper links in theme, for each of these caustic, sharply documented tales turns on imposture, self-deception, change and—in a sense—

growing up. When the sequence is complete I am sure it will stand out as one of the most notable individual commentaries of our time on the vanity of human wishes, a lesson anyone could learn willingly through this unique combination of historical detail and universal feeling. (pp. 3199-200)

> *Margery Fisher, "Placing People in the Past," in*
> Growing Point, *Vol. 16, No. 5, November, 1977, pp.*
> *3198-200.*

No writer can convey the spirit and sheer liveliness of the eighteenth century as can Leon Garfield. His longer novels are masterpieces and in this series of stories of the apprentices of London he has proved that he can write just as skilfully for younger children. [In *The Fool*,] "Bunting—the fool" is apprenticed to his uncle Israels, the clock maker, whose minx of a daughter Rachel is always playing tricks on Bunting and so indeed earning him the title fool. With the coming of the Passover feast the family gather to celebrate but it is Bunting who unwittingly allows old Levy the tramp who travels the land buying and selling watches to be admitted to the house and the feast. A lively account of the rough and tumble of city life before the days of social services and modern sanitation. Garfield has traced back his apprentices in eighteenth century books and manuscripts and no detail is omitted, no subtlety of plot missed. A rare masterpiece. . . . (pp. 25-6)

> *J. Russell, in a review of "The Fool," in* The Junior
> Bookshelf, *Vol. 42, No. 1, February, 1978, pp. 25-6.*

Leon Garfield's *Apprentices* are self-sufficient stories of the eighteenth-century London he has made his own. Indeed, it is Mr Garfield's London to the same extent as it was Balzac's Paris. We now have a veritable "Comédie Humaine" unfolding, with a lengthy list of titles still to come.

[In *The Cloak, Moss and Blister, Rosy Starling*, and *The Fool*, characters] crop up from one tale to the next—like the birdcage lady and the link-boy (joke)—while the tales appear to be centred around the yearly festivals, pious or pagan, Gentile or Jewish. Few of the actors are downright evil and few are wholly good. Eighteenth-century London is no more or less of a devil's paradise than the world of today; and there are no fewer chances for doing good or evil.

But Mr Garfield suffuses the mean, petty world of jaundiced apprentices and penny-pinching masters with burlesque humour and extravagant similes as thick as chintz in a Victorian drawing room. . . . The stories are shot through with opposing tensions—from the brightness of the Mayday to the blackness of the chimney sweeps; sickness and health, worldliness and joy.

Wise saws and quirky old testaments garnish the text in surprising disguises. In *Moss and Blister* the midwife's apprentice ("with sticking-out ears and saucer eyes") longs to give birth to the Son of God during his second coming. She is thus mortified when a gypsy girl bears a child in the stable of the New Star Inn. " 'ere I am," she whimpered. "Blister! It's me you're lookin' for! Me! Down 'ere! Me wiv the big ears . . ." By oscillating between the Sublime and the Cor Blimey, Mr Garfield composes a fine celebration of life in each one of these bubbling morality playlets.

> *Peter Fanning, "Sublime to Cor Blimey," in* The
> Times Educational Supplement, *No. 3269, Febru-*
> *ary 2, 1978, p. 42.*

Leon Garfield's twelve short books published under the label

"Garfield's Apprentices" are deceptive. At first sight, their brief span of approximately forty-eight pages, together with the plentiful illustrations, would suggest that these are books for younger children who may lack the stamina for his weightier work. Nothing could be further from the truth; the books may be short but they demand as much from the reader as do his longer novels and, although these stories may well lead children to Garfield's other books, they are not for apprentice readers.

The Dumb Cake, Tom Titmarsh's Devil, The Filthy Beast and *The Enemy* draw the series to a close and, like their predecessors, present an authentic and distinctive view of life in eighteenth-century London. . . .

These stories, like those which preceded them, are linked by their background: the teeming streets and alleys of eighteenth century London with their shifting population of link-boys and vagrants, merchants and gravediggers, hangmen and flower sellers. The ritual festivals of the time often act as a focus for the stories: Bartholomew Fair in *The Filthy Beast*, Passover Eve in *The Fool*, the Mayday and Michaelmas fairs in *Rosy Starling* and *The Enemy*. Such scenes offer not only a convenient peg on which to hang a plot but also a specific contemporary background for characters and themes that are timeless. For Garfield is concerned above all to show that human nature has changed little in two hundred years. The failings of his characters—their pride and vanity, self-deception and ambition—will be easily recognized by readers today.

The mood of the stories is not entirely sombre, though. All the books are lightened by humour, none more so than *The Dumb Cake*, which is a small comic masterpiece. Parrot's master, the hypochondriacal apothecary Chambers, is a brilliant creation, noting his symptoms in a calf-bound notebook as he subsides into a drunken stupor occasioned by liberal draughts of Camomile in White Wine, Tincture of Aloes and Cinnamon (steeped for nine days in gin), and Wintergreen in Rectified Wine. And the ritual of the baking of the "dumb cake" itself is observed with a wealth of the humorous imagery that is one of Garfield's characteristic skills.

Now that the sequence is complete, "Garfield's Apprentices" can be seen to be a remarkable combination of precise historical detail and timeless characterization. Despite the misleading format of the books themselves, the series as a whole is an achievement that matches the best of Leon Garfield's more prestigious work.

> *Lance Salway, "Apprentices' Progress," in* The
> Times Literary Supplement, *No. 3979, July 7, 1978,*
> *p. 772.*

THE HOUSE OF HANOVER: ENGLAND IN THE EIGHTEENTH CENTURY (1976)

The intentions of this book and the series of which it forms a part, are excellent. A short, well-illustrated and attractively presented outline of the cultural history of England, with the emphasis on a young, popular market, is entirely commendable, and earlier titles in the series have amply answered their purpose. Unfortunately this cannot be said in the present case. . . . It is a short book, but the approach is self-indulgent, with lengthy accounts of conversations between the author and a garrulous attendant, and a good deal of trivial jocularity. It is page forty before we actually reach the age of Hanover, though the result hardly justifies the effort of getting there. Each character is treated in a few superficial words, which convey Leon Garfield's prejudices, such as they are, but little of interest or consequence. There is no attempt to relate the artists and writers discussed to the major cultural, let alone social developments of the period, no attempt to transmit the essential flavour and character of Hanoverian England, no attempt to impose any kind of framework.

> *Paul Langford, "Georgian Stroller," in* The Times Literary Supplement, *No. 3879, July 16, 1976, p. 886.*

The 'Mirror of Britain' series, in which distinguished historical novelists write about periods of history, got off to a good start. I am a little doubtful about this one. Mr. Garfield is, at best, an instinctive historian, which makes his romantic novels so splendidly uninhibited by preoccupation with facts. When he turns to the facts he becomes rather dull, struggling a little too hard to inject personality into this portrait gallery of the Georgian age.

> *M. Crouch, in a review of "The House of Hanover," in* The Junior Bookshelf, *Vol. 40, No. 4, August, 1976, p. 226.*

The value of any guided tour will necessarily depend on the guide. It hardly needs saying that when Leon Garfield takes us through his chosen areas of the National Portrait Gallery, the experience is delightfully entertaining. As a writer with a unique, keen eye for the infinite suggestiveness of people's appearances, he revels in a feast of humorous, stimulating and enlightening observations on the faces of the eighteenth century. To offset any extravagant eccentricities, he has the occasional company of the attendant whose commonsense philosophy we learn has been enhanced by attendance at evening classes.

Lavishly illustrated with photographs of the portraits and attractively presented, the book could nevertheless prove deceptive to hard-pressed catalogue purchasers. If it is not, as the main title might suggest, a traditional view of history as the potted biographies of a series of royals, neither is it, as its sub-title hints, a more comprehensive focus on the various strands—social, political and economic—that weave the closest tapestry we have telling how it was. (pp. 252, 255)

> *Gordon Parsons, in a review of "The House of Hanover: England in the Eighteenth Century," in* The School Librarian, *Vol. 24, No. 3, September, 1976, pp. 252, 255.*

THE PLEASURE GARDEN (1976)

Leon Garfield has produced another rich meal from his sub-Smollett/Hogarth/Dickens recipe, and as a heavily decorated thriller it is very impressive. The cameos and grotesques are all alive—the staymakers, beggars, blackmailers, half-innocent urchins, the whores. But this time, his packed world is paralleled by an equally packed symbolism, centered on the microcosm of Mrs Bray's Mulberry Pleasure Garden with its masks, confessions, and dubious redemptions. Thus the Reverend Justice Young's search for a murderer is also a search for his own salvation; the trouble is that he often seems to be wading knee deep in symbols as well as red herrings.

Perhaps it is all too much of a good thing, for Mr Garfield's cleverness is also his Achilles' heel. His verbal dexterity does

as much to create his atmosphere as do his scenes, and for most of the time it works well. Thus the noise of children on cellar steps "suggested that a small-sized hailstorm had got inside the house and panicked". But to say that "the revellers go out of the pleasure garden, out into the black garden of pain" is to go out into pretentiousness. It is not that the allegory is inappropriate, or that the ambivalence of everything (including, centrally, sex) is not well conveyed. It is more that Garfield is too insistent; his overstressing of the cosmic leads to overwriting, almost to self-parody, so that episodes such as Martin Young's struggle with the flesh (in the form of Fanny Bush) collapse under the weight of biblical significance.

But at least Mr Garfield's clichés are his own, and on this showing he remains someone to set standards by. Thus when Jenny Oldfield takes her pale Victorian heroine out among gypsies and tokens and wicked stepmothers and black-cloaked writers, we can manage without universal symbolism, but not so well without richness, or more of a sense of style.

> *Peter Hunt, "The Microsmic Past," in* The Times Literary Supplement, *No. 3879, July 16, 1976, p. 880.*

Leon Garfield's latest major offering includes transvestism, prostitution, blackmail and murder. Meat for the kiddies? On the one hand Mr. Garfield has always maintained his contention that there are no books for children, only books; on the other his view of Georgian London is so enriched by imagination, persuasive detail, humour and dazzling wit that children and adults alike have no option but to surrender to his appeal. (p. 226)

The complex and flawlessly constructed plot unfolds with adequately sustained suspense.

There are too many good things here for full enumeration. One may mention briefly the brilliant character-drawing which is never very deep but always colourful, and the writing, which offers, literally, never a dull moment. . . . In this, as in his mastery of colour and his control of a crowded canvas, Mr. Garfield is the Dickensian writer of our times. (p. 227)

> *M. Crouch, in a review of "The Pleasure Garden," in* The Junior Bookshelf, *Vol. 40, No. 4, August, 1976, pp. 226-27.*

In 1971 Frank Eyre made some perceptive comments about Garfield, noting, of **Black Jack,** "the almost frenzied 'come along quickly, let's get on with action and not bother too much about what is really supposed to be going on' that is the special mark of his manner"; and of **The Drummer Boy,** "there is too much in this book that strikes false notes". These are precisely the problems with **The Pleasure Garden.** The variable narrative stance implies clearly that action is not the primary concern of the book; therefore, the author has a duty first to the book, and perhaps more to the implied audience to make these other concerns coherent. If one is concerned with the audience, then a symbol, an undertone, a resonance, is a serious (although not necessarily solemn) business. If you are going to lead someone along a path merely to leave them in a bog of frustration, disillusion, or incoherence, then it might be better not to lead them at all. To say that *value*—in terms of depth and honest interaction between surface and depth—is inappropriate to a children's book is merely to suggest that the second-rate is appropriate to children; it seems to me unlikely that even the most child-centred critic would admit that.

Therefore it may be hard to suggest that Garfield has deliberately produced a book which sells short the potential of his readers, in which case it is difficult to defend him in terms of art or audience; or that he is not capable of producing a better book, in which case his publishers should look to their standards. Yet it is clear that Garfield has produced, and can produce the book of value which **The Pleasure Garden** points towards. The confusions in the minds of publishers and critics, who have been reluctant to look at the *book,* appear to have affected the author with a vengeance. (p. 240)

> *Peter Hunt, "The Good, the Bad and the Indifferent: Quality and Value in Three Contemporary Children's Books," in* The Signal Approach to Children's Books, *edited by Nancy Chambers, Scarecrow Press, 1980, pp. 225-46.*

THE CONFIDENCE MAN (1978)

Obscurity for its own sake is fortunately very rare in children's literature, but to be unwittingly obscure is still reprehensible, and too often it passes without comment: no adult reader cares to admit that he cannot understand a book written for people half his age, particularly if the author is respected and admired, as Leon Garfield most certainly is.

His latest novel, **The Confidence Man,** is an allegory which, after two careful readings, I still understood only in part. It tells of the journey of a group of eighteenth-century German Protestants from persecution at home to freedom in America, and at a much deeper level it tells of the journey of a boy's soul. The boy is Hans Ruppert, fourteen-year-old shoemaker's son from a street inhabited entirely by small tradesmen—a Protestant ghetto in an aggressively Catholic town. The story begins in vintage Garfield style with the decapitation of a German soldier. Though the Rupperts know it to have been an accident, this gruesome death is fuel to the Catholic fire. Reprisals are inevitable: Protestant homes are burnt and it becomes necessary to escape.

Into this scene of crisis comes Captain von Stumpfel, the mysterious black hussar. It is he who persuades the whole street to undertake the formidable flight to Virginia, where he promises them peace and freedom to build a new life. It is on his identity that the entire story must hinge. Is he God or the Devil; saviour or confidence man; swindler or Gentleman of Death? Clues are thrown out in quick and crazy succession. The evidence mounts up in a manner which would confuse a High Court judge. Blandly the blurb asserts that "all is finally explained". To me it is not, nor, I suspect, will the average fourteen-year-old reader easily solve the book's central enigma.

The actual account of the long journey does not compensate for the elusiveness of its underlying truth. The narrative is often tortuous, there are too many minor characters and Garfield's exuberant Dickensian style is inhibited by the device of letting author and hero take turn and turn about as storyteller. Despite its faults, however, this is a significant and rewarding book, the more so because of the demands it makes on its reader.

> *Ann Evans, "Enigmatic Journey," in* The Times Literary Supplement, *No. 4000, December 1, 1978, p. 1395.*

Trust and deceit, doubt and determination, are illustrated seriously but with panache in the relationship between Hans Ruppert, who is twelve, and the black-clad Hussar von Stumpfel, who seems at times to be Grandfather Death himself. Developing his fiction from a nexus of fact—the plight of a group of Protestants, refugees from Catholic Germany, stranded in London in the mid-eighteenth century—Leon Garfield describes [their] journey . . . with a heady blend of laconic dialogue, and macabre description. He divides his narrative between Hans's first-person, perplexed, touchingly brave comments and an all-seeing, powerfully imagistic authorial chronicling, binding the parts together by the repetition of motifs and by a visual alternation of light and darkness that dominates the book and isolates the inexplicable personality of the tormented, plausible pied piper of a hussar.

> *Margery Fisher, in a review of "The Confidence Man," in* Growing Point, *Vol. 18, No. 1, May, 1979, p. 3525.*

Garfield begins this with characteristic flamboyance and a lavish cascade of startling similes—as he vividly introduces the tough poverty of an 18th-century German town; the petty shopkeepers (petty in spirit, as well) who inhabit its Protestant ghetto; 14-year-old Hans Ruppert who dreams only of getting rich; and (with fanfare), the mysterious Captain von Stumpful, who arrives in town dressed all in black with a death's head on his skull and a little black notebook in which he keeps accounts of lives and deaths. The captain wins Hans' special regard when he spirits off an accidentally severed head that would have meant trouble for the Rupperts, and soon the "black hussar" is leading the whole Protestant community away from raiding Catholics . . . and on to his plot in America. . . . After the flashing start Garfield settles down to the rigors of the journey, but the mysterious captain—seen variously by the company as God, devil, Grandfather Death, straw man, and impostor—continues to intrigue. And Garfield's juggling and balancing of the meanings of "confidence" is as virtuoso a performance as we've come to expect.

> *A review of "The Confidence Man," in* Kirkus Reviews, *Vol. XLVII, No. 10, May 15, 1979, p. 579.*

THE APPRENTICES (1978)

Between 1976 and 1978 Garfield wrote twelve stories about different eighteenth-century London apprentices. . . . Since then, two of the titles have gone out of print, so their reappearance now, all together in one comparatively inexpensive volume, is most welcome. While all the pictures [by Antony Maitland and Faith Jaques] have sadly had to go, Garfield is such a graphic author that his readers can always visualize for themselves what is going on without much trouble. And if it is true that illustrations in books can put off older audiences, then this present volume could also win Garfield some new, grown-up fans, particularly in America, where **The Apprentices** has already been marketed as adult fiction.

Whoever finally reads it, though, will discover that Garfield has once again used London's past history to dazzling effect, disinterring the forgotten skills that went into undertaking, midwifery or mirror-silvering, filling his pages with menacing darkness through which only the lamp-lighter and his linkboy—here a symbolic leitmotif—can find their way, and bringing out the former significance of city street names now incongruously attached to yards of office blocks. All this is described with the author's usual eloquence, so that when even he occasionally falls back on a tired phrase ("As white as a sheet") the contrast is all the greater for what has come before. Regular salvoes of Garfield's inexhaustibly fertile imagery quickly create characters who become real through the relentless insistence of the metaphors surrounding them. To disbelieve would be to reject images that are too brilliant to go away quietly and unheeded, even though the literary overkill involved can at times be fatiguing. If follows, therefore, that all Garfield's apprentices are nonpareils, since even those who lack personality tend to do so in quite startling degrees of vacuity. Minor characters are sometimes pinned down so closely by this heavy literary fire that they barely have a chance to breathe, let alone spring from the page. Yet even they often lodge in the imagination afterwards; no mean achievement in stories less than thirty pages long.

Cramming them all into one volume reveals a more fundamental repetitiveness, however, and there are times when reading, **The Apprentices** is like eating a rich twelve course meal: ingredients that thrill in the hors d'oeuvres or entice in the entrée become harder work dished up once again as a savoury. The structure of each tale is too similar: each apprentice eventually finds truth rather than treasure through a reconciliation of opposites, with the ugly revealing inner beauty and the dark finally drawn towards the light. In previous novels, Garfield has also dealt with such themes, but more subtly, given the greater elbow room at his disposal. Here, individual stories occasionally become at best parables and at other moments something like sermons, even down to passages of pulpit pomposity ("For to him who expected there was nothing given", as a way of describing the failure of a child to pay his shilling entrance fee to a doorkeeper.)

As parables, the stories certainly have power, reinforced by artfully woven-in Biblical texts coming from the mouths of characters themselves. This Christian emphasis has been increased in this present volume which does not always follow the original text. In one story, for example, about a feud between a house-painter and his smoother rival in a silk-mercer's shop, the original line: "You filthy beast up there . . . anointing me head with oil!" now appears as *"Thou anointest my head with oil. . . . You filthy beast up there!"* Our own age, like any other, should always be grateful for effective moral tales illustrating the need for greater love and understanding, yet the problems and temptations facing the apprentices as described in these pages are not, on the whole, those which confront young people now. In this sense, urging compassion through the medium of stories in exclusively Georgian settings is rather like preaching sermons in eighteenth-century costume and language: spectacular, perhaps, but curiously remote.

Garfield's penchant for the past, at one time the apparent key to his great narrative and stylistic gifts, now sometimes seems more like a final obstacle to his overall achievement as a novelist. It would be fascinating, for example, to see what he could manage in a modern setting, where the extravagant imagery he uses so confidently to clobber his Hogarthian characters into line would, as it now stands, risk carrying less conviction applied to individuals we know better from our own times. The vivid detail he is so good at unearthing from history may also have to be replaced by something even more carefully selected in order to illumine scenes from today with any-

thing like the same effectiveness. But if the attempt came off, and Garfield was able to invest the present with the same colour and urgent sense of moral metaphor found in his current books, the result would indeed be impressive, given the drab literary times in which we now live, both as children and as adults.

On the other hand, faults and all, Garfield is still worth a good deal, and we should be grateful for a such a highly skilled practitioner. If he is never going to try anything radically new, so be it; if anyone remains curious about what a Garfield description of modern life would read like, this may either have to remain a mystery or, at the very least, perhaps the subject of a small literary competition somewhere in the future.

Nicholas Tucker, "Powerful Parables," in The Times Literary Supplement, *No. 4156, November 26, 1982, p. 1301.*

The stories in this collection were originally published, in twelve separate and elegant volumes with illustrations by Faith Jaques, between 1976 and 1978. Now they appear, with equal elegance but without the illustrations, in a single big volume. Good as Miss Jaques' drawings were, they may have served to distract attention from the singular excellence of Mr. Garfield's writing. Now we can concentrate on the stories, and very good they are.

Mr. Garfield presents a picture of eighteenth-century London through the activities, briefly glimpsed, of the apprentices, active, idle, solemn, jolly, meek and aggressive. Despite their pitiable lack of privilege they were at the heart of the life of the city, and, seeing them, we see also the whole of urban society, but viewed through this most unflattering glass. There is plenty of sentiment, lots of fun, some heartache, and more than a hint of tragedy.

Here then are twelve tales incomparably well told. We may sometimes find the sheer exuberance and virtuosity of Mr. Garfield's writing a little overwhelming in the long novels. In **The Apprentices** he has submitted to the disciplines of the short-story. His prose is as rich and colourful as ever, but it is more taut, in firmer control. If all the rest were lost, we could be comforted with the thought that here is the best of him, and a very good best it is. (pp. 40-1)

M. Crouch, in a review of "The Apprentices," in The Junior Bookshelf, *Vol. 47, No. 1, February, 1983, pp. 40-1.*

These twelve stories sparkle with scintillating imagery, much of it drawn from the Garden of Eden and Song of Songs, as they follow the linked destinies of twelve variously grimy, wretched, but chipper London apprentices through the cycle of the year and the cycles of adolescent love and hope. Only Garfield could combine so much tenderness with so much glittering wit and verbal dash. (pp. 305-06)

Michele Landsberg, in a review of "The Apprentices," in her Reading for the Love of It: Best Books for Young Readers, *Prentice Hall Press, 1987, pp. 305-14.*

BOSTOCK AND HARRIS: OR, THE NIGHT OF THE COMET (1979; U.S. edition as *The Night of the Comet*)

In addition to [having learned to enjoy wit as well as humor, readers] will need a certain power of concentration when they read *Bostock and Harris* if they are to follow the plot; in fact, readers who really want to know what happens might make a graph of the movements of the actors in this Regency masquerade. But perhaps a certain feeling of confusion is useful, for it is essential to comedy that it should be steered far enough into absurdity to ensure that reason cannot break in. This book is best thought of as a round dance in which the various couples are separated and reunited in a series of accidents arranged by the author in a very formal shape. Cassidy, an itinerant handyman, locates his love, Mary Flatley, in Brighton after a long search, but their union is interrupted because of his roving eye; Bostock, yearning after Harris's fourteen-year-old sister Mary, is rehearsed by his clever friend in the rudiments of courtship (which Harris has studied in birds rather than in people); her older sister Dorothy makes more than one false identification of a mysterious unknown lover. The movements of the dance are complicated by the well-meaning efforts of the two boys, whose hopes of reviving classical myth gave rise to *The Strange Affair of Adelaide Harris.* The sequel to that matchless tale, if perhaps less spontaneous in tone, is neatly constructed, the various events all leading up to a final scene on the Devil's Dyke, where everyone has gone ostensibly to view Piggott's Comet but in fact to try to resolve the confusions of a few days and to achieve the satisfaction of true love and friendship.

> *Margery Fisher, in a review of "Bostock and Harris: Or, the Night of the Comet," in* Growing Point, *Vol. 18, No. 4, November, 1979, p. 3600.*

All's well that ends well in Garfield's new comedy of errors. . . . [The characters] all weave a neat net of plots and sub-plots. Events evolve at a rapid clip like a good Virginia reel, until the entire cast of appealing characters does a deft dance on Devil's Dyke, when the long awaited comet of the title finally arrives "in the guise of a speedy Cupid, showering arrows down on the town." The most felicitious collection of mishaps since the author's equally *Strange Affair of Adelaide Harris.*

> *Laura Geringer, in a review of "Bostock and Harris: Or, the Night of the Comet," in* School Library Journal, *Vol. 26, No. 3, November, 1979, p. 87.*

With each successive book the author shows his manifold talents; not even his preoccupation with the eighteenth century restricts him, for he has worked its various aspects into novels of many moods. The two young conspirators of *The Strange Affair of Adelaide Harris* return in a book that echoes the high comedy and opera buffa of the period. . . . To carry the farce and to resolve the plot—almost mathematical in its intricacy and symmetry—other more or less lovelorn characters [besides Bostock and Harris] are important links in a long chain of mistaken identities: Cassidy, a roguish, philandering Irishman searching all England for his runaway sweetheart; pretty Mary Flatley, "who'd made an honest man of Cassidy by the contrary means of stealing away with his heart"; Andrews, the fishmonger's son; Dorothy, Harris's older sister, who ended up enamored of her timid music master; and sharp-tongued Maggie Hemp, "who couldn't keep a lover for more than a week because she couldn't help telling him things for his own good." A delicious literary concoction bubbling along with the author's perfect sense of dramatic timing and with his mixture of earthy humor and effervescent wit.

> *Ethel L. Heins, in a review of "Bostock and Harris:*

Or, the Night of the Comet," in The Horn Book Magazine, *Vol. LVI, No. 1, February, 1980, p. 60.*

JOHN DIAMOND (1980; U.S. edition as *Footsteps*)

Leon Garfield, word wizard extraordinary, virtuoso of the convoluted plot that is also a fast-moving adventure story, conjurer-up of times past and master of the macabre, is back; back with the best novel he has written since *Smith*. . . .

Most years since 1967 have seen new Garfields; some of his work, like *The Pleasure Garden* and *The Prisoner of September* have been well outside the children's field; some, like the "Apprentices" series, have been novelettes; slender, colourful (often over-colourful) evocations of individual eighteenth-century trades and occupations seen through the well-skinned eyes of the artful young.

Only last year, *Bostock and Harris,* a short frolicsome sequel to the major comic novel *The Strange Affair of Adelaide Harris,* had one pondering on whether Leon Garfield's gifts for burlesque and florid turn of phrase would ever again be channelled into a story that combined gripping plot with a graphic prose spiced, but not dominated by, verbal wit. In *John Diamond* Leon Garfield hits the gong dead centre; it will reverberate through the Eighties.

William Jones's father is dying. He had been in coffee—"not like a spoon, but in the way of buying and selling it". Only William Jones knows that his father, whose footsteps grow ever more halting through the long restless nights before he dies, was also in debt—a swindler, no less. The story Leon Garfield tells so brilliantly in his new novel is how young William Jones sets out from rural Hertfordshire for London all alone—to find Diamond, his father's partner, and to lay his father's ghost by righting paternal wrongs. . . .

John Diamond, in human terms as an exploration of guilt and love, as well as in the narrative terms of plot and excitement, is a great achievement. It brings the literary adventure story right back into the arena of children's reading for pleasure. And that, today, is a feat.

> *Elaine Moss, "Settling Old Scores," in* The Times Literary Supplement, *No. 4018, March 28, 1980, p. 355.*

Electricity has killed the classic adventure-story as surely as modern communications have. True, electricity has its own special glare of terror, but the shadows thrown by candlelight, the dark corners of rooms, the terrifying twitch of our sense of sound that comes from movement unseen (properties responsible for the atmosphere of, for instance, *The Prisoner of Zenda* or Weyman's *Abbess of Vlaye*) no longer have a place in adventures set in our time. In books that prove his inheritance of a great tradition, Leon Garfield has borrowed from that tradition the contrast of light and darkness which is partly a writer's trick and partly a far more meaningful metaphor. Of all his London romance-adventures, *John Diamond* is most skilfully governed by this particular narrative device. It is the story of a boy leaving a comfortable home in the airy country of Hertfordshire to follow the quest for his dead father's former partner and victim (though the object of his search turns out to be not benevolent father but flawed son) through the murky alleyways of London-past, in dingy tenements, on rooftops seamed with shadows thrown by the moon. William Jones's quest is dark because he has no idea how to identify 'John Diamond' and because the experience of twelve years has hardly warned him of the dark side of man's nature. His bizarre and alarming experiences in the streets of Holborn and Limehouse instruct him, brutally, not only in the darkness of hate, vengeance, violence, but also in the puzzling fact that darkness and light can be interchangeable. The charming and elegant Mr. Robinson proves an enemy, his whistled tune a menace. The ragged urchin called Shot-in-the-Head, whose knife seemed to threaten William, proves a loyal protector.

This mystery of hidden identities and (seemingly) hidden treasure is intensified by the alternations of darkness and light in background descriptions which are not merely a matter of atmosphere (though this is, as always with Leon Garfield, enormously important) but significant mirror-images of events. When William finally catches up with the elusive John Diamond (realising he has been with him all the time), it is on London Bridge after midnight, with the distant spires and poles of shipping 'sticking up out of the mist like a giant's pincushion' and with unseen lanterns producing 'cloudy yellow eyes'. Earlier, when the lad is sheltering from street-riots in a house whose importance to him he does not yet realise, he sits down to a bowl of soup 'entirely curtained in' by Mrs. Branch's washing. The booths in the Sun of Splendour are dark behind the central lights of the inn; the tunnel-like lair on the roof where Shot-in-the-Head lurks is dimly lit by a brazier and by the sparkles of the stolen brooches and rings which the wizened boy hoards like a magpie. The dark climax of the book is intensified by the flames of a burning house, an image of John Diamond's burning hatred of the Jones family.

Inevitably Dickens is invoked in this alternation of light and darkness and there are echoes of Dickens also in the way minor characters are created in one or two vivid strokes— Mrs. Branch who 'seemed to make soup as the rain makes mud, absolutely without thinking about it', or domineering Uncle Turner (the immediate cause of William's decamping from home) with his reiterated cry 'Give him to me for six months . . . and I'll make a man of him!', or the dwarfish Mr. Seed who has his own way of increasing his stature by drawing attention to his lack of it. Leon Garfield must by now be well accustomed to being compared with Dickens. But though echoes, especially of *Bleak House* and *Our Mutual Friend*, are heard everywhere in **John Diamond,** the author's voice emphatically sounds its own unmistakeable music. The puzzling double identity of John Diamond looks back to **Jack Holborn,** the use of weather in city streets to **Smith;** the teasing, bizarre images are unmistakeable Garfield (though in this book more than in any other they are exactly attuned to the character of the young narrator). Above all the story has that sustained, light, compassionate irony that gives his stories their special significance. . . . Drawn into the intricacies of mistake and misunderstanding, beguiled by quirky dialogue and by the comic-serious reflection of old wrongs, lured also into a vivid past through Antony Maitland's visualisation of odd folk and teeming London, I emerged from two readings of this superbly crafted tale with that sense of disorientation from the present which is the sign of satisfied imagination. This is surely the most brilliantly devised of all Leon Garfield's secondary worlds. (pp. 3742-43)

> *Margery Fisher, in a review of "John Diamond," in* Growing Point, *Vol. 19, No. 3, September, 1980, pp. 3742-43.*

This latest Garfield is a kind of staging post on the writer's

creative journey. The novel includes all the familiar elements of mystery, confidence trickery, search for identity, and moral strength emerging from the vulnerability of youth. It is all done with consummate skill and characteristic stylish elegance and wit.

The story of William Jones's breathless and dangerous quest through Garfield's London for an omnipresent shadow of evil intent going under the name of John Diamond, in order to make possible amends for his dead father's dishonesty and thereby to lay his restless ghost and ease his own tender conscience, is indeed so finally complete and masterly that one feels the author must now move on once more. . . . Put this one down half-way through if you can!

> *Gordon Parsons, in a review of "John Diamond," in* The School Librarian, *Vol. 28, No. 3, September, 1980, p. 289.*

FAIR'S FAIR (1981)

Leon Garfield is one of the best writers for children ever. His subtleties may not always be easily appreciated and the historical settings of all his books may set some children at a distance but his sense of story overcomes all. It is particularly refreshing therefore to have this big picture book with its full page colour illustrations [by Margaret Chamberlain] setting the Dickensian scene superbly to introduce a whole new generation to his work.

Just before Christmas, bitter cold on the streets of London and Jackson is out in it, an orphan, who survives by scrubbing doorsteps. Along comes a black dog, big as a donkey with eyes like street lamps. Hello—an iron key heavy enough to open a church is round its neck. The dog and the key lead Jackson to the discovery of a mysterious house where he finds another orphan, a girl, already installed. They have everything for their comfort—food is left for them but they never catch a glimpse of any person. But *"fair's fair"* so the children do what they can in return and when their own charity is tested prove that they too can be generous. In every sense a good book for children.

> *A review of "Fair's Fair," in* Books for Your Children, *Vol. 16, No. 3, Autumn-Winter, 1981, p. 22.*

Christmas, a time for warm hearts and generous impulses, belongs most of all to Dickens, as Leon Garfield has recognised in his tale of two street-urchins whose lives are dramatically changed through the benevolence of a rich gentleman and his lawyer. Jackson, 'thin, small and ugly', who 'stank like a drain' and the 'small, thin, dirty, tattered, angry little girl' whom the boy finds feasting in a seemingly empty house, come to their new life through the agency of a huge black dog. This in itself is enough to make an old story fresh and inviting. Leon Garfield's quirky phrases and sharp dialogue confirm the restatement of old values. Finally, Margaret Chamberlain's choice of a curiously offbeat, mildly grotesque manner of depicting children and adults and her dashing use of paint to suggest contrasts of cold and warmth, poverty and luxury, help to make a superb picture-story book.

> *Margery Fisher, in a review of "Fair's Fair," in* Growing Point, *Vol. 20, No. 4, November, 1981, p. 3972.*

Although some may object to the ungrammatical (but realistic) dialogue of the children, the story would be an excellent read-aloud. . . . The book is in no way another version of *Annie,* but in fact has a freshness and originality that makes it hard to put down.

> *Jean Hammond Zimmerman, in a review of "Fair's Fair," in* School Library Journal, *Vol. 30, No. 2, October, 1983, p. 176.*

KING NIMROD'S TOWER (with Michael Bragg, 1982)

King Nimrod's Tower uses a Biblical story creatively. Here is the building of the Tower of Babel seen from ground level, as it were, through the activities of a boy and his dog. As the boy struggles to instil some discipline into his wilful pet, foremen, architects, craftsmen and labourers, and the great King himself, raise the tower even higher. But God looks down from the clouds more interested in the boy than in the antics of men. When their work puts the safety of the boy in hazard God acts and the work grinds to a halt through a confusion of tongues. King Nimrod abandons his tower, but the boy has at last taught his dog to sit and stand. The last word is left with God. Every word counts in Leon Garfield's brief text, which moves the action forward smoothly through Michael Bragg's dramatic and humorous drawings. An original picture-book of quite outstanding quality, for its idea and for its performance.

> *M. Crouch, in a review of "King Nimrod's Tower," in* The Junior Bookshelf, *Vol. 46, No. 5, October, 1982, pp. 182-83.*

Though simple, Garfield's text has great impact: strong poetic images like 'and threw up their hats and handkerchiefs and dinner bundles, till the tower looked like a tree with blossoms tossed up in the wind' imprint vivid pictures in the mind. The parallel stories are sensitively illustrated with Brueghel-like paintings; and such is the design of the book that there is a perfect balance between text and pictures. I hope this one will reach a wide audience: it deserves to.

> *Jill Bennett, in a review of "King Nimrod's Tower," in* The School Librarian, *Vol. 31, No. 2, June, 1983, p. 128.*

THE WRITING ON THE WALL (with Michael Bragg, 1983)

The Writing on the Wall is Leon Garfield's second picture book version of an episode from the Bible, and, as in *King Nimrod's Tower,* the events are seen through the eyes of a child. Garfield uses rich poetic images and rippling rhythms with stirring eloquence. As in *King Nimrod's Tower,* the message in *The Writing on the Wall* is clearly that the meek shall inherit the earth; while Belshazzar is brought to justice for daring to eat out of God's holy golden bowl, a hungry cat. "tattered, one-eared, smelly old Mordecai", is allowed to drink cream from the same bowl. . . . Garfield's brand of heroic story-telling is a long distance away from the type of modern whimsy presented by Helme Heine [in *The Most Wonderful Egg in the World*], but what they have in common is the ability to communicate directly with children without falseness.

> *Kicki Moxon Browne, "The Child Within: Picture Books 1," in* The Times Literary Supplement, *No. 4200, September 30, 1983, p. 1050.*

A message mysteriously appears on the wall stating that Bel-

shazzar's days are numbered; Daniel is the only one who can interpret the message. Garfield relates these events through Sam, a Babylonian kitchen boy, and there is a subplot involving Sam and a scruffy cat, Mordecai. The commotion at the feast after the appearance of the writing allows Sam to feed Mordecai under the table, using one of the sacred gold dishes Belshazzar has taken from the Lord's sanctuary. Daniel appears and gives his judgment; most of the people flee. He then discovers Sam, and assures him that he was not responsible for what happened by feeding the cat. This gloss gives a puzzling sense of Garfield's intent. By reducing Belshazzar's sins to simple greed, he has lost the meaning of the story. His version of Sam and Mordecai seems disjointed and it does not stand well on its own. As a Bible story, it is incomplete, and as a story of a Babylonian kitchen boy, it lacks characterization and a meaningful structure of its own. (pp. 54-5)

> *Elizabeth Bruce, in a review of "The Writing on the Wall," in* School Library Journal, *Vol. 30, No. 4, December, 1983, pp. 54-5.*

GUILT AND GINGERBREAD (1984)

Heart-transplants—with a difference—provide the motif for Leon Garfield's new fantasy. Young Princess Charlotte is renowned for the heart of gold with which she dispenses hospitality to strangers and rules her Rhineland principality of Oberweselberg, a fairytale city of quaint streets and brightly painted shutters looking so exactly as it does on stamps that you "half-expect to see Twenty Pfennigs engraved on a cloud". Along with its air of enchantment it has up-to-date sanitation, an excellent public transport system, early closing on Thursdays and steamers calling twice a day. The best of both worlds, indeed.

Thither goes, Giorgio, a good-looking but impecunious philosophy student of Padua, who has already absorbed the important lesson that it is better to be rich than poor, and that marriage may be the easiest route to that end. With his sagacious old horse (unnamed, an odd omission in a children's story) he crosses the Alps on one of those quests which are a favourite Garfield device to symbolize the search for truth and permanent values.

Nearing his destination, he has the traditional wayside encounter with a witchlike old woman, whose one desire in life is the princess's golden heart. She asks Giorgio to get it for her. When he shrinks from the ghoulish commission she gives an alarming demonstration of how deftly she can, with her magic scissors, needle and thread, slit open his arm and stitch it up again without trace or tremor. Afraid to refuse, but with no intention of fulfilling her horrific instructions, he accepts the needlework case pressed upon him, together with the necessary replacement heart of finest china, and resumes his journey.

He is warmly received at the castle, which, like the princess, is all it has been cracked up to be, with its peacocks, Italian fountains and formal French gardens "like an impossible problem in green geometry". Now, as we are all fully expecting with delicious dread, his good resolutions weaken. Temptation lures him on, step by fatal step, not greed but vanity, over-estimating (as which of us does not?) his own capacity for self-restraint. As he stands over the sleeping princess, still intending no action, the demonic scissors uncontrollably take charge (no prizes offered for interpretations) and in a trice the golden heart is laid bare and detached. Dumbfounded, he drops and smashes the china replica and snatches up a bedside apple to fill the space. The princess does not wake. With the witch's needle even Giorgio's stitchery achieves invisible mending. . . . Only when, after a succession of nocturnal transplants, Giorgio is driven to restore the original heart of gold, is the parable worked out to its happy ending. Even then, there are tantalizing ambiguities. . . . This is cool, Mozartian Garfield, with no violent action or gusty garlic-flavoured characterization, but all the usual verbal felicities, quick-witted dialogue, humorous incongruity, new-minted similes, and his inimitable quick-silver fancy.

Geoffrey Trease, "Delicious Dread," in The Times Literary Supplement, *No. 4252, September 28, 1984, p. 1106.*

Like all students in pursuit of truth, Giorgio finds that lack of money forces him to search for fortune. So he sets off to win the hand of the rich and beautiful Princess Charlotte who rules the land with a golden heart. As in all good fairy tales he meets an old woman on his journey, but this is no fairy godmother. In return for Giorgio's success she demands that he give her the golden heart. This witty and in some ways poignant story maps Giorgio's futile attempts both to secure his fortune and preserve the golden heart. Leon Garfield handles the fairy tale with much skill. While working through the repetitions of the genre (Giorgio is compelled to take the heart and replace it with totally unsuitable substitutes three times) he sows his text with neat maxims and amusing dialogue.

As an adult reader used to the conventions of the fairy tale and understanding the jibes against philosophy and academe, I thoroughly enjoyed this story. But would a young reader? Both adult and child can experience Giorgio's quest. The 'guilt and gingerbread' need to be combined in a mutual enjoyment of the text. *Share* this book with a child.

Joan Foley, in a review of "Guilt and Gingerbread," in The School Librarian, *Vol. 33, No. 1, March, 1985, p. 35.*

THE KING IN THE GARDEN (with Michael Bragg, 1984)

This book has a strange and haunting quality weaving in and out of the immense pathos aroused through Leon Garfield's text and Michael Bragg's atmospherically beautiful illustrations.

This [is a] rather special book. . . .

The story begins with the mystery of the dishevelled and wandering king behaving in a strange manner inside Abigail's garden. From then on, skilfully using a flashback technique and rich allegory, Leon Garfield unfolds the mystery surrounding the king.

The lyrical text is not at all biblical considering, perhaps, the nature of the story. Instead, there is a down-to-earth poetic quality, aided by shots of humour from the earthy Abigail. This is one illustrated book that has, I believe, enduring quality.

Ron Morton, in a review of "The King in the Garden," in Books for Your Children, *Vol. 20, No. 1, Spring, 1985, p. 17.*

Bible stories have it all—royalty, revenge, high drama, pa-

thos. In Leon Garfield and Michael Bragg's **King in the Garden,** a wonderful retelling of the Old Testament tale of King Nebuchadnezzar's madness, Abigail, a determined-looking little girl, has spotted the lunatic king grazing on grass behind her house. The practical-minded child is outraged that a slobbering, filthy creature should be gobbling up her flowers and crying into her lily pond, and she simply isn't going to put up with it. Unfortunately, Babylon's smug elders won't help out, declaring that the king is in his palace—neat as a pin, well fed and "grand as God."

Abigail realizes that she has to take matters into her own hands. She shrieks at the king, orders him off her property and finally seizes him by the hair and shouts, "I hate you! . . . Go away, you mad, sad king! Go back to your home!"

But this is just what the king cannot do. "Home?" he says. "What's that?"

"Why, it's where you can eat and drink and cry to your heart's content!" the down-to-earth Abigail explains. "Everybody knows that!"

"But I am nobody," the repulsive monarch says. "I am nothing. I am neither fish, flesh, nor fowl."

Abigail knows better, as usual, and she sees a solution to the king's problem—and hers. Armed with a brush, comb and scissors, she untangles, washes and clips the king's hair until he emerges in his glory again.

Now that he is looking better, he feels better, but he realizes to his horror that he has neglected his kingdom, which he thinks must have been destroyed during the seven years of his madness. Wrong again, Abigail explains as she leads him home: "Everything is just as it should be." . . .

[Now] a changed Nebuchadnezzar can return to lead his well-ordered kingdom, and Abigail, vindicated, can go home for tea. They have both realized the story's point—people can get along just fine without a king, but neither people nor a king can get along without the help of God. This is a sensible, unpretentious, handsomely illustrated book with a text so beautifully cadenced that it flows off the tongue as trippingly as "Nebuchadnezzar." **The King in the Garden** is a delight.

Elizabeth Crow, in a review of "The King in the Garden," in The New York Times Book Review, *April 14, 1985, p. 42.*

SHAKESPEARE STORIES (1985)

A collection of stories based on plays may seem an essentially untheatrical enterprise, a translation from the public, first-person enactment of events by a whole company of players to a private, third-person recounting of them by a single voice: a movement away from the stage to the study. That is how Mary and Charles Lamb presented their selection of twenty *Tales from Shakespeare.* It was "an introduction to the study of Shakespeare" for young persons, and especially for "young ladies". . . . The Lambs' preface does not mention the theatre.

Leon Garfield and his illustrator, Michael Foreman, make no statement of intent, but the dedication of their book to the Royal Shakespeare Company points to an essential difference between Garfield's method and the Lambs'. Whereas the

Lambs provide a simplified reading experience as a preparation for a more complex and difficult experience of the same kind, Leon Garfield seeks to convey in prose narrative the experience, not of reading the twelve plays that he includes, but of seeing them performed. . . .

[Throughout] these stories the theatrical imagination is evident. Sometimes, indeed, the action that Garfield visualizes as an accompaniment to the dialogue could be used as stage business: Falstaff "sat down and regarded his countenance in the diminishing bowl of a spoon" before saying "Why, my skin hangs about me like an old lady's loose-gown"; Polonius reads his list of the multiple kinds of entertainment offered by the actors who visit Elsinore "from the company's extensive advertisement, which reached down, like a paper apron, almost to his knees"; and after the enraged Claudius has stopped the play and stormed out of the chamber, "the bewildered Player King crept back to recover his tinsel crown. Then he went away, sadly shaking his head. The performance had not gone well." It might almost be William Hazlitt writing about Edmund Kean.

Longer episodes, too—such as that in which Falstaff and Prince Hal successively assume the role of King Henry IV—are narrated with a vivid sense of their theatrical impact. But Garfield writes like one who has not merely imagined the plays theatrically but has also mastered their structural principles, with the result that he can transmute their essential features into the medium of the short story. He can deftly sketch in as much of the plot as is necessary to his narrative purpose: "Fortinbras, the Prince of Norway, was aiming to seize back the lands that the dead King had boldly conquered": it gives us all we need to know. He can offer penetrating comment that takes us to the heart of a situation: Gloucester (in *King Lear*), having seen Edgar disguised as Poor Tom, "no more knew his son naked than he had really known him in his best attire". And Garfield's sense of overall structure makes for a wonderfully successful articulation of all elements of the plot. . . . [His] selection seems dictated always by a sense of the demands of the whole story. Narrative suspense is delicately manipulated—"Before you hear of the shipwreck . . .", begins *Twelfth Night*—the transitions are brilliantly effected by the analytical drawing of parallels: "While one Harry was idly dreaming of the glory that would be his, the other Harry was much concerned with the glory that *was* his"; and "Even as the casket that Jessica had thrown down from Shylock's window had contained her father's treasure, so one of the three closed caskets in Belmont contained another father's treasure". Such comments have the quality of good criticism as well as good story-telling.

Whereas Mary and Charles Lamb aimed as far as possible to use Shakespeare's words in both narrative and dialogue, Garfield does so only in dialogue. He selects judiciously, never indulging in set pieces simply for their own sake. His own narrative is written in a crisp, sharply metaphorical style, often employing bold images: Juliet stares down from her balcony "with her willow hair weeping"; when Kate, the shrew, stormed through her father's house in a bad temper "doors kept going off like exploding chestnuts"; in Illyria, thatched cottages are "neat as well-combed children". Garfield's prose is mannered, but it succeeds remarkably in providing an acceptable alternative to Shakespeare's poetry. Ariel, indeed, is more poetical in Garfield's prose than he often is in theatrical realization: "with a flash and a whirl and a quick unwinding of air, Prospero's servant appeared"; and when Shakespeare's

effects are visual rather than verbal, as in the banquet episode in *The Tempest,* Garfield can rise to the occasion with a vivid prose counterpart.

Though the presentation of the volume suggests that it is intended primarily for young readers. Leon Garfield's uncondescending tone gives the stories a wider appeal: they are not pale reflections of the plays, not introductions to the study of Shakespeare, but fresh creations with a life of their own.

Stanley Wells, "The Theatre of the Page," in The Times Literary Supplement, *No. 4282, April 26, 1985, p. 478.*

The value of this book will depend upon the intended use. From the deep orange endpapers, through generous margins and clear print, to the multitude of evocative illustrations, the volume is a delight. Foreman's intense watercolors and lively ink-wash illustrations go far to help create the moods of the stories. The storytelling is uneven—Garfield is able to evoke the heartbreak of *King Lear* but fails to convey the crazy humor of *Twelfth Night*—but it is generally competent enough. However, Garfield's visual descriptions are so specific and so lavish; his line interpretations so absolute that he almost guarantees that any given production will seem inadequate after such a buildup! Libraries that have Lamb's *Tales from Shakespeare* or Chute's *Stories from Shakespeare* probably don't need to add this luxury item. Garfield covers only 12 of the best-known plays, while the Lambs tell 20 tales and Chute leads the pack with 36. While Garfield's style is more accessible to modern readers and covers the plays more completely than the evasive Victorianisms of the Lambs, he must take a back seat when compared with the lucid straightforward prose in Chute's book.

Sally T. Margolis, in a review of "Shakespeare Stories," in School Library Journal, *Vol. 32, No. 5, January, 1986, p. 66.*

Telling the story of a Shakespeare play is an exacting test of understanding and imagination. It is far easier to recount *The Iliad,* the plays of most other playwrights, *Don Quixote* or even "The Brothers Karamazov" than to give someone an adequate narrative of *Hamlet, The Merchant of Venice* or *The Tempest.* In performance even the most complicated of Shakespeare's plays leave the impression that the emotions and actions of dozens of characters come together to give one a clear, direct comprehension of life. It is only when one tries to tell one of these well-known tales that he knows how subtle an artist, and how cunning an illusionist, Shakespeare was.

Leon Garfield's performance in **Shakespeare Stories** is masterly. In narratives of remarkable clarity the British writer tells the stories of a dozen plays—five tragedies, four comedies, two histories and *The Merchant of Venice.* That last one and *The Taming of the Shrew, Twelfth Night* and *A Midsummer Night's Dream* best reveal the virtuosity Mr. Garfield has developed in many years of writing dozens of children's books and historical novels. The injuries done to, or by, such characters as Lear, Richard II, Othello and Macbeth are easier to present without distorting the play than the sufferings of Malvolio in *Twelfth Night,* Shylock in *The Merchant of Venice* or Kate in *The Taming of the Shrew.* In Mr. Garfield's deft narratives the laughter is the same that one finds in the plays, but so is the uneasiness—brought on by the angry departure of Malvolio who, fool that he is, is not unpitiable, the pain of Shylock, not all of it brought on himself; or the unsettling transformation of Kate into a dutiful wife. He gets the balances right.

Possibly just as important for the audience of young teen-agers the book seems meant for primarily (although it can be a pleasure for anyone older than that to read these versions), he holds each story to about 5,000 words. His choice of words is more important than their number. With Shakespeare that choice is never easy. Mr. Garfield limits direct quotations to key sentences that reveal character or define the action, but he does weave a certain amount of Shakespearean language into his own throughout, so the reader of his tales gets some notion of the richness, and occasionally the oddity, of the playwright's expressions. The method does not make all these stories easy to read, but with a few exceptions it heightens the dramatic interest of them in a way that should make young-sters stay with them, and learn something new about English at the same time.

A few of the stories are problematical. It is unlikely that American readers will enjoy *King Richard the Second* as much as Mr. Garfield's English readers might, and his deci-sion to recount only the first part of *King Henry IV* must leave readers wondering how it all came out. And I think the one play in which Mr. Garfield fails to achieve his customary clarity is *Hamlet,* his treatment of the ghost of the prince's father and of Ophelia introduces complications that are not necessarily in the play. Nonetheless, his success in telling the majority of these stories is admirable.

> *D. J. R. Bruckner, in a review of "Shakespeare Sto-ries," in* The New York Times Book Review, *Janu-ary 26, 1986, p. 32.*

THE WEDDING GHOST (1985)

The Wedding Ghost is, I think, [Garfield and illustrator Charles Keeping's] most remarkable production to date. Dif-ficult to classify, it has a picture-book format, with a large page and many monochrome drawings, but neither words nor pictures are particularly directed to children. A book for Garfield and Keeping and for like minded people in fact. . . . Mr. Garfield offers a gloss on the story of the Sleep-ing Beauty. Beauty is awakened not by a prince but by Jack Best, son of a builder's merchant ('Why go elsewhere when we are Best!). It all happens just before Jack's wedding day, and what will the beauteous Gillian think? Mr. Garfield puts some of his most atmospheric writing into the account of Jack's quest and discovery of Beauty's palace. Superb stuff this, full of characteristic wit but with more restraint than usual. . . . Altogether, in absolute terms, a most notable achievement, and for the right reader, meeting it at the right moment, a powerful experience.

> *M. Crouch, in a review of "The Wedding Ghost," in* The Junior Bookshelf, *Vol. 49, No. 4, August, 1985, p. 176.*

Haunting in both art and narrative, this sophisticated mod-ern elaboration on "Sleeping Beauty" will appeal to adults as much as it will to precocious juvenile readers. . . . Keeping's black pen-and-wash drawings are mysterious and sinister, projecting the power of Garfield's densely packed writing with a relentless force of their own. The book is deceptively formatted in the size of a large picture book. Illusions of time, allusions to literature, and some terrifying graphic images

make it a supernatural tour de force for an audience with a taste for the Gothic.

> *Betsy Hearne, in a review of "The Wedding Ghost," in* Bulletin of the Center for Children's Books, *Vol. 40, No. 8, April, 1987, p. 144.*

This illustrated story for the older reader achieves rich sym-bolism through the blending of two distinct sources: Shake-speare's *Twelfth Night* and the traditional tale of the Sleeping Beauty. The result is a haunting, short story, narrated with the sensuous imagery for which Garfield is rightly praised but with a plot drawn from the nineteenth-century gothics. . . . Garfield's rapid flow of words, listing of details, and uncanny descriptions of characters create the feeling of a play—drawing the reader into the scene as spectator. The nuances of the relationship between Jack and Jill, the somewhat less than genteel quality of the latter's family, the skillful fore-shadowing of what is to come are so artfully handled that their significance is apparent only in retrospect. . . . An un-forgettable experience. (pp. 611-12)

> *Mary M. Burns, in a review of "The Wedding Ghost," in* The Horn Book Magazine, *Vol. LXIII, No. 5, September-October, 1987, pp. 611-12.*

THE DECEMBER ROSE (1986)

Absalom Brown, better known as Barnacle from his amazing powers of holding on, is, like Tom in *The Water Babies,* a Vic-torian sweep's boy who falls down the wrong chimney. He lands in the middle of a dark and devious plot, flees in terror clutching by accident its key, a golden locket, and is then pur-sued relentlessly throughout the book by Inspector Creaker, "a dark and terrible figure, shaped like a coffin, with enor-mous square-toed boots".

The book was recently a BBC1 television serial; it is, in fact, a children's version of the currently fashionable *Edge of Darkness*-type thriller, in which the righteous individual or group confronts an evil and corrupt establishment, which is misusing justice and the force of law. Here the good, the side of the individual and his private conscience, is represented by Tom Gosling, master of the Thames barge Lady of the Lea. "The policeman inside his head was paid his wages by a dif-ferent government from the one who paid the policeman on the corner of the street", remarks the author, and Gosling himself, repeating the sentiment, bangs the nail through the wood: "There's a law inside of us all that we has to abide by, and sometimes it's a different law from the law of the land." He takes Barnacle in, feeds him, washes him—making him temporarily unrecognizable—reforms him, humanizes him, teaches him self-sacrifice, and in the end is saved by him, when this new Barnacle goes alone to meet the dread Inspec-tor Creaker. . . .

The December Rose is a colourful, ebulliently lively book, which is by turns amusing, exciting and touching. It is narrat-ed in the third person, but in that subjective, impressionistic manner which tends to empathize with rather than describe. Do children prefer this to the staider, old-fashioned, more ob-jective narrative voice? If not, they probably should. At the same time the book is, in its own way, no less moralistic than Kingsley's Victorian tale, and—despite a veneer of social re-alism—even perhaps shares some of its predecessor's senti-mentality. For a clear, cold, hard look at life and death in a children's book one still has to turn to Beatrix Potter's *The Tale of Mr. Tod.*

> *T. J. Binyon, "The Policeman Inside," in* The Times Literary Supplement, *No. 4334, April 25, 1986, p. 458.*

The December Rose is the one book under review which *will* be read time and again. (p. 36)

The December Rose runs true to form, brimming over with much 19th-century fog and gloom. . . . The chase that follows [Barnacle's escape from Inspector Creaker] is worthy of its counterpart at the beginning of *The Water Babies:* it could hardly have been bettered. (pp. 36-7)

The December Rose is not quite on a par with *The Apprentices,* Garfield's masterpiece to date. But its many strengths owe much to his masterly gifts as a story-teller drawing on oral as well as literary traditions. As the Colonel says to Barnacle, 'Stories, my child, are like candles in the mind. They comfort and show us wonders.' Garfield's candles will never be extinguished. (p. 37)

> *John Horder, in a review of "December Rose," in* The Spectator, *Vol. 256, No. 8233, April 26, 1986, pp. 36-7.*

Here is a first rate adventure story in the pattern Leon Garfield has used so successfully in *Smith* and *John Diamond.* . . .

The exciting and dramatic story is set in the environment the author uses to such effect, Victorian London, where the abyss between the rich and the destitute is so marked, where there is thoughtless cruelty and rough kindness. . . .

It is Barnacle, however, who is the masterpiece of characterization. A foundling and a sweep's boy, he appears at first meeting as little more than an animal—in fact he bites! Gradually under the influence of Thomas Gosling he shows his true worth as a resourceful, brave and affectionate boy, whose respect and utter loyalty are for one person 'Mister Goslin".

The end is deeply moving and 'right' for a book which is not only compulsive reading but has that underlying window on real life that all the best adventure stories have.

Surely this is a Medal book.

> *E. Colwell, in a review of "The December Rose," in* The Junior Bookshelf, *Vol. 50, No. 3, June, 1986, p. 114.*

THE EMPTY SLEEVE (1988)

Born in Hope Sufferance Wharf in Rotherhithe, as the clock strikes on a Saturday in January, Paul Gannet is a chime-child who has communications and dealings with the devil. His younger and weaker twin brother Peter comes into the world after the clock has stopped sounding the hour and so avoids this dubious privilege. When he is fourteen the older, "Well-timbered" twin is apprenticed to a locksmith in Covent Garden, while his younger, "chapel-eyed" brother stays at home—being a ship-chandler's.

On the morning of Paul's departure the evil-smelling Mr. Bagley gives each twin a model ship, carved out of a mutton bone, in a bottle: each ship contains a bit of its owner's soul and the state of the vessels reflects the state of each twin's

moral being. The first twist in Leon Garfield's accomplished study of duality comes when the sweet-natured Peter secretly swaps the ships about and keeps Paul's for himself. Soon, as Paul learns the tricks and wiles of the rowdy apprentices of Cucumber Alley up in town, where he works for Mr Woodcock and his craftsman Mr Shoveller (a shoveller is a kind of duck), his ship begins to decay. Paul's desperate search for money to enable him to escape from his present life leads him into the trade of lending out the key to the alley to other apprentices for a small fee, and finally into the clutches of the sinister Lord Marriner. Paul's ship is wrecked, but Peter, who has anxiously watched its decay, comes to the rescue and the antagonistic twins become fast and affectionate friends.

Leon Garfield creates a Victorian world of coincidences, reflections, doubles, revenants, doppelgängers, secrets and of the occult with practised and fluent ease; he manages to be chilling without being frightening, mysterious without being ludicrous. The mutual dislike, but essential similarity of the twins, the one pale and delicate, the other felt by those older than him to be a coarse lout, is particularly well done. Paul's view of other people is pleasantly harsh and cynical and his life as a locksmith's apprentice realistically described, without sentimentality or exaggeration. His future trade supplies the genesis for the novel's secrecy: " 'In a locksmith's house" ', says Polly, the kindly maid who keeps him supplied with food, " 'things has to be kept locked up. And that means everything: spoons, jools, *and* tongues!" ' Paul lives among the blacksmith's tools and fire which turn iron and steel into keys and locks. But essentially he is a bolter, who longs at first to escape from himself to sea and then from his adolescence into the arms of plump Ruby Stint, the jeweller's daughter (a stint is a small sandpiper). . . .

Like other birds, Paul Gannet dives and swoops, but he falls into petty crime, deceit, drunkenness, the snow his unlucky presence always seems to conjure up, and finally into his own guilty shadow—the beckoning devil whose empty sleeve has haunted him throughout his life in London. Wishing to run away from all this to a ship which will sail to Zanzibar and the China Seas he falls into the arms of Lord Marriner, sells him his brother's ship, finds out something of the more grown-up transgressions of adultery and murder, but in return is reconciled to his own personality, which turns out not to be as nasty as everybody else had always made it out to be.

Lord Marriner is the only weak point in *The Empty Sleeve,* a jealous husband too obviously drawn and improbably placed in such a subtle and intelligent book. Marriner is a strange lapse, for Garfield's strength lies in creating memorable minor characters, a vivid sense of time and place, and a distinctive atmosphere of smells and tastes, with great skill and economy.

> *H. R. Woudhuysen, "Dealing and Double-Dealing," in* The Times Literary Supplement, *No. 4447, June 24-30, 1988, p. 716.*

The ambiguities of human behaviour and of fraternal interdependence provide the theme for *The Empty Sleeve;* the story of twin brothers trapped in love and hate, of life and of one another, takes one back to that very first Garfield extravaganza, *Jack Holborn.* Ships in a bottle, made by an old ship's carpenter, reflect the pattern and in a mysterious way contain the souls of these two interdependent lives; misfortune causes the rigging of one model to break—but which brother owns this ship? The reader is teased all through this period-adventure with doubts and contradictions, misled by the assumption that Peter Gannet, locksmith's apprentice, is the 'bad' twin and Paul, sickly stay-at-home, is the 'good' one. Round the brothers is arranged a typical group of Garfield eccentrics, from murderous Lord Marriner and his shabby usher Mr. Velonty to Jay and Dawkins, whose thievish proclivities lead Peter astray, and fat Ruby, the jeweller's daughter, an unlikely romantic light in Peter's life. Together with this cloud of witnesses there is a conglomeration of suggestive images—fog in the Dickensian streets, wild storm, apparitions and sinister shifting handprints—while old Mr. Bagley's prediction that 'Saturday's child, born on the chime, will surely see ghosts and have communications with the devil' acts as a refrain and a kind of compulsion on Peter, who is not as thick as he appears and who enjoys a wry kind of triumph after he has been beset by enemies and temptations. Whether the reader concludes that Peter and Paul were governed by Fate or whether they seem to create events by the operation of their dual natures, the author has as always declined to do more than set an intriguing problem in heredity and environment and leave it to us to make up our minds about this latest of the line of uniquely mannered and compelling period-adventures. (pp. 5066-67)

> *Margery Fisher, in a review of "The Empty Sleeve,"* in Growing Point, *Vol. 27, No. 4, November, 1988, pp. 5066-67.*

A master of epigrammatic, figurative writing, the author draws the reader, with the opening paragraph, straight into the novel. The period—eighteenth or early nineteenth-century—is never precisely indicated, nor does it need to be; far more important is the sense of suspense and the almost palpable atmosphere of foreboding and doom. . . . Leon Garfield, as usual, is an irresistible virtuoso at hyperbole—in language, in characterizations, and in plot.

> *Ethel L. Heins, in a review of "The Empty Sleeve,"* in The Horn Book Magazine, *Vol. LXV, No. 1, January-February, 1989, p. 78.*

BLEWCOAT BOY (1988)

Why do some child readers feel at home in "historical" novels, and others find them alien? How does a writer achieve this sense of sameness and distance both?

Leon Garfield seems to solve the matter, I would say, not only by the sheer vitality of his writing, but by being wholly *within* his chosen time and place—something admirably shown in *Blewcoat Boy.* If he has clearly learnt from Dickens, Mayhew, Gay of the "Beggar's Opera", perhaps Mark Twain, the resulting voice is unmistakably his own. Here we have two orphaned urchins, brother and sister, ten and nine, "a bony, ragged, runaway pair, with bottle-green eyes and foxy looks", living rough on the wild side of St. James's Park. Young Nick is obsessed by the need to get his sister a dowry—or she'll be on his hands for life.

Chance puts them in the way of the Blewcoat School, a bygone 18th-century charity. "You must bring your father along," they are told. Quick! They must find a temporary Dad. They rummage about the alleys and end up with Old Parrot-face, a lightfingered Welshman with a splendid vocabulary and a heart of gold. The characters crackle with life; the words remain in the mind. This may be small-scale Garfield, but it's vintage none the less.

> *Naomi Lewis, "Back to the Past," in* The Times Educational Supplement, *No. 3778, November 25, 1988, p. 31.*

Not only should good children's historical fiction give an accurate account of the facts, it should also give us the feel of a period, its smells and tastes and sounds. No one does this better than Leon Garfield, and in *Blewcoat Boy* he transports us to the filthy slums of Victorian Westminster. . . . It is a good story, short and straightforward enough to be accessible to slower readers, and a vivid introduction to a visit to the Blewcoat School. (p. 37)

> *Juliet Townsend, "The Way It Was for the Moment," in* The Spectator, *Vol. 261, No. 8370, December 10, 1988, pp. 37-8.*

Paul Goble

1933-

English-born American author and illustrator of fiction and reteller.

Devoting himself to presenting grade school readers with works which focus on native American legends and customs, Goble is celebrated for successfully capturing both the attributes and spirit of his subjects; critic Jon C. Stott has called him "the foremost contemporary interpreter for children of native myths and legends." Writing primarily of the Sioux, Blackfoot, and Cheyenne peoples, he reflects the way of life of the Plains Indians through stories of famous battles, porquoi and trickster tales, popular legends, and narratives of episodes in Amerindian history. Goble is often noted as a writer who emphasizes the nobility of American Indian culture. In *Beyond the Ridge* (1989), for example, he offers young readers a sensitive portrayal of Amerindian rituals and spiritual beliefs. Picturing a family as it prepares the body of their grandmother for burial, he simultaneously shows the woman on her journey into the afterlife, ascending a hill to the ridge where her ancestors wait for her to join them. Goble has been enthralled by Indian culture since boyhood; as an adult, he traveled to the Great Plains several times and lived with native American tribes, two of which have adopted him. Not only critically acclaimed, his works are also welcomed by native American readers for their insightful handling of such themes as the harmony between people and nature, friendship with animals, and admiration for bravery in battle. Goble delineates his themes in the formal poetic style of Indian storytelling, often including Amerindian songs and poems as well as bibliographies of suggestions for further readings. He sees himself, however, as an interpreter, not a reteller, and purposely enhances his subjects with personal style and perspective.

Goble's distinctive approach also extends to his illustrations. In his first two books, *Red Hawk's Account of Custer's Last Battle: The Battle of the Little Bighorn, 25 June 1876* (1969) and *Brave Eagle's Account of the Fetterman Fight, 21 December 1866* (1972), which he coauthored with his first wife Dorothy, Goble relates the story of two legendary battles through the narration of fictional Sioux warriors. In his drawings for these works, Goble employs a method based on the ledger book art used by native Americans during the 1870s. These Indians, taken prisoner and transported to the southern United States, tried to preserve Amerindian historical events through the pictures they created in ledger books given to them by their captors. Goble's illustrations echo these drawings in their intense colors, stylized forms, and two-dimensionality. In subsequent works, he increasingly integrates elements from ledger book art with his own details, a style he would develop fully in *The Girl Who Loved Wild Horses* (1978), the tale of a girl whose passion for horses is so strong that she is transformed into a beautiful mare. In this and succeeding titles, Goble's illustrations include such symbols of Amerindian culture as the circle to signify unity and wavy lines to depict lightning while accurately utilizing motifs found on teepees, shields, hides, and other items decorated by tribes of the Great Plains. He then takes these tradition-

al symbols and invests them with some of the components of contemporary art: vigorous, rhythmic design, sophisticated composition, and copious, dramatic use of white space. In this way, he has been credited with creating an image of native American life and legend that is wholly veracious and remarkably personal. Goble is also the illustrator of a collection of Indian legends transcribed and edited by Richard Erdoes. *The Girl Who Loved Wild Horses* was awarded the Caldecott Medal in 1979.

(See also *Something about the Author,* Vol. 25 and *Contemporary Authors,* Vols. 93-96.)

GENERAL COMMENTARY

JOSEPH EPES BROWN

I first heard of Paul Goble during the war years through our mutual British friend Marco Pallis, the distinguished Tibetan scholar best known perhaps for his important book *Peaks and Lamas.* As Pallis was throughout his life a champion of Tibetan peoples and cultures, he undoubtedly foresaw in the young Paul Goble a potential champion of the American Indians, since their traditional beliefs and cultures were similarly oppressed by peoples of alien beliefs and life-ways. Knowing of my own writings and relationships with American Indians, Pallis asked me to contact Paul to add what I could to the warm encouragement he had always offered this unusual young person. Following a period of correspondence with Paul in the late war years and the shipments to England of Indian books and artifacts, I finally met him and his family at Greatstones, their home outside Oxford. Paul was a sensitive youth with a strong passion and ear for everything relating to North American Indians; with bows and arrows which he had beautifully made, we scouted the English countryside, where lawns became the Dakota plains, British hares became bison, and neighbors' horses were there to be taken with courage and honor. Around our camp fire we talked of the old Lakota sage Black Elk, with whom I had been living and learning, and of the wisdom of his people, which he had been willing to share with the outer world through the two books, *Black Elk Speaks* and *The Sacred Pipe*. Indeed, later in life Paul was to write: "It was the books concerning the wisdom of Black Elk which finally determined my life's orientation."

Paul became a student who not only read everything he could find on American Indian history and sacred lore but sought to integrate what he learned into his person; and in keeping with his own art heritage, he applied this learning to his growing understanding of American Indian art forms, examples of which he assiduously sought out in British museums and private collections. At one time Paul was particularly helpful in making for me beautifully executed copies of Plains Indian depictions of animals and birds, a facility now so evident in his numerous books. It is the quality of Paul's understanding of the inner spirit of the Indian, intensified in later years by his travels to America and by direct contacts with Indians, which lends to his writing and painting something of the Indians' own spirit and perspective. At the same time he retains the integrity of his own style and perspective and discipline, which spring from his own background, not the least part of which was his distinguished work in art and design in England.

In becoming an American citizen, in taking up residence in the sacred *Pa Sapa*—Black Hills—of South Dakota, and in placing himself closer to his adopted Indian families, Paul Goble has come home. It is clear that we may now anticipate a continuity resulting from a growing maturity in his writing and illustration, for in his visual and verbal translations of the Native American vision of life, there is a message which speaks to our times and certainly to all ages. *Hechetu welo!* (pp. 400-01)

Joseph Epes Brown, "Paul Goble," in The Horn Book Magazine, *Vol. LV, No. 4, August, 1979, pp. 399-401.*

J. C. STOTT

Thanks to a series of studies which have appeared during the last decade, non-native readers of children's materials have become more sensitive to stereotyping of native peoples. We are now in a far better position to reject inadequate, racist depictions of native peoples. However, there has not been a corresponding development of awareness about the realities of traditional and contemporary native physical and especially cultural life. Such an awareness is necessary if we are to be better equipped not only to reject erroneous materials, but also to understand more completely the truths of those books which present accurate pictures of various aspects of native lives. Certainly if we are to come closer to such fine picture

books as Gerald McDermott's *Arrow to the Sun,* Beverly Brodsky McDermott's *Sedna,* or Paul Goble's *The Girl Who Loved Wild Horses,* we must increase our awareness of the traditional cultural backgrounds which these writer-artists have assimilated and integrated into their stories.

In this essay, I shall concentrate on only one historic culture, that of the Northern Plains, and the works of one modern writer-artist, Paul Goble. (pp. 117-18)

The Plains Indian, riding horses to hunt buffalo and make war, bedecked in elaborate headdress, living in tipis, and speaking a formal, poetic language, has become a symbol in North America and Europe for all native peoples. (p. 118)

But what was the reality of the Plains Indians who were represented in these stereotypes? In the first place, the culture so depicted existed for a relatively brief time. The "Horse Culture," as it is often called, extended from the middle of the eighteenth century to the later part of the nineteenth, from the time when the majority of Plains bands had domesticated the horse to the time when the extinction of the buffalo and repressive governmental policies effectively terminated the hunting, nomadic way of life. (p. 119)

If we were to choose words to summarize the physical and cultural reactions of the Plains native peoples to the horse, we could say *familiarity* on the one hand, and *wonder, awe,* and *reverence* on the other. These people knew their horses intimately as physical beings: they knew how to breed, care for, and train them so that these animals became an integral part of their daily lives; yet they continued to marvel at them, finding in them powers that they only vaguely understood, but deeply worshipped. (p. 120)

Not native himself, Paul Goble brings to his picture books the fruits of his life-long study of native peoples and his deep respect for their customs and beliefs. (p. 121)

Both *The Girl Who Loved Wild Horses* and *The Gift of the Sacred Dog* are based on traditional narratives; however, Goble's retellings are his own, being, as he has noted, syntheses from many sources. What distinguishes each of these books is not only the excellence of the illustrations, but the ways in which they reflect historic cultural elements behind the story and infuse meanings into the stories which reinforce these cultural elements.

The underlying theme of *The Girl Who Loved Wild Horses* is the unity of all creatures. It expresses, Goble has written, "the Native American rapport with nature." A young woman noted for her ability to tend the horses is carried away with them during a summer thunder storm. When she is discovered sometime later by the members of the village, she is leading a young colt. Unhappy in her village, she rejoins the wild horses she has befriended, and, after several years, she disappears; her people see the wild stallion running with a magnificent mare who, it is implied, is the girl. She has found fulfillment in nature. "Today," the closing lines state, "we are still glad to remember that we have relatives among the Horse People. And it gives us joy to see the wild horses running free."

On first examining the pictures, one notices their accuracy to nineteenth century Plains' culture. This is seen most clearly in the depiction of the village with its tipis. Tipi placement and design were of great cultural and religious significance to the Plains people. As the pictures show, they are all facing the sun, the source of life. . . . It is interesting to note that there are no depictions of horses on the center section of the tipis and that the stallion is shown in the picture far above the village, silhouetted on a mesa. At this point, the horse and the girl are separated; the union is not complete.

Other visual elements of the story reflect the theme of a movement toward union, toward completeness. The half-title page depicts a girl riding a spotted stallion against a background of a Black War Bonnet design. This design was a widely used Plains symbol of completeness, depicting as it did the circle, the emblem of completeness which pervaded every element of Plains life. However, in this picture, the union of girl and stallion is not fulfilled; they maintain their separate identities of human being and horse. The title and dedication pages also reflect this incompleteness. In each of them are found the girl and five horses. The stallion is the odd one; he is without a mate. During the story, the girl's first sight of the stallion prefigures the conclusion. Spring flowers abound and a rainbow indicates the end of a storm; new beginnings are at hand. The union completed, the Black War Bonnet Design is reintroduced. However, there are now two horses, the arches of their necks encompassing the sun, the source of life. Nearby, small animals and birds, in pairs, reinforce the concept of fulfillment.

The Girl Who Loved Wild Horses is a strange, mystic story which, whatever psychological interpretations Freudians might wish to give it, reflects in text and pictures the spiritual significance which was given to horses by the Plains Indians. The importance of the horse is more specifically stated in *The Gift of the Sacred Dog,* Goble's version of the pourquoi myth about the origin of horses.

Like *The Girl Who Loved Wild Horses, The Gift of the Sacred Dog* begins with a sense of incompleteness. The pedestrian people cannot find the buffalo and the tribe is starving. The half-title page shows two men on foot looking into an empty landscape, the only sign of buffalo being the stylized hoofprints below them. On the title page, a lone figure stands amongst five tipis facing the sun his arms raised in supplication. The dwellings appear to be small in scale as were tipis in the pre-horse era. (Dogs could not drag long tent poles or the longer heavier skin coverings.) On the dedication page, the band files down a hill toward a long, dry valley, while buzzards circle above.

After buffalo dances have failed to discover the herds, a young boy travels alone up a hill hoping to receive a vision which will aid the tribe. This he does: thunderbirds swoop towards him and a buffalo-masked figure astride a horse tells him of the forthcoming gift of sacred dogs. In his vision the boy sees a group of many colored horses circling the sky in whirlwind fashion, and, as he descends the hill on the next morning, he sees dozens of horses emerging from a cave mouth on the hillside. They follow him to his village where the people offer them food.

Goble's illustrations for this section of the book reflect the depth of his research into traditional Plains oral narratives. The boy has engaged in a classic rite of passage. Alone, in a state of extreme hunger, he has received a vision, one the Plains Indians believed foretold his future. As he begins his hilltop supplication, a giant War Bonnet design surrounds the sun, a prefiguration of the fulfillment to come. As the thunderbirds approach, waving lines on their wings and from the hillside are seen. In traditional iconography these lines

were used to depict personal visions. The swirling configuration of the horses were typical in depictions of horse-origin accounts. The point in drawing attention to these items is not merely to indicate the accuracy of Goble's visuals, but rather to indicate that he has used them implicitly to enhance the intense, visionary experience he is recounting.

As the boy leads the horses to his village, the landscape is depicted as springlike. Seeds hang from the trees, flowers are on the shrubs, and butterflies abound. A new life is beginning in the world and for his people. The conclusion of the story depicts the celebration of the buffalo hunt, made successful in large part because of the horses. As two buffalo-hunting ponies look on, two members of the band dressed in sacred ceremonial regalia hold a buffalo skull towards the sun while behind them in a circle other buffalo skulls rest on piles of green leaves emblematic of the new life that has come from their death. Now their spirits are being thanked. The circle of life is being completed. Once again through his illustrations, Goble has integrated facts of nineteenth century Plains cultural life into his narrative, thereby emphasizing the spiritual emotions associated with the legend.

We should finally notice that both the specific forms of Goble's illustrations and narrative are his own. There is a distinctive Paul Goble style, one that is, if we may borrow the often used T. S. Eliot phrase, a blend of "tradition and the individual talent." Goble does not invent, he reinterprets; better still, he gives new life to the old stories using his knowledge of the old ways to vitalize beliefs which were at the center of Plains life during the period of the Horse Culture. This in itself is in keeping with the Plains Indians. As Hartley Burr Alexander has noted, Indian art was "in a curious sense a private possession. . . . Certain patterns were revealed to the owner in dream or vision, and therefore they were for his person, or clothing, or dwelling, and might not be copies or appropriated by any other, at least not without a proper transfer." Like the people he writes about, Goble has drawn from the shared wealth of images and themes, has internalized them in his own unique vision, and in so doing has established a personal relationship with the people and with the world around him. Thus Goble's artistic method is parallel to the cultural life of the past he both depicts and reveres. (pp. 121-24)

Certainly most children will not recognize the cultural elements which have been discussed above, and even if they did recognize the visual aspects, it is highly unlikely that they would understand their symbolic significances and relationships to the narrative. Whether children can or cannot consciously understand these elements is not the issue; although my experience is that a surprising number of them can. The fact is that any book which purports to deal with a traditional culture must be completely accurate in its depiction of that culture, materially and spiritually. Children do not realize that they are looking at stereotypes; but if they see enough of them, stereotypes will very naturally become a part of their world view. Conversely, when they see historic cultures honestly and fully depicted in books, they will, in the course of time, make these pictures of the cultures part of their world view. They will understand that this is an element of a great culture, but a culture which no longer exists in that form. Living in tipis, riding horses, and hunting buffalo is a way of the past. In fact, after they have learned that the books of Goble come very close to showing how things were, they must be led to understand that just as the people of the Plains adapted to the appearance of horses in their midst, so too they have adapted to the developments of the twentieth century.

However, when the presentations of the historic culture are as richly multi-dimensional as those found in Paul Goble's depictions of Plains Indian oral narratives, children will have planted within them seeds which will send roots deep into their beings and which will bloom in good time, making them fuller, and it is to be hoped more sympathetic—that is humanistic—individuals. (p. 124)

J. C. Stott, "Horses of Different Colors: The Plains Indians in Stories for Children," in American Indian Quarterly, *Vol. 8, No. 2, Spring, 1984, pp. 117-25.*

JON C. STOTT

Like most Englishmen, Paul Goble enjoys working in his garden. But he's not that interested in the vegetables and flowers he grows; instead, he's fascinated with the Indian arrowheads he uncovers while he's hoeing and weeding! You see, this native son of Haslemere, England lives outside Deadwood City, South Dakota, in the sacred Black Hills. There, in addition to hoeing and finding arrowheads, he writes and paints the stories which have made him the foremost contemporary interpreter for children of native myths and legends. (p. 867)

He can't remember not having been interested in the Indians of America. "When I was quite small, my mother read and reread the books of Grey Owl and Ernest Thompson Seton to me, and after that I read just about everything on native peoples I could lay my hands on." One of these books included the most famous American Indian autobiography, *Black Elk Speaks,* the life story of the visionary Sioux healer.

Paul Goble was fortunate that the man who introduced him to the writings and philosophies of Black Elk was Joseph Epes Brown who had met the Sioux holy man in 1947 and who was to publish *The Seven Rites of the Oglala Sioux,* based on these meetings, in 1953. Thus, instead of receiving the biased stereotyped notions of American Indians found in juvenile fiction and Hollywood movies, Paul early learned of the rich spiritual qualities of their lives. In fact, in his picture books Goble has re-created this rich spirituality.

"I came from a religious family, so I suppose that helped me to get closer to Black Elk. But the reverse is true as well. I can never be an Indian, but their spirituality has helped me understand myself. It's difficult to explain, but Indian thought does add an extra dimension for me. It's good to look at the Moon and to know that she is the wife of the sun; to know that moths are not just a nuisance at open windows, but bring good dreams; that the coyote (who is hated by white people) is the central figure in all the Plains stories; that you never kill a spider without telling him the Thunder is doing it. These aren't superstitions, but real explanations of our surroundings, real understandings."

In 1959, after having read, thought, and talked about native peoples for so many years, Paul Goble came to the United States for a long summer vacation. . . . [He] visited Sioux, Crow, and Shoshoni villages. . . .

Goble visited the Great Plains again in 1972, 1975, and 1976. . . .

During his visits, and since his permanent move to South Dakota in 1977, he experienced a great deal of native life, learning about and participating in many of the traditional activities which have been revived during the past two decades. "I've been in sweat baths (traditional purification rites), smoked the sacred pipe, participated in the building of the Sun Dance lodge, and witnessed the Sun Dance." (p. 868)

In 1969, Paul Goble published his first children's book, *Red Hawk's Account of Custer's Last Battle,* a fictionalized retelling of the 1876 battle of the Little Bighorn. Living in England, Goble had been watching a TV account of the event with his son, Richard. "What struck me was how biased the show was. But when I tried to find my son a book with the native point of view, I couldn't; and so the idea for the book was born." Told by an Oglala Sioux who was fifteen years old in 1876, the story is notable for the fairness with which both sides are treated. As was indeed the case, the native fighters had great respect for the bravery of their opponents. For the illustrations, Goble chose an appropriate style: Indian ledger book painting. Based on historical paintings found on buffalo robes, ledger book painting had been developed by Indian prisoners who, shipped to the southern states, far from their ancestral lands, had depicted past and contemporary history on the ledger books supplied to them by their captors. His second book, *Brave Eagle's Account of the Fetterman Fight,* recounts the events of a Wyoming battle of 1866, and uses similar techniques: ledger book style art and fictionalized autobiographical narrative of a young Indian fighter.

Lone Bull's Horse Raid and *The Friendly Wolf* are, in a sense transition books, linked artistically to the earlier ones and anticipating visually and thematically his later interpretations of native legends. While accurate to the culture of the nineteenth century, *Horse Raid* is a purely fictional autobiography. Bravery and the possession of horses were closely linked in Plains society; and in this story, the hero is fourteen years old and impatient to prove himself in a raid. . . . What follows is an exciting and dangerous raid of a Crow camp. For the illustrations, Goble depicts the horses and riders in the manner of ledger book painting; but the portrayals of landscape and villages contain the vibrant colors and intricate details of his later works.

The Friendly Wolf was written, Goble noted in his Caldecott Acceptance Speech, "because I was distressed at how wolves in Alaska were being hunted to extinction by helicopter. No Indian story I had ever read had anything but fine things to tell of wolves. The Indian understands the language of the birds and animals and seeks to learn their wisdom." Wandering away from a berry-picking expedition, two small children become lost in the hills. There they are protected by a wolf who, in the morning, leads them back to the tribe. "And ever since that day the wolves have been their [the people's] friends." While the pictures of the village are in the ledger book style, those of the children alone emphasize their relationship to nature. The boy and girl are integrated into the landscape, a symbol of the harmony which exists between the two-leggeds (human beings) and their four-legged brothers.

During the period of the mid-1970s, after the publication of his first four books, and those of the later part of the decade, Paul Goble's stature as an artist was growing rapidly. (pp. 869-70)

The style he developed over that period is seen at its best in the four retellings of Plains legends he has published in the last five years: *The Girl Who Loved Wild Horses, The Gift of the Sacred Dog, Star Boy,* and *Buffalo Woman.* Each of them reflects the Sioux expression, *mitakuye oyasin,* "we are all related"; each also reveals a technique of visual communication which is at once intensely personal and an expression of the spiritual values of the Plains people.

As did all native peoples, those about whom Goble writes—the Sioux, Blackfoot, and Cheyenne—viewed the universe holistically. All beings were created equal by the Wakan Tanka, the Great Spirit; all possessed spirits, even the rocks. All had equal rights to live on their Mother the Earth, and so were brothers and sisters. The sacred stories of the Plains people embodied these beliefs and Goble reproduces them faithfully in his books.

The prefatory note to Goble's most recent book, **Buffalo Woman,** indicates how fully he understands the spiritual views of the traditional native peoples and how he has chosen his stories to reflect these:

> The story of Buffalo Woman comes from the tribes who followed the buffalo herds on the Great Plains. The buffalo was the source of life for the people, giving them food, hides for robes and tipi covers, as well as many other things. The lives of both were closely interwoven, and the story teaches that buffalo and people were related. . . . These stories were not simply for entertainment; they had power to strengthen the bond with the herds, and to encourage the herds to continue to give themselves so that the people could live. It was felt that retelling the story had power to bring about a change within each of us; that in listening we might all be a little more worthy of our buffalo relatives.

This relationship is reflected in Goble's Caldecott Medal winning **The Girl Who Loved Wild Horses,** in which a girl who feels very close to the horses eventually is transformed into one, becoming the wife to the leader of the wild herd. In **Buffalo Woman,** the idea is the same although the sexes are reversed. When a buffalo turns herself into a woman, she is married to a young man whom she tells: "You have always had good feelings for our people They know you are a good and kind man. I will be your wife. My people wish that the love we have for each other will be an example for both our peoples to follow." At the legend's conclusion, the young man is turned into a buffalo, a symbol of the relationship between the human and the buffalo people.

In **The Gift of the Sacred Dog,** Goble created his own version of a pourquoi story found throughout the plains, the tale of how the people got the first horses. The horse revolutionized the culture of the Plains Indians during the eighteenth and nineteenth centuries, making the people greater hunters and warriors, and greatly facilitating their mobility. More important, however, than the physical benefits of the sacred dog or sacred elk, as it was called, were the spiritual qualities it possessed. In the true sense of the word, it was viewed as a godsend, a miraculous gift. The people hoped that they could acquire some of these powers from their horses. In his story, Goble captures this spiritual quality. (pp. 870-71)

Star Boy is Goble's interpretation of the most widely known legend of the northern Plains, the story of the boy who journeyed to the sun and brought back the secrets of the Sun Dance Lodge the sacred edifice of the great annual festivals. Just as the scarfaced boy was renewed through his journey to the sun, so too the people hope that through their observance of the rituals, they will be physically and spiritually renewed.

If the texts of Goble's books capture the spiritual beliefs of the peoples he portrays, the illustrations do so to an even greater extent. For native peoples, decorative art, art for art's sake, did not exist. The physical adornments found on nearly all of the articles they created embodied their view of themselves and the cosmos in which they lived. Goble accurately reproduces the designs found among the Plains peoples and he does so to impart spiritual symbolism to the stories he tells. An example can be found in the radiating circle design found on both the half-title page and the final double-spread of *The Girl Who Loved Wild Horses.* This symbol represented not only the life-giving power of the sun, but also the circle of unity and harmony the native peoples believed existed in life. In the first picture, the circle incorporates the neck of the male horse, but the girl is not a part of it. At the beginning of the story, the unity between the human beings and animals has not been achieved. At the end of the story, the girl has been transformed into a horse, and her neck is now included as part of the radiating circle: the unity is complete.

In *The Gift of the Sacred Dog,* the illustrations of the boy's vision quest contain a number of flowing, wavy lines. In traditional iconography, these lines were used to depict the lightning, an important supernatural element of vision quests. By including these in the illustrations, Goble implicitly emphasizes the intense spiritual nature of the boy's mission.

This brief survey of Goble's books will emphasize the fact that they are the results of years of artistic training and of study of the peoples they depict. He, in fact, has remarked that each book is the product of hundreds of hours of careful labor. Speaking of the story he's now working on, *The Great Race,* he says, "To come up with the final draft of three typed sheets, double-spaced, I had to work through 170 pages of typed and hand-written drafts." Add to that the painstaking care given to the illustrations, the hours spent "hanging around" reservations listening, and the research in anthropological and historical studies, we can understand why the results are so uniformly excellent.

The books have all been highly acclaimed critically. But do they pass the acid test—are they well received by the native peoples themselves? The answer is an unqualified yes! At talks he has given, native peoples have come up to congratulate him on being so true to their culture. "One woman even told me that she was surprised to discover that I wasn't Sioux, let alone American!" In a way, he creates his books for native children, as a kind of gift to them. "For hundreds of years Europeans have been taking away from the native peoples—their land and, more important, their culture. So many native children don't know anything about the great traditions of their past. I hope that the books will help them rediscover some of these. The books aren't really gifts at all; all I'm doing is giving back to these people the things that are really theirs, after all."

But Paul Goble does not pretend that he is giving back to native peoples exact replicas of traditional culture. "I'm a reinterpreter, really, I'm sure that if Indian children had been presented with my books seventy-five years ago, they probably wouldn't have felt that the stories reflected their culture that well. So much has changed for native peoples, and of course, I'm influenced by the modern world I've grown up in. Modern design and the vividness of modern colors seem to appeal to all my readers, native or white. However, native people also see echoes of older times which are not present reality."

From Brave Eagle's Account of the Fetterman Fight, 21 December 1866, *by Paul and Dorothy Goble.*

All of this discussion brings us back to that garden outside of Paul Goble's home. He does grow vegetables and flowers; but when he finds the arrowheads, he's learning from the land. And he's giving back to it as well. The animals that feed in the valley or at the feeding stations around the house are sharing with him the bounties he's received from the earth. And he's creating stories from that earth. As his wife told a local reporter: "He imagines how the arrowhead might have broken off in a bird or rabbit. Then he imagines the Sioux chipping on the arrowheads, or sitting here on the hillside above the creek waiting for game. And pretty soon, he has created the valley again just as it must have been."

Paul Goble may be an Englishman working in his garden, but who could come closer to the spirit of the native people, living among the creatures of nature, treating them with reverence and respect, experiencing their spirituality, and then embodying that spirituality in words and pictures which help others to get closer to it as well? (pp. 871-73)

Jon C. Stott, "Profile: Paul Goble," in Language Arts, *Vol. 61, No. 8, December, 1984, pp. 867-73.*

MARY STEELE

[**Buffalo Woman** and **Star Boy**] are based on careful scholarship and dedicated to an expression of the Indians' kinship with the natural world. Buffalo Woman marries a hunter who returns with her to the Buffalo nation. Star Boy's father is the morning star and, with help from a mortal woman, he brings the Sun Dance to the Indians. These love stories are also the mythology of a nation and form a living memorial to a way of life that has disappeared. In striking illustrations Goble choreographs the shape of feathers, hair, tents, the forbidding sight of a herd of buffalo, or the abstraction of the planets. Another Amerindian tale, the Ojibway *Star Maiden*, retold by Barbara Juster Esbensen and illustrated by Helen K. Davie provides a more lyrical visualizing of legendary material.

Mary Steele, "Folk & Fairy Stories," in The Signal Selection of Children's Books 1988, *edited by Nancy Chambers, The Thimble Press, 1989, p. 73.*

RED HAWK'S ACCOUNT OF CUSTER'S LAST BATTLE: THE BATTLE OF THE LITTLE BIGHORN, 25 JUNE 1876 (with Dorothy Goble, 1969)

Painted-robe figures charge across spacious white pages as Red Hawk, a stand-in for those who were there, tells of the Battle of Little Bighorn: "Why had the soldiers come to kill us? I was only a boy and did not understand but I felt like a man and I did not care whether I lived or died." The "why," such as it was, is provided at the outset; italicized insertions explain what "Red Hawk" would not have known or thought to tell. As a dramatized reconstruction this has immediate visual and narrative impact but beyond the event there lingers a sense of honor (those who "say that the soldiers were drunk" or cowardly were not there, "I never saw such brave men") and particularly of pride mingled with regret: "We won a great victory. But when you look about you today you can see that it meant little. The White Men, who were then few, have spread over the earth like fallen leaves driven before the wind." From the picture map on the title page to the lists of sources and suggested readings, an unusual volume that is at once handsome, stirring and historically anchored (and thus worth the trouble of being unusual). (pp. 879-80)

> *A review of "Red Hawk's Account of Custer's Last Battle," in* Kirkus Reviews, *Vol. XXXVIII, No. 16, August 15, 1970, pp. 879-80.*

My first reaction to this book was that I disliked its attempt to speak through the mouth of a Sioux Indian boy warrior in the formal poetic manner of Indian storytelling. Then I realized that I was at fault by considering it from a point of view too accustomed to conventional military history. The eyes of a junior school child will see it in a different light and I think with approval. The illustrations particularly will appeal: rather primitive and so very much after the style of the Plains Indians from whom the illustrators drew their inspiration.

The military side of the story intermingles with the boy's personal account in a sort of counterpoint; the device succeeds very well without interrupting the flow of the narrative.

The authors obviously have a deep affection for the Plains Indians and succeed in presenting a sympathetic picture of them. A valuable list of books for further reading completes the book.

> *Gilbert Dowdall-Brown, in a review of "Red Hawk's Account of Custer's Last Battle," in* The School Librarian, *Vol. 18, No. 3, September, 1970, p. 369.*

Custer's last battle is an experiment as regard form and content, and a most interesting one; the battle of the Little Bighorn on 25 June, 1876, is presented in picture-book format. Paul Goble . . . has an understandable desire to strike a balance between truth and legend, between General Custer's reputation and the true motives and natures of his Indian opponents. He uses as narrator a boy of fifteen belonging to the Oglala nation who plays a small part in the action but sees a great deal more. As Red Hawk tells his story, referring to personalities in the tribe and to its customs in peace and war, italicised passages are inserted in which the authors summarise the American army's actions and motives. There is no hysteria in the analysis of how and why Indian land was exploited by the American Government; the whole picture seems a very fair one. The illustrations are an integral part of the book. Based on the descriptive techniques of Indian art, they are formalised in a way that makes the course of the battle entirely clear and their smooth colour and firm design give enormous pleasure to the eye. Here is yet another example of how the scope of the orthodox picture-book is being extended in our time.

> *Margery Fisher, in a review of "Custer's Last Battle," in* Growing Point, *Vol. 9, No. 5, November, 1970, p. 1619.*

BRAVE EAGLE'S ACCOUNT OF THE FETTERMAN FIGHT, 21 DECEMBER 1866 (with Dorothy Goble, 1972)

"Give me 80 men and I will ride through the whole Sioux Na-

tion," boasted young Captain William Fetterman. He did not live long enough to fulfill the pledge. On December 21, 1866, he and his entire command of 82 men, were killed in a battle known to whites as the Fetterman Massacre and to the Sioux as the Battle of the Hundred in the Hand.

Paul and Dorothy Goble have told the story of this event, with the background that led up to it, in a beautifully-produced book, *Brave Eagle's Account of the Fetterman Fight.* In look and layout it is similar to the Gobles' *Red Hawk's Account of Custer's Last Battle.* There is an illustration on almost every page, often a double spread, and the figures of Indians and ponies, cavalry men and foot soldiers are complete in minute detail, with action in every line.

On the book jacket we learn that Mr. Goble is an Englishman who was inspired by the work of George Catlin. Catlin would be proud to know he had such a talented disciple.

The story itself, when finally I tore myself away from the art to read it, is a brief account of Chief Red Cloud's six months war against the United States Government, the only war in which this country ever negotiated for peace on the enemy's terms. The book concludes with the Fetterman battle, but it is so matter-of-factly told that it is not likely to bring on nightmares. The saddest note is the death of a small dog on the battlefield, and for the sake of some small readers I wish that could have been omitted.

At the time, the event stirred up violent feelings throughout the nation. Now, 106 years later, young readers of *The Fetterman Fight* will probably decide that the captain had asked for it. Like Custer, he disobeyed orders and led his men into direct combat with the outraged Sioux and Cheyenne, who were well aware of his boastful claims.

Since there were no white survivors, the Gobles have wisely told their story in the words of Brave Eagle, a young Oglala-Sioux warrior. And while there will never be another Mari Sandoz, they do a creditable job. I was especially reassured of authenticity by the story of the bravest white man. Indians, unlike some other races, always singled out an enemy who had been exceptionally brave in battle. In their lodges, at story-telling time, they kept his memory alive with that of their own heroes. Thus the valor of the unknown soldier with hair on his face is included in the book.

The illustrations may lead doting grandmothers to buy the volume for much younger children, who will not understand the text but will love the pictures. It's a good book to grow into.

> *Evelyn Sibley Lampman, in a review of "Brave Eagle's Account of the Fetterman Fight," in* The New York Times Book Review, *September 24, 1972, p. 8.*

Drawn from published Indian statements, Red Cloud's speeches, and the information of white historians, the account in the book amalgamates all the material for a smooth description of the battle from the Indian point-of-view. But all too often the book serves only as a glorification of warfare and a glorification of the Indian because he could win wars. Consequently, the telling does not present frequently enough the truly beautiful religious and cultural attitudes of the Indian tribes. The book is certainly attractive; the illustrations moving and vivid; the writing excellent. But those who praise the book for presenting a new slant on American history may be missing the impact of the second in a series of books devoted, so far, to battles the Indian won. To elevate the Indians because they also won battles is to praise them in imperialistic terms—those who win are superior. Sadly missing from the book are eloquent, moving Indian statements, like those of Black Elk [*Black Elk Speaks* by John Neihardt]: "When I look back now from this high hill of my old age, I can still see the butchered women and children lying heaped and scattered all along the crooked gulch as plain as when I saw them with eyes still young. And I can see that something else died there in the bloody mud, and was buried in the blizzard. A people's dream died there. It was a beautiful dream." In remarks like these, one finds the true superiority of the Indian mind: an understanding of nature and the world which has its counterpart in the knowledge of the poets and writers—not of the warriors—of America. (p. 606)

> *Anita Silvey, in a review of "Brave Eagle's Account of the Fetterman Fight," in* The Horn Book Magazine, *Vol. XLVIII, No. 6, December, 1972, pp. 605-06.*

The Gobles have drawn from both Indian and U.S. Army primary sources. Brave Eagle's account is both vivid and sympathetic: in the midst of battle he takes time to note that " . . . they [white soldiers] fought bravely." The full-color illustrations, done in the style of Plains Indian painting, are profuse and lavish. Throughout, the fighting men on both sides resemble toy soldiers—perhaps the English artist's interpretation that these wars carried on by the white men resembled a child's game. The moving, authentic text combines with the striking illustrations to create an outstanding book.

> *Alice Miller Bregman, in a review of "Brave Eagle's Account of the Fetterman Fight," in* School Library Journal, *Vol. 19, No. 4, December, 1972, p. 60.*

LONE BULL'S HORSE RAID (with Dorothy Goble, 1973)

When that strange beast which neighed and ran like the wind and could bear men was first traded into the northern American plains by the Shoshoni Indians around the turn of the 18th century, the relations between the tribes living there—Blackfoot, Assiniboin, Cheyenne, Gros Ventre, Crow and Sioux—changed dramatically. Buffalo could be shot from horseback instead of having to be chased over cliffs in chancy, organized drives. Tipis could be loftier, for now horses and not dogs dragged their poles. Life was richer and wealth was tallied in mounts. With guns and beads came leisure and refinement of high costume art. And then, most importantly, flowered the warrior etiquette of intertribal feuding, with horses and scalps and war honors as principal booty.

Artist/writer team Paul and Dorothy Goble have chosen this heyday of the northern plains Indians—whose feathered and beaded image would become synonymous with Indianness the world over—for their authentic and thrilling story of the first horse-stealing raid undertaken by a 14-year-old Oglala Sioux boy named Lone Bull. It is a distillation of countless accounts buried in anthropological writings, however the Gobles tastefully exploit the new ethnic candor and still bring fictional intimacy to the tale.

Young Lone Bull yearns for the test of manhood through a raid on the Oglala blood enemy, the Crow. His grandparents conspire to sneak him out of camp, with his companion Charging Bear, to catch up with his father's war party already bent on horse-stealing. Coming upon a Crow camp,

they all wait until nightfall, then stealthily cut tethers until an edgy horse makes the Crow camp burst alive. In the ensuing chase, Charging Bear is wounded and Lone Bull "counts coup" on a Crow lad. As with the traditional accounts, Lone Bull's rite-of-passage adventure climaxes with a ritual parade through his home village, after returning with no lives lost and a thundering herd of stolen horses.

Although a prefatory section on horse-raiding is delivered in the impersonal style which in the past infected writing about Indians, as if tribal customs were as predictable as an anthill's, in the narrative itself dramatic involvement and cultural authenticity are nicely balanced. (However, it is entirely baffling and out of place to have a preliminary page of quotes from famous white Indian fighters, all generals, praising Indian horsemanship and fighting ability, when the book describes that period before the unique plains Indian world was undone by the expansion of the white frontier.)

Most splendid are Paul Goble's illustrations, which were inspired by his research into both plains painting style and study of plains ethnography. Style—people and horses drawn in profile or from the back, overlapping to emphasize congestion, an insistent two dimensionality and super-realistic exactitude—he has borrowed from numerous sources: the Oglala pictographic chronicle produced by Amos Bad Heart Bull from 1890 to 1913, but perhaps even more heavily—though unacknowledged in the book's bibliography—from the southern plains tradition which, oddly enough, flourished during the captivity of Cheyenne and Kiowa warriors in Fort Marion, Fla., in the 1870's. There artists like Lame Man and Howling Wolf adapted the realistic approach of men's hide painting—as distinguished from the abstract decoration done by women—to their cheap paper notebooks.

Goble has derived his content from a wide knowledge of plains apparel, horse gear, shield and tipi decoration; the connoisseur of oft-reproduced choice pieces can here see them excitingly introduced into their real-life settings. Goble revels in colorful accuracy: the Crow can be detected by their brush-tuft hair style, their women by their elk-teeth dresses, the Sioux by their wide beaded blanket strips, and so on delightfully.

Both tale and picture in *Lone Bull's Horse Raid* offer young people a fine introduction to the warrior ethic and native heraldry of the plains Indian.

> *Peter Nabokov, in a review of "Lone Bull's Horse Raid," in* The New York Times Book Review, *November 11, 1973, p. 8.*

This is the third of these beautifully-illustrated books that the Gobles have produced. . . . As with the other books, the text is short and highly-charged, but it is in the illustrations that the true glory lies. Inspired by Plains Indian paintings of the late nineteenth century, a fine example of which can be found in the last pages of the Time-Life *The Indians,* they provide a wealth of strong colour and stylised detail. Opening after opening is fraught with multi-patterned blankets, decorated braids, streaming war-bonnets, feathered lances and coup sticks, painted tipis, and charging horses. The pictures recreate a world in which one can linger, and, while lingering, appreciate a now-faded culture. They combine immediacy and timelessness.

> *C. E. J. Smith, in a review of "Lone Bull's Horse*

Raid," in Children's Book Review, *Vol. III, No. 6, December, 1973, p. 188.*

By the same British collaborators who produced *Custer's Last Battle* and *The Fetterman Fight,* another book with simple, direct prose and handsome color illustrations. . . . The author's note provides background for an understanding of the significance and excitement of such raids: the "fierce competition among the warriors to win personal glory"; the "traditional way for a young man to gain a good reputation in the tribe." Based on the art of the Plains Indians, the detailed panoramic spreads and smaller scenes of horsemen and tipis are full of rhythmic design and driving movement.

Virginia Haviland, in a review of "Lone Bull's Horse Raid," in The Horn Book Magazine, *Vol. L, No. 2, April, 1974, p. 158.*

THE FRIENDLY WOLF   (with Dorothy Goble, 1974)

The authors have collaborated before to give some admirably illustrated and well told stories of the Indian race, and their art is not diminished in this latest book. The story tells of the wanderings of Little Cloud and his small sister Bright Eyes as they leave the band of berry pickers and ultimately become lost. A wolf who at first frightens them eventually leads them to home and safety. There is rather more text than in most picture books, and the tale, a re-telling of an existing legend combined with other native lore, is a thoughtful and purposeful one, drawing attention to the friendship between animal and man which exists amongst Indian tribes, and is in danger of being lost as man becomes more sophisticated. The style of writing is well in keeping with the traditional tale and displays a poetic lilting quality which is echoed in the positive but delicate and exquisitely attuned illustrations. They have the character of an Indian type of painting peculiar to that race in the second half of the nineteenth century, and the author-illustrators embellish this style with a thematic sequence of colours to each page, the colour as well as the manner evoking the feeling of that part of the story. A most charming and commendable book. (pp. 38-9)

E. A. Astbury, in a review of "The Friendly Wolf," in The Junior Bookshelf, *Vol. 39, No. 1, February, 1975, pp. 38-9.*

By itself, the tale is sober and rather deliberately unfanciful. But the Gobles concentrate the action in the flat, clean edged designs which are reminiscent of *The Fetterman Fight* and *Custer's Last Stand* but more varied. Animals are hidden everywhere among the patterned rocks and berry bushes and scenes of camp life are richly decorated. It's unfortunate that, in such an attractive volume, the print looks, as it perhaps is, secondary. Still, the progress of Little Cloud and his sister across the keenly stylized landscapes is worth following.

A review of "The Friendly Wolf," in Kirkus Reviews, *Vol. XLIII, No. 24, December 15, 1975, p. 1377.*

The clear text builds and sustains interest and is complemented by colorful, full-page, uncluttered illustrations which present accurate, richly detailed information about Indian life. Although the text is set in small type and the specific tribe depicted is not identified, these drawbacks are minor when compared with the overall excellence of this book. A splendid resource for children studying American Indian units.

Marily Richards, in a review of "The Friendly Wolf," in School Library Journal, *Vol. 22, No. 6, February, 1976, p. 38.*

THE GIRL WHO LOVED WILD HORSES   (1978)

AUTHOR'S COMMENTARY

[The following excerpt is from Goble's Caldecott Medal acceptance speech, which was originally delivered on 26 June 1979.]

I have been interested in everything Indian since I can remember. The books of Grey Owl and Ernest Thompson Seton are well known in the United States. Before television days my mother read the complete works of these two authors to my brother and me. Many other books too, but I loved best Grey Owl and Ernest Thompson Seton because both wrote about Indians and both were true naturalists. The world they wrote about was so different from the crowded island where I lived. And yet perhaps growing up so far from this country sharpened my need to know more. Over many years I acquired a considerable library of the better books concerning Native Americans, and I really studied those books.

In 1959, after I had finished three years of training in industrial design at the Central School of Art and Design in London, I was fortunate to be given a long summer visit to this country. I accompanied Frithjof Schuon, the eminent Swiss writer on comparative religion. He had contacts among Sioux and Crow Indians, and the summer was spent on reservations in South Dakota and Montana.

Love of Indians and love of nature have always been my priorities, but they never seemed a combination likely to support a family. For the next eighteen years, from 1959 to 1977, I kept it as a serious hobby and put my main energies into industrial design, with the eighteen years about equally divided between practicing and teaching the subject. Nearly two years ago the hobby took over completely when I left England to live in the Black Hills as a painter.

As a teacher in England I had long summer vacations, and in recent years I spent four summers in the United States. My son Richard came with me on most of those visits. We would bring a small tent, hire a car, and spend the summer with Sioux friends in South Dakota and Crow Indian friends in Montana. During those summers I was privileged to take part in ceremonies, to be present at their sacred Sun Dances. I have taken part in building the Sun Dance lodge and have helped to pitch tipis. Knowing that I loved their ways, my Indian friends have told me much about their folklore and beliefs. They have given me new perspectives, and really all my travels were spiritual journeys.

I do not know what is a valid reason for writing a book. *The Friendly Wolf* came about because I was distressed at how wolves in Alaska were being hunted to extinction by helicopter. No Indian story I had ever read had anything but fine things to tell of wolves. The Indian understands the language of the birds and animals and seeks to learn their wisdom. He knows they were here long before we were and being older, deserve our respect. We have been subjected to Walt Disney and his many followers. I have a horror of the havoc they have created with literature, art, and the blunting of our attitudes towards nature. Children grow up with the idea that bears are huggable, woodpeckers are destructive, coyotes and tomcats mean; and that whales and dolphins are happiest when being made to clown in a marina. Respect and inspiration are not there at all.

Similarly, in *The Girl Who Loved Wild Horses* I tried to express and paint what I believe to be the Native American rapport with nature. The Indian does not feel afraid or alone in the forests and prairies; he knows many stories about ancestors who turned into the seven stars of the Big Dipper and others who became the Pleiades. Indians tell about a girl who married the Morning Star and of their son who, coming from the Sky but living on Earth, did many wonderful things. Knowledge of this relationship with the universe gives them confidence. They have no thought to reorganize nature in a way other than that in which the Great Spirit made it. Indeed, it would be sacrilegious to do so.

The Girl Who Loved Wild Horses is not a retelling of any one legend but a synthesis of many. Psychological interpretations should not be read into it. Simply, the girl loves horses, and perhaps she becomes one. If we think about something long enough, maybe we will become like that thing. I believe children will easily understand this. By the time we are grown up we might think some thought-doors have been opened, but perhaps others have been closed.

I hope that Native Americans will approve of the book and will feel sympathy for the illustrations. At a recent autographing party in a small South Dakota community, it gave me great joy when an Indian gave me a beautiful feather in a fold of red felt. And there was a sixth-grade Sioux boy who, while having breakfast, heard on the radio that I was to be at the Rapid City library that day. He told his mother he was not going to school, and so it was we met. It gives me a warm feeling when Indians respond to my books. Some will speak no English, and yet the lively discussions amongst themselves which the illustrations provoke tell me they are happy that a white man has admiration for their culture. (pp. 396-98)

Paul Goble, "Caldecott Medal Acceptance," in The Horn Book Magazine, *Vol. LV, No. 4, August, 1979, pp. 396-98.*

A story of an Indian girl who feels such a strong kinship with the wild horses grazing near her village that she eventually becomes one of them. During a thunderstorm she is carried away on the back of one of the horses and agrees to stay among them in the hills. When members of her tribe discover her whereabouts and bring her home, she is so unhappy that she becomes ill; and her family realizes where her true home must be. Brilliantly colored illustrations are similar in style to those in *Custer's Last Battle, The Fetterman Fight,* and *Lone Bull's Horse Raid,* but much less restrained. Elaborate double-page spreads burst with life, revealing details of flowers and insects, animals and birds. The swirling thunderstorm is dramatically shown with zigzags of yellow lightning against black skies. Often creatures are drawn in pairs—woodchucks, rabbits, lizards, and owls—and the concluding scene shows two wild horses magnificently framed against a burning red sun. The story is told in simple language, and the author has included verses of a Navaho and a Sioux song about horses. Both storytelling and art express the harmony with and the love of nature which characterize Native American culture. (pp. 631-32)

Karen M. Klockner, in a review of "The Girl Who Loved Wild Horses," in The Horn Book Magazine, *Vol. LIV, No. 6, December, 1978, pp. 631-32.*

We do not always see eye to eye with the American Caldecott Medal committee, but here surely they have chosen a picture book of outstanding merit. It is not often that we are privileged to see such controlled power, such mastery of overall design and detail. (p. 17)

The story is told with quiet eloquence, but it is the pictures that matter most. They are strongly stylized but always anchored to natural forms. They stride boldly and colourfully across the double-spreads, using with great skill the confines of the page and the areas of white paper. We are reminded a little of the best American picture books of the pre-War period, but then we should have had a larger format, and Mr. Goble might have enjoyed the additional space. And of course he would have had the benefit of board covers and a jacket, not this nasty laminated plastic! But let us not carp. This is a book in a thousand. (p. 18)

M. Crouch, in a review of "The Girl Who Loved Wild Horses," in The Junior Bookshelf, *Vol. 44, No. 1, February, 1980, pp. 17-18.*

Paul Goble's illustrations . . . contain the stylized shapes of animals, which are similar to those of prehistoric cave paintings. The simplicity of the art of the cave painters, however, is absent in the overabundant patterns which repeat throughout the compositions of these illustrations. Though the bold hues of these full-color pages reflect the story's content, they also serve to create disharmony rather than cohesiveness of composition, often distracting the eye in several directions at once.

The dramatic style which Goble employs helps heighten the suspense of the story at times, especially as the black, stormy sky swirls over the stark white of the pages, but the drama begins to lose its effect page after page. Perhaps the most successful full-page spread is that in which the darkness of night dominates. With only a spattering of circular stars, the tinted golden moon, and the figures of horses and rider, the picture seems serene in comparison to the remainder of the book.

Words to Native American songs from the Navaho and Oglala Sioux tribes find inclusion at the book's close and help authenticate and reinforce the importance of the horse to the peoples in the story. Though Goble's work is nothing less than creative and skillful, it may be too powerful, visually, to appeal to most children. (p. 369)

Linda Kauffman Peterson, "The Caldecott Medal and Honor Books, 1938-1981," in Newbery and Caldecott Medal and Honor Books: An Annotated Bibliography, *by Linda Kauffman Peterson and Marilyn Leathers Solt, G. K. Hall & Co., 1982, pp. 235-378.*

The Girl Who Loved Wild Horses . . . is unique in its artistic vibrancy and in its reverence for nature, humankind, and the fragile mystical kinship between the two. A synthesis of many stories, it provides a stunning exhibition of flat space, shape, and color used for figures of Indian people, wildlife, landscape, and weather itself. Like [Verna Aardema's *Why Mosquitoes Buzz in People's Ears,* illustrated by Leo and Diane Dillon], Goble's illustrations are a beautifully stylized wedding of old and new art, here inspired by Indian hide paintings and ledger-book art such as that found in *A Cheyenne*

Sketchbook by Cohoe. In Cohoe's book, primitive shapes in earthy colors document battles and hunting expeditions; in *Wild Horses,* similarly bold and colorful shapes document a girl's life in the wilderness, the tribal village she left behind, and the rugged, cathedrallike terrain of the plains' high buttes where the Horse Nation ran free.

Goble had been an industrial designer in England before coming to live in America near the Indian people he had admired since childhood, and like Lent in *The Funny Little Woman* he is faithful to cultural motifs. Tepees in *Wild Horses* have schematized animal designs on them that are much like animals in the plot itself, and authentic colors and patterns are used throughout. Goble's white highlighting of compositions is like that of Lent's aboveground illustrations of the little woman's house on the hill. Goble uses the technique to focus attention on such symbolic representations as the vivid red sun, the Great Spirit's finest creation; proud stances for human and horse alike (to prepare the viewer for the story's transformation of one into the other); and a particularly fine waterside scene. . . . (pp. 212-13)

> Lyn Ellen Lacy, "Space," in her Art and Design in Children's Picture Books: An Analysis of Caldecott Award-Winning Illustrations, *American Library Association, 1986, pp. 178-216.*

Though some of the varied [Caldecott] winners do demonstrate technical competence and others have an ingratiating personality, little can be said for the 1979 selection, Paul Goble's pseudo-Plains-Indian *The Girl Who Loved Wild Horses.* The story is a thin, maudlin conceit, shallowly rooted in Indian folklore (the Animal Husband motif) but more in keeping with a romantic, Western theme, the prepubescent girl's infatuation with horses. Goble's illustrational style, modeled after the flat planes and silhouetted forms of Plains-Indian skin painting, produces some bold design effects in scenes of running horses, the sort of scenes for which the originals are famous. But once the horse leaves the herd, and the setting and tenor of the story change, the illustrations become stilted, arbitrarily stylized, art-modern absurdities. Native American art gains nothing by such misconceived and vacuous emulation, well-intended as it may be. (pp. 291-92)

> Barbara Bader, "The Caldecott Spectrum," in *Newbery and Caldecott Medal Books: 1976-1985, edited by Lee Kingman, The Horn Book, Incorporated, 1986, pp. 279-314.*

THE GIFT OF THE SACRED DOG (1980)

Goble's handsome paintings, vigorous in composition and often delicate in style, often stylized, always reflect his identification with the Native American way of life and his empathy with their respect for natural things. Here he uses fiction to dramatize the importance of the horse in the Indian culture; although a prefatory note states that the horse was brought to this continent by the Spanish, it is a herd of wild horses that comes to the boy protagonist who has gone alone into the hills to ask the Great Spirit to help his hungry people. Like other Goble books, this is handsome, with good page layout and good integration of print and picture. The writing style is a bit stiff, the book's focus being on how the horse improved the Indian way of life and the ability to hunt—especially to hunt buffalo. The text, which can be read aloud to younger children, ends with Sioux songs about horses and buffalo, capping a tale of the wild horses who came after the

boy's vigil, delighting those who acquired and tamed them. (pp. 133-34)

> A review of "The Gift of the Sacred Dog," in Bulletin of the Center for Children's Books, *Vol. 34, No. 7, March, 1981, pp. 133-34.*

Paul Goble's *The Gift of the Sacred Dog* powerfully combines pictures and words. As author and illustrator, Goble has created a world of striking images. Drawings as brilliant as Indian beadwork help tell the ancient story of how the horse, or "sacred dog," appeared to the Indians as a blessing from their Great Spirit.

Goble is refreshingly unsentimental in his portrayal of Indian life. *The Gift of the Sacred Dog* begins with a description of suffering in the days before horses: "The people were hungry. They had walked many days looking for buffalo herds. . . . the dogs could no longer be urged to carry their heavy loads."

What is particularly joyous about Goble's treatment of this legend is that he makes a child the link between the people's need and the powers of the Great Spirit. . . .

Like Goble's Caldecott Medal winner *The Girl Who Loved Wild Horses, The Gift of the Sacred Dog* offers young readers a glorious sense of the unity between man and nature. Goble's interpretations are graceful and powerful. (p. 62)

> Nancy Bell Rollings, "Children's Books Open Bright Frontiers," in The American West, *Vol. XVIII, No. 2, March-April, 1981, pp. 62-3.*

Paul Goble . . . is at the height of his powers in this noble picture-book. . . .

The words have great dignity, but the strength of the book lies in its designs. These are strongly stylized without ever becoming false to the true natures of the creatures depicted. The theme unfolds quietly and inevitably as mountains and forests and a tide of horses spill across the page. There is something admirable here for everyone.

> M. Crouch, in a review of "The Gift of the Sacred Dog," in The Junior Bookshelf, *Vol. 46, No. 2, April, 1982, p. 61.*

STAR BOY (1983)

Each summer when the Sun reaches its peak, the Blackfeet perform the sacred ritual of the Sun Dance. How and why that ritual became part of their lore is presented for children in a handsomely designed picture book with resplendent illustrations. The language is simple, dignified, and rhythmic and emphasizes the drama inherent in the story of the young man whose commingled natures—the human and the divine—ultimately bring great blessing to his people. Born of an earthly mother and the Morning Star, he lived in the heavens as the infant Star Boy, honored as the grandson of the Sun and the Moon, until his mother's curiosity impelled her to harvest a forbidden plant. Exiled to earth with her, he grew to manhood as Scarface, for his countenance bore an ugly reminder of the Sun's displeasure. Then, through love of the Chief's beautiful daughter he found the courage to seek out his grandfather, beg forgiveness, and request that the scar be removed as a sign of blessing. Not only did the Sun comply; he also promised that if the people built a lodge in his honor each summer, he would restore health to those who were ill. And it is this promise which the Blackfeet celebrate in the annual ceremony of thanksgiving. Sources for the retelling are indicated. The brilliantly colored, stylized art is at once transcendent and comprehensible, for the symbols integrated into the design enhance and extend the power of the story.

> *Mary M. Burns, in a review of "Star Boy," in* The Horn Book Magazine, *Vol. LIX, No. 4, August, 1983, p. 431.*

Star Boy is Paul Goble's retelling of the Blackfeet story that was written down by George Bird Grinnell as "The Legend of Scarface" and on which Jamake Highwater based *Anpao: An American Indian Odyssey.* Its purpose is to tell how the Sun Dance was given to the Blackfeet people. A publisher's release on the book quotes Goble as inspired by a "rare and valuable portfolio of Blackfeet tipi designs and the stories of their origin." An apologia on the back of the title page cites Grinnell and something called *The Old North Trail* by Walter McClintock (1910) as sources. No mention is made of any current Blackfeet sources. Goble says that the story is "retold here, with respect, in its narrative form for children," which does cause one to wonder if he was entirely sure that he had made it work. Certainly he has had to omit a great deal in adapting the material to the picture-book format. The illustrations are lovely, as usual, and pretty authentic, although I am always bothered that Goble's people never have real faces. Also, the large colored polka-dots, running along the tops and bottoms of some of the pages, are a bit distracting.

As with his other books, Goble closes with a poem, in this case a Sun Song by Black Elk. Maybe it would have made his book stronger if he had said that Black Elk was not Blackfeet but Oglala, and that the Sun Dance is a sacred time shared by many of the plains Nations.

It is hard to resist the beauty of the book, and the story, if taken just for what it is, is coherent and does no violence to the spirit of the original. I would not object to using this with very young Native children, particularly those growing up away from their homelands. **Star Boy** would also, if used by a knowledgeable adult, be a good way to introduce non-Native children to a spiritual concept that is central to the lives of a large number of Native North Americans.

> *Doris Seale, in a review of "Star Boy," in* Interracial Books for Children Bulletin, *Vol. 15, Nos. 1 & 2, 1984, p. 38.*

Paul Goble won a Caldecott Medal nearly ten years ago for **The Girl Who Loved Wild Horses. Star Boy** is in the same manner. It is another Red Indian tale derived from folk-lore, and the author/artist uses Indian motifs to give a powerful unity to his book. . . . The story is told with due gravity, if a little wordily. What is more important is the quality of Mr. Goble's pictures which are of the greatest beauty, both in strength of design and richness of colour. They are disposed on the page in a way which is an example to all picture-book makers. Each opening is a delight in itself and an incentive to explore further the treasures of an outstandingly lovely book. (p. 182)

> *M. Crouch, in a review of "Star Boy," in* The Junior Bookshelf, *Vol. 52, No. 4, August, 1988, pp. 181-82.*

BUFFALO WOMAN (1984)

Glowing colors, bold figures, and brilliant decorative detail mark another of the author-illustrator's retellings of a Native American legend. In a story of transformation that stems from the tribes of the Plains Indians, a young brave discovers and marries a beautiful woman who has been sent from the "Buffalo Nation." The two have a child; but disturbed by the antagonism of her husband's people, she departs with her young son. Despite a warning that her family will kill him, the husband follows and joins a gathering of her tribe. He bravely faces the thundering wrath of the leader and correctly identifies both his son and wife in their newly acquired buffalo shapes. Having passed this test, he then submits to his own metamorphosis from man to animal, thus symbolizing the age-old bond of the Indian and the buffalo. Each page sparkles with the lupins and yuccas of the Southwest and teems with native birds, butterflies, and small animals, the richness of detail never detracting from the overall design of the handsome illustrations. The author-artist successfully combines a compelling version of an old legend with his own imaginative and striking visual interpretation.

> *Ethel R. Twichell, in a review of "Buffalo Woman," in* The Horn Book Magazine, *Vol. LX, No. 4, August, 1984, p. 457.*

There is eloquent beauty in this story of a young hunter who marries a woman from the Buffalo Nation. . . . The ink and watercolor paintings tell their own story of the Indian environment and way of life. As the young hunter leaves the peaceful serenity of his countryside (shown through pastel panoramas) to enter the strong, powerful Buffalo Nation, the colors change to rich, bold browns, reds and blues. In text and illustrations, Goble's story exhibits a quiet simplicity, respect for nature and the power of love. (pp. 59-60)

> *Candy Bertelson, in a review of "Buffalo Woman," in* School Library Journal, *Vol. 30, No. 10, August, 1984, pp. 59-60.*

Author Goble says that the story comes from "the tribes who followed the buffalo herds on the Great Plains," and he cites a number of sources from museum literature and collections such as Grinnell's *By Cheyenne Campfires.* As usual, the material is treated with respect, which is appreciated. Also as usual, the illustrations are lovely. Goble's art has been criticized as static, and to an extent, I can see that. But, if you compare the work in this book to that found in, say, Goble's **The Friendly Wolf,** you can see change and motion, subtle, but there. For some time now, gifted Native artists have been exploring other modes of expression than the traditional. It *would* be nice to see what Paul Goble might do, should he also decide to expand his horizons.

> *Doris Seale, in a review of "Buffalo Woman," in* Interracial Books for Children Bulletin, *Vol. 16, No. 1, 1985, p. 8.*

THE GREAT RACE OF THE BIRDS AND ANIMALS (1985)

This simply told "pourquoi" tale, taken from Cheyenne and Sioux mythology, draws on Indian motifs in the detailed, stylized illustrations. Using a bold range of colors and generous white space, Goble's compositions are particularly evocative of South Dakota's Black Hills, where the story is set. Freely adapted from original sources cited on the verso, the tale may provoke questions not answered in the text, such as: If men and birds were aligned in the race, why do humans eat fowl? (One source, *Sweet Medicine* [University of Oklahoma Pr, 1969] specifies, "After this [people] never ate the flesh of the birds who sided with [them] in the Great Race. The magpie, crow, swifthawk and eagle all eat meat because they sided with the man who was given authority to eat the buffalo." Goble's retelling would have been stronger were he more specific on this issue. Notwithstanding, the tale will make a fine read-aloud supplement to units on Sioux and Cherokee culture, especially to a group small and close enough to perceive the delicate detail of the illustrations. (pp. 117-18)

> *Susan Patron, in a review of "The Great Race of the Birds and the Animals," in* School Library Journal, *Vol. 32, No. 1, September, 1985, pp. 117-18.*

The Cheyenne and Sioux myth comes to life through Goble's striking paintings full of deep color and dramatic movement. The artist's style is as eye-catching as ever, though the rhythm of the spreads is interrupted by an occasional change of style. In terms of story, this is one of Goble's strongest offerings; even though the pictures do not quite reach his previous heights, they are a familiar pleasure and just right for the tale.

> *Denise M. Wilms, in a review of "The Great Race of the Birds and the Animals," in* Booklist, *Vol. 82, No. 2, September 15, 1985, p. 132.*

The moral, that Man must be worthy of his power over the beasts and birds, brings to the close a brief, supple text well integrated with pictures in which motifs and colours from Plains art provide exquisite patterns and sequences on each page, with a rare sense of space and movement in the picturesque style.

> *Margery Fisher, in a review of "The Great Race of the Birds and the Animals," in* Growing Point, *Vol. 26, No. 6, March, 1988, p. 4952.*

DEATH OF THE IRON HORSE (1987)

A fine example of pictorial history recounts the only incident when Indians wrecked a train—a Union Pacific freight derailed by Cheyennes on August 7, 1867. The brief introduction dispels the movie myth that trainwrecking was a constant Native American activity and sets the stage for the story, which begins with a Cheyenne prophet's dream of whites stripping the earth and covering it with iron bands. The ensuing settlers' and soldiers' destruction bears the dream out; when several villages are burned and scouts bring word of an Iron Horse threatening their camp, a group of warriors determines to destroy it. Their raid has both humorous and tragic aspects: they derail the train without realizing quite how they've done it, leave several of the crew dead, and raid the shipment of many products that have been withheld or sold too dearly to them by traders. They keep the coins for decoration and throw away the paper money, galloping wildly across the plain with bolts of cloth streaming behind them in a game long remembered by their people. Their triumph, of course, is shortlived, and the last picture makes a telling statement with an Amtrak train speeding across a littered landscape surmounted by fighter jets. Goble's art is all the better for a new infusion of non-folkloric subject matter. The landscapes here are stunning, one double-page spread green with a stippling of locomotive smoke rising among the trees, the next dawn gray with silhouetted shapes of the war party facing a white circle of light from the engine. The angles of

the wrecked cars are echoed in the body of the dead crewmen, while later, the flowing cloth flies as wildly as the warriors' excitement. A different view of history, socially and aesthetically.

> *Betsy Hearne, in a review of "Death of the Iron Horse," in* Bulletin of the Center for Children's Books, *Vol. 40, No. 8, April, 1987, p. 145.*

History remembered is the stuff of legend in this dramatically illustrated incident from the post Civil War period. Sometimes that legend is exaggerated to the point where it becomes not simply a cliché but also a stereotype, as implied in the author's prelude to his retelling: "There have been many trains wrecked by Indian people in the pages of fiction, but it really happened only once." . . . Their act was not capricious but rather a desperate act of bravery. Like the warriors of old, they were defending their traditions, attempting to stave off the tragedy foreseen by the Cheyenne prophet, Sweet Medicine. That legendary figure had not only foretold the coming of the "strange hairy people . . . from the East" but had also seen them tear open the earth, exposing her bones and binding her with iron bands. To the Cheyenne the construction of the railroad brought the desecration that the prophet had predicted. Thus their foray against this fearsome monster, using tomahawks and knives to pull up the road on which it traveled, is an adventure of epic proportions, when viewed in the context of the times. Written as if narrated by a participant, the memoir is bittersweet, ending on a note of triumph as the young men return to their people laden with the spoils of victory. But on the horizon, a dark smudge of smoke presages still another wave of invaders. Although the art is recognizably that of Paul Goble, he has combined the stylized, brilliantly colored portrayal of the Cheyennes with a more literal rendering of the train, thus restating the juxtaposition of legend and reality found in the text. And while there are some lighter touches—such as the Cheyennes' delight in exploring the contents of the boxcars—for the most part, this is a somber tale, a sad commentary on the often ignored, less happy consequences of progress. (pp. 329-30)

> *Mary M. Burns, in a review of "Death of the Iron Horse," in* The Horn Book Magazine, *Vol. LXIII, No. 3, May-June, 1987, pp. 329-30.*

Mr. Goble . . . is a very fine artist. In colorful double-page spreads he sets out the story in stylized images. There is a dark and haunting center spread where the Cheyenne braves, after a night spent freeing Mother Earth of the iron bands—the rails—that imprison her, see a point of light hovering on the awakening horizon and cannot tell whether it's the Morning Star rising or the Iron Horse returning. But the book is marred on the last page, when Mr. Goble, in a confused attempt to reconcile the past with the present, shows an Amtrak train crossing a prairie littered with Coke and Pepsi cans accompanied by the fatuous words, "Whoever could have imagined that . . . the Iron Horse would become the train on which we all ride?" Some things are better left unreconciled.

> *Gregory Blake Smith, in a review of "Death of the Iron Horse," in* The New York Times Book Review, *November 22, 1987, p. 44.*

HER SEVEN BROTHERS (1988)

This latest book in Goble's much-respected series of Indian

stories is a Cheyenne legend about the creation of a group of stars the white man has called the Big Dipper. It begins with a young Cheyenne girl being helped by the spirits to become highly skilled at embroidering clothes with porcupine quills. She creates seven sets of men's shirts and moccasins and then journeys north to give them to seven brothers who have been revealed to her in her mind and whom she has chosen as her own brothers. She is welcomed as a sister, especially by the youngest brother, who is also endowed with special powers. When buffalo threatened to destroy them all, the boy uses his powers to create a pine tree that extends higher and higher to the sky, where he and the others escape to become the group of stars known as the Big Dipper in the Great Bear constellation. The boy becomes the famous eighth tiny star (known elsewhere as Alcor) that stands beside the middle star of the Dipper's "handle" (Mizar), which in this legend the girl has become.

As in texts for all his books, Goble imparts true Indian qualities, such as an easy acceptance of natural spirituality, the goodness of sisterhood/brotherhood, and an unquestioning respect for an individual's need to do what must be done. The girl's mother does not understand her daughter's vision and weeps to see her go but nonetheless helps her set out on her journey.

Similarly in his pictures, Goble faithfully recreates stylized Indian artistic qualities, such as use of flat bright colors, flat shapes, and flat spatial orientation remniscent of hide paintings or ledger-book art. To this oldest of Indian art, Goble adds his personal contemporary touch of softened watercolors for details of flowers and grasses or distant hills seen through a haze. The illustrations in this book present us with traditional Cheyenne designs for painted tipis, shirts, dresses, moccasins, pipe bags, backrests, and parfleches (rawhide pieces that are folded and painted to make envelopes for carrying things), all of which were meticulously researched in museums and photographs.

The artist's use of the picture-book format demonstrates thoughtful planning. The wraparound book jacket depicts the girl and her chosen brothers in a scene not repeated within the book itself. Underneath the jacket, the book's cover is dark blue with an imprint of the familar eight-star Dipper configuration. On the half-title page, the girl is shown walking to find her brothers, who are pictured waiting on the title page that follows. The artist's dedication to his young son Robert is found on the copyright page with a quillwork design used again later on the lining of the girl's family tipi, and an acknowledgments page is decorated with little porcupines to prepare us for the Porcupine spirit's part in this story. All but the final illustration are double-page spreads that are well-balanced left to right in use of white space, colors, and text placements, with little or no interference by the gutter.

In his acceptance speech for the 1979 Caldecott Award for *The Girl Who Loved Wild Horses,* Goble mentioned an Indian story "about ancestors who turned into the stars of the Big Dipper," a story that obviously stayed in his mind to retell and illustrate one day. For children and adults alike, it is fortunate that the day has arrived. (pp. 76-7)

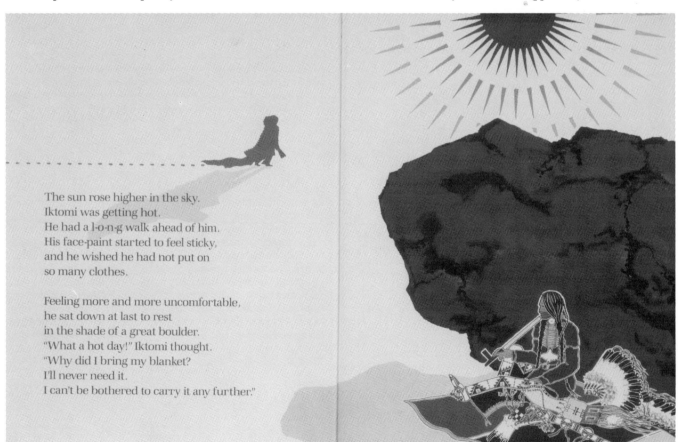

The sun rose higher in the sky.
Iktomi was getting hot.
He had a l-o-n-g walk ahead of him.
His face-paint started to feel sticky,
and he wished he had not put on
so many clothes.

Feeling more and more uncomfortable,
he sat down at last to rest
in the shade of a great boulder.
"What a hot day!" Iktomi thought.
"Why did I bring my blanket?
I'll never need it.
I can't be bothered to carry it any further."

From Iktomi and the Boulder: A Plains Indian Story, *written and illustrated by Paul Goble.*

Lyn Lacy and Sally Hunter, in a review of "Her Seven Brothers," in The Five Owls, *Vol. II, No. 5, May-June, 1988, pp. 76-7.*

Goble once more combines a respectful retelling of a Cheyenne legend with dynamic paintings depicting both traditional Indian life and the beauty of the natural world. . . . Goble's adaptation is distinguished by its restraint; he resists the temptation to dramatize the tale, choosing instead the quiet, matter-of-fact voice of the traditional Indian storyteller. The illustrations, by contrast, are boldly graphic, with dynamic patterns, brilliant color, and strong line dramatically imposed on the white of the page. While the elements are all from the natural world, Goble stylizes and idealizes them, creating fields of texture, merging from realistic foliage and animals to abstract, flattened shapes. Like the story, the characters are never particularized. Goble keeps the human characters at a distance and flattens their faces, removing all individuality. At the same time he lingers over the design of the clothing and the painted tipis. Once again Goble's admiration for the Plains Indians has been combined with his considerable gifts as a painter to produce a seamless whole.

Eleanor K. MacDonald, in a review of "Her Seven Brothers," in School Library Journal, *Vol. 35, No. 9, June-July, 1988, p. 97.*

The story is lovely: the retelling echoes its delicate and gentle charm. The illustrations, although executed in Goble's distinctive style, emphasize the flora and fauna associated with hope and spring. The pages are filled with detail, yet they do not seem busy but rather representative of nature's magnificent bounty—a romanticist's view of the world. The author's note not only gives the sources for his art and for his retelling but also describes the particular techniques employed for the illustrations: pen and India ink outlines filled in with watercolor, leaving thin white lines "to try and achieve the brightness of Indian bead and quillwork, and to capture something of the bright colors that one sees in the clear air of the Great Plains." Like the stars it celebrates, the whole book scintillates. (pp. 506-07)

Mary M. Burns, in a review of "Her Seven Brothers," in The Horn Book Magazine, *Vol. LXIV, No. 4, July-August, 1988, pp. 506-07.*

IKTOMI AND THE BOULDER: A PLAINS INDIAN STORY (1988)

This is just what the doctor ordered for Paul Goble: a change of tone from stories of dignified weight to a trickster tale adapted and illustrated with mischief. Iktomi is so vain that he struts off toward the next village in his best clothes and blanket. When the sun shines too hot, he gives the blanket to a boulder; but when the rain falls he takes it back, infuriating the boulder so that it rolls after him and pins him down. Finally, Iktomi tricks some bats into destroying the rock, after which he sets off again, battered-looking but jaunty as ever. The basic story is in large black print, the narrator's periodic remarks to the audience in gray italics, and the trickster's comments ("That rock has a terrible temper") in small print in the midst of the pictures. These are simply composed against lots of white space that allows a smooth, amusing blend of diverse design and color elements. The picture of Iktomi completely enveloped in his isolated, tent-shaped blanket with rain and lightning aiming at its peak is particularly funny, as are his lies to the bats ("He said that you sleep up-side-down because you don't know your 'up side' from your 'down side.' ") The last depiction of Iktomi, showing one leg in traditional garb and the other in an athletic sock to go with his baseball cap, steps the story right into modern times. With source and background notes and an attention-grabbing cover that portrays Iktomi upside down under the rock ("Help!"), this is a coup. (pp. 228-29)

Betsy Hearne, in a review of "Iktomi and the Boulder: A Plains Indian Story," in Bulletin of the Center for Children's Books, *Vol. 41, No. 11, July-August, 1988, pp. 228-29.*

The text consists of three continuously running threads: the story itself, the comments that an Indian storyteller would add as asides (printed in italics), and the words of Iktomi himself, which appear in the illustrations beside his head as they might in a comic strip (but without the balloons). Goble's striking artwork turns this amusing folktale into a memorable picture book. On white pages, the brilliant reds, blues, and yellows of Iktomi's magnificent clothes glow brightly, their colors defined and intensified by fine black lines. The animals, mountains, and clouds are depicted with simplicity and, often, monumentality. Goble uses silhouette effectively and white space with sensitivity. On the last page, Iktomi, his clothes tattered, wearing a modern baseball cap on his head and an athletic sock on his front foot, strides forward musing "Let me think: what shall I do now?" leading readers to wonder what present-day troubles we might blame on the mischief-making Iktomi. A wonderful read-aloud for school-age children.

Carolyn Phelan, in a review of "Iktomi and the Boulder: A Plains Indian Story," in Booklist, *Vol. 84, No. 22, August, 1988, p. 1924.*

Iktomi is the trickster figure in Plains Indian folklore. Stories about him appear in slightly different versions in many collections of Native American folk tales; the most common is "Iktomi and the Ducks," a *pourquoi* tale which explains why ducks have red eyes. Goble has chosen a lesser known story and has judiciously pruned it of extraneous material; the result is a brief and lively tale suitable for the youngest listener. . . . Goble indicates in his notes that Iktomi is both clever and stupid; the author effectively conveys the varied qualities of the character's personality in a variety of techniques. Iktomi's thoughts are printed in small type, and, in contrast to the bold black print used for the bulk of the third-person text, italic gray type offers comments from the narrator on the duplicity, absurdity, or uselessness of Iktomi's actions. Both approaches encourage participation by the listener and attempt to re-create the informal, ever-changing nature of Native American storytelling. In keeping with the abbreviated character of the text, Goble's distinctive flat, bright India ink and watercolor illustrations focus only on the essential elements of the story. Humor is inherent in trickster tales, and Goble has perfectly captured Iktomi's shenanigans for the amusement of young readers. (pp. 638-39)

Ellen G. Fader, in a review of "Iktomi and the Boulder: A Plains Indian Story," in The Horn Book Magazine, *Vol. LXIV, No. 5, September-October, 1988, pp. 638-39.*

BEYOND THE RIDGE (1989)

Although LC calls this wonderful, consoling book fiction, it is more truly a prayer, a moving affirmation of death as a natural part of life—and a tribute to the wisdom and culture of the Plains Indians.

Quoting several of their memorable poetic prayers, Goble notes that he has "embroidered upon a few of the thoughts which Plains Indian people express. Dying, they say, is like climbing up a long and difficult slope towards a high pine-covered ridge of the Great Plains." Responding to her mother's call, an old woman makes such a journey as her family grieves by her body; from the top, she views a surpassingly beautiful country, burgeoning with flowers and herds of animals, peopled with long-dead loved ones. Meanwhile, her living family follows their traditional ceremony for the dead, mourning yet recognizing that while "the body goes back to the earth . . . the spirit lives forever . . . the dead, and the living, and those who will one day be born are part of a great circle."

The meticulously detailed illustrations, joyously celebrating the earth's poignant loveliness, are in a style similar to the one used in **Her Seven Brothers,** with white outlines used to brighten the images. Goble explains that he has left faces blank to allow readers to imagine in their own way. This outstandingly beautiful book should indeed free imaginations to soar.

> *A review of "Beyond the Ridge," in* Kirkus Reviews, *Vol. LVI, No. 24, December 15, 1988, p. 1811.*

Goble, whose **The Girl Who Loved Wild Horses** won the Caldecott Medal and whose **Iktomi and the Boulder** presented an Indian folktale with wit and panache, takes his Plains Indian subject matter in a totally new direction. The theme here is death; the treatment is unusual, the message comforting. . . . Throughout the book quotations from Indians resonate with the story and artwork to create an aura of acceptance of death and a celebration of all creation. Goble's full-color paintings sing with vibrancy and confidence. The wide double-page spreads vary in composition and in palette. Re-creating the present world in the clear, heraldic colors for which he is best known, Goble depicts the after world in other ways. Deep, contrasting shades of gray and slate blue define the ridge, giving way to a sky brightened with white and the freshest of pastels. In an intriguing glimpse of how the illustrator approaches his work, Goble's notes detail his method of creating the artwork and his reason for leaving the faces of the characters relatively featureless. Inspired by thoughts about death expressed by Indians, the author-artist's work is part story, part reverent expression of belief, and a wholly original picture book.

> *Carolyn Rhelan, in a review of "Beyond the Ridge," in* Booklist, *Vol. 85, No. 13, March 1, 1989, p. 1191.*

Once again Goble has created a stunning picture book interpretation of an aspect of Plains Indian tradition. . . . The art work is Goble at his best. Clear colors and meticulous details make his paintings come alive. Clouds break like waves across the expanses of sky. The Great Plains shimmer with changing light, and there is a pervading sense of the unity of all creation. The story is bracketed by several passages in italics on life and death written by traditional native Americans. Attributions are made only in small print on the back of the title page, and so the individual voices seem to merge with the voice of the storyteller. Unfortunately, these sections are too repetitive to read out loud in one sitting; a wise librarian will be selective in reading these passages. Nonetheless, this book is a wonderful acquisition. Goble's portrayal of native American beliefs is accurate and respectful. And the universal wisdom the book contains will give comfort and insight on a subject that troubles readers of all ages.

> *Carolyn Polese, in a review of "Beyond the Ridge," in* School Library Journal, *Vol. 35, No. 9, May, 1989, p. 84.*

Gail E(inhart) Haley

1939-

American author and illustrator of picture books, fiction, and nonfiction, and reteller.

Recognized for manifesting the traditions and techniques of the storyteller in books for preschoolers and primary grade readers which evince her interest in both the magical and instructional features of myth and folklore, Haley is commended for creating fanciful plots which include messages of social or moral relevance, for the read-aloud quality of her works, and for the appropriateness, lavishness, and vitality of her illustrations. Intrigued by the mystical, imaginative nature of folktales, she has also delved into the lessons taught by the narratives of oral legends. *A Story, A Story: An African Tale* (1970), for example, recounts how Kwaku Ananse, the Spider trickster of Ashanti lore, procures the stories of the Sky God for the people on earth by accomplishing three difficult tasks which the god sets for him. Acknowledged as the first book to introduce the concept of a black God to children's literature, *A Story, A Story* describes how the aged and powerless Ananse outsmarts his adversaries through narration which includes poetic, repetitive phrases and words of African origin in the manner of the initial oral versions of the tale. *A Story, A Story* was named a *Boston Globe-Horn Book* honor book for its illustrations in 1970 and was awarded the Caldecott Medal in 1971. Haley's retellings draw upon a variety of sources, including the Brothers Grimm and the Bible. In *Noah's Ark* (1971), she transports the tale to a contemporary setting where pollution has made the world so uninhabitable that Noah sets sail until the air is purified. In 1976, Haley became the first illustrator to win both the Caldecott and Greenaway Medals when she was awarded the latter for *The Post Office Cat* (1976), a work which informs young readers about the basis of the British custom of employing cats as mouse catchers in postal offices.

Despite her thought-provoking themes, it is for her pictures that Haley has received the most accolades. In an attempt to exemplify the respective cultures of her stories, she diversifies her illustrations to suit the nature of each work. Haley employs an art nouveau style to capture the feel of Victorian England in *The Post Office Cat,* for example, while representing *A Story, A Story* in vibrant woodcuts and *The Green Man* (1980), the tale of a prince who lives in the forest as a fugitive, in pictures which incorporate flat perspective and stylized poses and evoke the texture of medieval tapestries. Haley has also illustrated the works of authors such as Francelia Butler and E. L. Konigsburg and has written a book of counting rhymes and an informational book about costumes and costume-making. In 1984, the Gail Haley Collection of the Culture of Childhood was established at Appalachian State University in Boone, North Carolina.

(See also *Something about the Author,* Vols. 28, 43; *Contemporary Authors New Revision Series,* Vol. 14; and *Contemporary Authors,* Vols. 21-22, rev. ed.)

AUTHOR'S COMMENTARY

[The following excerpt is from a speech Haley originally delivered at the Claremont Reading Conference in 1972.]

During the past year I have talked to thousands of children. I enjoy talking to them, . . . and to all who are interested in children's literature. But I haven't done all the talking. I've also done a great deal of listening. And what I've heard makes me feel very concerned about the future of the culture of childhood. The most encouraging thing I have found is that children—my own, and those who crowd round when I speak in libraries and schools—are still relatively immune from the child hostile environment we are creating for them. . . .

We read and hear a great deal about the pollution of our environment. We know what it does to our children's health. (p. 72)

Imagine the probable reaction of children in the year two thousand, who'll discover that the plants and animals pictured in their literary heritage have gone the way of the Brontosaurus. Their elders will tell them that they still existed in their childhood. And the children of tomorrow are likely to ask, "What have you done to our animals?" What answers will we give them?

Other, more immediate, though less visible aspects of our children's environment are threatened. The very concept of active play, curiosity, experimentation, manipulative doing and reading are being extinguished. Is it not equally possible that children of tomorrow may ask "Daddy, what is a book?" or "Mommy, what does reading mean?" We may be killing yet another species—children—as we alienate them from active cultural participation. (pp. 72-3)

Mass culture and passive consumption are antithetical to the idea that childhood is a special stage of human development requiring shelter, care, and nurturance. (p. 73)

If we are to retain and recapture a loving child culture, we must be parents to all children. We must be considerate of the individual differences and needs of each, and of the special nature of childhood.

We cannot view children as material to be conditioned for consumption. We must stop exploiting them as soon as they can sit before a TV set. We must discourage the media oriented merchandisers from using the child audience as a market. (p. 74)

A little more than one hundred years ago "The pratfalls of Wilhelm Busch's Max and Moritz" included torturing chickens by feeding them morsels tied together with string. The confused fowl, unable to disgorge their fodder, flutter about, and become entangled in the branches of a tree. The following lines describe the chicken's death throes, and reflect a brand of humor that kept generations of incipient concentration camp guards in stitches:

> On the tree behold them dangling,
> In the Agony of Strangling!
> And their necks grow longer and longer,
> And their groans grow stronger and stronger.

Today's put-on, put-down versions of literary violence, and the pathological fantasies of children's books, comics, and TV shows have identifiable roots in this heritage. Some authors of children's literature admit to, and pride themselves upon this ancestry. And the latter day Max and Moritzes enmesh our children in the branches of their perverse and perverted culture.

Our children know that something has changed for them. They are deeply troubled by anguish and hopelessness that differ from the youth unrest of former generations. They suffer the debilitating apathy common to all vanishing species. (pp. 74-5)

I write, draw, paint, and cut wood blocks like every other artist, painstakingly and sometimes painfully. My skills are a means and not an end. I enlist them in the fight for survival and restoration of childhood.

These goals can be reached by many different paths and viewpoints, as represented by a great variety of authors and artists. They are needed to assure the diversity that speaks with many voices to different children. I caution only against perverse uniformity of the mass culture that threatens the survival of childhood.

We must not lose hope. Cultural survival has much in common with physical survival. Each depends on the other. Even in evolutionary terms, the human characteristic of hope is an expression of the instinct of survival in lower species. Without hope, there can be no survival, no striving for, and no vi-

sion of the future. Hope is the thread I weave through my work. It's not the sugar coated hope of a plasticized world of tomorrow. It is hope that finds beauty in being alive today. It does not look back over its shoulder to a nostalgic past that never was. It is the hope that there will be a tomorrow. It is the hope for a survival of childhood. Such hope is an act of faith that may yet divert our children from following the media oriented pied pipers into a world from which they may not return. Or if they do, they are likely to be less human and humane than they might have been if we had given them proper guidance. (pp. 75-6)

> *Gail Haley, "Children—the Vanishing Species," in* Claremont Reading Conference, *36th Yearbook, 1972, pp. 72-6.*

GENERAL COMMENTARY

EARLY YEARS

"I had a make-believe playmate when I was five. I remember this absolutely vividly," Gail Haley told us. "Also, I used to see fairies and talk to little creatures all the time. **The Green Man** is someone I saw in the woods when I was a kid. Yes, I still talk to fairies." (p. 24)

Gail Haley is the only author/illustrator of children's books to win both the Caldecott award and its English equivalent, the Kate Greenaway medal, which she won for her book, **The Post Office Cat**. "Awards are important," she says, "because they help build a market for my books. I'd do books whether I won awards or not, however, because I love to do children's books!"

There is a bit of the crusader in Gail Haley. "I saw a lot of prejudice in the south when I was growing up," she says. Indicating she'd like to right wrongs, she volunteered that "Most of the books I've done have espoused some cause. I try not to put the message too strongly, but the message is there. For example, **A Story, A Story** was the first book to have a black God," she said with quiet pride. "If one of my books doesn't have a cause, it may tell children something significant from folklore, something I feel kids should know."

Anyone who talks to fairies and sees green men in the forest would find it easy to become an expert on folklore, and Gail Haley qualifies. She has become particularly knowledgeable on mountain folklore, which she has traced back to Europe and Elizabethan times. Her hope is that someday she will be able to live for several months in Rumania, "where villages have gone almost untouched by modern times. Living in a village in Rumania would be like stepping back in time into something that just doesn't exist anywhere else in the world." She has already done enough research to know such a culture will be rich in folklore.

As one begins to see inside today's Gale Haley—and it doesn't take long—one sees glimpses of the person whom her grandfather liked to call "wild-eyed Gail." One also sees a determined spirit and a far-out imagination. One watches as today's Gail fails to suppress the exuberance, the mischievous qualities, the kooky imagination of yesterday's Gail. It is, in fact, that spirit of yesterday, alive and well in today's Gail, which spawns books such as **A Story, A Story; Go Away, Stay Away; The Green Man** and now her latest, **Birdsong**.

From A Story, A Story: An African Tale, *written and illustrated by Gail E. Haley.*

Nowhere, of course, is the Haley free spirit more noticeable than in her art. (pp. 24-5)

She works in whatever medium fits her fancy or mood. One book will be done in woodcuts, another in linoleum blocks, another painted on wood. Her imagination leads her in many directions and the finished books seem to capture some of her own inner excitement. (p. 25)

> *"Gail Haley . . . a Whimsical Visionary," in* Early Years, *Vol. 16, No. 3, November-December, 1985, pp. 24-5.*

ONE, TWO, BUCKLE MY SHOE: A BOOK OF COUNTING RHYMES (1965)

If one can successfully combine the alphabet and Mother Goose, (Joan Anglund's *In a Pumpkin Shell*), why not as well numbers and poems? Rhymes with numbers in them (but not really counting rhymes) have been assembled in this oversized, 64-page picture book. There are more than enough to satisfy any child who must listen to them or the adult who has to read them out loud. The bright, two dimensional, rather nondescript illustrations often act as a divider between poems since titles are not given. For purchase where a large variety of counting rhymes is needed.

> *Suzanne M. Glazer, in a review of "One, Two, Buckle My Shoe: A Book of Counting Rhymes," in* School Library Journal, *Vol. 11, No. 5, January, 1965, p. 96.*

Miss Haley has had the pleasant idea of collecting together a great many counting rhymes and arranging them numerically. This brings together a lively collection of the familiar and unfamiliar. To these she adds her own agreeable, but on the whole not very distinguished, drawings. Here, one feels, is a good idea not wasted but not exploited quite well enough. (p. 276)

> *A review of "One, Two, Buckle My Shoe," in* The Junior Bookshelf, *Vol. 29, No. 5, October, 1965, pp. 275-76.*

This agreeable picture-book from America contains rhymes for each figure from one to ten and further cumulative jingles dealing with numbers, like *The twelve days of Christmas* and the nonsense-piece describing such marvels as "One old Oxford ox opening oysters". The illustrative style is amusing, occasionally a little ostentatious in its jokes, with fondant colours disposed in elegant designs alternating with a combination of black, grey and brick red which is less distracting than full colour when you want to explore fully the small pertinent details.

> *Margery Fisher, in a review of "One Two Buckle My Shoe," in* Growing Point, *Vol. 12, No. 6, December, 1973, p. 2298.*

A STORY, A STORY: AN AFRICAN TALE (1970)

AUTHOR'S COMMENTARY

[The following excerpt is from Haley's Caldecott Award acceptance speech, which she delivered in June, 1971.]

Live storytelling, reading to preschool and early-grade children, and the discussion of picture books with them are perhaps more important today than at any time since Comenius. In the days before mass literacy, the oral tradition prepared children for later life. The give-and-take between storyteller and child was a vital educational experience. It provided incentives for speech and for self-expression. This oral tradition has all but vanished; but the book is a natural extension of the storyteller. It takes the place of folk memory. And the picture book, especially, is a bridge from speech to literacy. It allows adults to whet a young child's appetite for finding out about a world that is beyond his experience. No "Right to Read" and no TV program can compensate children for a lack of exposure to stories and books. Instead, they encourage—rather than reverse—the trend toward autism and functional illiteracy, even when they succeed in drilling children to recite letters and numbers.

Deprive a child of love and he will reach for affection or clamor for attention at the expense of all other aspirations. Deprive him of fantasy and he may try, on his own, to make up even for that deficit. But children who are not spoken to by live and responsive adults will not learn to speak properly. Children who are not answered will stop asking questions. They will become incurious. And children who are not told stories and who are not read to will have few reasons for wanting to learn to read.

The advocates of electronic shortcuts to literacy do not understand the storyteller's function. My interest in African folk tales stems in large part from the role they play in the education of children. The African storyteller, like the live reader of children's books, invites questions and he answers them. He adapts his tales to the understanding and experience of his audience, and he repeats or explains what is difficult. He is an imitable example. He is marvelously well informed and he has a prodigious memory. He recalls heroic deeds of whole dynasties of chiefs, back through three or more centuries. He is the keeper of the tribe's traditions, conscience, and identity. He is the poser of riddles and conundrums. He is the spontaneous teacher of the young. He chronicles the exploits of his contemporaries and he adds them to the stories that are memorized by his successors. He plays with the sound of language, and he weaves witticisms, sly barbs, and criticism of tribal members and chiefs into the fabric of the classic stories he tells. No two renditions of the same story are ever alike. Each evokes new contributions from his audience. The African folk tale and the modern children's book are very closely related.

An adult book requires only two participants—the author and the reader. But a picture book, like the folk tale, needs three—the author, the story-reader, and the child. Any live reading of a picture book, like the telling of a folk tale, requires interpretation. The reader must adapt it to the child-listener's experience, and no two versions need ever be the same. (pp. 364-65)

A picture book, like a good toy, invites participation. (p. 366)

The leisurely daydreams of childhood, stimulated by stories and picture books, are not mere pastimes for children. Children expect, from babyhood onward, human and humane responses from everything with which they come into contact. And they need to be able to respond, actively and spontaneously, to people, animals, objects, and ideas. Seen in this light it becomes obvious that children need anthropomorphic fantasies for proper development. They make it possible for the child to interact with his world. Children live in a world in which they are "so small, so small"—the smallest in the family. Most of their choices are made for them: what they will eat and wear and when they have to go to bed. Their earliest independence is gained only in fantasy. At first, these fantasies may be merely rebellious. But they help children learn to cope. Children's dreams allow them to come to terms with the necessary limitations on their freedom and impulses.

Eventually, this sheer resistance to authority is displaced by idealized heroic yearnings. And these permit a child to try out who and what he would like to become. No one who learned to enjoy a rich, imaginative life in childhood need ever lose this faculty. As children mature, their fantasies are converted into ideals and into goals. Such children stand a good chance to turn longings into reality—at least in part. The exercise of a child's fantasies give him foresight and prepare him for a fearless and hopeful future.

Yet, we seem determined to choke learning that is "species specific" to human beings. Laughter, imaginative play, curiosity, self-expression, and language are among the skills that are peculiar to our kind. They cannot flourish unless our young practice them actively. And so the picture book, among other essential early learning experiences, is pitted against the lavishness of the motion, color, imagery, and sound of television—a presentation that makes no demand on the audience. But the picture book's esthetic economy is much more valuable for the child. It demands that he fill in the void between the peaks represented by succeeding spreads. He is required to make his own contribution.

More than a personal catharsis, my work is an effort designed to stimulate verbal and visual responses, and a preparation for literacy. My books are for children. They are also frames of reference for the story-reader who needs to dramatize, explain, and discuss the ideas I express, the pictures I draw, and the words I use. My object is to involve adult and child. Both are my collaborators. Telling stories and illustrating them is my invitation to children to join me in a world of fantasy I envision and to elaborate on what I present to them. My aim is not to manipulate children, but to encourage them to be active, imaginative, whimsical, and curious. These, more than fact gathering or rote memorization, are the specific appetites that lead to learning which is essential for human survival. Chief among such appetites is the hunger to read. (pp. 366-68)

Gail E. Haley, "Caldecott Award Acceptance," in The Horn Book Magazine, *Vol. XLVII, No. 4, August, 1971, pp. 363-68.*

Outside of West Africa, it is just not true that "Most African stories, whether or not they are about Kwaku Ananse the 'spider man,' are called 'Spider Stories.'" And of course this is only one variant of "how that came to be" (cf. Courlander, *The Hat-Shaking Dance*). But as story, and especially as picture story, **A Story, A Story** is terse, pungent and dramatic. In words that repeat rhythmically, hypnotically—"So Ananse tied the leopard / by his foot / by his foot / by his foot / by his foot, with the vine creeper"—or strike suddenly—"and (the hornets) flew into the calabash—fom!"—Anase pays the price of Nyama the Sky God and secures the golden box of stories for the people on earth. Also in woodcuts that are expressively patterned, subtly but strikingly colored, and boldly designed—so much so that they show to advantage at a distance. For most black children in America, the route of their forebears *is* the root of the story, and it's perfectly rendered for sharing.

A review of "A Story, A Story," in Kirkus Reviews, *Vol. XXXVIII, No. 5, March 1, 1970, p. 241.*

One of the most appealing of African stories has here been given an extremely handsome setting. Woodcuts developed from African design motifs employ brilliant blues, oranges, yellows, pinks, greens, and purples to give vigorous visual form to a witty tale. . . . The tale appears in several collections (Radin, Feldmann, Courlander), all harking back to the definitive collection of Ashanti lore gathered by R. S. Rattray during his service early in this century as a British colonial officer in the Gold Coast. Haley has retold her story from Rattray's collection, freely borrowing the language of the Ashanti storytellers as Rattray so faithfully recorded it. It is unfortunate that she has not chosen to acknowledge her debt to this pioneer folklorist. It is also less than accurate to assert, as is done in the introduction, that "Most African stories . . . are called 'Spider Stories'," for this is a term unique to the Ashanti people. Nor is it correct to state that "This story begins as do all African stories." The formulaic opening here used is a bastardized combination of the beautiful "We do not really mean . . . " of the Ashanti and the equally poetic "A Story, a Story . . . " which Rattray identified as a Hausa formula in his earlier collection of Hausa stories. The elegance of the illustrations make this book distinguished; its inaccuracies about its African sources are lamentable.

> *Gertrude B. Herman, in a review of "A Story, A Story," in* School Library Journal, *Vol. 17, No. 1, September, 1970, p. 148.*

Although this gets off to a slow start with an explanation—and a generalization about the genre—it soon moves to cadenced prose, the author adeptly using repetition at points of emphasis. The woodcut illustrations, busy with detail, are sometimes overcrowded and almost garish, but they have vitality, humor, and a good sense of design.

> *Zena Sutherland, in a review of "A Story, A Story," in* Bulletin of the Center for Children's Books, *Vol. 24, No. 4, December, 1970, p. 59.*

Gail Haley's *A Story, A Story,* the pictorial rendering of one of the African Anansi tales, is an unexceptional book—effective for reading to a group, commonplace as art. The spread represented in this volume perfectly illustrates its utility—the large scale, the clear-cut flat forms, the manifest action, the vivid coloring—and, equally, its deficiencies. What exists in African art as expressive simplification is here facile stylization, without meaning or force. The tree, for instance, is not an idea of a tree but a wallpaper pattern; and a similar lack of precise observation, variety or modulation is marked throughout. (p. 281)

> *Barbara Bader, "Picture Books, Art and Illustration," in* Newbery and Caldecott Medal Books: 1966-1975, *edited by Lee Kingman, The Horn Book, Inc., 1975, pp. 276-90.*

Heavy with African motifs, native costumes, and rich colors and patterns, the woodcuts of this Medal Book help communicate the symbolism of the story. Repeating patterns and designs cover the pages of the book, and, though abstract, they create recognizable shapes. If the basic elements of the text were memorized, the book could function effectively if the story were *told,* rather than read, allowing the oral origins of the tale to become more evident.

The emotional use of color and patterns draws attention to the ethnic backgrounds of the tale, but the universal elements of the story are amazing. Like the trials of Hercules and the mythical motif of Pandora's box full of intangible sorrows, Haley has brought the universality of the contents of children's books to light, as well as the traditions of a culture which commands respectable exposure in its books. (p. 346)

> *Linda Kauffman Peterson, "The Caldecott Medal and Honor Books, 1938-1981," in* Newbery and Caldecott Medal and Honor Books: An Annotated Bibliography, *by Linda Kauffman Peterson and Marilyn Leathers Solt, G. K. Hall & Co., 1982, pp. 235-378.*

NOAH'S ARK (1971)

[*Noah's Ark*] is another message-freighted tale for young listeners—this one about a contemporary Noah, up-tight about civilization's headlong flight toward ecological doom. Dreaming one night that all the animals on earth have become extinct, Noah tries to forewarn his fellow men. Failing this, he builds a latter-day ark complete with ship-to-shore radio, deep freeze for Arctic animals and solarium for warm-blooded guests. Miss Haley's art work, rendered in a style midway between Henri *Le Douanier* Rousseau and Mexico's proletarian muralists of the 1930's, is unrelievedly earnest. So is the plot, its lightest moments dependent upon contrast with the Genesis original. (Miss Haley's dove, for example, is a helicopter piloted by Noah's son.) Pure air ultimately lures the ark to port. And thus endeth Miss Haley's lesson.

> *Selma G. Lanes, in a review of "Noah's Ark," in* The New York Times Book Review, *September 19, 1971, p. 8.*

A luxurious production—outsized, with full-color work on special paper. The heavily burdened didactic tale is based on Genesis: "Every beast of the earth/ . . . every fowl of the air/ . . . into your hands are they delivered." . . . Opulent and panoramic the art tends to be conventional with its "cute" children and stiffly postured Noah, and the treatment of ecology is simplistic and idealized.

> *Virginia Haviland, in a review of "Noah's Ark," in* The Horn Book Magazine, *Vol. XLVII, No. 5, October, 1971, p. 471.*

An appealing, thoughtful picture book on the theme of our upset ecology. . . . A hint of greeting card influence, discernible in the slightly anthropomorphized animals and the cherubic children, does not detract significantly from the ambitious illustrations, which were painted on wood in many dusky but deep colors. The succession of carefully designed double-page spreads brings to mind a series of stately murals, painted to tell a story, which these do quite well. (pp. 102-03)

> *Melinda Schroeder, in a review of "Noah's Ark," in* School Library Journal, *Vol. 18, No. 2, October, 1971, pp. 102-03.*

JACK JOUETT'S RIDE (1973)

In 1782 Jack Jouett, "the Southern Paul Revere," rode 40 miles from Cuckoo to Charlottesville, Virginia, to warn Thomas Jefferson, Patrick Henry, and other revolutionaries that the British Green Dragoons were coming to capture the town. Then he led the enemy on a diversionary chase and rode off shouting, "When men need to be free from tyrants, they will always find a way." Haley tells the story straight, aiming not to humanize a hero as in Jean Fritz's *And Then What Happened Paul Revere?* but to promote one, and she illustrates it with harsh, prosaic linoleum cuts. Strictly for patriots and Virginians.

From The Post Office Cat, *written and illustrated by Gail E. Haley.*

A review of "Jack Jouett's Ride," in Kirkus Reviews, *Vol. XLI, No. 20, October 15, 1973, p. 1153.*

Haley has resurrected and stunningly restored to history Jack Jouett. . . . The spare, even text and vividly designed, hand-tinted linoleum block prints tightly mesh to capture the historical mood and the sense of urgency in Jouett's ride. And for readers too young for the particulars of history, the adventure alone will sustain.

A review of "Jack Jouett's Ride," in The Booklist, *Vol. 70, No. 6, November 15, 1973, p. 339.*

Jack Jouett's heroism may not mean much to English readers. They should nevertheless find the story exciting enough, especially when supported by the author's bold and mannered linocuts. If they have a slightly old-fashioned air about them, this is all to the good in this context. They encompass a wide range of mood and action, and the use of colour is restrained and effective.

M. Crouch, in a review of "Jack Jouett's Ride," in The Junior Bookshelf, *Vol. 38, No. 5, October, 1974, p. 270.*

THE ABOMINABLE SWAMP MAN (1975)

Even as a parody of allegorical fantasy this would be insipid, but the sad truth is that Haley is serious. Between the tritely compassionate beginning (heroine Edwardina sets out to save Grundelwich, a faun-like swamp creature whom the sheriff and others decide should be killed) and the tritely visionary ending (Edwardina brings a dormant magical world to life by unlocking the Chamber of Dreams), Haley throws in some borrowed motifs and traditional trappings (a singing key, a talking tree), some fanciful companions (a griffon, St. George the Dragon, blonde Princess Merrily . . .) and some silly, derivative agents of good and evil (a three-headed lion [!] vs. Kremunkin, King of the Dark Domain and his Sniveling Snitches, Creeping Gnauves and prehistoric Deceptadon). The dialogue is muddied with confused pontification ("people create the things they fear" says the Swamp Man of his persecutors) and vague, entirely unsupported hints of large significance. (Says Edwardina in her candyland paradise, "Now I feel that what I missed and the answer to every question I ever asked are right here.") And, Caldecott or no, Haley's illustrations are as crude and banal as her pretentious, amateurish story.

A review of "The Abominable Swamp Man," in Kirkus Reviews, *Vol. XLIII, No. 21, November 1, 1975, p. 1229.*

Haley seems to have set out to write a book which contains every possible fanciful creature and situation. This story has monsters, human-like vegetation, castles, fruit salad trees, a carnival, elves, a living carousel, prehistoric animals, moving statutes, a princess, secret passages, and, of course, your basic three wishes. The title itself is an instant attention getter, and the book maintains a heady pace to the last page. Unfortunately, the pictures, reminiscent of Charles Folkard or Arthur Hughes, are a let down: they come off dull and coarse next to the extremely lively text. Still, this Gothic plum pudding is rich enough to appeal to many early and middle grade readers.

Merrie C. Cohen, in a review of "The Abominable Swamp Man," in School Library Journal, *Vol. 22, No. 5, January, 1976, p. 37.*

THE POST OFFICE CAT (1976)

Inspired by a 19th-century London postmaster's correspondence, this commonplace story of Clarence, a country cat who goes to the city and finds employment as a post office mouse catcher, is so peremptory in its plotting that it seems designed chiefly as travelogue commentary for Haley's stiff, clichéd views of Victorian London and its cats. But the street scenes compare unfavorably with those on low-budget wallpaper or gift wrap, and Clarence belongs with the corniest of nursery decals.

> *A review of "The Post Office Cat," in* Kirkus Reviews, *Vol. XLIV, No. 13, July 1, 1976, p. 726.*

The story is humdrum; the glory of the book is in Haley's splendidly constructed illustrations from quiet country life to the bustling world of public service in the capitol city. The poster-like watercolors are strongly influenced by La Belle Epoque artists, e.g., a Lautrec housemaid doing a Can-Can kick, a rolling Van Gogh sky and many other stylish art nouveau touches.

> *Merrie C. Cohen, in a review of "The Post Office Cat," in* School Library Journal, *Vol. 23, No. 1, September, 1976, p. 100.*

Readers should ignore the tweeness of the dedication and read the historical note before commencing this witty, beautifully illustrated story. The atmosphere of Victorian London is captured superbly in stylish paintings which follow the tale of an itinerant cat's adventures in the raucous city. Eventually, the cat finds security as Official Cat to the Post Office (hence the historical note). The illustrations of the East End with its gaunt-faced inhabitants are particularly effective as are the pictures of moonlit rooftops which expertly use page-size and shape.

The text, too, is full of stimulating verbal imagery which shows none of the trickiness too often employed by writers of animal stories for the five to seven-year-olds. It is most highly recommended both as a book to read aloud and for children to read for themselves. (pp. 8-9)

> *Gabrielle Maunder, in a review of "The Post Office Cat," in* Children's Book Review, *Vol. VI, October, 1976, pp. 8-9.*

The concise text accompanies a sequence of most distinctive drawings, beautifully stylised, true to period, and full of sharp

observation. We already know Gail Haley, who has now adopted this country—and very warmly welcomed too—but here she adds a new dimension to her work.

> *M. Crouch, in a review of "The Post Office Cat," in* The Junior Bookshelf, *Vol. 40, No. 5, October, 1976, p. 263.*

[**The Post Office Cat**] is the story of Clarence, the post office cat. It is set in Victorian England and is based on historical fact and therefore can be used as an information book as well as a good storybook. The pictures are very striking and are ideal on two levels—an individual child looking at the book will be thrilled by the detail and the muted colours, while a group will also find that the pictures are clear and precise even from a distance. The child will also come away with lots of information e.g. that to this day cats employed in the Post Office receive a Maternity Allowance. Altogether this is the complete picture book.

> *Anne Reilly, in a review of "The Post Office Cat," in* Book Window, *Vol. 5, No. 2, Spring, 1978, p. 9.*

GO AWAY, STAY AWAY! (1977)

The story is on the utilitarian side, though children will no doubt enjoy the spirit names ("Kicklebucket") and want to make up some for their own failings. The pictures, however, are splendid—vigorous, multi-textured blockprints, colored in soft hues, with the spirits amusingly painted into the scenes. The title page double-spread of black silhouettes in the style of Swiss paper-cuttings, with a backwash of moss-green and highlights in tan and rose, acts as a lively cast of characters and preview for the handsome contents.

> *Ruth M. McConnell, in a review of "Go Away, Stay Away!" in* School Library Journal, *Vol. 24, No. 3, November, 1977, p. 47.*

Gail Haley follows her Kate Greenaway Medal book with another distinguished by fine craftsmanship and a sharp sense of humour. Here is an artist who does nothing the easy way. Her strong stylised woodcuts illustrate a story with a universal theme, the need for a scapegoat. . . . Miss Haley has de-

From Jack and the Bean Tree, *written and illustrated by Gail E. Haley.*

vised a simple and effective means of distinguishing between her real villagers and the unreal goblins, and the whole book is a triumph of good sense, good taste and superb artistry.

M. Crouch, in a review of "Go Away, Stay Away!" in The Junior Bookshelf, *Vol. 42, No. 1, February, 1978, p. 16.*

During the course of an early spring day in a European mountain village, mother upsets her spinning wheel, young Peter discovers a plate full of sugar lumps missing, the cow kids over Maria's milking pale, and Ivan discovers that while he's been napping the cheese he'd been carrying home has broken. Father, who is wise and patient, explains that these accidents are the result of winter goblins who are angry at the coming of spring. Accordingly, the family joins with the rest of the village in the ritual exorcism of these demons. We have in this book a presentation of what author Gail Haley calls a "spring cleaning of the soul." Not willing to blame themselves for their mistakes, people have created demons who are to shoulder the blame. This, she explains, is the origin of many spring rituals around the world. As we might expect from a Gail Haley book, the drawings are excellent. Not only do they realistically reflect the Alps environment, but also they present the humor and comedy of the characters. Color is never too vivid, thus the delicacy of mountain spring is conveyed, as is the imaginary quality of the supernatural beings these people have created.

Jon C. Stott, in a review of "Go Away, Stay Away!" in The World of Children's Books, *Vol. III, No. 1, Spring, 1978, p. 30.*

COSTUMES FOR PLAYS AND PLAYING   (1977)

A vivacious dust-jacket showing romping children in fancy dress indicates the verve and variety of the contents and the text quickly demonstrates the author's expertise in assembling useful details of period costume and devising designs to help the young to make their own patterns. The emphasis throughout the book is on improvisation from materials "found in the home or school". A friendly book, with exhilarating illustrations.

Margery Fisher, in a review of "Costumes for Plays and Playing," in Growing Point, *Vol. 16, No. 6, December, 1977, p. 3229.*

Though presented within a somewhat pretentious framework of the mystique of mime, the suggestions put forward here for making a most astonishing variety of costumes are excellently comprehensive. They are arranged, practically, under basic shapes and functions: button-up clothes, hats, shoes, cloaks, collars, button-on ears and so on. Useful skills are described simply, with beautifully clear diagrams and illustrations, showing methods for reducing adult-size clothes, with thoughtful allowance for possible poor needlework by decorative cover-ups or the alternative use of safety pins or sellotape. An astonishing number of ways is found of deriving costumes from paper or papier-mâché. A section on make-up is well adapted for young readers into popular rather than technical terms; others deal with home-made jewellery, dyeing and the type of shop which will stock materials named. The purpose of the costumes hovers between a super dressing-up box, "fancy dress" and (the area in which the book should prove most useful) amateur theatricals. A good point of the presentation is the emphasis on using the suggestions,

full as they are, merely as points of departure from the reader's own invention in costume and design.

M. Hobbs, in a review of "Costumes for Plays and Playing," in The Junior Bookshelf, *Vol. 41, No. 6, December, 1977, p. 365.*

THE GREEN MAN   (1980)

Haley's appended note refers to several legends (Robin Hood, Arthur's knights, a 12th-century story of Danish Prince Amleth), but sheds no light on their connection or their darker origins; nor does it relate to the story she tells of a prince who serves his term as the Green Man after a forest swim when his clothes and horse are snitched. Claude, who till now has been "arrogant, vain, and selfish" and has mocked the common folks' belief in the Green Man, is transformed by his stay in the forest, where he gathers wild food and cares for the animals. Then one day Claude comes upon another fine young man splashing in the water and takes *his* clothes and horse to return home, kind and generous. Why didn't he go home sooner? At first, he was ashamed to return without his clothes; then, later, he felt "needed in the forest." But why do the animals need a human caretaker? And why do children need such arbitrary, pious "legends"? And it's all lifelessly related—though at times Haley's stagy imitations of medieval tapestry project a verdant, emblematic vitality that the story badly needs. (pp. 906-07)

A review of "The Green Man," in Kirkus Reviews, *Vol. XLVIII, No. 14, July 15, 1980, pp. 906-07.*

The tale has all the symmetry of a medieval morality play, particularly in the closely drawn parallel between the action and the cycle of the seasons: fall (from grace) turns to winter (banishment) turns to spring (return and rebirth). But the effect is curiously static, a sensation that is reinforced by the illustrations, which rely on stylized emblematic details, flattened perspectives, fabric-like textures, and (too) carefully posed figures. Even more unfortunate, the faces have a distinctly contemporary appearance—a big-eyed Keene quality—that reduces the carefully created settings to the level of mere staging. Overall, from the opening disclaimer ("The story you are about to read may have happened just this way—or perhaps it came about in some other place entirely . . .") to the denouement, the story is overburdened with "significance." (pp. 59-60)

Kristi L. Thomas, in a review of "The Green Man," in School Library Journal, *Vol. 27, No. 1, September, 1980, pp. 59-60.*

Gail Haley's illustrations, which resemble mediaeval tapestries, depict the various stages of the hero's adventures. Facial expressions depict the transformation of the arrogant young man into a humble and helpful believer. The stylized designs enhance the folk-like qualities of the story. Another outstanding book from a major author-illustrator.

Jon C. Stott, in a review of "The Green Man," in The World of Children's Books, *Vol. VI, 1981, p. 25.*

BIRDSONG   (1984)

Birdsong tells a traditional story of good and evil. The "good" is Birdsong, a delicate waif with a gift for creating music of such beauty that birds flock to add their voices to it. The "evil" is Jorinella, a bird-catcher determined to exploit the musical gift of Birdsong.

In a sense, the story is also an exploration of free choice. The decision to follow good or evil is Birdsong's alone. She is helped in her decision by the device of magical feathers which enable her to see she is at a crossroads: she can exploit her gift and follow the road of "evil," like Jorinella, or she can respect it and follow the path of "good." Of course, in the tradition of folktales, Birdsong shows strength and integrity and reestablishes our belief in the supremacy of "good."

The real strength of this tale lies in the illustrations. They are magnificent! Every page is filled with images of birds. For example, the hair and clothing of Birdsong and Jorinella resemble exotic plummage and everything flows and moves, creating an impression of birds in flight.

> *Margot Filipenko, in a review of "Birdsong," in* Language Arts, *Vol. 61, No. 7, November, 1984, p. 744.*

The distinguished author and illustrator of *A Story, A Story* has come up with another winner. . . . . Haley's use of birds as the vehicle to move her tale also provides for the opulence of their plumage whether on the birds themselves or as decorations on Jorinella's magic cloak or Birdsong's dress and hair. Each stained glass window-like illustration fills two-thirds of the page, and the figures are so full of movement that their dark outlines burst through the heavy dark borders of each painting. The settings in which the characters move are artfully and lushly crowded with color and detail, whether they are the interior of Jorinella's cottage, the medieval marketplace or the Garden of Eden-like forest. Haley's beautiful use of a clean watercolor palette is enhanced by the pen and black or white inked details in each illustration. The result is an opulent visual experience for story hour or individual enjoyment.

> *Patricia Homer, in a review of "Birdsong," in* School Library Journal, *Vol. 31, No. 4, December, 1984, p. 71.*

A distinguished and prolific author and illustrator, Gail E. Haley has taken the theme of a fairy tale by the Brothers Grimm, in which a witch lures and cages birds, beasts and innocent maidens into an enchanted forest, and adapted the story for her new book, *Birdsong.* In it she brilliantly transforms the skeletal idea into a dramatic tale of love and its triumph over greed and wickedness. She embroiders rich imagery into both her prose and poetry. . . . . The illustrations, which work beautifully with the text, are just as rich as the story. The brushwork and pen strokes are a blend of delicate detail and bold washes. The colors are bright and the textures intricately overlap, weaving across the pages. There is drama and energy in the movements and gestures of the figures, and the expressive faces can even startle and disturb. Miss Haley has perfected the use of the semi-bordered picture separated by text. The format works. The pictures are a visual feast, though I especially loved reading *Birdsong* aloud.

> *Beverly Brodsky, in a review of "Birdsong," in* The New York Times Book Review, *January 6, 1985, p. 24.*

JACK AND THE BEAN TREE   (1986)

Joseph Jacobs' "Jack and the Beanstalk" is retold and illustrated with a southern Appalachian setting. . . .

Haley's variation on the familiar text is in the best storytelling tradition. Framed within a story about mountain neighbors gathering to hear a master teller, the central tale is artfully embellished with incident, characterization, and regional cadence that add humor and local color while respecting the boundaries of the original. It begs to be shared aloud. And the author's bold illustrations, painted on wood in brilliant tones, are also suitable to share with a group—although closer examination reveals careful attention to a wealth of detail, from the voluptuous vegetation that dances and twines across the pages to the chaotic, over-abundant feast magically produced for the giant. The faces, whether Mother's, monstrous giant's (the kids will love this one), dark giant's wife's in cornrows or towhead Jack's, are variants on one face, Haley's own—a suggestion that we are all one, whether good or bad, real or fantastic.

A fine tribute to Appalachia's heritage of story; a treasure to share.

> *A review of "Jack and the Bean Tree," in* Kirkus Reviews, *Vol. LIV, No. 12, June 15, 1986, p. 930.*

An Appalachian version closer to the English than to the Richard Chase tale with which some storytellers will be familiar, this is framed within a family gathering in which an old woman, Poppyseed, explains how she magically came by her stories. In this one, Jack trades the cow (absent in Chase), climbs the stalk, and finds himself in a Greco-Romantic setting with a giant named Ephicophilus. He steals tablecloth, hen, and harp (rifle, knife, and coverlet in Chase) and escapes with the giant crashed to a grease spot and Matilda, the giant's wife who took such a liking to Jack, left up in Skyland. (In most versions, the giant's wife is assumed to suffer the fate of all suckers—in Chase, to be "smashed up when the house landed.") It's too bad there are no notes to the story. The art consists of heavily textured, page-and-a-half-spread paintings with text in the other half page. The deep colors work best in green landscape scenes; they get a bit jarring in the giants' palace. This is a fairly elaborate version, and the long text and heavy palette best suit it to children already familiar with the tale. (pp. 208-09)

> *Zena Sutherland, in a review of "Jack and the Bean Tree," in* Bulletin of the Center for Children's Books, *Vol. 39, No. 11, July-August, 1986, pp. 208-09.*

While not entirely successful, Haley's *Jack and the Bean Tree* is more than a good try. Her lively retelling has illustrations to match—energetic paintings with movement and humor. This retelling of *Jack and the Beanstalk* has a Southern Appalachian air. Haley uses the device of Poppyseed, a storyteller, to frame the opening and closing of her tale. Poppyseed goes on for two pages about how she became a "story-tellin' woman" before she finally gets on with it, and the delay does not add to the story, but the tale itself moves along rapidly. There are some variations on the traditional motifs. A disconcerting note is Matilda, the giant's wife, telling Jack that her husband is accusing the other giants of theft. The inclusion of a community of giants in Haley's "sky-land" is extraneous and jarring. . . . . The attempt at regional dialect sometimes falls into the precious, as does the device of Poppyseed. There is one double-page, vertical spread of the giant climbing down the bean tree—there is no text on these pages, and they interrupt the narrative at a climactic moment—but it is such an exciting visual it is easily justified. Haley's paintings have enormous power, almost surging off the pages, and lush greens and connecting foliage provide continuity throughout.

Janice M. Del Negro, in a review of "Jack and the Bean Tree," in School Library Journal, *Vol. 33, No. 1, September, 1986, p. 122.*

JACK AND THE FIRE DRAGON (1988)

In a companion to **Jack and the Bean Tree,** the Caldecott-winning illustrator retells another English/Appalachian folktale with her usual wit and verve.

Jack and his two brothers, just back from the army, are building themselves a new cabin on the mountain when the Fire Dragaman comes and steals their dinner; it's Jack, the youngest, who outwits him, follows him down a hole to his home, rescues three maidens, defeats the Dragaman (now a dragon) and finds his way happily back—in spite of his brothers, who have tried to trap him in the hole. Both the back-country scenes and the flamboyant dragon are depicted in vigorous, bold linoleum cuts and harmonious, vivid color. Good for storytelling or reading aloud; fine for kids who want illustrations of scary monsters: these have the additional value of having merit as art.

A review of "Jack and the Fire Dragon," in Kirkus Reviews, *Vol. LVI, No. 10, May 15, 1988, p. 761.*

Linocut pictures drenched in watercolor reveal the mythic adventures of Jack, of beanstalk fame, who must fight the Fire Dragaman, and wins the love of Jenny, the Dragon King's daughter. Related in a dialect of the Appalachian mountains, this story is garnished with folksy descriptions and the prankish good humor that characterizes oral storytelling. A note on the back of the jacket explains many of the references for modern readers; the heroic elements meld with hearty illustrations, making this an unusual offering for folklore fans.

A review of "Jack and the Fire Dragon," in Publishers Weekly, *Vol. 233, No. 23, June 10, 1988, p. 79.*

Haley's spirited and dramatic retelling of this Appalachian folktale reads as if it has been polished from many oral tellings. (A similar version appears in Richard Chase's *Jack Tales* [Houghton, 1943] as "Old Fire Dragaman.") . . . Colloquial, expressive language ("If ye kill me, I'll come back to haint ye, Jack") is reinforced by dazzling full-color linocut illustrations. Text and art are handsomely composed on double-page spreads that carry the dramatic tension as well as the humor of the story. Deep, inky blacks, and fiery yellows and oranges vibrate on the page; the bold pictures project well. Children will love the scary metamorphosis of giant to dragon and the mysterious trappings of the underground house. A tale sure to attract a following among both tellers and enthralled listeners.

Susan H. Patron, in a review of "Jack and the Fire Dragon," in School Library Journal, *Vol. 35, No. 1, September, 1988, p. 177.*

Joyce Hansen

1942-

Black American author of fiction.

Commended for writing uplifting books with strong-willed, convincing characters, Hansen creates works with both contemporary and historical settings which propose messages of hope and social and personal responsibility to her readers. Her first three books, realistic fiction for middle graders, draw on her experiences as a child in New York City and a teacher of students with learning problems to depict life in the Bronx, where her young protagonists battle against great odds and succeed through their own perseverance, the love of their families, and the loyal assistance of their friends. In *The Gift-Giver* (1980) and its sequel *Yellow Bird and Me* (1986), fifth grader Doris learns compassion and resiliency from resourceful Amir and later assists a classmate who is struggling with an undiagnosed learning disability. *Home Boy* (1982) follows Marcus, a high school student from the Caribbean, whose feelings of alienation prompt his degeneration into drug dealing and violence until he resolves to reform through the influence of his parents and his supportive girlfriend. Investing these works with what observers consider a fluent use of black English, Hansen explores such themes as accountability for one's life, loyalty, and the necessity for love and understanding, especially under difficult circumstances. Her next two books, *Which Way Freedom?* (1986) and its sequel *Out from This Place* (1988), reflect a major variation in Hansen's subject matter but not in her message; in these historical novels for young adults about Civil War America, she again portrays the redemptive virtues of true friendship and the need for adaptability. Offering her audience an awareness of the contributions of black Americans to the Civil War, Hansen describes how teenaged Obi, an escaped slave, and his companion Easter labor to obtain their freedom. Through Obi's service to his country as a soldier and Easter's determination to learn to read in order to teach the children in her community, Hansen points out the significance of altruism as well as the victory of her characters over adversity. *Which Way Freedom?* was given the Coretta Scott King Award honorable mention for literature in 1987.

(See also *Something about the Author,* Vols. 39, 46 and *Contemporary Authors,* Vol. 105.)

AUTHOR'S COMMENTARY

I teach reading in a special education school for adolescents who have learning problems. The student body in this New York City school is almost entirely Black and Hispanic. Reading is a painful and difficult task for many of these youngsters; however, I've seen comprehension and interest rise dramatically when they're given literature with characters, themes and settings that they can identify with. (p. 9)

Brian, for example, was a "non-reader." He was eighteen years old and tested at a fourth grade reading level. One day he picked up a copy of *The Days When the Animals Talked,* which is about the original Brer Rabbit folk tales. This is not easy reading. Half the book gives the historical background of the tales; the other half consists of the stories themselves, written in dialect. (Often even students who read fluently have problems understanding dialect.)

Brian chose this difficult book without any prompting from me. As a matter of fact, I thought that he was doing an exercise out of a workbook until I heard him laughing quietly to himself. When I realized he could read the folk tales, I took the workbook away.

"You just graduated," I told him. For the rest of the term that became his reading book. Brian also read **Home Boy,** a young adult novel that I wrote about a teenager from the Caribbean who moves to New York City. Because his experiences were similar, he identified with the main character.

Brian had to struggle through these books, but he *wanted* to read them. I noticed that he, as well as many of my other students, preferred to tackle a novel than read a hi-lo book (a high interest-low reading level book). Though the hi-lo's are easier to read, the stories don't hold students' interest. Brian reminded me of something that teachers sometimes forget— the aim of the lesson is not answering the ten comprehension questions correctly in the workbook, but to enjoy a real book. (pp. 9-10)

Literature can be a great teacher, yet large numbers of Black and other youngsters of color never have a chance to explore themselves or their lives through the literary process. Those who attempt to meet this need can not yet get enough material. (p. 10)

We need more black literature for children—and what's already in print should be far more accessible than it presently is. All of our young people are miseducated when the literature they're exposed to represents only a segment of the society. White children should learn that they're not the whole scene, but one of the parts that form the complete picture. A great deal of Black popular culture—music, dance, dress styles, even speech patterns—is co-opted by white youth. Why would a good story with Black characters, told from a Black perspective, be incomprehensible to anyone but Blacks and therefore limited in audience?

All children need sound, solid literature that relates to their own experiences and interests; this holds particularly true for children who, for whatever reason, have learning difficulties. Maybe the inclusion of different voices would add the sparkle that would keep our kids reading. (p. 11)

> *Joyce Hansen, "Needed: Quality Literature for Reluctant Readers," in* Interracial Books for Children Bulletin, *Vol. 15, No. 4, 1984, pp. 9-11.*

THE GIFT-GIVER (1980)

Fifth-grader Doris tells the story of Amir, the new boy who has just joined her class. Amir is slight, quiet, and mature; he doesn't join the boys' games, yet—Doris can't understand why—he is accepted; he doesn't feel a need to conform, yet he belongs. This is in Black English, sometimes with discrepant usages, and believably an account by a ten-year-old. It conveys effectively the atmosphere (the Bronx) and has strong characters, particularly Amir, who helps a lonely old woman, helps Doris when she has to take on new responsibilities at home, and is more understanding than any of the other children when one of their classmates runs away from a foster home. This hasn't a strong story line, but it has well-developed plot threads that are nicely knit, a memorable depiction of a person whose understanding and compassion are gifts to his friends, and a poignantly realistic ending: Amir, whose own experience of foster homes has given him his compassionate understanding, is sent to another place yet again, leaving Doris and his other friends sadly aware of the loss they have suffered. A substantial first novel.

> *Zena Sutherland, in a review of "The Gift-Giver," in* Bulletin of the Center for Children's Books, *Vol. 34, No. 5, January, 1981, p. 94.*

In her first book, the author not only tells a good story but also paints an effective, inside picture of childhood in a New York ghetto. . . . Hansen does not stint on action or dialogue, revealed through easy, natural dialect. Although moments of interest are sometimes passed by or treated too briskly, the total picture is drawn with depth and cohesiveness.

> *Judith Goldberger, in a review of "The Gift-Giver," in* Booklist, *Vol. 77, No. 9, January 1, 1981, p. 624.*

The theme of responsibility dominates the book, but Doris' growth arises naturally from the plot. Amir's wisdom seems excessive in a fifth grader but he explains it as a matter of survival as a foster child. The story is low key and slow moving

in spite of the occasional violence of its inner city setting. But it is effective, and valuable for its portrait of a loving family in that setting. Doris is like the character in Nikki Giovanni's poem, "nikki-rosa," who wrote that "Black love is Black wealth." (p. 145)

> *Carolyn Caywood, in a review of "The Gift-Giver," in* School Library Journal, *Vol. 27, No. 7, March, 1981, pp. 144-45.*

HOME BOY (1982)

The downward path to wisdom, as pursued by Marcus—who's called "Jamaica" at his Bronx high school though he's really just come from St. Cruz. Taunted and challenged by the other boys at school, Marcus beats two in a fight and then becomes friends with one of them, the red-eyed Ron. But drunken, surly Eddie won't let it be, and Marcus, always impulsive and short-tempered, ends up knifing him in the stomach. The book alternates between that incident, followed by Marcus' frantic flight by subway around the city, and flashbacks showing his troubles at school and with his father, his overworked parents' breakup, his level-headed girlfriend's attempts to steer him straight, his lucrative job selling dope with Ron until the boss dealer gets shot up, and his return to school determined to reform on the very morning of the knifing. When the memories trail back to St. Cruz toward the end, the one-on-one switch between past and present gets in the way and the story bogs down, despite the island ambience and glimpse of Rastifarian culture. But the end, at the police station with both parents, is a fitting one of reconciliation and good resolutions. And the depiction of the city's pressures on a "home boy" has readers empathizing with Marcus at his rashest and wrongest moments. (pp. 1195-96)

> *A review of "Home Boy," in* Kirkus Reviews, *Vol. L, No. 21, November 1, 1982, pp. 1195-96.*

Hansen does a good job of portraying the alienation and despair of the newcomer who is adjusting to a radical change in life style, environment, and parental conflict; her writing style is capable and her insight impressive. What weakens the book is that Marcus, struggling with guilt (he has been a pusher, knifed another boy, and run away) and with anger at his father, goes back and forth in his memory, back from the present to both his first days in New York and to events in his life on the island, so that there is little flow to the story, which is choppy and at times confusing.

> *Zena Sutherland, in a review of "Home Boy," in* Bulletin of the Center for Children's Books, *Vol. 36, No. 5, January, 1983, p. 89.*

In a series of neatly juxtaposed chapters of flight and island flashback, Hansen reveals a character who is at once vulnerable and exasperating, often caring, yet capable of deceit and violence. Marcus, the **Home Boy,** is as unpredictable and, ultimately, as tragic as the ruined South Bronx that is his home.

Hansen's second novel (as did **The Gift Giver,** her first), revolves around Blacks and inner city life, but touches on catholic truths and themes; quests for dignity, pursuits of familial and personal love, and the search for individual understanding. It is, frankly, a memorable story, craftily drawn from simple incident; a very readable, very credible tale.

> *Kevin Kenny, in a review of "Home Boy," in* Voice

of Youth Advocates, *Vol. 5, No. 6, February, 1983, p. 36.*

YELLOW BIRD AND ME (1986)

In a sequel to *The Gift-Giver,* its gentle hero, Amir, is still missed by his friend Doris, the narrator, who is black and bright. Doris is in sixth grade, and so is Yellow Bird, who clowns in class and irritates Doris by asking for her help with his lesson preparation. Two plot threads are capably meshed; one is the mounting of a play in which Bird is given the lead thanks to an astute visiting playwright/director, and the other is the fact that Doris realizes that Bird is intelligent but has a learning disability. The author, a teacher, paints a hard picture of her fictional counterpart, who refuses for too long to recognize the fact that Bird is handicapped, even when Doris points it out. However, her characterization is certainly believable, and the children are depicted with insight and their personalities and changing relationship developed logically and positively. (pp. 148-49)

> *Zena Sutherland, in a review of "Yellow Bird and Me," in* Bulletin of the Center for Children's Books, *Vol. 39, No. 8, April, 1986, pp. 148-49.*

In a sequel to *The Gift Giver,* Doris helps the class trouble-maker find a better outlet for his talents, and discovers the rich rewards of friendship. . . .

How she helps Bird redeem himself in the eyes of his teacher, with the help of a special improvisational theater program, and how she reaffirms her closeness to Amir despite their physical distance make a lively and heartwarming story.

Smoothly written and easy to read; the language, with touches of colloquial black English, has strength and vitality. Rich with the distinctive personalities in Doris' world, the story is particularly valuable for its emphasis on friendship, generosity of spirit, and seeing what's below the surface.

> *A review of "Yellow Bird and Me," in* Kirkus Reviews, *Vol. LIV, No. 7, April 1, 1986, p. 545.*

Joyce Hansen creates a vivid portrait of the neighborhood and a sensitive study of its people. She deals realistically with Doris's growing maturity and self-esteem and with the evolving friendship between Doris and Yellow Bird. The theme of a boy and girl being best friends without the element of romance that was central to the first book is not as strong in the sequel. Instead, the reader has a sense of that issue having been settled and of moving beyond it to new ground. As Doris gains maturity, she is better able to act on Amir's urging that she look "inside of Bird to see who he really is" and is instrumental in having Yellow Bird's dyslexia recognized. The setting and colloquial speech used in the dialogue add depth to the story as do the minor characters, briefly but clearly sketched. Joyce Hansen has written a warm, satisfying book with an underlying positiveness that will not be lost on the reader.

> *Elizabeth S. Watson, in a review of "Yellow Bird and Me," in* The Horn Book Magazine, *Vol. LXII, No. 6, November-December, 1986, p. 745.*

WHICH WAY FREEDOM? (1986)

This new volume in Walker's American History Series for Young People focuses on the Civil War and the years from 1861 to 1864. The protagonist is Obi, an escaped slave who joins a black Union regiment just before fighting begins at Ft. Pillow, Tenn. Most of the story is flashbacks to the tobacco farm in South Carolina, from which Obi flees, and his search for his mother. Unfortunately, the most riveting page in this fiction is the foreword.

It seems the author sincerely wants to share this important slice of history, but what could be a powerful telling, just doesn't come through. Characters are stiff with bulky adjectives, their dialogue so flat that it's like watching actors read their lines for the first time on an empty stage. The Ft. Pillow massacre must have been horrible, but to find there "was so much noise, smoke and confusion," is a loose description. Youngsters need *specific* details to visualize such tragedy. Also, there must be less monotonous ways to draw blacks besides saying Obi has a "smooth, black face," Thomas has a "rich, brown face," or the sergeant "scanned the black and brown faces of his men."

Some of the difficulty here may be the dialect, which seems authentic, but, at times, makes the reader stumble. "She eyes sit deep inside her face like yours," is how old Buka describes Obi's mother to him. . . . "She cry fierce when the man take you from her to put you on the boat." Now *there* is the emotion that could have made this into a real story.

> *Kristiana Gregory, in a review of "Which Way Freedom?" in* Los Angeles Times Book Review, *July 13, 1986, p. 6.*

Hansen has made Obi real, emphasizing his tenacity and courage by showing it rather than declaring him a cardboard hero. He is himself, but he also exemplifies the commitment of all those who fought to be free, just as he illustrates the contribution made by many black soldiers in the Civil War. (pp. 209-10)

> *A review of "Which Way Freedom?" in* Bulletin of the Center for Children's Books, *Vol. 39, No. 11, July-August, 1986, pp. 209-10.*

In spite of its deceptively short length, **Which Way Freedom?** covers a good deal of ground. The historical detail never overwhelms but seems to grow naturally from the story. There is sufficient action to sustain readers' interest, but it is in the book's characterization that the chief strength lies. Obi is a sympathetic but fallible young man, often at odds with others and himself over the importance of freedom and loyalty. Obi's relationships with those close to him are subtly depicted; indeed at times in an almost too understated fashion. A sensitive, thought-provoking historical novel.

> *Ruth Reutter, in a review of "Which Way Freedom?" in* School Library Journal, *Vol. 32, No. 10, August, 1986, p. 100.*

What a stirring adventure! . . .

Hansen's skill with black dialect and gift for storytelling as displayed in **The Gift Giver** and **Home Boy** provide new insight as these fictional characters unfold documented circumstances and events, recount unfamiliar details of everyday activities, portray life in the First South Carolina Volunteers as one of the original black regiments of the Union Army, depict a slave's struggle to gain and understand his own freedom during this brutal and confusing time, and relate this saga of America's history from an Afro-American perspective.

This thin novel with a suspenseful jacket and highly visible print will attract less able readers while the Gullah dialect will offer a fascinating challenge to bright readers and older teens who often need black history book reports. Significantly, the quotes from various sources involved in the Civil War which introduce each chapter offer additional information and understanding for application in Social Studies classrooms.

Virginia B. Moore, in a review of "Which Way Freedom?" in Voice of Youth Advocates, *Vol. 10, No. 1, April, 1987, p. 30.*

OUT FROM THIS PLACE (1988)

This sequel to **Which Way Freedom** follows Obi's companion in escape, Easter. She joins a group of slaves (including her beloved Jason) who are running away from their former master. They escape to the islands off the coast of South Carolina, where they work on a plantation for pay and, reportedly, will have the opportunity to buy their land. Easter learns to read, then must make a decision: wait for Obi to come for her and continue to make inquiries about him or go to a real school in Philadelphia. Hansen has written another wonderful tale, showing the unfairness of the situations in which freed slaves often found themselves. The use of black dialect may slow down some readers at first, but it adds tremendously to the novel, making Easter spring to life. Although a familiarity with the first book isn't required, it does give readers a better background for the incidents to which Easter refers. Fans of the first book will enjoy it, and will be excited about the epilogue, which seems to suggest a third book will be coming.

Elizabeth M. Reardon, in a review of "Out from This Place," in School Library Journal, *Vol. 35, No. 4, December, 1988, p. 121.*

As in Hansen's earlier story, history is the main point. Easter's experiences in the sea island community shed light on a little-known aspect of the Civil War. Her hunger for education and her determination to keep control of her life carry a strong message for modern readers. Characters here are more carefully developed than in the previous book, and themes emerge in a credible manner. Interesting and instructive, this novel will support history curriculums and please readers as well. (p. 872)

Denise M. Wilms, in a review of "Out from This Place," in Booklist, *Vol. 85, No. 10, January 15, 1989, pp. 871-72.*

Hansen has again created an impressive historical novel depicting the injustice of broken promises to the newly-freed slaves, whose hard work and tenacity are apparent on every page. Readers will gain insights into Civil War and post-war life for Blacks through this moving narrative of real-life situations. At the same time, it's captivating to watch Easter's growth and maturation as she changes from a young girl concerned only with herself to a young woman who can give help and support to others. **Out from This Place** ends with a flash to Obi, who is still looking for Easter, leading us to expect, or at least suspect, another sequel. If handled with the skill of these first two books, it will be a very welcome addition.

Marijo Grimes, in a review of "Out from This Place," in Voice of Youth Advocates, *Vol. 11, No. 6, February, 1989, p. 285.*

Brian Jacques

1939-

English author of fiction.

The creator of *Redwall* (1987) and its prequel *Mossflower* (1988), two volumes of a projected trilogy of epic fantasies for middle and upper graders which describe how peace-loving woodland animals defeat the evil creatures that attempt to destroy their community, Jacques is praised as a writer of rich, inventive, and exciting books which reflect his mastery of narrative and characterization. Often compared to such works as *The Wind in the Willows, The Lord of the Rings,* and *Watership Down,* the novels are lengthy, intricately structured works which combine humor, warmth, and romance with descriptions of violent battles, mutilations, and death as they explore the struggle between good and evil. Both *Redwall* and *Mossflower* have quests at their centers. In *Redwall,* Jacques describes how a monastic order of mice preserve Redwall Abbey from the vicious rat Cluny the Scourge with the help of the peaceful animals who have taken refuge within its walls. However, until the mice find the sword belonging to Martin, the legendary champion who founded and defended the abbey, victory cannot take place. When the novice mouse Matthias embarks on a search for the sword, he discovers that he is the true descendant of the great hero. *Mossflower* focuses on how Martin becomes the leader of a band of animals resisting their crazed wildcat queen, Tsarmina. In order to overthrow her, Martin embarks on a journey to enlist the help of a badger, the powerful Lord Boar. When Tsarmina is displaced, Martin and the rest of the triumphant animals plan to destroy her fortress and build Redwall Abbey in its place. An adult playwright and scriptwriter who is also a professional comic and broadcaster on radio and television, Jacques has noted that a successful book for children includes both a good story and a strong moral sense, elements which observers often recognize in his own works. *Redwall* has received both parent and child-selected awards.

(See also *Contemporary Authors,* Vol. 127.)

REDWALL (1987)

[*Redwall* is] a long, densely detailed account of a siege in which animals play the roles which, in a different kind of book, might have been taken by Cavaliers and Roundheads. The romantic aura of the story means that though events take place in a country setting realistically described and though most of the actions of the animals are more or less possible in nature, the division into good and bad (mice as heroes, helped by otter, hedgehog, vole, badger and squirrel, with stoats, weasel and ferret as the enemy and fox, sparrow and adder playing one side against the other) is reminiscent of the fabular characters imposed by storytelling Man on the animals of his environment. This impression is fostered also by the idiom allotted to the characters—ethnic phrases for the sparrow, comic slang in public school vein for the Jack hare and military briskness for the badger. *Redwall* itself is an ecclesiastical foundation and the hero of the tale, excitable Matthias Mouse, is a novice in a community ruled by wise Abbot Mortimer, who though he reveres the legends of Mar-

tin, the champion who in earlier days had defended the Abbey from 'foxes, vermin and a great wild cat', still bases his rule on peaceful co-existence with the neighbours. Much of the point of the story, an obvious topical point, lies in the difficulty of distinguishing between defence and offence. When Cluny the Scourge, a rat reputed to be Portuguese, and his five hundred scabby, ferocious followers, cast covetous eye on the well-provisioned Abbey, many local animals hurry to defend the place, bringing differing strategies and talents to a conflict which almost at once produces its hero. For Matthias is found by various signs and remembrances to be the true descendant of the valiant Martin and his discovery of his true self, his dedicated efforts to keep the Abbey vow and still preserve it from harm, runs through the tale as a theme to link the well-devised episodes. The comedy of incongruity and the humour of assorted personalities (Warbeak the sparrow foremost among them) mesh together, with a background of dark forest and Gothic cloisters which is so cunningly described that the animal actors never seem out of place in what is essentially a chivalric adventure. The book will almost inevitably be compared with *Watership Down* but with all the similarities of idiom, alert sophisticated narrative and neat humanisation, *Redwall* has an intriguing and unusual flavour of its own and no young reader capable of sustained effort (for this is a long, substantial and maturely written book) should miss the memorable reading experience it offers. (pp. 4756-57)

Margery Fisher, in a review of "Redwall," in Growing Point, Vol. 25, No. 6, March, 1987, pp. 4756-57.

What on the surface appears to be just another medieval fantasy peopled with animals enacting the fight to the death between good and evil is actually a rich and thought-provoking novel on the nature of good and evil. The peaceful life of the mice of Redwall Abbey is shattered by the onslaught of the fierce rat, Cluny the Scourge, and his army of rats, weasels, and other vermin. The mice and the other peaceful animals take refuge in the Abbey's strong walls while Cluny lays seige. Advantage is with the besieged (as long as food and supplies last), and the Abbey defenders are able to withstand numerous attacks. Cluny cannot be completely defeated, however, until the sword of Martin, the legendary warrior who founded Redwall Abbey, can be found. A young novice, Matthias, embarks on a quest and ultimately finds it, but a wise cat reminds him that it is just a sword. . . . Just as Martin's sword is neither good nor evil, the characters avoid being simply personifications of attributes. The defenders, even Matthias, have faults, while even Cluny displays characteristics which make him not likable, but at least deserving of a grudging admiration. The book is violent, and at some times downright gruesome, but the quality of the writing, the rich cast of characters, the detailed accounts of medieval warfare, and Jacques' ability to tell a good story *and* make readers think all earn **Redwall** a place on library shelves.

Susan M. Harding, in a review of "Redwall," in School Library Journal, Vol. 33, No. 11, August, 1987, p. 96.

The decline in the American taste for blockbuster fantasies, no matter how good, seems to have discouraged American authors. Such lengthy but acclaimed works as *Watership Down* or *Hounds of the Morrigan* are by British authors; American authors tend to break up long works into volumes—Le Guin's Earthsea trilogy, for example. We have in **Redwall** another long, beautifully written, exciting British fantasy. . . . The scenes of combat are quite fascinating, with the strategy and counter strategy cleverly and clearly worked out. The book offers an immense cast of distinctive characters, including the redoubtable Constance the badger, extremely strong and utterly fearless; Basil Stag Hare, a satirical replica of the regimental British officer; the sparrows, notably Warbeak, who speak a gutter language reminiscent of that of the seagulls in *Watership Down;* and Abbot Mortimer, the epitome of goodness and gentleness. The flaw in the book, if there is one, is that the lines drawn between good and evil are never ambiguous, not allowing for that shiver of doubt and wonder about the outcome. But the book is splendid, with a delightful hero and a smooth, charming style.

Ann A. Flowers, in a review of "Redwall," in The Horn Book Magazine, Vol. LXIV, No. 1, January-February, 1988, p. 71.

It is no mean feat to produce an animal fantasy that bears comparison with *Watership Down,* but **Redwall** has proved impossible to put down and wonderful to read aloud. It's a fast-moving saga of siege and struggle. . . . The story is packed with dramatic incident, the climax satisfying—victory snatched in the nick of time from the very jaws of defeat—the narrative style forceful and flowing. Dialogue is superb, each character finding a distinctive voice. Brian Jacques

has a tremendous sense of fun, but does not spare his readers the inevitable tragedies of violent conflict. His creatures are true first and foremost to their animal natures, whatever symbolic and human attributes they may also have. A rich and memorable book, extraordinary as a first novel, which will appeal to a very wide age range—9 to 90, at a guess.

Jane Inglis, in a review of "Redwall," in Books for Your Children, Vol. 23, No. 1, Spring, 1988, p. 31.

MOSSFLOWER (1988)

In a prequel to **Redwall,** the peace-loving woodland animals—mice, rabbits, moles, otters, badgers, squirrels—defeat the evil rats, stoats, and weasels and their wildcat queen, destroying their grim fortress and planning an abbey refuge in its place.

Like its predecessor, this installment is packed with action and imbued with warmth by its well-individualized characters and the homely details of their lives, including a delectable-sounding array of vegetarian fare. Jacques' narrative is more skillful here; switching adroitly from one plot strand to another (sometimes only a sentence here, a paragraph there), he keeps them all spinning swiftly and without confusion, an astonishing feat considering the number of his characters and the complexity of the story. He doesn't always find the *mot juste*—it's hard to imagine a cat "slumped moodily," for example—but readers enthralled by the richly inventive story aren't likely to notice.

Philosophically, Jacques' work remains firmly in that conventional, simplistic world where the enemies are not only totally evil but stupid, while the clever heroes are models of valor and selfless cooperation; where peace may be an honorable goal, but war provides the intense and exciting experiences. For fantasy with more complexity and depth, see Lloyd Alexander's *Westmark* books.

A review of "Mossflower," in Kirkus Reviews, Vol. LVI, No. 21, November 1, 1988, p. 1605.

[With] **Mossflower** Brian Jacques gives us a prequel to last year's **Redwall.** In it he aims at a slightly younger age group: maybe that's why he feels free to expand on an old-fashioned kind of heroism, all action, plot and bravery—though he, too, tempers it with an egalitarian approach. There are female villains, leaders and warriors here, as well as cosily medieval "goodwives" who are a dab hand with rustic cakes and homemade ale.

Mossflower is a kind of junior *Lord of the Rings* crossed with *The Wind in the Willows.* Martin the Warrior (a "sturdy young mouse") arrives in the kingdom of Kotir only to be taken prisoner by the power-crazed female tyrant, the wildcat Tsarmina. A cartoon villainess, she grinds down the humble local folk—hedgehogs, squirrels, badgers and moles—with her army of assorted evil rodents.

Once Martin escapes from prison, with the help of a scamp called Gonff (a thief mouse), he joins forces with the woodland animals who have formed a kind of resistance band under the leadership of old Bella the badger.

All the Tolkien essentials are here: magic swords, long journeys, skirmishes and set-piece battles, wild creatures who speak in distinctive Gollum-style languages, quaint dialect-speaking little animals who burst into song and a hero who humbly accepts the mantle of destined greatness.

It's an immensely long epic read, and Jacques keeps up a brisk pace by jumping back and forth between opposing camps. (His good guys, though, with their friendly enthusiasms and plucky schemes, are more convincing than the monotonous baddies, who screech, posture and snarl, especially at each other, with B-movie predictability.)

For the less-experienced reader who hungers for a clear, winnable contest of good and evil, *Mossflower* may satisfy with its sheer bulk and colorful detail. For those who have read the real thing—Kenneth Grahame and J.R.R. Tolkien—the derivative echoes on every page will seem as pesky as flies buzzing around the jam.

> Michele Landsberg, *"Robin Hood Rides Again," in* Book World—The Washington Post, *November 6, 1988, p. 15.*

In *Mossflower* we have, in the publisher's happy word, a 'prequel' to [*Redwall*]. . . . Whether the mixture has therapeutic value each reader must decide for himself. (p. 304)

Brian Jacques handles the complex strands of his narrative with much skill. I feel that I ought to have enjoyed his story more than I did. There are two main obstacles to that enjoyment. First—length. A book should be as long as it needs to be. Mr. Jacques' trouble is that he cannot bear to leave anything out. Every detail of every operation is faithfully reported, not to mention every bit of tedious backchat between the characters. Greater selectivity would have resulted in a tighter story, more tension, more conviction, and a book perhaps half its present length. Secondly—style. It is not just that many of the components of the story are narrative clichés. The language in which they are recorded is tired, lacking in 'snap, crackle and pop'. Much the same goes for the characters, which are mostly stereotypes. I leave to others the question of violence, a fundamental and unavoidable element and one described in telling detail.

Many children, I fear, will love it. (pp. 304-05)

> M. Crouch, *in a review of "Mossflower," in* The Junior Bookshelf, *Vol. 52, No. 6, December, 1988, pp. 304-05.*

Robin Klein

1936-

Australian author of fiction, picture books, short stories, and nonfiction; poet; and editor.

One of Australia's most popular contemporary writers for children, Klein presents young readers with portrayals of middle class urban Australia in which perspicacious young girls, often misfits, triumph over common problems with tenacity and spirit. In her works of fiction for upper primary grade through high school readers, as well as in her picture books for an early primary grade audience, Klein displays what observers consider a particularly sensitive understanding of children and an ability to depict young people realistically by representing their thoughts and conversations with precision and humor. A self-professed proponent of tolerance, Klein often addresses this theme in her writings. In *People Might Hear You* (1983), religious fanaticism and narrow-mindedness leads to insufferable oppression for twelve-year-old Frances; in *Junk Castle* (1983), a group of children build an edifice of scrap materials on public property, then face the opposition of outraged neighbors. But, in a variation of the theme that is perhaps more pertinent to the everyday lives of most young readers, Klein encourages consideration and understanding between friends or, as in *Hating Alison Ashley* (1984), the acceptance of someone once regarded as an enemy or competitor. Although critics have noted the predictability of some of Klein's plot lines, she has also been credited with rescuing her books from tedium by her wit, the appeal of her self-reliant, successful characters, and her dramatic presentation of the universal, often commonplace, experiences of childhood. Klein writes her books in an unadorned style enlivened by animated dialogue, and often employs what reviewers regard as unusual methods of composition. In her popular "Penny Pollard" series, for example, Klein's ten-year-old protagonist speaks her mind through a composite of diary entries, letters, newspaper articles, and other writings. *Laurie Loved Me Best* (1988) is told in chapters which alternate between two narrators, fourteen-year-old best friends who both think a teenage con artist loves her most; in turn they offer their impressions, spiced with comical observations about each other. *The Lonely Hearts Club* (1986), which Klein coauthored with Max Dann, concerns the attempts of two youths to captivate girls; the book also contains letters written by fictional counterparts of Klein and Dann, offering a unique view of the disparate personalities of the writers' personas and the architecture of their collaboration. Among other works, Klein has written a science fiction novel, a book of short stories in which each tale focuses on an eccentric character, and a collection of poems about the vicissitudes of life as a child; she has also edited a selection of letters written to her by young readers. *Thing* won the Australian Children's Book Award as Junior Book of the Year in 1983, an award won by *Penny Pollard's Diary* in 1984 as Book of the Year Highly Commended. In addition, Klein has won several child-selected awards.

(See also *Something about the Author,* Vols. 45, 55 and *Contemporary Authors,* Vol. 116.)

GENERAL COMMENTARY

STEPHANIE NETTELL

Robin Klein believes fiercely in three things: tolerance, laughter and children. You don't need to hear her talking in her amazingly fast, self-deprecating Strine to know this, for the message is clear from her nine books that have appeared over here. In all of them, the world is seen to be a cheerier place when everyone, old or young, is free to be his or her harmlessly quirky self, and in all of them she reveals an uncanny empathy with children.

> My kids say it's a case of arrested development, but I happen to like things that children like. I like to stare and listen—I never read on public transport! I was hopeless as a teacher because I never kept order: they'd come and put an arm round my shoulder and we'd end up with a chat session. It's quite possible to have an involved philosophical discussion with even a small child—adults forget that it's a *privilege* to be with children. . . .

She is a marvellously gutsy writer who relishes the drama of everyday life. For her youngest readers, it's no holds barred as her central characters fight off their pompous, snobbish, egotistical, boringly conventional enemies with joyously unorthodox tactics. ***Thing,*** a loving little dinosaur with a self-protective ability to freeze into other shapes, is totally content to live with Emily and her taxi-driver mum, watching TV in the flat while they're both out, and even the youngest reader can somehow see that it is his and Emily's innocent integrity that wins round the no-pets landlady and defeats the loathsomely spoilt Stephanie Strobe.

Junk Castle is a paean to the triumph of the imagination over stultifying gentility, to the revitalising of dead urban scenes, to the rejuvenation of the spirit. Is that a pile of old rubbish on the Beatrice Binker Reserve (a tiny triangle of cropped grass in a jungle of concrete), or a glitteringly exciting castle? This is a favourite theme of Klein's, a sort of personal war on tidy suburbia—perhaps because 'I used to live in a ghastly middle-class suburb that I absolutely loathed. Now I live miles from anywhere out in the bush, in a tolerant, dotty area.'

She aims not to obliterate the enemy but to liberate them, to show that appearances aren't everything. So the tough-talking Erica, who escapes from her own uncertainty into brazen fantasies, learns to her humbled surprise that nauseatingly perfect ***Alison Ashley*** turns out to have her own griefs as well as valuable talents.

Erica is in the ***Penny Pollard*** mould. We watched Penny finding out about life in, first, her ***Diary*** (as she touchingly discovers that old people are not all tedious wrinklies but individuals with fascinating memories and passions), then her ***Letters*** (which reveal that babies may not be as boring as she thought, and, in postscripts, a grudging but growing interest in a certain Alistair who can't help his name); and soon we'll share her experiences as a monstrously reluctant bridesmaid, to be followed by a visit to England. There will, I hope, be no stopping our Penny. She's a sturdy, delightful character, with a message for girls in particular that 'you don't always need Daddy or big brother to solve your problems—she can solve her own problems, though she's not tough all the way through. All the little boys in Australia are in love with her, and write to her as if she exists.' . . .

It's an irony of the can't-win situation of a writer that while it's been hard work importing Penny into Britain, and even harder into the States, because of her Australian background and slang, my own reviewer on the *Guardian* complained at the lack of good strong Aussie details! In fact, children aren't as fussed by either as editors imagine, as long as the characters and plot bowl along.

Penny and Erica are classic Klein, writing in the voice of an engagingly anti-social tomboy who nevertheless conceals an intelligent and affectionate soul. A sort of wise-cracking, female William. I can think of no contemporary writer who does it better: Klein herself wishes she could write like Jan Mark, and one can respect this, for the affinity is clear, but in her ability to speak directly in the child's persona, with no apparent sophistication, and still allow a young reader to see the joke or the pathos from the outside—in this she can stand alone with pride.

Her one novel for over-elevens so far is ***People Might Hear You,*** a powerful story of a girl imprisoned, quite literally, in a sinister household obsessed by religious fanaticism, told with a controlled simplicity that heightens both the emotion and the suspense. . . . She is struggling now to complete another serious work . . . , one she feels must be written, on drug addiction (a criminal offence in Australia), both inspired and hampered by the agony of seeing her own beautiful and gifted 22-year-old daughter's harrowing fight with heroin. 'I could have come to terms with it more if I'd had a child with leukaemia,' she says, and for one fleeting moment even Robin Klein is not laughing.

Stephanie Nettell, "Stephanie Nettell Introduces Robin Klein," in Books for Keeps, *No. 34, September, 1985, p. 26.*

ANNE HAZELL

It may seem to North American readers that life in Australia is full of exotic animals and danger but for most of us that is far from the truth. To a suburbs dweller such as myself wombats, koalas and kangaroos are seen mainly in zoos (or sad to say dead by the roadside in the country). Penny Pollard, the doughty heroine of ***Penny Pollard's diary*** and ***Penny Pollard's letters*** is just one such urban dweller whose daily round more closely resembles life in Vancouver than in Alice Springs. Author Robin Klein perfectly captures the spirit of a lively, independent 10 year old girl whose outlook on life is bound to bring her into conflict with the adults around her. Slapstick humor, plenty of illustrations and a very readable style have made Penny's stories great favorites with Australian children who are eagerly awaiting the next in the series. (p. 24)

Anne Hazell, "All Right Vegemite! Down Under Australiana," in Emergency Librarian, *Vol. 13, No. 4, March-April, 1986, pp. 23-5.*

DEBORAH SINGMASTER

The Australian writer Robin Klein has written fifteen books for young adults; the two reviewed here [***People Might Hear You*** and ***Hating Alison Ashley***], although very different, are both eminently readable. The plots move rapidly; the spare style is peppered with snappy dialogue; and the main characters are misunderstood rebels guaranteed to evoke teenage sympathies. Rebellion is forced on Francis, in ***People Might Hear You,*** when her Aunt Loris marries the hateful Finley Tyrell and takes her to live with him and his three daughters. The Tyrells are members of some unspecified crank religion. . . . The Tyrells' house is an oppressive fortress barricaded against the Outside. . . . When Francis protests against a way of life that she sees as imprisonment she is threatened with banishment to the Temple for a crash course in obedience. If this fails to convert her she will be sent to "that place" from which no one returns. The atmosphere of the house, with its locked windows and the garden surrounded by high walls and barbed wire, is vividly conveyed and suspense is maintained to the last page. There are some gruesome moments: Mr Tyrell kills a cat that Francis lets into the house (he has previously squashed a canary), and although Francis is about thirteen, readers of this age may find the book distressing. There is no attempt at a comfortable happy ending and the book leaves an unpleasant taste in the mouth.

"Yuk" in ***Hating Alison Ashley*** is a compulsive liar, a hypochondriac and a snob. She conceives an uncontrollable hatred for Alison Ashley, a new girl at her school who is everything that she, Yuk, is not. But by Drama Night at the school summer camp, her hatred has been translated into best-friendship, with both girls' advantages and disadvantages neatly balanced. Yuk's chief advantage is her chaotic family and home which are entertainingly and even affectionately described, from the clutter on the kitchen table—including fake eyelashes and the cat—to her hippomaniac younger sister Jedda who has converted her half of their shared bedroom into a pretend stable and race course.

My chief criticism of Robin Klein's books, and this is strengthened by reading her earlier *Games,* is her lack of emotional warmth: the orphan Francis in *People Might Hear You* never gives a thought to her dead parents and her aunt seems devoid of any love for her; the Tyrell children never refer to their dead mother and exhibit no filial feeling for their tyrannical father. In *Hating Alison Ashley,* Alison's mother's lack of affection for her is glossed over, compensated for, we must suppose, by the friendship of the ghastly Yuk. Characters bristle with anger and resentment in a hard world where the softer human qualities play little part. This imbalance is not likely to worry the avid young adult reader for whom Robin Klein is writing so successfully.

> *Deborah Singmaster, "Cold Confinement," in* The Times Literary Supplement, *No. 4391, May 29, 1987, p. 589.*

JUDITH ELKIN

Robin Klein is an Australian writer of great versatility and wit. Imaginative and talented, her work over the past three or four years has successfully spanned the age range from young reader to teenager. Her writing is not heavily demanding of the reader but it can be original, thought-provoking and very funny.

One of her earliest picture books, *Thing,* a humorous exploration of the monster in the garden theme, . . . has been a great favourite here with younger readers.

Junk Castle is a fast-moving story for a slightly older age group. It follows the exploits of a gang of children who create an ingenious and complex castle from junk materials and, when they arouse the anger of local residents, determine to defend the castle in true military fashion.

Halfway Across the Galaxy and Turn Left, ie the instructions for reaching the Earth from the planet Zyrgon, is a highly inventive science fiction story which turns upside down our general understanding of responsibility and seniority, in a very amusing way. From the zany characters of *Halfway,* Robin Klein seems to have matured as a writer as she moves towards the psychological, in-depth exploration of human relationships, in her three newly published novels for teenagers.

Hating Alison Ashley is an absorbing novel about bright, precocious Erika Yurken or "Yuk" who has always been queen of downtown Barringa East Primary School. She knows she is superior in every way to all the other kids in school, until the immaculate, beautifully behaved, rich, clever Alison Ashley arrives. Yuk hates her on sight. The story is somewhat predictable in outcome as the two girls probe each other's weaknesses and finally come to a mutual understanding and respect. But the story has considerable depth of character, is at times highly perceptive and very realistic. Above all, it is very readable and many younger teenagers will identify closely with these young adolescents.

Games is about another loner, Patricia, invited along, unexpectedly, to an isolated cottage for a weekend with the two most popular girls in school. The weekend turns nasty, as what begins as an attempt to make Patricia believe that the house is haunted, turns into a compellingly chilly and believable "haunting". Robin Klein manages to hold a very tightly

constructed, eerie story extremely well, until the final denouément.

People Might Hear You is the least satisfactory of the three, largely because the ending is unresolved and leaves too many unanswered questions and problems. Again, however, this is a readable and compelling story of conflict in relationships. . . .

All three books have an immediate appeal to teenagers of around 13 +. The main characters are all girls and it is girl readers who will largely respond to them. They are all fast-moving and readable, well within the reach of the average reader but containing more substance and challenges than many of the lighter weight teenage novels of recent years.

> *Judith Elkin, "Inclined to Klein," in* The Times Educational Supplement, *No. 3701, June 5, 1987, p. 56.*

THE GIRAFFE IN PEPPERELL STREET   (1978)

Another giraffe story, this one is a nonsense poem about the giraffe who

> Followed me home from school one day,
> vertical, patterned and neat.
> I suppose it was rather irregular
> a giraffe in Pepperell Street.

The light hearted verses . . . describe the trials and tribulations of having a giraffe. After all what would you do if you had a giraffe with its head stuck up the fireplace?

Humorous, sophisticated, not everyone will accept the gullibility of the adults in the book, but anyone who has owned a wayward pet will appreciate the problems.

> *J. Russell, in a review of "The Giraffe in Pepperell Street," in* The Junior Bookshelf, *Vol. 43, No. 4, August, 1979, p. 196.*

THING   (1982)

Thing is a variation of a well-worn theme dealt with in a light-hearted and humorous fashion, if at times a little wordy. Emily, desperate for a pet of her own, finds an attractive-looking stone to take home with her. Overnight, it hatches into an attractive apple-green baby stegosaurus, which she calls Thing. Pets are not allowed in Emily's flat and thing has to learn very quickly to avoid detection by 'freezing' into an instant cactus plant, decorative fence, coffee table or whatever the situation demands. When the landlady finds Thing protecting her valuables from thieves, she has a change of heart about pets! The humour of the story is well captured in the charming illustrations [by Alison Lester].

> *Judith Elkin, in a review of "Thing," in* British Book News Children's Books, *Autumn, 1982, p. 12.*

An appealing story woven round the ever popular theme of a child's longing for a pet in an environment where pets are forbidden. . . .

The author and artist have created an appealing creature, both in words and pictures. The moods and feelings of this shapeless lumpy creature from the past are revealed most skilfully and Thing becomes an endearing character.

E. Colwell, in a review of "Thing," in The Junior Bookshelf, *Vol. 46, No. 5, October, 1982, p. 182.*

This is an illustrated story rather than a picture book, though there is a picture on each page and every third or fourth spread is in colour. The story should appeal to, and hold the interest of, new solo readers, but judicious editing of the text in places could have heightened the drama of the tale. (p. 322)

Jill Bennett, in a review of "Thing," in The School Librarian, *Vol. 30, No. 4, December, 1982, pp. 321-22.*

Although Klein uses a familiar device (the pet under threat of banishment foils a burglary and is accepted) her engaging fantasy is so deftly written that it has, despite some British spelling or terms that may puzzle our young readers, great appeal. . . . What makes the story particularly enjoyable is the blandness with which others accept the stegosaurus; the police who come to get the burglars, for example, say "But would you kindly ask your dinosaur to step out of the way?" This is a good choice, too, for reading aloud to younger children.

Zena Sutherland, in a review of "Thing," in Bulletin of the Center for Children's Books, *Vol. 37, No. 3, November, 1983, p. 52.*

The book shows its Australian origins in vocabulary and spelling, but such variations will not cause major problems. A greater consideration is the book's resemblance to other dinosaur tales, including *Jethro's Difficult Dinosaur* (Pantheon, 1977), in which a boy brings home a dinosaur egg from Central Park and *Dinosaur My Darling* (Harper, 1978), which tells of a dinosaur, Big Thing, unearthed by a construction worker. But Klein is a competent storyteller, and the plot is helped greatly by the illustrations of whimsical and appealing Thing, who freezes into disguises such as a cactus to avoid detection. Dinosaur lovers will enjoy Thing's exploits.

Kathy Piehl, in a review of "Thing," in School Library Journal, *Vol. 30, No. 7, March, 1984, p. 146.*

PEOPLE MIGHT HEAR YOU (1983)

The picture of fanaticism in *People might hear you* is an extreme one but entirely believable. Finley Tyrell controls his 'temple' congregation, and his family, through fear. Believing that he and his followers have been chosen to lead a new civilisation after inevitable nuclear war, he has retreated from the world behind high walls and a rigid denial of pleasure and freedom. When Frances's lonely aunt and guardian is persuaded to take instruction as a suitable subject to join the community, and to bind herself in marriage to its leader, the girl finds herself virtually a prisoner, forbidden to raise her voice (for Finley's three daughters must not be contaminated by the outside world and therefore must be hidden from school attendance officials), robbed of her own clothes and private treasures and forced into a straitjacket of observance meaningless to her and offering none of the warmth and affection she needs and deserves. Worst of all, the fearful whisperings of the Tyrell girls, the tightly closed windows and locked doors, the warnings about a polluted and threatened world, begin to have an effect on Frances. But before she can be bullied out of the normal impulses of adolescence she is encouraged by the secret misery of Helen, who has not yet been turned into an inhuman prig. The two girls escape from the beleaguered house into the dangers of the city. It is left for the reader to decide whether they will be able to hold on to a precarious freedom and, a more serious doubt, whether Helen's warped personality can ever adjust to the world outside. The evil of religious fanaticism, as great as that of any enslaving political doctrine, has seldom been more clearly demonstrated than in this bitter look behind one colourless dwelling in an Australian city.

Margery Fisher, in a review of "People Might Hear You," in Growing Point, *Vol. 22, No. 6, March, 1984, p. 4208.*

Internal evidence suggests that the book is set in Australia, and the sect bears resemblances to groups such as the Children of God and the Moonies. Presumably the intention is to warn teenagers about such groups, though it is hard to see how those likely to be personally attracted would either read or be influenced by a 'cautionary tale' identified with a younger age group. On the other hand, I found myself deeply disturbed by the sort of effects that the book might have on a child who *would* be able to identify—a foster child, for instance, coming into a family of new or more intense religious faith, though of a completely wholesome kind.

This is a book that I would never wittingly allow to fall into the hands of adolescents—though I suspect that many, happily, would not get beyond the first chapter. My copy went on the fire.

Allan Wainwright, in a review of "People Might Hear You," in The School Librarian, *Vol. 32, No. 2, June, 1984, p. 157.*

In Robin Klein's *People Might Hear You,* a strict religious sect try to solve today's problems by shutting them out behind a high wall and living in a state of siege, in preparation for a war they have been conditioned to expect. . . . It is a nightmare world, and on the whole the characters are only too credible: the tension is well maintained, though the plot is so slight, and there is a tremendous relief when at the end, Frances and Helen succeed in breaking free (we leave them at that very moment, which one feels may not be the end). Is there any point, however, in rousing such prolonged terror over what for almost every reader will be a remote set of circumstances and emotions? Perhaps one may see it as a catharsis, symbolic of a release from other forms of repression. (p. 185)

M. Hobbs, in a review of "People Might Hear You," in The Junior Bookshelf, *Vol. 51, No. 4, August, 1987, pp. 184-85.*

JUNK CASTLE (1983)

Klein's narration keeps up a breakneck pace without slighting the story's engaging, strongly individual characters. . . . Mandy, Irene, Con and Splinter live in a block of flats and attend the same class in school with a draconian teacher. Timid Irene is spared the need to give a talk to the students by a dental emergency and her meeting with a group of construction workers gives her the idea of building a castle in the disused Beatrice Binker Memorial Park near home. The four friends enthusiastically construct the "junk castle" that enrages Mr. Drake, donor of the park, and the children lock him in the dungeon to prevent his tearing down their edifice. When Irene sneaks back to rescue the prisoner, the results are heartening and unexpected, adding a hint of poignancy to the fresh comedy.

> *A review of "Junk Castle," in* Publishers Weekly, *Vol. 225, No. 12, March 23, 1984, p. 71.*

There is a special authenticity behind the hyperbole of this tale of an Australian city where, on a small piece of waste ground in the centre of a square, a group of children decide to build a castle for their imaginative games. . . . Children against bureaucracy, a congenial theme, interpreted in sparkling comic scenes, in an engaging tale for nine-up readers.

> *Margery Fisher, in a review of "Junk Castle," in* Growing Point, *Vol. 23, No. 1, May, 1984, p. 4266.*

PENNY POLLARD'S DIARY (1983)

Penny Pollard finds lots of things yucky—the dress an aunt gave her, community singing by pupils in her school grade, visiting an Old People's Home. To escape these she dodges into the garden of the Home when taken there on a social work project.

In the garden she meets eighty year old Edith Bettany, possessor of a robust individuality. Friendship springs up, and Penny's obsession with horses slips into second place as she takes Mrs. Bettany on a visit to her old house—only to find it has been demolished—and devises eighty-first birthday celebrations.

In fact this is a sentimental story of do-gooding, reasonably successfully tricked out with unfeminine sub-plots and tomboyish language to confuse those likely to regard the basic theme as "yucky". (pp. 129-30)

> *R. Baines, in a review of "Penny Pollard's Diary," in* The Junior Bookshelf, *Vol. 48, No. 3, June, 1984, pp. 129-30.*

Although this has a few Australian expressions that may baffle American readers, it's a book that should have universal appeal, especially to horse lovers. That's what Penny is, and she complains in her diary that nobody ever really looks at her collection of horse pictures. . . . The writing is breezy, just a bit too obviously look-I'm-a-tomboy at first but that wears off, and the story is economically structured and believable as the diary of a child.

> *Zena Sutherland, in a review of "Penny Pollard's Diary," in* Bulletin of the Center for Children's Books, *Vol. 38, No. 1, September, 1984, p. 9.*

PENNY POLLARD'S LETTERS (1984)

Australian Penny Pollard resembles a female version of Adrian Mole. Here her mother is in hospital awaiting a baby, and Penny is sent to stay with great-aunt Winifred. She keeps up a constant stream of letters to everyone she knows at home, and these form the text of this book.

Some subjects feature in several letters. Dad is requested to take the dead rat from Penny's wardrobe and place it in the freezer, and Jason Taylor, purveyor of the rat, is bombarded with messages demanding compensation for a bad buy. Twelve year old Alistair, originally encountered on the train, develops from a despised egghead into a friend and possible

first romantic interest. The prospect of a baby at home becomes more endurable.

> *G. Bott, in a review of "Penny Pollard's Letters," in* The Junior Bookshelf, *Vol. 49, No. 3, June, 1985, p. 129.*

Students might not appreciate how fascinating letters can be—until they read Penny's hilarious correspondence with her friends and enemies. Penny reveals certain strong dislikes—such as babies and boys—but she also reveals tenacity, humor, and a willingness to change and grow.

> *A review of "Penny Pollard's Letters," in* Learning, *Vol. 15, No. 4, November-December, 1986, p. 56.*

RATBAGS AND RASCALS: FUNNY STORIES (1984)

Although occasional settings and words (swagman, dugong, bunyips) betray the Australian origin of these seventeen minigiggles, the sense of humour to which they appeal is universal. The subtlety of presentation and the effectiveness of the sting-in-the-tail technique are by no means of uniform quality, but the development and pace of most of the stories ensure they hit their prime target—to amuse.

Most of the pivot characters are, as the title suggests, rascals or ratbags ("an eccentric person, an unpleasant person, troublemaker—slang, chiefly Australia and New Zealand" O.E.D.). On parade are a kidnapped girl who takes charge of the gang; Parker-Hamilton, a superior robot, who bullies the Brown family into total submission; bossy Annabel whose seance goes awry; Captain Gnash, the pirate, who moves into a profitable career in advertising; Brother Ninian, who spills ink and invents the decorated Latin manuscript; irritating Irma who tames a dragon.

Homely or extra-terrestrial, outrageous or astute, these zany tales are fashioned by an appreciation of juvenile humour—simple incongruity, a splash of slap-stick, unexpected triumphs, imaginative impossibilities.

> *G. Bott, in a review of "Ratbags and Rascals: Funny Stories," in* The Junior Bookshelf, *Vol. 49, No. 3, June, 1985, p. 129.*

Both the language and the humor in these Australian imports have traveled well. . . . The simple blend of fantasy and reality is enchanting. Some of these stories are more accessible than others; some are better read aloud, when a quick explanation can be inserted. The silly line drawings [by Alison Lester] complement the book perfectly. When kids beg for new humor and librarians pine for a tantalizing read-aloud, think of this one.

> *J. Alison Illsley, in a review of "Ratbags and Rascals: Funny Stories," in* School Library Journal, *Vol. 32, No. 10, August, 1986, p. 94.*

Australian writer Robin Klein has given us a refreshing book with a difference, a collection of pithy tales, each with an unusual twist or outcome. . . . Most exciting of all, there isn't a weakness anywhere in the collection. It's not a book whose messages need explanation—there are no attempts to impress (and, therefore, perhaps to confuse!) and no strident excesses.

In classroom terms, the immediacy of its impact means that it can—and should—be read widely by fourth and fifth-year pupils—girls *and* boys, of course.

Nigel Spencer, in a review of "Ratbags and Rascals: Funny Stories," in Books for Keeps, *No. 45, July, 1987, p. 18.*

THINGNAPPED! (1984)

The sequel to *Thing* will set readers tingling with indignation at iniquitous Stephanie Strobe. Rich though she is, Stephanie envies Emily Forbes her pet stegosaurus, Thing, and steals the little green fellow because his like is not to be bought for any price. The captive shrinks where the beastly girl hides him to starve in her bathroom. When Thing is smaller, Stephanie gloats, Emily won't be able to identify him. Bullying Mrs. Strobe, the schemer keeps her out of the bathroom until the day of reckoning. The mother finds Thing and is so outraged that she gets the upper hand on her daughter and keeps it. Emily and Thing are reunited as Klein's piquant comedy closes and the villain is properly punished.

A review of "ThingNapped!" in Publishers Weekly, *Vol. 228, No. 9, August 30, 1985, p. 423.*

A quirky, original and very funny picture book which will be enjoyed by sixes to tens. I like this author's assured and witty style, as well as the ability (too rare) to create convincing and assertive girl characters.

Emily's beloved stegosaurus, Thing, is kidnapped by the odious Stephanie Strobe: there's some well paced and punchy writing in the recounting of how he endures the ordeal.

Colin Mills, in a review of "ThingNapped!" in Books for Keeps, *No. 44, May, 1987, p. 20.*

HATING ALISON ASHLEY (1984)

Erica Yurken, known as Yuk, compensates for her rough and ready homelife and attending a school officially graded Disadvantaged by behaving like a hypochondriac and fantasising about the doings of her family. Life is changed by a revised zoning, which brings the elegant and correct Alison Ashley to Barringa East Primary School.

Alison is beautifully dressed, well mannered and good at everything. Even the most brutal of the boys in school modifies his behaviour to impress her. All Yuk's boasts and dreams collapse in failure. It is not until the trip to summer camp that she achieves any success, and then in an unexpected way.

Robin Klein tells a conventional story, in which the two girls feud and quarrel unable to see that they not only like but also envy one another. However, this author writes with style and wit, creating characters who are both credible and sympathetic.

R. Baines, in a review of "Hating Alison Ashley," in The Junior Bookshelf, *Vol. 51, No. 4, August, 1987, p. 183.*

This very funny, very astute story brings the two girls together with such compassion and wit that it doesn't matter a whit that the rapprochement has been inevitable from the start. First published in Australia, this is a gem of a school-and-camp story.

Zena Sutherland, in a review of "Hating Alison Ashley," in Bulletin of the Center for Children's Books, *Vol. 41, No. 4, December, 1987, p. 68.*

Although school stories about misfits are hardly a rare commodity, the author has created vivid characters with such skill and apparent ease that her novel deserves a look. . . . Distinguished by the snappy dialogue and believable characterization that have elevated Robin Klein to enormous popularity in Australia, the story is absorbing and provocative. While flecked with humor the book is also effectively touched by the sad reality of unsatisfactory family relationships. (pp. 202-03)

Karen Jameyson, in a review of "Hating Alison Ashley," in The Horn Book Magazine, *Vol. LXIV, No. 2, March-April, 1988, pp. 202-03.*

HALFWAY ACROSS THE GALAXY AND TURN LEFT (1985)

X and her family are in self-imposed exile from their planet of Zyrgon after Father had aroused suspicion in the minds of the authorities by winning the government lottery twenty-seven times in a row. X, the officially recognized Organizer in the family, is faced with the task of settling her decidedly odd relations into the scheme of things on planet earth. This is not easy with a sister who is apt to levitate at odd moments, and an infant prodigy of a brother, (recently nominated for a full professorship to the Knowledge Bank back on Zyrgon). Hopefully, thinks X, they won't have to be away for long.

It is an entertaining story, but one in which, I felt, a good plot has become confused by too many disparate elements. What should be a racy read for nine-year-olds became, for me, a book difficult to finish.

Margaret Banerjee, in a review of "Halfway Across the Galaxy and Turn Left," in British Book News Children's Books, *June, 1986, p. 27.*

Ms. Klein's visitors from another planet are superficially not very different from the earthlings they encounter although some have mental powers which would guarantee instant entry to Mensa. . . . X's efforts to settle them all in a fairly humdrum earthly environment without their attracting undue attention or getting under the feet of authority prove wearing for her and amusing for the reader with muted satire in most instances unobtrusively present. Altogether this is a happy change from alien/earthling confrontations of the close encounter kind. (pp. 116-17)

A. R. Williams, in a review of "Halfway Across the Galaxy and Turn Left," in The Junior Bookshelf, *Vol. 50, No. 3, June, 1986, pp. 116-17.*

This is a typical family story, with some flimsy space trappings. The middle child is simply named X, which is going a bit far to show that she feels like a non-entity. Father continues his borderline crooked ways, not the most desirable role model to present to children. After numerous small adventures in adjusting to life on Earth, the family decides on permanent residence. A nice idea, but the execution does not live up to the promise.

Li Stark, in a review of "Halfway Across the Galaxy and Turn Left," in School Library Journal, *Vol. 33, No. 2, October, 1986, p. 177.*

SNAKES AND LADDERS: POEMS ABOUT THE UPS AND DOWNS OF LIFE (1985)

The 'ups and downs of life' recorded in Robin Klein's collection of poems may refer immediately to the author's Australian background, but they have a universal quality in them. Kids are like that here and everywhere. Miss Klein writes neatly and with wit, capturing the awful moment (she lands mostly on snakes, not ladders) in well-constructed formal verses. Her picture is reinforced by Ann James, whose strong scribbly line is just right. The whole book seems to have sprung from a single creative impulse. New poets are rare indeed; to meet one in this attractive form, and at such a reasonable price, is both pleasure and privilege.

> *M. Crouch, in a review of "Snakes and Ladders," in* The Junior Bookshelf, *Vol. 50, No. 4, August, 1986, p. 149.*

Robin Klein is as keen an observer, but her eye is for the comedy of everyday life. Her verse technique is a bit crude, but she makes up for that in sparkle. Worth keeping this little book on hand for that spare five minutes at the end of the school day.

> *Marcus Crouch, in a review of "Snakes and Ladders," in* The School Librarian, *Vol. 34, No. 3, September, 1986, p. 283.*

Klein gets right to the heart of middle-grade children's trials and tribulations in this collection of funny, bouncy rhymes. Messy bedrooms, miseries of classwork, insomnia, problems of baby-sitting, and thoughts on running away are some of the subjects the poet deftly scrutinizes with wit and candor. . . . Librarians who read a couple of the selections aloud, however, will probably not encounter any difficulty in getting youngsters to check out this title. Klein, an Australian, easily leaps the Pacific with these amusing universal traumas. (p. 513)

> *Barbara Elleman, in a review of "Snakes and Ladders," in* Booklist, *Vol. 83, No. 6, November 15, 1986, pp. 512-13.*

THE ENEMIES (1985)

Fans of Robin Klein's other books will not be disappointed by **The Enemies.** Mary-Anna and Sandra are two girls who hate each other, and spend a lot of time at school scoring points and arguing. Then Mary-Anna finds that she has to spend a weekend at her enemy's house. One might think that a *rapprochement* is inevitable given such a plot set-up, and it does happen. But that doesn't matter, for it is adversity that brings the girls together, and helps them to learn important lessons about co-operation and being friends. Robin Klein's strength, too, is her ability to get inside an eight-or nine-year-old's skin and produce really believable dialogue and descriptions of emotion. A good, albeit short, read for the over-eights.

> *Tony Bradman, in a review of "The Enemies," in* British Book News Children's Books, *Autumn, 1986, p. 33.*

Australian author Klein has a gift for exploring youthful friendships and enmities, as in the well-received **Hating Alison Ashley**; in this brief, pungent story, a weekend together transforms the longstanding animosity between two ten-year-olds. . . .

It's not clear why the two girls are so at odds; their mothers seem too sensible to have forced them on each other. Still, young readers should be amused to recognize themselves in Klein's humorous report on their vigorous hostility and its believable resolution.

> *A review of "Enemies," in* Kirkus Reviews, *Vol. LVII, No. 7, April 1, 1989, p. 549.*

GAMES (1986)

Games can be harmless or sinister, innocent or calculating, depending upon who is playing them. Children learn the value of deception early, and by the time they have reached their teenage years, have honed their gaming skill down to a fine cutting edge.

Kirsty and Genevieve were used to winning any malicious game they happened to have invented, and Patricia usually played whichever game she was told to. They were an ill-assorted threesome who elected to spend a night in an old country house: the beautiful, mendacious Kirsty; cool, aloof Genevieve; and unpopular Patricia—three teenagers who found themselves unwittingly engaged in a game whose rules were unknown.

Kirsty had deceitfully planned a wild weekend in Aunt Maude's house, but was disgruntled when the boys from school failed to show up. Her insistence that they conduct a seance in order to while away the evening had some unexpected results, for it soon became obvious that a strange "presence" had materialised in the house. Was it the ghost of Dorothea Jacklin, or was it just someone playing some nasty pranks? With Robin Klein orchestrating the action, the games were bound to be inventive and the characters thoroughly credible. As the story progresses we gain a cumulative insight into the three girls' characters, with some cunningly descriptive passages. For instance, Genevieve is described as having "rain-coloured eyes that gave nothing away, but looked at you like the screen of a computer waiting for input. But unlike a computer, she gave nothing back". Kirsty is the tyrannical queen of every school playground; beneath her vacuous prettiness and her beguiling ways, there is a heart of pure steel.

Patricia, like all of Robin Klein's "heroines", is a captivating mass of insecurities. Her depressing home-life is gradually revealed as the source of her constant efforts to ingratiate herself with school friends; her father's untimely death and her mother's consequent agoraphobia provide sufficient incentive for Patricia's efforts to "overcompensate". As the story progresses, she makes some valuable discoveries; she learns that some friends simply are not worth having, and that she has sterling qualities of her own.

The clever chapter headings derived from traditional word games, such as "Three Blind Mice" and "Simon Says", act as a framework for the action, which is fast paced and suspenseful. Robin Klein has made a thriller out of an ordinary teenage escapade—a testimony to her already proven ability to combine masterful storytelling with a penetrating analysis of the child psyche. (pp. 49-50)

> *Robyn Sheahan, in a review of "Games," in* Reading Time, *Vol. 31, No. 1, January, 1987, pp. 49-50.*

Relationships are crucial in **Games**; the irrational behaviour of the characters provokes action as they are moved by the confusions within their peer group. . . . The gradual building of suspense is expertly done, always depending on the fluctuating moods of the three girls. When events (which the reader must come to without previous knowledge) come to a head, the despised, tormented Patricia proves to be equal to a crisis which has sent the other two running to the station in selfish terror. The cruelty of teenagers with class pretensions provides a theme for the story and the importance of personality as the impetus to action is notably demonstrated in this compact, tense, well managed story. (pp. 4878-79)

> *Margery Fisher, in a review of "Games," in* Growing Point, *Vol. 26, No. 4, November, 1987, pp. 4878-79.*

The games played by three teenage girls at an illicit party at an apparently empty and isolated house in the Australian bush are many. The mindless malicious games of the adolescent bully and a simulated séance that raises uncontrollable and menacing spirits dominate, their chilling effects heightened by the ironic nursery-rhyme chapter heads. Beneath the suspense, Klein charts a rough rite of passage that reveals an unctuous outsider's real nature and exposes that of her tormentors.

> *Nancy Chambers, in a review of "Games," in* The Signal Selection of Children's Books 1988, *edited by Nancy Chambers, The Thimble Press, 1989, p. 67.*

PENNY POLLARD IN PRINT   (1986)

Followers of Penny Pollard probably know that the worst day of her life was when she was made to be a flowergirl at her Aunty Janice's wedding. And this, the third Penny Pollard book, begins with our hero receiving an invitation to Simone Norris's sister's wedding as, you guessed it, a flowergirl. Simone is naturally delighted at the prospect of dressing up in a pink frock, but not so Penny. She devises a number of imaginative plans to escape, to no avail. Mrs. Norris has a will of iron and no one is getting out of this, Kurringa's wedding of the year. Meanwhile Penny's interests have diversified, and she is relentless in offering her peculiar view of life to the Kurringa Gazette in asorted unsolicited articles of local interest. Horses still rank, as do Amazonian cannibal plants and chicken hypnosis techniques. But it is Penny's inspired account of the wedding which finally captures the headlines.

Like the first Penny Pollard book, this uses the diary format to bring us a swag of new characters, as well as some of the old. But something tells me that Penny, while still as stubborn and rebellious as ever, might be softening just a little around the edges.

> *Margot Nelmes, in a review of "Penny Pollard in Print," in* Reading Time, *Vol. 31, No. 2, 1987, p. 50.*

Through her diary entries, readers meet an independent, spirited, and determined Australian girl with an unusual assortment of interests. Although **Penny Pollard in Print** is the third in a series, each book stands alone. . . . Australian slang is not distracting and, although not defined, will be understood by American readers within the context of the story. Most readers will enjoy Penny's humorous view of life

around her and will marvel at her crazy schemes. Fast, easy, and entertaining reading.

> *Jeanette Larson, in a review of "Penny Pollard in Print," in* School Library Journal, *Vol. 35, No. 8, May, 1988, p. 98.*

THE LONELY HEARTS CLUB   (with Max Dann, 1986)

Something interesting is currently going on in the writing of literature for the young. Students of literature know that writers for adult audiences have been exploring, with increasing ingenuity, the challenges readers can meet in complex narrative. Abstruse theories are written about it and a sizeable part of the Ph.D. industry lives on these artistic developments.

What has this to do with this collaboration of Robin Klein and Max Dann? Well, in this romp through the difficulties of male growing-up when young male adolescents decide that girls are the all important centre of attention, Klein and Dann present an interesting example of artistic collaboration by becoming, in a sense, dramatic participants in their own work. They do this by including letters exchanged between fictional versions of themselves and written apparently while working together to finish the work. The young reader finds that one of them appears conscientious and hard-working (Klein) and the other is the sort of person who is pleased to have finished a work but not excited about foregoing the pleasures of leisure in order to complete the task. The letters, typed in significantly different ways, are couched in language which reveals the characters of the fictional authors very vividly. Max is not good at making his excuses consistent or believable and Robin has a shrewd notion of the kinds of errors and excuses he will make.

What we have here is an experiment in writing a story, a collaboration, in which the letters tell us a little about the efforts required in writing. The book includes also, for each chapter, an epigraph drawn from a fictional boarding school's manual on etiquette and good behaviour. This school, run by a set of religious brothers, is the location for the story of boarders, Donovan and Scuff. The epigraphs comment ironically on the behaviour and fortunes of the pair in the accompanying chapter. This combination of written forms suggests that the work will provide quite an interesting narrative model for young writers in late primary and junior high school.

The story centres around Donovan and Scuff's efforts to arrange to meet some girls—thus the title. They use all the commonly observed techniques of young adolescent males to hide their lack of confidence. They are inept exhibitionists, they lie, boast and exaggerate. Above all, they are accident prone, since they never quite see the likely consequences of the actions.

The story has, given the writing team, the expected vivacity in plot, language, broad characterization and insight into the sense of humour of the young adolescent. For the adult reader, especially the teacher, it has an attraction because of the model it provides for combining writing forms and as an example of how literature for the young has shown, in recent years, a willingness to experiment in refreshing ways with the arts of narrative.

> *A review of "The Lonely Hearts Club," in* Magpies, *Vol. 2, No. 4, September, 1987, p. 26.*

[Klein] is capable of notably perceptive books as well as considerable wit; here, the wit predominates. The pratfalls, while predictable, have universal appeal; but the repartee is so heavily Australian that its humor will be lost on all but the most facile readers. The interpolated correspondence with the reputed co-author (the letters imply that he never actually contributed a deletion, much less a sentence) is more accessible—and funnier—than the book itself, but so irrelevant to it that it seems like a misplaced joke.

Of very limited use.

> *A review of "The Lonely Hearts Club," in* Kirkus Reviews, *Vol. LVI, No. 1, September 1, 1988, p. 1324.*

This is a very funny story. . . .

Unfortunately the book has two major flaws. The language is so totally British as to be incomprehensible to American children. For example, the students make "galahs of themselves," play "footy" on "House teams," are described as "dags" and given "bin duty" as punishment. Such colloquialisms and slang expressions abound throughout the book. The second major flaw is the inclusion of the co-authors' letters to each other. These missives have been inserted at irregular intervals, often in the middle of a chapter. They completely break readers' train of thought and ruin the flow of the story. Adults might find the co-authors' exchange of ideas and insults which were part of the story's creation amusing, but children will be lost.

> *Nancy P. Reeder, in a review of "The Lonely Hearts Club," in* School Library Journal, *Vol. 35, No. 3, November, 1988, p. 112.*

BOSS OF THE POOL (1986)

In a brief novel by the author of last year's fine **Hating Alison Ashley,** Shelley is furious because her mother, Anne, has taken an evening job as occupational therapist at a hostel for the mentally and physically handicapped. Shelley may stay with a boring baby-sitter or come along and have the use of the pool (she's a champion swimmer). When the baby-sitter's absence forces her to accompany her mother, Shelley is outspoken in her antipathy to the hostel's inmates, makes no effort to be accommodating, and responds to the interest of Ben, full grown but mentally a toddler, with outrage. Ben likes her, but is terrified of the water; in spite of herself, and without ever completely dropping her defensive rudeness, Shelley cajols him into the pool, rewards his courage, teaches him rudimentary swimming, and even gives him a new swim suit.

This is an extraordinary book in honestly depicting the fear and cruel taunts that are common and perhaps natural in children who confront people who are different before they understand their humanity. Cleverly, Klein makes her readers sympathize with Ben before Shelley does; with their own consciousness raised, they will applaud her concluding turnaround.

> *A review of "Boss of the Pool," in* Kirkus Reviews, *Vol. LVI, No. 4, February 15, 1988, p. 280.*

This somewhat predictable but heartwarming story is obviously set in England given the periodic use of unfamiliar verbal expressions. This fact, however, will not detract one's en-

joyment of the book. The novel's targeted age group is notoriously self-conscious and self-centered one minute, sensitive, caring, and open the next. Young adolescents will understand Shelley's initial repugnance for and fear of mentally handicapped people. Although at first she scorns and ridicules the disabled people her mother enjoys working with, Shelley eventually achieves a new level of maturity and learns the personal satisfaction of helping others.

> *Iona R. Malanchuk, in a review of "Boss of the Pool," in* Children's Book Review Service, *Vol. 16, No. 9, April, 1988, p. 101.*

Shelley is not a sympathetic character—she's sulky, whiney, and mean-spirited. Although readers are expected to witness her transformation, all that Klein shows are tears in Shelley's eyes when she sees Ben swim after giving him a new bathing suit and a swimming medal. . . . Despite Klein's good intentions, this book is just too dreary to be enjoyable.

> *Janet DiGianni, in a review of "Boss of the Pool," in* School Library Journal, *Vol. 35, No. 9, June-July, 1988, p. 105.*

BIRK THE BERSERKER (1987)

Another book from the prolific Robin Klein, this one is reminiscent of Ferdinand the Bull or The Reluctant Dragon. Birk is a Viking who does not want to fight. He would rather lie in a field and smell the flowers. The men of his village together with his mother are absolutely ashamed of him and do everything in their power to get him into battle, until one day he gets left behind during a fight and imprisoned in a cage. How Birk manages to overcome his reluctance and yet remain true to himself takes up the remainder of the story.

All is related in a humorous vein, with an occasional little comment from the artist, Alison Lester, thrown in in the illustrations. A pleasant, fun-filled book that middle primary students should enjoy.

> *Kelsey Taylor, in a review of "Birk the Berserker," in* Magpies, *Vol. 3, No. 1, March, 1988, p. 28.*

LAURIE LOVED ME BEST (1988)

Though 14-year-old Julia and Andre are best friends at the posh Australian school where both are misfits, neither knows about the other's difficult home life. Julia imagines that Andre has the perfect well-heeled nuclear family, unaware that Andre's father's miserliness and constant carping have forced her brother to leave home. Andre idealizes Julia's hippie mother and their casual life-style; she's never seen the discomforts of their latest communal ménage.

The two fix up an abandoned cottage as a haven, where one day charming Laurie (18) appears, wounded and hungry. His flattering words make each girl think she's the object of his affection, though their alternating narratives make it clear that they are being conned. Meanwhile, life at home deteriorates for both; but instead of comforting one another, they quarrel about Laurie—until Julia happens to discover that he's not only a fraud but actually quite ordinary.

Klein . . . writes well; her images are arresting, her dialogue crisp, her characters sharply individual. But though it makes a telling symbol, it's not plausible that the girls have kept their private lives secret for four years; and there's no hint that Laurie, a stranger, might prove dangerous. The conclusion—each taking control of her relationship with her own family—is well motivated, yet the final scene—both suddenly falling for the same new boy—tends to undermine the book's more serious insights. Still, like Klein's other novels, well told and entertaining.

A review of "Laurie Loved Me Best," in Kirkus Reviews, *Vol. LVI, No. 23, December 1, 1988, p. 1740.*

Klein eloquently conveys a poignant story by allowing each girl to narrate alternate chapters. This complex handling of point of view masterfully dovetails each character's development and moves the plot in a remarkably smooth and suspenseful manner. Klein is at turns breezy, humorous, pensive, and ironic, but never boring. Her story transcends its Australian setting to make universal statements about friendship and love at all ages.

Cindy Darling Codell, in a review of "Laurie Loved Me Best," in School Library Journal, *Vol. 35, No. 5, January, 1989, p. 94.*

When writing about themes of adolescent envy, misunderstanding, and insecurity, Robin Klein's periscope provides a remarkably clear and vivid picture. Although the adults in her latest novel as well as some of the peripheral characters are somewhat weak, the two girls and their conflict come across with painful clarity. Yet humorous moments emerge through the first-person narration, as chapters alternating between the two main characters give one girl a chance to wryly comment on the other.

Karen Jameyson, in a review of "Laurie Loved Me Best," in The Horn Book Magazine, *Vol. LXV, No. 1, January-February, 1989, p. 79.*

DEAR ROBIN: LETTERS TO ROBIN KLEIN (1988)

I am never sure just what is the intended audience for collections of kids' letters—whether to God, Father Christmas or, in this case, Robin Klein. Here is a collection of brief excerpts (most are just one sentence) from kids' letters to one of Australia's most popular authors. In addition the book is decorated with kids' drawings. There are compliments and complaints, questions are asked and advice freely given. A number of letters have obviously been written grudgingly at a teacher's behest. Most of the extracts could be described as charming or amusing; there are no examples of really unhappy writers, nor of distressing personal problems. I feel sure that Robin must receive these, so I believe their omission is a deliberate one, to make the book light hearted and "suitable" for young readers. Thus we are only given half the picture. I find it hard to assess this book: it is not a genre that appeals to me, but may amuse other readers, child and adult.

Jo Goodman, in a review of "Dear Robin: Letters to Robin Klein," in Reading Time, *Vol. 33, No. 1, 1989, p. 34.*

The temptation when reviewing this book is simply to give lots of quotes. . . .

The letters are classified under various headings: openings, family gossip, hobbies, confessions, ambitions, classroom gossip, praise, and flattery (and several others). My favourite opening is "Dear Ms. I have to admit to ignorance about you and your work." A couple of other quotations will be enough to give the flavour of this book. Scoldings: "All your books have fantastic illustrations but your writing doesn't suit them." Praise: "Our teacher read us your Penny Pollard books. It [sic] was an oases [sic] in a desert of boredom," and, finally some Advice: "If you want a tip for Caulfield Guineas it's Red Ancor" [sic].

All Robin Klein's many fans, both child and adult, will enjoy this book and it will amuse even those few who, like her correspondent, are ignorant of her and her work.

Margot Tyrrell, in a review of "Dear Robin: Letters to Robin Klein," in Magpies, *Vol. 4, No. 1, March, 1989, p. 34.*

James Marshall

1942-

(Also writes as Edward Marshall) American author and illustrator of picture books and fiction and reteller.

A prolific author of distinctive picture books for preschool to early primary grade readers, Marshall is regarded for creating works distinguished by their genial wit and themes relevant to childhood. He is credited with devising broadly humorous yet genuinely lifelike characters and, while featuring them in a sequence of titles, retaining the essence of their individual personalities. This is clearly indicated both in Marshall's first book, *George and Martha* (1972), and in his subsequent works about the two hippopotamuses. Composed of brief narrative sketches, the "George and Martha" series treats subjects that touch young lives: recognizing true friendships, getting along with others, and attempting to soothe hurt feelings. Through understatement and irony, Marshall depicts the efforts of his characters to help and to understand each other, thereby subtly and playfully teaching lessons in compassion and consideration to young readers. In a similar vein, Marshall has written series headlined, among others, by such animals as Carruthers the bear, whose loyal friends valiantly try to help him; Emily the pig, who battles her gluttony and its attendant weight gain and indigestion; and the wily but innocuous Fox, whose folly leads him into typical juvenile dilemmas. While Marshall has won praise for the inventiveness and freshness of the plots for these works, he has also been lauded for his retellings of Mother Goose rhymes and such fairy tales as "Little Red Riding Hood" and "Goldilocks and the Three Bears." Critics appreciate Marshall's ability to sustain the traits of the original stories while integrating them with unique qualities, such as making Red Riding Hood's grandma spunky, the wolf persuasive and engaging, and Goldilocks cocky and headstrong.

In addition to his own publications and those he has written under the pseudonym of Edward Marshall, Marshall has co-authored several notable books with Harry Allard. While functioning as illustrator, Marshall has stated that he also assists Allard in devising the story lines and has called their work together "a real collaboration." Once again, the books are designed to follow their characters through a variety of comical situations. In the popular "Miss Nelson" series, a sweet-tempered but ineffectual teacher disguises herself as Miss Viola Swamp, whose dictatorial approach subdues the unruly students of Horace B. Smedley School, who gladly welcome Miss Nelson back after they repent for their actions. In "The Stupids" series, readers are presented with the chronicles of Stanley Q. Stupid and family, pleasingly benevolent and gracious but laughably moronic. While they stumble through adventures like mistaking death for the darkness from a blown fuse, children are made to feel proudly superior in intelligence and experience. In his own works and those done with Allard, Marshall has been praised for the significant contribution of his illustrations, through which he imbues the books with a wealth of good-natured merriment. A self-taught artist whose work is executed in a naïve and informal style, Marshall is considered a master at capturing the humor of a situation through farcical details and the person-

ality of his characters through candid facial expressions. His drawings, characterized by bold outlines and flat spaces filled with vivid color washes, also enhance the texts through sight gags and ludicrous incongruities. From the delineation of an enormous hippo perched on a chandelier to the depiction of Mrs. Stupid's dress of live chickens, Marshall has exhibited a zany view of life that has captivated critics and young readers since George and Martha's first appearance. Marshall has also illustrated numerous books by authors such as Jakob and Wilhelm Grimm, Jane Yolen, Russell Hoban, and Norma Klein and has written a mystery for older primary grade readers. *Miss Nelson Is Missing!* was named a runner-up for the Edgar Allan Poe Award in 1978 and *Goldilocks and the Three Bears* was a Caldecott honor book in 1989.

(See also *Something about the Author,* Vols. 6, 51; *Contemporary Authors,* Vols. 41-44, rev. ed.; and *Dictionary of Literary Biography,* Vol. 61.)

AUTHOR'S COMMENTARY

[*The following excerpt is from an interview by Leonard Marcus.*]

For nearly 20 years, the prolific author and illustrator, who received a 1989 Caldecott Honor for his buoyantly tongue-in-cheek *Goldilocks and the Three Bears,* has been bringing down the house not just with readers in the upper reaches of the picture-book age, but also with younger kids and more than a few of their parents. . . .

Marshall was born in 1942 in San Antonio, Tex.—"across the street from the Alamo," he recalls. . . . Lone Star State flags, windmills and "clear blue Texas skies" are among the tokens of his affection for the region that turn up regularly in his drawings. . . .

[When Marshall was in his mid-20s he] admired the work of a handful of illustrators—Maurice Sendak, Tomi Ungerer, Arnold Lobel, Edward Gorey and the Italian artist Domenico Gnoli, whose baroquely elegant *The Art of Smiling* was among the first picture books to capture his attention. "Like a fool," Marshall recalls, "I looked at that book, and at Sendak's *Where the Wild Things Are,* and said, I can do that."

The day after taking his portfolio—"on napkins and all sorts of things"—to Houghton Mifflin's children's book editor Walter Lorraine, he was offered his first illustration assignment, a Byrd Baylor manuscript called *Plink Plink Plink,* which Houghton published in 1971. (p. 202)

The following year, two Marshall books appeared, including the first of a series that is well on its way to classic status, the George and Martha books—of which there are presently seven.

Marshall was back in Texas visiting his family when the winsome hippo friends first made their appearance in a sketchbook. "They started out as two little dots—imperfections in the paper" that metamorphosed into one of the corpulent characters' pin-point eyes. Such improvisation has always been basic to the way Marshall works. A story idea often emerges from a sketch in which he has placed a character in an unlikely predicament. He then keeps drawing until both he and the character find their way out.

While people often suppose that George and Martha are namesakes of the nation's original First Family, Marshall says this is not so. "My mother," he explains, "was watching *Who's Afraid of Virginia Woolf?* on television while the sketches were in progress." Albee's gladiatorial marriage partners are a far cry from the gently prankish hippo pals that Marshall describes as "innocent, crafty and courtly" with "exquisite manners and a sense of fun." But many of the stories, which are marvels of terse understatement and of an oddly endearing kind of tact, do concern the difficulties of getting along with others. George cannot resist sprinkling Martha with the hose. Martha can't help unwrapping a box that George has marked "Do not open." It is hardly surprising that younger school-aged children, who are just learning to make their way in the world of their peers, laugh audibly at the pair's endless pratfalls and misunderstandings.

Marshall sees the "dear friends" as being quite distinct from each other. "George bumbles into things. Martha gets a little grand in places. I guess they are probably two sides of my own personality." (pp. 202-03)

In conversation with the artist and in letters, Marshall's young readers often refer to incidents that aren't to be found anywhere in the books. One reason that kids so freely add to the stock of George and Martha lore, Marshall thinks, is that the stories themselves take an open-ended view of experience

that is neither sentimental nor predictable. When George drags Martha to a scary movie, it is he who ends up cowering under the seats. When George pretends to enjoy Martha's homemade pea soup (while actually pouring it into his loafers when she's not looking), he bungles the deception. Martha, who, it turns out doesn't like making pea soup nearly as much as George had thought, is relieved rather than insulted. She is also touched by his good intent. The emotion is real, even if the situation is always a trifle ridiculous. Most of the laughs Marshall garners are heartfelt laughs of recognition.

Much of the fun of any Marshall book derives from the sense of theater that the artist brings to the goings-on. In part, this is achieved by formal graphic means that readers aren't apt to notice. "Scale is important," Marshall says. "There is only one point where the character should be in relation to the frame, the viewer and the back wall. It's like focusing in and out. I like to play with the margins. Anyone who loves Japanese prints, as I do, will [understand that] it's a whole technique that does wonderful things dramatically."

A more apparent hint of theater comes in the way Marshall characters typically dress. George and Martha, Fox and the Stanley Q. Stupids are among the quick-change artists whose outfits are as outlandish as anything they say or do. "They're very broad characters acting out very broad humor." The children who put on Marshall-inspired school plays are not alone in the unfettered, let-'er-rip delight they take in this aspect of the author's art. . . .

[Marshall's frequent collaborator, Harry Allard,] who lives in Mexico, is perhaps best known as the inventor of the Stupids, a family of noodleheads whose talent for getting backwards what every four-year-old can plainly understand is matched only by their boundless *joie de vivre.* "The Stupids always have a good time," Marshall observes, even when their sundaes consist of mashed potatoes topped with butterscotch syrup. In *The Stupids Take Off* . . . , the gang celebrates Pattie Stupid's sixth birthday with a cake with eight candles on it. "Why are there eight candles on the cake?" asks brother Buster. "Because I didn't have six," says Pattie. Typically, no one questions her incongruous explanation. If the Stupids' lives resemble an enviable state of grace, it is largely due to such unconditional acceptance, given and received by one and all, an arrangement that leaves everyone's pet quirks and incorrigible selves blissfully intact.

Among Marshall's recent projects have been picture-book retellings of traditional fairy tales. . . . Approaching these time-honored stories without undue reverence, Marshall has, he says, tried to make them "light but without losing the truth in them." His characteristic solution has been to present his protagonists as players—comic masks—and the stories' backdrops as elaborate stage sets. "The forest in *Red Riding Hood* is meant to look artificial. I don't know why I keep wanting things to look artificial. I guess because the artificial has a much more poetic resonance. Many times my stuff has been called 'cartoony.' I think that's wrong. I think of books as theater—and in theater, the more artificial, the truer it is."

Picture books remain the main focus of his prodigious comic art. As Martha, in a different context, once observed, "It's hard work." For his part, Marshall believes that "it gives people a great sense of well-being to look at a book that is put together well. That alone," he says, "just to be able to do that, is something." (p. 203)

Leonard Marcus, "James Marshall," in Publishers Weekly, *Vol. 236, No. 4, July 28, 1989, pp. 202-03.*

GENERAL COMMENTARY

KICKI MOXON BROWNE

James Marshall could hardly be accused of a deliberate effort to appeal, with his extraordinary squat creatures, tiny eyes set close together. But his stories about the two hippopotamuses George and Martha are very likeable, because the author is instinctively on the same wavelength as children. *George and Martha Rise and Shine* consists of five very short sketches in which the characters come to life beautifully, in a minimum of well chosen words: Martha is bossy, impetuous and inventive, George is boastful, gentle and a little lazy.

We also see James Marshall at work in *Three By the Sea.* a new title in the Bodley Beginners series. It is three short stories within one—three children at a picnic each tell a story involving a cat and a rat. One of the stories is a nice little satire of a traditional reading book: "The rat saw the cat and the dog. 'I see them' said the rat. 'I see the cat and the dog.'" The stilted tone is underlined by some hilarious drawings of the animals posing stiffly and pointing awkwardly at one another.

Kicki Moxon Browne, "On the Right Wavelength," in The Times Literary Supplement, *No. 4121, March 26, 1982, p. 346.*

GEORGE AND MARTHA (1972)

"Five stories about two great friends"—a pair of hippos named George and Martha. The stories are as diminutive as their principals are gross, and there's nothing heavy about the moral verities tucked in among the nonsense. Thus George learns after pouring Martha's pea soup into his loafers (because "I just can't stand another spoonful") that "friends should always tell each other the truth," and when he peeks through Martha's bathroom window she crowns him with the tub to teach him that "there is such a thing as privacy." The pictures—of George trying to roller skate or to ascend in a balloon, of Martha gazing into the mirror—hold up their end of the "lovable blimp" load, and though this George and Martha won't go down in history, they are worth looking in on.

A review of "George and Martha," in Kirkus Reviews, *Vol. XL, No. 6, March 15, 1972, p. 321.*

Five stories about a couple of hippos living together and demonstrating their friendship through scenes that display lively bad taste and some innuendo in showing the stout animals dressed in skirt, slippers and so on, wielding toothbrushes and clumsily simulating humans. Will children smile, will adults be titillated, by these sick little tales and the equally sentimental pictures?

Margery Fisher, in a review of "George and Martha," in Growing Point, *Vol. 13, No. 6, December, 1974, p. 2541.*

Five simple but funny and pertinent stories about the friendship of two endearingly childlike hippos. Marshall has a gimlet eye for the small conflicts that lead to wounded feelings between friends, and for the affectionate honesty that can heal the hurt. The drawings amplify the plot with broad comic details. (p. 258)

Michele Landsberg, in a review of "George and Martha," in her Reading for the Love of It: Best Books for Young Readers, *Prentice Hall Press, 1987, pp. 258-59.*

WHAT'S THE MATTER WITH CARRUTHERS? A BEDTIME STORY (1972)

Carruthers is a grumpy bear, but one of the most lovable characters in many a season of children's picture books. His stanch friends wonder and worry about him in *What's the Matter With Carruthers?*. . . . They serenade him with tuba and tambourine, feed him honey cakes, even take him to an amusement park. Nothing seems to cheer Carruthers till he falls headfirst into a pile of autumn leaves—and his friends finally understand his need to hibernate. Emily and Eugene carry the huge bear to his bed, tuck him in and set the alarm for spring. Ingenuous line drawings, fresh colors and humorous dialogue make this compassionate tale every bit as delightful as Marshall's first book, *George and Martha.*

Ellen Raskin, "Bears and Forebears," in The New York Times Book Review, *December 24, 1972, p. 8.*

Emily and Eugene (a pig and a turtle) can't understand what's wrong with their usually amiable friend Carruthers, a large and gloomy bear. . . . There is humor in the situation, and the text and illustrations share a blithe, ingenuous tone; the story is somewhat weakened, however, by the slightness of the story line.

Zena Sutherland, in a review of "What's the Matter with Carruthers? A Bedtime Story," in Bulletin of the Center for Children's Books, *Vol. 26, No. 7, March, 1973, p. 110.*

YUMMERS! (1972)

Whereas in *George and Martha* Marshall portrayed a pair of loveably blimpy hippopotami without overt reference to their proportions, here he confronts the subjects of overweight and compulsive eating head on. Emily Pig perceives her weight gain as a problem which she resolves to attack with exercise. But when her friend Eugene Turtle suggests a walk Emily turns the outing into an occasion for consuming sandwiches, corn, scones with jam, eskimo pie, cookies, milk, pizza, all sorts of soda fountain concoctions . . . which understandably make her so sick that she has to take a taxi home. "It must have been all that walking" is Emily's explanation. Though they might recognize others here it's unlikely that small children will apply the object lesson to their own exercises in self-deception. Still Marshall carries Emily's gastronomical orgy to such preposterous lengths that even at this level it will be hard to miss the indulgent irony of his closing lines. And Eugene is a model straight man.

A review of "Yummers!" in Kirkus Reviews, *Vol. XLI, No. 3, February 1, 1973, p. 110.*

[After Emily Pig takes a walk, overeats, and gets a stomachache] Eugene drops by to see how she is feeling: "'It must have been all that walking,' replied his friend. Eugene smiled. 'Maybe you should stay in bed and eat plenty of good food.'

'Oh, yummers,' said Emily." The simple, amusing text and pictures make their point painlessly (for readers if not for Emily); children will delight in their superior understanding because poor Emily hasn't yet seen the light as she sits in front of a heaping plate of pancakes.

Marilyn R. Singer, in a review of "Yummers!" in School Library Journal, *Vol. 20, No. 1, September, 1973, p. 115.*

MISS DOG'S CHRISTMAS TREAT (1973)

A tract on dieting in the form of an animal fantasy won't get a glance even from youthful Weight Watchers. *Miss Dog's Christmas Treat* is more trick—what became of the candy canes?—than promised treat. For the eat-drink-and-be-merry season, James Marshall serves up the bland tale of a dog who tries to put the bite on her sweet tooth by stashing the confections she craves. Of course, the exercise Miss Dog gets finding hiding places makes her hungry; she seeks out and compulsively consumes all the candy she'd been saving for friends—except for a box of candy canes her tail had swept from tabletop to the interior of a vase. Any fun in figuring that out or in the author-artist's whimsical red, green, and mustard illustrations is outweighed by the book's "for shame" attitude and the flimsiness of the gimmick. What separates this from Marshall's winning portrayal of another overeater, Emily Pig, is the difference between *Yummers!* and bummers!

From Miss Nelson Is Missing! *by Harry Allard and James Marshall.*

Pamela D. Pollack, in a review of "Miss Dog's Christmas Treat," in School Library Journal, *Vol. 20, No. 2, October, 1973, p. 96.*

The theme is Christmas, and the illustrations echo it, but the story really could be a gentle lesson in sharing at any time of year; what weakens the story is that it is neither an effective lesson nor a funny one, so that the slight plot seems pointless—yet the book has a pleasant style and the triple appeals of animals, Christmas, and gorging on candy.

Zena Sutherland, in a review of "Miss Dog's Christmas Treat," in Bulletin of the Center for Children's Books, *Vol. 27, No. 6, February, 1974, p. 98.*

GEORGE AND MARTHA ENCORE (1973)

Children will enjoy viewing another round of *George and Martha*, as the hippos, for all their apparent weight, daintily romp through pages decorated in pen-and-ink and light watercolors. Unfortunately, the highs and lows of hippopotami friendship portrayed in most of the five slight stories are less amusing in this sequel. Such pronouncements as " . . . George never said 'I told you so.' Because that's not what friends are for." and " 'I would much rather have a friend like you than all the gardens in the world.' " would make more sense to older children, but even the youngest will cotton to the visual humor created by a hippo disguised as an Indian, doing a Mexican Hat Dance, taking a Swan dive, or sick in bed with a sun burn.

Susan Roth Morris, in a review of "George and Martha Encore," in School Library Journal, *Vol. 20, No. 3, November, 1973, p. 42.*

What is there about James Marshall . . . and his style that invites not just laughter but exegesis? If last year's *George and Martha* and *What's the Matter With Carruthers?* were about vanity and sloth respectively, and if *Yummers!* is—surprise—about gluttony, then for *George and Martha Encore* that would seem to leave a choice of four of the seven mildly deadly sins. George does plant a smooch on Martha's hippo cheek. Can *this* be lechery?

"Tee-hee," says Martha.

In his earlier appearance, you will remember, George tripped skating and broke his favorite tooth. With his buttercup-golden one he is, in Martha's word, distinguished, and, elegant as ever, continues to live on an apparent independent income. Some Marshall animals do work, mostly in the food trades or in transportation, and of course George's dentist Buck McTooth, D.D. (Doctor of Divinity?) is a professional; but so far the vocation of the main characters has been for friendship. . . .

Like their fellow-Americans, Marshall animals believe in culture, recreation and perfectibility. Emily and Eugene play musical instruments, joyfully, loudly and badly. George and Martha not only dance, but, suitably costumed, they also swim and learn French. Each episode is a blend of formality and farce, kindliness and foolishness. In response to the compliment, "My, how lovely your fur looks today," Carruthers the bear once remarked, "I've never cared for it." Here, when in her literalness, Martha unwittingly demolishes one of George's fantasies, her apology is: "I would never have recognized you if it hadn't been for your bright smiling eyes." The poky polka dot eyes being roughly a constant, it probably takes a hippo to know when hippo eyes are smiling; but since George and Martha are more real and for that matter more comprehensible than my neighbors, this is as plausible as the illustration that indicates that while he droops, George happens to be perched on a swing.

> *Nora L. Magid, "Formality and Farce," in* The New York Times Book Review, *November 18, 1973, p. 8.*

The humour of this book revolves around the nature of the characters—hippos—and the unsuitability of their activities. These include learning ballet, learning French ('voolay-voo mom-brars-ay'), and gardening. Each page of text contains no more than half-a-dozen lines of simple words, but is accompanied by a whole-page illustration, which both partners and marvellously adds to the stories. Children will be enchanted by a hippo in a leotard, doing barre-practice, and another of his female companion languishing in bed with sunstroke, while her formidable friend, George, stands solicitously by, determinedly not 'telling her so'. (pp. 222, 225)

> *Gabrielle Maunder, in a review of "George and Martha Encore," in* The School Librarian, *Vol. 24, No. 3, September, 1976, pp. 222, 225.*

THE STUPIDS STEP OUT (with Harry Allard, 1974)

Allard's deadpan delivery leaves the clowning to the slapstick cartoons. Marshall, with his keen sense of kids' humor, will do almost anything for a laugh—the dog inexplicably wears an Indian headdress; Grandpa dodders around in a sailor suit on backwards. Although his faces are familiar (Mrs. S. is a dead ringer for the dot-eyed, potato-nosed Mama in **All the Way Home** [written by Lore Segal and illustrated by Marshall] and the Stupids' décor looks a lot like the hippo home in **George and Martha Encore,** the humor is fresh and flipped-out, e.g., the framed paintings of flowers, boats, etc. are all idiotically mistitled. Even youngest listeners will laugh with smug superiority as they follow these good-natured *dumbkopfs* from departure time to journey's end (flopping into bed, the Stupids fall asleep the second their feet hit the pillows).

> *Jane Abramson, in a review of "The Stupids Step Out," in* School Library Journal, *Vol. 20, No. 8, April, 1974, p. 48.*

We've met them in folklore as sillies or dumkopfs but, in truth, survival as folklore would require more of a story than Allard provides to link his string of moron jokes. Some of the behavior of Stanley Q. Stupid and family has the logical sort of absurdity found in traditional foolishness—the children climb onto the lower end of the banister and wonder why they don't slide up, and they take a dry bath together fully dressed ("if we fill up the tub, our clothes will get wet"), but much of this is indeed on the level of kids' top-of-the-head humor that they themselves call stupid—Mrs. Stupid wears the cat for a hat, Mr. Stupid wears his new socks on his ears, and they all eat mashed potato sundaes. Even Marshall seems at a loss for his own organic kind of whimsy or any interesting variety, but he does make the best of it by putting Grandfather in a little boy's sailor suit, mislabeled pictures on the wall, etc. And then that last shot of the Supids "all tucked into bed" with five pairs of feet (one pair is the dog's) sticking out from the top end of the blanket should send children off

laughing. In short, though one feels that the Stupids are not performing up to their potential, they deserve a chance.

> *A review of "The Stupids Step Out," in* Kirkus Reviews, *Vol. XLII, No. 7, April 1, 1974, p. 359.*

In this best of all possible worlds, if it's not nice to fool Mother Nature, it's certainly not nice to refer to anyone as stupid. Still, it's a favorite kid term, and these particular Stupids are so safe, snug and amiable in their context as to make the condition enviable. Harry Allard's minimal text is amplified by the Marshall illustrations. . . . [The] wonderful Stupid dog Kitty looks like a relative of the Stupid children. (As Marshall says, "My children look like my animals. I just transpose the little dots.") The Stupid's grandfather wears a child's sailor suit and after a lovely visit says, "Come again, whoever you are." The Stupids, in their modest fling, are notably cordial and considerate as well as dense, and their standards of decorum are high.

> *Nora L. Magid, in a review of "The Stupids Step Out," in* The New York Times Book Review, *May 5, 1974, p. 19.*

The Stupid's Step Out won't ruffle adult sensibilities, but it too employs a finger-pointing form of humor that proper grownups have put behind them. In an original story that draws on the dummkopf-moron tradition still being revamped and handed on from child to child like ancient skiprope rhymes, the Stanley Q. Stupids wear cats on their heads or socks on their ears, eat mashed potato sundaes, take a family bath in a dry tub so as not to get their clothes wet, and tuck themselves head first into bed with their feet on the pillows. The Stupids will of course make even stumbling new readers look brilliant, and it's already clear that James Marshall's quirky childlike illustrations—full of mislabeled paintings, misplaced provisions (jam and tuna in the bathroom soap rack) and incongruous costumes—are breaking them up.

> *Sada Fretz, in a review of "The Stupids Step Out," in* Book World—The Washington Post, *May 19, 1974, p. 4.*

WILLIS (1974)

All that unhappy Willis, a sort of potbellied crocagator, needs to cheer him up is a pair of sunglasses so that he can open his eyes and take in the fun on the beautiful beach, but though his new friends Bird, Snake, and Lobster are eager to help, they can only come up with ten cents toward the 29¢ glasses. To raise the difference, Marshall's unlikely and, it would seem, inept quartet bungle through a number of jobs and money raising projects: then when lethargic Lobster wakes up long enough to remind the others that "everyone is good for something and you will always be good at what you like to do most," the four friends are inspired to get up a talent show that earns them enough for sunglasses all round. Again the buoyant blimpiness of Marshall's open-hearted creatures is paralleled in the disarmingly goofy delivery of his message.

> *A review of "Willis," in* Kirkus Reviews, *Vol. XLII, No. 17, September 1, 1974, p. 940.*

The green, blue, and orange illustrations wittily depict Willis (in bathing cap and trunks) and his entertaining friends. A pleasant picture book, the only drawback is that the story is too long for reading aloud and the difficult vocabulary is beyond just-beginning readers.

Kristin E. Hammond, in a review of "Willis," in School Library Journal, *Vol. 21, No. 2, October, 1974, p. 106.*

THE GUEST (1975)

Maurice and Mona aren't the perfectly matched couple that *George and Martha* were. Maurice is a snail with a shocking pink shell, and Mona is . . . well, no one ever says what Mona is, but she looks like a moose in hippo's clothing. Of course they share the same sort of endearing friendship George and Martha had, with the affecting difference being the size disproportion between big, lonely Mona and tiny Maurice as they play hide and seek, cook (Maurice's favorite hobby) and share their French toast breakfast. Then Maurice disappears and Mona is disconsolate until he returns with his new family—Jean Pierre, Brigitte, Monique, etc. etc.—in tow. One would think that all those new arrivals might throw a wrench into even the most perfect friendship, and sunny harmony here is a bit thick. This is patently a variation on Marshall's last successful matchmaking job, though as usual his cheerfully costumed blimps make a visual splash.

A review of "The Guest," in Kirkus Reviews, *Vol. XLIII, No. 8, April 15, 1975, p. 447.*

Not as hilarious as other Marshalls—more of a smile than a laugh. But the illustrations of huge Mona in assorted smart skirts and dainty pumps and Maurice carrying his house on his back like a piece of pink bubble gum are delicious. (p. 49)

Marjorie Lewis, in a review of "The Guest," in School Library Journal, *Vol. 21, No. 9, May, 1975, pp. 48-9.*

A lightweight tale of hippo-ish, moosey Mona and her snail friend Maurice. . . . The pictures, jolly as usual, are done in pink, grey, green, and yellow. At his worst, Marshall is mildly funny and comfortingly logical—still better than mediocre. But perhaps his inspirational snail has left him, and, like the moosopotamus' boss, we feel constrained to say "You're getting sloppy, Mona."

A review of "The Guest," in The Booklist, *Vol. 71, No. 20, June 15, 1975, p. 1076.*

FOUR LITTLE TROUBLES (1975; includes *Eugene; Sing Out, Irene; Snake: His Story; Someone Is Talking about Hortense*)

[*Someone Is Talking about Hortense was written by Laurette Murdock.*]

With indifferently reproduced three color drawings and soft paper covers, this boxed package of four puny variations on a minimal theme is better suited to toting to the sandbox than returning to the library. In *Eugene* a turtle just starting school finds that the "real meanie" of a teacher he's been warned against is really the kind lady he saved from a bug just that morning; in *Sing Out Irene* a bulldog finds that being cast as a toadstool in the spring pageant is special after all, for all the other children are flowers who can't be told apart; in *Snake* the title character uses his ability to hear, which had made him unhappily different from his peers, to

foil a bank robbery; and in *Someone Is Talking About Hortense* a white raccoon, upset about her friends' secretive behavior finds out most predictably of all that they've been planning her birthday party. But it takes more than furnishing all the dumpy looking animals with clothes and cozy homes to make these very little fabrications worth the trouble.

A review of "Four Little Troubles," in Kirkus Reviews, *Vol. XLIII, No. 20, October 15, 1975, p. 1177.*

A box of four tiny paperbacks illustrated and bound in the author-artist's familiar orange-lemon-and-lime palette. Each story conveys that sense of kindness and good humor which are as characteristic of Marshall as his fruit basket colors. . . . It seems mean to quibble with so pleasant a package, but pleasantries alone are not the stuff of which good stories are made. Probably conceived as an item for the Christmas stocking trade, *Four Little Troubles* is too flimsy in content and format for library consumption.

Janet French, in a review of "Four Little Troubles," in School Library Journal, *Vol. 22, No. 4, December, 1975, p. 48.*

SPEEDBOAT (1976)

Just when we'd had it with both easy-reading animal friendships and James Marshall's schleppy creatures, along come Jasper Raisintoast and Jack Tweedy-Jones, canine companions of complementary dispositions and discrete charms. While Tweedy-Jones, the homebody, stays behind (though his day does have its "ups and downs," as he puts it later without mentioning the bubblegum bubble that carried him into the sky), rip-roaring Raisintoast is off making a racket in his speedboat. You can't help feeling gratified when the stew he cadges turns out to be laundry water, when a mean, mustached lady (beaver) demands a kiss as a bridge toll, and especially when, showing off more recklessly than usual, he is at last waved in to join the "lovely creature" for whom he's performing—who then introduces herself as Sheriff Mackenzie and writes out tickets for "river speeding, foolishness and disturbing the peace of the river." But you can be sure that Raisintoast will rally . . . and ride right over Mole and Troll, Gus and Buster, and all those other poor copies of the matchless Frog and Toad.

A review of "Speedboat," in Kirkus Reviews, *Vol. XLIV, No. 4, February 15, 1976, p. 198.*

The plot meanders like an abandoned ship, but Marshall does well at setting up opportunities for open-faced slapstick. As usual, his two-color pictures catch, however carelessly, the tickle in the tale.

Judith Goldberger, in a review of "Speedboat," in The Booklist, *Vol. 72, No. 18, May 15, 1976, p. 1338.*

GEORGE AND MARTHA RISE AND SHINE (1976)

George and Martha, friendly hippopotamuses whose daily actions culminate in minor epiphanies, return in five vignettes corresponding roughly to vaudeville sketches. The appeal of this whimsical hippo couple who tame snakes, watch scary movies, and plan surprises increases with acquaintance: so wise, unpretentious, and filled with love is this pair that they unobtrusively instill an understanding of true companionship. The illustrations, predominately in yellows, greens, and maroons provide a gentle, homey feel.

> *Allene Stuart Phy, in a review of "George and Martha Rise and Shine," in* School Library Journal, *Vol. 23, No. 2, October, 1976, p. 100.*

George and Martha, James Marshall's irrepressible hippopotamus friends, are back in *George and Martha Rise and Shine.* The story lines are thin in these five episodes, but it's hard not to love the hefty pair, who show how good it is to have a friend, someone to hold your hand or be a secret fan. Where James Marshall really shines is at the drawing board.

> *Barbara Karlin, in a review of "George and Martha Rise and Shine," in* The New York Times Book Review, *November 14, 1976, p. 39.*

MISS NELSON IS MISSING! (with Harry Allard, 1977)

Miss Nelson's class takes advantage of her leniency by misbehaving—"They were even rude during storyhour." Then Miss Nelson disappears and is replaced by the strict Miss Swamp (really Miss Nelson in disguise). The kids get their beloved teacher back after they learn their lesson. The story is not up to the standard of broad humor set by Allard and Marshall's *The Stupids Step Out* and the off-beat pictures lack the dash of *George and Martha.* But, a classroom of Marshall's leering, lumpish kids flying paper airplanes is still good fun.

> *Andrew K. Stevenson, in a review of "Miss Nelson Is Missing," in* School Library Journal, *Vol. 23, No. 8, April, 1977, p. 52.*

What is not necessary here, it seems to me, is that this book be so large in size, have color illustrations and cost so much. The story itself is pleasantly modest and gentle. . . . This is a story whose humor and moralizing are unpretentiously low-key, and it should have been placed in a less pretentious setting. At about half its size, *Miss Nelson Is Missing* could have been swell. But such overblown productions aren't necessary.

> *A review of "Miss Nelson Is Missing!" in* The New York Times Book Review, *April 17, 1977, p. 51.*

Humor and suspense fill the pages of *Miss Nelson Is Missing.*

The mystery of Miss Nelson's disappearance is helped along not at all by Detective McSmogg. Other characters have names that would have been the envy of Charles Dickens.

On one page I found the drawings a treat and the text great. Then I turned the page to find the drawings great, and the text a treat.

Appreciation of teachers shines through it all with imagination and great good humor.

> *Gene Langley, "The Care and Feeding of Hippos" in* The Christian Science Monitor, *May 4, 1977, p. B4.*

A SUMMER IN THE SOUTH (1977)

Marshall's first "novel" for young readers, a kookie murder mystery, is more like an extended easy reader, with no pretense to the dimension you'd associate with the label even at this level. It takes place at a summer hotel visited by disagreeable Foster Pig, complaining Don Coyote, detective Eleanor Owl and her cat assistant Mr. Paws, Miss Marietta Chicken from the circus, and a family of "cooties" who arrive in the mail in envelope number two. (Envelope number one contains a note alerting the turkey proprietor to their presence.) There's not much interaction, and the only mystery consists of strange sights and sounds that begin shortly after the arrival of four unmusical female baboons who check in as a string quartet. What are they up to? Eleanor, enlisting the cooties as spies, discovers that the baboons are seeking a treasure stolen from the Egyptian King Kluck whose tomb they guard; all that's left, then, is to pick out the perpetrator of an offstage, previously accomplished crime—and Eleanor shortly fingers the hotel's rotten cook and maid-of-all-work, a goose named Maxine. To us it seems more thin than whacky; perhaps a young reader in the summer sun would reverse the judgment. (pp. 1144-45)

> *A review of "A Summer in the South," in* Kirkus Reviews, *Vol. XLV, No. 21, November 1, 1977, pp. 1144-45.*

Marshall has elated lovers of nonsense, young and old, with his hit picture books. Now he has brought off his first novel, a hilarious mystery. The fun comes partly from the author's deadpan narration and partly from his comic cartoons. . . . The end of the story is a real zinger.

> *A review of "A Summer in the South," in* Publishers Weekly, *Vol. 212, No. 22, November 28, 1977, p. 51.*

The satire in *A Summer in the South* is somewhat . . . sophisticated and this book might be best read aloud (perhaps during a wet seaside holiday) to an assortment of children from seven or so upwards. The point of the book is to present human types in animal guise—a snob as Foster the aristocratic pig, Don Coyote a boring hypochondriac, a scatty goose as cook in the turkey's seaside boarding house. . . . The story, extended in sections and enlivened by snappy dialogue, keeps the suspense right up to the last pages, while black and white illustrations in a style reminiscent of Steig's help to establish the points of character which are, in a way, the vital part of a most accomplished romp.

> *Margery Fisher, in a review of "A Summer in the South," in* Growing Point, *Vol. 18, No. 2, July, 1979, p. 3543.*

THE STUPIDS HAVE A BALL (with Harry Allard, 1978)

Unlike *The Stupids Step Out,* the family's second appearance is less consistently a string of moron jokes than a mixture of dumb behavior, odd taste, and bad puns; but there's no doubt that they're as stupid as ever. To celebrate the children's straight-F report cards, Mr. and Mrs. Stupid invite their relatives to a costume ball. ("Oh dear," says Mrs. Stupid, "I don't know how to spell cousin Dottie Stupid's last name.") Mr. Stupid goes as General George Washing Machine, his wife wears "beautiful" spaghetti, the dog is dressed in a Bone Ranger cape, and the visiting relatives look even stranger. (Grandfather Stupid, dressed as the Easter Bunny and carrying a pumpkin, comes down the chimney with a "Ho ho ho.") The big joke—" 'Oh dear,' said Mrs. Stupid. 'I forgot to mention that it would be a costume ball! The other Stupids came

From The Stupids Have a Ball, *by Harry Allard and James Marshall.*

in their everyday clothes.' " More groaners for the Stupids' guaranteed following.

> *A review of "The Stupids Have a Ball," in* Kirkus Reviews, *Vol. XLVI, No. 6, March 15, 1978, p. 297.*

Marshall's watercolor cartoons—of Mother at the door with each foot firmly planted in a bucket or with spaghetti wrapped around herself for a mummy costume; Mr. Stupid dressed as General George Washing Machine; the family cat blowing up party balloons—aid and abet the zany, incongruous goings-on. Children who appreciate slapstick situations and nonsensical word plays (Grandfather Stupid compliments his dancing partner: "You sure can polka, Dot.") will find the book a lark.

> *Judith Kronick, in a review of "The Stupids Have a Ball," in* School Library Journal, *Vol. 24, No. 8, April, 1978, p. 65.*

I have to stipulate at the beginning that I am a pushover for James Marshall's cheerfully stolid drawings. . . . What gossip columnist could describe the Stupids' lovely home, adorned with such works of art as "Mount Stupid," a masterful rendering of a flat green field, and helpful signs like, "Please Don't Lick the Walls"? I would much rather linger

with the Stupids than deal seriously with the other . . . books reviewed here—and if I were a 6-year-old, by gosh, I would.

> *Georgess McHargue, in a review of "The Stupids Have a Ball," in* The New York Times Book Review, *May 21, 1978, p. 25.*

___

GEORGE AND MARTHA, ONE FINE DAY (1978)

Another quintet of minitales, filled out by the blimpy shapes of Marshall's inseparable hippopotami. During the course of one day George learns to encourage Martha at her tightrope walking (a typical Marshall stunt), not to tell icky stories at the table (she can retaliate with worse), and that if snooping won't get him a look in her diary, neither will a polite request. The last two tales are impishly paired: first, George scares Martha with a BOO and waits on edge all day for her revenge . . . and she gets it that night at the amusement park in the darkened tunnel of love. " 'Have mercy!' screamed George." Another winner.

> *A review of "George and Martha One Fine Day," in* Kirkus Reviews, *Vol. XLVI, No. 17, September 1, 1978, p. 947.*

When a genre, or mode, or type of story establishes itself with a readership, a given example's fidelity to that form becomes a matter of virtue to its admirers. This is another George and Martha book; and it is every bit as agreeable as its predecessors.

> *Joan W. Blos, in a review of "George and Martha One Fine Day," in* School Library Journal, *Vol. 25, No. 2, October, 1978, p. 136.*

[*Turtle Spring* by Lillian Hoban] is full of amusing touches which help to overcome any trace of coyness. The same is true for **George and Martha One Fine Day.** There is no good reason why two hippopotamuses behaving like a small boy and girl should be comic, but it is so; there is a Babar-like quality to the incongruity of these short tales of the tricks the two play on one another, with Martha always having the last word.

> *Ann Martin, "The Morality of the Menagerie," in* The Times Literary Supplement, *No. 4086, July 24, 1981, p. 841.*

PORTLY McSWINE (1979)

"What if my party isn't amusing enough? . . . What if my refreshments aren't tasty enough? . . . What if my dancing isn't up to snuff?" And finally, waiting in his top hat, white tie, tails, and bare pig feet, "What if no one comes?" Portly needn't worry of course; his guests charge in like the pigs they are and head straight for the food—leaving their host, when it's over, with an even greater worry: "What if next year's party isn't so good as this year's?" The concept is as lightweight as the hero isn't, but Portly's anxious behavior and his visions of disaster make him a perfect target for Marshall's familiar treatment. Fetchingly ludicrous.

> *A review of "Portly McSwine," in* Kirkus Reviews, *Vol. XLVII, No. 6, March 15, 1979, p. 324.*

Although there's a modicum of humor in the situation, it never changes or develops; while the writing style is adequate, there's little action, most of the story being devoted to Portly's fussing. The illustrations are mildly amusing, but a bit repetitive. (p. 197)

> *Zena Sutherland, in a review of "Portly McSwine," in* Bulletin of the Center for Children's Books, *Vol. 32, No. 11, July-August, 1979, pp. 196-97.*

A sub-acid commentary on human nature, whose point may or may not be clear to the children who are drawn to the robust cartoon-style of the fable. A socially conscious pig worries over the party he is giving, brushing off the gallant attempts of his secretary to reassure him. . . . Chalk and pencil suit the broad joke but I find the book brash beside the subtleties of William Steig's somewhat similar use of animal fable. (pp. 3907-08)

> *Margery Fisher, in a review of "Portly McSwine," in* Growing Point, *Vol. 21, No. 1, May, 1982, pp. 3907-08.*

JAMES MARSHALL'S MOTHER GOOSE (1979)

There are too many Mother Gooses. No, I don't mean on the market (though that's probably true, too), I mean in my house. I can think of five or six offhand, and James Marshall's new version makes no claim to being bigger, more historic,

more comprehensive or a funnier shape than any other. Why, then, make room for this one?

For one thing, it's my hypothesis that Mother Goose illustrations have to help immunize the reading-aloud grown-up from succumbing to an attack of screaming during the umpteenth command performance of "Hey, Diddle Diddle" or "To Market, to Market." Therefore, you may find it useful to defend yourself against boredom with an Elsie Marley who peeps nervously from under the bedclothes at a windowful of irate, unfed swine, or a tongue-twisting swan who swims over the sea to receive her accolade ("Well swum, swan!") from none other than a jowly Queen Victoria. One might also note that by my highly informal count, 16 of the 34 rhymes in this book do not appear in any of the other collections I happen to have. The main point, though, is that many people think James Marshall is just plain funny and though this may not be his funniest book, it's still funnier than many or even most Mother Gooses. And that ought to be enough.

> *Georgess McHargue, in a review of "James Marshall's Mother Goose," in* The New York Times Book Review, *December 2, 1979, p. 41.*

Although numerous editions of Mother Goose have appeared over the years, James Marshall's will need no defense. In his inimitable style he has filled the pages with a hilarious and memorable cast of characters. Peter pumpkin eater's wife is about to escape from her pumpkin shell, a hefty pig awaits a shave in the barber's chair while reading a copy of *Snout and Stream,* Queen Victoria congratulates the swan who "swam over the sea," and an intent Betty Botter vigorously beats her batter. Many familiar verses are included as well as a few lesser known, and the illustrator seems to have contributed his own variant of **"Hey diddle diddle."** Reds, yellows, and greens predominate in the pictures, most of which are framed in squares, rectangles, or circles. The book is a subtle and funny treatment of traditional material in which the characters—whether animal or human—tell stories all their own.

> *Karen M. Klockner, in a review of "James Marshall's Mother Goose," in* The Horn Book Magazine, *Vol. LVI, No. 1, February, 1980, p. 48.*

Many very familiar rhymes are included here, but the chief attraction of this collection is the many rhymes and verses which are not so often quoted, and which do not appear so frequently in collections of this kind. The illustrations of human faces are less appealing than those of the animals, and the repetitive use of pinks, greens and yellows is effective.

> *B. Clark, in a review of "Mother Goose," in* The Junior Bookshelf, *Vol. 45, No. 2, April 1, 1981, p. 72.*

TROLL COUNTRY (1980)

The matter-of-fact looniness James Marshall is famous for fits Edward Marshall's spacey story to a tee-hee. Drawings overlaid with russet and green tones illustrate the story of little Elsie Fay Johnson, fond of reading about trolls. When Mrs. Johnson tells about meeting and fooling a troll when she was a child, her husband pooh-poohs the recital, as usual. "Trolls don't exist!" he declares. Then Elsie Fay goes off on an errand and takes a short-cut through Troll Country where she meets the same troll her mother had outsmarted years earlier. Using a ploy of her own, Elsie Fay escapes and comes home with a memento of Mrs. Johnson's unforgotten encounter—proof that butters no parsnips with Mr. Johnson. He still insists trolls don't exist. The book is a delightful addition to the fine Dial Easy-to-Read line.

A review of "Troll Country," in Publishers Weekly, *Vol. 217, No. 8, February 29, 1980, p. 136.*

Though somewhat long-winded, the author handles a limited vocabulary well while providing enough kick to a time-honored subject to keep things rolling. . . . Conversation with the troll is droll, and James Marshall exercises his usual ability to tickle readers (though they may wonder why the "odd little man" is at least a head taller than anyone else).

Judith Goldberger, in a review of "Troll Country," in Booklist, *Vol. 76, No. 16, April 15, 1980, p. 1211.*

Although weakened by a diffuse ending, this is simply written for the beginning independent reader, is mildly humorous, and has the appeal of any story in which a child outwits another creature. . . . Not substantial, but mildly amusing.

Zena Sutherland, in a review of "Troll Country," in Bulletin of the Center for Children's Books, *Vol. 33, No. 11, July-August, 1980, p. 219.*

GEORGE AND MARTHA, TONS OF FUN (1980)

In this latest George and Martha quintet, the gold-toothed George is still trying to tell the truth at the risk of offending Martha; but she gets over it by playing her saxophone. Then she tries to reform his sweet tooth by threatening to take up cigar smoking. And George is still stomping on her vanity: she gives him a photo of herself that thrills her with its beauty, while George only sees the humorous side to it. Since the original *George and Martha,* there have been slight changes in the presentation: the text is briefer and has more punch; the shapes of the drawings and their arrangement on the pages seem more sophisticated; but the pictures still have their endearing buoyancy, which is ironic considering the title—*Tons of Fun*—and the characters—hippopotami.

Marilyn R. Singer, in a review of "George and Martha, Tons of Fun," in School Library Journal, *Vol. 27, No. 2, October, 1980, p. 137.*

Misunderstandings, twinges of guilt, petty deceptions, and the loss of a birthday gift are winningly overcome in this latest set of five brief tales about Marshall's ludicrously buoyant hippos. Marshall must have had great fun dreaming up poses for the two: George in fuzzy slippers raiding the refrigerator, Martha smoking an ugly cigar as a counter to his overeating, Martha eating up all the cookies while perched atop the repentant George, the two of them overhanging the seat of a playground merry-go-round. Best of all is the photography-booth photo Martha has taken in story number three. "I've never looked prettier," says Martha of the odd, cut-off snout shot. But the last story ends with her joining George in a laugh at the picture. "She saw that the photograph was pretty funny after all"—a concession that pretty well illustrates why this picture-book friendship endures.

A review of "George and Martha, Tons of Fun," in Kirkus Reviews, *Vol. XLVIII, No. 20, October 15, 1980, p. 1352.*

The five stories are short and dumb, the illustrations utterly uniform, but there's a lazy good humor to the large floating

gray shapes—though I doubt we can take many more of the series. Whatever psychosocial hippo dynamic existed in the first books is missing from the recent ones. Mr. Marshall ought to give the beasts a rest; an uninspired hippo is a sad thing to behold. (pp. 49, 64)

Harold C. K. Rice, in a review of "George and Martha, Tons of Fun," in The New York Times Book Review, *November 9, 1980, pp. 49, 64.*

SPACE CASE (1980)

Featuring a cast of appealing and zany characters limned in expressive cartoonlike drawings overlaid with bright colors, the story adds an unexpected fillip to conventional Halloween fare. A round-eyed creature from outer space arrives during the annual trek of the trick-or-treat brigade, whose members assume that its natural shape is simply a great costume. Adapting readily to native customs, the "thing" quickly learns the magic phrase and becomes a participant in the evening's revelry. Hankering after more loot, it follows a boy home, much to his delight, and the next day accompanies him to school, where the children skillfully manage to preserve the stranger's secret. The open ending of the brief story is as satisfying as it is original, for the small space traveler is thoroughly childlike in its insouciance, curiosity, and concern for self-gratification. The text is an economical, tongue-in-cheek accompaniment to the various levels of humor depicted in the illustrations. Transcending the particular holiday, the picture book should be a marvelous vehicle for story hours.

Mary M. Burns, in a review of "Space Case," in The Horn Book Magazine, *Vol. LVI, No. 5, October, 1980, p. 509.*

The spare, matter-of-fact text is expanded by the artist's typically zany, vividly hued cartoons, full of details and sight gags. A fun story reminiscent of Allard and Marshall's *Miss Nelson Is Missing!* that should be as popular as the illustrator's other books—especially with a character like something from *Star Wars.*

Elaine Fort Weischedel, in a review of "Space Case," in School Library Journal, *Vol. 27, No. 4, December, 1980, p. 54.*

The combination of a favorite holiday and an outer space visitor will no doubt appeal to the read-aloud audience, but they may find the ending a bit flat and inconclusive. The story is adequately told and has humor (as do the bright, simply drawn and colored illustrations) but even within the parameters of a fantasy, it isn't quite believable that most of the characters, children or adults, express little interest or curiosity—let alone disbelief—at the appearance of a yellow dome with antennae that walks, talks, and does mathematical calculations at the blackboard when it visits school.

Zena Sutherland, in a review of "Space Case," in Bulletin of the Center for Children's Books, *Vol. 34, No. 7, March, 1981, p. 136.*

THE STUPIDS DIE (with Harry Allard, 1981)

This hilarious picture book has nothing to do with actual death; the Stupids *assume* they're dead when the lights go off one evening, leaving just their beady, roaming eyes visible in the darkness. It's a good thing their dog and cat know how to change fuses; they return things to "normal," much to the disappointment of Petunia. " 'Oh, heck, I'm going to bed,' " she says, and we last see the family serenely snoozing *under* the bed, near a framed picture of beach balls, entitled "The Pyramids." With Mrs. Stupid going a step beyond punk to wear a dress made of live chickens, their antics are sure to please. Excellent pacing, concise, witty prose and artwork perfectly suited to the (" 'cluck, cluck' ") text.

> *Sally Holmes Holtze, in a review of "The Stupids Die," in* School Library Journal, *Vol. 27, No. 6, February, 1981, p. 53.*

The Stupids are at their best—or worst, if you see it that way—in this ultrasilly string of one-liners. The loose, nonsensical plot has the Stupids thinking they've died when their house lights go out and gone to heaven when they come back on. Jokes along the way range from being genuinely funny to terribly flat—so flat that you laugh anyway. There's a dash of adultish humor: "Oh, wow!" say the Stupid kids constantly; and when Grandfather Stupid stops by and is welcomed into heaven, he replies, "This isn't heaven. . . . This is Cleveland." The pictures are in typical Marshall style and have plenty of visual gags to augment the text's humor.

> *Denise M. Wilms, in a review of "The Stupids Die," in* Booklist, *Vol. 77, No. 14, March 15, 1981, p. 1025.*

THREE BY THE SEA (1981)

Sam, Spider and Lolly—who, with her harlequin sunglasses and avant-garde bathing bloomers looks like the lead singer in a punk rock band—are spending the day on an idyllic tropical beach. Too full from hot dogs and lemonade to go swimming and disgusted by the idea of napping, they tell each other stories. The boys dismiss Lolly's story as "dull," and Sam's story rates a "very sweet" and a "dumb" from his harsh critics. (It shows you what adults know: A small rat making a pet of a huge cat, who sweetly holds his tail à la the Cowardly Lion, is my idea of fun.) Spider, determined to best his friends, conjures up a monster who tiptoes around a highly familiar beach looking for kids to slap between two slices of toast for a quick lunch.

Three by the Sea hardly ranks with "The Monkey's Paw" in the scary campfire department, but it's a lot funnier. The beach vignettes—for instance, the greased-up rat playing the slob conked out on a towel surrounded by litter—are grand, but James Marshall's eccentrically simple drawings may remind some readers of art found hanging on proud parents' refrigerator doors.

> *Susan Bolotin, in a review of "Three by the Sea," in* The New York Times Book Review, *May 3, 1981, p. 40.*

What fun, within an easy reader, to find a story that pokes fun at easy readers. . . . The mild lunacy of the illustrations (an almost vertical hill, a neatly striped cat) with their ungainly, comical figures is nicely matched with the bland directness of the writing. This is good-humored and amusing, good practice for the beginning reader, and unusual in its presentation of storytelling within the story.

> *Zena Sutherland, in a review of "Three by the Sea," in* Bulletin of the Center for Children's Books, *Vol. 34, No. 10, June, 1981, p. 199.*

I cannot help but laugh every time I open *Three by the sea.* In this witty send-up of the banality of many reading schemes, Lolly's friends demonstrate their skill at storytelling, using the same characters as those in her reader—a cat and a rat—but supplying the vital ingredients: humour, suspense, and a touch of irony. A book to be read by teachers as much as by children.

> *A review of "Three by the Sea," in* The School Librarian, *Vol. 30, No. 4, December, 1982, p. 321.*

TAKING CARE OF CARRUTHERS (1981)

Marshall begins with Eugene the turtle, who's written a story, reading it to grumpy Carruthers the bear. And Eugene's story begins when a seasick swan gives Marshall's three old friends her rowboat in return for a ride on Emily the pig's motorcycle. And so Carruthers, Emily, and Eugene set off down the river, stopping for tea with famous cookbook author Ambrosia Suet, running into a number of nefarious characters as they row through Skunk County ("Very few Skunk County folks can be trusted," reads the guide book, "for they are profoundly greedy, mean, and hateful"), and stopping off in Stupendousberg where Carruthers is a big hit as replacement for the sick Baby Bear in a Goldilocks production. The return trip nicely ties up all the early encounters that had seemed like throwaway loose ends. And that's about all it takes to fit the wiggy, free-floating charm of Marshall's picture books to a longer come-what-may riverboat jaunt. A restorative tonic for the grumpiest bear.

> *A review of "Taking Care of Carruthers," in* Kirkus Reviews, *Vol. L, No. 1, January 1, 1982, p. 3.*

Carruthers, in James Marshall's charming little book, is a bear. I mention this, together with the fact that Emily is a pig and Eugene a turtle, because their animal-ness is not emphasized in the text. Reading the story hastily and ignoring the pictures—but how could you?—you might think it a rather episodic tale of human adventures. In the words there is a quiet humour and a gentle irony. The sheer fun comes in the author's own strongly simplified illustrations. Never were word and picture more closely complementary. Admittedly some of the jokes are of a sophisticated kind, but listening children will pick up most of them, and they will be a welcome bonus to a reading-aloud parent.

> *M. Crouch, in a review of "Taking Care of Carruthers," in* The Junior Bookshelf, *Vol. 47, No. 6, December, 1983, p. 247.*

Any book whose characters include a pig called Emily, a turtle called Eugene and a bear called Carruthers is in difficulties. I have trouble suspending disbelief from the start and there had better be something there to make it worth the trouble. . . .

Everyone has a funny name, there is a lot of food about, the illustrations are frequent and naive, the print large and the chapters short. Children of an age to read this book would be likely to find it wet.

> *Dorothy Nimmo, in a review of "Taking Care of Carruthers," in* The School Librarian, *Vol. 32, No. 2, June, 1984, p. 137.*

FOX AND HIS FRIENDS (1982)

The chief characteristic of the Marshalls' Fox is not slyness but a less than assiduous attention to duty. First, while Fox sulks in the park over being stuck with little sister Louise and no friends to play with, Louise slips off to the top of a telephone pole—and Fox, who hates high places, has to bring her down. There's a similar incident at the swimming pool: this time, Louise leads Fox up to the high diving board and shames him into jumping off after her. Finally, Fox leaves his patrol post at the corner to go to the beach with his friends . . . but his conscience acts up in the form of a dream that sends him hurrying back in time to cross old Mr. Dog. James Marshall makes these doings as fetchingly ridiculous as others he has pictured, but the straight story hasn't the teasing wit of this pair's *Troll Country* or *Three By the Sea.*

> *A review of "Fox and His Friends," in* Kirkus Reviews, *Vol. L, No. 6, March 15, 1982, p. 344.*

Three stories about *Fox and His Friends,* and how Fox's responsibilities thwart his attempts to be alone with them and have a good time. . . . The sibling exchanges and situations are comically true to life, as is Fox's duty/pleasure conflict. The red, green and black illustrations, showing a defiant Louise, a beleaguered Fox, a wonderful assortment of creature friends and a hilariously feeble group of old hounds pick the story up and add character embellishment and humor.

> *Nancy Palmer, in a review of "Fox and His Friends," in* School Library Journal, *Vol. 28, No. 9, May, 1982, p. 77.*

Fox has one objective—having fun with his motley group of friends. . . . The result is a humorous blend of familiar situations with unexpected consequences: Louise, independent and fearless, hankers after heights—which he detests—and visions of elderly canines venturing into traffic without his sharp-eyed guidance mar his idyllic romp at the beach. Although easy-to-read, the text is witty and ingenious. The boxed illustrations, in bright shades of green and orange-red, are marked by the artist's skillful use of line and flair for characterization. Appropriately scaled to the three appealing narrative vignettes, the pictures extend the story and provide additional insight into the nature of Fox's personality and dilemmas.

> *Mary M. Burns, in a review of "Fox and His Friends," in* The Horn Book Magazine, *Vol. LVIII, No. 4, August, 1982, p. 396.*

FOX IN LOVE (1982)

Three humorous stories portray Fox and his romantic escapades. Fox has better things to do than take his sister Louise to the park, but when Mom gives him "one of her looks," he reluctantly goes along. There he meets a pretty white fox named Raisin, and the next day it is Fox who practically drags an unwilling Louise back to the park. In the second story Fox takes four girls to the fair on different days, and each time the happy couple gets its picture taken. But when the pictures fall out of Fox's pocket, Raisin sees them and tells the other girls. "And on Saturday Fox went to the fair . . . all alone." Finally, Fox asks Raisin to be his partner in a dance contest, but at the last moment he ends up with his sister Louise. There is subtle humor in the concise, easy-to-read text as well as in the well-placed illustrations done

primarily in shades of orange and green. Likable Fox, in his assorted hats and sunglasses, tries hard to be debonair—but doesn't always succeed. Text and pictures complement each other as the author and illustrator once again combine their talents.

> *Nancy Sheridan, in a review of "Fox in Love," in* The Horn Book Magazine, *Vol. LVIII, No. 5, October, 1982, p. 515.*

There are plenty of pictures in colour and the text is set out in simple sentences five or six words to a line. The vocabulary is limited but not stilted. Words and phrases are repeated which helps the young reader to feel at home in the text. It makes a refreshing change in the usual diet of Reading Schemes which are thought by some to be lacking in imagination if not downright stodgy.

> *D. A. Young, in a review of "Fox in Love," in* The Junior Bookshelf, *Vol. 47, No. 6, December, 1983, p. 246.*

Though published in the Bodley Beginner series as an 'easy reader', these stories have a text that is elegant and sophisticated, yet simple, while the pictures speak loud and clear of big brother Fox's first encounter with love. Rebellious, Fox consents to take little sister Louise to the park—a monumental bore, as he makes plain—until Raisin, a comely white female fox, puts in an appearance. 'You are sweet to bring your little sister to the park,' said Raisin. 'I love to do it,' said Fox.

> *Elaine Moss, in a review of "Fox in Love," in her* Picture Books for Young People 9-13, *revised edition, The Thimble Press, 1985, p. 17.*

MISS NELSON IS BACK (with Harry Allard, 1982)

After a long gap, a sequel to *Miss Nelson Is Missing,* an amusing tale of a teacher who played a trick on her class; here Miss Nelson really *is* out of school for a minor operation, and the class dreads the return of the substitute, Miss Swamp (Miss Nelson in disguise) but finds that having the principal fill in is even worse than Miss Swamp. En masse, they play hookey; they are spotted by Miss Nelson as they pass her house, and that precipitates the return of "Miss Swamp." And, again, the return of Miss Nelson. The disguise is a bit less believable here, and the depiction of the principal, Mr. Blandsworth, is quite unconvincing, as he spends all the class time doing bird calls and card tricks or showing slides of his goldfish. Not as funny as the first book, but mildly amusing.

> *Zena Sutherland, in a review of "Miss Nelson Is Back," in* Bulletin of the Center for Children's Books, *Vol. 36, No. 6, February, 1983, p. 101.*

FOX AT SCHOOL (1983)

Fox, star of *Fox and His Friends* and *Fox in Love,* returns for more buffoonery in this Easy-to-Read, in which he brings his silliness to school. In the first story, Fox is slated to be the handsome prince in the class play, but neglects to learn his lines, because he's too busy bragging, and is replaced by goody-goody Dexter. Then Fox holds up the school's fire drill because he's afraid to slide down the escape chute. In the third tale, our hero is put in charge of the class while Miss Moon steps out for a minute, and troublemaker Dexter incites the class to go hogwild, but finally gets his comeup-

From George and Martha, Tons of Fun, *written and illustrated by* James Marshall

pance. The shenanigans are, once again, depicted hilariously in the zany drawings; the Marshalls have themselves another winner.

A review of "Fox at School," in Publishers Weekly, *Vol. 223, No. 11, March 18, 1983, p. 71.*

Three more foible-filled tales of Fox. . . . As always, Fox's indomitable confidence sees him through . . . and simple justice surfaces every time. James Marshall's cast of portly animals is perfectly goofy but with a dead-on accuracy of expression that makes everyone—from Carmen, the fat frog in Hollywood shades, to the simply bovine Miss Moon—absurdly real.

Nancy Palmer, in a review of "Fox at School," in School Library Journal, *Vol. 29, No. 9, May, 1983, p. 88.*

Ebullient Fox, introduced in ***Fox and His Friends*** and ***Fox in Love,*** returns in another humorous, easy-to-read book featuring three episodes centered on familiar school situations. . . . Fox triumphs under the worst conditions and fails under the best. The framed, cartoon illustrations, depicted in vigorous colors, encapsulate and extend the stories' *joie de vivre.*

Nancy C. Hammond, in a review of "Fox at

School," in The Horn Book Magazine, *Vol. LIX, No. 4, August, 1983, p. 438.*

FOX ON WHEELS (1983)

The fourth appearance of the Marshalls' less-than-dutiful Fox is a little pale, a little stale, a little limp. In the first and snappiest episode, little sister Louise takes a tumble while Fox, lost in TV, isn't looking after her; and he guiltily does everything she asks (even "Rub my toes") until, hailed by her friends, she quickly recovers. In the second sketch, Fox once again overcomes his fear of heights—only to find, when he's joined friend Millie on a scary tree limb, that *she* "doesn't know how to get down!" Finally, Fox wins a mad grocery-cart race through the supermarket—but winds up, after his mother's had a complaint call, behind a hand-mower: an ancient/antiquated put-down. But the droll pictures will probably keep the pages turning, regardless.

A review of "Fox on Wheels," in Kirkus Reviews, *Vol. LI, No. 17, September, 1983, p. 158.*

Whether he is outmaneuvered by his little sister Louise or merely outsmarted by his friend Millie, Fox again finds himself in small difficulties that loom large in his young life. . . . The easy-to-read vocabulary sustains a lively pace, and the amusing cartoonlike drawings reflect the good nature of Fox and his neighbors. Young readers will enjoy the natty appearance of Fox in his jogging suit and echo his heartfelt " 'Rats!' " when Mom's punishments are meted out.

> *Ethel R. Twichell, in a review of "Fox on Wheels,"* in The Horn Book Magazine, *Vol. LIX, No. 6, December, 1983, p. 705.*

Fox's latest scrapes carry on in the funny, sharply witty tradition of Marshall's (the schizophrenically crafty James, who is also Cousin Edward) earlier Fox titles. . . . Marshall's acerbic humor lends itself perfectly to the quick, comic justice of these tales, while the wonderfully simple drawings catch facial expressions precisely and add quirky detail. Wheels or no, Marshall is on a roll.

> *Nancy Palmer, in a review of "Fox on Wheels," in* School Library Journal, *Vol. 30, No. 4, December, 1983, p. 79.*

RAPSCALLION JONES (1983)

A lazy unemployed fox is Rapscallion Jones, who decides that in order to pay the rent he will become a writer. The illustrations have Mr. Marshall's usual air of joyful abandon—with a couple of lumpy crocodiles thrown in—but the story is quite seriously about the price a writer must pay for having to invent. This might even be a sort of autobiography, sly fox that Mr. Marshall himself can be.

> *Christopher Lehmann-Haupt, in a review of "Rapscallion Jones," in* The New York Times Book Review, *November 30, 1983, p. C29.*

Rapscallion, a fox, is being pressed for his rent by the tough female bulldog who runs his boardinghouse. Rather than take a job, which is not his style, Rapscallion decides to become a writer. Skeptical friends goad him into telling a story, in which a joy-riding, deceitful fox, pretending to be a doctor, robs an alligator couple. That evening Rapscallion takes ill, and the doctor and the minister are called to his bedside. There is an exchange of pieties ("Crime does not pay") as Rapscallion tries to clear his conscience and the next day he is fully recovered, although still as scheming as ever. If all this sounds like *non sequetur* nonsense, it is. It is also confusing, unfocused, loaded with stereotypes, stilted in style and feverishly busy. Similarly, the illustrations are hoked up with distractingly patterned clothes, and the watercolors rely heavily on fuchsia, green and yellow. While the illustrations for the story-within-a-story are quite thoughtfully designed and attentively drawn, the others are slapdash and dull. (pp. 66-7)

> *Mary B. Nickerson, in a review of "Rapscallion Jones," in* School Library Journal, *Vol. 30, No. 5, January, 1984, pp. 66-7.*

James Marshall's text is amusing and sophisticated, with perhaps more jokes for parents than children, but his drawings will surely please everyone. His water-colours have great charm and skill; he has a gift for conveying much in the simplest of lines, the villainy of his anti-hero and the mild helplessness of his victim as well as the homely world in which they live. (p. 119)

> *M. Crouch, in a review of "Rapscallion Jones," in* The Junior Bookshelf, *Vol. 48, No. 3, June, 1984, p. 118-19.*

GEORGE AND MARTHA BACK IN TOWN (1984)

Marshall's latest lighthearted George and Martha collection again captures the illogical antics of two charming hippos. In five engaging stories, Martha leaps to catch jumping beans; George loses his nerve on the highdive, so Martha flings herself from it; George tries out lifeguarding; Martha finally pulls a trick on George; and in the final story, a very sentimental George learns things are not always what they seem. These George and Martha stories, once again, offer cozy drawings (Marshall is a master at eye expression) and warm tales that simply make readers feel good.

> *Peggy Forehand, in a review of "George and Martha Back in Town," in* School Library Journal, *Vol. 30, No. 9, May, 1984, p. 68.*

It is a pleasure to welcome back George and Martha. In five more comic vignettes they demonstrate by turns the qualities which have endeared them to readers. Martha still has a red tulip stuck nonchalantly behind her ear; her ebullience and capacity for self-delusion complement George's self-doubts and delight in practical jokes. Although admirably honest in their assessment of each other, they exhibit exemplary tact in moments of strain, their ponderous bodies presenting a delightful foil for the delicacy of their understanding.

> *Charlotte W. Draper, in a review of "George and Martha Back in Town," in* The Horn Book Magazine, *Vol. LX, No. 3, June, 1984, p. 320.*

The buck-toothed hippos who've pranced their way through earlier George and Martha books are seen here in five very brief vignettes about the vicissitudes and nuances of a peer relationship. Typical of the brevity, wit, and pithiness of all the stories is the first one: Martha finds a box marked "Do Not Open," and is taken aback when she opens it and then has to pick up George's entire collection of Mexican jumping beans. "You seem out of breath," George comments. "You don't think I opened that little box, do you?" asks Martha, giving herself away with an innocence most of the lap audience will recognize ruefully. Again, beguiling.

> *Zena Sutherland, in a review of "George and Martha Back in Town," in* Bulletin of the Center for Children's Books, *Vol. 38, No. 2, October, 1984, p. 31.*

FOX ALL WEEK (1984)

Yes, an episode-a-day in the life of young slyboots Fox—and a better lot of stories than this series has seen in some time. On Monday, when the class fieldtrip looks to be rained out, Fox develops a sore throat: " 'But I will go to school anyway.' 'Oh, no.' said Mom. 'You will go straight to bed.' 'If you say so,' said Fox." (But, just when he's congratulating himself, his class files past the window, undeterred. " 'It isn't funny,' said Fox.") Tuesday brings a snafu with tuna fish sandwiches, Wednesday a laugh at the library, Thursday some passing discomfort with cigars. On Friday, Fox offers to cook dinner (" 'Oh, goody,' said Mom"—who's not "a good cook"), and ceremoniously serves forth peanut butter and jelly sandwiches. Saturday he gets an understanding nod from Grandma; Sunday brings comforting words for friend Carmen (hiding under a paper bag) and all kids who wear braces. Varyingly humorous, then: not according to formula, not tediously tied to a single trait.

> *A review of "Fox All Week," in* Kirkus Reviews, *Juvenile Issues, Vol. LII, Nos. 10-17, September 1, 1984, p. 68.*

[This book] has seven brief episodes. They are mildly amusing, variable in structure, busily illustrated. Fox emerges as a bumbling but well-meaning character. Beginning independent readers will probably enjoy this as they have earlier books about Fox, but they may detect a note of contrivance in some of the episodes. (p. 90)

> *Zena Sutherland, in a review of "Fox All Week," in* Bulletin of the Center for Children's Books, *Vol. 38, No. 5, January, 1985, pp. 89-90.*

THE CUT-UPS (1984)

This is the first of cut-ups Spud Jenkins and Joe Turner, but it apparently won't be the last: at the book's close the neighborhood terrors are headed for school, where "little did they know" that their latest victim, kid-hating Lamar J. Spurgle, awaits them. Meanwhile, between scapegrace pranks (like tying Spud's little brother to a kite, turning the bathroom into a deep-sea tank), they meet up with their match, red-haired demon Mary Frances—possessor of a sports car and a rocket ship (the vehicle that gets them into trouble with Mr. Spurgle). But it's all mindless, aimless mayhem: sheer illustration of what devils kids can be.

> *A review of "The Cut-Ups," in* Kirkus Reviews, *Juvenile Issue, Vol. LII, Nos. 18-21, November 1, 1984, p. 90.*

James Marshall fans know that they're guaranteed laughter when they read his books, and they won't be disappointed by his newest offering. . . . The cut-ups are the sort of mischievous trouble-makers that children love to read about. Their escapades are very funny and not malicious. The watercolors are reminiscent of Marshall's illustrations for *Miss Nelson Is Missing.* This book may not show the subtle wit of Marshall at his best (as in the *"George and Martha"* stories) but it is good-humored fun that will certainly entice readers and listeners.

> *Jean Hammond Zimmerman, in a review of "The Cut-Ups," in* School Library Journal, *Vol. 31, No. 4, December, 1984, p. 74.*

The story's high jinks and its deliciously nasty curmudgeon will strongly appeal to elementary audiences. Marshall's pen-and-wash cartoons play the action for lots of broad laughs. This should be a pleaser for older picture-book readers.

> *Denise M. Wilms, in a review of "The Cut-Ups," in* Booklist, *Vol. 81, No. 13, March 1, 1985, p. 986.*

FOUR ON THE SHORE (1985)

For all the kids who've ever asked for "a scary story" that they could read alone. Not that this is that spooky, but it has all the elements that young fright fans demand: ghosts, a witch, a haunted house and, best of all, a vampire. *Four on the Shore* reads like a story kids would concoct for themselves and, indeed, the tales here are told by the crowd from

Marshall's *Three by the Sea:* Lolly, Spider and Sam. This time they're making up stories to frighten away tag-along little Willie, but it's Willie, of course, who comes up with the story that terrifies the others. The escalating degrees of spookiness as each child adds on to the story make for mounting fun and tension, and the full-color drawings depict a hilariously creepy blue-winged, green-fanged vampire and a cast of matter-of-fact creatures and kids. The flights the stories take are crazy and clever—and always brought back to reality by the sardonic commentary of this crew—" 'That story wouldn't scare a chicken,' said Sam,"—as they finesse each other's stories. Stock up. Kids will kill for this one.

> *Nancy Palmer, in a review of "Four on the Shore," in* School Library Journal, *Vol. 31, No. 9, May, 1985, p. 107.*

Full-color illustrations depict the ruddy-cheeked foursome and the shenanigans in their stories with energy and amusing touches. The surprise ending and the simple, clever dialogue are equally successful. As in *Three by the Sea,* the zesty blend of humor and drama is exceptional.

> *Karen Jameyson, in a review of "Four on the Shore," in* The Horn Book Magazine, *Vol. LXI, No. 3, May-June, 1985, p. 309.*

Stories within a story make this appropriate for the beginning independent reader because of the brevity of segments; the vocabulary is undemanding, the print large and set off by ample space. . . . The tales (including Willie's) are slight, the appeal being in the concept rather than the execution of the story line; the exaggeration and humor of the line and wash drawings add to the book's potential for popularity.

> *A review of "Four on the Shore," in* Bulletin of the Center for Children's Books, *Vol. 39, No. 2, October, 1985, p. 32.*

MISS NELSON HAS A FIELD DAY (with Harry Allard, 1985)

With her talon-tipped fingers and eyes like shotgun pellets, the ever-terrifying Viola Swamp is back at the Horace B. Smedley School. This time she is summoned to whip the football team into shape. When Coach Armstrong cracks under the outrageous shenanigans of the Smedley Tornadoes, he is shipped home in a taxi for a nice long rest. Panicky because the Thanksgiving game against the Werewolves from Central is coming soon, Principal Blandsworth, with his usual ineptness, attempts to fill in while disguised as the one and only Viola. "The guys" are not fooled for a minute. But Miss Nelson, heroine of *Miss Nelson Is Missing* and *Miss Nelson Is Back,* comes to the rescue. Once again she sets Viola Swamp in action, and there is no mistaking *her* in a black sweat suit with "COACH AND DON'T YOU FORGET IT" emblazoned on her chest. Marshall subjects his urchins to Viola's brand of punishment—for their own good, of course. Scratchy, bouncy, funny drawings and a deadpan text combine in a case study in teacher's daydreams and children's nightmares. The plot is somewhat sketchy, but children of any age will relish the raucous carrying-on at what has to be the most gloriously awful school in the entire state of Texas. (pp. 297-98)

> *Ethel R. Twichell, in a review of "Miss Nelson Has a Field Day," in* The Horn Book Magazine, *Vol. LXI, No. 3, May-June, 1985, pp. 297-98.*

Staff and pupils at the Horace B. Smedley School are equally dejected; not only is their football team inept, but also the coach has cracked up—and the big Thanksgiving Day game is looming. Pretty Miss Nelson comes to the rescue in the guise of the dreaded, dour Viola Swamp. But there's one thing different here; unlike the other Miss Nelson books, in which it's clear that the teacher is in disguise, the two appear at the same time! Allard's explanation is pat, but children will probably enjoy the contrivance just as they have enjoyed the ebullience and exaggeration of text and pictures in the earlier stories. Anyway, it's hard to take seriously a story in which a struggling team is so quickly made to shape up that they defeat a strong team seventy-seven to three.

> *Zena Sutherland, in a review of "Miss Nelson Has a Field Day," in* Bulletin of the Center for Children's Books, *Vol. 38, No. 11, July, 1985, p. 200.*

Allard and Marshall have combined talents once again in this crazy addition to the ever hilarious escapades of the students and faculty at the Horace B. Smedley School. . . . Allard's tongue-in-cheek text is full of the colloquialisms that make these stories so delightful, while Marshall is in top form as he shows his flair for capturing the spirit of a story in illustrations. There is a surprise peek into the Nelson/Swamp mystery on the last page which should leave young readers happily satisfied; the story itself will leave them screaming for more. (pp. 51-2)

> *Laura Bacher, in a review of "Miss Nelson Has a Field Day," in* School Library Journal, *Vol. 31, No. 10, August, 1985, pp. 51-2.*

WINGS: A TALE OF TWO CHICKENS (1986)

Wings gets off to a flying start as Winnie, a bored chicken, takes off in a stranger's balloon basket, so she can "live a little." Foolish, uneducated Winnie never realizes until the tale's end that the stranger is a fox planning a chicken dinner. But her sensible sister Harriet (who knows about foxes) recognizes the danger and, in a clever disguise, outfoxes the abductor after some madcap shenanigans. But there is more here than just a hilarious plot—very real characters, a plug for reading, a warning about strangers and, above all, animated, breezy art full of detail, expression and humor. Marshall is in top form here.

> *A review of "Wings: A Tale of Two Chickens," in* Publishers Weekly, *Vol. 229, No. 17, April 25, 1986, p. 71.*

This crisply cautionary tale about the dangers of not reading is Marshall at his medium-best, which is far ahead of most others in the field. . . .

A bit overlong, this shaggy-fox story does have some nice touches: Winnie's eyes remain stubbornly unfocused throughout, and Mr. Johnson is a sporty villain. Smart young readers will figure out the ending several pages before they're supposed to, but all is forgiven at the sight of Winnie's expression when she finally figures out what has been going on. Satisfying suspense.

> *A review of "Wings: A Tale of Two Chickens," in* Kirkus Reviews, *Vol. LIV, No. 10, May 15, 1986, p. 788.*

In a zany series of events, Winnie escapes while her captor is picking up a package of instant dumplings, is recaptured by the fox disguised as a chicken, and is rescued by Harriet disguised as a fox. Marshall's pictures are even roomier and more expressive than usual in a story perfectly suited for the young audience who has just discovered the difference between chickens and foxes and who will therefore delight in these sly reversals. Theatre of the absurd at its most basic level, with vivid color sets.

> *A review of "Wings: A Tale of Two Chickens," in* Bulletin of the Center for Children's Books, *Vol. 39, No. 10, June, 1986, p. 190.*

MERRY CHRISTMAS, SPACE CASE (1986)

James Marshall, who illustrated Edward Marshall's **Space Case,** has written and illustrated this sequel. As it promised at the conclusion of its Halloween visit, the thing from outer space returns for Christmas. But its friend, Buddy McGee, has been taken to Grandma's house for the holidays. The thing follows directions left for it, encountering various difficulties. Meanwhile, neighboring twin bullies threaten Buddy as he waits impatiently.

The story lacks the subtlety and drollness of the original. Christmas is cynically portrayed as a materialistic competition. The ability of the thing to turn people into snowmen adds a fantastic element that seems out of place. The illustrations, however, continue the quality and tone of the original. The best scenes are when the thing is coping with unfamiliar earthlings. The dynamic and scientifically-inclined grandmother defies stereotypes; she seems like a character one would like to know better.

Despite some disappointing features, this new story will be welcomed by those who loved the small alien during its first visit.

> *A review of "Merry Christmas, Space Case," in* Kirkus Reviews, *Vol. LIV, No. 14, July 15, 1986, p. 1121.*

Some children will find this highly entertaining, but there's one thing lacking—Christmas spirit. A hostile world greets Buddy and the thing at every turn, and Christmas is more of an excuse here than an integral part of the plot.

> *A review of "Merry Christmas, Space Case," in* Publishers Weekly, *Vol. 230, No. 13, September 26, 1986, p. 75.*

YUMMERS TOO: THE SECOND COURSE (1986)

Emily Pig and Eugene Turtle continue their anarchic adventures in this third book about them, the second to concentrate on Emily's dedicated gluttony.

When Eugene appears with a Popsicle cart, Emily has eaten three before Eugene informs her that she was supposed to pay for them. Since Emily is broke from previous gastronomic adventures, she must work off her debt, but her attempts to do so only worsen the problem until she inadvertently rescues a wedding cake from thieves and is offered a reward which will return her to solvency. Or a box of chocolate éclairs. Emily's fans will anticipate her decision.

Ramshackle yet entertaining, the story is carried by Emily's resolutely greedy character and Marshall's slyly detailed, cartoon-like illustrations. Although not on the level of his *Wings,* the book will nonetheless be welcomed by Marshall's fans.

> *A review of "Yummers Too," in* Kirkus Reviews, *Vol. LIV, No. 16, August 15, 1986, p. 1291.*

The colorful watercolor cartoon illustrations are unmistakably Marshall and are really very funny. They are, in fact, largely responsible for any chuckles produced by this lightweight story. While lacking the charm and warm messages of friendship found in his **"George and Martha"** stories, *Yummers Too* is a funny sequel and will not disappoint Marshall's many fans. Tailor-made for story hours.

> *Luann Toth, in a review of "Yummers Too: The Second Course," in* School Library Journal, *Vol. 33, No. 3, November, 1986, p. 80.*

THREE UP A TREE (1986)

Spider, Sam and Lolly of *Three by the Sea* are back, with some competitive storytelling in a tree house. The boys don't want to let Lolly up because she didn't help with construction, so she bribes them with a story. It has a monster, but "The end was too sweet." Spider's story, about a fox who tries to horn in on a hen's dinner plans, isn't bad, but Sam tops both by including the characters from the two previous stories and introducing a robbery. Then, more important than agreeing whose story was best, they decide to ". . . hear them again."

The snappy dialogue should keep new readers chuckling; the threesome's example may even start them debating the merits of stories they read. Marshall's lively, cartoon-like illustrations are just right.

> *A review of "Three Up a Tree," in* Kirkus Reviews, *Vol. LIV, No. 18, September 15, 1986, p. 1448.*

Marshall is at his best in this funny beginning reader that incorporates the trio familiar from *Three By the Sea,* plus two of his recent favorite characters, a chicken and a fox, *plus* everychild's favorite green monster. These appear variously in a story-within-a-story pattern with ebulliently silly pictures and lines: says a hungry fox sidling up to a disguised hen waiting with her groceries for a bus, "I can smell that you're having chicken tonight." And she, seeking to dissuade him from coming to dinner, explains that she will cook it "in sour chocolate milk with lots of pickles and rotten eggs. . . . " "It sounds delicious," says the fox. A treat for students struggling from one word to the next. (pp. 71-2)

> *Betsy Hearne, in a review of "Three Up a Tree," in* Bulletin of the Center for Children's Books, *Vol. 40, No. 4, December, 1986, pp. 71-2.*

The stories the three tell here have Marshall's child-like weirdness and non-sequitery to them, but there's less substance and cohesive continuity than before. The stories are still refreshingly bizarre, and the full-color watercolors hilarious, but the genuine wit—vs. contrived cuckooness—of much of Marshall's other work is missing here. This seems tossed off, the stories *too* childishly rambling; it will be popular, but we've heard better from these three.

> *Nancy Palmer, in a review of "Three Up a Tree,"*

> *in* School Library Journal, *Vol. 33, No. 4, December, 1986, p. 124.*

RED RIDING HOOD (1987)

Some people are born to be funny; James Marshall can't help himself. Fortunately. Here he extends his high humor to a Perrault/Grimm tale with a serious past. Sticking to the basic plot formula, he reduces the text to the minimum, with a few choice bits of dialogue ("It is I, your delicious—er—darling granddaughter," says the wolf, and later, "I'm so wicked . . . So wicked"). Most of the high jinks are pictorial, however, and played out against some of the boldest color compositions the artist has done. When the wolf comes to the door, we are treated with a view of Granny's feet, replaced, ominously enough, by a pair of gray clawed paws when Red Riding Hood knocks on the door. On the last page, as proof that R. R. H. keeps her promise never to speak to another stranger, she spurns the overtures of a large green crocodile. Marshall's version may be counterproductive to the moral, however; this is one wolf not to be missed.

> *Betsy Hearne, in a review of "Red Riding Hood," in* Bulletin of the Center for Children's Books, *Vol. 41, No. 1, September, 1987, p. 8.*

This irresistible retelling of the familiar tale will rank high in popular appeal while still maintaining the integrity of the Grimm Brothers' version, with both Grandma and Red Riding Hood eaten and later rescued by a hunter. Through simple words and a restrained use of line in the art, Marshall masterfully imbues his characters with humorous personality traits. The heroine is a considerate, bouncy sort of kid; Grandma, an avid reader, is feisty; and the wolf, a charming villain, is just a *bit* guilty about his behavior—after his second meal he admits, "I'm so wicked . . . so wicked." With just a flick of the whiskers even Grandma's heavy-set feline looks both outraged and scared. The cartoon styled ink and watercolor illustrations play harmoniously along with the spare story, and as the drama heightens viewers are treated to fresh perspectives and enticing peeks into Grandma's bedroom. Cheery colors predominate, with a judicious use of black effectively conveying tense moments. Throughout, comic touches are understated (a box of empty imported afterdinner mints lay discretely beside the snoring wolf). A marvelous offering that begs to be added to everyone's storytelling repertoire.

> *Caroline Ward, in a review of "Red Riding Hood," in* School Library Journal, *Vol. 34, No. 1, September, 1987, p. 176.*

An utterly felicitous retelling of the old classic will have both children and their parents gripped with the drama and amused by the up-to-date dialogue. Those enamored of the traditional plot will find nothing to distress them. . . . The humorous, slightly sinister illustrations display Marshall's wacky style to its best advantage. Funny and wonderful for reading aloud. (pp. 747-48)

> *Ann A. Flowers, in a review of "Red Riding Hood," in* The Horn Book Magazine, *Vol. LXIII, No. 6, November-December, 1987, pp. 747-48.*

From Goldilocks and the Three Bears, *written and illustrated by James Marshall.*

THE CUT-UPS CUT LOOSE (1987)

Those mischievous pals, Spud and Joe, are back for more hi-jinks after their first outing in *The Cut-Ups.* It's a new school year, and Spud and Joe are more than ready with a full supply of spitballs, stink bombs, and the like. Unfortunately, their old nemesis, Lamar J. Spurgle, is also prepared . . . and he's the new principal. When the cut-ups find that life under Spurgle's heavy thumb is too restraining, their friend Mary Frances comes to the rescue with her secret weapon—"Big Al," otherwise known as Sister Aloysius of St. Bridget's School, who once taught young Lamar Spurgle and still has the power to subdue him. Marshall's sly watercolor illustrations are the perfect foil for this rollicking tale which will have adults rolling their eyes in recognition and children giggling over Spud and Joe's goodnatured pranks. Have the cut-ups learned their lesson? Not a chance. Will this book find an ample audience? You bet! (p. 117)

> *Kathleen Brachmann, in a review of "The Cut-Ups Cut Loose," in* School Library Journal, *Vol. 34, No. 2, October, 1987, pp. 116-17.*

Although the boys' pranks are not as awe-inspiring as those in *The Cut-Ups,* the lively cartoonlike drawings, bubbling with Marshall's zany humor, and the entirely satisfactory conclusion—as Spurgle is brought to heel by his former grade school teacher—more than compensate. Shuddering adults can be grateful that Spike and Joe don't live in their neighborhood, but children will thoroughly enjoy the downfall of the infamous Lamar J. Spurgle in a world where mischief approaches mayhem, but justice prevails. (pp. 727-28)

> *Ethel R. Twichell, in a review of "The Cut-Ups Cut Loose," in* The Horn Book Magazine, *Vol. LXIII, No. 6, November-December, 1987, pp. 727-28.*

While he's probably best known for the bland, "what, me worry?" effrontery of his illustrations, Marshall's ear for the quirks and cliches of the American language has always been an important contribution to his peculiar sense for what is funny. Those two, Spud and Joe, "a couple of *real* cut-ups," are back, and eager for the first day of school, "the biggest challenge of all." . . . Marshall's easy handling of simultaneous deadpan drollery and outrageousness is unique, demonstrated especially well here by the boys' friend, "that nice Mary Frances Hooley," and her benefactress, Sister Aloysius, who takes on Spurgle with practiced ease: "Shame on you." As Mary Frances says, "Nobody messes with Big Al."

> *Robert Strang, in a review of "The Cut-Ups Cut Loose," in* Bulletin of the Center for Children's Books, *Vol. 41, No. 4, December, 1987, p. 71.*

FOX ON THE JOB (1988)

In a fast-paced and funny Easy-to-Read, Fox wrecks his bike while showing off and asks his mother for a new one. When she suggests that he get a job, Fox tries to oblige her, and in the succeeding chapters pursues a number of employment opportunities. In most occupations Fox seems a hopeless misfit. To a lady buying shoes he says of her feet, "Those are the biggest!" Hired as a ticket seller at the amusement park's haunted house, Fox is frightened and declares, "That's no place for little kids! I quit!" His next job is delivering pizza, which lasts until he mixes up a box of pizza with a box of pet mice. Finally he finds a job for which he's perfectly suited: bed testing (sleeping) in a store window. The drawings are zingy and sly; fans of Fox will take comfort in the idea that not everyone is cut out for hard labor, but that there are jobs for everyone.

> *A review of "Fox on the Job," in* Publishers Weekly, *Vol. 233, No. 10, March 11, 1988, p. 104.*

The words are easy, the stories funny, the watercolor cartoons absurdly suited to Fox's antics, which are calculated (correctly) to appeal to youngsters who need all the humor they can get for the serious business of decoding.

> *Betsy Hearne, in a review of "Fox on the Job," in* Bulletin of the Center for Children's Books, *Vol. 41, No. 8, April, 1988, p. 161.*

Fans of the five previous books will once again appreciate Marshall's light touch both in words and pictures. Word choice and sentence length put this squarely at a second-grade level, though the colorful pencil-and-watercolor art is so amusing that younger children may be tempted to pick this up and find out what's so funny. (pp. 1355-56)

> *Ilene Cooper, in a review of "Fox on the Job," in* Booklist, *Vol. 84, No. 15, April 1, 1988, pp. 1355-56.*

GOLDILOCKS AND THE THREE BEARS (1988)

With the same delightfully irreverent spirit that he brought to his retelling of *Little Red Riding Hood,* Marshall enlivens another favorite. Although completely retold with his usual pungent wit and contemporary touches ("I don't mind if I do," says Goldilocks, as she tries out porridge, chair, and bed), Marshall retains the stories well-loved pattern, including Goldilocks escaping through the window (whereupon Baby Bear inquires, "Who *was* that little girl?"). The illustrations are fraught with delicious humor and detail: books that are stacked everywhere around the rather cluttered house, including some used in lieu of a missing leg for Papa Bear's chair; comically exaggerated beds—*much* too high at the head and the foot; and Baby Bear's wonderfully messy room, which certainly brings the story into the 20th century. Like its predecessor, perfect for several uses, from picture-book hour to beginning reading. (pp. 976-77)

> *A review of "Goldilocks and the Three Bears," in* Kirkus Reviews, *Vol. LVI, No. 13, July 1, 1988, pp. 976-77.*

"Once there was a little girl named Goldilocks. 'What a sweet child,' said someone new in town. 'That's what *you* think,' said a neighbor." From the very first sentence this book takes off in typical Marshall style. Goldilocks is a self-satisfied girl used to doing exactly as she pleases. So when signs around the entrance to the shortcut read "DANGER," "TURN BACK," "VERY RISKY" and even "GO THE OTHER WAY," the undaunted lass tromps headlong into adventure. Once inside the house of the three bears, Goldilocks notices a lot of coarse brown fur and thinks, "They must have kitties." She thrashes her way through the bears' domain. Eventually, they return and scare the girl off, but whether or not she has learned her lesson is left to the imagination. Marshall's wonderfully unique characters are as offbeat and self-propelled as ever; the book boasts many jolly details and the pictures burst with color.

> *A review of "Goldilocks and the Three Bears," in*

Publishers Weekly, *Vol. 234, No. 5, July 29, 1988, p. 232.*

This retelling is a Victorianesque version of a chubby, blond-hair strong-willed "naughty little girl" who takes a shortcut through the woods on her way to buy muffins in the next village, and invades the home of the three sophisticated bears. While the basic storyline may be recognizable to young listeners, sight gags and ironic wit are whimsically employed for those who already know the tale and/or Marshall's other works (for example, a white hen perches atop the bears' house). The tone is straightforward and droll. Marshall is careful to include basic motifs from the original tale: the bowls of porridge, the chairs, and the beds, but he takes liberties in his commentary: "She walked right in without *even* bothering to knock" and in the characters' exclamations, like "Patooie!" and "Egads!" His playful watercolor illustrations fill the pages in their comic portrayal of these well-known figures. Whether shared in a lap or with a group, this one's a winner.

Marianne Pilla, in a review of "Goldilocks and the Three Bears," in School Library Journal, *Vol. 35, No. 2, October, 1988, p. 134.*

Marshall's Goldilocks, the naughty little girl who disrupts a placid bear household, is no adorable blond moppet led more by curiosity than by mischievous intent. Instead, she is a sturdy, brazen, mini-hussy who stomps over the doorsill with a determined set to her mouth and a confident bounce in her step. She spits out the first taste of hot porridge with a disgusted " 'Patooie,' " puts her feet up on the table to enjoy the one bowl that is just right, and isn't the least bit repentant over breaking the little bear's rocking chair. The big cartoon-like pictures depict a cozy modern setting for the respectable, suburban bears with snug rooms cluttered with books, bulbous upholstered furniture and a messy little bear's room. While lacking the outrageous zaniness and the fresh interpretation in both pictures and text of Marshall's earlier ***Red Riding Hood,*** the story contains a genuine enjoyment of Goldilock's adventures as they are reflected in Marshall's usual slapdash and rollicking illustrations. (pp. 774-75)

Ethel R. Twichell, in a review of "Goldilocks and the Three Bears," in The Horn Book Magazine, *Vol. LXIV, No. 6, November-December, 1988, pp. 774-75.*

Hans Peter Richter

1925-

German author of fiction, scriptwriter, and editor.

Hailed for dramatizing in microcosm the turmoil in Germany during Hitler's reign, Richter is best known in the English-speaking world as the author of three first-person autobiographical works of fiction for middle grade through high school readers which recount the experiences of German youth during the Third Reich. *Friedrich* (1970), the first of these novels, commences in 1925 with the birth of the narrator, a gentile, and his best friend Friedrich Schneider, a Jew. The story then describes the fate of Friedrich's family during the next seventeen years: Frau Schneider is murdered, Herr Schneider is consigned to a concentration camp, and Friedrich is killed during a bombing when he is denied entrance to an air raid shelter because of his religion. In the course of the tragic events, the narrator matures, haunted by uncertainties and moral quandaries. The book concludes without promise; rather, in a final note of harsh reality, Richter appends a chronological list of laws and regulations enforced against Jewish people. In the second work, *I Was There* (1972), Richter details the experiences of the narrator and his two friends during their childhoods, culminating with their teenage years as Nazi soldiers. Through these three characters, Richter explores the motives of the young who joined the Hitler youth movement, then traces their early enthusiasm and later disillusionment as they endure the suffering and barbarity of battle. Richter again adds a historical chronology at the conclusion of the book as a stark reminder of the events of World War II. In the last book of Richter's trilogy, *The Time of the Young Soldiers* (1976), the narrator is a young man giving his impressions of the Second World War as well as relating his perceptions of the German soldiers of his acquaintance. Throughout, there is a condemnation of both Nazism and war in general; the book begins with the well-known quotation from Benjamin Franklin: "There never was a good war or a bad peace." With candor that is admired by critics, Richter's narrator admits to his naïve conviction that his actions were sound because no one publicly disputed them. It has been noted, in fact, that each book of the trilogy bears this forthright, unembellished style; in a stark documentary approach, Richter unemotionally presents a humanistic message through explicit presentation of the grim facts of war and the atrocities of Nazism. The impact of these books, it is conceded, is a direct result of the youthful frankness of Richter's narrators. In addition to his trilogy, Richter is also the author, reteller, and editor of stories for preschoolers, middle graders, and young adults, most of which have not been translated into English, as well as nonfiction for adults and a number of radio and television scripts. *Friedrich* received the Jugendbuchpreis Sebaldus-Verlag in 1961, was a runner-up for the German Children's Book Prize in 1964 (both under its original title *Damals war es Friedrich*), and was presented with the Mildred L. Batchelder Award in 1972.

(See also *Something about the Author,* Vol. 6 and *Contemporary Authors,* Vols. 45-48.)

GENERAL COMMENTARY

SHEILA A. EGOFF

Not surprisingly, the greatest difference between English-language novels and those from Europe are seen when they treat of the more momentous themes, such as war. British and American writers such as Jill Paton Walsh, Alan Garner, Nina Bawden, Penelope Lively, Bette Greene, and T. Degens have all used World War II as a setting and a means. They probe deeply into the personal lives of their children, but one senses that the war itself does not matter that much; *any* traumatic interruption in the children's lives would have served just as well to portray their writers' main intent—an insight into the minds of their protagonists and whether maturation results.

Conversely, the European novels tend to stem from a more immediate, everyday connection with war. They are in every sense war novels, being at once more concerned with actual events—the German writer Hans Richter, for example, includes a chronology of events in an appendix to both *Friedrich* and *I Was There*—and yet more mythically charged, mythic in the sense of a larger story enveloping the immediate tale. The major power in these German novels arises from the fact that we know the ending to the actual events. They therefore create both a catharsis and an irony that is lacking in the more personal war stories in English literature. (pp. 283-84)

Sheila A. Egoff, "The European Children's Novel in Translation," in her Thursday's Child: Trends and Patterns in Contemporary Children's Literature, *American Library Association, 1981, pp. 275-96.*

FRIEDRICH (1970)

Death and doom pervade the pages of these two shattering novels set in Nazi Germany [*Friedrich* and James Forman's *Ceremony of Innocence*]. Both books are superb, sensitive, honest and compelling, symbolizing juvenile fiction at its best.

First published in Germany, **Friedrich** is a simple but terrifying tale of the destruction of a single Jewish family, the Schneiders. Friedrich Schneider is a buddy of the narrator. Their families are friendly until the Nazi plague poisons the relationship. Before Hitler, there is affection and innocence—a family visit to an amusement park, two boys sharing the same bathtub. In 1933, the signs are clear: "Don't buy from Jews"; "The Jews are our affliction." The landlord tries to evict the Schneiders; Herr Schneider is fired from his civil service job; Friedrich is forced to transfer to a Jewish school; Frau Schneider loses her maid. The wave of prejudice swells to a pogrom, to the death of Mrs. Schneider, to the imprisonment of her husband and, finally, to the death of Friedrich in an air raid after he is bounced from a bomb shelter. "His luck that he died *this* way," said Herr Resch, the landlord. The microcosm is complete; the solution, final.

Robert Hood, in a review of "Friedrich," in The New York Times Book Review, *January 10, 1971, p. 26.*

First published in Germany in 1961, an unusual—and disturbing—first-person, documentary novel of Germany from 1925-1942. It is charged with the growing awareness of a boy developing from childhood to maturity in a period of social and political chaos. Generally, books dealing with the consequences of racism and war have been narrated by the victims—or rather, by the obvious victims. In their reminiscences, the one shining theme is the indomitable spirit of those who refuse to be spiritually debased even when denied the most elementary creature comforts. In contrast, Friedrich's tragic fate is described by another kind of victim—the bewildered observer, who is ostensibly protected by the regime in power, but is ultimately persecuted by self-doubt and tormented by the memories of weakness. Beginning with the narrator's first childhood recollections of the relationship between his family and Friedrich's, the chronicle becomes a microcosmic study of a society's dissolution when humanitarian values are forgotten or ignored. Subtle changes in diction corresponding to the changes in the narrator's age add realism to a novel which reaches a devastating climax when Friedrich, once the petted only child of a competent civil servant, now parentless and terrified, is denied access to an air-raid shelter—because he is a Jew. As remarkable for the details it omits as for those it includes, the novel leaves the reader with neither happiness nor hope—only the terrible realization that the decrees, laws, and regulations listed in the chronology appended to the final chapter are not—nearly four decades later—merely historical facts but were once a series

of fateful sentences meted out to living human beings whose sole crime was being "different." (pp. 173-74)

Mary M. Burns, in a review of "Friedrich," in The Horn Book Magazine, *Vol. XLVII, No. 2, April, 1971, pp. 173-74.*

Friedrich offers . . . didactic zeal, with the result that an intended novel is reduced to a documentary. This wooden translation from West Germany relates through the mouth of a non-Jew the fate of his Jewish friend, Friedrich, who lives with his family in the flat upstairs. At first disjointed and episodic, the account gathers force, and even horror, as the Nazi persecution of the Jews intensifies and Friedrich and his family are hounded to death. The author's concern to drive home the message of Nazi inhumanity overwhelms any attempt to draw his characters or their situation in the round, and there is incongruity between the story's grim import and the naive style of its narration. This makes it a difficult book to place in a British context, and there lingers the suspicion that it will remain the hopeful, but largely unread, stimulant of classroom discussion.

"Episodes of Adolescence," in The Times Literary Supplement, *No. 3640, December 3, 1971, p. 1512.*

This is a gripping story of the growing ostracism of Jews in Nazi Germany. The story is poignant because it shows the quandary faced by Germans, former friends of Jews, who find themselves having to make decisions in a time of growing viciousness which affects them and annihilates their friends. . . .

First, Friedrich's father is fired and then the family is asked to leave the apartment. They refuse to leave, but later the apartment is ravaged and the family is beaten. This scene exposes the viciousness which has swelled like a tide among the German populace. . . .

This is the story of the building of social systems upon which the horrors of destruction are often founded. (p. 141)

Binnie Tate Wilkin, "Religion and Politics," in her Survival Themes in Fiction for Children and Young People, *The Scarecrow Press, Inc., 1978, pp. 137-47.*

In the last two decades the ironic mode—the depiction of the human condition as limited by realistic historical time and space—has made definite encroachments on children's literature, particularly in stories about familial or social trauma. Though reviewers often question if works about child abuse, family disintegration, sex, violence, drug addiction, and prejudice can still be called children's fiction, perceptive adults would agree that such works can both have therapeutic value for young victims and raise the consciousness of youngsters whose environment is stable. There is, however, another category of the ironic mode in young people's literature: literature about historical trauma.

The nightmare of history is de-creation by adults, a nightmare that always includes children, be they enslaved Africans, Nazi holocaust victims, or survivors of Hiroshima. Historical trauma is a collective inundation of a culture; it affects the life, not just of the individual or the small group, but of the entire social order, its past, present, and future. The reader of literature about such traumas can no longer comfortably apply us/them dichotomies, for this literature universalizes moral problems, choices, and consequences. The image of the child in such literature, as recalled by a survivor-witness, is often a devastating ethical challenge, for children have often been singled out to suffer special brutalities.

We are loathe to shape our collective sin and guilt through the genre of children's literature. Perhaps we fear that to depict the children within the nightmare of history will both taint our own image of innocence and deny young readers trust in the future we shape; for is not children's literature a seduction of children into our symbolic structures and values? Yet children have lived and do live in historical time and voice their concerns today about the next possible nightmare—global nuclear war.

Three works that confront the themes and horizons of historical trauma in children's literature are Paula Fox's *The Slave Dancer,* Hans Peter Richter's *Friedrich,* and Toshi Maruki's *Hiroshima No Pika.* . . . [The] three cardinal sins of Western civilization—the enslavement of Africans, anti-Semitism and the holocaust, and the atom bomb as apocalypse—affect the child characters in these stories, and . . . might influence the young reader's reaction to our civilization's discontents, crimes, and guilts. I contend that if such literary works are shared within a context where youngsters can voice their concerns and where adults are ready to engage in dialogue rather than diatribe, rationalization, and assuagement, they cannot but be therapeutic. They define and thereby set limits to the anxieties of young readers.

In each narrative the main character is a victim-survivor. In *The Slave Dancer* and *Friedrich* the narrator writes a confession because he witnessed and participated in historical crimes. (p. 20)

In Hans Peter Richter's *Friedrich* . . . the narrator and his family . . . remain nameless, for this narrator cannot even experience the memory of guilt—he has implicated himself too much. There is safety in remaining nameless, and the anonymity adds a universality of guilt to the story, which could be the story of many a German family. The victims here are named, as if to rescue them from the vast anonymity of the millions who were murdered.

Friedrich is the story of the friendship between two boys during the time of the Third Reich, but Richter does not show a child being led to the gas chamber. There has been no depiction of the final solution in a book written for children, though there are many accounts, poems, and drawings by children who were in the camps. As of now the ultimate extremity is censored by adult writers as too horrible to depict. Because writing is as therapeutic for the writer as reading can be for the reader, the writer, especially of children's literature, may even be afraid of subliminally expressing aggression against children.

Friedrich Schneider and his parents, who live in isolation in their urban apartment, believe that they are accepted as Germans, and are thus caught in the "illusion of reprieve." When the narrator's father, a Nazi for expediency's sake, advises Herr Schneider to flee Germany, Schneider cannot imagine slavery and injustice, much less pitiless murder in twentieth century Germany: "Perhaps we will put an end to our wandering by not seeking flight any more, by learning to suffer, by staying where we are." Bettelheim's criticism in *Surviving* of Anne Frank's family for wanting to maintain the *status quo* is corroborated in Richter's book. The author's emphasis is always on individual human suffering resulting from human choices. He reveals graphically the ransacking of the Schnei-

ders' apartment, the death of Frau Schneider, and the arrest of Herr Schneider by the Gestapo.

Present or not, the Schneiders will always be the focus in the narrator's world, even as his consciousness splits, objectifies conflicting worlds, and finally allows itself no reflection. Caught in the historical moment he becomes a member of the *Jungvolk,* yet still maintains his friendship with Friedrich. Awareness of otherness begins harmlessly enough when the narrator's mother notes while bathing both boys: "Well, Fritzchen! You look like a little Jew." The word *Jew* will be repeated with increasing vehemence on placards, on park benches, and in speeches and songs of the Nazis. Still, the narrator tries to get an eager Friedrich into a *Jungvolk* meeting, where Friedrich is made to say, "The Jews are our Affliction." Occasionally there is a humane teacher or righteous judge, but anti-Semitic myths turn more and more into gruesome reality. During the famous night of broken glass, the narrator finds it "strangely exhilarating" to be drawn into the crowd. Almost accidentally he picks up a hammer, almost casually he breaks a glass pane; then he immerses himself in an orgy of vandalism, until spent, tired, and disgusted, he walks home to find that the Schneiders' apartment, too, has been demolished. His tears come too late.

While Friedrich grows in moral courage and self-awareness, the narrator is infantilized by the totalitarian system, in which ego and superego identify with the state. At the end he can no longer express his feelings for Friedrich. After Friedrich is refused entry into the shelter and dies during the air raid, the narrator can only clutch "the thorny rosebush" in front of the apartment house to let physical pain somehow replace the anguish he dare not express. The Nazi landlord notes, "His luck that he died *this* way," implying the other end that would have been likely for Friedrich. The book ends with this "lucky" death and only Richter's chronology at the end shows that the Third Reich collapsed on May 8, 1945. Richter wants to show the young reader that we do make choices and even have the choice to give up our freedom to choose until there is no choice left. (pp. 21-2)

[*Friedrich, The Slave Dancer,* and *Hiroshima No Pika*] do not project survival fantasies onto the nightmare of history, for each survivor-victim receives lasting physical, moral, or psychological damage. Each of the three child characters is denied wholeness through the process of individuation. We, who live in the fearful symmetry of the world of experience, would like our children to sing songs of innocence, but it is difficult to delude children who have intimations of nuclear war. By breaking with the convictions of children's literature, these stories open spaces or blanks for the young readers' thoughts. Young readers will fill the blanks and appropriate the text in ways not necessarily acceptable to adults. Yet, the damage will not come from books, for these books impress order on historical chaos. Stories that we hear or read are stories that can be told. While on the outer limits of children's literature, these books, too, share the subversiveness of children's literature written by adults. Through them we communicate to the child our suffering, sins, and guilts. A child character is central in each, and bears much of the burden, as a young scapegoat whose consciousness and conscience is to awaken to what our civilization lacked. Do we still expect children to redeem us even after we dropped [the atomic bomb] "Little Boy" on Hiroshima? (p. 22)

Hamida Bosmajian, "Nightmares of History—The Outer Limits of Children's Literature," in Children's Literature Association Quarterly, *Vol. 8, No. 4, Winter, 1983, pp. 20-2.*

I WAS THERE (1972)

The four decades which separate the present moment from the years of the Hitler regime have provided the perspective which transforms newspaper headlines from history-in-the-making to historical events. In the same vein, many juvenile novels dealing retrospectively with that era have changed substantially from quasi-thrillers into subtle studies of human motivation, and thus have the intensity, if not the form, of poetry. It is this quality one senses in the introduction to the book: "I am reporting how I lived through that time and what I saw—no more. I was there. I was not merely an eyewitness. I believed—and I will never believe again." In the spare, restrained style which so masterfully heightened the tension of *Friedrich,* the author offers another perspective on Hitler's rise to power. Autobiographical in tone, the first-person novel focuses on the narrator himself and his friends Heinz and Günther. Friedrich, the central figure of the earlier book, plays only a minor role, for it is the author's intent to explore the diversity of reasons which compelled youngsters to join the Hitler youth movement and to delineate the extent to which that movement both dictated and reflected the life style of the Third Reich. Thus, historical events are frequently handled as staccato preludes to the personal agonies they induced: "In January 1933 Adolf Hitler became Chancellor of the German Reich; in February the Parliament building burned; in March there were elections; in April actions against Jews began; in May the unions were dissolved; in June the political parties started dissolving on their own; in July it became illegal to found new parties; in August, vacation time, things were quieter; in September the Nazi 'Party Convention of Victory' was celebrated in Nuremberg; in October Germany left the League of Nations—and now, in November, there were more elections." And the cycle—from Hitler youth parades to military service, from exhilaration to disillusion—is completed as the three friends are reunited at the front, and youthful dreams are destroyed in the nightmare of an artillery barrage. An unforgettable and compelling reading experience given added significance by means of the appended historical chronology. (pp. 600-01)

Mary M. Burns, in a review of "I Was There," in The Horn Book Magazine, *Vol. XLVIII, No. 6, December, 1972, pp. 600-01.*

Simple, moving—as commonplace as the history of any Boy Scout troop. Young Richter and his friends grow up along with Hitler's rise to power in the Germany of the 1930's. As his father points out: "He (Hitler) has accomplished quite a bit . . . I now work again . . . we have enough to eat."

Shreds of disillusionment weave their subtle way into the fabric of days occupied with Jew-baiting, sadistic "toughening" punishments, and finally, climaxing in the "rumblings, roars, bursts, explosions, crashing, fizzing, hissing, burning-bodies odors, screams, whimpers, moans, tremblings that form the pattern of war."

The reader is uneasy as thoughts rise from the obvious parallels between Germany and other countries, our own included. Signs are read differently, depending on where a person stands. The tightly structured autobiography flows swiftly on a fine-honed writing style—plain language that needs no vul-

garity, no embellishment to shine with the icy glare of death. Highly recommended. (pp. 446-47)

Mrs. John G. Gray, in a review of "I Was There," in Best Sellers, *Vol. 32, No. 18, December 15, 1972, pp. 446-47.*

Hans Peter Richter's brilliant and austere novel traces the progress of a group of German boys from 1933, through their membership of the Hitler Youth, to the final horror of the front in 1943. The author tells us: "I am reporting how I lived through that time, and what I saw—no more. I was there. I was not merely an eyewitness. I believed—and I will never believe again." This note well conveys the quality of the book. It is written with simple directness. It makes no open comments. It describes the boys' reluctant, uneasy participation in the Hitler Youth; their nervous response to the crazed fanaticism of others; the shiftiness of the adults, cowed by fear, or full of fascist ambition. Life is full of speeches; the boys' attention wanders as they are harangued. Every shade of reaction to the situation is charted with an appearance of accuracy and truth.

Beneath the surface the author's restrained emotion gives the book immense and sinister force. Naturally enough, it is easy to convey the compulsion to join in, to conform, that a society such as Nazi Germany brought to bear on the young. It is natural to feel more sympathy than revulsion for the reluctant member of the Hitler Youth. Hans Peter Richter makes us feel such sympathy. But in the character of Heinz he has achieved much more. Heinz is the son of a Nazi; he is a willing and keen member of the youth movement. But he is decent and kind. He helps the others. He is disgusted when they torment a Jew. He takes responsibility for his group. It is in showing us what becomes of Heinz that Mr Richter makes the main point of his book.

This book can be earnestly recommended for children; with all its other merits it is as gripping as a thriller. But it is a pity if its publication for children restricts its readership to those too young to remember the war. For those English readers who are the contemporaries or near contemporaries of Mr Richter's characters, and whose secret prejudice is often their only war-wound, his portrayal of Heinz offers a healing education of the heart.

"Pawns of War," in The Times Literary Supplement, *No. 3709, April 6, 1973, p. 380.*

THE TIME OF THE YOUNG SOLDIERS (1976)

Benjamin Franklin's unequivocal view that there never was a good war or a bad peace is quoted by Hans Peter Richter to round off his novel and underline its message. He wants to convey the experience of being a German soldier in the Second World War without glamour or heroic rhetoric; he is eager to emphasize that wars are fought in ignorance and that the military machine brutalizes the individual. His foreword makes his own position clear: "When the war broke out, I was fourteen years old; when it ended I was twenty. I was a soldier for three years. I thought that the things I saw and the things I did were justified because no one spoke out openly against them."

His book, the final part of a trilogy, uses a narrative technique familiar from documentary television. It splits the experience of a boy who volunteered for the Army at seventeen and served in France, Poland and Denmark into a series of short, visually vivid scenes, seldom more than a page long, often disconnected. Whether the narrator is describing bayonet training, a bombing raid by the RAF, the humiliation of a recruit who is ordered to crawl on muddy ground like a seal, or a medical inspection for venereal disease, the writing is spare and austere and in Anthea Bell's unobtrusive translation suggests a resolute integrity.

The narrator records each new happening squarely and stoically, even the amputation of his arm. He is commissioned as an officer after this severe wound, an indication of the shortage of German manpower during the latter half of the war. Such indications, however, are few and never openly stated. The young soldier seems totally unaware of any events outside his own small section of the Army. Hitler and his policies are never mentioned.

The strongest passages in the book trace the transformation of a boy civilian into an Army officer. They shade in the eighteen-year-old's initial embarrassment at giving orders to men old enough to be his father and his subsequent satisfaction as he imposes humiliations he has himself once endured. All this is observed without humour or irony but with an impressive honesty. Yet because the book evades any consideration of Nazism its integrity seems flawed, and young readers with no background knowledge of the war from the German side may find the impressionistic style of the narrative disconcerting.

> *Sylvia Clayton, "Men at Arms," in* The Times Literary Supplement, *No. 3864, April 2, 1976, p. 387.*

In this quiet story one sees a nation passing from pride to despair, a boy losing his arm, his innocence and any objective in life but survival. It is the more moving because it avoids heroics or any overstatement. The boy sees his friends killed, his mother suffering extreme poverty and loss of dignity, his

country disintegrating. He records everything in the same terse, almost objective manner. Only an irony so unobtrusive that it is almost unnoticed points to the incongruity of this boy who loses an arm before he has seen action, and who then becomes an officer and leads a platoon of cripples, jailbirds and shirkers into the disasters of the final retreat.

Only in the youth of the central character can this be considered a children's book. It pulls no punches, dodges none of the harsh issues of war. It is a man-sized book. Teenagers who come to it may find that this is the book they have been looking for, which treats them seriously and refuses to fob them off with quarter-truths. They will recognise the integrity of this reporting in which words are treated with due respect for their real meaning. A very remarkable book.

> *M. Crouch, in a review of "The Time of the Young Soldiers," in* The Junior Bookshelf, *Vol. 40, No. 3, June, 1976, p. 171.*

Propaganda . . . directs **The Time of the Young Soldiers**. . . . The quiet indictment of Nazism is, more broadly, an indictment of war itself, as he describes, in plain, unemotional terms, the effects of military discipline, of conflicting rumour and growing despair, on a young man who has been trained to accept without question a barbarous system. There is no squeamish mitigation of horror in the book and the grotesque humour that cuts into it from time to time only makes the picture blacker. The intention of the book is obvious: its effect on young readers can only be surmised. (pp. 2906-07)

> *Margery Fisher, in a review of "The Time of the Young Soldiers," in* Growing Point, *Vol. 15, No. 2, July, 1976, pp. 2906-07.*

E(lwyn) B(rooks) White

1899-1985

American author of fiction.

The following entry presents criticism of *Charlotte's Web*.

Distinguished as an essayist, poet, and humorist for adults who is recognized as one of the world's foremost writers of prose, White is the author of three stories for middle graders, *Stuart Little* (1945), *Charlotte's Web* (1952), and *The Trumpet of the Swan* (1970), in which he blends fantasy and realism to present profound themes to young readers in narratives which reflect his personal philosophy and characteristically succinct style. Although all of his contributions to juvenile literature have been critical and popular successes, *Charlotte's Web* is generally considered not only White's best book for children but also the finest achievement of his career. Acknowledged as a landmark in children's literature for White's honest yet sensitive treatment of the subject of death, *Charlotte's Web* is often lauded as the classic American children's book of the twentieth century. The story focuses on how Wilbur, an insecure, vulnerable pig, is saved from slaughter through the efforts of his barnyard friends, especially the ingenious and heroic spider Charlotte, who, after miraculously spinning the words "some pig," "terrific," "radiant," and "humble" into her web and spinning a sac in which she deposits her eggs, dies alone of exhaustion and old age. With Charlotte's help, Wilbur achieves both fame and maturity, understanding the meaning of true friendship as well as the place of death in the continuity of life; after Charlotte dies, Wilbur nurtures her children and becomes a good friend to them and their descendants. White further demonstrates his theme of growth and change through his portrayal of eight-year-old Fern Arable, Wilbur's first protector, who convinces her father to spare the pig's life. Initially, Fern spends much of her time in the barn owned by her uncle, Homer Zuckerman, where she can understand the conversation of Wilbur and the other animals that live there; later, however, her interests shift to the attentions of a neighbor boy, Henry Fussy. She becomes increasingly disinterested in the barn and its inhabitants, and finally misses Charlotte's noble acts and Wilbur's triumph because she has chosen to be with Henry.

White was inspired to write *Charlotte's Web* by his observations of the animals on his farm in North Brooklin, Maine: a celebration of nature and country life, the book is, he wrote "a straight report from the barn cellar, which I dearly love." Intending to create a story which accurately represents the facts of nature while stressing its beauty and joys, he emphasizes the natural world and the attributes of his animal characters while portraying his human characters less sympathetically. Although *Charlotte's Web* is narrated in an amiable tone, White draws a satiric picture of several of his adult characters which reflects his distaste for their ignorance, pride, and greed. He refuses to pass similar judgment on Fern, despite her abandonment of Wilbur and his friends; however, her portrayal has received a mixed reaction from critics: though some consider her a secondary character and dismiss her for losing interest in the barnyard characters, others note her importance both as a figure with whom young readers can identify and a representation of how the mutabili-

ty of nature affects humans as well as animals. *Charlotte's Web* is usually considered a work of both pathos and humor in which White delicately combines sadness and happiness to create a positive, affirming, and ultimately reassuring world view. *Charlotte's Web* was named a Newbery Medal honor book in 1953 and was given the Lewis Carroll Shelf Award in 1959. It has also received several child-selected awards.

(See also *CLR,* Vol. 1; *Something about the Author,* Vols. 2, 29, 44; *Contemporary Literary Criticism,* Vols. 10, 34, 39; *Contemporary Authors,* Vols. 13-16, rev. ed., Vol. 116 [obituary]; *Contemporary Authors New Revision Series,* Vol. 16; and *Dictionary of Literary Biography,* Vols. 11, 22.)

AUTHOR'S COMMENTARY

[The following excerpt is from a letter dated 12 January 1971 to Gene Deitch, a director who wanted to make an animated film of Charlotte's Web. *A film adaptation of the book, not directed by Deitch, was released by Paramount in 1972.]*

It was generous of you to send me such a detailed report of your scheme for the picture. This afternoon I sent you a few more photographs—they were taken in Canada, but they are close to New England in form and spirit.

You said in your letter (about my script) "how I wish I had the whole thing." You have everything I wrote; there wasn't any more.

I've studied your letter very carefully and find myself in sympathy, or agreement, with most of it. I do hope, though, that you are not planning to turn *Charlotte's Web* into a moral tale. It is not that at all. It is, I think, an *appreciative* story, and there is quite a difference. It celebrates life, the seasons, the goodness of the barn, the beauty of the world, the glory of everything. But it is essentially amoral, because animals are essentially amoral, and I respect them, and I think this respect is implicit in the tale. I discovered, quite by accident, that reality and fantasy make good bedfellows. I discovered that there was no need to tamper in any way with the habits and characteristics of spiders, pigs, geese, and rats. No "motivation" is needed if you remain true to life and true to the spirit of fantasy. I would hate to see Charlotte turned into a "dedicated" spider: she is, if anything, more the Mehitabel type—toujours gai. She is also a New Englander, precise and disciplined. She does what she does. Perhaps she is magnifying herself by her devotion to another, but essentially she is just a trapper. . . .

As for Templeton, he's an old acquaintance and I know him well. He starts as a rat and he ends as a rat—the perfect opportunist and a great gourmand. I devoutly hope that you are not planning to elevate Templeton to sainthood. . . .

An aura of magic is essential, because this is a magical happening. Much can be done by music of the right kind, as when the moment arrives when communication takes place between the little girl and the animals in the barn cellar. This is truly a magical moment and should be so marked by the music. (I hear it as a sort of thrumming, brooding sound, like the sound of crickets in the fall, or katydids, or cicadas. It should be a haunting, quiet, steady sound—subdued and repetitive.)

Even more can be done by *words,* if you are able to use them. (You'll have to forgive me for being a word man, but that's what I am.)

In writing of a spider, I did not make the spider adapt her ways to my scheme. I spent a year studying spiders before I ever started writing the book. In this, I think I found the key to the story. I hope you will, in your own medium, be true to Charlotte and to nature in general. My feeling about animals is just the opposite of Disney's. He made them dance to his tune and came up with some great creations, like Donald Duck. I preferred to dance to *their* tune and came up with Charlotte and Wilbur. It would be futile and unfair to compare the two approaches, but you are stuck with my scheme and will probably come out better if you go along with it. Both techniques are all right, each in its own way, but I have a strong feeling that you can't mix them. It just comes natural to me to keep animals pure and not distort them or take advantage of them.

Interdependence? I agree that the film should be a paean to life, a hymn to the barn, an acceptance of dung. But I think it would be quite untrue to suggest that barnyard creatures are dependent on each other. The barn is a community of rugged individualists, everybody mildly suspicious of everybody else, including me. Friendships sometimes develop, as between a goat and a horse, but there is no sense of true community or cooperation. Heaven forfend! Joy of life, yes. Tolerance of other cultures, yes. Community, no.

I just want to add that there is no symbolism in *Charlotte's Web.* And there is no political meaning in the story. It is a straight report from the barn cellar, which I dearly love, having spent so many fine hours there, winter and summer, spring and fall, good times and bad times, with the garrulous geese, the passage of swallows, the nearness of rats, and the sameness of sheep. . . . (p. 614)

> *E. B. White, in a letter to Gene Deitch on January 12, 1971, in his* Letters of E. B. White, *edited by Dorothy Lobrano Guth, Harper & Row, Publishers, 1976, pp. 613-14.*

EUDORA WELTY

[*Charlotte's Web*] has liveliness and felicity, tenderness and unexpectedness, grace and humor and praise of life, and the good backbone of succinctness that only the most highly imaginative stories seem to grow.

The characters are varied—good and bad, human and animal, talented and untalented, warm and cold, ignorant and intelligent, vegetarian and blood-drinking—varied but not simple or opposites. They are the real thing.

Wilbur is of a sweet nature—he is a spring pig—affectionate, responsive to moods of the weather and the song of the crickets, has long eyelashes, is hopeful, partially willing to try anything, brave, subject to faints from bashfulness, is loyal to friends, enjoys a good appetite and a soft bed, and is a little likely to be overwhelmed by the sudden chance for complete freedom. . . . [He] is the hero.

Charlotte A. Cavitica ("but just call me Charlotte") is the heroine, a large gray spider "about the size of a gumdrop." She has eight legs and can wave them in friendly greeting. When her friends wake up in the morning she says "Salutations!"—in spite of sometimes having been up all night herself, working. She tells Wilbur right away that she drinks blood, and Wilbur on first acquaintance begs her not to say that.

Another good character is Templeton, the rat. "The rat had no morals, no conscience, no scruples, no consideration, no decency, no milk of rodent kindness, no compunctions, no higher feeling, no friendliness, no anything." "Talking with Templeton was not the most interesting occupation in the world," Wilbur finds, "but it was better than nothing." Templeton grudges his help to others, then brags about it, can fold his hands behind his head, and sometimes acts like a spoiled child. . . .

What the book is about is friendship on earth, affection and protection, adventure and miracle, life and death, trust and treachery, pleasure and pain, and the passing of time. As a piece of work it is just about perfect, and just about magical in the way it is done. What it all proves—in the words of the minister in the story which he hands down to his congregation after Charlotte writes "Some Pig" in her web—is "that human beings must always be on the watch for the coming of wonders." Dr. Dorian says in another place, "Oh, no, I don't understand it. But for that matter I don't understand how a spider learned to spin a web in the first place. When the words appeared, everyone said they were a miracle. But nobody pointed out that the web itself is a miracle." The author will only say, "Charlotte was in a class by herself." . . .

Charlotte's Web is an adorable book.

Eudora Welty, " 'Life in the Barn Was Very Good', " in The New York Times Book Review, *October 19, 1952, p. 49.*

P. L. TRAVERS

I am sure there is a special formula for writing books for children. But it is like poetry. You have to be born with it. You can't learn it the way you can learn the alphabet or that two and two make five. Every Christmas I find myself playing a sort of literary "Who's got the slipper?" among the children's books. Not you, not you, not you—but YOU! And out comes the slipper with the author's name. Once it was J. R. R. Tolkein, who wrote one of the best children's books of the century, *The Hobbit.* . . . Twice and in quick succession, too, the name on the slipper has been E. B. White. . . [His books] fulfill as many requirements of that special formula as can reasonably be expected of one man.

First of all, he never explains. He begins his story right in the middle, which, of course, is the proper place. "Mrs. Frederick C. Little's second son," we read in *Stuart Little,* "was no bigger than a mouse and the baby looked very much like a mouse in every way." What a satisfying statement! No clinical details, no surprise. It is all in the order of things. Magic, the author blandly tells us, without stooping to put it into words, is nowhere else but *here,* as real as a morning bowl of cereal, the star being in the grain.

So, too, with *Charlotte's Web.* We no sooner learn that Mr. Arable (a suitable surname for a farmer) has given the runt of the pig family to his daughter, Fern (a country girl from her name onwards), than we realize that the smallest pig, like the youngest prince, is in for an unusual destiny. Troubles arise—how could they not?—for with runts, as with Ugly Ducklings, the way is always uphill. But with that inevitability that the formula requires he is saved from becoming breakfast bacon by his friend Charlotte, the Spider. *How* this is done, I shall not say, for twice-cooked magic is like Shepherd's Pie, heavy in the eating. You must get it straight, with its first fine flavour, from Mr. White himself. But Wilbur the Pig's story, is not merely a success story and in making it something more the author is adhering to that element in the formula which insists that the function of the heart is to feel and the function of a door—at least, in this connection—is to open. Stuart Little's quest for his flown bird differs in terminology only from the quest of every fairy-tale prince for his lost princess. Love is at the core of it.

We are not told the end of the story for no true story has an ending but we feel the door swinging wide as the Mouse steers towards the North. For the ends of the earth have many names and North perhaps is as good as any. The same with Wilbur. He, too, loses a precious friend, experiences the pain of it and the joy that follows after pain when he hatches her spider children. His end of the earth is a barn cellar and his door opens upon the seasons, on birth and ripening, fall and birth. "It was the best place to be" (he thought) "this warm delicious cellar, with the heat of the sun, the passage of swallows, the nearness of rats, the love of spiders, the smell of manure and the glory of everything." This sense of delight in daily things is as strong in *Charlotte's Web* as it was in *Stuart Little.* There is goodness and meaning in simply being alive.

Such tangible magic is the proper element of childhood and any grown up who can still dip into it—even with only so

much as a toe—is certain at last of dying young even if he lives to be ninety. (pp. 1, 38)

P. L. Travers, "Tangible Magic," in New York Herald Tribune Book Review, *November 16, 1952, pp. 1, 38.*

CHARLOTTE S. HUCK AND DORIS A. YOUNG

This is a story that has humor, pathos, wisdom, and beauty. It speaks to all ages; the adults who read it to their children enjoy it as much as the children fortunate enough to hear it. Much of our fantasy is of English origin. *Charlotte's Web* is as American as the Fourth of July and should be just as much a part of our heritage. (p. 298)

Charlotte S. Huck and Doris A. Young, "Children Enjoy Folk, Fun, and Fancy," in their Children's Literature in the Elementary School, *Holt, Rinehart and Winston, 1961, pp. 272-318.*

A. K. D. CAMPBELL

[*Charlotte's Web*] is notable both for its opening, which can be guaranteed to capture attention in almost any household, and for its ending, in which sadness and joy are wonderfully blended into serenity. The plot of this story hinges on the quite conventional idea of a condemned pig striving to escape his fate, but in Mr. White's hands the situation becomes a drama in which each character has a distinctive part to play and almost every incident has the sparkle of novelty.

Among the animals, Wilbur the pig, Templeton the rat, and Charlotte the spider are an unforgettable trio; while of the more lightly-sketched humans, the dreamy Fern Arable and her boisterous brother Avery should be greeted as kindred spirits by most readers. One or other of these individuals is usually at the centre of the stage as the action advances from crisis to crisis, although there are occasional planned interludes when the author moralises to his readers in half-humorous vein, or expands on some point of natural history which happens to have arisen.

Among all the good things in this book, nothing perhaps is better than the delicacy and good taste with which Mr. White approaches the death of Charlotte:

> "Maybe," said Charlotte quickly. "However, I have a feeling I'm not going to see the results of last night's efforts. I don't feel good at all. I'm beginning to languish, to tell you the truth."

From this point onwards the ideas of mortality and of continuing generations are brought forward together, so that there is no likelihood of undue distress for any young reader. If one function of children's literature is to prepare for the stresses of adult life, this particular episode in *Charlotte's Web* deserves the highest praise. (pp. 12-13)

A. K. D. Campbell, "The Stories of E. B. White," in Books for Your Children, *Vol. 7, No. 3, 1971, pp. 12-13.*

SELMA G. LANES

In White's *Charlotte's Web,* far more rounded and satisfactory a modern fairy tale [than *Stuart Little*], the pig hero, Wilbur, has only one dream in life: to keep from being turned into smoked bacon and ham when the cold weather sets in. . . . [Neither] freedom nor adventure is as important to him as comfort, friendship and the magic of simply living from day to day in a barn that "had a sort of peaceful smell—as though nothing bad could happen ever again in the world." A thoroughly post-World War II pig in attitude, Wilbur is enabled to achieve his dream when his wise friend, the spider Charlotte, applies the magic of modern American advertising technique to his plight. Here . . . , the fairy tale reflects a new American attitude. Unbounded faith in the future is replaced by satisfaction with a comfortable and familiar *status quo.* An imperfect reality is magic enough for Wilbur. (pp. 105-06)

> *Selma G. Lanes, "America as Fairy Tale," in her* Down the Rabbit Hole: Adventures & Misadventures in the Realm of Children's Literature, *Atheneum Publishers, 1971, pp. 91-111.*

LAURENCE GAGNON

One type of model which can be used with great success in interpreting works of children's literature and adult fantasy is a Heideggerian model. By associating parts of Martin Heidegger's philosophy with certain parts of these literary works, we can achieve a novel, if not profound, understanding of them. Two cases in point are *The Little Prince* by A. de Saint Exupéry and *Charlotte's Web.* . . .

Stated as simply and untechnically as possible, the particular Heideggarian model appealed to here is one concerned with persons and their capabilities. Now persons are capable of many things, of flying planes and watering flowers, of eating leftovers and killing insects. Yet these are rather superficial capabilities, not being characteristic of persons as such but rather only of persons as pilots or gardeners, omnivores or killers. Among the more fundamental capabilities are those of being aware of oneself, of being concerned about things in the world, of dreading one's death, and ultimately of living authentically. Since each person as such is unique and irreplaceable, this ultimate capability is also the ultimate personal obligation: to live authentically. Under the present interpretation, *The Little Prince* and *Charlotte's Web* are about various personal struggles to live authentically. In each of these works there are characters who find themselves thrown into existence, as it were, amidst other beings with whom they end up being concerned, all the while being confronted with the difficult and inescapable task of truly becoming what they alone can be—even unto death. This is precisely the task of living authentically. The ever-present danger here is that of losing one's sense of personal identity by becoming part of the crowd or by becoming overly concerned with other beings. (p. 61)

In *Charlotte's Web,* a rat, a pig, and a spider find themselves thrown into existence together, inescapably confronted with the task of truly becoming what they can be—even unto death. The rat, Templeton, commits himself to an inauthentic existence. In a miserly fashion he acquires things without thereafter tending to them. Merely storing rotten eggs like banking stars does not involve taking care of one's possessions. Not having developed even this capacity, he cannot develop his capacity of caring for others. He must be enticed to go to the fair and bribed to pick up the egg sac. He could care less whether Wilbur, the pig, died of a broken heart or whether Charlotte, the spider, died of exhaustion and old age. Nor does he really confront the possibility of his own death. He lives for the present, especially when it is "full of life" in the form of feasting and carousing. Of course, his death will come sometime. But he sees it as coming in the distant future,

as the end of his life, rather than as a distinctive part of his life. "Who wants to live forever?" he sneers.

Wilbur, on the other hand, is not committed to inauthentic existence but he is tempted in a variety of ways to live inauthentically. As a young pig, he does not have an especially strong personality. His attitudes and opinions can easily be swayed by outside influences: a few words from the goose, a pail of slops, a rainy day, the bad news from the old sheep, the reassuring promise of Charlotte. As a result he is always in danger of becoming a people-self rather than a distinctive person. If Charlotte's web says that he is "some pig" and people believe it, Wilbur believes it. If it says that he is "terrific" and people believe it, he not only believes it but also really feels terrific. If it's "radiant," then radiant Wilbur is. (Only with the last, prophetic message is there a genuineness in Wilbur's attitude—he has finally become more of himself, a humble pig.)

Wilbur refuses to face the fact that he might be killed next Christmas-time and turned into smoked bacon and ham. " 'I don't *want* to die . . . ' " he moans, " ' . . . I want to stay alive, right here in my comfortable manure pile with all my friends' ". He does not see his dying as an integral part of his life. He sees it as the end of it all.

Left to his own devices, the selfish and insecure Wilbur would remain a people-self. But "out of the darkness, came a small voice he had never heard before. . . . " 'Do you want a friend, Wilbur?' it said. 'I'll be a friend to you' ". Charlotte tames him. From the ties thus established, Wilbur gradually grows to care for the large grey spider, who lives in the upper part of the barn doorway. Since he naturally tends toward being a people-self, his initial reaction is to identify himself with his new found friend by imitating her. So he tries in vain to spin a web, ignoring Charlotte's profound observation, " ' . . . you and I lead different lives' ". When Charlotte says she's glad she's a sedentary spider, Wilbur replies, " 'Well, I'm sort of sendentary myself, I guess' ".

Gradually Wilbur realizes that he and Charlotte are different, even though friends. They are different not merely generically, as pig and spider, but also individually, as distinctive persons. But persons are beings-unto-death. So Wilbur and Charlotte must also differ in their dying.

It is only after the Fair has ended, the crowd dispersed, and Wilbur's hour of triumph over that he turns his attention away from himself toward his dying friend. " 'Why did you do all this for me? . . . I don't deserve it. I've never done anything for you' ". With her characteristic wisdom, Charlotte replies, " 'You have been my friend . . . That in itself is a tremendous thing' ".

Now more than ever, Wilbur wants to preserve the ties that have been established between him and the lovely grey spider. He throws "himself down in an agony of pain and sorrow," sobbing " ' . . . 'I can't stand it . . . I won't leave you here alone to die' ". But Wilbur is being ridiculous. He can't stay with Charlotte. For if he stayed, he would not be true either to Charlotte or himself. His call of conscience is to return to the farm with Charlotte's egg sac. With amazing agility (for a pig) Wilbur accepts this call to authenticity. "All winter Wilbur watched over Charlotte's egg sac as though he were guarding his own children".

In the spring the young spiders came. But there is sorrow in this resurrection. Being unique themselves, none can live the life Charlotte did. So Charlotte's children sail away. "This is our moment for setting forth". However, Wilbur is not left totally alone. Three of them stay. To them Wilbur pledges his friendship, "forever and ever". Yet "Wilbur never forgot Charlotte. Although he loved her children and grandchildren dearly, none of the new spiders ever quite took her place in his heart. She was in a class by herself ". From the beginning Charlotte had resolutely advanced toward her own solitary death, all the while taking care of her magnificent web and caring for her humble friend. She saves Wilbur from an undistinctive death and gives him both the situation and the time to heed his own call of concern. (pp. 63-5)

> *Laurence Gagnon, "Webs of Concern: 'The Little Prince' and 'Charlotte's Web',"* in Children's Literature: Annual of the Modern Language Association Seminar on Children's Literature and The Children's Literature Association, *Vol. 2, 1973, pp. 61-6.*

URSULA NORDSTROM

[*An editor at Harper & Row, Nordstrom edited the manuscript of* Charlotte's Web.]

One day in the early spring of 1962 I was sitting in my Harper office and the receptionist came in to tell me E. B. White was outside. I went out to the elevator and greeted him, and he said, "I've brought you a new manuscript." I hadn't known he was even close to finishing a second book and I was overwhelmed. Thinking immediately that it was already pretty late to get it illustrated and printed and bound in time for the fall list, I said, "Have you given me a carbon copy too, so I can rush it off to [illustrator Garth Williams]?"

"No," he said, "this is the only copy; I didn't make a carbon copy." And he gave me the only copy in existence of *Charlotte's Web,* got back on the elevator and left.

An editor seldom has the luxury of enough time in the office to read manuscripts, but I decided I would have to give myself just that luxury that afternoon. There were no Xerox machines in 1952, and I didn't dare take a chance on losing the manuscript on the train home, or whatever. So I sat down and began to read.

I couldn't believe that it was so good! I came to the chapter in which Wilbur the pig, so lonely and frightened in the barn, hears "a small voice he had never heard before. It sounded rather thin, but pleasant. 'Do you want a friend, Wilbur? I'll be a friend to you. I've watched you all day and I like you.' " Then in the next chapter, the following morning, Wilbur says "in a loud firm voice, 'Will the party who addressed me at bedtime last night kindly make himself or herself known by giving an appropriate sign or signal?' " At that, I knew that this was one of the great ones, and I reached for the telephone to call Mr. White at the New Yorker.

Book salesmen are usually not eager to hear a detailed synopsis of a book, but when *Charlotte's Web* was presented to the sales conference in June of 1952, the men honestly wanted to hear as much of the story as we could tell them. They circulated the pictures, expressed great enthusiasm and seemed truly touched. During the summer, one of them wrote me that he had been painting his porch and hadn't been able to do a completely good job because he couldn't bring himself to disturb a spider's web on the ceiling. I must have shared this with Mr. White, for I have a note saying: "Spiders expect to have their webs busted, and they take it in their stride. One

of Charlotte's daughters placed her web in the tie-ups, right behind my bull calf, and I kept forgetting about it and would bust one of her foundation lines on my trips to and from the trapdoor where I push the manure into the cellar . . . After several days of this, during which she had to rebuild the entire web each evening, she solved the matter neatly by changing the angle of the web so that the foundation line no longer crossed my path. Her ingenuity has impressed me, and I am now teaching her to write SOME BOOK, and will let Brentano have her for their window." (pp. 8, 10)

> *Ursula Nordstrom, "Stuart, Wilbur, Charlotte: A Tale of Tales," in* The New York Times Book Review, *May 12, 1974, pp. 8, 10.*

EDWARD C. SAMPSON

[*Charlotte's Web*] is touching, with death and sadness, but also continuity and renewal. The main story—the saving of Wilbur and Charlotte's death—has clear progress; what helps to give it additional depth and unity is Fern, who is really the key to the structure. It is ironic that Fern is absent when Wilbur reaches his highest triumph, and when Charlotte dies. Yet, given the real-life situation of Fern, her absence is almost inevitable. She is no stock figure for the telling of the story, or for getting the attention of the young reader, although a child can identify with her. She is a girl growing up, and her growth is a counterpoint to the main plot.

White doesn't dwell on Fern's growth, and we should not try . . . to find profundity and complication where none exists. I doubt if most children think much about Fern at the last; their attention is on Wilbur and Charlotte. Still, every good children's story has something for the adult as well as for the child, and Fern is part of the story for the adult. With Wilbur and the yearly spring-born spiders, the world of childhood continues; with Fern there is growth and transition to a world where it is not the spider's life, but man's, that can't help being something of a mess. It is also a world where the miracle of love and courtship supplements the miracle of the spider's web. (p. 103)

> *Edward C. Sampson, in his* E. B. White, *Twayne Publishers, Inc., 1974, 190 p.*

ROGER SALE

[*Charlotte's Web*] is probably *the* classic American children's book of the last thirty years. White's is rather an odd case. On the one hand he is the one author considered here who has made a full and lasting reputation as a writer of other kinds of literature, the essays and sketches that for so many years distinguished the pages of *Harper's* and the *New Yorker.* On the other he is the author of three children's books— *Stuart Little* and *The Trumpet of the Swan* are the other two—and neither, it seems to me, is even good enough to be called a distinguished or considerable failure. One might conclude that White is just not a writer of books, except that *Charlotte's Web* is full, sustained, serene, a *book* in ways that perhaps only the great Potters and *Kim* rival or exceed among all those discussed in [the essays in this book]. One surmises that he seldom tried to think of himself as a writer of whole books, which is perhaps just as well, given his talents. But with *Charlotte's Web* he worked hard to get it to come right, and he did not let himself be satisfied until he had. *Stuart Little,* by comparison, is terribly bored during many of its episodes, and *The Trumpet of the Swan* seems explainable as a book that White wrote for personal reasons that he never could get to square articulately with his materials. But *Charlotte's Web* is a gem. . . . (p. 258)

White calls *Charlotte's Web* a "hymn to the barn," and it is the word "hymn," and the sense of celebration and praise, that is important here, though the way the book is a hymn is not clear at the outset. [The author of the *Freddy* books, Walter R.] Brooks's way with his barn is from the beginning detached, amused, and dedicated to the proposition that the barnyard has problems, that problems have solutions, and that nothing essentially ever changes. There are no seasons in the Freddy books, the barnyard activities are assumed rather than described, and no one ever grows a day older. White's way is different; with him process and change are all, because only buildings and tools are unchanging, and the essential celebration is of the beautiful things change brings or can bring. But the key change, the one upon which our sense of all the others hangs, comes early, before we are fully aware of White's way with realism and with animals. By the third chapter, by the twentieth page, White has played his one magical trick, because of which he can show in a nonrealistic way what the life of a barn is really like.

The opening pages are all realism. A sow has littered, and one of her piglets is a runt, and Mr. Arable is going to kill it "because it would probably die anyway." His daughter Fern is outraged:

> "But it's unfair," cried Fern. "The pig couldn't help being born small, could it? If I had been very small at birth, would you have killed *me*?"

> Mr. Arable smiled. "Certainly not," he said, looking down at his daughter with love. "But this is different. A little girl is one thing, a little runty pig is another."

This is a variation that none of [the books considered in this study] so far has faced: human beings value animals less than they do human beings, and farmers tend to treat animals as conveniences and necessities rather than as fellow creatures. White next does all he can to make his reversal of Lewis Carroll's "Pig and Pepper" seem a joke at Fern's expense. Her father agrees to let Fern keep the runt, and Fern gives it a bottle, names it Wilbur, puts it in a baby carriage, and we are told "he liked this." But the moment Wilbur's appetite begins to increase, Fern's father insists he must be sold, and Fern's efforts at motherhood come to an end: pigs are not human, and they mature much faster too. The best that can be done for Wilbur is to sell him to Uncle Homer Zuckerman, whose farm is not far off.

So first we thwart the "natural human" tendency to want to treat animals like people. Next we put Wilbur into Zuckerman's barn and make Fern into nothing more than an occasional bystander; Uncle Homer won't allow Fern into Wilbur's pen, but she comes every afternoon: "Here she sat quietly during the long afternoons, thinking and listening and watching Wilbur. The sheep soon got to know her and trust her. So did the geese, who lived with the sheep. All the animals trusted her, she was so quiet and friendly." The sentences are all peaceful, but they are building a bridge. Wilbur "liked" being in Fern's baby carriage, and now the animals "trusted" Fern. If it will not work to deny the possibility of animals' liking and trusting, then it can make "Wilbur happy to know that she was sitting there, right outside his pen," and in the context of that trusting happiness, we learn "But he never had any fun—no walks, no rides, no swims." Are we

over the line yet, the one we usually draw between thoughts and feelings we easily imagine intelligent animals having, and those we seriously doubt them having? Can Wilbur remember his treatment as an infant by Fern? Can he stand "in the sun feeling lonely and bored"? Can he say "I'm less than two months old and I'm tired of living"? He can, of course, and he does, but White has also moved across his bridge to the unrealistic quietly and without fuss, as though Wilbur's thoughts and speaking were available to him and us because Fern has sat watching him in ways more patient than the rest of us offer animals.

Once Wilbur can speak and know he is two months old, then the gander can tell him about a loose board in his pen, and he can seek the outside world. From this point on White never shifts his bearings; having given himself this much magic on page 16, he uses it to sing his otherwise realistic hymn to the barn. This is Selma Lagerlöf's way too, and White's intentions are similar, if softer. Both want to imagine it is only human egotism and busyness that prevents us from seeing the lives of animals that are lived all around us, lives that could, they say, be understood in human terms. Wilbur can be bored and lonely, plan out his day in advance, and be disappointed when that day comes up raining. As I write this I watch my cat, staring out the window on a rainy morning. Usually he goes outside and sniffs about in the yard at this time, but he hates rain. Is he lonely, bored, disappointed? Randall Jarrell's mermaid would say no, and certainly if he feels something like these feelings, he does not respond to them with the same impatience or mournfulness that I would. But when I read about Wilbur's loneliness I think I don't understand my cat very clearly because my patience and imagination are weak. Think what a long day it would be—"I have no real friend here in the barn, it's going to rain all morning and all afternoon, and Fern won't come in such bad weather". The goose can't play because she is sitting on her nest, the lamb won't play because she is not interested in pigs, Templeton the rat won't play because he hardly knows the meaning of the word: "I prefer to spend my time eating, gnawing, spying, and hiding". So the same circumstances concerning the lives of pigs which amused Walter Brooks into making Freddy an amateur and thus his central figure are those which make time and loneliness so oppressive for Wilbur. Pigs, as he is soon to learn, are given nothing to do except eating and growing fat.

But before he learns that, he finds his friend, a voice from the rafters as he goes asleep one night, Charlotte A. Cavatica as she introduces herself the next morning, a spider about the size of a gumdrop. As if to make sure he realizes what Templeton was telling him the day before—some creatures around here get fed by farmers, and some just have to make their own way—Charlotte first shows Wilbur how she traps flies, then stuns them, then drinks their blood; "I love blood," she says; " 'Don't say that!' groaned Wilbur"; "Why not? It's true." No blood, no spiders; no spiders, no friend for Wilbur. White then drops a stitch, as it were, and ends this chapter with a needless reassuring note about Charlotte's true kind heart, "and she was to prove loyal and true to the very end." It is as though White knows to his own satisfaction why he wants to introduce Charlotte as a lover of blood—to get that over with so he can ignore it—but is nervous his young readers will not see this. As always, when a writer fixes on children as the audience, a mistake is almost sure to follow. Beatrix Potter never makes such mistakes, and White, fortunately, makes very few.

Having established his cast, White is ready to begin singing his hymn:

> The early summer days on a farm are the happiest and fairest days of the year. Lilacs bloom and make the air sweet, and then fade. Apple blossoms come with the lilacs, and the bees visit around among the apple trees. The days grow warm and soft. School ends, and children have time to play and to fish for trouts in the brook. Avery often brought a trout home in his pocket, warm and stiff and ready to be fried for supper.
>
> Now that school was over, Fern visited the barn almost every day, to sit quietly on her stool. The animals treated her as an equal. The sheep lay calmly at her feet.

Then we have the farmers in the field, the bird songs, including the song sparrow, "who knows how brief and lovely life is," and says, "Sweet, sweet, sweet interlude; sweet, sweet, sweet interlude." The interlude is the moment of singing, the early summer days, and all of life, and all three at once. "Everywhere you look is life; even the little ball of spit on the weed stalk, if you poke it apart, has a green worm inside it. And on the under side of the leaf of the potato vine are the bright orange eggs of the potato bug."

White does not imagine the song sparrow understands its song as White asks us to understand it; it takes a human mind to know fully the meaning of "sweet interlude." Nor is it beauty White is concerned with, but the acknowledgment that the love of life, especially the love of early summer days, includes the knowledge of transience and death. For the problem is Wilbur, eating three times a day and getting fat. . . . (pp. 258-62)

[After Wilbur learns that he is being fattened up because he is going to be killed,] he runs to Charlotte. She might have told him that just as she needs blood to live, farmers need smoked meat to get them through the winter. Instead she says, "If she says they plan to kill you, I'm sure it's true. It's also the dirtiest trick I ever heard of. What people don't think of !" She then tells Wilbur she will save him, somehow. Charlotte, then, assumes the position Fern took at the opening of the book: she becomes the protester against injustice, though she has no court of appeal. Then, later, after he has had a chance to calm down, Wilbur can offer the real reason, or at least White's real reason, for not wanting to die:

> "Charlotte?" he said softly.
>
> "Yes, Wilbur?"
>
> "I don't want to die."
>
> "Of course you don't," said Charlotte in a comforting voice.
>
> "I just love it here in the barn," said Wilbur. "I love everything about this place."

So White's first hymn, in praise of early summer days, has come to this; the more one loves life, the less one wants to leave it; Wilbur hears the seven goslings whistling, "like a tiny troupe of pipers," and listens "with love in his heart." So he too has taken over part of Fern's position.

One summer afternoon Fern and her brother Avery are playing on a rope swing in Zuckerman's barn when Avery spots Charlotte's web hanging from the rafter next to the swing. He decides to do the human thing and get rid of it, but as he climbs above Wilbur's pig trough he stumbles, falls, and lands on the by-now rotten egg Templeton has been saving. The smell immediately drives him away, and Charlotte and her web are saved. None of this is lost on Wilbur—"It was that rotten goose egg that saved Charlotte's life," he says, and that night he remembers to leave a little extra of his food so Templeton can scavenge it: "Then he remembered that the rat had been useful in saving Charlotte's life, and that Charlotte was trying to save *his* life. So he left a whole noodle, instead of a half." We are back, though by a very different route, to Walter Brooks's sense of the barnyard as a place of mutual cooperation, though White sounds this note in a different key. A whole noodle instead of a half is not a lot, but it is quite a bit. At this point White and Wilbur are ready for Charlotte's "miracle."

Actually, it takes a human perspective to call it a miracle, and White has been urging us for some time to take a somewhat different one. But there it is; Zuckerman's hired man, Lurvy, comes to the barn one morning and sees, distinctly, the words SOME PIG written in Charlotte's web. Clearly, if Wilbur and Charlotte and the others can speak English, it is only a short step to their being able to write it, so there is no reason why we should be surprised at all at the message in Charlotte's web. But of those who first see it, only Mrs. Zuckerman concludes that the extraordinary one is not the pig but the spider. We are to presume Charlotte had counted on that, and there follows some not altogether satisfactory satire about the gullibility of human beings, all of whom think Wilbur is or has become miraculously SOME PIG because Charlotte's web says so. So Charlotte makes another message, the single word TERRIFIC. Wilbur has become Zuckerman's famous pig, and he is to be sent to the county fair for show, and it seems clear that although the people now own the pig and all the publicity attendant upon Charlotte's "miracle," Wilbur is safe.

But if human beings are fools, what of Fern? She has become the one her mother worries about when she talks about the conversations in the barnyard, and White does not want to lose her, though he clearly has, since early in the book, wanted to keep her in the background. One night, after Charlotte sings Wilbur to sleep with a lullaby with its own barnyard lyrics—"Rest from care, my one and only, Deep in the dung and the dark"—White adds, "When the song ended, Fern got up and went home," though he had not said she was even there. In the next chapter Mrs. Arable goes to see the genial and bearded Dr. Dorian, who immediately says it is fine if Fern spends all her time in the barn and asks if anyone has noticed that the ability of a spider to spin a web is itself a miracle, message or no message. What Dr. Dorian is doing in the book at all is, unfortunately, too obvious: he is the wise one who will say that Fern too can expect change, just like Charlotte and Wilbur, because it is only the obdurate adult human beings who truly resist changes and changing. Fern fought to keep Wilbur alive, and then became a silent watcher of the barn; the next step, White and Dr. Dorian assure us, is boys: "Let Fern associate with her friends in the barn if she wants to. I would say, offhand, that spiders and pigs were fully as interesting as Henry Fussy. Yet I predict that the day will come when even Henry will drop some chance remark that catches Fern's attention. It's amazing how children change from year to year." So at the county fair Fern is off with Henry Fussy, while the central drama is played without her, or her attentiveness.

The hymn begins again: "The crickets sang in the grasses. They sang the song of summer's ending, a sad, monotonous song. 'Summer is over and gone,' they sang. 'Over and gone, over and gone. Summer is dying, dying.' " The children know school opens soon, Lurvy knows it's time to dig potatoes, "Charlotte heard it and knew that she hadn't much time left." It's time for her to lay her eggs, and she must build an egg sac, and she tells Wilbur she should not leave her web to go to the county fair. But she decides Wilbur may need her, and she gets Templeton to come along to run errands; in addition, says the old sheep, "a fair is a rat's paradise." So Charlotte and Templeton hide down in the bottom of Wilbur's van and go with him to the fair, where Fern finds Henry Fussy, where Wilbur is not given the blue ribbon but gets a special award anyway because he is SOME PIG, where Templeton gorges himself as he never has before, where Charlotte weaves her last message, HUMBLE, over Wilbur's pen, and also makes her own egg sac, "made of the toughest material I have," where five hundred and fourteen spiders will gestate until the following spring. It is Charlotte's magnum opus, as she says, but partly because she will make only one in her life, and the end of summer means the end of living for her. The hour of Wilbur's triumph comes when he receives his award, but the book's climax comes a little later:

> For a moment Charlotte said nothing. Then she spoke in a voice so low Wilbur could hardly hear the words.
>
> "I will not be going back to the barn," she said.
>
> Wilbur leaped to his feet. "Not going back?" he cried. "Charlotte, what are you talking about!"
>
> "I'm done for," she replied. "In a day or two I'll be dead. I haven't even strength enough to climb down into the crate. I doubt if I have enough silk in my spinnerets to lower me to the ground."

Consciousness, we may often feel, is a debilitating and isolating capacity; it keeps us from having the simple dignity of animals. White gives Charlotte the knowledge that she is dying, but retains the simple dignity of which consciousness usually deprives us. "After all," she tells Wilbur when he asks why she did so much for him, "what's a life, anyway? We're born, we live a little while, we die. A spider's life can't help being something of a mess, with all this trapping and eating flies." The speech is a trifle too pat, but it is hard to know how White might have improved it, because what makes it pat is not so much the words themselves but its being offered as an obviously climactic and concluding attitude. "By helping you," Charlotte goes on, "perhaps I was trying to lift up my life a trifle." That *is* awkwardly said, because White can have Charlotte say "We're born, we live a little while, we die," only if she can add what he has insistently shown: she is SOME SPIDER.

On the one hand White wants us to move into the barn and to imagine the lives of pigs and spiders as being much more interesting than we know. But on the other he wants to tell the story of an extraordinary spider, so that the next time we are tempted to clear out a spider's web we may pause, but know as we do so that that spider is no Charlotte. Charlotte has done more than "lift up" her life "a little." It is a ticklish situation for White, and perhaps one should not mind if he does not handle it as deftly as we could wish. He does much better at the end, after Wilbur has talked Templeton into getting Charlotte's egg sac for him so he can place it under his tongue and bring the spider eggs back to the barn: "She never moved again. Next day, as the Ferris wheel was being taken apart and the race horses were being loaded into vans and the entertainers were packing their belongings and driving away in their trailers, Charlotte died. The Fair Grounds were soon deserted. The sheds and buildings were empty and forlorn. The infield was littered with bottles and trash. Nobody, of the hundreds of people that had visited the Fair, knew that a grey spider had played the most important part of all. No one was with her when she died." The country fair is over just as the summer is over, and it does not matter much if anyone is with Charlotte when she dies. But she did play the most important part of all, she performed the one less than fully natural and heroic act of being Wilbur's friend and saving his life and creating his fame. No need here to insist we should not cry if we feel like crying; it is more important that the simple dignity be Charlotte's than White's, more important that he be dignified than we.

Wilbur, Charlotte's one and only, "came home to his beloved manure pile," deep in the dung and the dark. He has now been guaranteed what, considering the lives of most pigs, is an unnaturally long life. After the autumn comes snow, and Fern and Avery go sledding:

> "Coasting is the most fun there is," said Avery.
>
> "The most fun there is," retorted Fern, "is when the Ferris wheel stops and Henry and I are in the top car and Henry makes the car swing and we can see everything for miles and miles and miles."
>
> "Goodness, are you still thinking about that ol' Ferris wheel?" said Avery in disgust. "The Fair was weeks and weeks ago."
>
> "I think about it all the time," said Fern, picking snow from her ear.

Avery has learned one of White's messages: time passes, things change, live with what comes. Fern, sentimental still, cannot think back to her saving Wilbur's life, but she can learn in her own way the other message: remember the best things, treasure them.

Spring comes, a new lamb is born and the goose lays nine new eggs, and Charlotte's tiny spiders crawl from the egg sac. There are dozens and dozens spinning little webs near the sac, but soon most have left, and only three, Joy, Aranea, and Nellie, are left to spin webs in the rafters above Wilbur's pen. At the end White sings his two hymns one last time. First:

> It was the best place to be, thought Wilbur, this warm delicious cellar, with the garrulous geese, the changing seasons, the heat of the sun, the passage of swallows, the nearness of rats, the sameness of sheep, the love of spiders, the smell of manure, the glory of everything.

Then:

> Wilbur never forgot Charlotte. Although he loved her children and grandchildren dearly, none of the new spiders ever quite took her place in his heart. She was in a class by herself. It is not often that someone comes along who is a true friend and a good writer. Charlotte was both.

White may not know here how to sing this hymn as well as the other, but no matter, because he has sung it well enough earlier. It is a sweet interlude of a book. (pp. 262-67)

Roger Sale, "Two Pigs," in his Fairy Tales and
After: From Snow White to E. B. White, Cambridge, Mass.: Harvard University Press, 1978, pp.
245-68.

PETER NEUMEYER

What makes a good children's book? The very question elicits
expressions of despair. Might as well ask, "What makes a
good book?" But the question is not impossible to answer.
Denseness of texture would be a simple and defensible reply.
And what is "denseness of texture?" It is close warp; close
woof. Many threads per inch. Denseness is allied to richness.
There's simply a lot there, a lot put into the book, by an author with many resources, and consequently a lot to consider
by a reader with developed capacities.

Take E. B. White's **Charlotte's Web,** and contemplate it,
from the discreet word all the way to the mythopoeic dimension.

The most discreet attribute in a book is the individual word.
The words of **Charlotte's Web** are distinctive and describable.
The book opens: " 'Where's Papa going with that ax?' said
Fern to her mother as they were setting the table for breakfast." The words are simple and basic. "Simple" and "basic"
are not terms to cover numinous impressions. They mean
that the words are not Latinate, but are short, commonplace,
and that they bespeak their homely Anglo-Saxon origins.

Book endings are almost as instructive as their openings.
Charlotte's Web ends: "It is not often that someone comes
along who is a true friend and a good writer. Charlotte was
both". "Charlotte was both" is the last sentence of the book.
Charlotte, the feminine of Karl, is, unlike Cher or Sherry,
both spawned antiseptically of electronic parents, a true, almost, a chivalric, name. "Was" and "both" bespeak their ancient lineage on their very face. And the antithesis, the longer
period followed by the almost shockingly short sentence, is
classic.

Point one, then, **Charlotte's Web** is a book in which much of
the language is distinctive for its pure and primordial pedigree.

The main characters in **Charlotte's Web** have, in good novelistic tradition, names suggestive of the characteristics of their
owners, and—in manner to be explored later—crucial to the
most basic nature of the book.

The farm family owning the famous pig is named Arable. The
plowable farm—arable. The Plowables own the land to be
plowed. One Arable child has an intimate relationship with
all natural creatures. Fern Arable, of course. The Fern is a
plant so ancient that its earliest evidences are fossilized, are
paleographic.

Mrs. Arable is simply Fern's mother, or Mrs. Arable. She
dreams of deep freezers, as any generic missus would. And
Mr. Arable is Mr. Arable simply, *The Farmer,* not further
distinguished, and thus a cousin of Lenski's pasteboard "Farmer Small."

The pig is Wilbur, with all respects to a possible Wilbur reader of this piece, an amiable if perhaps somewhat lumpish
name. About Charlotte's name, or Templeton, the rat's, I
have no more to say, for the reader can, if he knows the per-
sonages involved, make inferences as plausible as mine.

White, then, uses simple English language, and gives his
characters names that are appropriate and suggestive. In addition he gives to those characters, human and animal, language such as is befitting to their person, or describes them
in language appropriate to character. Thus Templeton, the
rat, incarnation of physical and moral putridness, is introduced first as he "crept stealthily along the wall and disappeared into a private tunnel that he had dug between the door
and the trough . . . ".

"Dug," "door," and "trough," are surreptitious and plough-
nosed words. Not open, clean, easy words with healthy pure
vowels and crisp consonants, but "ough" words, of off sound,
and deceptive in their very spelling. "Dung," "Dugs," "Din-
giness"—we can make a catalogue of such words.

Later, still about Templeton, White says, "A rat can creep
out late at night . . . [eating from] . . . discarded lunch
boxes containing the foul remains of peanut butter sandwiches". The word "creep" is one of White's deceptively simple
felicities, reminding us of Swift's use of the same word in describing the Lilliputians' groveling sycophancy—"leaping
and creeping," cowering and fawning.

How pure, how simple, by contrast, the straight-forward address of simple Wilbur (like Squire Allworthy in *Tom Jones*).

> "Attention please!" he said in a loud, firm voice.
> "Will the party who addressed me at bedtime last
> night kindly make himself or herself known by giv-
> ing an appropriate sign or signal!"

The bull-horn sensibility of the opening, and the ingenuous
covering of all bases—"himself or herself [affirmative action!] . . . sign or signal"—betoken a cerebral circuitry in pig
that has all the convolutions of a railroad track in arable
Kansas. Truly, "by their words ye shall know them." And
this is the manner in which the true dramatist, the real negative capability, delineates character.

One may pursue the subtlety of White's play with individual
words one degree further. In fact, one must do so to understand all that is happening in this seemingly simple book.

Templeton, who, as he told Wilbur, prefers to spend his time
"eating, gnawing, spying, and hiding," eats Wilbur's food
from the trough during the rainstorm, sending Wilbur into
a fit of depression which makes Lurvy, the hired man, force
medicine down the ailing pig's throat. A sad, a bitter day indeed!

"Darkness settled over everything," White begins the next
paragraph—a sentence not suited so much to a medicated
porker, as fitting to the description of chaos the first night before creation, or to the interstellar void mirroring God's
wrath following the revolt of the angels.

The sentence, "Darkness settled over everything" has the
tone of Haydn's *Creation,* and tells us we shall have to do
with an epic, even if a mini-epic like a rape of the lock, for
example. Or, a close call for a pig. The phrase foreshadows,
and we shall return to the matter of epic later.

To continue with the subject of wordplay by the author: when
Wilbur learns how the seemingly cruel spider, Charlotte, puts
her net-caught prey out of its misery:

> Wilbur admired the way Charlotte managed. He
> was particularly glad that she always put her victim
> to sleep before eating it.

"It's real thoughtful of you to do that, Charlotte," he said.

Note, a book that begins "Where's Papa going with the ax?", a book preferring always to see the real world *there,* and eschewing all obfuscation—such a book using the doily and antimacassar euphemism, the genteelism, "put to sleep" for the simple word "kill" or "dead", and juxtaposing the phrase outrageously with the eating of the "deceased." ("Would you like to view the cremains?" Charlotte might now ask.) (pp. 66-9)

When White is serious, his words are serious and to the point. There are no circumlocutions, no euphemisms, no fancy talk when there's writerly work to be done, as when, at the beginning of Chapter XIII, White has to set the stage naturalistically, explaining economically and precisely the web of a spider, with its orb and radial lines. No verbal high jinx here. . . . (p. 69)

And finally, fittingly, on the matter of words, the plot itself is to turn on a simple word, and the tension and the suspense regarding the identity of a single word.

Wilbur, at the fair, turns out not to win the blue ribbon, not to be the largest, biggest, fattest pig. Again there rises the spectre of his being slaughtered for bacon. Clearly, as we know must be the case in stories such as this, rescue must come from somewhere. But from where? Templeton, the rat, creeps once again, and typically, into the garbage and the foul remnants scattered about the fairground. There, among deviled ham sandwich and wormy apple, he finds a bit of old newspaper from which he tears a—*the*—word. What word? It will be the talisman, the instrument of Wilbur's salvation as sweet Charlotte in her dying last act weaves neatly into the center of her final web the great word, HUMBLE. Similarly to the manner in which comparable situations are handled in *Winnie the Pooh* ("trespassers," or "North Pole") nobody is completely certain of the word's proper use. They have the dictionary definition all right—more or less—"Not proud," and "near the ground." How fitting for Wilbur, says Charlotte. He is indeed not a proud pig, and he is, physically speaking, "near the ground."

White renders with enormous skill the very slight misconstrual of words, as such misconstrual takes place among children and students, and occasionally foreigners, when they look up a word in the dictionary and use it, but have not the custom of the word, and therefore slightly, only slightly, mistake, using, more or less, the dictionary equivalents, but in a manner in which one who is *really* in possession of the word would not.

And the joke continues with the human beings in the next chapter. Next morning everyone climbs out of the truck at the Fair Grounds:

> "Look!" cried Fern. "Look at Charlotte's web! Look what it says!"
>
> The grownups and the children joined hands and stood there, studying the new sign.
>
> " 'Humble,' " said Mr. Zuckerman. "Now ain't that just the word for Wilbur!"

and later an admiring woman, looking at the livestock, points out that Wilbur

> "isn't as big as the pig next door, . . . but he's cleaner. That's what I like."

"So do I," said another man.

"He's humble, too," said a woman reading the sign on the web.

The glorious non-sequitur is authorial genius of a sort almost to defy analysis. Wilbur is not *not* humble; nor is Humble the word anyone would think to describe him. The word is simply askew for the occasion, a good and literally "found" joke. The magic word is itself common and unpretentious, simple, yet misunderstood, and it turns out, in all its—not wrongness, but simply irrelevance—to be the "open sesame" that clinches Wilbur's salvation and sinecure.

White is artist of the word. He is also artist of the sentence. The marvelous dictional simplicity of the opening has been commented on. That the first sentence, "Where's Papa going with that ax?" is almost as simple an interrogative as is possible in our language is noteworthy. And between that exemplary opening and the closing, White continues play with syntax. . . . (pp. 69-71)

[More] stunning even than White's first sentence is the conclusion to *Charlotte's Web.* " . . . It is not often that someone comes along who is a true friend and a good writer. Charlotte was both". This penultimate sentence has the neoclassical poise, balance, distance, and decorum: the proverb-like conclusiveness, of a line from, say, Johnson's "The Vanity of Human Wishes." It stands classically, drawing its credibility from the clarity of its expression. Exegesis would be but a diminution of the impact of its brevity: *Charlotte was both.*

Beyond matters of diction and syntax, further expertise is demonstrated by White in his control of basic authorial techniques, such as plotting. *Charlotte's Web* is a skillfully plotted tale, a well-told tale using forshadowing, and standing up to the old Scheherazade test—will you leave the story teller's head on one more night to hear the outcome? "Will loveable pig Wilbur be left alive or butchered? Can Charlotte save him?"

" 'Hello!' " says a dumb bumbling sheep to Wilbur at the outset. " 'Seems to me you're putting on weight. . . . Well, I don't like to spread bad news . . . ' ". Like the first rejection of Lear by Goneril, such a note bodes ill. From then on in *Charlotte's Web,* the incidents follow inevitably, fate seems inexorable, and, in fact, we have no cheap romance, but tragicomedy in which salvation comes hand in hand with the cathartic ending in which Charlotte is sacrificed for the continuity of her species. (pp. 71-2)

As for White's authorial stance, it is omniscient, as when he says of the newly introduced spider, Charlotte, "[u]nderneath her rather bold and cruel exterior, she had a kind heart, and she was to prove loyal and true to the very end". No doubt, then, that White has in mind the total shape and the outcome of the story. Occasionally, too, White permits himself an aside to the audience, either to children reading the tale, or to their parents, as when Charlotte, explaining webs to Wilbur, says "Did you ever hear of the Queensborough Bridge?" "What do people catch in the Queensborough Bridge—bugs?" asks Wilbur, and you must note the felicitous little touch of "in," not "on" the Queensborough Bridge, since Wilbur is thinking still syntactically about webs (*in* webs), not bridges (about which one, of course, says "on"). The grace of White's ironical asides may be fully appreciated when compared with similar attempts by no less than Thackeray in *The Rose and the Ring,* archly addressing the parents over the heads of children so that the effect is really none other than the author breaking faith with his audience.

The matter of authorial stance is complicated, too, when White successfully violates that first injunction for children's authors "Don't have talking animals." For the first two chapters, indeed, only the human beings talk. Then, later, when the animals do seem to talk, the stunt is pulled off so neatly that, even with the text in front of one, one is hard put to decide whether Fern can actually understand the animals. We never do hear a conversational exchange between Fern and the beasts.

Having noted White's artistry, ranging from diction to sentence structure, to rhetorical and authorial stance, there remains only the analysis of the largest dimension of the tale, the demonstration that this seemingly slight children's story flows in the mainstream of Western literary tradition, drawing for its names, themes, even its plot, from rich classical backgrounds, and, insofar as these themselves mirror deepest archetypical truths, drawing on primordial human manifestations.

First, the epical connotations of "Darkness settled over everything", and of Mr. Zuckerman's first name, Homer, have been suggested. *Charlotte's Web,* both according to the author's oft-stated intent, and from ample internal evidence, is in the mainstream of the Western literary tradition, a tradition traceable at least three millennia, beginning in the ninth century B.C. with Hesiod's *Works and Days,* and carried on through Virgil's *Eclogues,* and then on through such 18th century achievements as Thomson's "The Seasons." And indeed, as in Thomson, and in Haydn, the book is interspersed with lyrical intermezzos in a minor key, celebrating the beauties of the rural year. Thus, mid-plot and action, in Chapter VI, we find:

> Early summer days are a jubilee time for birds. In the fields around the house, in the barn, in the woods, in the swamp—everywhere love and songs and nests and eggs. . . . On an apple bough, the phoebe teeters and wags its tail and says "Phoebe, phoebe!": The song sparrow, who knows how brief and lovely life is, says "Sweet, sweet, sweet interlude. . . ."

Note in this excerpt not only the exaltation of the seasons, but the melancholy theme of *et in arcadia ego*—in the midst of life, there comes death. Moodful contemplations of the time—of year or of day—pervade the book, as when Fern is at the barn and, though knowing it is suppertime, cannot bear to leave.

> Swallows passed on silent wings, in and out of the doorways, bringing food to their young ones. From across the road a bird sang "Whipoorwill, whipoorwill!' . . . he [Lurvy] loved life, and loved to be a part of the world on a summer evening.

Such a passage is kindred to Collins's odes, to Young's "Night Thoughts," and, by way of them, to the Roman, and through them, to the Greek pastoral. (pp. 72-3)

White himself, (the letter to me notwithstanding) was fully aware of what he was about, as we may see in his recently published *Letters,* in which repeatedly there occur such statements as White's telling Gene Deitch, who intended to film the book, " . . . the film should be a paean to life, a hymn to the barn, an acceptance of dung." Ten years earlier, writ-

ing to Louis de Rochemont, White had already called *Charlotte's Web* a "hymn to the barn . . . pastoral, seasonal. . . ." And if further supporting evidence of the arcadian sources of the book is needed, note merely the name of the one understanding choral interpreter of the relationship of nature's beasts to the natural child, and to the lapsarian adults—Dr. Dorian.

Secondly, as significant as the generic placement of the book, is its clear place in the archetypical tradition: Life out of Death; Birth and Renewal out of the Ashes. Out of the winter earth springs new life, and out of the death of Charlotte comes her progeny and her immortality. "We're leaving here on the warm updraft," the ballooning spiders call to Wilbur. "This is our moment of setting forth." And we readers may ponder back to the long history of settings forth in literature—Adam and Eve at the end of *Paradise Lost,* Gawain, the Grail questers, Huck on his river, and Stuart Little, White's mouse creation of five years earlier. In Stuart's book, *Stuart Little,* the last sentence reads " . . . he peered ahead into the great land that stretched before him . . . the sky was bright, and somehow he felt he was headed in the right direction."

The dying first, and the setting forth, were crucial to White as he worked and contemplated his book. We have again the evidence in the *Letters* of White's repeated exasperation with those who would trivialize the story, making it meaningless by altering the conclusion, eliminating Charlotte's death, and giving the book a happy ending. As White well knew, the great theme of the book was its core. As he wrote in 1973, "*Charlotte* was a story of friendship, life, death, salvation."

To set forth such a historically and anthropologically basic and primal theme, using authorial resources but a few of which I have adumbrated, is to write with denseness of texture on a subject of sufficient magnitude. And to do that is to write greatly. Written perhaps with children in mind, *Charlotte's Web* is a great book. (pp. 73-5)

Peter Neumeyer, "What Makes a Good Children's Book? The Texture of 'Charlotte's Web'," in South Atlantic Bulletin, *Vol. XLIV, No. 2, May, 1979, pp. 66-75.*

A drawing by White of Zuckerman's barn in Charlotte's Web.

BOBBIE ANN MASON

I did not know about *Charlotte's Web* until after I was grown—after I had become an admirer of E. B. White's clear-headed, sensible, witty style and outlook. I discovered that *Charlotte's Web* has the same personal directness, unfailing clarity, and economical humor one finds in his essays and letters.

It occurs to me that his children's stories are so much appreciated by adults because he makes few allowances for children. The vocabulary in these stories is simpler, and because there is fantasy they *seem* to be children's stories—tales about swans that play jazz trumpet, spiders that write, mice that drive cars. (p. 692)

Using the same comic, straightforward style in *Charlotte's Web* that he uses in his essays, he diminishes the distance between child and adult. He brings out the child in his adult readers, and he elicits the capacity for maturity in the child. He asks adults to renew their sense of wonder, and he asks children to try to understand the nature of reality. In the end, actually, he is asking adults to understand reality, since they usually don't understand it any better than children do—unless they have the presence of mind to omit needless words, hold on to a suitable design, use concrete language, and avoid affecting a breezy manner.

The key is clarity. White's mentor, Will Strunk, is omnipresent, directing the show. If we see things clearly, perhaps it is because we say them clearly, or vice versa. In *Charlotte's Web,* the reader is asked to confront the necessity of death. White gets straight to the point. Most pigs get butchered and spiders die in the autumn. White's humor in the reporting is as blunt as these hard facts. His humor, his direct style, and his vision of the world are all blended in a manner that is unmistakable, whether in his children's stories or in his *New Yorker* essays.

Part of what is so appealing about White—the writer, the humorist, the stylist, the man—is that he makes so much sense; his words have authority. We trust his sensible view of things. And because he is so straightforward, he is amusing. Children must sense that clarity and humor too, even when he treads into unpleasant territory. He never ducks or blinks, and he never tries to hide plain facts. So when he gets to the truly troubling things—destruction, death, change—he sails right into them with the clear voice of reason. That's the way it is, folks. White's revolutionary view of what is right for children's literature—the spider dies, the charming mouse leaves, the swan steals—has caused librarians a lot of fuss. White says he has encountered two taboos—death and monstrosity.

> Apparently, children are not supposed to be exposed to death, but I did not pay any attention to this. In *Stuart Little,* an American family has a two-inch mouse. This is highly questionable and would be, I guess, bad if it were stated in any other than a matter-of-fact way.

His bluntness is a dominant characteristic, even in his carefully written letters, themselves masterpieces. White refused to give speeches because he thought he was a writer, not a speaker. He sent a collect telegram to the Harvard *Crimson* declining an offer: "SORRY CANNOT SPEAK DO NOT KNOW HOW MANY THANKS". Telegrams are blunt by definition, but White could be equally forthright at any time.

He wrote to a reader that there is no allegory in *Charlotte's Web.*

> *Charlotte's Web* is a tale of the animals in my barn, not of the people in my life. When you read it, just relax. Any attempt to find allegorical meanings is bound to end disastrously, for no meanings are in there. I ought to know.
> Sincerely,
> Andy White

His matter-of-fact style reflects his realistic vision. He sacrifices a few facts to fancy in order to make an entertaining tale, but his common sense is unswerving. (pp. 693-95)

His approach is always direct. Another reader had apparently asked where he got the idea for Charlotte's writing. He answered:

> The idea of the writing in *Charlotte's Web* came to me one day when I was on my way down through the orchard carrying a pail of slops to my pig. I had made up my mind to write a children's book about animals, and I needed a way to save a pig's life, and I had been watching a large spider in the backhouse, and what with one thing and another, the idea came to me.
> Sincerely,
> E. B. White

Yet in his essays White often characterizes himself as a bumbler, at odds with the quirks of the social and mechanistic world. Like the child dealing with confusing reality, White documents the confusion of contemporary adults who must deal with xerography, stapling machines, the IRS. The perplexities of society sharply contrast with the real issues at hand—sheep shearing, raising geese, buying a cow, a pet's death. The natural world is less obstructed by needless words, social subterfuges, injustice. That White clarifies the real and the true is comforting, reliable. That he is awkward in the social world is also comforting; it was never meant to be taken seriously anyway.

White's plain, economical speech is the essence of his humor. In *Charlotte's Web,* the goose hatches seven eggs, but the eighth is a "dud." Wilbur the pig lives in a manure pile. "But he never had any fun—no walks, no rides, no swims." Wilbur is bored. "I'm less than two months old and I'm tired of living".

Most of the characters assume White's own voice. Mr. Arable, for example, tells his son he can't have a pig. "I only distribute pigs to early risers . . . Fern was up at daylight, trying to rid the world of injustice. As a result, she now has a pig. A small one, to be sure, but nevertheless a pig. It just shows what can happen if a person gets out of bed promptly. Let's eat!" A no-nonsense reply. White's characters are lovably irascible. (p. 695)

Charlotte is the practical, patient leader of the barnyard. She gives orders, thinks up the trick to save Wilbur, speaks wisely, prepares for her inevitable death. When she starts writing words in her web, she says, "People believe almost anything they see in print". Her views on human nature are outspoken. The Queensborough Bridge, which took eight years to build, is in her estimation a poor attempt at a web. And people are always rushing back and forth across the bridge, instead of hanging patiently upside down.

"I have to say what is true," Charlotte says, when Wilbur objects to her saying that she drinks the blood of flies, which she finds "delicious." "I love blood," she remarks. Wilbur thinks Charlotte is blood-thirsty, but he likes her and comes to understand how necessary her work is. "I have to live, don't I?" she asks. Charlotte puts her victims to sleep before she eats them, and Wilbur thinks this is kind. She replies, "I always give them an anesthetic so they won't feel pain. It's a little service I throw in". Charlotte says her ancestors were trappers.

In White's works, you can almost hear Will Strunk shouting, "Omit needless words!" By direct speaking, you can hit the truth more often than not. At least the errors will be out in the open. The scene between Fern's mother and the doctor . . . is funny because of the one-liners and because the doctor sees clearly.

> "What's miraculous about a spider's web?" said Mrs. Arable. "I don't see why you say a web is a miracle—it's just a web."
>
> "Ever try to spin one?" asked Dr. Dorian.

By omitting needless words, White avoids sentimentality and rationalization. Humor is the only deception allowed. If humorists seem to be clowns crying on the inside, it's because "Humorists fatten on trouble". But humor musn't preach— "it need only speak the truth". And it does speak the truth. It is the means by which White communicates his deepest sense of the world. White's vision—trained by Thoreau's economy of effort and Strunk's economy of words—is far from simplistic. These disciplines just clear the way for a direct look at essential issues: Creatures die in the fall, but what they do beforehand is wondrous. White doesn't protect children from uncomfortable realities, though adults have a way of doing just that to themselves—with hazy concepts and hazier language. White doesn't. Enough said. (pp. 695-96)

> *Bobbie Ann Mason, "Profile: The Elements of E. B. White's Style," in* Language Arts, *Vol. 56, No. 6, September, 1979, pp. 692-96.*

JOHN GRIFFITH

Charlotte's Web expresses as poignantly as anything E. B. White has written his bright and whimsical but fundamentally melancholy sense of life. In this story of Wilbur, a goodhearted but lonely and vulnerable pig, White creates a consoling fantasy in which a small Everyman survives and triumphs over the pathos of being alone. (p. 111)

Charlotte's Web is the consolation White offers to the child who has lived and continues to live in the presence of [what he calls this] "lady of infinite allure, this dangerous and beautiful and sublime being," freedom, and in the lonely realization of one's individuality. He approaches that task by creating a character and set of circumstances which dramatize the anxieties of that situation. (p. 112)

White . . . establishes Wilbur in a desperate existential situation: he is scared of dying; he faces *ennui,* and he is starved for friendship and love. These are the psychic problems attendant on [what White calls] the "haunting intimation" that one is ultimately alone. Wilbur's loneliness is the emotional counterpart of the philosophical perception that between oneself and others lies an unbridgeable gap. Since on this level one becomes the sole measure and standard of his own world—becomes "all things to himself," as White put it— then everything depends on his being fulfilled. Boredom is

simply the enervating sense that this is not happening. One comes to believe that nothing matters. Doing novel things can allay this feeling temporarily, but novelty wears out. To find significance that appears permanent, the individual must find a context larger than himself to give purpose to his actions. Without it one is prey to the debilitating state of mind in which the only important question is "Am I being fulfilled?"

In this state of mind, the thought of death has keen edge. The person whose sense of himself is governed by a feeling of communality—of being most importantly a member of a family or a tribe or a people or a cause—can see his own death as less than absolute. To one who lives in and for himself, death must be the ultimate end and terror. Herein the prospect of death combines thoughts of boredom and loneliness. (p. 113)

Wilbur of course is not a philosopher meditating on alienation and morality; on the contrary he is an eager and gregarious child wishing to live and to be loved and happy. White is the philosopher; through Wilbur he addresses the anxieties which a child in a modern, fragmented culture might feel. White says, in effect, "Once upon a time there was a youngster who was bored, lonely, and afraid of dying." The story which follows like a fairy tale soothes these anxieties.

To disarm boredom, White offers a vision of a rich and various world—a world filled with dramatic experiences like winning a prize at the county fair, riding the Ferris wheel, swinging on the big rope in the barn, sledding, listening to stories, and making new friends. Even without such events, the world of *Charlotte's Web* resembles Mr. Zuckerman's barn—full of splendid ordinary things: "ladders, grindstones, pitch forks, monkey wrenches, scythes, lawn mowers, snow shovels, ax handles, milk pails, water buckets, empty grain sacks, and rusty rat traps. It was the kind of barn that swallows like to build their nests in. It was the kind of barn that children like to play in". In this world the variety of experience is practically inexhaustible. . . . Of course the best antidote to boredom is Charlotte. . . . Once Charlotte appears, Wilbur is free from boredom.

White's story speaks soothingly to loneliness. When Wilbur complains, "I'm very young, I have no real friend here in the barn, it's going to rain all morning and all afternoon, and Fern won't come in such bad weather. Oh, *honestly!*"—there comes an answer. "You can imagine Wilbur's surprise when, out of the darkness, came a voice he had never heard before. It sounded rather thin, but pleasant. 'Do you want a friend, Wilbur?' it said. 'I'll be a friend to you' ". It is, of course, Charlotte, the perfect friend, at once confidante, instructor, protector, and mother.

White's handling of death is more complicated but nonetheless firm. He implies that if a child (like Wilbur) is frightened at the thought of death, he should be assured that reliable adults (like Charlotte) will see to it that he does not die. Children may be vulnerable, but grownups will protect them. "I don't want to die!" screams Wilbur. "You shall not die," says Charlotte. What she means is that Wilbur the young pig will not die; death is for the old and not the young. By the time one is old, the story shows, one will accept and perhaps even welcome death, like Charlotte dying alone at the fairgrounds. By then one will have lived out his life, wearied himself in the fulfillment of purpose, and be ready to rest. Dying in season evokes no terrors. And since, for the child, that season is a long time off, he need not worry about it.

In the center of this consoling fantasy is Charlotte. On one hand, she is the perfect adult. Yet she is also a fantastic character from fairyland. . . . In White's writing for grownups, the "experts" or sages are usually threatening, irrationally headstrong creatures, whose way it is best to stay out of. Only in his fantasy-writing, where spiders talk lovingly to pigs and spell out words in their webs, can someone like Charlotte exist. She is needed there; and need, rather than reality, is the operative principle in fantasy.

It may seem perverse to lay such stress on fantasy in *Charlotte's Web* when compared with other more patently fantastic stories like *Alice in Wonderland* or *Peter Pan*. In the fantasies of Carroll and Barrie, the prospect of growing up and growing old holds terrors which send the authors' imaginations into spasms of rejection. Adulthood in *Alice in Wonderland* is a mixture of mystery and madness; in *Peter Pan*, it is a dull round of routine through which flirts sexuality. Next to these stories, *Charlotte's Web* stands as a wise and fatherly discourse, acknowledging mutability and mortality but nevertheless reassuring the reader.

White's story acknowledges that people change when they grow up—and the change is not entirely for the better. Fern, who begins as Wilbur's devoted friend, grows up, falls in love, and loses interest in him. White acknowledges, too, that people die as Charlotte dies tired and alone. White stresses, however, that it is right for Fern to grow up and lose interest and for Charlotte to die. These events are natural parts of life's order. But psychologically more important is the fact that, lovable as they may be, Fern and Charlotte are not Wilbur. Fern changes, and Charlotte dies, but Wilbur is allowed to live a long life without the permanent changes or trauma. He finds interests outside himself, primarily in Charlotte and the endless succession of her descendants who live with him in the barn, without causing him any responsibility. He never has to arrange their lives in the way Charlotte has arranged his. He finds love without the complications of sex or parenthood. Essentially he remains a child: "Mr. Zuckerman took fine care of Wilbur all the rest of his days". Strictly speaking, he never even dies. That phrase "all the rest of his days" is as close as White comes to suggesting Wilbur's death. Since Wilbur is the character with whom the reader is invited to identify, and since to him none of the problems of boredom, loneliness, and death prove insoluble, the story assures the reader that, though sad things do happen, they may not happen to him.

White's craft and gentle humor mute all sadness and, at the same time, control the tendency toward sentimentality. When the going gets sticky, the narrator reminds us that the story is only a story. The final paragraph is a masterpiece of semi-sweet, semi-serious humor, expressing a melancholy sentiment without tears. "Wilbur never forgot Charlotte. Although he loved her children and grandchildren dearly, none of the new spiders ever quite took her place in his heart. She was in a class by herself. It is not often that someone comes along who is a true friend and a good writer. Charlotte was both". The tone here is vintage White: wry, amiable, and softly arch. It is sad that Charlotte is gone, but it's funny to think of her as a good writer, since her entire published canon was only five words.

In an important way, this is the right epitaph: a true friend and a good writer. Charlotte talked to Wilbur, sang to him, and wrote advertising copy for him. Their contact was verbal. One of the clearest marks of *Charlotte's Web* as the fantasy of a lonely, yearning imagination is the importance it places on language as the means through which "spirit is laid against spirit." The highest and best love, in this story, is that which expresses itself through words. Language is pure, a process in which "all animal heat and moisture may have a chance to evaporate," as Thoreau put it. Wilbur has talked to Charlotte; she has talked to and for him; and her descendants will talk to him forever in White's idyllic barnyard. (pp. 114-17)

John Griffith, "Charlotte's Web: 'A Lonely Fantasy of Love'," in Children's Literature: Annual of the Modern Language Association Seminar on Children's Literature and The Children's Literature Association, *Vol. 8, 1980, pp. 111-17.*

HELENE SOLHEIM

My purpose [in this essay] is to show that in *Charlotte's Web* are brought together the concerns and the method that are consistent in White. It is too often true that critics discussing the work of a writer who produces children's books as well as grown-up writing toss off rather as an addendum, "He also writes children's stories," as though it were a hobby, or a bad habit. In White, and particularly in *Charlotte's Web,* there is nothing in his children's stories inconsistent with or unlike the substance of his articles or essays or poems for adults. White's only sustained fictions are in his three children's books. *Charlotte's Web* is the best of the three, and it seems to me that the best of White is there: rather than being incidental, *Charlotte's Web* is central to White's work. . . .

The cycles and circles which are important thematically in White's work, as in *Charlotte's Web,* are manifest, too, in his style, as in [his essay] "Death of a Pig." [Edward C. Sampson] observes, "with a technique he has often used, White summarizes the events first . . . and then turns back and relates the whole matter in more leisurely detail." (p. 391)

In "Death of a Pig," as in White's other essays, his poetry, and *Charlotte's Web,* his tenor is often almost humorlessly intense; at the same time his vehicle is light and informal and filled with humor. White's essays often express "a deadly seriousness that may be richly compounded with humor," and that compound seriousness is at work in "Death of a Pig." "Contrast is at the heart of White's style," Edward C. Sampson rightly notes, though he also finds a "tonal dualism" that works against rather than for White. "And just as there is a dualism in White about the city and the country—his love for Maine and his love for New York City—so there is a tonal dualism in White. If he found it hard to write anything long or sustained, he seems also to have found it hard to maintain a consistent tone of seriousness or of lightheartedness."

But it is exactly this constant contrast of tone—not the inability to sustain one, but the agility to maintain two—that enables White in "Death of a Pig" first to see the event as farce and then to pull meaning from farce. "I discovered, though, that once having given a pig an enema"; this is ridiculous, and one expects the sentence to continue so. Instead, it shifts: "there is no turning back, no chance of resuming one of life's more stereotyped roles." The shift is abrupt but not disruptive; it is compelling. The reader is compelled to share White's perspective, and his dualism. Paying attention to the untimely death of a pig is absurd, a colonic carnival, but we come to see it is the untimely death itself, rather than its victim, which occasions a greater loss—a disruption in the community of things.

In earlier times and different perspectives man's rhythms are analogues of God's. In a finely concise expression of the medieval view, "since earthly things are joined to celestial things, the cycles of their times join together in an harmonious succession as if in universal song." But White muses to a different calliope, and what leads to immortality in the work of other writers is in his vision a sequential mortality, as in his poem **"Subway People,"** which was first published in the *New Yorker* December 5, 1925,

> Sitters, waiters,—riders to eternity,
> Shuffling in the shadow world, all day long;
> Standers, thinkers,—joggers to eternity,
> Swaying to the rhythm of the sad loud song.

Sampson finds its rhythm "strongly suggestive of Vachel Lindsay and Stephen Vincent Benet," and that "White captures in this poem something of the aimlessness of life, and something of its pathos." There is pathos, though it is the everyday, pre-nine, post-five pathos of the quiet desperation crowd. Rather than aimlessness, I see the repetitive sameness of the trip, and the hint of the theme of the circularity of time which White later develops in **"The Ring of Time"** and in *Charlotte's Web.* The poem's rhythm echoes the rhythm of the ride, and while the identical rhyme is weak, it echoes commuter boredom. Here, eternity is no more than your stop, and that caesura is—of course—somebody else's. (pp. 393-94)

White carried in his pocket, he says, for many years a copy of Thoreau's *Walden;* he read it often, quoted from it almost involuntarily, and wrote about it in several essays. In his centenary essay **"Walden—1954,"** he says that *Walden,* "encountered" at the proper time (a similar time to that of its writing in Thoreau's life) of one's life, can be like "an invitation to life's dance." (And for a spirit as capable of "new, radiant action" and remarkable feats as Wilbur's, *Walden*'s different drummer plays a catchy, syncopated beat.) In an earlier letter about the animated film project, White wanted to make very clear that the animals on Zuckerman's farm not appear to live in "community"; that they be seen as an aggregation of "rugged individualists," each out foremost for its own interests, and working together in compromise only when pushed to the wall. "Interdependence? I agree that the film should be a paean to life, a hymn to the barn, an acceptance of dung. But I think it would be quite untrue to suggest that barnyard creatures are dependent on each other. The barn is a community of rugged individualists, everybody mildly suspicious of everybody else, including me. Friendships sometimes develop, as between a goat and a horse, but there is no sense of true community or cooperation. Heaven forfend! Joy of life, yes. Tolerance of other cultures, yes. Community, no." But White isn't quite right about the farm, or about communities—the best kind of community is that made up of rugged individualists. In a sense, Stuart Little shares the snobbish individual anarchism Thoreau has, and though he is too urban and urbane (and too dependently small) to be a rugged individualist, in heading north at the end of the book, Stuart is avoiding the commitment and responsibility that participation in community demands. It is those who, like Wilbur, seek to retain individualism while staying in one place, who become, finally, the most solid citizens—if that term means full participants in the life of the community. Beginning with his brutely selfish instincts to stay alive despite the usual routine, Wilbur grows and, with more than a little help from his friends, learns to enjoy his unique, exceptional nature, and at last can drop back to the supporting role of foster parent to newer, shinier lives. And in that he has achieved some resolution of individual expression and community welfare. (pp. 398-99)

Of the traditional "classics" for children, of which *Charlotte's Web* may be the last, there are, of course, girls' books and boys' books. I don't believe the difference I see in the girl and boy protagonists need be sex-related, but it falls that way in the books. The girls are dreamy and existential things, and observers, knowing the rules but waiting for time to give them the apparatus to take part in the game. Like George MacDonald's Princess Irene, they pursue the thread of life. The boys, on the other hand, are having adventures (and a surprising number of them playing at pirates). It would be simplistic to say the boys are active and the girls passive (Alice, after all, is awfully busy, and rather aggressive, too), and equally simplistic to call the girls thoughtful and the boys rash (Tom Sawyer plots childhood like chess). Instead, the boys learn to be adults by imitating adult (if fantastic) action—"as if his whole vocation / were endless imitation," Wordsworth says—while the girls try to figure out what is going on. It is only after time, and some loss, that the girls are able to participate in adult activity. And, traditionally, these options for boys and limits for girls have been sex-related.

Avery and Fern Arable demonstrate this difference clearly (and it is suggested in their names). "That morning, just as Wilbur fell asleep, Avery Arable wandered into Zuckerman's front yard, followed by Fern. Avery carried a live frog in his hand. Fern had a crown of daisies in her hair". Avery is timely and insensitive. Fern, for some moment, is timeless, and hypersensitive. She is all eyes and ears, and as we see in the violent fight against the injustice of killing the runt piglet Wilbur with which the book opens, even her emotions are a sense.

The addition of Fern to the story of life in the barnyard was an after-thought, and it makes all the difference. Fern is an observer of life in the barn, rather than a participant, and in fact she is not mentioned at all from page 16 through page 43. As in so many children's books, the little girl Fern is the character who makes the trip from the real world into the fantasy world, but unlike many other heroines, Fern takes the fantasy world back into the real one.

She grows up a great deal during the year of this story and puts away "childish" concerns. . . . After Wilbur's life is saved, Fern's interest turns, as though her vision were altered by confinement in the ring of time, to another future promise in Henry Fussy. . . . Though the reader begins *Charlotte's Web* with great sympathy for Fern and her cause, when Fern's concern shifts, the reader's sympathy stays with Wilbur. She forfeits our sympathy when she ceases to care.

It might well be asked how White gets away with devoting so much of *Charlotte's Web,* a children's book, to death. Somehow, it is not enough to say that death is a part of life—or life's dance. Art makes its own demands, and in this case the issue is the audience, and decorum. It seems to me White gets there, and gets the reader there, by a sequence of images, and by "image" here I mean an object which is at the center of an action. After White's fashion, I will summarize, and then look to the detail. The first image is the rope swing, then Charlotte's painstakingly constructed web, next the Ferris wheel, and finally Charlotte's last web.

We are prepared for the pleasure of the barn swing, if not by memory, by Wilbur's expectation that, if he wants to and tries to spin a web, he will have a filament like Charlotte's strand extruding from his rear. He is wrong, but we begin to see possibilities. Then, in the rope swing passage, we are virtually forced to become imaginatively involved in swinging through the insistent second-person address (twelve "you's," in fact). As Charlotte plans and constructs her "Terrific" web (Wilbur's hoped-for filament having become the child's rope, and that in turn become Charlotte's rope-like web strands), we see her enthusiasm and effort and determination in a creation which is only transitory and briefly functional. (It is, of course, Wilbur whom the web advertises as "Terrific." But what is confusion and disagreement among the characters becomes the critic's ambiguity: the web and Charlotte are terrific, too.) The same roundish shape of the web recurs in the Ferris wheel—another childish joy, and Fern's happiest memory—and the wheel, too, is a passing pleasure. On the day the Ferris wheel is taken down, Charlotte dies, having begun the renewal of life by planting her egg sac and her last, wheel-shaped, web.

I have laboriously connected what rests easily independent in the book. But if we can see that Wilbur's hoped-for filament is like the rope swing, and the rope swing like the elements of Charlotte's web, and the shape of that web like that of the Ferris wheel (that other symbol of child-like, if temporal, joy), and that the Ferris wheel—never for long a closed circle—is like Charlotte's last life-nurturing web, then we can see that the magic of the web of this story encompasses both what is permanent—death, and the memory of joy—and what passes—life, and sorrow. "The song sparrow, who knows how brief and lovely life is, says, 'Sweet, sweet, sweet interlude; sweet, sweet, sweet interlude' ".

The spring is Fern's season: the book opens with her story, in that time. The summer, radiantly, belongs to Wilbur, though his growth and development are a motif, if not more, throughout the whole. In the fall and the harvest fair, our attention, though not the crowd's, turns to Charlotte: autumn is, to borrow a metaphor from another part of the kingdom, Charlotte's swan song. In winter Fern has outgrown her interest in the barnyard, and so we lose interest in her. Wilbur is mature now and is taking on the uninteresting manners of parents. Charlotte is gone. And so, as the year comes full circle we see here, too, that time is not circular at all. It is the time for new heroes, and for a new story. The final chapter is, really, an epilogue. Perspective draws back to take the larger view—life, rather than lives—and to celebrate life in the barn, and the glory of everything. There are three stories in *Charlotte's Web:* Fern's, Wilbur's, and Charlotte's. The three are joined in the miracle of the web, which, like time and like comedy, brings renewal and new life. *Charlotte's Web,* like *Walden,* is an invitation to life's dance.

Sampson says, "Except for his three children's stories, White has been above all a writer of his times, and interpreter of the contemporary scene; and, as such, it has seemed not only wise but necessary to consider his writing against the changing background of his times." The contemporary scene, the changing background of the times, are a part of White's children's stories as well as his other work: there is no reason to except them. "Fiction," says Virginia Woolf in *A Room of One's Own,* "is like a spider's web, attached ever so lightly perhaps, but still attached to life at all four corners." My aim has been to show that *Charlotte's Web* is not on the periphery of White's work but at its center. And when we see in *Char-*

lotte's Web how White weaves together the themes, the tone, the style that recur in his work, we see it is a winter's tale, a romance, a curious interlude when comedy and tragedy seem to cohere. And how. (pp. 402-05)

Helene Solheim, "Magic in the Web: Time, Pigs, and E. B. White," in South Atlantic Quarterly, Vol. 8, No. 4, Autumn, 1981, pp. 391-405.

SHEILA A. EGOFF

Both Kenneth Grahame's *The Wind in the Willows* and E. B. White's *Charlotte's Web* are . . . an unfolding of "other worlds." The former . . . takes place in the closed world of an English riverbank and the latter, in the equally separate world of an American Midwest barnyard. Both writers link fantasy and reality, animal life and human life, in their evocation of friendship, love of home, spirit of adventure, and the cosmic cycle of birth and death. Grahame's animals are more highly anthropomorphized than those of E. B. White, but still his technique is that adopted by most animal fantasists. Grahame takes the quite legitimate characteristics of a certain animal that have overtones of a certain type of human being (pompous Toad) who in turn exemplifies more general human characteristics often attributed to a certain type of animal. Thus there is a circular "feed-back" between animal and human. Of course, the wonder really is that the technique works so well.

E. B. White keeps his animals "in their place" to a greater extent than Grahame. The concerns of White's animals are far less philosophical and so more closely attuned to natural animal life. Knowing nothing more than the barnyard, they would not dream of a life beyond their own, as does Rat in *The Wind in the Willows.* But, like Walter de la Mare, White succeeds in creating a fantasy world that has universal applications. Grahame, with all his perception of small animals, their behavior, and their habitats, remains chiefly a commentator about his own time. (pp. 108-09)

Sheila A. Egoff, "The New Fantasy," in her Thursday's Child: Trends and Patterns in Contemporary Children's Literature, American Library Association, 1981, pp. 80-129.

REBECCA J. LUKENS

Classics are books that have worn well, attracting readers from one generation to the next. They cross all genre lines; they are historical fiction, regional literature, and high fantasy. What seems to keep them in continuous circulation may be the significance of theme, the credibility of character, the continuing reality of the conflict, or the engaging quality of style. . . .

A work may be popular for a time, as were *A Dog of Flanders* and *Seventeen,* and then fade. What seemed the height of ingenious wordplay at one time may at another seem dull and trite; the wit in *The Peterkin Papers,* for example, seems now to be heavy-handed and dull. *Alice in Wonderland,* on the other hand, remains an incomparable work of nonsense; readers have never outgrown Carroll's wit, and his playful inventiveness remains unsurpassed. If the diversified family farm becomes extinct, E. B. White's finest novel *Charlotte's Web* may come to be seen as a piece of historical fiction. But White's thorough portrayal of character, his choice of life and death conflict, his affectionately humorous tone, and his universal themes about friendship, satisfaction, and death are elements that identify classics. The classics of one generation may be supplanted by later works, but the appeals of other books may remain for a surprisingly long time. (p. 23)

There are certain terms that describe the degree of character development and that refer to change or lack of it in a character in the course of a story. Briefly, a *round character* is one that we know well, who has a variety of traits that make him or her believable. A *flat character* is less well developed, and has fewer traits. A *dynamic character* is a round character that changes, while a *static character*—either round or flat—is one that does not change in the course of the story. . . .

Fern in **Charlotte's Web** . . . is a flat character, a child with an intense interest that absorbs her for a time. She treats Wilbur like a doll, listens to the animals' conversations, and reports them to incredulous parents. She plays and quarrels, loves the Ferris wheel, and the freedom of the Fair. However, Fern has few traits that distinguish her from other little girls. She remains a believable little girl but not a special one with extraordinary traits that distinguish her from the large class of characters known as "little girls." Wilbur's relationships and worries are the focus of the story, and the conflict goes on without Fern's being totally aware of all that spiders and pigs mean to each other. Because this is Wilbur's story not Fern's, she needs no greater development. (p. 35)

In **Charlotte's Web** Lurvy is an example of a stereotype—in this case of a hired man. Lurvy has only the expected traits and does only the expected things. He nails down the loose board on Wilbur's pen, he slops Wilbur, he discovers the exploded dud. Lurvy is neither eloquent nor imaginative:

> "I've always noticed that pig. He's quite a pig."
> "He's long, and he's smooth," said Zuckerman.
> "That's right," agreed Lurvy. "He's as smooth as they come. He's some pig."

As Lurvy's speech shows, stereotypes describe themselves by what they say as well as how they say it. (p. 36)

In children's literature there are a great many round characters that we may feel we know. However, in order to help us see clearly what is meant by a round character, compare the many traits of Wilbur, for example, to the few traits of Fern, or the stereotype Lurvy. From the first words of the first page when Fern asks where her father is going with the ax, we are anxious about Wilbur's fate. We soon discover that Wilbur's struggle is the conflict, and that he is therefore the *protagonist,* or central character. Tiny, dependent Wilbur has almost no life of his own at the opening of the story, except to amuse himself like a toddler, finding the mud moist and warm and pleasantly oozy. When he goes to live in the barn, he is bored, unable to dream up anything exciting to do. Friends must introduce themselves to him. When he squeezes through the fence and is pursued, he has no idea what to do with freedom; and his constant appetite makes him captive again, since Lurvy's pail of slops is irresistible. Wilbur plans his day around his body: sleeping, eating, scratching, digging, eating, watching flies, eating, napping, standing still, eating. On the day that Wilbur wants love more than comfort and food, he has grown. But now he wonders uncertainly about friendship, which seems such a gamble. After Wilbur makes a friend, life becomes more exciting and he becomes confident enough to try spinning a web. Cheerfully, he tries and fails; humbly he admits that Charlotte is brighter and more clever. Wilbur's innocence and dependence are clear when he pleads for a story or a song, for a last bedtime bite, a last drink of milk, and calls out the series of quiet good-nights to Char-

lotte. Panic is Wilbur's reaction to news of his destiny—the Arable's dinner table. But once he is assured that Charlotte can perform miracles, he calms down to be patient, trusting, and humble. The congratulatory words in Charlotte's web make Wilbur an exemplary pig; he decides that if he is called "radiant," he must act radiant, and in his way he becomes radiant. Despite all the admiration Wilbur attracts, he remains modest. Happy and confident, he honestly admires Charlotte's peach-colored egg sac and gazes lovingly into the faces of the crowd. He looks both grateful and humble. Wilbur has enough traits to classify him as a round character. (pp. 37-8)

When the word *dynamic* is used in ordinary conversation it may mean forceful, or perhaps exciting. However, in the context of literature, the word has special meaning, since a *dynamic character* is one who changes in the course of the action. . . . The variety of possibilities for change is huge. (p. 38)

Wilbur changes. He is a believable character early in the story, although he is young and immature. The experience of receiving selfless friendship makes him able to give selfless friendship. Slowly, as we watch this change occurring, Wilbur is altered by his part in the action, by his receiving so much. Now he is the same Wilbur, and yet not the same. To his early qualities of humility and naiveté are added dependability and steadfastness, sacrifice and purpose. Even Wilbur's vocabulary matures. When first he hears the bad news, he is a panicky child:

> "I can't be quiet," screamed Wilbur, racing up and down. "I don't want to die. Is it true . . . Charlotte? Is it true they are going to kill me when the cold weather comes?"

By the end of a summer of maturing, Wilbur responds to news that his dearest friend will die, and he knows that he must save the egg sac. Notice how his vocabulary has changed to adult words, and his tone has changed to reasonable persuasion:

> "Listen to me! . . . Charlotte . . . has only a short time to live. She cannot accompany us home, because of her condition. Therefore, it is absolutely necessary that I take her egg sac with me. I can't reach it, and I can't climb. You are the only one that can get it. There's not a second to be lost. . . . Please, please, please, Templeton, climb up and get the egg sac."

Wilbur does not scream; he uses "please" liberally. His desperation does not arise from his own need, but from the need of another. Once Charlotte had said to the screaming Wilbur that he was carrying on childishly. The new Wilbur tells Templeton to "stop acting like a spoiled child." Wilbur—who once planned his day around his slops—can now, out of deep concern for Charlotte, promise solemnly that Templeton may eat first and take his choice of all the goodies in the trough.

During winter Wilbur warms the egg sac with his breath in the cold barn. By the end of the story, it is Wilbur who offers the first mature greeting, a cheerful Hello! for the baby spiders. The change is significant, and it occurs slowly. It is convincing. Little by little events have molded a self-centered child into responsible maturity; we believe in Wilbur's maturity just as we believed in his childishness. (pp. 38-9)

A *static character* is one that does not change in the course of the story. . . .

Although Charlotte is not the center of Wilbur's story, we know her consistent nature very well. Charlotte is not only motherly, but hard-working, and her web words prove it. She is the same wise and selfless character at the end of the story that she was at the beginning, and we therefore call her a static character. (p. 41)

From the first line in the first chapter of *Charlotte's Web*— "Where's Papa going with the ax?"—we know that Wilbur's fate is uncertain, and from that initial moment White holds us in *suspense,* a state that makes us read on. By tears, sobs, cries, and yells, Fern wins temporary reprieve for Wilbur and he becomes Fern's baby. Wilbur's brothers and sisters are all sold and it becomes Wilbur's turn. There goes Wilbur. But, see if Uncle Homer Zuckerman will buy Wilbur so Fern can visit him at the nearby farm. Wilbur is lonely, finding his life boring without Fern as constant companion. When he finds a friend, loneliness vanishes. Then, electrifying news comes: An old sheep spitefully tells Wilbur he is being fattened for Christmas slaughter. Charlotte to the rescue. She weaves the words "Some Pig" into her web; people come from miles around to see Wilbur. Mr. Zuckerman now admires him, and no celebrity was ever made into sausage.

As the excitement wears off, our worries revive. Charlotte, however, sends Templeton to the dump for more words. When each of the woven words miraculously appears, we have new hope. Then Wilbur's protector announces regretfully that she cannot accompany Wilbur to the Fair. Catastrophe looms again, but a ray of hope glimmers: "We'll leave it this way: I'll come to the Fair if I possibly can." Our security lasts only until we overhear Arable and Zuckerman talking about the fine hams and bacon he'll make. A huge pig called Uncle is appallingly stiff competition: "He's going to be a hard pig to beat." Wilbur's doom is sealed. Suddenly, an unprecedented award, but Wilbur faints and "We can't give a prize to a *dead* pig. . . . It's never been done before." No prize. Then Templeton bites Wilbur's tail, and Wilbur revives and wins the prize.

But Charlotte is languishing. Can Wilbur survive without Charlotte? Charlotte spins her final Magnum Opus and dies, and Wilbur, now mature, takes responsibility for Charlotte's egg sac. When spring comes, Wilbur is still alive and hearty, and life continues.

Suspense, the emotional pull that keeps us wanting to read on, involves us in conflict up to the climax in the final pages. These moments of suspense are not panic points in the story; nor at any point do we know the outcome with certainty. White controls the suspense to keep it peaking and leveling, and at every point we remain not only curious but concerned for the outcome, because either success or failure looms and we cannot be completely certain which will prevail.

Suspense has kept us reading, but White has carefully led us with optimism and never despair. Throughout the suspense, even in spite of it, we feel that all will be well, somehow. The author skillfully builds the story so that nowhere is the ending too predictable, lest we lose interest, nor too frightful, lest we give up. At the end of the book, the adult or child reader feels that the ups and downs of "perhaps he'll win, perhaps he'll lose" are finally settled. Suspense does not go beyond the story's ending. White, as he pulls us to the satisfactory end of the story, makes us heave a final, relieved sigh. The feeling

that all will be well, even after the final page, results from White's skill in handling suspense. Our optimism has been justified. (pp. 61-2)

The *denouement* begins at the climax, at the point where we feel that the protagonist's fate is known. From here the action of the plot is also called the *falling action.* In the denouement of *Charlotte's Web,* Templeton and Wilbur, the two survivors of the original trio, reach a bargain about who eats first at Wilbur's trough. Wilbur returns the egg sac to the barn, and its presence sustains the feeling that Charlotte is still there. Finally, warmed and protected by Wilbur's breath, the eggs hatch. Joy, Aranea, and Nellie, three of Charlotte's tiny progeny, stay on in the barn to keep Wilbur company, and to learn from him the ways of barn life. The seasonal cycle continues; everything is resolved. There is no question left unanswered. We say there is a resolution.

When the reader is assured that all is well and will continue to be, we say that the denouement is closed, or that the plot has a *closed ending.* In this case, the tying of the loose ends is thoroughly optimistic and satisfactory, a good conclusion for a small child's story. There is no anxiety for reader or listener on the last page of *Charlotte's Web.* The sigh is not a breath of anxiety, but one of regret that so good a story is over. (p. 68)

> *Rebecca J. Lukens, in her* A Critical Handbook of Children's Literature, *second edition, Scott, Foresman and Company, 1982, 264 p.*

SCOTT ELLEDGE

Charlotte's Web is a fabric of memories. . . . It is a pastoral fiction written when, more than ever before, White's vision was retrospective and his sense of life was sharpened by his having seen many things come to an end. . . . [For] White, the most important things that had passed were the sensations and images of infancy, childhood, and youth; and if he could remember them clearly, he could remember the self that had experienced them. If he could evoke that self and keep in touch with it, he could imagine a fiction, write a story, create a world that children would believe in and love. . . .

Perhaps White was especially able to write for the child that was himself because he had never stopped communicating with it. He had in fact, never stopped trying to win the approval of the self he once referred to as "a boy I knew." The integrity of White's view of the world owed much to the boy he kept in touch with despite his own loss of innocence. And the clarity and grace of his writing derived in part from the clarity of his vision of that ideal young self. . . . (p. 300)

About what he discovered when he got in touch with himself, we should take White at his word. To a reader of *Charlotte's Web* he wrote: "All that I hope to say in books, all that I ever hope to say, is that I love the world. I guess you can find that in there, if you dig around." (pp. 300-01)

Most of what White loved in the world is represented in *Charlotte's Web.* Essentially it consists of the natural world of creatures living in a habitat filled with objects, animate and inanimate, that White enjoyed seeing, hearing, feeling, smelling, and tasting. The most lyrical passages in the story are celebrations of what's out there—things and actions. (p. 301)

[The] book makes clear that the world White loves is more than a collection of things, natural and man-made, or a fascinating organization of reassuring cyclical, ongoing processes:

it is a world in which the motive for creating, nurturing, teaching, encouraging, singing, and celebrating is love. Charlotte sang away Wilbur's loneliness and his fear of death by persuading him that his world was cuddling him in the warmth and protection of its dung and its darkness. But her power to convince him of this benevolence came from her love for him, whom she called her "one and only." It was the love implied in "Sleep, my love" that cured Wilbur's depression and anxiety, that saved his life, and that taught him how to live out the rest of his life.

White discovered Charlotte, to be sure, when he was looking for a way to save Wilbur, but in making her the savior he served more than the needs of his plot. By making her an admirable creature, he helped readers free themselves from prejudices against spiders. He wanted to write a children's story that was true to the facts of nature and that, by reflecting his own love and understanding of the natural world, might help others to lift up their lives a little. His story turned out to be more than an idyll. It is a fable that subtly questions the assumption that homo sapiens was created to have dominion over every other living thing upon the earth. It also affirms that heroism is not a sexually determined characteristic, nor is it identical with self-sacrifice. Charlotte does not save Wilbur by dying; she saves him by following her instincts, by using her intelligence, and by being true to her individual self without being false to her general nature. Heroes, Charlotte reminds us, have from ancient times been people in a class by themselves because they used their unusual gifts to protect others. (p. 303)

White does not make Charlotte a victim of anything—even fate. She obeys sensibly the imperatives of being a female spider, knowing that she "has to," and she sounds, in fact, as if she were proud of her part in the great natural scheme, proud of the "versatility" of someone who can write and can also produce five hundred and fourteen eggs—save a friend's life as well as create new lives.

Children's books in the past had seldom faced up so squarely as did *Charlotte's Web* to such truths of the human condition as fear of death, and death itself; and they had not implied the courageous agnosticism that disclaimed any understanding of why life and the world are the way they are. In 1952 few children's books had made so clear as *Charlotte's Web* that the natural world of the barn does not exist to serve the world of the farmers who think they own it. And few children's books have so clearly embodied a love that can cure fear, make death seem a part of life, and be strong without being possessive. Charlotte was "in a class by herself." She was braver and more capable of friendship than Wilbur because she was older and more experienced, and probably because she was a superior individual—that is, a hero. Among heroes, of course, she was *sui generis.*

All of which is to suggest that *Charlotte's Web* was and probably will continue to be a modern book based on the integrity of a humble and skeptical view of the natural world and of the human beings in it. It gives no support to prejudice in favor of the superiority of human beings, or of one sex over another. It does celebrate a child's generous view of the world and a child's love of that world.

Charlotte's Web is a kind of fable, of course; but it is also a pastoral—an eclogue that takes its readers back to an early vision of an arcadia. It is itself a pastoral game, a form of play, and its effects are partly, perhaps heavily, nostalgic. If adults still possessed the world of the barn, they would not be so moved by a description of it. They love its memory because they have lost the original. They also love it because in loving it they are persuaded of its truth and perhaps of its perpetuity. *Charlotte's Web* can be "explained" in Wordsworthian, Blakean, or Proustian ways. As we grow older we lose the vision, but not beyond recall; in the vision of innocence is contained the wisdom of experience; the act of remembrance of things past affirms their value, affirms our value, and creates a sense of man freed from the clutches of time. Readers of *Charlotte's Web* momentarily enjoy this freedom because White succeeded in getting in touch with himself, with "the child that is himself." (p. 305)

Scott Elledge, in his E. B. White: A Biography, *W. W. Norton & Company, 1984, 400 p.*

JANICE M. ALBERGHENE

My acquaintance with *Charlotte's Web* was long delayed. I first read it at 25, an age at which many of my contemporaries were anticipating the pleasures of rereading it with the infants they at present cradled in their arms. . . . I turned then to the book's last page and read, "It is not often that someone comes along who is a true friend and a good writer. Charlotte was both." The child reader in me nodded familiarly at the words "true friend"—most children's books got around to this topic one way or another—but when I saw "good writer," I resumed my role of adult critic. Even the co-author of *The Elements of Style* would, I thought, be hard pressed to explain to children what the term "good writer" signified. Surely White had used that last phrase lightly; he could not have meant to explore what it means to be a "good writer" in a children's book. But he could, and he did.

At first glance then, it seems odd that few critics have commented on Charlotte's writing. More importantly, if skilled readers pay little conscious attention to Charlotte as a writer, what attention do children pay? Dr. Dorian, a character who appears midway through *Charlotte's Web,* offers a broad hint during a conversation with Mrs. Arable. She is worried about eight-year-old Fern's claim that "animals talk to each other." Asked his opinion, he says that he has never heard an animal talk, "But that proves nothing. It is quite possible that an animal has spoken civilly to me and that I didn't catch the remark because I wasn't paying attention. Children pay better attention than grownups."

The attention Fern pays to the animals' talk is a deep absorption. She is reflective, but she is not self-conscious—she is thinking, but she isn't thinking that she's thinking. Readers of *Charlotte's Web* are sometimes startled to discover Fern at the end of Chapter 13 ("Good Progress"). The chapter falls into two halves, with the break signaled by a space of several blank lines as well as by a brief change in scene to the dump where Templeton scavenges advertising slogans for Charlotte's campaign to save Wilbur. The remainder of the chapter concerns Charlotte's review of the slogans, Wilbur's audition for the word "radiant," and Charlotte's soothing Wilbur with two stories followed by a lullaby. Only then does White mention Fern: "When the song ended, Fern got up and went home." Although White does not state the exact time of Fern's arrival, the reader knows that she has heard the song, and White's use of the word "when" indicates that Fern has been present for some time—for the mulling over of words, for checking the chosen word's match with the living being it is meant to describe, and for the storytelling before the lullaby. And in fact, the next chapter begins with Fern's telling her mother, " 'Charlotte is the best storyteller I ever heard'." Fern follows up her praise of Charlotte by telling her own versions of the stories.

I would like to suggest that the child reader's experience with words and storytelling is similar to Fern's, not only in this chapter, but throughout the book. Starting with the moment the reader first meets Charlotte as a "small voice" invisible in the darkness, she prompts the reader to consider and experience language in increasingly sophisticated ways, from the literal meanings of words to casting words into stories and speeches. Please note, in this connection, that the child reader's experience of language is *similar* to Fern's, but it is not identical. For some readers, Wilbur provides an even closer parallel. Wilbur is Charlotte's first pupil—he is the character addressed out of the darkness by the "small voice." As he matures under Charlotte's guidance, so does his use of language, until he too can make a speech worthy of a "good writer." By saying this I am not claiming that children become good writers by the time they finish *Charlotte's Web.* Children do, however, have numerous opportunities to experience language from the inside out—from the perspective of storyteller or writer. Charlotte's role in that process is the subject of the rest of this article.

Charlotte's Web is as distinctly American as the county fair its characters attend. Yet Charlotte does not conform to many of American society's widely held presuppositions about writers. Despite their being condoned or even admired as the price of creativity, the traits the presuppositions refer to characterize the writer as eccentric at best. At his worst, he is a self-centered egotist who is "fierce, brutal, scheming, bloodthirsty" in the service of his art. These adjectives are, of course, the ones Wilbur uses to describe Charlotte at the beginning of their friendship. The narrator, however, immediately tells the reader that Wilbur is "mistaken about Charlotte. Underneath her rather bold and cruel exterior, she had a kind heart, and she was to prove loyal and true to the very end." Charlotte's altruism is commendable, but encouraging the child reader to identify closely with her is problematic, because, among other things, Charlotte dies at the end of the book. Rather than being the reader's second self, Charlotte is the reader's inspiration. One of the reasons this occurs is because Charlotte is Wilbur's inspiration. Right from the beginning of the book, the child reader is encouraged to sympathize with Wilbur's point of view; he is just a little pig and he does not want to die.

The reader's sympathies for Wilbur are first enlisted by Fern, who is "only eight." She stands in for the reader who is old enough to nurture something more helpless than herself, but young enough to know what it is like to be subject regularly to someone else's control, no matter how benevolent that control may be. On hearing that her father plans to kill Wilbur because he is little and a weakling, Fern cries: "The pig couldn't help being born small, could it? If *I* had been very small at birth, would you have killed *me*?" Fern's championing the weak and powerless Wilbur is an action children fervently support. Some of the readers of *Charlotte's Web* have questioned why at the end of the book Fern forgets Charlotte and Wilbur and runs off with Henry Fussy at the County Fair. One reason is that the reader simply does not need Fern anymore. The reader's involvement with Wilbur and Charlotte is so complete that seeing Fern's reactions to the more private events of the fair (Fern does witness Wilbur's public

triumph) would be superfluous to the point of distraction. The reader's own sensitivity to words, a sensitivity coached by Charlotte, is what counts. (pp. 32-4)

Charlotte's first contact with Wilbur is his introduction to the most easily appreciated extraliteral quality of words: how they sound. Charlotte is heard, not seen: ". . . out of the darkness, came a small voice. . . . It sounded rather thin, but pleasant." In the morning Charlotte adds meaning to sound with her greeting of "Salutations!" Wilbur's response is slightly hysterical:

> "Salu-*what*?" he cried.
>
> "Salutations!" repeated the voice.
>
> "What are *they,* and where are *you*?" screamed Wilbur. "Please, *please,* tell me where you are. And what are salutations?"
>
> "Salutations are greetings," said the voice. When I say 'salutations,' it's just my fancy way of saying hello or good morning. Actually, it's a silly expression, and I am surprised that I used it at all."

In this one short exchange, Charlotte both explains the meaning of a word and says something about it as language—"it's a silly expression." Although she says that she is surprised that she used the word, the reader is not. Silly expressions are fun to use, especially when one knows how to pronounce them. In this connection, note that Wilbur's "Salu-*what*?" breaks the word in half and makes the reader pause to sound it out.

"Salutations" is just the first of a series of words that Charlotte defines for Wilbur. "Untenable," "sedentary," "gullible," "versatile," *"magnum opus,"* and "languishing" also become a part of his, *and the reader's,* vocabulary. This results each time from Charlotte's using the word and Wilbur's asking what it means. Wilbur's reactions to the successive words show his emotional maturing and his increasing sophistication regarding language. . . . In this sequence of terms, Wilbur's early babyish excitability gives way respectively to relaxation, curiosity, and consideration for someone else's well-being.

Having a large vocabulary and using it in her conversation is by no means Charlotte's only claim to being a writer. She demonstrates her skill with words in two other, and very important, ways. One involves the selection and actual writing of words in her web. This is Charlotte's public authorship. Her private storytelling also shows that she is a writer. Public and private authorship alternate throughout the book in ways that artfully encourage the reader to imitate each kind of composing.

As the distinction suggests, Charlotte's public authorship is the more striking of the two kinds of composing. Ironically, however, only the reader, the animals, Fern, and one very singular adult character know or believe that Charlotte is special because she is the author of the words which appear in her web. These words refer to Wilbur and are a trick that Charlotte plays on the gullible humans in order to save Wilbur's life. Charlotte figures, quite rightly, that the humans will see the words as a sign that Wilbur is very special and should not meet the ordinary pig's fate of becoming bacon and sausage links. . . . The exclusion of adults (with the exception of the pro-child Dr. Dorian) from the group of believers in Charlotte serves to strengthen the child reader's involvement with the words in the web—the child knows that *she* knows the *real* story.

The reader in fact has participated in the choosing of the words for the web. Charlotte chose the first slogan, "Some Pig," by herself. For the second slogan, Charlotte calls together the barn animals and asks for suggestions. As the suggestions are put forward, it is hard for any reader not to start thinking of suggestions of her own. . . . The word "terrific" . . . meets with Charlotte's approbation even though Wilbur objects that he is not terrific: "That doesn't make a particle of difference. . . . People believe almost anything they see in print." Charlotte later softens this cynical bit of advice by telling Wilbur, "You're terrific as far as *I'm* concerned, . . . and that's what counts." The reader learns several things here. She learns that the connotations of words are important, but she also learns that most people are not conscious or critical enough of what they see in print. Sensitivity to language is important in both the sending and receiving of words.

Wilbur demonstrates his sensitivity to the words in the web by discovering that he feels sensations or emotions appropriate to the various words. Although Wilbur at first objected that he was not actually "terrific," by the time Charlotte has finished writing the word in her web and people have come to marvel over seeing it, ". . . Wilbur, who really *felt* terrific, stood quietly swelling out his chest and swinging his snout from side to side." Charlotte tests the aptness of the next word, "radiant," by asking to see Wilbur "in action." The pig obliges by racing, jumping, and doing a back flip. Charlotte decides to use the word even though she has reservations, whereupon Wilbur announces, "Actually, . . . I *feel* radiant." Although his outward appearance belies the adjective, the word does describe Wilbur's inner self. The italics in the above quotations are White's. They emphasize that Wilbur subjectively feels the words' applications. The pig's reaction shows that a good writer affects her audience. Charlotte is careful to mull over the meanings of the next (which is also the final) word she writes. Satisfied that "humble" is "Wilbur all over," she incorporates the adjective into the center of her web. Wilbur reacts by looking "very humble and very grateful." The team of Wilbur and Charlotte provides a model of responsive reader and responsible author.

Charlotte concretely delineates artistic responsibility in the scene in "Good Progress," where the reader sees her weave "terrific" into her web. Charlotte has no audience as she writes, but for the witnessing reader. Her isolation emphasizes her close connection to the word she is actually drawing out of her own body. Charlotte only uses words that are literally a part of her, and her craftsmanship is clearly evident as she labors in the dark—an apt metaphor for the artist at work. Earlier in the story, Mrs. Zuckerman's "It seems to me we have no ordinary *spider*" implied what readers already knew: the author of "Some Pig" was "Some Spider." The adjective she chose referred to herself as well as to her subject. The same applies to the word she writes now and to the words she will write in the future. Charlotte *is* "terrific." She fits Webster's definition: "exciting, or adapted to excite, great fear or dread." Wilbur, for example, is horrified when he sees Charlotte wrap a fly and then listens to her discussing her love of blood. Yet Charlotte is also "terrific" in the colloquial sense of being wonderful. "Radiant" certainly describes both Charlotte and her weaving: eight legs radiate out from her body, and radial lines emanate from the center of her web.

Finally, the last word Charlotte writes is the most telling of all. She writes with no desire for personal fame; she wants to focus attention on Wilbur, not herself. "Humble" aptly characterizes this goal. It is, moreover, a wonderfully understated reference to what Wilbur once called Charlotte's "miserable inheritance" through generations of spiders of trapping and weaving as a way to make a living. In a discussion of *Stuart Little,* Peter Neumeyer states that "White always uses established classic themes,". . . . Considering this information, it is therefore not unreasonable to suggest that White may have recalled the story of Arachne when he decided on "humble" as the last word for Charlotte's web. Arachne was a young Lydian weaver who boasted that her work rivalled that of Athena, goddess of crafts. Although warned by Athena about her presumption, Arachne shrugged off the advice. Athena then wove a tapestry depicting mortals punished for their arrogance by the gods. Arachne retaliated by portraying some of the gods' scandals. Enraged, Athena struck the girl with a shuttle and turned her into a spider (hence the zoological classification Arachnida to which spiders belong). Ever since that time, spiders have crept into corners to spin their webs. (pp. 35-9)

"Humble" is Charlotte's reversal of Arachne's hubris. She does play a trick on *her* gullible Olympians, the Zuckermans et al., but she plays the trick out of love, not pride. Her writing fools adults into seeing the truth about Wilbur, a truth that child readers did not need to be fooled into seeing. Neither do they *need* to know the story of Arachne to understand that Charlotte's position as a writer is a humble one: "Some Spider" was overlooked in the excitement about "Some Pig." I specifically mention Arachne, then, not as an example of a connection that a child reader is likely to make, but rather as an example of the kind of connection that *Charlotte's Web* prepares him to make. The "Some Pig" incident clearly raises for even very young children the issue of writing as self-expression. This is an issue that becomes more and more complicated as one becomes literate, as can one's interpretation of "humble."

The trick is to keep a sense of perspective, as well as a sense of humor. White's sense of perspective and his sense of humor are in full swing in the passage where Charlotte works on her second slogan. The physical act of writing, routine that it is to adults, is enormously complicated to young children. For them, forming letters is analogous to Charlotte's spinning. Charlotte must think carefully about every move she makes. She begins by deciding what kind of thread (dry or sticky) to use. This is very like choosing among pen, pencil, or crayons. Charlotte next decides to write double-lined figures so that they will stand out. This is a favorite device of children shortly after they have mastered the basic shapes of letters. . . . The concentration that distinguishes Charlotte's work also characterizes the effort of any novice printer who with fat pencil in hand leans over a sheet of wide-ruled manila practice paper. Note too that following the . . . description of the "R's" creation further implicates the reader in Charlotte's writing. Really following White's description means visualizing to the point of tracing with a finger or a pencil the movements the spider made.

Interesting or intriguing as this imitation may be, it is only one of two kinds of imitating that *Charlotte's Web* inspires. The second kind of imitating is much richer, for here the reader is invited to do no less than tell stories herself. Fern,

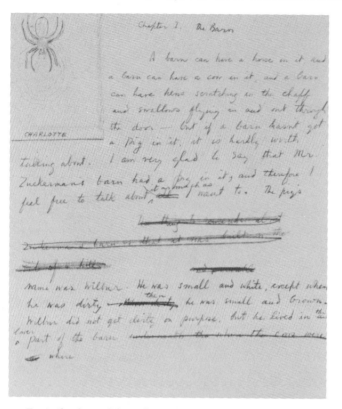

Facsimile of one of the earliest versions of the first page of Charlotte's Web.

and then much later, Wilbur, provide the reader with examples of following Charlotte's lead. The first instance of Fern's imitating Charlotte is the occasion of Charlotte's making a speech to welcome the new goslings to the barn. (pp. 39-40)

The second occasion of Fern's repeating what Charlotte has said even more clearly shows Fern's excitement in storytelling. After his try-out for the word "radiant," Wilbur asks Charlotte to tell him a story. She begins "Once upon a time," but what follows is a fish tale delivered in the frenetic style of a ringside announcer. A cousin of hers found a small fish in the web she had built over a little stream:

> "There was the fish, caught only by one fin, and its tail wildly thrashing and shining in the sun. There was the web, sagging dangerously under the weight of the fish."

> "How much did the fish weigh?" asked Wilbur eagerly.

> "I don't know," said Charlotte. "There was my cousin, slipping in, dodging out, beaten mercilessly over the head by the wildly thrashing fish, dancing in, dancing out, throwing her threads and fighting hard."

Like many a child, Wilbur then begs for another story. Charlotte complies, but this story is much shorter—only two sentences, compared with the previous narrative, which runs about three paragraphs in its entirety. Once again Charlotte talks about a cousin, this time one "who was an aeronaut. . . .'A balloonist. . . . My cousin used to stand on her head and let out enough thread to form a balloon. Then she'd let go and be lifted into the air and carried upward on the

warm wind'." These are the stories Fern had in mind when, in a passage mentioned earlier, she praises Charlotte's storytelling. Charlotte *is* a fine storyteller, one who can spin a fish tale as well as she can spin a web.

The effect the story has on Fern is still more evident in the version she gives her mother. . . . (pp. 40-1)

Fern was so affected by the story, and is so effective in retelling it that her mother, a woman who believes that "Spiders can't talk," wants to hear the end of the story. Mrs. Arable even agrees, after hearing the aeronaut story, that being a balloonist would be quite pleasant.

As is only fitting, Wilbur provides the reader with a final example of Charlotte's inspiring language that heightens one's awareness of the life around and within oneself. Charlotte is now dead, and all but three of her children have ballooned off to find new homes. At their suggestion, Wilbur has collaborated in giving each of the three a name. Naming is sacral; it demonstrates that the speaker identifies and knows the spirit and essence of the person or object named. The collaborative aspect of Wilbur's naming emphasizes the power of language to create community and shared understanding. This is a power which can transcend death and make the past come alive in the present. The following speech "on this very important occasion" shows how much of this power Wilbur owes to Charlotte:

> "Joy! Aranea! Nellie!" he began. "Welcome to the barn cellar. You have chosen a hallowed doorway from which to string your webs. I think it is only fair to tell you that I was devoted to your mother. I owe my very life to her. She was brilliant, beautiful, and loyal to the end. I shall always treasure her memory. To you, her daughters, I pledge my friendship, forever and ever."

Wilbur's speech closely echoes the cadences of Charlotte's greeting to the goslings, but the substance of the text is Wilbur's response to the present. Whereas Fern repeated Charlotte's speech with minor variations, Wilbur shows that he has learned how to make new speeches for new occasions. Wilbur owes not only life, but also language, to the grey spider. The reader owes White not only her glimpse of the humble experience of one writer, but also her (the reader's) own initiation into a community of writers. *Charlotte's Web* does not merely tell about the writer's experience; it shows and creates that experience right before the willing reader's eyes. (pp. 41-2)

Janice M. Alberghene, "Writing in 'Charlotte's Web'," in Children's literature in education, *Vol. 16, No. 1, Spring, 1985, pp. 32-44.*

NORTON D. KINGHORN

From the time of its first appearance in 1952, reviewers and critics have heralded E. B. White's *Charlotte's Web* as a children's classic, but they differ widely on the question of what it is about. . . .

On the question of who the book is about, there is even less agreement. . . .

[While] *Charlotte's Web* is about Fern, there is probably not a case for Fern as the protagonist of the story, for, as Rebecca Lukens maintains, Fern's character is left quite flat and undeveloped. After the beginning, when she saves the runt pig with her child's argument for justice, Fern soon becomes unobtrusive in the story of Wilbur and Charlotte and the barn, almost invisible, to become visible only occasionally to remind us that the story is, after all, partly hers, and to represent the evolution of the species human beings. . . . Fern is important in White's tale in the way that Gatsby is important in F. Scott Fitzgerald's *The Great Gatsby,* or that Willie Stark is important in Robert Penn Warren's *All the King's Men,* or Kurtz in Joseph Conrad's *Heart of Darkness.* She is not the protagonist of the story, but the point cannot be made without her.

Rebecca Lukens identifies Wilbur as the sole protagonist of the story, for Wilbur's character develops, Wilbur changes. (p. 4)

In fact, the book is centrally about Charlotte—Charlotte the artist, the friend, the writer and rhetorician. If the book has a protagonist she is it. For she effects the outcome of the series of events; she is the one who acts heroically and unselfishly; she expresses or draws together all the themes of the book; it is she upon whom we fasten our attention from the time she first appears and for the duration of the book.

Above all, it is the web Charlotte weaves that most essentially expresses the meaning of the book. The web is a means of catching food, a medium of communication, a means of transportation. Symbolically, the web is the passage, the threshold, between one existence and another, between life and death, between the innocent (but wise) world in which all living creatures are equal and equally deserving of a place in the sun or the barn, and the world of "commonplace human life" [in John Rowe Townsend's words], in which every creature not human is either food or profit—a world populated by the species H. L. Mencken called "homo-boobiens." As a symbol of transition, the web is central because **Charlotte's Web** is about change—inevitable, irresistable, implacable change—change in two worlds: the world of the barn, of the seasons, all of nature; and the world of humans, who appear in the novel as interlopers, creatures lost to the mysteries of nature, no longer able to fathom the miracle of a spider's web or the chirping of crickets or the coming of spring.

The "hymn to the barn," White's description of **Charlotte's Web,** does much more than simply celebrate and praise; it serves as the emotional accompaniment to the plot. If **Charlotte's Web** is about change—passage from one existence to another—then the hymn, with its lyrical interludes, chronicles and choruses that transition. . . . [It] is one of many webs in the novel, securing the reader's emotional participation in the life-death-rebirth cycle and in the loss of paradise. (p. 5)

The hymn to the barn . . . provides the lyrical background to the unfolding drama. From a celebration of life in the barn, of all of nature, of the changing seasons, to the elegy for the passing of Charlotte, the cycle is complete, life returns with the spring. That is, much returns. But Charlotte is gone, and while her daughters and granddaughters, a few of them at least, take her place in the doorway of the barn, no one can really replace her in Wilbur's heart: "She was in a class by herself."

The hymn provides the lyrical background for still another change, another passing—something else, too, has been lost with the falling leaves of autumn and the snows of winter. The hymn to the barn is in part a lament for Fern's lost childhood, or rather the loss of the mystical tie that exists between a sensitive child and the earth and all the creatures and things of the earth. . . .

White is quite specific about this change in Fern; it is more than just growing up. It is the fall from innocence, the loss of paradise—a paradise in which every living creature has a *raison d'etre,* in which all life exists on an equality absolute. This paradise is Edenic and primitive. It is the world of Indian myth and legend, of the one-ness of all life. Fern's prelapsarian state—her rapport with nature—is not perfect, for though she understands the animals of the barn and follows their conversations with apparent ease, she never talks *to* them, nor they to her. They accept her presence, assume her friendship and trust her to come near, but they do not acknowledge her presence in any other way.

From this imperfect Eden, the world of the barn, Fern falls into adulthood (or at least stumbles a step in that direction—she is only eight) or into the real world, in Townsend's words "that of commonplace human life." Townsend is philosophical about Fern's fall: ". . . that is life. . . . Childhood passes." But the fall is neither so simple nor to be tossed off so easily. The reader must sense the quality of the change—must feel the loss of paradise.

What then is the nature of Fern's passing? . . .

For one thing Fern's passing, her fall, is into a world peopled by the species *homo sapiens;* and White is quite specific about human beings in this book—his images, his metaphors, depict human life in less than honorific terms. This is the satire of the novel. . . .

Once again, the web is the key to the satire, the informing symbol, which introduces a series of analogies between the two worlds, animal and human. The first of these analogies is from Charlotte herself as she begins to form a plan to save Wilbur. Her logic is irrefutable:

> Charlotte was naturally patient. She knew from experience that if she waited long enough, a fly would come to her web; and she felt sure that if she thought long enough about Wilbur's problem, an idea would come to her mind.

> Finally, one morning toward the middle of July, the idea came. "Why, how perfectly simple!" she said to herself. "The way to save Wilbur's life is to play a trick on Zuckerman. If I can fool a bug," thought Charlotte, "I can surely fool a man. People are not as smart as bugs."

The proof is in the web, in its message. Lurvy is the first to read the message, "SOME PIG!" and he is so frightened that he utters a prayer and then runs to fetch Zuckerman. In one of the funniest scenes in the novel, Lurvy and Zuckerman consider the web; they are helpless in the snare of Charlotte's prose—frightened and trembling. Zuckerman tells his wife: "A miracle has happened and a sign has occurred here on earth, right on our farm, and we have no ordinary pig." Mrs. Zuckerman, the one bright hope for human beings at this point, seems to know that the real miracle is not the pig but the spider, but soon she too succumbs to the spell of Charlotte's prose. Of course, the web only confirms the belief of the men about the pig. They knew it all along.

Zuckerman takes his news to the minister for spiritual guidance. The minister counsels secrecy and promises to turn his powers to an interpretation. "There can be no doubt," says the minister, "that you have a most unusual pig. I intend to speak about it in my sermon and point out the fact that this community has been visited with a wondrous animal." The minister speaks truth, but is no more open to miracles than the farmer; the truly wondrous animal escapes his notice—the web; *as web,* is beyond his feeble imagination. (p. 6)

Charlotte's trick—Charlotte's web—spreads to trap everybody for miles round. The tourists arrive by the hundreds to see the amazing pig. The Zuckermans are so busy promoting their miracle pig that the farm begins to go to smash, a piece of information that White drops in so unobtrusively that one could easily miss it. On Sunday the minister, true to his word, offers his interpretation to a church full of people: ". . . that the words on the spider's web proved that human beings must always be on the watch for the coming of wonders." As for Fern, " . . . she found that the barn was not nearly as pleasant—too many people. She liked it better when she could be all alone with her friends the animals."

Fern's preference for the barn and the animals of the barn, and her talk of their conversations cause her mother some concern. . . . When she takes her questions about Fern's suspected abnormality to Dr. Dorian, the conversation turns naturally to the pig and the spider's web—the miracle. The doctor proposes that the real miracle is the web itself and the spider that made it. When Mrs. Arable disagrees, Dr. Dorian draws a comparison between the spider and Mrs. Arable, as seamstresses—to Mrs. Arable's humiliation.

Mrs. Arable is not convinced that spiders can be the purveyors of miracles, and as for the web: "I don't understand it, and I don't like what I can't understand." And there we have it: fear or dislike for the unknown—one of the differences between the two worlds, characteristic of human beings. . . . To understand the meaning of the web we, like Dr. Dorian, must at least believe it possible that animals can talk, and might do so, if only we had the ability to pick up on it.

Dr. Dorian's function in **Charlotte's Web** is not immediately clear. He has nothing really to do with the narrative of the barn or with Wilbur's story. He does not affect the outcome in any way. Rather, he is a kind of choral figure, commenting on the story of Fern, clarifying the satire against human beings. He exists only on a level above story. And he is puzzling for another reason: he would seem to be the only human in the novel with a foot in both worlds, an example of a human not blind to the true miracles of the earth. But that is only partly the case, for while Dr. Dorian the scientist has an open mind on the question of communications among animals, Dorian the man "has never heard one say anything." Perhaps Dr. Dorian represents the best that is possible for a member of the species that has lost paradise. (p. 7)

The dominant symbol of the change in Fern is the web, not Charlotte's web but several images of webs, most of them man-made. Charlotte herself provides the clue that readers are supposed to look for other, less obvious webs. . . . The Queensborough Bridge is one of man's webs. While Charlotte's web satisfies her basic need for food, man seeks "something better on the other side." The spider's web is the mark of her patience; the bridge represents man's impatience ("rush, rush, rush, every minute") perhaps his materialism (time is money, the saying goes).

Wilbur's ludicrous attempt to spin a web with Templeton's string tied to his tail, which precedes, by a chapter only, the passage describing the swing in Zuckerman's barn, perhaps foreshadows the play of Avery and Fern on the swing. The swing in Zuckerman's barn is also an inferior web, for, like the Queensborough Bridge, it is man-made, and, like the bridge, traffic on it goes back and forth; no one ever simply hangs and waits for "something good to come along." What else White has in mind is difficult to say. There is of course the parents' fear that a child will fall. But fall to what? Its starting point is the hay loft; at its apogee the view is of sky and clouds (freedom?); its perigee is the north barn door (the passage?). That is about all one can say with certainty. Perhaps the sky and clouds represent one world, a world of imagination in which all things are possible. The children always wind up, after several trips to and fro, back on the barn floor—not the basement, where the animals live, but the floor above, apart from the peace and certitude of "the dung and the dark."

The rest of the webs appear at the fairground, that version of the world of "commonplace human life" that Townsend calls "imaginatively regressive," and which is obviously a symbol of man's materialism. The webs of the fairground share characteristics of earlier man-made webs. The merry-go-round is a sign, to humans, of growing up:

> The children grabbed each other by the hand and danced off in the direction of the merry-go-round, toward the *wonderful* music and the *wonderful* adventure and the *wonderful* excitement, into the *wonderful* midway where there would be no parents to guard them and guide them, and where they could be happy and free and do as they pleased. Mrs. Arable stood quietly and watched them go. Then she sighed. Then she blew her nose.
>
> "Do you really think it's all right?" she asked.
>
> "Well, they've got to grow up sometime," said Mr. Arable. "And a fair is a good place to start, I guess." (italics mine)

So the fair, with its merry-go-round and its midway, is an approved route to maturity. But White is very careful to inform us of what sort of passage this is that leads into the midway, through the almost nauseous repetition of the empty word "wonderful." The merry-go-round, like the swing, leads nowhere but around and around. And the children are drawn to this gaudy world much as flies are attracted to Charlotte's web.

The merry-go-round is only a small version of a larger web, the Ferris wheel. True to Dr. Dorian's prediction, Henry Fussy catches Fern's attention and together they ride the Ferris wheel. Like the rope swing, the Ferris wheel affords glimpses of sky and clouds and even of distant vistas; but like the swing and the Queensborough Bridge, always returns the rider to the place from whence he began.

After the Ferris wheel and Henry Fussy, Fern does not think of Wilbur and Charlotte again. She is forever arrested in the world of bright lights, jangling music, the wonderful midway, and the web of the Ferris wheel. And there can be little doubt that this world is not only commonplace and imaginatively regressive, it is also crassly materialistic. To Charlotte, the saving of Wilbur is an artistic and moral achievement, and the ultimate act of friendship. But in the world of human beings, Wilbur receives his award for promoting the tourist trade, for "attracting many valuable tourists to our great State." "A pig shall be saved" from the fate of becoming bacon, porkchops, and ham hocks, not out of any goodness or tenderness or creativity in man, but out of pride that a miracle should occur "right here on our farm," and for the profit motive. Pride and profit—two motives that have always made humans a prey to the confidence game—now prove them vulnerable to the stratagems of a selfless, heroic spider who can write.

Because Charlotte can write, there is one further aspect to the meaning of her web. Ultimately, it is a symbol of language. . . . (pp. 7-8)

The chief commentary on language in *Charlotte's Web* is from Charlotte herself—Charlotte the writer, the lexicographer, the rhetorician. While her web catches flies, the words that she weaves into it catch man. "If I can fool a bug," she thinks, "I can surely fool a man. People are not as smart as bugs." The rhetoric she uses on this inferior creature is of his own invention, as ancient as the written language, as prestigious as Aristotle, Quintilian, and Cicero. . . .

Charlotte is not only a skilled rhetorician, but also a sensitive manipulator of words; her knowledge of connotations is considerable. (p. 8)

But it is in her web that Charlotte best expresses herself. The web symbolizes the persuasive capability of language, as it points up human helplessness before the printed word. It never occurs to anyone but Fern, and to a lesser degree Mrs. Zuckerman and Dr. Dorian, that it is just possible (if miraculous) that other creatures might have language, too. Even when one of those creatures does send a message *in human language,* humans do not think to write back or talk back, they are so taken in by the message itself and by its referent. How ironic that man's one distinguishing feature is also his most vulnerable spot. Charlotte's real web is language, stuck together by rhetoric; and man, pathetic fly that he is, in his fallen state, is trapped in this most ingenious web.

So are readers of the book. The ultimate strategy of any book is to align its readers with one or more of its characters or ideologies, in a way to ensnare them in the web of its fiction. *Charlotte's Web* would seem to have succeeded too well, for the critics—the best of readers—fall in with the humans of the story and miss all the real miracles of it. One loss that accompanies the fall from innocence is the loss of the ability to believe in miracles—call it faith perhaps—the ability to believe, or perceive, that spiders can write—or, more precisely, the ability to perceive the miracles of nature as opposed to miracles from nowhere. (pp. 8-9)

[The] key to understanding a literary text is experience. . . . Writers write for the "hidden child within" them (at least the ones worth reading do); therefore it follows that adults should read for the hidden child within them. And this goes for teachers who would hope to lead children to the rich meaning that is literature.

Teachers and critics alike should have the wisdom to ask questions about the experiences of children—experiences and feelings analogous to those in the fiction. Do you ever talk to animals? Has an animal ever talked to you? The answers to those questions will allow teachers, critics, and children to explore the real miracle of *Charlotte's Web.* (p. 9)

> Norton D. Kinghorn, "The Real Miracle of 'Charlotte's Web'," in Children's Literature Association Quarterly, *Vol. 11, No. 1, Spring, 1986, pp. 4-9.*

BETTY LEVIN

Although child psychologists tell us that children see the world with themselves at its center, we know that they can respond to literature which suggests otherwise. Even if the Zuckerman barnyard in *Charlotte's Web* is seen as a microcosmic universe, its center isn't easily fixed. The reader may begin with the child Fern, the heroine and listener; but then the reader moves on. To Wilbur, innocent and anxious; to Charlotte and her life-giving web which is also, importantly, a killing web. In this book people take action and appear to be in charge of their lives (or, anyhow, the life of a runty pig), until the animals themselves take charge, each according to its nature and supernature. Who disturbs the universe? Fern, charging in to rescue Wilbur from the ax? Wilbur himself, striving to overcome the ordinary fate of a farm pig? . . . Or was it Charlotte, who tells Wilbur, " 'I was never more serious in my life. I am not going to let you die, Wilbur' "?

I think that on one level, very much a child's level, all three of these characters dare to disturb the universe. But on a deeper level, the author's inmost Heart of the Wood, none of them can disturb the universe, not really. The pig is born and for a while lives, and for a while more is famous, is "SOME PIG." But the world goes on—Fern to the Ferris wheel, Charlotte to dust. And when the novelty wears off, Wilbur's future is not all that certain. I think this is a powerful and consuming idea for the child-centered world of the storybook, especially when it comes through as perspective, not explicit message.

The other side of the coin is equally true, of course—that we cannot help disturbing the universe. It's what Ged tells Arren in [Ursula K. Le Guin's] *The Farthest Shore:* " 'When that rock is lifted, the earth is lighter, the hand that bears it heavier. When it is thrown, the circuits of the stars respond, and where it strikes or falls the universe is changed.' " It is the tension between these opposites that sets the predicament of choice and action for the protagonist in most fiction. The responsibility and dilemma of the children's writer is to show the protagonist taking charge and pressing past the easy or passive development while at the same time showing some effectiveness on the part of the individual. E. B. White uses this tension in *Charlotte's Web* by creating and sustaining a balance between action and the universe. (pp. 104-05)

While almost all adults love *Charlotte's Web,* only occasional children may enjoy **"Death of a Pig,"** for there is no hero in the story, no suspense or hope—only trying, caring, and failing. Charlotte herself accomplishes what White would have done if he could have. Instead, he brings the pig to life in the character of Wilbur. Where Charlotte spun her web, White spins a yarn; he, too, sets his words in it where they count. It is the same old story of life and death, love and commitment, freshly told—a miracle. (p. 106)

> Betty Levin, "The Universe and Old MacDonald," in Innocence & Experience: Essays & Conversations on Children's Literature, *edited by Barbara Harrison and Gregory Maguire, Lothrop, Lee & Shepard Books, 1987, pp. 102-15.*

CHARLES FREY AND JOHN GRIFFITH

Although it is only a bedtime story, *Charlotte's Web* expresses as poignantly as anything E. B. White ever wrote his bright and whimsical but fundamentally melancholy sense of life. In this story of Wilbur a pig—lonely, vulnerable, good-hearted, and decent but incapable of making the world conform to his wishes—White created a consoling fantasy in which a small porcine Everyman survives and triumphs over the pathos of being alone. White was writing for children here, but he expressed the same attitude toward life and death that he expressed in his writing for adults. He may have been having fun with *Charlotte's Web,* but he was not joking.

Charlotte's Web was published in 1952. Twelve years earlier White had written an essay on freedom which provides a valuable commentary on the story's essential meaning.

> Intuitively, I've always been aware of the vitally important pact which a man has with himself, to be all things to himself, . . . to stand self-reliant. . . . My first and greatest love affair was with this thing we call freedom. . . .
>
> It began with the haunting intimation (which I presume every child receives) of his mystical inner life; of God in man; of nature publishing herself through the "I." This elusive sensation is moving and memorable. It comes early in life: a boy, we'll say, sitting on the front steps on a summer night, thinking of nothing in particular, suddenly hearing as with a new perception and as though for the first time the pulsing sound of crickets, overwhelmed with the novel sense of identification with the natural company of insects and grass and night, conscious of a faint answering cry to the universal perplexing question: "What is 'I'?" Or a little girl, returning from the grave of a pet bird, leaning with her elbows on the windowsill, inhaling the unfamiliar draught of death, suddenly seeing herself as part of the complete story. Or to an older youth, encountering for the first time a great teacher who by some chance word or mood awakens something and the youth beginning to breathe as an individual and conscious of strength in his vitals. . . .
>
> This is the beginning of the affair with freedom.

That is to say, sometime early in life, every child experiences a mildly mystical sense of his participation in a vast natural order as a separable, individual part. This experience provides the true basis for his sense of himself, the indispensable first part of the answer to the question, "What is my self?"

But more than White's explicit point, notice the particular atmosphere with which he dramatizes the moment of insight into the link between the self and the cosmos: a boy sitting alone, musing aimlessly, not thinking of anything; or a girl whose pet bird has died, feeling for the first time the nearness of death; or a student making his first acquaintance with a skilled teacher. These situations, for White, contain the intuited clues, the intimations of the depths of one's inner life. They all take place in one's youth; White presumes that all children experience them in some form. They are abstracted, unsocial moments of personal isolation. In two of the three, the child is alone, and in the third—the youth who meets for the first time with a powerful teacher—the experience is again essentially a lonely one, not a reciprocal transaction but a receiving of "some chance word or mood" from without, impinging, for once, on the youth's sensibilities. This realization of one's self in the universe, then, has something to do with the impact of language—the chance word of a teacher; it has something to do with idleness and aimless musing; and it has something to do with the thought of death.

Charlotte's Web is the consolation White offers to the child

who has lived and continues to live in the presence of the beautiful but rather forbidding and unsociable personage, freedom, and in the lonely realization of one's individuality. He approaches the task by creating a character and a set of circumstances that dramatize the anxieties of that situation. (pp. 219-20)

White . . . establishes Wilbur in a desperate existential situation: He is bored, he is starved for affection, and he is scared of dying. These are precisely the psychic problems attendant on the haunting intimation that one is ultimately alone. Wilbur's loneliness is the emotional counterpart of the philosophical perception that between oneself and others lies an unbridgeable gap. Since on this level one becomes the sole measure and standard of his own world (becomes all things to himself, as White puts it) everything depends on his being fulfilled. Boredom is simply that enervating sense that this is not happening. One comes to believe that nothing he does really matters. Doing novel things can allay this feeling temporarily, but novelty wears out. To find significance that appears permanent, the individual must find a context larger than himself to give purpose to his actions. Without it, one is prey to the debilitating state of mind in which the only important question is "Am I being fulfilled?"

In this state of mind, the thought of death has a keen edge. The person whose sense of himself is governed by a feeling of communality—of being most importantly a member of a tribe or a family or a people or a cause—can see his own death as less than absolute. To one who lives in and for himself, death must be the ultimate terror, the end of all that matters. Indeed, the thought of death in this situation often combines thoughts of ultimate boredom and ultimate loneliness. Death appears as a vast emptiness, where no one else is and where there is absolutely nothing to do. (p. 221)

Wilbur of course is not a philosopher meditating on alienation and mortality; on the contrary, he is an eager and gregarious child wishing to live and to be loved and happy. White is the philosopher; through Wilbur he addresses the anxieties that a child in a modern, fragmented culture might feel. White says, in effect, "Once upon a time there was a youngster who was bored, lonely, and afraid of dying." The story which follows, like a fairy tale, soothes these anxieties.

To disarm boredom, White offers a vision of a rich and various world, a world filled with dramatic experiences such as winning a prize at the county fair, riding the Ferris wheel, taking dizzying swings on the big rope in the barn, sledding, listening to stories, making new friends. Even without such events, the world of *Charlotte's Web* resembles Mr. Zuckerman's barn—full of splendid ordinary things: tools and equipment and farm machinery and scraps and clutter and odds and ends—a place good for nesting in, for poking around in, for playing in. In this world the variety of experience is practically inexhaustible. (pp. 221-22)

And of course there is Charlotte, the articulate spider. . . . Once Charlotte puts in her appearance, Wilbur is free from boredom forever.

The book speaks just as soothingly to the fear of loneliness. When Wilbur voices his complaint, and cries out that he is young and friendless and depressed by the rain and devoid of any happy prospects whatsoever, there comes an answer. A small voice that Wilbur has never heard before issues out of the darkness, rather thin but comforting. "I'll be a friend to you," the voice says. It is of course Charlotte, the perfect friend: confidante, instructor, protector, mother. A tacit message of the book is this: If you feel lonely, do not despair; look for love and companionship, and you will find it.

The book's answer to the fear of death is a bit more complicated but nonetheless firm and unambiguous. The book says that if you (like Wilbur) are panic-stricken at the thought that you may suddenly and horribly die, be assured that clever, solid, reliable adults (like Charlotte) will see to it that this does not happen. Children may feel vulnerable, but they need not fear the worst, for grown-ups can protect them. When Wilbur screams that he doesn't want to die, Charlotte promises him that he won't have to. In a strict sense, of course, she is lying; but she is telling a truth true enough for Wilbur, because what she really means is that Wilbur, the young pig, will not die; death is for the old, not the young. And by the time you are old, you (like Charlotte, dying alone at the fairgrounds) will accept and perhaps even welcome death. By then you will have lived out your life, wearied yourself in the fulfillment of your mortal purpose, and you will be ready for the sleep of death. By then death will be seen as one of the elements in the wholesome natural cycle of existence; dying in season will create no special terror. The old don't mind dying, White's argument runs, and since it will be a long time before you are old, you need not worry about it now.

In the center of this consoling fantasy is Charlotte, the radiantly perfect adult—completely reliable, completely considerate, completely competent, completely right. In availing himself of her services, White has engaged in an act of fantasy, of wishful thinking. The world of modern individualism has sweepingly outlawed the idea of the sage who knows the answers. White's hero Thoreau, for example, was strident on this point.

> I have lived some thirty years on this planet, and I have yet to hear the first syllable of valuable or even earnest advice from my seniors. They have told me nothing, and probably cannot tell me anything, to the purpose. Here is life, an experiment to a great extent untried by me; but it does not avail me that they tried it.

There speaks the true individualist—and there speak most of the classic children's authors, the Mark Twains and Lewis Carrolls and James M. Barries and Hans Christian Andersens, to whom adulthood is seldom much more than a stultification of the genius and vitality of childhood. In the face of this august company sits White's Charlotte, an adult who has actually lived and learned, and who uses her wisdom to save the child Wilbur. She embodies a very old-fashioned notion ("Hear, my son, your father's instruction, and reject not your mother's teaching; for they are a fair garland for your head, and pendants for your neck," Proverbs 1:8-9); but in White's handling she is a figure of fantasy, for she is there not because the world has really provided a way for her to exist, but because Wilbur (and White and the reader) needs her to be there.

In White's writing for adults, the experts or sages are usually threatening, irrationally headstrong creatures whose way it is best to stay out of. Only in his fantasy writing, where spiders talk lovingly to pigs and spell out words in their webs, can someone like Charlotte exist. She is needed there; and need, rather than reality, is the operative principle in fantasy.

It may seem perverse to lay such stress on fantasy in *Charlotte's Web* when compared with other more patently fantas-

tic stories like *Alice in Wonderland* or *Peter Pan.* In the fantasies of Carroll and Barrie, the prospect of growing up and growing old holds terrors which send the authors' imaginations into spasms of rejection. Adulthood in *Alice in Wonderland* is a mixture of mystery and madness; in *Peter Pan,* it is a dull round of routine through which flirts the ghost of serious sexuality. Next to these stories, **Charlotte's Web** stands forth as a wise and fatherly discourse acknowledging the sadness of mutability and mortality, but reassuring the reader all the same.

White's book acknowledges that when people grow up they change, and the change is not entirely for the better. The little girl Fern, who begins as Wilbur's devoted friend and protector, grows up, and loses interest in Wilbur. Early in the story, when Fern's mother is worried about the girl's spending so much time "alone" in the barn, wise old Dr. Dorian assures her that the company of animals is healthy enough. He even avers that animals may talk, may have spoken to him on occasion, and that he missed hearing their remarks because he wasn't paying attention. "Children pay better attention than grown-ups." By the end of the story, Fern, who no longer comes to the barn, has stopped paying attention. She has found a boyfriend named Henry Fussy. In this way White acknowledges that one of the things that will draw one away from childish concerns is the awakening of sexual interests. At the height of Wilbur's triumph, just as he is to be awarded the special prize at the fair, Fern runs off through the midway crowd, looking for Henry.

The book acknowledges, too, that people die. Charlotte dies, tired and alone. The account of her death is the only undisguisedly sad scene in the novel. But White stresses that it is right for Fern to grow up and lose interest and for Charlotte to die. These events are natural parts of life's order. Even more important than this, psychologically, is the fact that, lovable as they may be, Fern and Charlotte are not Wilbur. Fern changes, and Charlotte dies, but Wilbur is allowed to live a long life without the permanent changes or trauma of maturation. He finds interest outside himself (primarily in Charlotte and the endless succession of her descendants who live with him in the barn) without the burdens of real responsibility for them. (He never, for example, has to arrange their destinies in the way Charlotte has arranged his for him.) He finds love without the complications of sex or parenthood (the nearest thing to reproduction he experiences is the adoption of the little spiders). Essentially he is allowed to remain a child for life: "Mr. Zuckerman took fine care of Wilbur all the rest of his days." Strictly speaking, he never even has to die. That phrase "all the rest of his days" is as close as White comes to suggesting Wilbur's death. Since Wilbur is the character with whom the reader is invited to identify, and since to him none of the problems of boredom, loneliness, maturation, or death proves insoluble, the plot serves to assure the reader that, though sad things do happen, they don't exactly happen to him.

The story soothes and consoles in even subtler ways. Its abundant humor and White's famous crafted style mute its sadness and control a troublesome sentimentality. When the going gets sticky, either by becoming too painful or cloyingly sweet, the narrator steps back rhetorically and reminds us that the story is, after all, only a story. It can be viewed with an aesthetic detachment we could not afford if its events were happening to real characters we really cared about. (pp. 222-24)

The final paragraph of **Charlotte's Web** is a masterpiece of semi-sweet, semi-serious humor, expressing melancholy sentiment without tears: "Wilbur never forgot Charlotte. Although he loved her children and grandchildren dearly, none of the new spiders ever quite took her place in his heart. She was in a class by herself. It is not often that someone comes along who is a true friend and a good writer. Charlotte was both." The play of tone here is vintage White: wry, amiable, softly arch. It is sad that Charlotte is gone forever, but it's funny to think of her as a good writer, since her entire published canon has consisted of five words in her web.

In an important way, this is exactly the right epitaph for her: a true friend and a good writer. What, after all, has been Charlotte's service to Wilbur? She has never touched him, never fed him, never sheltered him. She has talked to him, sung to him, and written advertising copy for him. Their contact has been purely verbal. One of the clearest marks of **Charlotte's Web** as the fantasy of a lonely, yearning imagination is the importance it places on language as the means through which spirit is laid against spirit. The highest and best love, in this book, is that which expresses itself through words, and words only. Language is pure, a process in which "all animal heat and moisture may have a chance to evaporate," as Thoreau approvingly puts it. Wilbur has talked to Charlotte, she has talked to and for him, her descendants converse with him—in the ambience of Wilbur's idyllic barnyard, these have found the best kind of friendship. When hearts make contact through language alone, they do so without invading each other's privacy. Approaching each other through the formal channel of words, they soften the pain of individuality without positively intruding. Hence, the truest friend must be a good writer. And that, of course, is Charlotte. (pp. 225-26)

Charles Frey and John Griffith, "E. B. White: 'Charlotte's Web'," in their The Literary Heritage of Childhood: An Appraisal of Children's Classics in the Western Tradition, *Greenwood Press, 1987, pp. 219-26.*

Valerie Worth

1933-

American poet and author of fiction.

Often praised for her originality and insight, Worth is best known for writing three volumes of poetry—*Small Poems* (1972), *More Small Poems* (1976), and *Still More Small Poems* (1978)—which capture the wonders of familiar subjects, experiences, places, and sensations in verse considered delicate yet solid. In these works, which are presented to middle graders in a small format designed to complement the content of the poetry, she provides her audience with opportunities to see the mystery and significance in the ordinary through free verse noted for its fresh images and internal discipline. The collections, which have been gathered into one volume in *All the Small Poems* (1987), are acknowledged both for the success of Worth's introspective vision and for the authenticity of her poetry as literature. Also a poet for adults, Worth is celebrated for investing her works for the young with a childlike quality and accessibility which aids her readers in recognizing the essential aspects of the world around them. In addition to her poetry, Worth has also created a story for the middle grades and two young adult novels which draw upon the genres of the fairy tale and the Gothic novel. With *Curlicues: The Fortunes of Two Pug Dogs* (1980; British edition as *Imp and Biscuit: The Fortunes of Two Pug Dogs*), Worth describes the adventures of a pair of pugs in the Edwardian era in language praised for its elegance. *Gypsy Gold* (1983) combines the attributes of a traditional tale with the more modern theme of adolescent maturation in the story of sixteen-year-old Miranda, who joins a family of gypsies and discovers a gift for fortune-telling after running away from her arranged marriage, while *Fox Hill* (1986) incorporates the poetry of John Keats in both its chapter headings and contents to describe how Lily, an orphan who comes to live in the country home of her spinster aunt, becomes obsessed with her aunt's ward, a deceased young man who died in a probable suicide.

(See also *Something about the Author*, Vol. 8; *Contemporary Authors New Revision Series*, Vol. 15; and *Contemporary Authors*, Vols. 41-44, rev. ed.)

GENERAL COMMENTARY

JUDITH GLEASON

Open the first of Valerie Worth's miniature poetry books [**small poems**]:

> On the front porch
> Chairs sit still;
>
> The table will receive
> Summer drinks;
>
> They wait, arranged,
> Strange and polite.
>
> On the back porch
> Garden tools spill;

> An empty basket
> Leans to one side;
>
> The watering can
> Rusts among friends.
>
> **("porches")**

What sort of a universe is this? We know the position of everything, with precision, but not its momentum. The transition from front to back porch is abrupt, discontinuous. It is a poetry of arrested motion, of disciplined particulars conveying structure: the neat and the messy, cultivated anticipation versus random process, an engraved invitation ("the table will receive") contrasted with an informal gathering ("rusts among friends"). Proceed from discrete poem to poem, twenty-four of them as alike in their tonalities as hours and yet as distinct as, say, six AM from four o'clock in the afternoon, as zinnias from crickets, and when you have heard all, ask again, what sort of a someone's universe is this I'm into? Infinitely witty, but never ostentatiously so, remote, because of the conscious control exerted upon flow of experience, and yet withal hospitable. Small creature comforts abound. Here's a pie wrapped in a soft dough blanket; there's a pebble, your own, to hold. How strangely sedentary this poetry is and how often somnolent! A second poem about chairs shows

219

them seated, settled down upon or into themselves ("Some even stretch out their arms to rest"); upon the floor even the violent, fiery sun lies down in (as if green pastures) "warm yellow squares" upon which a sleepy cat may curl. In the shed a tractor "rests," momentarily asleep or dead, waiting to bound from its high rear tires like a giant grasshopper. A dog sleeps "all afternoon / in his loose skin." Another cat ritually "slips in the ends, front paws, / tail, until she is readied, / arranged, for sleep." Equally silent, entire within themselves, here are the jewels of the *symboliste* universe in the homely guise of coins, pebbles, marbles. Held in a human hand they weigh it earthward down, but not too much; their gravity is their grace. Today a quantum of daisies opens eyes where yesterday were blind weeds. A forgotten hollyhock in an "uncut field" conjures up an appropriate reverie of cottage. This is a book of hours within which the Clock has stopped.

With good reason. Things, plants, animals—all are enchanted by contemplative mind. This poet but seems to be observing "objects" with a precise, unblinking eye; in reality she is re-dreaming old intimacies. Author of her solitude, to paraphrase Bachelard, the dreamer brackets time; the world opens itself to her openness immediately; there is no distance between them; gestalt-ground, phenomenal-field are invisible; a single image becomes a sign foretelling the whole. In the poet's state of reverie the world reposes. Because she feels deeply at home in the elsewhere, the poet's images are not only tranquil, they are accommodating. The quick, furtive fires of sorcery have returned to slumber in the heart.

Quiet, gentle, but not complacent. In her second volume [*more small poems*] Valerie Worth explores a state of being equally rare this hectic age. A derivative of reposeful reverie is happiness in slow motion—a euphoria most appropriately choreographed in a playful mode. The kitten, replacing the cat, dances, spins, pounces on a ridiculous piece of fluff. . . . Weeds sprout irrepressibly in rough out-of-the-way places and in time produce for themselves (no horticultural audience) "a few / dim stars of flowers." Discrete moments (phases) of things become transformations, as one twists the nozzle of the garden hose, as a sleeping safety pin opens "and looks / at the sharp / point with a surprised eye." Fireworks go off. A pumpkin begins to glow from inside. Christmas lights in this volume are strung because festivities affirm the playful intensity of cosmic existence as reflected in the perennial childhood of the poet. The book ends with a praise of the soap bubble, with the transient magnificence of a flexible wholeness.

"Childhood solitudes leave indelible marks on certain souls," says Bachelard. "Their entire life is sensitized for poetic reverie, for a reverie which knows the price of solitude. . . . These solitudes of today return us to the original ones." Which is why it is possible for a poet like Valerie Worth to write her best when she writes for children, for children, that is, who have not been so obtruded upon by the false society of television as to have forgotten what solitude purely is. Such solitude is like the toy magnet in *more small poems.* In the beginning it is offered pins to pick up. Then interest diminishes. Finally left alone, the magnet "leads its own / life, trading / secrets with / the North Pole, / reading / invisible messages / from the sun." It is not unusual for an imaginative, productively lonely child to become an animist, mystical, a psychic.

In her third volume [*still more small poems*] Valerie Worth presents several images of the solitary child's imagination:

Kite, Bell, and most notably, compass: "According to / the compass, / wherever you happen / to stand, / North, south, East and west, / meet in the palm / of your hand." This is an oriented imagination which contains the everywhere. As the sleeper of the lullabies is guarded by a directional angel at each bed post, so in dreams his shadow may range freely through time and space—or so the "folk" of all nations have believed. Combining the enchanted somnolence of the first volume with the exuberant animation of the second, Valerie Worth in *still more small poems* produces paradigms of inspiration. Beginning to work in a state of attentive quiescence, the imagination is seized by the wind.

> Sun in the back yard
> Grows lazy,
>
> Dozing on the porch steps
> All morning,
>
> Getting up and nosing
> About corners,
>
> Gazing into an empty
> Flowerpot,
>
> Later easing over the grass
> For a nap,
>
> Unless
> Someone hangs out the wash—
>
> Which changes
> Everything to a rush and a clap
>
> Of wet
> Cloth, and fresh wind
>
> And sun
> Wide awake in the white sheets.

                ("back yard")

But even the back yard as a whole is too big for the child's private imagination, which prefers to live like Mice, finding "places in places," a hidden world inside the wide. Shy, like Turtle "shawled in the shade of his shell," its self-image, centered, psychically whole, is small as an amulet, plain, ostensibly homely as toad or frog, and it has an elective affinity for the publicly discredited (Slug, Rags, Garbage). But actually this spotted or warted amphibian is a prince; this imagination is so wide, so luminous that all things become transcendently recycled in its poetry. No soul in things is lost. All are redeemed along this slice of roadside, even "a shivering spirit of lost cellophane." *still more small poems* concludes with a meditation upon the uniqueness of a snowflake, now, on creation's coat-sleeve, an eternal second before it dissolves. (pp. 74-8)

> *Judith Gleason, "That Lingering Child of Air," in* Parnassus: Poetry in Review, *Vol. 8, No. 2, 1980, pp. 63-82.*

SMALL POEMS (1972)

Valerie Worth's small, solid poems are consistently accessible but never condescending or compromising, and as different from the usual rhyming twaddle as her spotted cat, "shaped for sleep," is from Smith's "frightfully hisskery" one. The observations are sharp, matter-of-fact, fresh but unforced ("chairs / Seem to / Sit / Down / On / Themselves, almost as if / They were people . . ."); the subjects couldn't be more prosaic (a duck, a stopped clock, a cow—"Her hoofs / Thump / Like dropped / Rocks"); the reading pleasure derives as often from the Swenson-like sound as the uninflated sense ("Goldfish / Flash / Gold and silver scales; / They flick and slip away / Under green week / But round brown snails / Stick / To the glass / And stay"). Valerie Worth is to be commended for respecting her self-imposed limits and her readers' sensibilities. . . .

> *A review of "Small Poems," in* Kirkus Reviews, *Vol. XL, No. 21, November 1, 1972, p. 1243.*

More modestly presented, but completely self-possessed and of a much higher order of poetry [than Karla Kuskin's *Any Me I Want to Be*] is **Small Poems,** by Valerie Worth, 24 descriptions of such things as a tractor, crickets, marbles, grass and raw carrots. These *are* small poems, but each one has the clarity, delicacy, and concreteness of a dried stalk of last summer's timothy.

> *Georgess McHargue, "How Now, Poetry Lovers?" in* The New York Times Book Review, *November 5, 1972, p. 32.*

A poet often highlights what is unnoticed by others—the insignificant and the small. The title for the volume may indicate the size of the book, the length of the poems, or the scope of each poem, but both [Worth and artist Natalie Babbitt] have imbued their subjects with such insight that the poems and the book itself transcend physical size. In twenty-four poems about such topics as raw carrots, cows, jewels, grasses, and crickets, the author gives each object dimensions to the object by a suggestive turn of phrase or an unusual perspective. . . . Both text and illustrations have been housed in a book in which the texture of the pages, the typography, the layout, and even the color of the binding are as understated, but as beautiful, as the text and illustrations.

> *Anita Silvey, in a review of "Small Poems," in* The Horn Book Magazine, *Vol. XLIX, No. 1, February, 1973, p. 64.*

Simple, unpretentious free verse is perfectly matched to the format (short poems on 5 ½ " × 7 ½ " pages), and the author focuses on minute details and makes pointed comparisons. For instance, zinnias are ". . . stout and stiff, / . . . their petals / Jut like clipped cardboard, / . . . they / Will hardly wilt—I know / Someone like zinnias; . . . "; a tractor is "Ready to leap— / Like a heavy / Brown / Grasshopper."; and a duck is ". . . like a toy / . . . on yellow rubber-skinned feet." The descriptions often involve the senses (e.g., the taste of raw carrots, the texture of jewels, marbles, and coins, and the warmth of the sun).

> *Ginger Brauer, in a review of "Small Poems," in* School Library Journal, *April, 1973, p. 72.*

MORE SMALL POEMS (1976)

Identical in its small (5½" × 7½") format to Worth's first poetry collection, **Small Poems** and containing a couple of dozen short compositions, this is a minor achievement all around. The freewheeling impressions of sundry familiar objects, animate and not, are studiedly artless, direct, and easily accessible to young minds—e.g., a safety pin is "The silver / Image / Of some / Small fish"). However, although there is an introspective sensitivity here akin to that of Charlotte

Zolotow's *All That Sunlight,* the poems lack the catchiness of James Tippett's *Crickety Cricket!* the joyousness of Marchette Chute's *Rhymes About Us* or the out-and-out humor of Bobbi Katz's *Upside Down and Inside Out.*

> *Daisy Kouzel, in a review of "More Small Poems," in* School Library Journal, *Vol. 23, No. 6, February, 1977, p. 59.*

It's not a loud book, but it makes you listen. In Valerie Worth, young readers have a writer who leaves herself alone long enough to find a good, uncontrived poem, free of banalities and pretensions alike. She works with words but not to show off; with meaning but not to dictate: "When the flowers / Turned clever, and / Earned wide / Tender red petals / For themselves, / When the birds / Learned about feathers, / Spread green tails, / Grew cockades / On their heads, / The toad said: / Someone has got / To remember / The mud, and / I'm not proud." Here, as in **Small Poems,** the subjects are common and the images uncommon. The verse has no forced meter or rhyme but generates a disciplined internal sound and form.

> *Betsy Hearne, in a review of "More Small Poems," in* Booklist, *Vol. 73, No. 11, February 1, 1977, p. 839.*

The author and the illustrator of **Small Poems** have created another miniature treasury of spontaneous, expressive verse. Homely, everyday items are endowed with unexpected new life in twenty-five short poems, accompanied by modest drawings. With economy of phrase, deceptive simplicity, and artless skill, the poet celebrates, among other things, a pumpkin, a toad, a safety pin, a kitten, weeds, earthworms, and sidewalks. An imaginative but meticulous use of metaphor is seen in the lion's "harsh gold / [s]mell," the caterpillar's "[l]ong caravan / [o]f bristles," and in the lines about the dead crab that "keeps a shape / Of old anger / Curved along his claws." And almost like an ancient riddle is the poem about a magnet: "This small / Flat horseshoe / Is sold for / A toy: we are / Told that it / Will pick up pins / And it does, time / After time; later / It lies about, / Getting its red / Paint chipped, being / Offered pins less / Often, until at / Last we leave it / Alone: then / It leads its own / Life, trading / Secrets with / The North Pole, / Reading / Invisible messages / From the sun." (pp. 182-83)

> *Ethel L. Heins, in a review of "More Small Poems," in* The Horn Book Magazine, *Vol. LIII, No. 2, April, 1977, pp. 182-83.*

For me, the best original collection [of the books reviewed here was] Valerie Worth's **More Small Poems.** Worth takes ordinary items—earthworms, a safety pin, a lawnmower—and reveals wonders in them. She is sharp-eyed and unpretentious: a haunted house has "aching stairs" and "doors gone stiff / At the hinges"; sea lions fall into water like "Soft boulders"; a magnet "leads its own / Life, trading / Secrets with / The North Pole." Much as I like the book, I'm dismayed to report that it went all the way up the age-ladder of the family without meeting a child who much cared for it. The children may lack taste, but Worth's perceptions are subtle and fine; and only the 4-year-old seemed at all engaged by subjects so little and ordinary. (p. 31)

> *X. J. Kennedy, "The Flat, Fat Blatt," in* The New York Times Book Review, *May 1, 1977, pp. 31, 33.*

STILL MORE SMALL POEMS (1978)

A pail, a bell (it "gives metal a tongue"), a mushroom, grand-mother's old beveled-glass door: again Valerie Worth turns humble and familiar objects into solid little poems that seem almost like pebbles held in the palm of the hand. Her thick sounds slow the tongue, mixing words and image: "Old Tom / Comes along / The room / In steps / Laid down / Like cards, / Slow-paced / But firm, / All former / Temptations / Too humdrum / To turn / Him from / His goal: / His bowl." Her subjects are all surface, but surface illuminated—just as the moon "silvers" her slug's trails of slime. If Worth's focus on the ordinary occasionally has her settling for the too-obvious reflection—"rags" are ". . . Poor sad gray wads // That once were faithful / Flannel pajamas, // Favorite pink- / Flowered underpants"—more frequently her perception transforms even relatively ordinary thoughts into delightful observations: "Somehow the hen, / Herself all quirk / and freak and whim, // Manages to make / This egg, as pure / And calm as stone." The only original poetry in a season of anthologies—and it's real poetry, rare in any season.

> *A review of "Still More Small Poems," in* Kirkus Reviews, *Vol. XLVII, No. 1, January 1, 1979, p. 11.*

Worth returns with **Still More** . . . striking thumbnail sketches, in free verse, of everyday objects, animals, places, sensations, and situations, from sounds a bell makes "By flat tink / Of tin, or thin / Copper tong, / Brass clang, / Bronze bong . . ." to a drowsy turtle's speculations ("Does he hope / Something / Will happen, / After a hundred / Naps?") to the miraculous ability of a hen, "all quirk / And freak and whim" to produce so pure and calm an item as an egg. Similes are surprising: a horse's face becomes "thin silk over / Bone: to be stroked / Carefully, like / Fine upholstery . . ." while laundry on the line takes on cosmic dimensions and moon rocks are brought down to earth. As well trimmed and tuned as mice finding ". . . space enough, / Even in / Small spaces," these tidy vignettes . . . are clean, airy, and not as simple as they seem.

> *Laura Geringer, in a review of "Still More Small Poems," in* School Library Journal, *Vol. 25, No. 6, February, 1979, p. 61.*

"According to / The compass, / Wherever you happen / To stand, / North, south, / East and west, / Meet in the palm / Of your hand." The last two lines of the poem contain a key to the inspiration behind many of the twenty-five poems in the book. The author has captured the wonder of the small and the mundane—holding them, as it were, in the palm of her hand for the reader to see. With fresh insight she views an old pail, a tiny mushroom, a sleeping turtle. And she lifts one's eyes to view a fluttering kite and the gleaming stars. The book is a companion volume to **Small Poems** and **More Small Poems**; the author and the illustrator have again worked together compatibly. The delicate line drawings are mere hints and suggestions, never limiting the imagination. Each object described becomes like the snowflake in the last poem: "None anywhere / Ever like / This one, this / Very one."

> *Karen M. Klockner, in a review of "Still More Small Poems," in* The Horn Book Magazine, *Vol. LV, No. 2, April, 1979, p. 203.*

CURLICUES: THE FORTUNES OF TWO PUG DOGS (1980; British edition as *Imp and Biscuit: The Fortunes of Two Pugs*)

Two pug dogs are purchased separately by two elderly Edwardian ladies, one who cares nothing for her dog and feeds him scraps, the other a dear-old-thing who treats her dog to loving care and fancy delicacies. In both homes there's an adversary. The nasty lady has a kindly housemaid who disobeys her mistress' orders and treats the dog tenderly. The other mistress has a contrary cook who dislikes preparing special meals for the pug. One can feel reasonably well-assured that the two dogs will be reunited, that the nice people will find each other, and so they are. But despite the predictability of the tale, there's an old-fashioned appeal extended through the sedate yet mellifluous narrative tone and quaint, detailed illustrations [by Natalie Babbitt] which transcends any lack of real suspense. Some readers may be put off by the period-piece style and lack of child characters. But there's definitely something here for dog-lovers and others who take pleasure in happy endings.

> *Marilyn Kaye, in a review of "Curlicues: The Fortunes of Two Pug Dogs," in* School Library Journal, *Vol. 27, No. 4, December, 1980, p. 62.*

Elegance ('tasteful correctness' or 'ingenious simplicity', as the dictionary has it) is not a virtue often attributed to books for the young: all the more reason why it should be sought after on their behalf, so that they come to recognise that style and content are not two separate things but partners in the quest for excellence. 'Tasteful' is a word much blown upon and most often used nowadays in inverted commas, but the phrase 'tasteful correctness' is apt enough respecting the witty shapeliness of **Imp and Biscuit.** 'The Fortunes of Two Pugs' are pursued in a narrative that has an almost geometrical pattern and a logic of reward and punishment that invokes the spirit of fairy tale. Two cold-hearted people (arrogant Miss Thorne, and Mrs. Downey's cook, Mrs. Pinch, who is 'large and starched and sometimes hot-tempered') are opposed to two stout and kindly folk (Miss Thorne's sentimental housekeeper-cook, Mrs. Hart, and fat, lonely Mrs. Downey, whose sole diversion is a game of cards in the evening with Jenny the housemaid). The two pugs, offered at reasonable price when an old pet-shop owner sells up, move to the two vastly differing households and, for ingeniously different reasons, bring about the resignation of Mrs. Hart and the sacking of Mrs. Pinch. A meeting in the park, delightful reunion for the pugs, brings a happy re-arrangement of one household and unites the two dog-lovers. Resisting the temptation to be too symmetrical, Valerie Worth comments only of 'mean Miss Thorne and cross Mrs. Pinch' that 'it is tempting to think that the paths of their own destinies might have wound together at last'.

This simple, shapely tale is told in a measured, sometimes rhetorical prose, with a light irony and with verbal repetitions (especially of the key-words 'destiny' and 'fortune') which give both moral and event a kind of traditional validity. The prose asks to be read aloud, so that the stately polysyllables of certain passages can be translated through the ear (a mysterious process which is far more difficult for children to achieve with the reading eye) and so that the bubbling humour which deftly defines the people and neatly personalises the enchanting little pugs may be properly appreciated. Then, time should be taken to admire the period flavour and the sly hints of personality in Natalie Babbitt's drawings, as elegant in their way as the prose, and finally, the attractively appropriate production of a small but notable book.

> *Margery Fisher, in a review of "Imp and Biscuit," in* Growing Point, *Vol. 20, No. 5, January, 1982, p. 3990.*

Compared to many books in this bookshelf this is a work of literature of the very highest kind. . . . Beautifully constructed, elegant in its thought and language it will, nevertheless, appeal strongly to bookish children as well as to adults. It's brevity and charming illustrations will attract from around the age of 9.

> *A review of "Imp and Biscuit," in* Books for Your Children, *Vol. 17, No. 1, Spring, 1982, p. 10.*

GYPSY GOLD (1983)

In her latest novel, poet Valerie Worth proves her talents as a storyteller. She successfully applies the adolescent growth motif to a story of supernatural gypsy traditions. When 16-year-old Miranda fails to show promise in her father's apothecary business, she is betrothed to a wealthy, but spiritless, older man. Enraged, she runs off to join a family of gypsies, certain that she can learn the art of fortunetelling. The gypsies take her in, fearing they will be accused of kidnapping if this obstinate girl does not get her way. In time, Miranda learns the gypsy ways and is accepted by her new family. The gypsies can see that her interest in fortunetelling is special—she has the gift of vision. As her vision matures, Miranda realizes that she can not take her true place among the gypsies until she has resolved the conflicts in her former life. The story's mystical elements are credible because of the believable and well-developed characters and setting. Historical time and place are vague, but there is a detailed picture of the gypsy life style without the expected stereotypes. Worth's portrayal depicts a humble group of people with strong family bonds, strong traditions and a strong moral code. The language is simple yet full of a richness that conveys the moods and tone of the book beautifully. She incorporates subtle humor throughout, but there are also passages of deep emotion. This is definitely a book for special readers, but those who start it won't be disappointed.

> *Heide Piehler, in a review of "Gypsy Gold," in* School Library Journal, *Vol. 30, No. 6, February, 1984, p. 86.*

In her first full-length novel the poet and author of *Curlicues* adopts the omniscient perspective and the vague long-ago-and-far-away setting of a traditional storyteller. . . . Although the novel has an unexceptional plot, its prose is polished yet unpretentious. Furthermore, the tone, the philosophical revelations, and the restrained romance harmoniously combine to counter the immediate gratification espoused in much contemporary realistic fiction.

> *Nancy C. Hammond, in a review of "Gypsy Gold," in* The Horn Book Magazine, *Vol. LX, No. 2, April, 1984, p. 205.*

[*Gypsy Gold* is] set in a misty long-ago, in an unnamed town and countryside. The language sounds archaic, with many a "nay" and "thus." Miranda, the heroine, is 16 and unappreciated. Her parents think her clumsy, selfish, only fit to be married off to a rich old boorish suitor. She leaves home, joins a band of gypsies, learns their ways, falls in love, discovers

that she is a seer—in short, has a more fulfilling time than young readers will.

The story is slender, the characters are stock. The main drama in the gypsies' lives was a fire, in the past, merely told about. Instead of action and excitement there are earnest disquisitions on the significance of various tarot cards. There are no surprises. The fortune-telling, prophetic tarot cards and apparitions in a crystal ball preclude any suspense that might have built as to whether Miranda will go home and do right by her mother, and marry her handsome dark-eyed gypsy in the end.

I do respect the fervor of this ambitious attempt. But the mysticism in this case fails. I think the author conveys her clear-sighted vision better when she looks at everyday creatures and objects—for instance, a mosquito, or a garden hose—and lights up their extraordinary aspects with a brilliance not to be missed, as in her three collections of poetry, *Small Poems,* *More Small Poems,* and *Still More Small Poems.*

> *Doris Orgel, in a review of "Gypsy Gold," in* The New York Times Book Review, *May 27, 1984, p. 21.*

FOX HILL (1986)

A Gothic novel with a touch of fantasy.

Left penniless and alone in the world, 17-year-old Lily dreads the prospect of living with misanthropic Aunt Ruth, her only relative. The one bright spot in Lily's new life is housekeeper Betty, who tells the girl about her aunt's sad past, which includes a lost love and the untimely death of Martin, a much beloved child raised in the household. Lily is fascinated by the stories about Martin, and she becomes obsessed with making contact with him. Her fancies lead her to imagine that he is trying to communicate with her—and she becomes lost in a world of mystery and melancholy. Lily is abruptly shocked out of her obsession when she almost falls from the window where Martin toppled to his death. In a classic happy ending, she develops a warm relationship with her aunt, and she is even provided with a potential love interest when the family of a handsome young gentleman who lives nearby invites her to tea.

This intriguing book is not entirely successful—the plot is thin and insubstantial, even for a novel of this type. It is written in the elegant and formal style of a 19th-century novel which, though it may be difficult for some readers, perfectly suits the mood of the story. And the style and use of poetry as chapter headings give the book an interest beyond the usual escapist fare of this genre. (pp. 54-5)

> *A review of "Fox Hill," in* Kirkus Reviews, *Vol. LIV, No. 1, January 1, 1986, pp. 54-5.*

This is not easy reading: Worth uses elaborate syntax and Latinized vocabulary, especially in the Gothic passages, and she integrates Keats' poetry at the head of each chapter and sometimes in the story. But story and poetry do capture that brooding adolescent mood of being "half in love with easeful Death," and good readers will be moved by Lily's exorcism of Martin's power and her own depression, and by her mature acceptance of love and purpose in the cycle of daily life.

> *Hazel Rochman, in a review of "Fox Hill," in* Booklist, *Vol. 82, No. 12, February 15, 1986, p. 862.*

Worth uses Keats' poetry to introduce each chapter. This effective technique creates just the right mood as the plot develops, and the result is a superb mix of Keats' poetry and Worth's prose. . . . A welcome addition for fans of gothic novels. (pp. 111-12)

> *Dorothy Lilly, in a review of "Fox Hill," in* School Library Journal, *Vol. 32, No. 9, May, 1986, pp. 111-12.*

SMALL POEMS AGAIN (1986)

A fourth collection of brief lyrics inspired by the poet's original vision of ordinary things that the less gifted take for granted. . . .

Worth's compact images are drawn with delicate precision; the carefully tuned nuances and echoes of sounds and meanings give the reader the delight of recognizing the familiar through newly perceptive senses: in the library, ". . . Listen to the / Silent twitter / Of a billion / Tiny busy / Black words." Some thoughts are mind-opening: of a seashell, "Why did / That little creature / Take so much trouble / To be beautiful?" Some are playful: the mantis—"Can it / Really be / Wholly / Holly, / Pretending / to pray, / While intending / To prey?" Some are touched by a bit of quizzical philosophy: the kaleidoscope likened to ". . . earth's / Rough muddle / Jostled to / Jewels and flowers." [Natalie] Babbit's drawings are quietly decorative, the perfect complement to these small bits of real poetry.

A lovely little volume to treasure and savor again.

> *A review of "Small Poems Again," in* Kirkus Reviews, *Vol. LIV, No. 24, December 15, 1986, p. 1866.*

The most uneven of [the books reviewed here is **Small Poems Again**]. . . . Too often, one finds here a self-conscious extravagance of language and a sentimentality that bypasses young readers and grates on adults. In **"jacks,"** for example (the book abandons capital letters in its titles), Worth writes about the way jacks "nest together in the hand" and the way they land "in a loose starry cluster":

> Seems luxury
> Enough,
> Without the
> Further bliss
> Of their
> Slender
> Iridescent
> Luster.

"Bliss" and "iridescent" may work in the parlor or the duck-pond, but as words for jacks they arouse suspicion. Yet, Worth's book also includes some distinguished writing. Her poem **"fleas"** offers a hilarious and vivid picture of a flea's life on a dog's back; the language is deft and clever. In **"tiger,"** she provides a darkly evocative portrait of that fine beast, while **"heron"** is marred only by a sentimental twist in the next-to-last line.

Worth's best poems leave space for children's minds to play, to wonder, to explore, to question—and so to arrive at their own lessons and morals, which are always the strongest ones. (p. 31)

> *Thomas Simmons, "Poems Introduce Children to*

the Wonderful World of Words," in The Christian Science Monitor, *May 21, 1987, pp. 30-1.*

With this publication of Valerie Worth's fourth collection of small poems, the word *small* acquires a significance of microcosmic proportions. As the reflection of woods in a tranquil pool can be richer and more lucent than the original, these poems help us to see the clear essence of things. The descriptions of nature are filled with striking and original images: in **"Water Lily,"** "A hundred / Shallow green / Questions pressed / Upon the / Silent pool"; in **"Tiger,"** "Black flames / Flicker through / His fur." The ugliness of telephone poles close up, "sweating / Black creosote," is transformed by distance to "Gestures of / Exquisite / Gossamer." A skunk is described with a feast of words which could have been uttered by Puck on a Midsummer Night. In this volume, as in the first three collections, the small objects of everyday life are celebrated: kaleidoscopes, coat hangers, a broom, frost on the windows, and jacks. . . . In a humorous play on words the duplicity of the mantis is captured, "Can it / Really be / Wholly / Holy, / Pretending / To pray, / While intending / To prey?" The variety of poetic forms, including internal rhymes and blank verse, are a welcome change from the more conventional rhyming patterns in much of children's poetry. . . . The poems sharpen our awareness and reveal new ways to see the world, fulfilling William Blake's admonition "to see a world in a grain of sand." They are direct and simple enough to be accessible to children, yet the images are so apt and fresh that adults will also find joy in them. (pp. 353-54)

> *Hanna B. Zeigler, in a review of "Small Poems Again," in* The Horn Book Magazine, *Vol. LXIII, No. 3, May-June, 1987, pp. 353-54.*

ALL THE SMALL POEMS (1987)

It's not necessarily safe to assume your children will discover poetry all by themselves; it's safer to leave subversively readable little books like this one where they will trip over them, even if they won't stand for you to read them aloud. What Worth's poems . . . do is force the reader simply to take another look at, to smell or touch or hear again, the little things—fireworks, bells, lawnmowers, mushrooms, coat-hangers, dandelions, doors, pies and pebbles—that we ordinarily take for granted. . . . Soon the urge to try one's own hand at a small poem may become irresistible.

> *A review of "All the Small Poems," in* Book World—The Washington Post, *February 7, 1988, p. 12.*

Many people espouse the idea that poetry for children must be brightly illustrated snippets of rhyme, jolly anapestic verse that elicits immediate laughter and instant gratification. Others believe children's poetry to be a treasure of Beauty, Truth and Wisdom garnered from some beneficent, idealized past. By contrast, Valerie Worth's **All the Small Poems** underscores the poet's heightened consciousness, artful skill and the power of imagination that offer the finest poetry for the young, markedly different from singsong versification and/or cloying sentimentality. . . .

The treasures Ms. Worth offers do not lie in some distant, golden land but in the everyday world. . . . Her ". . . round jewels, / Slithering gold" are marbles poured into their bag. A hose "Can rain / Chill diamond / Chains / Across the yard . . ." or ". . . hang / A silk / Rainbow / Halo / Over soft fog." In the garbage she finds "Hammered-gold / Orange rind, / Eggshell ivory, / Garnet coffee- / Grounds, pearl / Wand of bared / Chicken bone." Riches to her are "satin sea lions," the "sleek velvets" on the back of a mosquito and the lions' "plush-covered clay."

Avoiding singsong meter and incessant end-rhyme, Ms. Worth brilliantly employs all aspects of the poet's craft. Through personification she notes the "soft skull" and "frail ribs" of a mushroom, a lawnmower that "Grinds its teeth / Over the grass / Spitting out a thick / Green spray"; with a head "too full / Of iron and oil / To know / What it throws / Away." Telephone poles sweat "Black creosote," and coat hangers "Clash and cling, / And fling them- / Selves to the / Floor in an / Inextricable tangle." . . .

Her rhythms mesh with subject: "This clock / Has stopped, / Some gear / Or spring / Gone wrong." She uses onomatopoeia to speak of "Hard leather heels, / Their blocks carved / Thick, like rocks, / Clacked down / Waxed wood stairs," and the "pale soles / Of sneakers." Alliteratively she observes the beetle's "lacquered / Coffer of / Curious / Compartments" or how "the slug / Slides sly." Employing synesthesia she writes of "The harsh gold / Smell of lions."

Like haiku, Ms. Worth's poems are written in the present tense of one thing keenly observed, inviting readers to complete the picture. Eminently pragmatic during her few lyrical forays, she believes that a sparrow "is as good a bird / As anyone needs." A magnet, she writes, "is sold for a toy . . . " and picks up pins, but

> . . .later
> It lies about
> Getting its red
> Paint chipped, being
> Offered pins less
> Often, until at
> Last we leave it
> Alone . . .

It is this amazing combination of practicality and the ability to view the commonplace in a variety of fresh ways that lifts this work beyond the ordinary. To call Valerie Worth's poems "small" is, indeed, indulging in no little measure of verbal irony.

> *Myra Cohn Livingston, in a review of "All the Small Poems," in* The New York Times Book Review, *March 6, 1988, p. 29.*

In the sixth grade the writing on the blackboard grew so fuzzy it was obvious I needed glasses. More than half a century later, I recall what happened the morning I first put them on. Suddenly I was looking at the world through a washed window pane. Everything now had edges and shape. I spent that whole day discovering what familiar things really looked like.

I thought of that long ago day when I first read **Small Poems**

by Valerie Worth and felt a delicious shock, a pleasure at the clarity with which real things were seen.

Small Poems and the three books that followed, modestly referred to as **Small Poems Again, More Small Poems,** and **Still More Small Poems,** have now been collected in a handsome and comfortable paperback called **All the Small Poems.** It is clearer than ever that these are not small poems, any more than the little stitched "packets" that Emily Dickinson left behind were small poems.

What we have in this collection is an unusual resource—an opportunity to share with children real poetry about the real world, to take them, as it were, on a field trip with special binoculars. (pp. 470-71)

The young person who reads and hears and becomes familiar with the poems of Valerie Worth meets a serene and contemplative adult who has retained or recovered the intense interest with which children look at the details of the world—at a bug, an earthworm, a dandelion. One is reminded of how artists like Klee have tried to capture the freshness with which a child first sees.

This poet is happily comfortable, as many children are, with all kinds of animals and creatures: cats and kittens, dogs and pigs, birds, sea lions that "fall like soft boulders into the water. . . . " The perceptions in these poems are revealed in language that is a gift to the reader. Sensory, precise, and fresh, it is language and imagery to feed the imagination. Kittens are "cactus-clawed"; grass in the fields "whistles, slides, / Casts up a foam / Of seeds"; young pigeons "sink and shift / Like beanbags heavy / With grain, and warm"; the turtle wakes "quietly / Shawled / In the shade / Of his / Shell"; and the zoo never loses "the harsh gold / Smell of lion." English to clear the palate! (pp. 471-72)

For those whom Worth calls "some-who-do" there is an interesting range in **All the Poems.** Which poems for which child? Adults have always had to use common sense about the readiness of children for the books we want them to read. We can't really know what goes on between the young person and the poem. More than we hoped? Less? We have to place our trust in the poetry we offer. What is important, therefore, is that there be some real poems to share.

"Not the poem which we have *read,*" said Coleridge, "but that to which we *return,* with the greatest pleasure, possesses the genuine power, and claims the name of *essential poetry.*"

For those who want poetry in the lives of children, **All the Small Poems** is a collection to return to with "the greatest pleasure." (p. 473)

> *Lilian Moore, "A Second Look: 'Small Poems'," in* The Horn Book Magazine, *Vol. LXIV, No. 4, July-August, 1988, pp. 470-73.*

Tim Wynne-Jones

1948-

English-born Canadian author of picture books, poet, playwright, and journalist.

Considered one of Canada's most popular authors for preschoolers and readers in the early primary grades, Wynne-Jones is recognized as the creator of works which capture the mystery, fantasy, and wonder of childhood while addressing such realistic concerns as the conquering of personal fears and the relationship of his audience with their parents. He is perhaps best known for writing the "Zoom" series, two picture books of a projected trilogy about the adventures of a small white cat and his enigmatic human friend, Maria. *Zoom at Sea* (1983) describes how Zoom, a spirited animal who loves the water and dreams of boundless seas and skies, has his fantasies realized in Maria's magical house. In *Zoom Away* (1985), Zoom and Maria climb the stairs of her home to the North Pole, where they solve the mystery of Zoom's missing uncle, a sea captain. Although Wynne-Jones has been a book and graphics designer as well as a visual arts instructor, he prefers to leave the illustrating of his books to others. Both "Zoom" books, for example, are illustrated by Canadian painter Ken Nutt, for whom Wynne-Jones created *Zoom at Sea;* Nutt's rich black-and-white pictures are often considered a perfect complement to Wynne-Jones's texts. With *I'll Make You Small* (1986), Wynne-Jones uses the format of the traditional fairy tale to describe how young Roland redeems his frightening next-door neighbor through kindness. *Architect of the Moon* (1988; U. S. edition as *Builder of the Moon*) is also recognized for echoing the elements of traditional tales; in this picture book, which has been compared to Maurice Sendak's *Where the Wild Things Are,* a small boy says goodbye to his mother and takes his homemade spaceship into space in order to rebuild the moon with his blocks before coming home for breakfast. Both *Madeline and Ermadello* (1977) and *Mischief City* (1986) explore the personalities of young children who have imaginary playmates. While *Madeline and Ermadello* is noted for its authentic and charming evocation of a preschooler's world, *Mischief City,* a collection of poems based on one of Wynne-Jones's plays for children, blends the real and imaginary worlds of childhood with wry humor in a theater motif. Throughout the poems, six-year-old Winchell provides young readers with a pointed perspective on his concerns and those of his imaginary friend, Maxine. An author of adult mysteries, scriptwriter, and composer, Wynne-Jones is also well known both as the lyricist for the television program *Fraggle Rock* and as a reviewer of children's books. *Zoom at Sea* was named the IODE Best Children's Book of the Year in 1983 and received the Ruth Schwartz Children's Book Award in 1984. Both *Zoom at Sea* and *Zoom Away* received the Amelia Frances Howard-Gibbon Award for their illustrations, in 1984 and 1986 respectively.

(See also *Contemporary Authors,* Vol. 105.)

AUTHOR'S COMMENTARY

[The following excerpt is from an interview by Dave Jenkinson.]

Tim's first experience at authoring a children's book occurred during his undergraduate days when a group of [University of] Waterloo Sociology students applied for an Opportunities for Youth Grant to examine racism and sexism in children's books. "At the last minute they decided that their application wouldn't look very good unless they had some kind of 'creative people', and so they hastily grabbed a couple of people in the visual arts, thinking we'd at least be able to find sexism in the pictures. It was an interesting experience, and certainly the best part was the seventy-five bucks a week we were getting, but I read an awful lot of contemporary children's books I had never read."

"Having looked at all these children's books and having found out what was good and what wasn't, the group decided that, because they knew what was wrong with children's books, they could then write good ones. It was a great lesson in how you do *not* write a children's book: you find a problem, and then fix it by writing a book. I just can't think of a worse way of writing a children's book, but these people did, and with no thought that writing was a skill." Though Tim was not with the group the next summer when further O.F.Y. funding allowed them to establish a publishing venture, Before We Are Six, "they did buy the manuscript I wrote,

226

Madelaine & Ermadello, for $90, and eventually I got $300 in royalties."

Seven years passed before Tim had another children's book published. "I didn't start writing children's books because I had children. I'd always had ideas for children's stories. I knew Ken Nutt as an acquaintance, liked his artwork and really wanted to see it in book form. I was inspired to find something he would illustrate. I was up writing early one morning. We had a cat called Montezuma, and 'Zuma was on the counter batting water out of the tap. The story, *Zoom at sea,* was written in 20 minutes. I don't quite know how those things happen." (p. 58)

Reflecting on *Zoom,* Tim says, "It's a book I can write a book about. There's so much going on in it, but luckily none of it occurred to me when I was writing it or I might have turned it into a novel. It's got its own little world."

Zoom next appeared in *Zoom away,* whose working title had been "Zoom on ice". (p. 59)

"Though we live in an age of sequels and despite the last page of *Zoom at sea* where Zoom asks Maria, 'May I come back?' followed by her reply, 'I'm sure you will', and the concluding words, 'And he did', in all honesty, I never intended to write another one. When the book was so successful, I thought, 'Oh, I've got to write another Zoom book, but I couldn't think of one until my mother-in-law wrote me the most wonderful letter about Maria's house and how it could lead anywhere in time or space. I'd been thinking about 'Zoom on the Farm'! And when she said that, I knew there were at least two places. I knew Zoom had to go up to the North, which would be in the attic, and he had to go south to Egypt, which would be the basement. That would encompass the whole house. In fact, when I was a guest at a literary evening of children in Nova Scotia, a little boy said as much. He stood up and said, 'May we presume that since Zoom has gone to the North and it was in the attic that he will go to the basement next and it will be war?' ".

"I've written the third one and it's called *Zoom upstream.* Ken likes it, and [editor Patsy Aldana] likes it with some changes. It was very hard to write. I always knew the title and that it was set in ancient Egypt. What self-respecting cat wouldn't go to that cat-loving society? Zoom and Maria would have to be reunited with Captain Roy. It's a book of reunion and probably a book about death, but I don't think any child will read that into it."

"I say I don't think any child will read death into the book, but I used to when I was young. Certainly when George Mac-Donald's Princess was running up the tower, there was a point where he had run too high and I knew he was in another place. I've always had that sense of children's books. There's a time when they go through a door into a new experience, and in that sense, *Zoom upstream* is the last of the Zoom books. There won't be anymore."

Montezuma, the cat, who provided an initial spark to Tim's writing the Zoom books, died in 1986. The books' illustrated feline, Tim explains, is a fictional character. "Whatever I wrote about 'Zuma was there, but Ken never 'met' 'Zuma until after *Zoom at sea* was written. Zoom had to be Ken's cat that he created."

In 1986, two new Tim Wynne-Jones children's titles were published with one, *I'll make you small,* also appearing in a collection of prose and poetry, *The window of dreams.* "I sent the editors, Mary Alice Downie and Elizabeth Greene, that story with the knowledge that it was going to the coming out as a book. For the purposes of the picture book by the same name, we cut down to the bone. Patsy Aldana at Ground-wood is a fine editor and had a lot of questions to ask. I think we actually cut a little too far. I would have liked three or four more sentences, but we were pushed by space at that point. When I'm 'reading' it to kids, I find myself adding the sentences without even thinking I'm adding them out of my head because I know they should be there."

Roland, a little boy, and his family live next door to old Mr. Swanskin, a grumpy recluse inhabiting a decrepit house. Attempting to retrieve his ball from Mr. Swanskin's yard, Roland is told by the old man, "You get away from here, or I'll make you small." Ultimately the little boy's kindness softens the old man's heart, but not before Mr. Swanskin does make Roland small. Swanskin also suggests that, when he was a child, his own mother had made him feel small for breaking his toys. "Children just break things. They can't do anything right."

"The thing we worked through most in the picture book was the actual act of Roland's getting small. For Patsy, it was imperative we know the answer to the question, 'Was he made small magically, or did Roland perceive Mr. Swanskin as very much larger?' We had to come to terms with that question. I wanted *not* to make that decision. Eventually, I think it was just about perception, and we sort of sidestepped the issue. There is no magic spell cast. Roland's just the same size; it's voice that makes children small. In the end, I knew how I was shocked at how small I could make my child when my voice grew and how big I must seem."

This idea of "huge adults" is also present in *Mischief City,* the second of Tim's books to appear in 1986, which, in one of the book's 25 poems, finds "Monster parents on the loose, they've grown twice their size". The book seems to polarize its readers who, principally on the basis of its illustrations, either adore or detest it. Says Tim, "I think people are confused by the theater motif which may, in all honesty, have been a mistake, but it was a mistake Patsy, Victor Gad, the illustrator, and I entered into together. Heaven knows, not many books are written with the thought of Brechtian alienation in them, but for me, that's what it was—the real and make-believe world of the child. The thing that came to mind for me was the theater. As far as I'm concerned, that choice, for better or worse, is justified by the cover in that you have this picture of a family group and in the background, not only are there theater flats, the parents are flat and there's Maxine, the imaginary friend, behind. To me, that says a tremendous lot about what the book is about."

"I also think that part of people's response is that we are not used to that European look, which is the very thing that Patsy and I adored when we saw Victor's work and those 'garish' colors. Victor's a political cartoonist, and there's all that kind of satire and stuff in it. The book just doesn't look like a North American children's book. It just doesn't work on that level, and what I have yet to find out is whether the poetry is being read. Certainly when I read it, I get a tremendous response. I'll be curious to see, as time goes by, whether any of the poems will be anthologized. I think many of them are very separate poems."

In the poems, six-year-old Winchell shares his amusing perspective on a world which is populated by, among others, an imaginary friend Maxine who is responsible for Mischief City, things that creep about "after the lights go down low", parents too busy talking to listen until "it's too late—I forgot", and by a baby sister about whom Winchell questions, "So do you think maybe now we could take her back?"

"The poems were written over a period of a couple of years." Richard Greenblatt, then Director of Toronto's Young People's Theatre, saw some of the poems and suggested to Tim that the poems become part of a 1985 theater workshop. "I said, 'Well, I do think that there's a context to them all, but I'm not going to have time to develop them before summer.'" Nevertheless, with Richard's encouragement, Tim took the poems to the workshop. "By the end of a week, I had written the first draft of a musical and also two or three other poems that are now part of *Mischief City.*"

At week's end, the actors sat around a table, "just reading the dialogue, the connective tissue. There was no music. It was the kind of thing where you get a sense that there had to be a song here. And the song I knew was titled 'I Wasn't Angry When I Thought About Maxine'. I hadn't written it, but that poem had to come into existence and that had to be the poem's title. The poem, when it was finally written, is the centerpiece of the book *Mischief City.* That poem means more to me than anything else, and I hope that it means something to other people".

"To me, it is a poem about all the years I drew as a child. Other people experience it in different ways. You learn how to do something. You get OK at it, and then one day, for no particularly good reason, you do it brilliantly. It just all comes together, and you draw a picture that is out of all proportion to your talent. The next day you are depressed because you can't do it again, but you know you *can* because you *have* done it. It gives you faith to go on. You've reached a plateau. There are those plateaus, and that's what the poem is about. I didn't know that until I had written it. But it's the day 'the eyes' come out the same size. Anybody who has drawn knows how hard it is. That poem is terribly important to me. There's a point you reach where you just don't care if anybody likes your books. That sounds very cynical, and it's not meant to. But there are things we write for different reasons. All my books are written selfishly in a sense."

The situation of two new Wynne-Jones books appearing in the same year almost reoccurred. *Zoom upstream* was tentatively scheduled for 1988 publication, but will not now come out until 1989. Meanwhile, Ian Wallace is preparing the illustrations for a 1988 release. "*The Architect of the Moon* is about a little boy, David Finebloom, who receives a message from the heavens, 'Help! I'm falling apart. Yours, The Moon.' David gets his Leggo bricks together, builds a spaceship, and goes and rebuilds the Moon. Of course, it takes him 28 days."

"I started to write a poem years ago about a little boy named David Finebloom who fades away. That had always been at the back of my mind, and then I heard that Ian would be interested in doing something with me. That put something in the air that I couldn't resist. I got up at four in the morning and wrote this little story. It is one of those stories that has something else that I don't know what it's about. That always gives me a sign that I've done something. It's funny and sweet, but there is an ineffable sadness to it. Ian, whenever he's mentioned thoughts he's had as an illustrator, I've just

been blown away, by how much further he's taken it." (pp. 59-61)

"I say constantly that I don't care about my audience. I don't say it nastily, but I do mean that I think that a writer has to do what he wants to do, and if there's an audience for it, the audience will find it out." And in so saying, Tim hasn't departed far from the idea found in his favorite poem from *Mischief City* where Winchell observes, "Sometimes when you draw, your pencil knows exactly what to do." (p. 62)

Dave Jenkinson, "Tim Wynne-Jones," in Emergency Librarian, *Vol. 15, No. 3, January-February, 1988, pp. 56-62.*

GENERAL COMMETARY

ADRIENNE KERTZER

That children's books often benefit when the lesson is not obvious is demonstrated by the work of Tim Wynne-Jones, although like [Mark] Thurman, Wynne-Jones also assumes that children need to hear that adults are peculiar and often foolish. Yet what does the protagonist learn in *I'll Make You Small*? Always bring a gift? In this intriguing story, Roland is frightened by his mysterious neighbour and the neighbour's equally mysterious, derelict house. As a child, Mr. Swanskin was terrible, "always breaking things," and now as an adult, he frequently threatens Roland; but when Swanskin disappears, Roland is sent to investigate. He discovers Swanskin repairing the toys he broke as a child. Yet if Swanskin regrets his own childhood behaviour, he still dislikes children, " 'Children! Children!' he shouted. 'They ruin everything!' " and does indeed turn Roland small. But like Odysseus and his magic moly, Roland is protected by his gift of a pie, and the horrific situation deflates into Swanskin and Roland sitting down together to eat the pie. Swanskin, the fixated adult making amends for his childhood behaviour; Roland, the child hero conquering his own dark tower with a monster who is still childlike in his love of food—*I'll Make You Small* echoes fairy tale patterns (including the ambiguities of those tales and the uncertainties of their lessons), and for once the illustrations [by Maryann Kovalski] support and add to the text.

[VictoR GAD's] illustrations in *Mischief City* are not as successful, often distracting the reader from the poems. Based on a play by Wynne-Jones, *Mischief City* tells its story through twenty-five poems that the author admits are indebted to Shel Silverstein, Edward Lear, Dennis Lee, and Frank Zappa. Although the quality is uneven, some of the poems and illustrations do capture the six-year-old's frustration with his parents. . . . (pp. 157-58)

There are also comic poems about art as therapy especially as the product of sibling rivalry. . . . Playing with nonsense and fantasy, exploring child-parent relations, appealing to the child's love of aggression, both physical and verbal . . . , *Mischief City* pleases for not taking itself too seriously. (p. 158)

Adrienne Kertzer, "Dummies & Children," in Canadian Literature, *No. 118, Autumn, 1988, pp. 156-58.*

JOAN McGRATH

In the last few years, there has been a wider, wilder choice of boldly attractive picture books for Canadian youngsters. If the tired stereotype of Canadian children's literature used to be that of stuffiness, our new breed of writers and illustrators include such thunderingly successful iconoclasts as Tim Wynne-Jones and Marie-Louise Gay.

Wynne-Jones's endearing *Zoom* books won him an army of young fans. Then in 1986, he produced two children's titles utterly different from his previous work and from each other.

[*I'll make you small*] is reminiscent of the traditional tale in which an adventurous lad challenges the ogre in his bone-littered den, to emerge successful and enriched by the experience; but there is less of bravado, and rather more psychological truth, in this 20th century semi-magical adventure for the very young. . . .

The story has a child's-eye perspective of wonder and awe, and is just scary enough to provide a delightful chill for youngsters of a "read-to-me" age. Older children may recognize the phenomenon of the childhood threat that dwindles into comfortable familiarity. . . .

Completely different in mood and appearance is *Mischief City,* a collection of verse for children. (p. 67)

The poems in the collection are about childhood's concerns, some of them slight and intentionally silly and smart-alecky; others addressing serious problems, especially of non-communication between parents (apparently obsessed with a new baby) and their resentful son, who takes the change out in brattiness and in his art, confiding only in Maxine, his imaginary friend. In the vivid title verse, Maxine rides a wrecker's ball over a "Mischief City" that is plainly Toronto gone mad, with jungle creepers climbing the CN Tower, the Sky Dome gaping like a giant frog, and the "Bad Year Blimp" soaring over a Dali-esque Toronto skyline enlivened by ducks, fish, giraffes and a wild array of unidentifiable wreckage. The fun is nihilistic, the bold and slashing illustrations a perfect match, and *Mischief City,* a place where a kid can unload all the ugly baggage, is plainly an invitation to put your worst foot forward. (pp. 67-8)

> *Joan McGrath, "Fantasy for the Youngest," in* Canadian Children's Literature, *No. 54, 1989, pp. 66-9.*

MADELINE AND ERMADELLO (1977)

Madeline has three friends—Ernie, her carpenter father, Barnell, her next-door-but-one neighbour, and Ermadello. Ermadello is special. She can be anything Madeline wants her to be, because she is imaginary.

This is a quietly charming story about a young girl's fantasies. Not much happens—the climax is a tea-party at which Madeline introduces Ermadello to her father and Barnell—but Madeline's thoughts and feelings are well depicted. [Lindsey Hallam's] illustrations, delicate charcoal sketches on a blue background, add to the appeal of the book.

While not for the literal minded nor the very young child, who may have trouble grasping the fact (never explicitly stated) that Ermadello is imaginary, this book should appeal to those among the older picture book audience who can understand and appreciate the fantasy and quiet humour in the book.

> *Linda Smith, in a review of "Madeline and Ermadello," in* In Review: Canadian Books for Children, *Vol. 12, No. 1, Winter, 1978, p. 70.*

Madeline's friend is Ermadello, who materializes in a variety of whimsical forms in this delightful picture book. Written in a way that captures the magical world of the child's imagination, *Madeline and Ermadello* is a charming story of friendship that younger readers are certain to enjoy.

> *A review of "Madeline and Ermadello," in* Children's Book News, *Toronto, Vol. 2, No. 1, June, 1979, p. 2.*

ZOOM AT SEA (1983)

Zoom is no ordinary cat. He loves the water and dreams fantastic dreams of limitless seas and boundless skies. Adventuresome mariner that he is, Zoom goes to the home of the mysterious Maria and there finds his fantasies realized. As the foamy sea surges around Zoom, Maria exclaims, "Go on. It's all yours." It proves an irresistible, exciting invitation to the cat and the reader alike.

Zoom at Sea . . . proves that a picture book can indeed be the perfect balance of text and illustration. Here, neither element overwhelms the other; both are complementary in their tone and texture. Ken Nutt's black-and-white pencil drawings are finely detailed renderings of surf and sea, cats, birds, and beams. The reader's imagination, spurred on by the text, supplies the additional colours.

The humour is wry: the Three Blind Mice Jazz Band, indeed! The book could easily be read aloud to toddlers or serve as a story for young readers who can also delight in the descriptive pictures.

Zoom's adventure is a reminder, to adults and children alike, of the power of the mind. "Go on. It's all yours." Oh, that someone would invite us—like Zoom—to live our dreams too!

> *Linda Granfield, in a review of "Zoom at Sea," in* Quill and Quire, *Vol. 50, No. 3, March, 1984, p. 72.*

ZOOM AWAY (1985)

Zoom is back! The spirited little cat, whose love of water first led him to Maria's door—and into our hearts—two years ago . . . has returned for another adventure.

This time, at Maria's invitation, he sets off for the High Arctic to help search for Uncle Roy (the sea-faring tomcat, remember?) who sailed for the North Pole but hasn't been heard from since.

And, again, it is Maria's house that magically transforms itself into a suitable setting for Zoom's quest. This time we go upstairs, and the description of the climb, both in word and picture, is a joy. "The way was very steep," the author tells us, as the accompanying illustration shows a tiny cat struggling to clamber up the steps. "The air grew cold . . . The windows on the landing were prickly with ice, and long icicles hung like teeth from the archway. The hallway was carpeted with snow. Zoom put on his ping-pong paddle snow shoes."

That last phrase has a wonderful ring to it and conjures up

an image that seems deliciously funny. Sure enough, there it is on the next page—Zoom and Maria trekking through the snow, he with ping-pong paddles strapped to his hind paws.

Text and illustration complement each other perfectly. . . . In *Zoom Away*, [Ken Nutt] again turns to detailed black-and-white drawings to create an expectant mood and a wondrous world where anything seems possible. The small, white cat, so full of *joie de vivre,* and the tall, voluptuous woman so generously giving him the chance to live life to the fullest, together seem destined to carve themselves a permanent niche in the world of Canadian picture-books.

Let's hope Wynne-Jones and Nutt continue to chronicle the adventures and that Maria's house is big enough to accommodate them.

Bernie Goedhart, in a review of "Zoom Away," in Quill and Quire, *Vol. 51, No. 8, August, 1985, p. 38.*

[*Zoom Away*] is designed for young reader-listeners (around four to seven years old). But even a story for young readers must possess depth in its simplicity. Unfortunately, *Zoom Away* does not. What is the relationship between Zoom and Maria? Are they equals or is she a benevolent mother/protector figure? Zoom's quest is to find a missing uncle; yet when he arrives at his destination, he cavorts on the ice, the search seemingly forgotten. And when he is alone, first in the tunnel and then on the ice, there is no sense of anxiousness or concern. Finally, when Zoom is back at Maria's he is in front of a fire (in summer?) dreaming of future adventure. Surely the adventure he has just completed would have had some impact on him; he would have been a changed individual. However, there is no indication that such is the case. The narrative is trivial, although pleasant.

Ken Nutt's illustrations, in black and white, are superior to the text, but even they do not give depth to the story.

Jon C. Stott, in a review of "Zoom Away," in Canadian Literature, *No. 112, Spring, 1987, p. 160.*

Zoom Away is one of those rare picture books that combines absolute simplicity with mythic resonance. The prose is straightforward, restrained, and sparing of metaphor. "Zoom lit his lantern. The doorway was very small. Too small for Maria." The story itself is clear and childlike, a small adventure such as the one in *Henry Explores the Jungle* or Pooh and Christopher Robin's on their "expotition" to the North Pole. Cozy touches such as Zoom's ping-pong paddle snowshoes and Maria's thermos of sustaining tomato soup keep the book grounded in a child's world.

But the story is bigger than its plot. Illustrator Ken Nutt invites comparison with Chris Van Allsburg not only because of Nutt's stunning use of black and white but also because of the monumental quality of his objects. Zoom is small and winsome, but Maria's house with its banisters and columns, its chandeliers and busts of bearded worthies, is grand. The arctic landscape with its ringed midnight sun is huge. The picture of Uncle Roy's deserted vessel suggests the title "The Wreck of the Catship." Maria herself is larger than life, particularly in the final picture as she lies odalisquelike on a chaise longue, lit in chiaroscuro from the fire.

Such illustrations do not overwhelm the text because behind the simple story of Zoom stands, it seems to me, a particularly Canadian myth. On one level Zoom's quest is for his uncle, but his route is via the Northwest Passage. The search for the Northwest Passage is such an essential story in Canadian history that Northrop Frye suggests it colors our culture to this day. The idea of Canada as a large malevolent land mass that is a barrier on the way to the riches of the Orient was a historical reality. The tragedy of explorer John Franklin, who died along with his crew of 129 on a Northwest Passage Expedition, is the tragedy of the North. But it is not the tragedy of *Zoom Away.* Maria appears to rescue Zoom, to build him a sled of two oars and some sailcloth, and to tuck him in, "nice and cozy." And when Zoom dreams of finding Uncle Roy when the ice melts, we are confident that he will. The satisfaction we feel at the book's safe ending goes beyond the satisfaction of putting a tired child to bed. (pp. 378-79)

Sarah Ellis, "News from the North," in The Horn Book Magazine, *Vol. LXIII, No. 3, May-June, 1987, pp. 378-81.*

I'LL MAKE YOU SMALL (1986)

[In *I'll Make You Small,* illustrated by Maryann Kovalski,] text and illustration complement each other perfectly. Readers familiar with the artist's previous, almost-too-cute offering, *Brenda and Edward,* will be pleasantly surprised at the scope of Kovalski's work in this book. Her illustrations have a haunting spookiness about them; she plays with perspective and size in wondrous ways.

Wynne-Jones's story is equally clever. A young boy, Roland, lives next door to eccentric, creepy Mr Swanskin who threatens to "make you small", when a child trespasses on his property. Then, for days, no one sees the man, and Roland's mother gets worried. She sends her son to see if Swanskin is all right and Roland asks if he can bring the neighbour a pie—a good move, it turns out.

Kovalski manages to extend the author's words by taking the questions posed by the text and infusing her art with the same sense of suspense and watchfulness.

The ending, as befits a child's picture-book, is suitably safe and happy. A child who likes scary stories, but is too young for Poe and Hitchcock, should enjoy this book. Particularly so if it's read to him or her by an adult who appreciates it, too.

Bernie Goedhart, "Kids' Books: Making Stories Live Up to Their Pictures," in Quill and Quire, *Vol. 52, No. 10, October, 1986, p. 16.*

MISCHIEF CITY (1986)

Tim Wynne-Jones's book of verse, *Mischief City,* is marred by the garish and distorted illustrations by Victor Gad. Some of Wynne-Jones's verses, **"Monster Parents,"** for example, are funny and strike close to home, but generally the text is overpowered by Gad's vivid reds and blues and, in particular, his nightmarish yellows. These verses are apparently part of a play for young people by Wynne-Jones, but the reasons for using a stage setting in the illustrations is not at all clear, and anyone seeking a coherent pattern to the poems will be confused. (p. 15)

Mary Ainslie Smith, "The Young and the Naked," in Books in Canada, *Vol. 15, No. 9, December, 1986, pp. 15-17.*

Mischief City is big, bold, and bright, a swirling circus of wild-looking people with multiple mouths, spiky hair, and odd, imaginary pets and friends. But Tim Wynne-Jones's poems seem like an adult's attempt to identify with a child's concerns: in this case, those of Winchell and his imaginary friend, Maxine. Unfortunately, the attempt doesn't convince. An adult voice is all too audible in lines such as "I sneak up on my mother / And frighten her as well" or "lately, when I start to speak, / I'm getting no response." The concerns are those of a child: parents not paying sufficient attention; not wanting a baby sister, etc. It's just that far too frequently the vocabulary and syntax are those of an adult.

Victor Gad's illustrations are wild-eyed and apocalyptic, a bit too strong for the thumpety-thumpety verse they accompany. To his credit, they are full of inventive detail. . . .

Throughout, the action is played to a houseful of empty theatre seats; the endpapers enclose the entire collection of poems in the vacant, popcorn-strewn auditorium. The visual device is an inadvertently apt comment on the book, wherein a self-conscious, adult entertainer is onstage, speaking with a child's voice, or a version thereof—but nobody is out there listening.

> Joan McGrath, "Poems for Kids Conjure Up a Cockeyed World," in Quill and Quire, Vol. 52, No. 12, December, 1986, p. 15.

ARCHITECT OF THE MOON (1988; U. S. edition as *Builder of the Moon*)

Here is yet another moon book to add to your shelves. *Architect of the Moon* is up against some steep competition, including Marie-Louise Gay's award-winning *Moonbeam on a Cat's Ear,* and Jirina Marton's *Midnight Visit at Molly's House,* to name only two. But author Tim Wynne-Jones and illustrator Ian Wallace make a strong contending team in the moon-book category.

In *Architect of the Moon,* David Finebloom, who sports turquoise-coloured goggles (moon glasses?), is a typical boy looking for adventure. One night he receives an urgent message by moonbeam requesting his immediate assistance. David whirls into action, kisses his mother goodbye, and jets into the night sky in his home-made spaceship. His mission? To build, block by block, a full-faced moon.

Wallace's delicately drawn illustrations of flying blocks and teapots in a vast indigo sky animate what might otherwise be a story too simple to be entertaining. Despite the art, the plot falls short when David flies home for breakfast. The ending is too abrupt and may leave the book's young readers wondering if they've missed a page or two. However, the classic read-aloud layout, with an image on one side of the spread and words on the other, is straightforward enough to encourage any beginning reader.

> Catherine Osborne, in a review of "Architect of the Moon," in Books for Young People, Vol. 2, No. 5, October, 1988, p. 10.

Builder of the Moon is a space odyssey for the very young, for all those tinkering with blocks and toying with "what if." . . . This book has all the compressed wish-fulfillment of a fairy tale. In many ways, it resembles our most famous modern fairy tale, *Where the Wild Things Are*: the journey motif, the transformation of objects, the bonding and breaking away of child and parent, and the reward of food at the end.

Ian Wallace imbues deeper meanings into the simple text by his elegaic wash of colors. On the cover, David sits on his homemade rocketship with sunset clouds providing a fiery combustion. The title page shows a window view of blocks and pyramids against a moonlit sky, as stark and timeless as a dream. The launching is an illumination of ordinary toys into extraordinary objects, a fantastic extension of the real. The colors are the magic that transports him into the night sky, a scene so joyous that the reader travels too.

Every page has details of surprise and wonder that extend the words beyond earthly confines. Wynne-Jones's text is spare, simple, poetic, weaving facts about the moon into fancy. A young reader might wonder about the "tranquil sea" and the topography, but that poetry of fact creates the curiosity that leads to other books and other journeys.

> Anne Lundin, in a review of "Builder of the Moon," in The Five Owls, Vol. III, No. 5, May-June, 1989, p. 72.

CUMULATIVE INDEX TO AUTHORS

This index lists all author entries in *Children's Literature Review* and includes cross-references to them in other Gale sources. References in the index are identified as follows:

CA: *Contemporary Authors* (original series), Volumes 1-130
CANR: *Contemporary Authors New Revision Series,* Volumes 1-29
CAP: *Contemporary Authors Permanent Series,* Volumes 1-2
CA-R: *Contemporary Authors* (revised editions), Volumes 1-44
CDALB: *Concise Dictionary of American Literary Biography,* Volumes 1-4
CLC: *Contemporary Literary Criticism,* Volumes 1-58
CLR: *Children's Literature Review,* Volumes 1-21
DLB: *Dictionary of Literary Biography,* Volumes 1-92
DLB-DS: *Dictionary of Literary Biography Documentary Series,* Volumes 1-6
DLB-Y: *Dictionary of Literary Biography Yearbook,* Volumes 1980-1988
LC: *Literature Criticism from 1400 to 1800,* Volumes 1-11
NCLC: *Nineteenth-Century Literature Criticism,* Volumes 1-27
SAAS: *Somthing About the Author Autobiography Series,* Volumes 1-8
SATA: *Something about the Author,* Volumes 1-59
TCLC: *Twentieth-Century Literary Criticism,* Volumes 1-36
YABC: *Yesterday's Authors of Books for Children,* Volumes 1-2

Author Index

Author Index

CUMULATIVE INDEX TO NATIONALITIES

Nationality Index

CUMULATIVE INDEX TO TITLES

Title Index

Title Index

Title Index

Title Index